The Prentice Hall *Reader*

The PRENTICE HALL *Reader*

SIXTH EDITION

GEORGE MILLER

University of Delaware

Upper Saddle River, New Jersey 07458

The Prentice Hall reader / [compiled by] George Miller. — 6th ed.
p. cm.
ISBN 0-13-022563-0 (pbk.)
1. College readers. 2. English language—Rhetoric—Problems, exercises, etc.
I. Miller, George.
PE1417.P74 2000
808'.0427—dc21 00-031347
CIP

VP, Editorial Director: Laura Pearson
Editor-in-Chief: Leah Jewell
Acquisitions Editor: Corey Good
Assistant Editor: Vivian Garcia
Development Editor: Mark Gallaher
AVP, Director of Manufacturing and Production: Barbara Kittle
Managing Editor: Mary Rottino
Production Liaison: Fran Russello
Project Manager: Nancy Land, Publications Development Co. of Texas
Manufacturing Manager: Nick Sklitsis
Prepress and Manufacturing Buyer: Mary Ann Gloriande
Art Director: Jayne Conte
Cover Designer: Bruce Kenselaar
Cover Art: Karen Sallatar
Director, Image Resource Center: Melinda Lee Reo
Manager, Rights & Permissions: Kay Dellosa
Image Specialist: Beth Boyd
Marketing Manager: Brandy Dawson

This book was set in 10/12.5 Janson by Publications Development Company of Texas and was printed and bound by R.R. Donnelley. The cover was printed by Phoenix Color Corp.

Printed in the United States of America
10 9 8 7 6 5 4

ISBN 0-13-022563-0 (student text)
ISBN 0-13-027692-8 (annotated instructor's edition)

Prentice-Hall International (UK) Limited, *London*
Prentice-Hall of Australia Pty. Limited, *Sydney*
Prentice-Hall Canada Inc., *Toronto*
Prentice-Hall Hispanoamericana, S.A., *Mexico*
Prentice-Hall of India Private Limited, *New Delhi*
Prentice-Hall of Japan, Inc., *Tokyo*
Pearson Education Asia Pte. Ltd., *Singapore*
Editora Prentice-Hall do Brasil, Ltda., *Rio de Janeiro*

For Valerie and Eric, their book

Contents

ONE

Gathering and Using Examples 39

TWO

Narration 90

THREE

Description 145

NINE

ARGUMENTATION AND PERSUASION 482

ALTERNATE

THEMATIC CONTENTS

AUTOBIOGRAPHY AND BIOGRAPHY

CHILDREN AND FAMILY

ALCOHOL, VIOLENCE, AND PUNISHMENT

Media and Computers

Stereotypes, Prejudice, and the Struggle for Equality

Women's Roles, Women's Rights

Growing Older

Humor and Satire

Men and Women

Race, Class, and Culture

Nature and the Environment

Psychology and Behavior

READING, WRITING, AND LANGUAGE

SCHOOL AND COLLEGE

Self-Discovery

PREFACE

The Prentice Hall Reader is predicated on two premises: that reading plays a vital role in learning how to write and that writing and reading can best be organized around the traditional division of discourse into a number of structural patterns. Such a division is not the only way that the forms of writing can be classified, but it does have several advantages.

First, practice in these structural patterns encourages students to organize knowledge and to see the ways in which information can be conveyed. How else does the mind know except by classifying, comparing, defining, or seeking cause and effect relationships? Second, the most common use of these patterns occurs in writing done in academic courses. There students are asked to narrate a chain of events, to describe an artistic style, to classify plant forms, to compare two political systems, to tell how a laboratory experiment was performed, to analyze why famine occurs in Africa, to define a philosophical concept, or to argue for or against building a space station. Learning how to structure papers using these patterns is an exercise that has immediate application in students' other academic work. Finally, because the readings use these patterns as structural devices, they offer an excellent way in which to integrate reading into a writing course. Students can see the patterns at work and learn how to use them to become more effective writers and better, more efficient readers.

WHAT IS NEW IN THE SIXTH EDITION

The sixth edition of *The Prentice Hall Reader* features 57 selections, 17 of which are new, and another 11 papers written by student writers. As in the previous editions, the readings are chosen on the basis of several criteria: how well they demonstrate a particular pattern of organization, appeal to a freshman audience, and promote interesting and appropriate discussion and writing activities.

The sixth edition of *The Prentice Hall Reader* includes a number of new features:

- *Visualizing.* Sections in each chapter show how the writing strategy is embodied in visual forms. A panel cartoon is a narrative, a technical drawing details a process, advertisements (even for products that do not exist!) show persuasion at work.
- *Writers on Writing.* Writers share their observations on the process of finding a subject, composing, and revising. We are not alone if we feel that writing is hard work.
- *Tips for Web Searching.* Type in a word or a subject on a Web search and get 100,000 matches? Get help in defining your search more narrowly.
- *Links to the Website. The Prentice Hall Reader* has a massive site at http://www.prenhall.com/miller. Additional materials for discussion, background information and reading suggestions, additional writing suggestions, and a group of hot-linked sites (just click your mouse!) are available for every reading in every chapter. Each chapter also has Web-based writing tasks—visit a site or a series of sites, gather information, and respond to a writing prompt. Use the *Reader* as you learn how to navigate the Web.

The sixth edition retains and improves some of the popular student features from earlier editions:

- *Writing in Other Disciplines.* Each chapter shows how the traditional patterns of organization are used in writing for other college courses.
- *Finding, Using, and Documenting Sources.* An appendix covers briefly every aspect of writing a research paper—including Web searches and documenting electronic sources. A new student research paper on "Ecotourism" is included.
- *Pre-reading Questions.* These questions help connect the reading to our experience and focus our reading attention.

- *A Revision Casebook.* Follow Gordon Grice's essay on the black widow spider from its first notebook entries through its first publication in a literary journal, to its edited version that appeared in *Harper's* magazine. In an exclusive interview, Grice discusses the writing and revising of the essay.
- *Writing Suggestions.* Having trouble finding a topic? Between the writing suggestions offered in the *Reader* itself and the additional topics you can find at the Website, the *Reader* has nearly 500 writing suggestions.

Other Distinctive Features of This Text

Prose in Revision

As every writing instructor knows, getting students to revise is never easy. Having finished a paper, most students do not want to see it again, let alone revise it. Furthermore, for many students revising means making word substitutions and correcting grammatical and mechanical errors—changes that instructors regard as proofreading, not revising. To help make the need for revision more vivid and to show how writers revise, the *Prentice Hall Reader* includes three features:

1. Chapter 10: Revising. A complete chapter with a lengthy introduction offers specific advice on how to revise. The chapter includes three examples of how professional writers revised their work. A case study of Gordon Grice's essay on the black widow spider documents the evolution of the essay from notebook entries to its original publication in a small literary journal, and then on to its appearance, revised again, in *Harper's* magazine.
2. The introduction to each chapter of readings include a first draft of a student essay, a comment on the draft's strengths and weaknesses, and a final, revised draft. These essays, realistic examples of student writing, model the student revision process.
3. The third writing suggestion after each selection is accompanied by prewriting and rewriting activities. In all, the text provides 170 specific rewriting activities to help students organize ideas and to revise what they have written.

Selections

The sixth edition of *The Prentice Hall Reader* offers instructors flexibility in choosing readings. No chapter has fewer than five selections and most have six or more. The readings are scaled in terms of length and sophistication. The selections in each chapter begin with a student essay and the selections from professional writers are arranged so that they increase in length and in difficulty and sophistication.

Writing Suggestions

Each reading is followed by four writing suggestions: the first is a journal writing suggestion; the second calls for a paragraph-length response; the third, an essay; and the fourth, an essay involving research. Each of the suggestions is related to the content of the reading and each calls for a response in the particular pattern or mode being studied. The material in the Annotated Instructor's Edition includes a fifth writing suggestion for each reading, bringing the total number of writing suggestions in the sixth edition to nearly 300. Even more writing suggestions can be found at the *Prentice Hall Reader* Website at http://www.prenhall.com/miller.

Introductions

The introduction to each chapter offers clear and succinct advice to the student on how to write that particular type of paragraph or essay. The introductions anticipate questions, provide answers, and end with a checklist, titled "Some Things to Remember," to remind students of the major concerns they should have when writing.

How to Read an Essay

The first introductory section offers advice on how to read an essay, following prereading, reading and rereading models. A sample analysis of an essay by Lewis Thomas shows how to use this reading model to prepare an essay for class.

How to Write an Essay

The section, "How to Write an Essay," offers an overview of every stage of the writing process, starting with advice on how to define a subject, purpose, and audience and an explanation of a variety of

prewriting techniques. The section also shows students how to write a thesis statement, how to decide where to place that statement in an essay, and how to approach the problems of revising an essay. Finally it contains a student essay as well as two drafts of the student's two opening paragraphs.

Annotated Instructor's Edition

An annotated edition of *The Prentice Hall Reader* is available to instructors. Each of the selections in the text is annotated with

- A Teaching Strategy that suggests ways in which to teach the reading and to keep attention focused on how the selection works as a piece of writing
- A suggested link to other writing and organizational strategies found in the reading
- Appropriate background information that explains allusions or historical contexts
- Specific class and collaborative learning activities that can be used with the reading
- A critical reading activity
- Links to Writing that suggest how to use the reader to teach specific grammatical, mechanical, and rhetorical issues in writing. These "links" provide a bridge between a handbook and *The Prentice Hall Reader.*
- Possible responses to all of the discussion questions included within the text
- Tips on "related readings" that suggest how to pair essays in the reader
- An additional writing suggestion

Instructor's Quiz Booklet

A separate *Instructor's Quiz Booklet* for *The Prentice Hall Reader* is available from your Prentice Hall representative. The booklet contains two quizzes for each selection in the reader—one on content and the other on vocabulary. Each quiz has five multiple-choice questions. The quizzes are intended to be administered and graded quickly. They provide the instructor with a brief and efficient means of testing the student's ability to extract significant ideas from the readings and of demonstrating his or her understanding of certain vocabulary words as they are used in the essays. Keys to both content and vocabulary quizzes are included at the back of the *Quiz Booklet*.

Teaching Writing with "The Prentice Hall Reader"

A separate manual on planning the writing and the reading in a composition course is available from your Prentice Hall representative. Primarily addressed to the new graduate teaching assistant or the adjunct instructor, the manual includes sections on teaching the writing process, including how to use prewriting activities, to conference, to design and implement collaborative learning activities, and to grade. In addition, it provides advice on how to plan a class discussion of a reading and how to avoid pointless discussions. An appendix contains an index to all of the activities and questions in *The Prentice Hall Reader* that involve grammatical, mechanical, sentence- or paragraph-level subjects, three additional sample syllabi, and a variety of sample course materials including self-assessment sheets, peer editing worksheets, and directions for small group activities.

"The Prentice Hall Reader" Website

The *Reader* has an extensive Website that includes additional resources for both the student and the instructor for every essay in the *Reader*. The Website is divided into sections on Related Readings (print or on-line documents that are related to the topic under discussion or to the author), Background Information, Web Resources (with hot-linked sites so that the students can immediately access these sites), and Additional Writing Suggestions. Each chapter also has writing tasks that involve examining Websites and documents. The Website adds a new dimension to the *Reader* and allows instructors to integrate the World Wide Web into their freshman English courses. Additional student essays are also available there and you can submit the best of your students' work for inclusion as well!

George Miller
University of Delaware

ACKNOWLEDGMENTS

Although writing is a solitary activity, no one can write without the assistance of others. This text owes much to many people: To the staff at Prentice Hall who have continued to play a large role in helping to develop this reader, especially Phil Miller, president, Humanities and Social Science; Leah Jewell, editor-in-chief; Corey Good, acquisitions editor; Vivian Garcia, assistant editor; Brandy Dawson, marketing manager; Fran Russello, production liaison; my production team at Publications Development Company, Nancy Land and Pam Blackmon; and Mark Gallaher, development editor.

To my reviewers, who wrote extensive critiques of the manuscript and made many helpful suggestions: Jan Worth, University of Michigan—Flint; Malcolm Hayward, Indiana University of Pennsylvania; Judith A. Burnham, Tulsa Community College; Brena B. Walker, Anderson College; C. Michael McKinney, Southwestern Oklahoma State University; Debra C. Boyd, Winthrop University; Randall L. Beebe, Eastern Illinois University; Jeffrey Knapp, Florida International University; Troy D. Nordman; John D. Conway, Central Connecticut State University; Candace Barrington, Southern Connecticut State University; Sally Bishop Shigley, Weber State University; Stephanie Westphal, San Jose State University; Denise Clark, Eastern Illinois University.

To the writing program staff at the University of Delaware and the students in my own writing classes, who tested materials, offered suggestions, and contributed essays to the introductions. To my wife Vicki, who makes everything possible. And finally to my children, Lisa, Jon, Craig, Valerie, Eric, Evan, Adam, Nathan, and Alicia and Eric Gray, who have learned over the years to live with a father who writes.

G. M.

THE NEW YORK TIMES SUPPLEMENTS PROGRAM

THE NEW YORK TIMES and PRENTICE HALL are sponsoring Themes of the Times; a program designed to enhance student access to current information of relevance in the classroom.

Through this program, the core subject matter provided in the text is supplemented by a collection of time-sensitive articles from one of the world's most distinguished newspapers, THE NEW YORK TIMES. These articles demonstrate the vital, ongoing connection between what is learned in the classroom and what is happening in the world around us.

To enjoy the wealth of information of THE NEW YORK TIMES daily, a reduced subscription rate is available in deliverable areas. For information, call toll-free: 1-800-631-1222.

PRENTICE HALL and THE NEW YORK TIMES are proud to co-sponsor Themes of the Times. We hope it will make the reading of both textbooks and newspapers a more dynamic, involving process.

The PRENTICE HALL *Reader*

How to Read an Essay

When your grade in most writing courses is determined by the papers that you write, rather than by examinations based on the essays that you read in the course, you might wonder why any instructor would assign "readings" in a writing course. How do these two seemingly very different activities fit together?

How Does Reading Help You Write?

You read in a writing course for three purposes: First, the essays are a source of information: you learn by reading, and what you learn can then, in turn, be used in your writing. Any paper that involves research, for example, requires selective, critical reading on your part as you search for and evaluate sources. Second, readings offer a perspective on a particular subject, one with which you might agree or disagree. In this sense readings can serve as catalysts to spark writing. Many of the writing suggestions in this text grow out of the readings, asking you to explore some aspect of the subject more fully, to reply to a writer's position, or to expand on or refine that position. Finally, readings offer models to a writer; they show you how another writer dealt with a particular subject or a particular writing problem, and they demonstrate writing strategies. Other writing suggestions in this text ask you to employ the same strategy used in a reading with a different subject in an essay of your own.

The first two purposes—readings as a source of information or as a stimulus to writing—are fairly obvious, but the third purpose might seem confusing. Exactly how are you, as a student writer, to use an essay written by a professional writer as an example or model? Are you to suppose to sound like Margaret Atwood or Bob Greene or Maya Angelou? Are you to imitate their styles or the structures that they use in their essays?

To model, in the sense that the word is being used here, does not mean to produce an imitation. You are not expected to use the same organizational structure or to imitate someone else's style, tone, or approach. Rather, what you can learn from these writers is how to handle information; how to adapt writing to a particular audience; how to structure the body of an essay; how to begin, make transitions, and end; how to construct effective paragraphs and achieve sentence variety. In short, the readings represent an album of performances, examples that you can use to study writing techniques.

Models or examples are important to you as a writer because you learn to write effectively in the same way that you learn to do any other activity. You study the rules or advice on how it is done; you practice, especially under the watchful eye of an instructor or a coach; and you study how others have mastered similar problems and techniques. A young musician learns how to read music and play an instrument, practices daily, studies with a teacher, and listens to and watches how other musicians play. A baseball player learns the proper offensive and defensive techniques, practices daily, is supervised by a coach, and listens to the advice and watches the performance of other players. As a writer in a writing class, you do the same thing: follow the advice offered by your instructor and textbooks, practice by writing and revising, listen to the advice and suggestions of your fellow students, and study the work of other writers.

How Does Writing Help You Read?

Reading and writing actually benefit each other: being a good reader will help you become a more effective writer, and being a good writer will help you become a more effective reader. As a writer, you learn how to plan an essay, how to use examples to support a thesis, how to structure an argument, how to make an effective transition from one point to another. You learn how to write beginnings, middles, and ends, and most especially you learn how essays can be organized. For example, through reading you learn that comparison and contrast essays can be organized in either the subject-by-subject or the point-by-point pattern, that narratives are structured chronologically, and that cause and effect analyses are linear and sequential. When you read other essays, you look for structure and pattern, realizing that such devices are not only creative tools you use in writing but also analytical ones that can be used in reading. By revealing to you an underlying organizational pattern, such devices help you understand what the essay says. To become an efficient reader, however, you need to exercise the same care and attention that you do when you write. You do that by becoming an active rather than a passive reader.

Active Rather than Passive Reading

Every reader first reads a piece of writing for plot or subject matter. On that level, the reader wants to know what happens, what is the subject, whether it is new or interesting. Generally that first reading is done quickly, even, in a sense, superficially. The reader is a spectator waiting passively to be entertained or informed. Then, if it is important for the reader to use that piece of writing in some way, to understand it in detail and in depth, the next stage of active reading begins. On this level, the reader asks questions, seeks answers, looks for organizational structures, and concentrates on themes and images or on the thesis and the quality of evidence presented. Careful reading requires this active participation of the reader. Writing and reading are, after all, social acts, and as such they involve an implied contract between writer and audience. A writer's job is to communicate clearly and effectively; a reader's job is to read attentively and critically.

Because as a reader you need to become an active participant in this process of communication, you should always read any piece of writing you are using in a course or on your job more than once. Rereading an essay or a textbook involves the same types of critical activities that you use when rereading a poem, a novel, or a play and demands your attention and your active involvement as a reader. You must examine how the author embodies meaning or purpose in prose. You must seek answers to a variety of questions: How does the author structure the essay? How does the author select, organize, and present information? To whom is the author writing? How does that audience influence the essay?

You can increase your effectiveness as an active and critical reader by following the same three-stage model that you use as a writer: divide your time into prereading, reading, and rereading activities.

Prereading

Before you begin reading an essay in this text, look first at the biographical headnote that describes the author and her or his work and that identifies where and when the essay was originally published, including any special conditions or circumstances that surrounded or influenced its publication. The headnote ends with two "Before Reading" questions that encourage you to connect aspects of the reading to your experiences and to anticipate the writer's thought. A careful reading of this material can help prepare you to read the essay.

Look next at the text of the essay itself. What does the title tell you about the subject or the tone? A serious, dignified title such as "The Value of Children: A Taxonomical Essay" (p. 232) sets up a very different set of expectations than a playful title such as "That Lean and Hungry Look" (p. 277). Page through the essay—are there any obvious subdivisions in the text (extra spaces, sequence markers, subheadings) that signal an organizational pattern? Does the paragraphing suggest a particular structure? You might also read the first sentence in every paragraph to get a general sense of what the essay is about and where the author is going.

Finally, look at the series of questions that follow each selection. These questions always ask about subject and purpose, structure and audience, and vocabulary and style. Read through them so that you know what to look for when you read the essay. Before you begin to read, make sure that you have a pen or pencil, some paper on which to take notes, and a dictionary in which to check the meanings of unfamiliar words.

Reading

When you begin to read a selection in this book, you already have an important piece of information about its structure. Each selection was chosen to demonstrate a particular type of writing (narration, description, exposition, and argumentation) and a particular pattern of organization (chronological, spatial, division and classification, comparison and contrast, process, cause and effect, definition, induction or deduction). As you read, think about how the author organized the essay. On a separate sheet of paper, construct a brief outline. That will help you focus your attention on how the whole essay is put together.

Remember that an essay will typically express a particular idea or assertion **(thesis)** about a **subject** to an **audience** for a particular reason **(purpose)**. Probably one reading of an essay will be enough for you to answer questions about **subject**, but you may have to reread the essay several times to identify the author's **thesis** and **purpose**. Keep these three elements separate and clear in your own mind. It will help to answer each of the following questions as you read and reread:

1. **Subject:** What is this essay about?
2. **Thesis:** What particular point is the author trying to make about this subject?
3. **Audience:** To whom is the author writing? Where did the essay first appear? How does its intended audience help shape the essay and influence its language and style?
4. **Purpose:** Why is the author writing this? Is the intention to entertain? To inform? To persuade?

Effective writing contains specific, relevant details and examples. Look carefully at the writer's choice of examples. Remember that the author made a conscious decision to include each of these details. Ideally, each is appropriate to the subject and each contributes to the thesis and purpose.

Rereading

Rereading, like rewriting, is not always a discrete stage in a linear process. Just as you might pause after writing several sentences and then go back and make some immediate changes, so as a reader, you might stop at the end of a paragraph and then go back and reread what you have just read. Depending on the difficulty of the essay, it might take several rereadings for you to be able to answer the questions posed about the writer's thesis and purpose. Even if you feel certain about your understanding of the essay, a final rereading is important.

In that rereading, focus on the essay as an example of a writer's craft. Look carefully at the paragraphing. How effective is the introduction to the essay? The conclusion? Have you ever used a similar strategy to begin or end an essay? How do both reflect the writer's purpose? Audience? Pay attention to the writer's sentence structures. How do these sentences differ from the ones that you typically write? Does the author employ a variety of sentence types and lengths? Is there anything unusual about the author's word choices? Do you use a similar range of vocabulary when you write? Remember that the writer of essays is just as conscious of craft as the poet, the novelist, or the playwright.

A Sample Reading

Before you begin reading in the sixth edition of *The Prentice Hall Reader*, you can see how to use these techniques of prereading, reading, and rereading in the following essay, which has been annotated over the course of several readings. Following the essay are the reader's prereading, reading, and rereading notes.

On Cloning a Human Being

Lewis Thomas

Lewis Thomas (1913–1993) was born in Flushing, New York, and received his M.D. from Harvard University. He served on the medical faculty at Johns Hopkins, Tulane, Cornell, and Yale before assuming the position of chancellor of the Memorial Sloan-Kettering Cancer Center in New York. Thomas published widely in his research specialty, pathology, the study of diseases and their causes.

In 1971 he began contributing a 1,200-word monthly column, focusing on current topics related to medicine and biological science, to the New England Journal of Medicine. *Titled "Notes of a Biology Watcher," the column proved highly popular with professionals who subscribed to the journal as well as nonspecialists. Several collections of these essays have been published, including* The Lives of a Cell: Notes of a Biology Watcher *(1974),* The Medusa and the Snail *(1979),* Late Night Thoughts on Listening to Mahler's Ninth Symphony *(1983), and* Fragile Species *(1992).*

In "On Cloning a Human Being," originally published in the New England Journal of Medicine, *Thomas sets out to analyze the effect that an experiment to clone a human being would have on the rest of the world.*

BEFORE READING

Connecting: What do you know about cloning, both in fact and from science fiction? Do you find cloning a positive technological development or a frightening one?

Anticipating: What seems to be Thomas's attitude toward cloning? As a scientist, does he express the opinion you expect?

1 It is now theoretically possible to recreate an identical creature from any animal or plant, from the DNA contained in the nucleus of any somatic cell. A single plant root-tip cell can be teased and seduced into conceiving a perfect copy of the whole plant; a frog's intestinal epithelial cell possesses the complete instructions needed for a new, same frog. If the technology were further

Definition of cloning

advanced, you could do this with a human being, and there are now startled predictions all over the place that this will in fact be done, someday, in order to provide a version of immortality for carefully selected, especially valuable people.

2 The cloning of humans is on most of the lists of things to worry about from Science, along with behavior control, genetic engineering, transplanted heads, computer poetry, and the unrestrained growth of plastic flowers.

Joking here.

3 Cloning is the most dismaying of prospects, mandating as it does the elimination of sex with only a metaphoric elimination of death as compensation. It is almost no comfort to know that one's cloned, identical surrogate lives on, especially when the living will very likely involve edging one's real, now aging self off to the side, sooner or later. It is hard to imagine anything like filial affection or respect for a single, unmated nucleus; harder still to think of one's new, self-generated self as anything but an absolute, desolate orphan. Not to mention the complex interpersonal relationship involved in raising one's self from infancy, teaching the language, enforcing discipline, instilling good manners, and the like. How would you feel if you became an incorrigible juvenile delinquent by proxy, at the age of fifty-five?

Two versions of the same person living at once—the original and the clone. Wild idea.

proxy: person acting for another person

4 The public questions are obvious. Who is to be selected, and on what qualifications? How to handle the risks of misused technology, such as self-determined cloning by the rich and powerful but socially objectionable, or the cloning by governments of dumb, docile masses for the world's work? What will be the effect on all the uncloned rest of us of human sameness? After all, we've accustomed ourselves through hundreds of millennia to the continual exhilaration of uniqueness; each of us is totally different, in a fundamental sense, from all the other four billion. Selfness is an essential fact of life. The thought of human

4-paragraph introduction sets up negatives about cloning

nonselfness, precise sameness, is terrifying, when you think about it.

5 Well, don't think about it, because it isn't a probable possibility, not even as a long shot for the distant future, in my opinion. I agree that you might clone some people who would look amazingly like their parental cell donors, but the odds are that they'd be almost as different as you or me, and certainly more different than any of today's identical twins.

Thesis: Cloning human beings is not really possible.

6 The time required for the experiment is only one of the problems, but a formidable one. Suppose you wanted to clone a prominent, spectacularly successful diplomat, to look after the Middle East problems of the distant future. You'd have to catch him and persuade him, probably not very hard to do, and extirpate a cell. But then you'd have to wait for him to grow up through embryonic life and then for at least forty years more, and you'd have to be sure all observers remained patient and unmeddlesome through his unpromising, ambiguous childhood and adolescence.

Reason 1: Time involved

"valuable person"

7 Moreover, you'd have to be sure of recreating his environment, perhaps down to the last detail. "Environment" is a word which really means people, so you'd have to do a lot more cloning than just the diplomat himself.

Reason 2: Environment would have to be created

8 This is a very important part of the cloning problem, largely overlooked in our excitement about the cloned individual himself. You don't have to agree all the way with B. F. Skinner to acknowledge that the environment does make a difference, and when you examine what we really mean by the word "environment" it comes down to other human beings. We use euphemisms and jargon for this, like "social forces," "cultural influences," even Skinner's "verbal community," but what is meant is the dense crowd of nearby people who talk to, listen to, smile or frown at, give to, withhold from, nudge, push, caress, or flail out at the individual. No matter what the genome says, these people have a lot to do with shaping a char-

To be the same, the clone would have to have the same environment

genome: genetic organism

acter. Indeed, if all you had was the genome, and no people around, you'd grow a sort of vertebrate plant, nothing more.

9 So, to start with, you will undoubtedly need to clone the parents. No question about this. This means the diplomat is out, even in theory, since you couldn't have gotten cells from both his parents at the time when he was himself just recognizable as an early social treasure. You'd have to limit the list of clones to people already certified as sufficiently valuable for the effort, with both parents still alive. The parents would need cloning and, for consistency, their parents as well. I suppose you'd also need the usual informed-consent forms, filled out and signed, not easy to get if I know parents, even harder for grandparents.

Casual chain: clone parents, grandparents, family, people outside the family who came in contact with the individual, the whole world.

10 But this is only the beginning. It is the whole family that really influences the way a person turns out, not just the parents, according to current psychiatric thinking. Clone the family.

11 Then what? The way each member of the family develops has already been determined by the environment set around him, and this environment is more people, people outside the family, schoolmates, acquaintances, lovers, enemies, carpool partners, even, in special circumstances, peculiar strangers across the aisle on the subway. Find them, and clone them.

12 But there is no end to the protocol. Each of the outer contacts has his own surrounding family, and his and their outer contacts. Clone them all.

Isn't this an exaggeration?

13 To do the thing properly, with any hope of ending up with a genuine duplicate of a single person, you really have no choice. You must clone the world, no less.

14 We are not ready for an experiment of this size, nor, I should think, are we willing. For one thing, it would mean replacing today's world by an entirely identical world to follow immediately, and this means no new, natural, spontaneous, random, chancy children. No children at all, except for the manufactured doubles of those now on the scene. Plus all those identical adults, including all of to-

He's really joking here

day's politicians, all seen double. It is too much to contemplate.

Moreover, when the whole experiment is finally finished, fifty years or so from now, how could you get a responsible scientific reading on the outcome? Somewhere in there would be the original clonee, probably lost and overworked, now well into middle age, but everyone around him would be precise duplicates of today's everyone. It would be today's same world, filled to overflowing with duplicates of today's people and their same, duplicated problems, probably all resentful at having had to go through our whole thing all over, sore enough at the clone to make endless trouble for him, if they found him. 15

With the world cloned, everything would be the same, leading to dissatisfaction

And obviously, if the whole thing were done precisely right, they would still be casting about for ways to solve the problem of universal dissatisfaction, and sooner or later they'd surely begin to look around at each other, wondering who should be cloned for his special value to society, to get us out of all this. And so it would go, in regular cycles, perhaps forever. 16

I once lived through a period when I wondered what Hell could be like, and I stretched my imagination to try to think of a perpetual sort of damnation. I have to confess, I never thought of anything like this. 17

I have an alternative suggestion, if you're looking for a way out. Set cloning aside, and don't try it. Instead, go in the other direction. Look for ways to get mutations more quickly, new variety, different songs. Fiddle around, if you must fiddle, but never with ways to keep things the same, no matter who, not even yourself. Heaven, somewhere ahead, has got to be a change. 18

The author's real purpose comes out here; ties to paragraph 4.

PREREADING NOTES

The headnote indicates that the author, Lewis Thomas, was a physician and medical researcher and that most of his essays—including this one—were written for the New England Journal of

Medicine. These facts and the title "On Cloning a Human Being" initially suggest that this will be a pretty serious, probably dry essay and that it may be full of a lot of technical information. However, scanning the essay by looking at the first sentence in each paragraph shows the tone to be fairly informal: paragraph 5, for example, begins, "Well, don't think about it. . . ." It is also clear from a quick scan of the essay that it is really on not cloning a human being. Thomas is focusing on the problems involved in cloning human beings and seems to say that it will never happen.

READING NOTES

Outline:

par. 1 Introduction to cloning and predictions that "especially valuable people" will be cloned

pars. 2–4 Worries about cloning

par. 5 Thomas says cloning "isn't a probable possibility"

par. 6 Reason 1: Too much time involved in any experiment with human cloning

pars. 7–15 Reason 2: Since individuals are shaped by their environments, to clone a person would require cloning his or her parents, grandparents, the whole family, "the world, no less." People are not ready to replace today's world with "an entirely identical world to follow immediately," so everyone would hate the original clonee for causing all the trouble.

par. 16 The cloning cycle would have to start again to duplicate someone who could "solve the problem of universal dissatisfaction" with the original cloning experiment.

par. 17 To Thomas, this would be worse than Hell.

par. 18 Instead of cloning, it would be better to experiment with "ways to get mutations more quickly, new variety, different songs."

After an initial reading, it is clear that Thomas's subject is cloning and predictions that "valuable people" will be cloned experimentally in the future. He states his thesis explicitly in paragraph 5: cloning "isn't a probable possibility, not even as a long shot for the distant future. . . ." Even though the essay was written for the New England Journal of Medicine, it would seem that Thomas intended to reach a general educated audience; for example, he includes very little specialized terminology and doesn't assume any particular medical or scientific expertise. His purpose seems to be basically to inform, to explain to his audience why cloning of human beings isn't likely to happen in the future.

But in explaining why human beings aren't likely to be cloned, Thomas gives reasons that seem exaggerated. Could it really be necessary to clone the whole world, as he says? Why would he want to suggest that the effects of cloning a single human being would be so drastic?

REREADING NOTES

Rereading the essay reveals that Thomas is deliberately pushing the idea of cloning a human being to the point of absurdity. His tone is humorous from the beginning: in paragraph 2, for example, he lists as some of our worries about science—"transplanted heads, computer poetry, and the unrestrained growth of plastic flowers." When he describes the effects of an experiment in cloning an important diplomat and what would really be required to clone a human being (pars. 10–13), he builds each paragraph up to its logical—and increasingly absurd—conclusion: "Clone the family." "Find them, and clone them." "Clone them all." "You must clone the world, no less." In paragraph 14 he pushes the absurdity one step further, imagining a world where there are no longer unique children who grow up to be unique adults but only identical doubles of those who already exist—"including all of today's politicians. . . . It is too much to contemplate." The next two paragraphs continue in this vein, ending with the most absurd idea of all: that another cloning would have to take place of the person who could get everyone out of this mess. "And so it would go," Thomas says, "in regular cycles, perhaps forever."

Thomas is saying that it is absurd to imagine that an exact replica of another human being could ever be cloned; given the fact that the clone would necessarily grow up under different influences, the two might look alike, but "they'd be almost as different as you and me, and certainly more different than any of today's identical twins" (par. 5). Moreover, an even more substantial point emerges on rereading: there can be no benefit from cloning human beings to begin with. "Precise sameness," Thomas says, "is terrifying" (par. 4), an idea that he returns to in his conclusion, where he suggests that it is better for humans to experiment with "mutations," "variety," and "change" than with clones.

Thomas's purpose, therefore, seems to be more than simply informing readers about the impossibility of creating a human clone; at the core, he is arguing for a view of human nature that recognizes the value of "variety" over some standard of "perfection," and his method is to do so in an entertainingly humorous way.

Each of the essays in the sixth edition of *The Prentice Hall Reader* will repay you for the time and effort you put into reading it carefully and critically. Each essay shows an artful craftsperson at work, solving the problems inherent in communicating experiences, feelings, ideas, and opinions to an audience. Each writer is someone from whom you, as a reader and as a thinker, can learn. So when your instructor assigns a selection from the text, remember that as a reader you must assume an active role. Don't assume that reading an essay once—to see what it is "about"—will mean that you are prepared to write about it or that you have learned all that you can learn from the essay. Ask questions, seek answers to those questions, analyze, and reread.

Some Things to Remember When Reading

1. Read the headnote to the selection. How does this information help you understand the writer and the context in which the selection was written?
2. Look at the questions that precede and follow each reading. They will help focus your attention on the important aspects of the selection. After you read, write out answers to each question.
3. Read through the selection first to see what happens and to satisfy your curiosity.

4. Reread the selection several times, taking notes or underlining as you go.
5. Write or locate in the essay a thesis statement. Remember that the thesis is the particular point that the writer is trying to make about the subject.
6. Define a purpose for the essay. Why is the writer writing? Does the author make that purpose explicit?
7. Imagine the audience for such an essay. Who is the likely reader? What does that reader already know about the subject? Is the reader likely to have any preconceptions or prejudices about the subject?
8. Isolate a structure in the selection. How is it put together? Into how many parts can it be divided? How do those parts work together? Outline the essay.
9. Be sure that you understand every sentence. How does the writer vary the sentence structures?
10. Look up every word that you cannot define with some degree of certainty. Remember that you might misinterpret what the author is saying if you simply skip over the unfamiliar words.
11. Reread the essay one final time, reassembling its parts into the artful whole that it was intended to be.

How to Write an Essay

Watching a performance, whether it is athletic or artistic, our attention is focused on the achievement displayed in that moment. In concentrating on the performance, however, we might forget about the extensive practice that lies behind that achievement. Writing is no different. Typically, writers rely on perspiration, not inspiration. An effective final product depends on careful preliminary work.

A Writer's Subject

The first step in writing is to determine a subject, what a piece of writing is about. The majority of writing tasks that you face either in school or on the job require you to write in response to a specific assignment. Your instructor, for example, might ask you to use the specific writing suggestions that follow each reading in this book. Before you begin work on any writing assignment, take time to study what is being asked. What limits have already been placed on the assignment? What are the key words (for example, *compare, analyze, define*) used in the assignment?

Once you have a subject, the next step is to restrict, focus, or narrow that subject into a workable topic. Although the words *subject* and *topic* are sometimes used interchangeably, think of *subject* as the broader, more general word. You move from a subject to a *topic* by limiting or restricting what you will include or cover. The shift from subject to topic is a gradual one that is not marked by a clearly definable line. Just remember that a topic is a more restricted version of a larger subject.

A Writer's Purpose

A writer writes to fulfill three fundamental purposes: *to entertain*, *to inform*, and *to persuade*. Obviously, those purposes are not necessarily separate: an interesting, maybe even humorous, essay that documents the health hazards caused by smoking can, at the same time, attempt to persuade the reader to give up smoking. In this case the main purpose is still persuasion; entertainment and information play subordinate roles in catching the reader's interest and in providing appropriate evidence for the argument being advanced.

These three purposes are generally associated with the traditional division of writing into four forms—narration, description, exposition (including classification, comparison and contrast, process, cause and effect, and definition), and argumentation. *Narrative* or *descriptive essays* typically tell a story or describe a person, object, or place in order to entertain a reader and re-create the experience. *Expository essays* primarily provide information for a reader. *Argumentative* or *persuasive essays* seek to move a reader, to gain support, to advocate a particular type of action.

A Writer's Audience

Audience is a key factor in every writing situation. Writing is, after all, a form of communication and as such implies an audience. In many writing situations, your audience is a controlling factor that affects both the content of your paper and the style in which it is written. An effective writer learns to adjust to an audience and to write for that audience, for a writer, like a performer, needs and wants an audience.

Writers adjust their style and tone on a spectrum ranging from informal to formal. Articles that appear in popular, wide-circulation magazines often are written in the first person, use contractions, favor popular and colloquial words, and contain relatively short sentences and paragraphs. Articles in more scholarly journals exhibit a formal style that involves an objective and serious tone, a more advanced vocabulary, and longer and more complicated sentence and paragraph constructions. In the informal style, the writer injects his or her personality into the prose; in the formal style, the writer remains detached and impersonal. A writer adopts whatever style seems appropriate for a particular audience or context. An effective writer does not have just one style or voice but many.

Some Things to Remember

Before you begin to prewrite, you need to think about your subject, purpose, and audience. Remind yourself of their importance in your writing process by completing the following sentences:

1. My general subject is _____________ .
2. My more specific topic is _____________ .
3. My purpose is to _____________ .
4. My intended audience is _____________ .

A Writer's Information

What makes writing entertaining, informative, or persuasive is information—specific, relevant detail. If you try to write without gathering information, you end up skimming the surface of your subject, even if you "know" something about it.

How you go about gathering information on your topic depends on your subject and your purpose for writing. Some topics, such as those involving a personal experience, require a memory search; other assignments, such as describing a particular place, require careful observation. Essays that convey information or argue particular positions often require gathering information through research. Some possible strategies for gathering information and ideas about your topic are listed here. Before you start this step in your prewriting, remember three things.

First, remember that *different tactics work for different topics and for different writers.* You might find that freewriting is great for some assignments but not for others. As a writer, explore your options. Don't rule out any strategy until you have tried it. Second, remember that *prewriting activities sometimes produce information and sometimes just produce questions that you will then need to answer.* In other words, prewriting often involves learning what you don't know, what you need to find out. Learning to ask the right questions is just as important as knowing the right answers. Third, remember that *these prewriting activities are an excellent way in which to find a focus, to narrow a subject, or to suggest a working plan for your essay.* As you begin to explore a subject or topic, the possibilities spread out before you. Try not to be wedded to a particular topic or thesis until you have explored a subject through prewriting activities.

Listing Details from Personal Experience or Observation

Even your most unforgettable experience has probably been forgotten in part. If you are going to re-create it for a reader, you will have to do some active searching among your memories. By focusing your attention, you can slowly recall more details. Ask yourself a series of questions about the chronology of the experience. For example, start with a particular detail and then try to stimulate your memory: What happened just before? Just after? Who was there? Where did the experience take place? Why did it happen? When did it happen? How did it happen?

Sense impressions, like factual details, fade from memory. In the height of the summer, it is not easy to recall a crisp fall day. Furthermore, sensory details are not always noticed, let alone recorded. How many times have you passed by a particular location without really seeing it?

Descriptions, like every other form of writing, demand specific information, and the easiest way to gather that detail is to observe. Before you try to describe a person, place, or object, take some time to list specific details on a piece of paper. At first record everything you notice. Do not worry about having too much, for you can always edit later. At this stage it is better to have too much than to have too little.

The next step is to decide what to include in your description and what to exclude. As a general principle, an effective written description does not try to record everything. The selection of detail should be governed by your purpose in the description. Ask yourself what you are trying to show or reveal. For what reason? What is particularly important about this person, place, or object? A description is not the verbal equivalent of a photograph or a tape recording.

Freewriting

Putting words down on a page or a computer screen can be very intimidating. Your editing instincts immediately want to take over—are the words spelled correctly? Are the sentences complete? Do they contain any mechanical or grammatical errors? Not only must you express your ideas in words, but suddenly those words must be the correct words.

When you translate thoughts into written words and edit those words at the same time, writing can seem impossible. Instead of allowing ideas to take shape in words or allowing the writing to stimulate your thinking, you become fearful of committing anything to paper.

Writing, however, can stimulate thought. Every writer has experienced times when an idea became clear because it was written down. If those editing instincts can be turned off, you can use writing as a way of generating ideas about a paper.

Freewriting is an effective way to deal with this dilemma. Write without stopping for a fixed period of time—a period as short as ten minutes or as long as an hour. Do not stop; do not edit; do not worry about mistakes. If you find yourself stuck for something to write, repeat the last word or phrase you wrote until a new thought comes to mind. You are looking for a focus point—an idea or a subject for a paper. You are trying to externalize your thinking into writing. What emerges is a free association of ideas. Some are relevant; some are worthless. After you have ideas on paper, you can then decide what is worth saving, developing, or simply throwing away.

You can also do freewriting on a computer. One technique many writers find effective is to use the contrast control to darken the screen until it is completely black. Then as you write you won't be distracted by errors and typos or be tempted to stop and read what you have already written. Freewriting in this way provides an opportunity to free-associate almost as you might when you are speaking.

Journals

A daily journal can be an effective seedbed of ideas for writing projects. Such a journal should not be a daily log of your activities (got up, went to class, had lunch) but rather a place where you record ideas, observations, memories, and feelings. Set aside a specific notebook or a pad of paper in which to keep your journal. Try to write for at least ten minutes every day. Over a period of time—such as a semester—you will be surprised how many ideas for papers or projects you will accumulate. When you are working on a paper, you might want to confine part of your daily journal entries to that particular subject.

Brainstorming and Mapping

Brainstorming is oral freewriting among a group of people jointly trying to solve a problem by spontaneously contributing ideas. Whatever comes to mind, no matter how obvious or unusual, gets said. The hope is that out of the jumble of ideas that surface, some possible solutions to the problem will be found.

Although brainstorming is by definition a group activity, it can also be done by the individual writer. In the center of a blank sheet of paper, write down a key word or phrase referring to your subject. Then in the space around your subject, quickly jot down any ideas that come to mind. Do not write in sentences—just key words and phrases. Because you are not filling consecutive lines with words and because you have space in which the ideas can be arranged, this form of brainstorming often suggests structural relationships. You can increase the usefulness of such an idea generator by adding graphic devices such as circles, arrows, or connecting lines to indicate the possible relationships among ideas. These devices can be added to your brainstorming sheet later, and they become a map to the points you might want to cover in your essay.

Formal Questioning

One particularly effective way to gather information on any topic is to ask yourself questions about it. This allows you to explore the subject from a variety of angles. After all, the secret to finding answers always lies in knowing the right questions to ask. A good place to start is with the list of questions presented here. Remember, though, that not every question is appropriate for every topic.

Illustration

1. What examples of ____________ can be found?
2. In what ways are these things examples of ____________?

3. What details about ____________ seem the most important?

Comparison and Contrast

1. To what is ____________ similar? List the points of similarity.
2. From what is ____________ different? List the points of difference.
3. Which points of similarity or difference seem most important?
4. What does the comparison or contrast tell the reader about ____________ ?

Division and Classification

1. Into how many parts can ____________ be divided?
2. How many parts is ____________ composed of?
3. What other category of things is ____________ most like?
4. How does ____________ work?
5. What are ____________'s component parts?

Process

1. How many steps or stages are involved in ____________?
2. In what order do those steps or stages occur?

Cause and Effect

1. What precedes ____________?
2. Is that a cause of ____________?
3. What follows ____________?
4. Is that an effect of ____________?
5. How many causes of ____________ can you find?
6. How many effects of ____________ can you find?
7. Why does ____________ happen?

Definition

1. How is ____________ defined in a dictionary?
2. Does everyone agree about the meaning of ____________?
3. Does ____________ have any connotations? What are they?
4. Has the meaning of ____________ changed over time?
5. What words are synonymous with ____________?

Argument and Persuasion

1. How do your readers feel about ____________?
2. How do you feel about ____________?
3. What are the arguments in favor of ____________? List those arguments in order of strength.
4. What are the arguments against ____________? List those arguments in order of strength.

INTERVIEWING

Typically you gather information for college papers by locating printed or electronic sources—books, articles, reports, e-texts. Depending on your topic, however, printed or electronic sources are not always available. In that case, people often represent a great source of information for a writer. Obviously you should choose someone who has special credentials or knowledge about the subject.

Interviewing requires some special skills and tact. When you first contact someone to request an interview, always explain who you are, what you want to know, and how you will use the information. Remember that specific questions will produce more useful information than general ones. Take notes that you can expand later, or use a tape recorder. Keep attention focused on the information that you need, and do not be afraid to ask questions to keep your informant on the subject. If you plan to use direct quotations, make sure that the wording is accurate. If possible, check the quotations with your source one final time.

A WRITER'S THESIS

For informative and argumentative essays, the information-gathering stage of the writing process is the time in which to sharpen your topic and to define first a tentative or working thesis for your paper and then a final thesis. Even narrative and descriptive essays may be strengthened by the development of a thesis at this stage.

Thesis is derived from a Greek word that means "placing" or "position" or "proposition." When you formulate a thesis, you are defining your position on the subject. A thesis lets your reader know exactly where you stand. Because it represents your "final" position, a thesis is typically something that you develop and refine as you move through the prewriting stage, testing out ideas and gathering information. Don't try to start with a final thesis; begin with a tentative thesis (also called a *hypothesis*, from the Greek for "supposition"). Allow your final position to emerge based on what you have discovered in the prewriting stage.

Before you write a thesis statement, you need to consider the factors that will control or influence the form your thesis will take. For example, a thesis is a reflection of your purpose in writing. If your purpose is to persuade your audience to do or to believe something, your thesis will urge the reader to accept that position. If your purpose is to convey information to your reader, your thesis will forecast your main points and indicate how your paper will be organized.

Your thesis will also be shaped by the scope and length of your paper. Your topic and your thesis must be manageable within the space you have available; otherwise, you end up skimming the surface. A short paper requires a more precise focus than a longer one. As a result, when you move from subject to topic to thesis, make sure that each step is more specific and has an increasingly sharper focus. To check that focusing process, ask yourself the following questions:

- What is my general subject?
- What is my specific topic within that general subject area?
- What is my position on that specific topic?

Writing a Thesis Statement

When you have answered the questions about your purpose, when you have sharpened your general subject into a topic, when you have defined your position toward that topic, you are ready to write a thesis statement. The process is simple. You write a thesis statement by linking together your topic and your position on that topic.

Subject: Violence on television

Topic: The impact that viewing televised violence has on young children

Thesis: Televised violence makes young children numb to violence in the real world, distorts their perceptions of how people behave, and teaches them how to be violent.

An effective thesis, like any position statement, has a number of characteristics.

1. A thesis should clearly signal the purpose of the paper.
2. A thesis should state or take a definite position. It tells the reader what will be covered in the paper.
3. A thesis should express that definite position in precise, familiar terms. Avoid vague, abstract, or complicated technical terms.
4. A thesis should offer a position that can be explored or expanded within the scope of the paper. Remember that in moving from a general subject to a thesis, you have narrowed and sharpened your focus.

Placing a Thesis in Your Paper

Once you have written a thesis for your paper or essay, you must make two final decisions. First, you have to decide whether to include that explicit statement in your paper or just allow your paper's structure and content to imply the thesis. Second, if you decide to include a thesis statement, you must determine where to place it in your paper. For example, should it appear in the first paragraph or at some point later in the paper?

If you look carefully at examples of professional writing, you will discover that neither question has a single answer. Writers make these decisions based on the type of paper they are writing. As a student, however, you can follow several guidelines. Most pieces of writing done in college—either papers or essay examinations—should have explicit thesis statements. Typically, those statements should be placed early in the paper (although the thesis for a narrative or descriptive essay may typically come at the end). The thesis will not always be in the first paragraph, as your introduction might be designed to attract a reader's attention. Nevertheless, placing a thesis statement early in your paper will guarantee that the reader knows exactly what to expect.

Every argumentative or persuasive paper should have an explicitly stated thesis. Where you place that thesis depends on whether the paper is structured deductively or inductively. A deductive argument begins with a general truth and then moves to a specific application of that truth, so such an arrangement requires that the thesis be stated early. Conversely, an inductive argument moves in the opposite direction, starting with specific evidence and then moving to a conclusion, an arrangement that requires that the thesis be withheld until near the end of the paper.

Similarly, whenever your strategy in a paper is to build to a conclusion, a realization, or a discovery, you can withhold an explicit statement of your thesis until late in the paper. An early statement would spoil the suspense.

Revising an Essay

The idea of revising a paper may not sound appealing in the least. By the time you have finished the paper, the last thing you want to do is revise it. Nevertheless, revising is a crucial step in the writing process, one you cannot afford to skip.

The word *revision* literally means "to see again." You do not revise a paper just by proofreading it for mechanical and grammatical errors, which is an expected final step in the writing process. Instead, a revision takes place after a draft of a whole paper or part of it has been completed, after a period of time has elapsed and you have had a chance to get some advice or criticism on what you wrote, after you can see what you wrote, not what you *think* you wrote. Revision should also involve an active, careful scrutiny on your part of every aspect of your paper—your subject, thesis, purpose, audience, paragraph structures, sentence constructions, and word choice.

Beginning a Revision

Revision should start not with the smallest unit—the choice of a particular word—but with the largest—the choice of subject, thesis, purpose, audience, and organization. A revision in its broadest sense involves a complete rethinking of a paper from idea through execution. Once you have finished a paper, think first about these five groups of questions—if possible, write out answers to each:

1. What is my *subject?* Is it too large? Too small? Is it interesting? Is it fresh or informative?

2. What is my *thesis?* Do I have a precise position on my subject? Have I stated that thesis in a single sentence? Do I see the difference between having a subject and having a thesis?
3. What is my *purpose?* Why did I write *this* paper? Have I expressed my purpose in my thesis statement? Is everything in the paper related to that purpose?
4. Whom do I imagine as my *audience?* Who will read this? What do these people already know about the subject? Have I written the paper with that audience in mind?
5. How is my paper *structured?* Have I followed the advice on structure given in the chapter introductions to this text? Is the organization of my paper clear and inevitable? Can it be outlined easily? Have I provided enough examples and details?

Using the Advice of Others

Another great help in revising is to find an editor or a critic. If your writing instructor has the time to look at your draft or if your college or university has a writing center or a writing tutor program, you can get the advice of an experienced, trained reader. If your paper or part of it is discussed in class, listen to your classmates' comments as a way of gauging how successful your writing has been. If your writing class uses peer editing, you can study the responses of your editors for possible areas for revision.

Peer evaluation works best when readers start with a series of specific directions—questions to answer or things to look for. If you are interested in trying peer evaluation, you and a classmate could start with an editing checksheet adapted from the "Some Things to Remember" section at the end of each introductory chapter in this book. Whenever you are responding to someone else's writing, remember that your comments are always more valuable if they are specific and suggest ways in which changes could be made.

It is often difficult to accept criticism, but if you want to improve your writing skills, you need someone to say, "Why not do this?" After all, you expect that an athletic coach or a music or dance teacher will offer criticism. Your writing instructor plays the same role, and the advice and criticism he or she offers is meant to make your writing more effective; it is not intended as a personal criticism of you or your abilities.

Judging Length

After you have finished a draft of a paper, look carefully at how your response measures up to your instructor's guidelines about the length of the paper. Such guidelines are important in that they give you some idea of the amount of space that you will need to develop and illustrate your thesis sufficiently. If your papers are consistently short, you have probably not included enough examples or illustrating details. Writing the suggested number of words does not, of course, guarantee a good essay, but writing only half of the suggested number because you fail to develop and illustrate your thesis can result in a lower grade.

Similarly, if your papers consistently exceed your instructor's guidelines, you have probably not sufficiently narrowed your subjects or you may have included too many details and examples. Of the material available to support, develop, and illustrate a thesis, some is more significant and relevant than the rest. Never try to include everything—select the best, the most appropriate, the most convincing.

Checking Paragraphs

The qualities of a good paragraph—things like unity, coherence, organization, and completeness—have been stressed in every writing course you have taken. When you revise your paper, look carefully at each paragraph to see if it exhibits those qualities. How often have you paragraphed? If you have only one or two paragraphs in a several-page essay, you have not clearly indicated the structure of your essay to your reader or your essay does not have a clear, logical organization. At the opposite extreme, if you have many short paragraphs, you are overparagraphing, probably shifting ideas too quickly and failing to develop each one adequately. A good paragraph is meaty; a good essay is not a string of undeveloped ideas or bare generalizations.

Is an Error-Free Paper an "A" Paper?

Although good, effective writing is mechanically and grammatically correct, you cannot reverse the equation. It is perfectly possible to write a paper that has no "errors" but is still a poor paper. An effective paper fulfills the requirements of the assignment, has something interesting or meaningful to say, and provides specific evidence and examples rather than vague generalizations. Effective writing is a combination of many factors: appropriate content, focused purpose, clear organization, and fluent expression.

Although perfect grammar and mechanics do not make a perfect paper, such things are important. Minor errors are like static in your writing. Too many of them distract your reader and focus the reader's attention not on your message but on your apparent carelessness. Minor errors can undermine your reader's confidence in you as a qualified authority. If you make errors in spelling or punctuation, for example, your reader might assume that you made similar errors in reporting information. So while revision is not just proofreading, proofreading should be a part of the revision process.

When you draft using a computer, always print out a hard-copy version of your paper for proofreading. Most writers find that they miss more errors when they proofread only on screen. Also keep in mind that while your word processor's spell-check function will catch many spelling errors, it won't identify mistakes that occur because two words sound alike but are spelled differently (*its* and *it's*, for example) or typos that result in a correctly spelled word (such as *the* for *they*). You need to proofread carefully yourself for mistakes like these.

A Student Writer's Revision Process

The writing and rewriting process as outlined in this section can be seen in the evolution of Tina Burton's essay "The Watermelon Wooer." Tina's essay was written in response to a totally open assignment: she was asked to write an essay using examples, due in three weeks. The openness of the assignment proved initially frustrating to Tina. When she first began work on an essay, she started with a completely different topic. That weekend, however, she went home to visit her parents. Her grandfather had died a few months before, and the family was sorting through some photographs and reminiscing about him. Suddenly, Tina had the idea she wanted: she would write about her grandfather and her ambivalent feelings toward him. Once she had defined this specific topic, she also determined her purpose (to inform about her grandfather and her mixed feelings, as well as to entertain through a vivid description of this unusual old man) and her audience (her instructor and classmates).

Tina's first written work on the assignment came when she made a list of about thirty things that she remembered about him. "The list had to be cut," Tina said, "so I marked off things that were too bawdy or too unbelievable. I wanted to portray him as sympathetic," she added, "but I was really afraid that the whole piece would come off as too sentimental or drippy."

At the next class meeting, the instructor set aside some time for prewriting activities. The teacher recommended that the students try either a freewriting or a brainstorming exercise. Tina did the brainstorming that appears next.

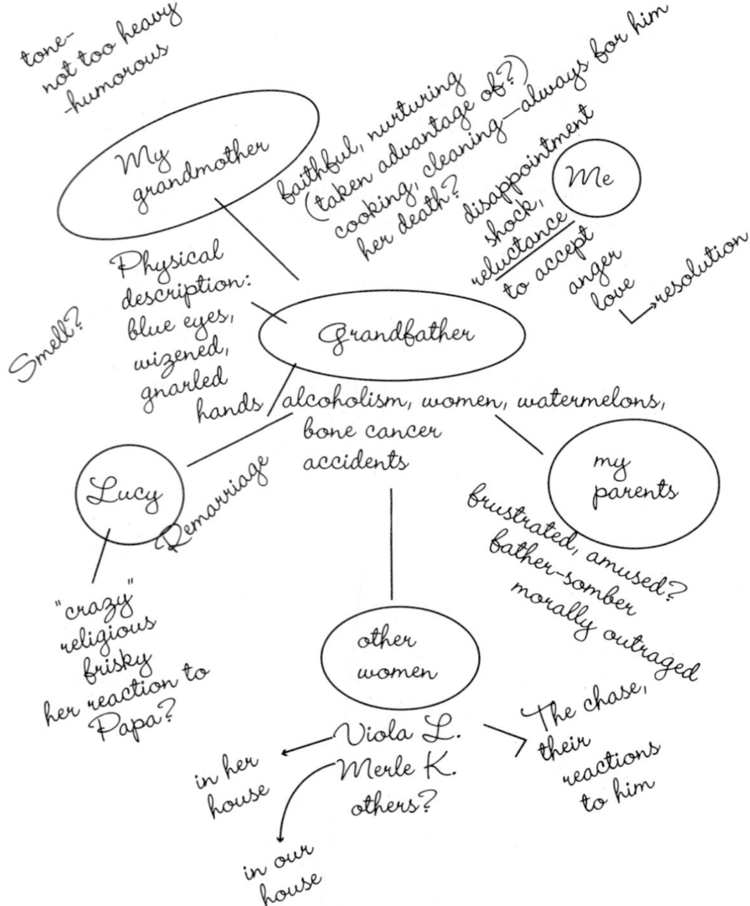

Earlier Draft

From here, Tina wrote a complete draft in one sitting. She had the most difficulty with the beginning of the essay. "I kept trying to describe him, but I found that I was including too much," she commented. The breakthrough came through the advice of two other students in the class. The first page of the first draft of Tina's essay follows. The handwritten comments were provided by Kathrine Varnes.

THE WATERMELON WOOER

When someone you love dearly behaves in a manner that offends you, do you stop loving that person? Do you lose all respect for that person because you cannot forget the repulsive [?] act that you judged as repulsive? Eventually,? On the contrary,* you might eventually fondly recall the once offensive behavior. Perhaps, in time, you might even understand why you found the behavior so? loathesome. Maybe, you will reach a point in time when you will be unable to think of your loved one without thinking of the once questionable behavior. Such is the case with my grandfather.

*I have a personal dislike for this 3-word transition

someway to condense?

Before I tell the story of how my grandfather behaved in ways that I could neither

understand nor tolerate, I must first (give some
introduce?
background information on) him. A wizened little man with dancing blue eyes and hands gnarled from years of carpentry work, "Papa" was a notorious womanizer and an alcoholic. Born and raised in Halifax County, Virginia, he spent most of his life building houses, distilling and selling corn liquor, and chasing women. After he and my grandmother had been married for thirty years or so, he decided to <u>curtail some of his wild behavior and treat her with more respect.</u> Actually, he remained faithful to her only after he discovered that she was ill and probably wouldn't be around to feed and nurture him for much longer. ~~So, as you can see~~, my grandfather didn't (does not) have a <u>spot</u>less, or even a remotely commendable reputation (record of personal achievements.)

both of these things? or respect by curtailing?

Use alternative diction to soften tone?

Revised Draft

"Kathrine wanted me to condense and to find a way in which to jump right into the essay," Tina noted. "She also said, 'You're trying to tell too much. Let the story tell itself. Try to think of one thing that might capture something essential or important about him.'" In a second peer edit, Tina sought the advice of Stephen Palley, another classmate. Stephen offered these comments on this first page of the second draft.

THE WATERMELON WOOER

characterize an essential part of his eccentricity

my grandfather never really (settled down)

Let me tell you a story about my grandfather ~~—and, I guess, me too~~. ~~I don't pretend to know whether my story will shock, offend, amuse, or bore~~. I only know that I feel the need to tell ~~the story~~ it.

Intro?

For a time he

~~Before I tell the story of how my grandfather~~ behaved in ways that I could neither understand nor tolerate, I must first introduce him.

but eventually

(I see him now) Let me introduce

introduce him. A wizened little man with ~~dancing blue eyes~~ and hands ~~gnarled from years of carpentry work~~, "Papa" was a notorious womanizer and an alcoholic. Born and raised in Halifax County, Virginia, he spent most of his life building houses, distilling and selling corn liquor, and chasing women. After he and my grandmother had been married for thirty years or so, he decided to show her some respect by curtailing his wild behavior. Actually, he remained faithful to her only after he discovered that she was ill and probably wouldn't be around to feed and nurture him for much longer. Papa didn't have a spotless reputation.

smell?

It's funny but when I think of my grandfather I think 1st of the way he smelled

Miller ponies, fertilizer

"Stephen offered me quite a few helpful suggestions," Tina recalled, "but he also suggested something that I just didn't quite feel comfortable with." As you can see in the revised draft, Tina had queried Stephen about possibly including her memories of odor. In a conversation Stephen urged Tina to substitute memories of smells for memories of sight. In the end, though, Tina observed, "I just couldn't do what Stephen suggested."

Final Draft

Before the three weeks were over, Tina actually wrote five separate drafts of her essay. "Everything here is true," she said, "but I worried so much about what I included, because I didn't want to embarrass anyone in my family. Throughout the process," she added, "I was also worried about my tone. I wanted it to be funny; I wanted my readers to like my grandfather and his watermelon adventures."

Reproduced here is Tina's final draft of her essay. Note that she concludes with a thesis that summarizes her main point.

THE WATERMELON WOOER

Tina M. Burton

I see him now, sprawled on our couch, clutching a frayed afghan, one brown toenail escaping his sock. His darting eyes are betraying his withered body.

Born and raised in backwoods Virginia, my grandfather spent most of his life building houses, distilling and selling corn liquor, and chasing women. After he and my grandmother had been married for thirty years or so, he decided to show her some respect by curtailing his wild behavior. Actually, he remained faithful to her only after he discovered that she was ill and probably wouldn't be around to feed and nurture him much longer. Papa didn't have a spotless reputation.

Because he'd been on the wagon for several years and hadn't had any affairs for the last ten years, my family thought that Papa would continue to behave in a "respectable" manner even after my grandmother died. I guess we were hoping for some sort of miracle. After my grandmother died in 1983, Papa became a rogue again: he insisted on reveling in wild abandon. When my father found out that Papa was drinking heavily again and crashing his car into mailboxes, houses, and other large obstacles, he asked Papa to move into our house. The fact that three of Papa's female neighbors had complained to the police about Papa's exposing himself probably had something to do with my father's decision.

The year that Papa lived with us rivaled the agony of Hell.

I was always Papa's favorite grandchild, his "gal," and I worshipped him from the time that I was old enough to spend summers with him on his farm. Until I saw him every day, witnessed for myself his sometimes lewd behavior and his odd personality quirks, I never really believed the stories about him that I had heard from my mother and father. Every morning, he baited my mother with comments like "the gravy's too thick," "my room's too cold," "your kids are too loud," and "the phone rings too often." Against my mother's wishes, he smoked in the house. In mixed company, he gleefully explained how to have sex in an inner tube in the ocean without getting caught and gave detailed physical descriptions of the women he'd had sex with. It surprised me how much my opinion of Papa changed in one year.

During this one year, Papa did many things that I thought were embarrassing and inexcusable. I came face-to-face with the "dark" side of his personality. One week after moving into my parents' home, Papa began to sneak the orange juice from the refrigerator and doctor it with Smirnoff's vodka. I knew he'd been pickling his brain with alcohol for years and that this was part of the disease, but he'd said that he'd gone dry. Besides, he was violating my father's most important rule: no alcohol in the house. I didn't know that his drinking was only the first of a long line of incredible acts.

The behaviors that ultimately endeared Papa to me, that made me forgive him his shortcomings, are also those which I recall with a great deal of sadness. These are the memories of him that I treasure, the stories that I will tell to my grandchildren when they are old enough to deal with graphic material. A year ago, I never would have believed that I could fondly remember, much less write about, these episodes.

For about a year, Papa engaged in what I refer to as the "watermelon affairs." Perhaps because he had lived on a vegetable farm for the majority of his life Papa had a special affinity for a wide variety of fruits and vegetables. Especially dear to him were watermelons. So, he assumed that other elderly people, particularly women, shared his proclivity for produce. One week after he moved into my parent's house, he embarked upon his mission—to woo with watermelons as many women as he could.

A shrewd man, possessed of a generous supply of common sense and watermelons, Papa decided to seduce a woman who lived very close to him. This woman happened to be my maternal grandmother who also lived in our house. Unaware of his lascivious intentions and bent on helping him assuage his grief over the loss of his wife. Grandmother Merle prepared special meals for Papa and spent long hours conversing with him about farming, grandchildren, and life in the "Old South." Merle assumed that the watermelons Papa brought to her were nothing more than a token of his appreciation for her kindness. When Papa grabbed a part of Merle that she preferred to remain untouched, these conversations came to an abrupt halt. Of course, we were mortified by his inappropriate behavior, but I suspect that my parents secretly were amused. While Papa's indiscretion with Merle was upsetting, at least no one other than members of my immediate family knew about the incident. His next romantic adventure earned him immediate notoriety in the neighborhood. One afternoon, huge watermelon in hand, he trotted over to visit Viola Lampson, a decrepit and cranky elderly woman with whom my family had been friendly for twenty years. Twenty minutes after Papa entered her house, the police came. Poor Viola was in a state of disrepair because my grandfather had been chasing her around her kitchen table demanding kisses. Fortunately, the policeman who arrived at the scene of the crime was quite understanding and polite; he advised my father to keep a careful watch on Papa at all times. My somber father was very embarrassed. Finally, we were all beginning to see the relationship between watermelons and women. He'd disappear with a watermelon and return with the police.

I was mortified by Papa's lecherous desire for other women. After all, wasn't he supposed to be grieving over the death of my grandmother, his wife of fifty years? I resigned myself to the fact that I never would love him or respect him in the manner that I once had. For a while, I avoided his company and refused to answer his frequent questions about why I was avoiding him. I didn't think about why he was behaving the way he was; I simply cast judgement on his behavior and shut myself off from him. Not until Papa remarried did I even try to understand his needs or his behavior.

Approximately one year after his wife died, Papa remarried. Finally, he found a woman who not only loved watermelon but also loved him and his frisky behavior. Lucy, often referred to as "crazy Lucy" by her neighbors who had heard her speak of miracle healings and visions of Christ, wed Papa and took him into her already jam-packed home. Amazingly, she convinced him to stop drinking and to refrain from molesting other women. She could not, however, convince Papa to "get the religion" as she called it. My family was nonplussed both by Papa's decision to remarry at age 77 and to stop drinking after all these years. We all were annoyed by the fact that Lucy convinced him to do in several months what we had been trying to get him to do for many years.

Not until I learned that Papa was dying of bone cancer did I try to understand why he needed to remarry and why I found that fact unbearable. Until this time, I harbored the feeling that Papa somehow was degrading the memory of my grandmother by remarrying. His attempted seductions of women disturbed me, but his decision to marry Lucy saddened me. Only after I spent many afternoons with Papa and Lucy did I realize that they truly loved each other. More importantly, I realized that Papa, devastated by his wife's death, was afraid to be alone in his old age. Perhaps sensing his illness, even though he knew nothing of its development at this time, he wanted to recapture some of his stamina, some of his youth. He really wasn't searching for someone to replace my grandmother: he simply wanted to have a companion to comfort him, to distract him from his grief.

Fortunately, I accepted Papa's actions and resolved my conflict with him before he died. Once again, I was his "gal" in spirit, and I even came to love and respect Lucy. Now, I find that I cannot conjure images of Papa without thinking of watermelons and his romantic escapades. The acts that once troubled me eventually allowed me to glimpse the frail side of my grandfather, to see him as a human being possessed of fears and flaws rather than a cardboard ideal.

Some Things to Remember When Revising

1. Put your paper aside for a period of time before you attempt to revise it.
2. Seek the advice of your instructor or a writing center tutor or the help of classmates.
3. Reconsider your choice of topic. Were you able to treat it adequately in the space you had available?
4. State your thesis in a sentence as a way of checking your content. Is everything in the paper relevant to that thesis?
5. Check to make sure that you have given enough examples to clarify your topic, to support your argument, or to make your thesis clear. Relevant specifics convince and interest a reader.
6. Look through the advice given in each of the introductions to this text. Have you organized your paper carefully? Is its structure clear?
7. Define your audience. To whom are you writing? What assumptions have you made about your audience? What changes are necessary to make your paper clear and interesting to that audience?
8. Check the guidelines your instructor provided. Have you done what was asked? Is your paper too short or too long?
9. Examine each sentence to make sure that it is complete and grammatically correct. Try for a variety of sentence structures and lengths.
10. Look carefully at each paragraph. Does it obey the rules for effective paragraph construction? Do your paragraphs clearly indicate the structure of your essay?
11. Check your word choice. Have you avoided slang, jargon, and clichés? Have you used specific words? Have you used appropriate words for your intended audience?
12. Proofread one final time.

ONE

GATHERING AND USING EXAMPLES

Effective writing in any form depends on details and examples. Relevant details and examples make writing interesting, informative, and persuasive. If you try to write without having gathered these essential specifics, you are forced to skim the surface of your subject, relying on generalizations, incomplete and sometimes inaccurate details, and unsubstantiated opinions.

Without specifics, even a paper with a strong, clearly stated thesis becomes superficial. How convinced would you be by the following argument?

> In their quest for big-time football programs, American universities have lost sight of their educational responsibilities. Eager for the revenues and alumni support that come with winning teams, universities exploit their football players. They do not care if the players get an education. They care only that they remain academically eligible to play for four seasons. At many schools only a small percentage of these athletes graduate. Throughout their college careers, they are encouraged to take easy courses and to put athletics first. It does not matter how they perform in the classroom as long as they distinguish themselves every Saturday afternoon. This exploitation should not be allowed to continue. Universities have a responsibility to educate their students, not to use them to gain publicity and to raise money.

Even if you agree with the writer's thesis, the paragraph does not go beyond the obvious. The writer generalizes, and probably distorts as a result. What the reader gets is an opinion unsupported by any evidence. For example, you might reasonably ask questions about the statement "At many schools only a small percentage of these athletes graduate." How many schools? How small a percentage? How does this percentage compare with that of nonathletes? After all, not everyone who starts college ends up graduating. To persuade your reader—even just to interest your reader—you need specific information, details and examples that illustrate the points you are trying to make.

Where Can You Find Details and Examples?

You gather details and examples either from your own experiences and observations or from research. Your sources vary, depending on what you are writing about. For example, *Life* magazine once asked writer Malcolm Cowley for an essay on what it was like to turn eighty. Cowley was already eighty years old, so he had a wealth of firsthand experiences from which to draw. Since nearly all of Cowley's readers were younger than eighty, he decided to show his readers what it was like to be old by providing a simple list that begins like this:

> The body and its surroundings have their messages for him, or only one message: "You are old." Here are some of the occasions on which he receives the message:
>
> —when it becomes an achievement to do thoughtfully, step by step, what he once did instinctively
>
> —when his bones ache
>
> —when there are more and more little bottles in the medicine cabinet, with instructions for taking four times a day
>
> —when he fumbles and drops his toothbrush (butterfingers)
>
> —when his face has bumps and wrinkles, so that he cuts himself while shaving (blood on the towel)
>
> —when year by year his feet seem farther from his hands
>
> —when he can't stand on one leg and has trouble pulling on his pants
>
> —when he hesitates on the landing before walking down a flight of stairs
>
> —when he spends more time looking for things misplaced than he spends using them after he (or more often his wife) has found them

—when he falls asleep in the afternoon

—when it becomes harder to bear in mind two things at once

—when a pretty girl passes him in the street and he doesn't turn his head

Much of what you might be writing about, however, lies outside of your own experiences and observations. David Guterson, for example, set out to write a magazine article for *Harper's* about the Mall of America in Minneapolis. He chose to begin his essay with a series of facts:

> Last April, on a visit to the new Mall of America near Minneapolis, I carried with me the public-relations press kit provided for the benefit of reporters. It included an assortment of "fun facts" about the mall: 140,000 hot dogs sold each week, 10,000 permanent jobs, 44 escalators and 17 elevators, 12,750 parking places, 13,300 short tons of steel, $1 million in cash disbursed weekly from 8 automatic-teller machines. Opened in the summer of 1992, the mall was built on the 78-acre site of the former Metropolitan Stadium, a five-minute drive from the Minneapolis–St. Paul International Airport. With 4.2 million square feet of floor space—including twenty-two times the retail footage of the average American shopping center—the Mall of America was "the largest fully enclosed combination retail and family entertainment center in the United States."

The accumulation of facts—taken from the press kit—becomes a way of catching the reader's attention. In a nation impressed by size, what better way to "capture" the country's largest mall than by heaping up facts and statistics.

As the examples in this chapter show, writers sometimes draw exclusively on their personal experiences, as Anna Quindlen does in "The Name Is Mine." At other times, though, writers mix examples drawn from their personal experiences with information gathered from outside sources. Leslie Heywood in "One of the Girls" draws upon her own experiences as a Division I track and cross country runner, but then adds the examples of the athletic achievements of Gertrude Ederle and Kathrine Switzer. Heywood also reflects on the impact that Title IX has had on women's athletics and on the dangers that young women athletes still face—from themselves and from society. Tina Kelley in "Whales in the Minnesota River," by contrast, draws all of her information and examples from outside sources. Although she has had experiences with the World Wide Web, she never introduces herself (through the use of "I," for example) or her own experiences into the essay. Remember that regardless of where you find them, specific, relevant details and examples are very important in everything you write. They add life and interest to your writing, and they support or illustrate the points you are trying to make.

How Do I Gather Details and Examples from My Experiences?

Even when you are narrating an experience that happened to you or describing something that you saw, you will have to spend some time remembering the event, sorting out the details of the experience, and deciding which examples best support the point that you are trying to make. The best place to start in your memory and observation search is with the advice offered in "How to Write an Essay" (pp. 16–38).

Many of the essays in this and later chapters begin with the writer's memories, experiences, and observations. Anna Quindlen, for example, draws only on a series of experiences in her married life to write "The Name Is Mine." Similarly, Bob Greene's "Cut" begins with his own experience. Even when writers add information from sources outside of their personal experiences—as Leslie Heywood in "One of the Girls," Tina Kelley in "Whales in the Minnesota River," and the writers of *U.S. News & World Report* in "Plugging the Kegs" do—observation and personal experience might still play a significant role in shaping the essay.

How Do I Gather Information from Outside Sources?

When you think about researching a subject, you might only think of going to a library to look up your topic in the on-line catalog or a database, consulting a CD-ROM encyclopedia, or logging on to the World Wide Web to "surf" for appropriate sites. As varied as these search methods are, you can also find information in many other ways. Tina Kelley in "Whales in the Minnesota River" and the writers at *U.S. News & World Report* in "Plugging the Kegs" both make extensive use of interviews with knowledgeable sources. That gathered information is mixed with or tempered by the writers' previous knowledge and experience. Leslie Heywood, for example, has written extensively about women athletes and modern culture; she has spent years not only directly experiencing what it is to be competitive athlete and a woman, but also studying, researching, and publishing in these areas. The experiences of other people can also be excellent sources of information. Bob Greene, for example, recounts the experiences of four men who were also cut from athletic teams when they were young.

When you use information gathered from outside sources—whether those sources are written texts, electronic media, or interviews—it is important that you document those sources. Though it is true that articles in newspapers and magazines do not provide the type of documentation that you find in a paper written for a college course, recognize that you are a student and not a reporter. Be sure to ask your instructor how you are to document quotations and paraphrases—is it all right just to mention the sources in the text, or do you need to provide formal parenthetical documentation? Additional advice and a sample paper can be found in the appendix, "Finding, Using, and Documenting Sources," pp. 604–632. Be sure to read that material before you hand in a paper that uses outside sources.

How Many Examples Are Enough?

It would make every writer's job much easier if there were a single, simple answer to the question of how many examples to use. Instead, the answer is "enough to interest or convince your reader." Sometimes one fully developed example might be enough. The advertisements for organizations such as Save the Children often tell the story of a specific child in need of food and shelter. The single example, accompanied by a photograph, is enough to persuade many people to sponsor a child. Anna Quindlen in "This Name Is Mine" focuses on a single example drawn from her own experience—using that example as a way to make her point about the significance and the consequences of keeping your own name.

At other times you might need to use many details and examples. Tina Kelley wrote about computers for *The New York Times* for several years; she has had extensive experiences with the World Wide Web. But she adds to that experience an extensive body of research. She cites the published research of experts and she interviews qualified professionals. The result is not a personal reaction to the Web, but a balanced, informative essay that draws upon a rich body of information. In "Cut," Bob Greene writes about how being cut from the junior high school basketball team changed his life. To support his thesis and extend it beyond his own personal experience, Greene includes the stories of four other men who had similar experiences. But why give five examples of the same experience? Why not three or seven? There is nothing magical about the number five—Greene might have used five because he had that much column space in the magazine—but the five give authority to Greene's assertion, or at least they create the illusion of authority. To prove the validity of Greene's thesis would require a proper statistical sample. Only then could it be said with some certainty that the experience of being cut makes men superachievers later in life. In most writing situations, however, such thoroughness is not needed. If the details and examples are well chosen and relevant, the reader is likely to accept your assertions.

SAMPLE STUDENT ESSAY

Frank Smite, recently divorced and recently returned to college, chose to work on an essay about the difficulties that older single or newly single people have in meeting people they can date. "Young college kids have it easy," Frank complained; "you are constantly surrounded by eligible people your own age. Try meeting someone when you're thirty-five, slightly balding, just divorced, and working all day." His first draft of the opening of his essay appears here:

MY SEARCH FOR LOVE

My wife and I separated and then quickly divorced a year ago. I figured that I would be able to forget some of the pain by returning to dating. At first, I was excited about the prospect of meeting new people. It made me feel young again. Besides, this time I'd be able to avoid the problems that led to my divorce. While I'm not exactly a male movie star—I'm thirty-five, a little overweight, kind of thin on the top, and have one daughter who I desperately miss seeing every day—I figured that romance was just around the corner.

It wasn't until I started to look for people to ask out that I realized how far away that corner was. Frankly, in my immediate world, there seemed to be no one who was roughly my age and unmarried. That's when I began to look at the various ways that people in my situation can meet people. I attended several meetings of the local Parents Without Partners group, but that didn't seem promising; I joined a computerized dating service; and, believe it or not, I started reading the "personals" in the newspaper.

When Frank came to revise his essay, he had his instructor's comments and the reactions of several classmates. Everyone agreed that he had an excellent subject and some good detail, but several readers were a little troubled by Frank's overuse of "I." One reader asked Frank if he could make his essay focus a little less on his own immediate experience and a little more on what anyone in his position might do. His instructor suggested that with the right type of revision, Frank might be able to publish his essay in the local newspaper—after all, she noted, many people are in the same situation. His instructor also suggested that Frank might eliminate the reference to his daughter and how much he misses her. Although those feelings are important, that is not where Frank wanted to center the essay. Frank liked the idea of sharing his experiences with a wider audience. His revised introduction—complete with a new title—follows.

LOOKING FOR LOVE

Ask any single or divorced adult about the problems of meeting "prospective partners" and you are likely to get a litany of complaints and horrifying experiences. No longer can people rely on introductions from well-meaning friends. After all, most of those friends are also looking for love. Matchmaking has become big business—even, in fact, a franchised business.

Today the search for love takes many forms, from bar hopping, to organizations such as Parents Without Partners, to computerized and videotaped "search services," to singles groups organized around a shared concern (for example, those who are concerned about the environment or who love books). A little more desperate (and risky and certainly tacky) is the newspaper classified. Titled "Getting Personal" in my local newspaper, advertisements typically read like this one running today: "Single white female, pretty, petite blond, 40's ISO [in search of] WM [white male] for a perfect relationship (it does exist!)."

Some Things to Remember

1. Use details and examples—effective writing depends on them.
2. For some subjects you can find the illustrations you need from your own experiences and observations. You will, however, probably need to work at remembering and gathering those specifics.
3. For some subjects you will need to do some type of research—interviewing people, looking up material in your school's library, using the Internet and the World Wide Web to locate relevant documents and sites. Remember as well that you are always connecting your observations with knowledge that you have acquired in other courses and other experiences.
4. Choose examples that are relevant and accurate. Quality is more important than quantity. Make sure your examples support your argument or illustrate the points you are trying to make. If you use an outside authority—an interview, a printed text, an electronic source—make sure that the source is knowledgeable and accurate. Remember also to document those sources.
5. The number of details and examples you need necessarily varies. Sometimes one will do; sometimes you will need many. If you want your readers to do or to believe something, you will need to supply some evidence to gain their support or confidence.

Gathering and Using Examples in Writing for Your Other Courses

Almost all the writing you do in college will require you to gather and use details and examples to support your ideas and to demonstrate that you have mastered the materials covered in the course. Here are some samples of the kinds of writing assignments you might complete that would require the use of examples.

- **American History.** For an assignment asking that you explore some aspect of slave life prior to the Civil War, you might draw on examples from slave narratives to support the thesis that despite the practice of slave owners separating slave families by selling individual members to sometimes far-distant owners, many families were surprisingly successful at maintaining close bonds extending among several generations.
- **Film Studies.** For an assignment asking you to explore an important theme running through the work of a film director of your choice, you might explore the theme of entrapment in the films of Alfred Hitchcock by looking in depth at four or five of his films.
- **Business Management.** For a paper on effective management styles, you might draw on examples you find in your reading, as well as from your own work experience, to illustrate some specific leadership qualities of strong managers.
- **Psychology.** For an essay exam question about how the different roles we play in our lives create problems of adjustment and psychological coherence, you might present real or hypothetical examples of particular individuals and their life roles to explain how such contradictions can be handled.
- **Environmental Science.** For an assignment asking you to explore the problems presented when a unique natural environment is threatened, you might, in choosing to write about the Florida Everglades, present a variety of examples of changes that have occurred in the plant and animal life of that ecosystem due to the effects of agricultural irrigation runoff.

VISUALIZING EXAMPLES

If you represent a land trust and you are trying to solicit donations from individuals, how do you make the value of your project vivid? Do you use a simple statistic? "We have 23,000 acres of conserved land under our permanent care." It's hard to imagine that much land and a photograph or two will hardly do the subject justice. Moreover, how do you convey a sense of those 23,000 acres, especially if they are located in heavily populated areas. After all, 23,000 acres in parts of the West, Midwest, or Southwest is different from 23,000 acres in the area around Philadelphia, Pennsylvania. Notice the strategy used here. By locating those areas held in trust on a map, the Natural Lands Trust makes the significance of those holdings much more vivid to the potential contributor. Here the individual pieces are represented by squares and circles; the aggregate, depicting all of the specific areas, is much more impressive and persuasive.

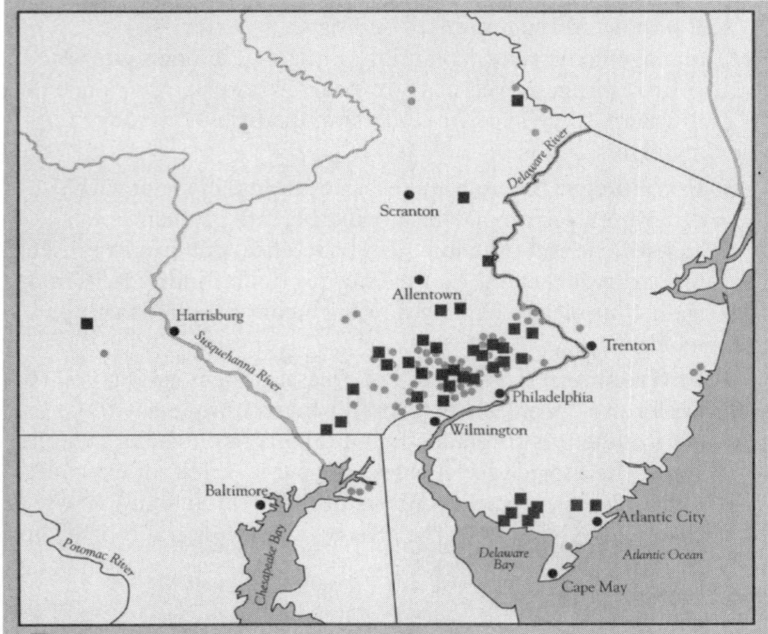

Natural Lands Trust

VISIT THE PRENTICE HALL READER'S WEBSITE

When you have finished reading an essay, check out the additional material available at the Reader's Website at www.prenhall.com /miller. For each reading, you will find a list of related readings connected with the topic or the author; additional background information; a group of relevant "hot-linked" web resources (just click on the site you want to visit); and still more writing suggestions.

GATHERING AND USING EXAMPLES

Ever tried reading an on-line newspaper? Most of the major newspapers have extensive Websites that include searchable archives. Visit four major newspapers and sample what's available. Then using the Web as your information resource, write a review of what you found. Your starting points can be found at www. prenhall.com/miller.

The Name Is Mine

Anna Quindlen

Born in 1953, Anna Quindlen attended Barnard College in New York City. She enjoyed a successful career at The New York Times, *where she wrote three different weekly columns, including her syndicated column, "Public and Private," for which she won the 1992 Pulitzer Prize for commentary. Since leaving the* Times, *she has published several successful novels. Her recent books include* Happily Ever After *(1997) and* Black and Blue *(1998). Her second novel,* One True Thing *(1994), was made into a film by the same name in 1998. In October 1999, she joined* Newsweek *magazine as columnist.*

This essay first appeared in "Life in the 30's," a weekly column that Quindlen wrote for the Times *from 1986 to 1988. Based on her own experiences as a mother, a wife, and a journalist, the column attracted millions of readers and was syndicated in some sixty other newspapers. She ended the column because of its personal nature: "It wasn't just that I was in the spotlight; it was like I was in the spotlight naked. . . . I became public property."*

On Writing: *Quindlen writes on a laptop computer and observes, "I listen to all those authors who say they write longhand in diaries they buy in London, and I say, 'Get a life.'" A perfectionist who "wants every sentence to be the best it can be," Quindlen notes, "I don't want anything to be loose or sloppy."*

BEFORE READING

Connecting: Can you remember times when your "identity" was defined not by yourself but by your association with someone else, when you were the child *of*, the sibling *of*, the spouse *of*, the parent *of*, the employee *of*? How did these occasions make you feel?

Anticipating: Every decision we make has consequences—some of which we are immediately aware of and some of which only emerge later. What are the consequences of Quindlen's decision not to take her husband's name?

1 I am on the telephone to the emergency room of the local hospital. My elder son is getting stitches in his palm, and I have

called to make myself feel better, because I am at home, waiting, and my husband is there, holding him. I am 34 years old, and I am crying like a child, making a slippery mess of my face. "Mrs. Krovatin?" says the nurse, and for the first time in my life I answer "Yes."

This is a story about a name. The name is mine. I was given it at birth, and I have never changed it, although I married. I could come up with lots of reasons why. It was a political decision, a simple statement that I was somebody and not an adjunct of anybody, especially a husband. As a friend of mine told her horrified mother, "He didn't adopt me, he married me." 2

It was a professional and a personal decision, too. I grew up with an ugly dog of a name, one I came to love because I thought it was weird and unlovable. Amid the Debbies and Kathys of my childhood, I had a first name only my grandmothers had and a last name that began with a strange letter. "Sorry, the letters, I, O, Q, U, V, X, Y and Z are not available," the catalogues said about monogrammed key rings and cocktail napkins. Seeing my name in black on white at the top of a good story, suddenly it wasn't an ugly dog anymore. 3

But neither of these are honest reasons, because they assume rational consideration, and it so happens that when it came to changing my name, there was no consideration, rational or otherwise. It was mine. It belonged to me. I don't even share a checking account with my husband. Damned if I was going to be hidden beneath the umbrella of his identity. 4

It seemed like a simple decision. But nowadays I think the only simple decisions are whether to have grilled cheese or tuna fish for lunch. Last week, my older child wanted an explanation of why he, his dad and his brother have one name, and I have another. 5

My answer was long, philosophical and rambling—that is to say, unsatisfactory. What's in a name? I could have said disingenuously. But I was talking to a person who had just spent three torturous, exhilarating years learning names for things, and I wanted to communicate to him that mine meant something quite special to me, had seemed as form-fitting as my skin, and as painful to remove. Personal identity and independence, however, were not what he was looking for; he just wanted to make sure I was one of them. And I am—and then again, I am not. When I made this decision, I was part of a couple. Now, there are two me's, the me who is the individual and the me who is part of a family of four, a family of four in which, in a small way, I am left out. 6

7 A wise friend who finds herself in the same fix says she never wants to change her name, only to have a slightly different identity as a family member, an identity for pediatricians' offices and parent-teacher conferences. She also says that the entire situation reminds her of the women's movement as a whole. We did these things as individuals, made these decisions about ourselves and what we wanted to be and do. And they were good decisions, the right decisions. But we based them on individual choice, not on group dynamics. We thought in terms of our sense of ourselves, not our relationships with others.

8 Some people found alternative solutions: hyphenated names, merged names, matriarchal names for the girls and patriarchal ones for the boys, one name at work and another at home. I did not like those choices; I thought they were middle grounds, and I didn't live much in the middle ground at the time. I was once slightly disdainful of women who went all the way and changed their names. But I now know too many smart, independent, terrific women who have the same last names as their husbands to be disdainful anymore. (Besides, if I made this decision as part of a feminist world view, it seems dishonest to turn around and trash other women for deciding as they did.)

9 I made my choice. I haven't changed my mind. I've just changed my life. Sometimes I feel like one of those worms I used to hear about in biology, the ones that, chopped in half, walked off in different directions. My name works fine for one half, not quite as well for the other. I would never give it up. Except for that one morning when I talked to the nurse at the hospital, I always answer the question "Mrs. Krovatin?" with "No, this is Mr. Krovatin's wife." It's just that I understand the down side now.

10 When I decided not to disappear beneath my husband's umbrella, it did not occur to me that I would be the only one left outside. It did not occur to me that I would ever care—not enough to change, just enough to think about the things we do on our own and what they mean when we aren't on our own anymore.

QUESTIONS ON SUBJECT AND PURPOSE

1. Why did Quindlen not change her last name when she married?
2. How does she feel about her decision now?
3. Since Quindlen does not plan to change her name, what purpose might she have in writing the essay?

QUESTIONS ON STRATEGY AND AUDIENCE

1. The essay could begin at the second paragraph. Why might Quindlen have chosen to begin the essay with the telephone call experience?
2. In paragraph 9, Quindlen returns to the incident at the hospital. How does this device help hold the essay together?
3. The essay appeared in a column headed "Life in the 30's." How might that affect the nature of the audience who might read the essay?

QUESTIONS ON VOCABULARY AND STYLE

1. At the beginning of paragraphs 2 and 9, Quindlen uses three very short simple sentences in a row. Why?
2. Twice in the essay (paragraphs 4 and 10), Quindlen refers to coming under her husband's "umbrella." What is the effect of such an image?
3. Be able to define the following words: *disingenuously* (paragraph 6) and *disdainful* (8).

WRITING SUGGESTIONS

1. **For Your Journal.** Do you have any desire to change your name? If so, why? If not, why not? In your journal, explore what changing or not changing your name might mean. Would "you" be any different?
2. **For a Paragraph.** In a paragraph, explore the meaning that you find in your name. You can choose your first or last name or even a nickname. How does that name define you?
3. **For an Essay.** In paragraph 6, Quindlen remarks, "There are two me's, the me who is the individual and the me who is part of a family of four." Everyone experiences such moments of awareness. Think about those times when you have been "two," and in an essay, explore the dilemma posed by being an individual and, at the same time, a part of a larger whole.

   Prewriting:

   a. Make a list of relationships that might have produced similar experiences (you and your family, you and your friends, you and a social group).

b. Select one of those relationships and freewrite about it, trying to focus on a significant and specific decision you made.

c. Remember that the experience will have to be narrated in a time sequence, either starting with the decision and then tracing the consequences or starting with the consequences and then flashing back to the decision.

Rewriting:

a. Try, if you have not already done so, to imitate Quindlen's strategy of "hooking" the reader into the essay.

b. Experiment with a different time sequence (as described in *c* under "Prewriting") for your essay. Does the other sequence work any more effectively?

c. Try to find someone to read your essay—a friend, roommate, classmate, or tutor in a writing center. Ask your reader for some constructive criticism, and listen to what you hear.

4. **For Research.** How widespread and recent is the phenomenon of women not taking their husbands' names? Research the phenomenon through the various databases that your library has. A crucial problem will be identifying the subject headings and keywords to use in your search. If you have problems, ask a reference librarian for some guidance. Remember as well that people make excellent sources of information. Then, using that research, write an essay for one of the following audiences:

   a. An article intended for a male audience

   b. An article intended for an audience of unmarried women who might be considering such a decision

   c. A traditional research paper for a college course

Website Link

What percentage of women in the United States choose not to take their husband's name? What socioeconomic factors influence that decision? Find out at www.prenhall.com/miller.

Cut

Bob Greene

Bob Greene was born in Columbus, Ohio, in 1947 and received a B.J. from Northwestern University in 1969. He has been a columnist for the Chicago Sun-Times, *the* Chicago Tribune, *and* Esquire, *as well as a contributing correspondent for "ABC News Nightline." A prolific writer, Greene has published numerous collections of his columns as well as other works. His most recent books include* Chevrolet Summers, Dairy Queen Nights *(1997) and* The 50 Year Dash: The Feelings, Foibles and Fears of Being a Half Century Old *(1997). In October 1999, he joined* Life *magazine as a columnist.*

On Writing: *Greene is, in many ways, a reporter of everyday events. He rarely tries to be profound but concentrates instead on "human interest" stories, the experiences that we all share. "Beyond entertaining or informing [my readers]," he has said, "the only responsibility I feel is . . . to make sure that they get to the last period of the last sentence of the last paragraph of the story . . . I feel I have a responsibility to make the story interesting enough for them to read all the way through." In this essay from* Esquire, *a magazine aimed at a male audience, Greene relates the stories of five successful men who shared the experience of being "cut from the team." Does being cut, Greene wonders, make you a super-achiever later in life?*

BEFORE READING

Connecting: Was there ever a time when you realized that you were not going to be allowed to participate in something that you wanted very much? Did someone tell you, "You're not good enough," or did you realize it yourself?

Anticipating: Writers recount personal experiences for some reason, and that reason is never just "here is what happened to me"; instead, writers focus on the significance of the experience. What significance does Greene see in these narratives?

I remember vividly the last time I cried. I was twelve years old, in the seventh grade, and I had tried out for the junior high school basketball team. I walked into the gymnasium; there was a piece of paper tacked to the bulletin board. 1

2 It was a cut list. The seventh-grade coach had put it up on the board. The boys whose names were on the list were still on the team; they were welcome to keep coming to practices. The boys whose names were not on the list had been cut; their presence was no longer desired. My name was not on the list.

3 I had not known the cut was coming that day. I stood and stared at the list. The coach had not composed it with a great deal of subtlety; the names of the very best athletes were at the top of the sheet of paper, and the other members of the squad were listed in what appeared to be a descending order of talent. I kept looking at the bottom of the list, hoping against hope that my name would miraculously appear there if I looked hard enough.

4 I held myself together as I walked out of the gym and out of the school, but when I got home I began to sob. I couldn't stop. For the first time in my life, I had been told officially that I wasn't good enough. Athletics meant everything to boys that age; if you were on the team, even a substitute, it put you in the desirable group. If you weren't on the team, you might as well not be alive.

5 I had tried desperately in practice, but the coach never seemed to notice. It didn't matter how hard I was willing to work; he didn't want me there. I knew that when I went to school the next morning I would have to face the boys who had not been cut—the boys whose names were on the list, who were still on the team, who had been judged worthy while I had been judged unworthy.

6 All these years later, I remember it as if I were still standing right there in the gym. And a curious thing has happened: in traveling around the country, I have found that an inordinately large proportion of successful men share that same memory—the memory of being cut from a sports team as a boy.

7 I don't know how the mind works in matters like this; I don't know what went on in my head following that day when I was cut. But I know that my ambition has been enormous ever since then; I know that for all of my life since that day, I have done more work than I had to be doing, taken more assignments than I had to be taking, put in more hours than I had to be spending. I don't know if all of that came from a determination never to allow myself to be cut again—never to allow someone to tell me that I'm not good enough again—but I know it's there. And apparently it's there in a lot of other men, too.

8 Bob Graham, thirty-six, is a partner with the Jenner & Block law firm in Chicago. "When I was sixteen, baseball was my whole life," he said. "I had gone to a relatively small high school, and I had

been on the team. But then my family moved, and I was going to a much bigger high school. All during the winter months I told everyone that I was a ballplayer. When spring came, of course I went out for the team.

"The cut list went up. I did not make the team. Reading that cut list is one of the clearest things I have in my memory. I wanted not to believe it, but there it was. 9

"I went home and told my father about it. He suggested that maybe I should talk to the coach. So I did. I pleaded to be put back on the team. He said there was nothing he could do; he said he didn't have enough room. 10

"I know for a fact that it altered my perception of myself. My view of myself was knocked down; my self-esteem was lowered. I felt so embarrassed; my whole life up to that point had revolved around sports, and particularly around playing baseball. That was the group I wanted to be in—the guys on the baseball team. And I was told that I wasn't good enough to be one of them. 11

"I know now that it changed me. I found out, even though I couldn't articulate it at the time, that there would be times in my life when certain people would be in a position to say 'You're not good enough' to me. I did not want that to happen ever again. 12

"It seems obvious to me now that being cut was what started me in determining that my success would always be based on my own abilities, and not on someone else's perceptions. Since then I've always been something of an overachiever; when I came to the law firm I was very aggressive in trying to run my own cases right away, to be the lead lawyer in the cases with which I was involved. I made partner at thirty-one; I never wanted to be left behind. 13

"Looking back, maybe it shouldn't have been that important. It was only baseball. You pass that by. Here I am. That coach is probably still there, still a high school baseball coach, still cutting boys off the baseball team every year. I wonder how many hundreds of boys he's cut in his life?" 14

Maurice McGrath is senior vice-president of Genstar Mortgage Corporation, a mortgage banking firm in Glendale, California. "I'm forty-seven years old, and I was fourteen when it happened to me, and I still feel something when I think about it," he said. 15

"I was in the eighth grade. I went to St. Philip's School in Pasadena. I went out for the baseball team, and one day at practice the coach came over to me. He was an Occidental College student who had been hired as the eighth-grade coach. 16

17 "He said, 'You're no good.' Those were his words. I asked him why he was saying that. He said, 'You can't hit the ball. I don't want you here.' I didn't know what to do, so I went over and sat off to the side, watching the others practice. The coach said I should leave the practice field. He said that I wasn't on the team, and that I didn't belong there anymore.

18 "I was outwardly stoic about it. I didn't want anyone to see how I felt. I didn't want to show that it hurt. But oh, did it hurt. All my friends played baseball after school every day. My best friend was the pitcher on the team. After I got whittled down by the coach, I would hear the other boys talking in class about what they were going to do at practice after school. I knew that I'd just have to go home.

19 "I guess you make your mind up never to allow yourself to be hurt like that again. In some way I must have been saying to myself, 'I'll play the game better.' Not the sports game, but anything I tried. I must have been saying, 'If I have to, I'll sit on the bench, but I'll be part of the team.'

20 "I try to make my own kids believe that, too. I try to tell them that they should show that they're a little bit better than the rest. I tell them to think of themselves as better. Who cares what anyone else thinks? You know, I can almost hear that coach saying the words. 'You're no good.'"

21 Author Malcolm MacPherson *(The Blood of His Servants)*, forty, lives in New York. "It happened to me in the ninth grade, at the Yalesville School in Yalesville, Connecticut," he said. "Both of my parents had just been killed in a car crash, and as you can imagine, it was a very difficult time in my life. I went out for the baseball team, and I did pretty well in practice.

22 "But in the first game I clutched. I was playing second base; the batter hit a pop-up, and I moved back to catch it. I can see it now. I felt dizzy as I looked up at the ball. It was like I was moving in slow motion, but the ball was going at regular speed. I couldn't get out of the way of my own feet. The ball dropped to the ground. I didn't catch it.

23 "The next day at practice, the coach read off the lineup. I wasn't on it. I was off the squad.

24 "I remember what I did: I walked. It was a cold spring afternoon, and the ground was wet, and I just walked. I was living with an aunt and uncle, and I didn't want to go home. I just wanted to walk forever.

"It drove my opinion of myself right into a tunnel. Right into a cave. And when I came out of the cave, something inside of me wanted to make sure in one manner or another that I would never again be told I wasn't good enough. 25

"I will confess that my ambition, to this day, is out of control. It's like a fire. I think the fire would have pretty much stayed in control if I hadn't been cut from that team. But that got it going. You don't slice ambition two ways; it's either there or it isn't. Those of us who went through something like that always know that we have to catch the ball. We'd rather die than have the ball fall at our feet. 26

"Once that fire is started in us, it never gets extinguished, until we die or have heart attacks or something. Sometimes I wonder about the home-run hitters; the guys who never even had to worry about being cut. They may have gotten the applause and the attention back then, but I wonder if they ever got the fire. I doubt it. I think maybe you have to get kicked in the teeth to get the fire started. 27

"You can tell the effect of something like that by examining the trail you've left in your life, and tracing it backward. It's almost like being a junkie with a need for success. You get attention and applause and you like it, but you never quite trust it. Because you know that back then you were good enough if only they would have given you a chance. You don't trust what you achieve, because you're afraid that someone will take it away from you. You know that it can happen; it already did. 28

"So you try to show people how good you are. Maybe you don't go out and become Dan Rather; maybe you just end up owning the Pontiac dealership in your town. But it's your dealership, and you're the top man, and every day you're showing people that you're good enough." 29

Dan Rather, fifty-two, is anchor of the CBS *Evening News*. "When I was thirteen, I had rheumatic fever," he said. "I became extremely skinny and extremely weak, but I still went out for the seventh-grade baseball team at Alexander Hamilton Junior High School in Houston. 30

"The school was small enough that there was no cut as such; you were supposed to figure out that you weren't good enough, and quit. Game after game I sat at the end of the bench, hoping that maybe this was the time I would get in. The coach never even looked at me; I might as well have been invisible. 31

32 "I told my mother about it. Her advice was not to quit. So I went to practice every day, and I tried to do well so that the coach would be impressed. He never even knew I was there. At home in my room I would fantasize that there was a big game, and the three guys in front of me would all get hurt, and the coach would turn to me and put me in, and I would make the winning hit. But then there'd be another game, and the late innings would come, and if we were way ahead I'd keep hoping that this was the game when the coach would put me in. He never did.

33 "When you're that age, you're looking for someone to tell you you're okay. Your sense of self-esteem is just being formed. And what that experience that baseball season did was make me think that perhaps I wasn't okay.

34 "In the last game of the season something terrible happened. It was the last of the ninth inning, there were two outs, and there were two strikes on the batter. And the coach turned to me and told me to go out to right field.

35 "It was a totally humiliating thing for him to do. For him to put me in for one pitch, the last pitch of the season, in front of all the other boys on the team . . . I stood out there for that one pitch, and I just wanted to sink into the ground and disappear. Looking back on it, it was an extremely unkind thing for him to have done. That was nearly forty years ago, and I don't know why the memory should be so vivid now; I've never known if the coach was purposely making fun of me—and if he was, why a grown man would do that to a thirteen-year-old boy.

36 "I'm not a psychologist. I don't know if a man can point to one event in his life and say that that's the thing that made him the way he is. But when you're that age, and you're searching for your own identity, and all you want is to be told that you're all right . . . I wish I understood it better, but I know the feeling is still there."

QUESTIONS ON SUBJECT AND PURPOSE

1. Greene's "cuts" all refer to not making an athletic team. What other kinds of "cuts" can you experience?
2. It is always risky to speculate on an author's purpose, but why would Greene write about this? Why reveal to everyone something that hurt so much?
3. How might Greene have gone about gathering examples of other men's similar experiences? Why would they be

willing to contribute? Would everyone who has been cut be so candid?

4. What can be said in the coaches' defense? Should everyone who tries out be automatically guaranteed a place on the team?

QUESTIONS ON STRATEGY AND AUDIENCE

1. Greene structures his essay in an unusual way. How can the essay be divided? Why give a series of examples of other men who were "cut"?
2. How many examples are enough? What if Greene had used two examples? Eight examples? How would either extreme have influenced your reaction as a reader?
3. Greene does not provide a final concluding paragraph. Why?
4. Are you skeptical after you have finished the essay? Does everyone react to being cut in the same way? What would it take to convince you that these reactions are typical?

QUESTIONS ON VOCABULARY AND STYLE

1. How would you characterize the tone of Greene's essay? How is it achieved? Through language? Sentence structure? Paragraphing?
2. Why does Greene allow each man to tell his own story? Why not just summarize their experiences? Each story is enclosed in quotation marks. Do you think that these were the exact words of each man? Why?
3. What do *inordinately* (paragraph 6) and *stoic* (18) mean?

WRITING SUGGESTIONS

1. **For Your Journal.** Greene attributes enormous significance to a single experience; he feels that it literally changed his entire life. Try to remember some occasions when a disappointment seemed to change your life by changing your expectations for yourself. In your journal, list some possible instances, and then explore one.
2. **For a Paragraph.** As children, we imagine ourselves doing or being anything we want. As we grow older, however, we

discover that our choices become increasingly limited; in fact, each choice we make seems to cut off whole paths of alternative choices. We cannot be or do everything that we once thought we could. Choose a time in your life when you realized that a particular expectation or dream would never come true. In a paragraph, narrate that experience. Be sure to make the significance of your realization clear to your reader.

3. **For an Essay.** Describe an experience similar to the one that Greene narrates. It might have happened in an academic course during your school years, in a school or community activity, in athletics, or on the job: we can be "cut," "released," or "fired" from almost anything. Remember to make your narrative vivid through the use of detail and to make the significance of your narrative clear to the reader.

   Prewriting:

   a. Make a list of some possible events about which to write.

   b. Select one of those events and brainstorm. Jot down whatever you remember about the event and your reactions to it. Do not worry about writing complete sentences.

   c. Use the details generated from your brainstorming in your essay. Do not try to include every detail, but select those that seem the most revealing. Always ask yourself, how important is this detail?

   Rewriting:

   a. Remember that in writing about yourself it is especially important to keep your readers interested. They need to feel how significant this experience was. Do not just *tell* them; *show* them. One way to do this is to dramatize the experience. Did you?

   b. Look carefully at your introduction. Do you begin in a vivid way? Does it make your reader want to keep reading? Test it by asking friends or relatives to read just the opening paragraphs.

   c. How effective is your conclusion? Do you just stop? Do you just repeat in slightly altered words what you said in your introduction? Try to find another possible ending.

4. **For Research.** Check the validity of Greene's argument. Is there any evidence from research studies about the psychological effects of such vivid rejections? Using print and

on-line sources (if they are available), see what you can find. A reference librarian can help you start your search for information. Use that research in an essay about the positive or negative effects of such experiences. Remember to document all sources. You might write your paper in one of the following forms (each has a slightly different audience):

a. A conventional research paper for a college course

b. An article for a popular magazine (for example, *Esquire*, *Working Woman*, *Parents'*)

c. A feature article for your school's newspaper

Website Link

Greene's essay originally appeared in *Esquire*, not *Sports Illustrated* or *Sporting News*. Want to see why?—compare the magazines (Hint: You can do it electronically).

ONE OF THE GIRLS

Leslie Heywood

Leslie Heywood (1964–), a former Division I track and cross country runner and currently a competitive powerlifter, is an associate professor of English and Cultural Studies at the State University of New York, Binghamton, where she also serves as a consultant to the Strength and Conditioning Program in Athletics. She has an M.F.A. in poetry from the University of Arizona and a Ph.D. in English and Critical Theory from the University of California, Irvine. Her books include Dedication to Hunger: The Anorexic Aesthetic in Modern Culture *(1996);* Third Wave Agenda: Being Feminist and Doing Feminism *(1997);* Bodymakers: A Cultural Anatomy of Women's Body Building *(1998); and* Pretty Good for a Girl: A Memoir *(1998), from which this selection is taken.*

The Preamble to Title IX of the Education Amendments of 1972 reads: "No person in the United States shall, on the basis of sex, be excluded from participation in, be denied the benefits of, or be subject to discrimination under any educational programs or activity receiving financial assistance." Among the many areas of gender inequality that Title IX has addressed are the opportunities for young women to participate in scholastic sports.

On Writing: *Asked about her writing habits, Heywood replied: "Some of my very best writing ideas come during a long run. Titles, an elusive piece of an argument, even a compelling voice often emerge in the cadence of my steps on a trail through the woods where there is nothing but quiet, deer, and wild turkeys. Something about physical movement, a steady heartbeat, the endorphin buzz, seems to catalyze my thinking."*

BEFORE READING

Connecting: The title of the book from which this essay is taken is *Pretty Good for a Girl.* Have you ever heard that phrase used in conversation? In what context might that expression be used? What does it seem to imply?

Anticipating: For Heywood, has it been enough just to provide equal opportunities for young women to participate in sports? Is anything more necessary?

When Gertrude Ederle swam the English Channel in 1926, two hours faster than any of the men who had preceded her, people began to think that women might not be so weak. Imagine her there, her hair cropped short like a flapper, looking into the water and saying *I will.* Imagine the pull of the water that day, the fierceness of the currents, her fearlessness as she greased up. For her, unlike the world that followed her swim, it wasn't a question of whether she could but how fast she would do it. Not wavering a bit, she coats herself from head to foot and heads out. As her face touches water and she takes her first stroke, what she feels is how a wolf feels setting in for an all-day run: she feels right. Her hand passes high above the water with precision and she feels the currents, rolling her over the way they would rough up a boat. Her heart opens with joy, it will be a fight, her muscles pulling the water for hours while exhaustion sets in and she keeps moving. Nothing can stop her, not the manta rays whose tentacles leave a blistering kiss around her throat, not the weather so bad there is an advisory for boats. Twelve hours in, nervous to see the waver in her stroke, the way her arms dip and weave, the way she floats in the seconds in between, her companions pace the deck, lean over the water, cupping their hands in a shout. Gertrude, they say, you should stop. But they're speaking another language, live different lives in which a body doesn't ask itself to dig itself in, to rally, to find an energy that simply doesn't exist, to explode from that gray space of silence and dread into a muscle that is supple, feeling blood beginning to tingle again, ready to bear itself on, to the limit, to the limit, to feel what *is*. No, she says, I have to go. 1

Forty-one years later, Kathrine Switzer knew she could go the 26.2 miles it took to run the Boston Marathon, knew the feel of the hills and the wind on her skin, knew where she had to dig to scale that inevitable wall, rising at mile 18, when her muscles start to sag and her back is tight far beyond the pounding of her heart stabbing like scabby birch bark. From training runs, she knew the breathing it takes to soar over that wall, the way she had to close her mind to the creeping exhaustion contracting her back, the ache that spreads and spreads like shooting stars of blood rushing through a limb too long compressed, iron spikes between the shoulders. She knew she was up to it. Every day she rose in the morning longing for that ache and the strength that would break in lemon waves, electric. Many times her feet kept moving, still in stride, the air sharp through her lungs past startled pines and leafless maples, through snow and ice, then rain and glittering sleeves 2 of summer green. And every time she scaled that wall and ran beyond those pressing hands along her spine, she opened up. Legs firm and sure, lungs silver-tanked, her strides taking the ground like a monster breathing. I *can do this. Here I am. Watch me run.* And Switzer wants to run like this in an official race, to see it, feel it measured. One for the girls, for the books.

3 But in 1967, women are not allowed to run. Still she needs to do it. She covers her body and her tracks. She enters the Boston Marathon, K. Switzer, number 261, and goes to the starting line thickened by sweats. A hooded head. No face. The gun goes off and she takes off with the pack, her training partners around her. They start at a decent pace, and breathing, settle in. The hood gathering her face and the top of her head makes her hot. Hothead. Sweat. Two miles in, she pushes it back, her chin-length hair falling free. She looks at her training partner and smiles. Her arms pump, her legs are steady.

4 But rushing at her from the corner is the race director, mid-sixties heavy in a long dark coat, stabbing his arms toward the number on her chest. *No girls allowed.* Her partner steps between them, and she pulls away, still running. They leave the race director behind. But then comes another, hips spread wide, rushing at her in heavy boots. Look at his lips curling back from his teeth, *a woman will not compete in this race, not ever, not if it is up to me.* His coat flies up as he grabs at her, his eyes narrowed to a slit. Her partner rushes between them again as Kathrine turns and slips away. For 24.2 more miles. Her heart beats even heavier, adrenaline strong. *I will do this.* And this time there is no wall rising at mile 18. This time, the four hours and twenty minutes it takes her to finish are a lime-long breeze. Pain in her ankles, ball joints of her hips, steel clamps on her neck, she breathes easy. Heart steadier than ever. When the newspapers mob the race director and ask him to speak, he says that he is "hurt to think that an American girl would go where she is not wanted. If that girl were my daughter I would spank her." So they turn to Switzer. Ask her why she runs. Because running makes her "strong, all there." It is another five years, 1972, before women are allowed to run, pound out the long roads laid by the still-grown trees. Stronger than strong. All there. They come. They run.

5 This is where I begin. Title IX of the Education Act of 1972, that law that made gender discrimination illegal, made athletes of millions of girls like me. No more female incompetence and physical weakness, *you throw like a girl, no girls allowed, why don't you just go home.* Not now, excuse me. Stepping out.

So now she is everywhere around us, staring back at you from the television screen, from women's magazines: a fierce babe with biceps, straight shoulders, a proud look, claiming the planet for her own. Gabby Reece. Lisa Leslie. Rebecca Lobo. Mia Hamm. She's given to us in blacks and in whites: you can see the stark beauty of her body like straight-line cords. She's no one you would mess with. She's someone you might like to become. She's beautiful. She's strong. She's proud. She's doing it for herself: you project on her all the strength you've never felt, all the invulnerability you've never mustered, all the desire for self-sufficiency and completion you've never owned. She has it. You want it. Look closer. 6

Are you the one she's looking at when she asks if you'll let her play sports? Are you the one who'll prepare her to win? Are you the one who follows, looks, watches her step out and stride? If she lets you touch her, is it because she wants to be touched? What if she turned from her chiseled silhouette, poised, and looked you in the face? What if she could speak? What if she could tell you a story you haven't heard, not yet, what if the image of perfection took on some blood and began to tell you? Would you listen? Would you follow her voice like a glistening chime? Would her story take you over, overcome where you need her to stay—way up there pedestaled, just out of reach , an image of hope and a goal that you can become—sometime soon, next month or next week? But who is she? How does she live? What does she think about, what does she eat? Who touches her, who does she touch? Her muscles, her body, her pillars of strength—what's inside her? Is her life like yours, like your best friend's? Look closer. 7

There are some great Nike ads out there that are a gateway to my vanished world, where I used to win races and everyone knew. In the black-and-white images, dreams, possibilities beckon to girls, welcome them into the world. Sports can give us that place, but a lot of work needs to be done before we've finished that race. Female athletes fight the same unrealistic images everyone fights, and researchers are only beginning to understand the relationship between those images and the "female athlete triad"—eating disorders and exercise compulsion, amenorrhea—that had me training until my bones fractured, my tendons ripped, and I stuck my fingers down my throat or simply didn't eat to stay lean. Nobody's been quite loud enough in saying that the female athlete triad is almost surely connected to all the old negative ideas about girls—girls trying to prove beyond a shadow of a doubt that they are not what those ideas say they are: weak, mild, meek, meant to serve 8 others instead of achieving for themselves. The ideas that made the race directors chase Kathrine Switzer away.

9 Are those ideas really gone? Let's face it—many of the images of female athletes out there are more about having a great butt or a great set of pecs than they are about winning races and feeling confident. If we really want a society where, as one of the young girls in the Nike ads says, "I can be anything I want to be," each of us will have to do everything we can to make this dream more than words sliding easily out of the mouth. We need to make sure Title IX is enforced so that as many girls as possible have the opportunity to play sports. We need to make sure girls are treated as athletes, not just pretty girls. We need to continue the research that's been started on all the different aspects of girls' and women's lives, which shows sports' potential to give us a sense of competence and power—like that feeling deep in my lungs as, running by, I dared the very cacti not to see me.

10 Because national attention has turned to female athletes, because we are no longer disparaged or scorned, or seen as exceptions to the woman-as-weakness rule, I know some things now I didn't know then. I belonged to the first wave of women in sports after Title IX, part of the gathering wave that ballooned the stats from 300,000 girls in interscholastic athletics to the 2.25 million who play today. Is it really safe now? Can we begin to try out some of the new ideas about competing, ideas I was struggling with competing against Sheila in the gym? Can we smile at each other without being fake? Can we find ways to get out there, still swallowing the world, still roaring like Tarzan swinging mightily on his vines, and not have to knock everyone else off the vines just so it looks like we're the one who soars best? Can we move toward what, in her new book, *Embracing Victory*, Mariah Burton Nelson names "the Champion" model of competition, which "respects all contestants, including the self"?

11 The old competitive model—what I did—led many of us from an earlier generation to the female athlete triad, and we missed out on the true benefits of sports. Can we revise people's ideas about girls enough so that my ghost will give up having to prove herself, and the other girls running in her place won't have to erase whole worlds inside themselves just so someone will notice them, just so they can stand out and win?

12 In spite of everything that happened I continued in sport. I knew instinctively what research is proving now: sports, if not played in the way I did, where everyone around you had to be stomped out with boots to their face because there was only one

winner and it had to be you—if played a little differently than this, sports help with depression. They help with what the books call self-esteem: feeling the sun on your warm face, walking across the field like a giant, feeling that just for a moment, the world belongs to you.

Running and lifting are as much a part of my life as is the quiet in-and-out of my steady chest. I write this book with hopes that other girls will have some support I didn't have and won't make the same mistakes. So here's to many, many more women's hockey teams and Picabo Streets—and to the women and men who'll work hard to make it possible for every young girl to burn bright as the sun without paying the price of self-destruction. And then when there are girls all around who are stronger and with better biceps than me, well, I just might be able to deal with it. 13

QUESTIONS ON SUBJECT AND PURPOSE

1. For Heywood, what benefits do sports hold for women?
2. Did Heywood herself only experience benefits from competing in sports? Were there any drawbacks or problems?
3. This essay forms the final chapter or epilogue to Heywood's memoir. What final thoughts does she want to leave with her reader?

QUESTIONS ON STRATEGY AND AUDIENCE

1. Why might Heywood have titled the essay "One of the Girls"?
2. Paragraph 7 is composed entirely of rhetorical questions—questions that provoke thought rather than require response. Specifically, to whom are those questions addressed? Define that "you."
3. As the headnote explains, this essay appeared in her memoir, not a magazine. What assumptions might Heywood have made about a book-reading audience rather than a magazine-reading audience?

QUESTIONS ON VOCABULARY AND STYLE

1. When Heywood writes of the "blistering kiss" (paragraph 1) of the manta ray or the "ache that spreads . . . like shooting stars of blood" (2), what type of language is she using?

2. In narrating Ederle's swim and Switzer's run, Heywood shifts to the present tense (for example, "she takes her first stroke" or "she takes off with the pack") rather than the past tense ("took"), even though the events occurred in the past. Why tell the story in this way?
3. Be prepared to define the following words: *flapper* (1), *supple* (1), *glistening* (7), *amenorrhea* (8), *disparaged* (10)

WRITING SUGGESTIONS

1. **For Your Journal.** How do you view women athletes? Are your images only positive? Do you stereotype women athletes? In your journal explore that idea—with reference to yourself (if you are a woman athlete) or to others.
2. **For a Paragraph.** How does our society seem to view women athletes? Look for advertisements, for example, that depict women athletes. Are they depicted in the same way as male athletes are? For a paragraph writing, pick a particular advertisement and explore the image that is projected.
3. **For an Essay.** Extend your analysis of the depiction of women athletes in our culture into an essay. If you are using advertisements, make sure that you gather them from a range of magazines. You might also use other visual examples—film, television, photographs, or drawings illustrating articles.

   Prewriting:

   a. Gather a representative visual sample. If you are using magazines, make sure that some of your examples come from magazines aimed at women and women athletes. Make photocopies of anything you use from your library—remember not to damage library copies!

   b. Formulate a thesis that will account for most (or all) of what you are seeing.

   c. Use your examples to substantiate your thesis. Select those examples that demonstrate the assertion(s) that you are making.

   Rewriting

   a. Look back at your working thesis—is it specific? Does it say something precise? Does it make a point that you could argue?

b. Ask your friends or classmates to read your essay. How do they react to your examples? Do they support your assertions? Use your readers' reactions to rethink your choice of examples.
c. Look again at your opening and closing paragraphs. Do you state your thesis early in the paper? Do you reiterate your thesis at the conclusion of the paper?

4. **For Research.** How did Title IX influence the women's athletic program at your school? Visit the Athletic Department and your school's library and archives and research the development of women's athletics since 1972. Then using that research—with specific facts and appropriate quotations—write an essay in which you trace that impact. Be sure to document your sources. You might want to submit your final paper to your school's newspaper for possible publication.

Website Link

What impact has Title IX of the Educational Amendments had on the education (not just sports participation) of young women in the United States? It's pretty amazing—see for yourself.

Whales in Minnesota River?

Tina Kelley

Tina Kelley (1963–) grew up in New Jersey and is a graduate of Yale University, where she majored in English and studied nonfiction writing with John Hersey. Currently a staff writer at The New York Times, *she has also written for the Philadelphia* Inquirer, *the Seattle* Post-Intelligencer, *and the Seattle* Times, *where she contributed a weekly column on outdoor adventures. She was a freelance writer for several years, working for the "Circuits" section of the* Times, *traveling 50 miles north of the Arctic Circle to do a profile of a Native American rights attorney for* People *magazine, and building a cedar sea kayak, which she wrote about several times. She has published a number of poems in journals such as* Poetry Northwest, Prairie Schooner, *and the* Journal of the American Medical Association.

On Writing: *Kelley notes: "I find ideas for stories at parties, on the Internet, and in the pursuit of my hobbies, which include beekeeping, birdwatching, and knitting." "One of the advantages of a full-time job in journalism," she continues, "is that it has all the benefits of college (you're always learning, meeting interesting people, and getting more proficient at what you do) with the added benefit of a paycheck!"*

BEFORE READING

Connecting: Have you ever used information for an academic paper that you obtained from a Website? Did you trust that information?

Anticipating: As you read, make a list of critical questions that you might use as criteria by which to evaluate Websites that you visit.

1 Tourists drove six hours to Mankato, Minn., in search of underground caves and hot springs mentioned on a Website. When they arrived, there were no such attractions.

2 People searching for a discussion of Amnesty International's views on Tunisia learned about human rights in that North African country—but from supporters of the Tunisian authorities,

not from the human rights group. The government supporters brought surfers to a site with a soothing Web address: www.amnesty-tunisia.org.

And bibliophiles who trust the grande dame of on-line retailers, Amazon.com, for suggestions under the headings of "Destined for Greatness" and "What We're Reading" were dismayed to learn that some publishers had paid for special treatment for their books—meaning a more accurate heading would have been "What We're Paid to Say We're Reading." (After the disclosure, Amazon added a note on its home page to make a subtle acknowledgement of the practice.) 3

On the World Wide Web, straight facts can be hard to find. After plowing through dense and recalcitrant search engines that offer more sites than you can point a mouse at, after enduring delays, lost links and dead ends and arriving at a site that looks just right, Web surfers must deal with uncertainty: Is the information true, unbiased and free of hidden sales pitches? 4

Even though it is easy to fall prey to parodies, politics, payola and ignorance on line, solid, watertight information can indeed be found on the Web. But experts on Internet research point out that the Web is largely unregulated and unchecked, and so they agree that it is wise to be skeptical: Consider the source. Reconsider the source. Is the information up to date and professional and traceable? Can it be verified, or the source checked, off line? And just who was that source again? 5

Don Ray, a freelance investigative reporter in Burbank, Calif., and the author of "Checking Out Lawyers" (MIE Publishing, 1997), has what he calls a J.D.L.R. test to apply to Web research. "There should be a switch in every Internet user that toggles when something Just Doesn't Look Right," he said, "to make them re-evaluate the credibility of the source." If a Web page has grammatical errors, sloppy spelling or a goofy design, that makes him distrust the content. 6

And people who are getting ready to spend money on the basis of Web information should, of course, approach their decisions with at least as much skepticism as they would use about a purchase off line. 7

Whoppers have found a home on the Web since the very beginning. Yet for many people, computers have generally been treated as authority figures, able to calculate compound interest in a single bound. A machine that has been perfected by institutions of higher learning and is relied on by the Government isn't likely to lie, is it? 8

9 "We've inherited this notion that if it pops up on a screen and looks good, we tend to think of it as fairly credible," said Paul Gilster, author of *Digital Literacy* (Wiley Computer Publishing, 1997).

10 Although the Web has come to resemble a monstrous library system where everyone has a printing press and all information is seemingly created equal, even the newest surfers come to it with useful information-sorting skills from the off-line world. They can differentiate among information from a trusted newspaper, a bulk mailing from a charity, a sales pitch from a stockbroker and a letter from a friend. They can distinguish commercial broadcasts from public television programs. They can skim over the pages in *Reader's Digest* with "Advertisement" printed at the top.

11 But on the Web, the clues for credibility are different, and so are the tools needed to assess the information. How can someone know if a favorite portal site is making a nanobuck in sales commission every time the person buys something at the florist featured on the page? Comments from people who are either touting or trashing a stock on the Web for their own financial gain have been investigated repeatedly by the Federal Government. And is that medical information on that site underwritten by a drug company or by someone on drugs?

12 Research specialists agree on the importance of determining who finances a site and what profit motives may be at work. While boundary between news material and advertising is fairly clearly marked in many print publications, on the Web the signals pointing to paid content are often subtle or nonexistent, or vary widely from site to site.

13 Amazon.com's practice is only the most visible of many arrangements between Internet companies—including one involving *The New York Times*. The Website of *The Times* includes on book review pages, links to Barnesandnoble.com; *The Times* receives commissions from the resulting sales.

14 Of course, off-line retail stores—including bookstores and groceries—have long accepted pay for product placement. And being a knowledgeable consumer is important on line as well as off line.

15 At Time Warner's Pathfinder Network, Andrew Weil's theories on vitamins and health are used to create a profile of your vitamin needs and—surprise, surprise—sell you vitamins at the end (cgi.pathfinder.com/drweil/vitaminprofiler). Or consider www.smokefreekids.com, which presents all kinds of information on smoke-free dining and how to kick the nicotine habit—and

won't let visitors miss out on the opportunity to buy No Smoke software to quit smoking.

Even outright spoofs can deceive the unwary Web traveler. Take the case of a site posted through Mankato State University by people fed up with the cold winters. The Mankato, Minn., Home Page advertised sunny beaches, an underwater city and whale watching on the Minnesota River (www.lme.mankato.msus.edu/mankato/mankato.html). Deep at the bottom of the disclaimer page one finds: "Mankato, as portrayed on these pages, DOES NOT EXIST! PLEASE do not come here to see these sites." Er, sights. (Of course, anybody looking at a map would probably be suspicious about the site's statement that "the winter temperature in many Mankato neighborhoods has never dropped below a balmy 70 degrees!") 16

That Mankato site "has caused some bad publicity for us," said Maureen Gustafson, head of the Mankato Area Chamber and Convention Bureau. "There was a guy who drove here from Canada with his son who was really ticked," she said. "And another one from Kansas." 17

She wrote the site's creator a letter—which he later posted, to her dismay—suggesting that he and his companions go play with Game Boys rather than undercut the city's promotional efforts. 18

Some Websites appear designed to mislead or even intercept surfers, sometimes for political reasons. For instance, to counter what it calls intentionally misleading information, Amnesty International, the human rights group, has posted www.amnesty.org/tunisia, which includes point-by-point refutations of the site at www.amnesty-tunisia.org, which Amnesty calls "official Tunisian Internet propaganda." The Internet addresses of the pages are, of course, very close, adding to the confusion. But most surfers who wanted impartial information about Tunisia would perhaps choose not to rely on a site that prominently features a quotation from the president of Tunisia, Zine el-Abidine Ben Ali. 19

In a medium where truth is so elusive, medical misinformation is all too easy to find. Beth Mark, a librarian at Messiah College in Grantham, Pa., said a friend had sent her husband, Ken, an article from a commercial Website (munkey.com/health/markle.html) about the health risks of the artificial sweetener aspartame. Mr. Mark, a diabetic, had recently suffered a mini-stroke, and he become worried after reading in the article that aspartame in the sodas he drinks could cause numbness, a claim that is generally not supported by scientific studies, although other questions have been raised about aspartame. 20

21 "It is sensational and contains unfounded claims regarding aspartame causing symptoms of M.S., numbness, etc.," Mrs. Mark said of the article, via E-mail. Soon after, a senior medical adviser to the Multiple Sclerosis Foundation, Dr. David Squillacote, posted a refutation of the article's claims (www.msfacts.org/aspartame.htm).

22 Deborah Cestone, head of the library and media department at the Pelham Memorial High School and Middle School in Pelham, N.Y., teaches students how to evaluate Web sources for their research papers.

23 "You'll find sites like the University of Pennsylvania Cancer Center, and you know that's good solid information, but then you'll find a paper done by some 10th grader as a project, and he's created a Web page from it," she said.

24 After all, anyone with an Internet service provider and a quarter to call it can set up a Web page that looks as official as a 1040 form, without the quality control that used to come from editors, fact checkers and large publishing houses. There are few barriers to bad information on line.

25 "If you wanted to publish a book that says 2 plus 2 equals 5, you had to go through a lot of effort and spend a great deal of money," said Tara Calishain, co-author of *The Official Netscape Guide to Internet Research* (International Thomson Publishing, 1998). "But the cost of putting up a Web page saying 2 plus 2 equals 5 is virtually nothing."

26 Genie Tyburski, a law librarian in Philadelphia, runs a site about reliable research on line (www.virtualchase.com), which includes pointers on how to avoid being duped. "Many of us who are my age, 41, grew up trusting print," she said. "If we read it, it must have been true. We translate that same comfort to the Web, where it's much more dangerous."

27 She recalled a Website about the medical uses of marijuana that had been run from a man's personal home page. It included copies of articles from medical journals but no mention of permission to reproduce them, she said.

28 "With the technology of the Web, there's no barrier to editing," she said. "An entire interview reproduced in the article on the bogus site was not in the original article at all, and there were graphs to support certain statements that weren't in the original article."

29 Rob Rosenberger, a computer security expert, set up a Website to dispel myths about computer viruses (www.kumite.com). "I just claim to be unaligned, but how do you know that?" Mr.

Rosenberger said in an interview. To encourage critical thinking, he has a link on his site titled "Learn About Rob *Before* You Start Taking His Advice," which dares people to treat his writing with the same skepticism he brings to virus scares.

Of course, it is hard to know who is paying whom for what 30
kind of Internet presence. "There are the ones we know about, like Amazon.com, which got caught," Mr. Rosenberger said. "But there are unscrupulous people in the securities industry who are trying to pump up or drive down stocks, to buy at low prices and sell at high prices, who may not be disclosing their fiduciary interests."

"People send out spams on the greatest I.P.O. on the Internet 31
this year, or trash an I.P.O. that's going to occur, so they can get in at the low end," Mr. Rosenberger said. "We know that goes on, too."

Mr. Gilster, the author of *Digital Literacy*, said Internet users 32
need to be trained to triangulate in on the truth.

"We need to set up content evaluation as part of the intellec- 33
tual superstructure here and explain it to kids," he said, "so we end up with students who can use the Web intelligently and know when to cast grave doubt on a particular Website. People have to be their own editors and take that upon themselves. Once you begin doing that, the habits become second nature."

But some questions about the validity of Web sources are 34
impossible to answer beyond a reasonable doubt without stepping outside the hermetic box of the Internet. In such cases, no combination of pixels is sure to help.

"When you want to check citations, your librarian is your 35
best friend," Ms. Calishain said. "There's a lot of stuff on line, but working with librarians is one of the best things you can do with research. They're trained to classify information, and they can help you out."

It is also true that many librarians are learning to navigate 36
the world of the Web, and they may just point an information-hungry consumer elsewhere.

Ms. Cestone, the Pelham school librarian, said she worked 37
hard teaching students how to evaluate what might be the best resource for a given research problem. "It may be the Internet is the best resource, or maybe a book, or maybe a person will be the best resource," she said.

QUESTIONS ON SUBJECT AND PURPOSE

1. When this essay first appeared in *The New York Times*, it carried, in addition to its title, a subtitle, "Only on the Web, Where Skepticism is a Required Navigational Aid." Why?
2. Throughout the essay, Kelley includes URL's, that is, Web addresses for the sites she is discussing. Why might she choose to include this information?
3. What purpose does Kelley seem to have in the essay?

QUESTIONS ON STRATEGY AND AUDIENCE

1. Why does Kelley begin the essay with examples? Are the examples different from one another in any way?
2. Why in paragraph 13 might Kelley disclose that even *The New York Times*, the publisher of this article, has a commercial link on its Website?
3. What strategy does Kelley use to end her essay?

QUESTIONS ON VOCABULARY AND STYLE

1. Judging from the vocabulary and the sentence structures used in the essay, what expectations do you think Kelley might have had about her audience?
2. At several points in the essay (for example, paragraphs 5, 8, and 11), Kelley makes use of rhetorical questions. What is a rhetorical question and why would a writer use one?
3. Be prepared to define the following words: *bibliophiles* (paragraph 3), *recalcitrant* (4), *payola* (5), *credible* (9), *refutations* (19), *fiduciary* (30), *spams* (31), *triangulate* (32), *hermetic* (34), *pixels* (34).

WRITING SUGGESTIONS

1. **For Your Journal.** Reflect on the role of computers in your life. You can focus on any aspect of that influence—your first experiences, your daily habits, your favorite computer activity. If you have not had much (or any) exposure to computers, reflect on the significance of that.
2. **For a Paragraph.** Using your journal as a prewriting exercise, focus on a single aspect of the interaction (or lack of interaction) between you and an increasingly "wired" world.

3. **For an Essay.** In an informational essay (perhaps one you might want to submit to your campus newspaper), describe the range of computer activity/knowledge that students at your school have.

   Prewriting:

   a. Interview a substantial number of your classmates—at least two dozen—about their use and knowledge of computers. Make notes so that you can use some of their responses in your essay.

   b. Check with your school's central computing office and with the Dean of Students' Office. What information do they have about undergraduates and their use of computers? For example, how many students at your school own computers? Most schools gather these statistics.

   c. Visit some of the computer sites on campus. What are the students typically doing? How much of the site's activity is devoted to course work and how much to personal use? The site supervisor might be able to provide some answers.

   Rewriting:

   a. Look carefully at how Kelley integrated quotations from her interviews into her essay. Check each quotation in your essay to make sure your quotations are handled smoothly and punctuated correctly.

   b. Arrange your examples in a variety of ways—you can cut and paste for example. Which order seems to work best? It is always best to try to think of alternative patterns rather than assuming that there is only one way in which the essay can be assembled.

   c. Remember that an effective introduction—one that both grabs your reader's attention and clearly forecasts what is to come—is crucial. Ask some classmates to critique the "interest level" of your opening paragraphs. Do they want to keep reading?

4. **For Research.** One of the current debates centered around the Web involves the use of advertisements on school classroom computers. For example, it is possible for schools to get free computers for student use if the school agrees that, while students are using the machines, the screens will display a constant stream of advertisements. Many districts, unable to fund computer purchases on their own, have

agreed to these conditions. Research the problem—newspapers and magazines (and Websites) will be more useful than books as informational sources. Try to get information that represents "both sides" in this debate. See if you can find classmates who have used these machines or schools that have them or have rejected them. Then write an informational essay discussing the phenomenon and the issues involved.

WEBSITE LINK

How do you know what to believe? The Website will point you to a variety of Web resources on evaluating information gathered from the Web. Check these sites before you write a research paper using Web resources.

Plugging the Kegs

U.S. News & World Report

Like its competitors Time *and* Newsweek, U.S. News and World Report *is a weekly news magazine, devoted, in the words of its Website history, to providing a "straightforward, issues-oriented approach to covering national and international news" and information useful to a broad range of readers. The publication was created in 1948 when* The United States News *(founded in 1940 as a magazine version of a weekly newspaper dating back to the 1920s) merged with* World Report *(founded in 1946) to better reflect the growing interconnectedness of national and international affairs. In recent years, the magazine has become particularly well know for its annual "best" guides, including "America's Best Colleges," "America's Best Hospitals," and "Best Jobs for the Future."*

The following essay originally appeared in January 1998 in a weekly section called "News You Can Use." It was based on a survey sent to 1,320 college presidents across the country (69% responded) asking them about policies and approaches concerning alcohol use on their campuses. The questionnaires were drafted in consultation with public-health experts associated with the Robert Wood Johnson Foundation and Mothers Against Drunk Driving.

BEFORE READING

Connecting: In what ways has alcohol touched your life as a college student? Touched the lives of your classmates?

Anticipating: Is the essay completely objective? Does it ever imply or make evaluative judgments about the behavior it describes?

Jason McCray remembers drinking shots at JB's in Tallahassee, 1
Fla., but after that the details of his 21st birthday fade. The college senior knows from photos his buddies took that, several pubs later, he forced down double shots of whiskey and later vomited under the bar. (They got photos of that, too.) "They had to carry me out," he says.

Thus ended McCray's Tennessee Waltz, a coming-of-legal- 2
age ritual in which Florida State University students celebrate

turning 21 with a free drink, in addition to those bought by friends, at each of the half-dozen or so bars along Tennessee Street.

3 McCray denies that his birthday binge is the way he typically drinks. But it does represent the manner of drinking that too many expect and experience at college. Surveys show that up to 85 percent of all college students imbibe and that nearly half drink heavily. In 1949, when the first thorough study of college drinking was made, undergraduates drank no more than others their age, and college life did not encourage excessive tippling. The same can't be said today. College students drink more because college officials are less strict and many young people drink in high school or before. The result is that students now encounter college cultures in which drinking is not only common but is done mainly to get drunk.

4 Schools tend to respond with hand-wringing, saying there is little they can do. Recent research, including a study by *U.S. News*, indicates that's not so. *U.S. News* got responses from 69 percent of the 1,320 presidents of four-year colleges and universities it surveyed to learn what makes a difference. The survey found that while college presidents try to highlight the evils of student alcohol abuse, many don't see how common binge drinking really is. Only 3 percent of the presidents responding to the questionnaire estimated a rate as high as that found by a Harvard University study and, remarkably, 21 percent couldn't say how common it was on their campuses. Some researchers argue that it is a good idea to teach students when to say when; others say it may be even better for schools to prohibit them from drinking. The *U.S. News* survey and follow-up reporting suggest that schools that allow drinking on campus are up to three times more likely to experience high numbers of binge drinkers.

5 College students don't just down more alcohol, experts say; many often swill stronger forms, such as "PGA" (pure grain alcohol) and potent concoctions of several alcoholic beverages—sometimes through funnels or directly from the keg taps, while hanging upside down. "When I was in school, if you got drunk once a week, you were thought to be somebody no one wanted to hang out with, never mind [getting drunk] three to four times a week," says Fran Cohen, 52, director of the Office of Student Life at the University of Rhode Island. Now she deals with students who don't seem to mind the drunken behavior, wooziness, vomiting, and passing out that accompany too much alcohol.

6 A late-fall fraternity bash at DePauw University in Greencastle, Ind., proves her point. Guests—many of whom had already

achieved a buzz at smaller parties and at the football game against rival Wabash College—tossed empty beer bottles from the balcony of the Delta Tau Delta house, watching them smash in the courtyard. Their target was the fraternity crest, and guests knew to walk far clear of the area when a big bash was going on. Inside, several hundred people, many of them riding on another's shoulders, screamed over the stereo's throbbing bass. Men and women waited their turns to lie on their backs and have beer or schnapps poured out of a bell, the trophy of that day's football victory, into their mouths. After each student gulped—be it one or 12—he or she rose to the cheers of the crowd and the clanking of the bell. Meanwhile, a nauseated woman leaned over a plastic trash can for several minutes, a man holding her so she wouldn't topple in headfirst.

Social scientists call this "binge drinking," defined as five or more drinks for a man at any one time within a two-week period, four or more drinks for a woman. This definition doesn't mean getting falling-down drunk, says Dr. Henry Wechsler, principal investigator in the Harvard study of college drinking. Instead, having five drinks in a row indicates problems associated with drinking. What's more, he found that few students who consume five fail to drink six or more. "It's right there, it's free, it's in front of you, and the next thing you know you've had 12 drinks in an hour and you can't move," one college senior explains. 7

The Harvard study showed that 44 percent of all undergraduates in the United States binge drink—a rate that has been fairly constant for almost 20 years. It also found that 23 percent of the men and 17 percent of the women were frequent binge drinkers—downing a bunch of drinks three or more times in two weeks. 8

This much drinking takes its toll. Tim Anderl, an Ohio University senior, says that typically, "By the end of the fall, you're broke and your grades are in the gutter." Indeed, many students spend more money in a semester on alcohol—over $300—than they do on books. There's also a correlation between drinking and grades. One study found that A students have, on average, three drinks a week, while those making D's and F's average 11 drinks a week. 9

Sex and violence. Problems with grades aren't the only ones plaguing binge drinkers. They are two to five times as likely as other drinkers to engage in unplanned or unprotected sex, get injured, damage property, argue, fight, or face trouble with the police. 10

And some die. Scott Krueger, 18, a high-achieving freshman at Massachusetts Institute of Technology, overdosed on alcohol at 11 a fraternity party in September, slipped into a coma, and died three days later. Leslie Anne Baltz was a 21-year-old honor student at the University of Virginia until November, when she drank too much at a pregame party, was left alone by friends to sleep it off, somehow tumbled down a flight of stairs, hit her head, and died. Alcohol poisoning or alcohol-related accidents killed a least five other undergraduates nationwide during the 1997 fall term. While no one counts the number of college students who die from alcohol use, Dr. David Anderson of George Mason University in Fairfax, Va., estimates that at least 50 die each year.

12 Binge drinkers also make life difficult for students who don't drink so heavily. At schools where more than 50 percent of the students binge drink, Wechsler found that a majority of the nonbingeing students complain of the secondhand effects of binge drinking, ranging "from assault to sexual assault to vandalism to just being a pain all the way around."

13 College administrators often identify student alcohol abuse as one of the biggest challenges they face. Yet, funding for prevention programs, on the increase until 1994, has never averaged more than a few dollars per student, not counting staff salaries. Experts complain that many alcohol education programs seldom involve more than a few posters, some brochures, and an Alcohol Awareness Week, all of which students say are largely ignored.

14 Bill DeJong, director of the Higher Education Center for Alcohol and Other Drug Prevention in Boston, thinks colleges have to change the way they recruit students. "If their view books show scenes of small groups socializing rather than football games, tailgate parties, and so on, they will attract a different kind of student," he argues. The *U.S. News* survey of college presidents suggests that when schools included their alcohol policies and the associated penalties in recruiting materials, they were about half as likely to have high numbers of binge drinkers.

15 That's the strategy being adopted by the University of Rhode Island, once rated a top party school. On a sunny fall afternoon, URI junior Denis Guay guides a tour of the campus for prospective students and their parents to a freshman dormitory room. After pointing out the route to the bathrooms, he states the school's alcohol policy: no drinking anywhere on campus by anyone under 21 and only one six-pack at a time per legal-age student in the dorm rooms. The first offense earns a fine of $50; the second, $100; the third, suspension.

16 Lee and Judi Kroll, on the tour with their son Jon, were glad to hear of the low-tolerance alcohol policy. Jon doubted the

measures were actually enforced. While a number of URI students said it was possible to discreetly drink on campus, more agreed with sophomore Kira Edler, who said, "If you get caught, there are prices to pay." As a result, URI is less of a party school. Since 1990, kegs have been banned from campus, alcohol prohibited from social events, and fines instituted and raised. While the number of violations for possessing alcohol is up, other violations involving alcohol, such as violence or vandalism, have fallen sharply.

The argument against such policies has always been that it pushes drinking underground. Harvard's Wechsler argues that administrators who say that are shunning responsibility. "If you let them drink on campus, it doesn't mean they'll only drink on campus," he says. He maintains that there is less binge drinking on campuses where students are encouraged to focus on other activities. One reason could be that schools with such tough antidrinking policies attract fewer students who want to party. 17

A number of students at Earlham College in Richmond, Ind., said that the school's dry policy influenced their decision to attend the liberal arts college. "One thing I like about it is that if you don't want to see drinking, you can avoid it," says student Roscoe Klausing. 18

Writing more-restrictive policies—which 30 percent of the campuses reporting to *U.S. News* did within the past two years—is no panacea. Consistent enforcement is key, as is filling students' days and nights with meaningful activities. Friday classes are a joke on too many campuses, and grade inflation has allowed students to spend even less time on coursework. "There's nothing else to do but drink" is a common lament among college students. 19

Keep them busy. In general, presidents of colleges in urban areas, where there are more recreational and cultural events to lure students, report lower binge drinking rates on campus than those running schools in less urban settings. In addition, schools with lots of older or part-time students report low binge-drinking rates, probably because those students have families, jobs, or responsibilities that keep them away from the party circuit. 20

Many experts agree that alcohol abuse is perhaps most rampant and causes the most trouble in places where colleges have little or no authority, such as the fraternity system. Studies show that residents of fraternity and sorority row are up to four times as likely to be binge drinkers as other students, and their leaders are the most likely of all. 21

But an organization doesn't have to be Greek to encourage drinking. At St. John's University, an all-male Catholic college in 22 central Minnesota, the school's unofficial rugby club initiated its new members one cold Saturday night at an off-campus party house known by the locals as the Far Side. The behavior is as bizarre as a Gary Larson cartoon. A chant of "Drink, [expletive]! Drink, [expletive]! Drink, [expletive]! Drink!" rings out. Two kegs of beer chill outside while inside a fifth of Jack Daniels waits on a table for the team's rookies—boys clad only in bras and panties. St. John's officials insist that the incident is not typical there, and they have met with the rugby team to plan alternatives for initiating new members.

23 Often, though, such behavior at most colleges has received little more than a "boys will be boys" response until student injuries or deaths, as well as lawsuits and rising insurance premiums, prompt some action. Nationally, two fraternities have committed to having dry houses by 2000. In December, all 66 member fraternities of the National Interfraternity Conference passed a resolution recommending alcohol-free chapter houses. URI's Carothers has moved all but two fraternities onto campus, where they must comply with school rules. The University of Iowa's interfraternity council has mandated that official Greek parties be alcohol free starting next fall.

24 **Cheap beer.** While some colleges and Greek organizations are making headway, the pubs and liquor stores near colleges tend to be much less cooperative. One Cornell University senior says, "I was 17 when I got to school and I could get a drink anywhere," including several bars and convenience stores near campus, where students often present false proof of age. Ads in college newspapers tempt students with "Nickel Beer," "Beat the Clock," and "Penny 'til You Pee" nights, where drinks are discounted or served free with a small cover charge. In the crowded parking lot outside Caesar's, an oceanside bar running a busy "Slug Fest" special about 5 miles from URI, senior Anthony Antorino was insisting that students there know their drinking limits when he had to interrupt himself. "Oh my God!" he exclaimed. "Well, there's an exception." He pointed to a young woman who had just squatted by the front wheel of a car to relieve herself.

25 Some college administrators have joined community leaders on "town and gown" councils to tackle this and other problems. Experts say that schools can wield their economic clout to compel local governments and alcohol control boards to action. The Presidents Leadership Group of the Higher Education Center for Alcohol and Other Drug Prevention goes a step further, urging their colleagues to work at the state level for more stringent laws. A peeved Bill Sheen knows such efforts work. After the Tallahassee

police started their weekend "Party Patrol," the sophomore business major was fined $195 for holding a cup of Coke and Jim Beam whiskey outside a rowdy apartment gathering. "It sucks. We can't have a party," he says.

Colleges and universities will never rid themselves of alcohol abuse completely, Wechsler says; instead, the goal is to change the norm. Look at what happened with smoking. "No Smoking" signs are obeyed with few complaints. The designated driver, an idea unheard of 15 years ago, is now a common practice, even for partying college kids. Alcohol education did reach some of the more moderate drinkers, experts say. Now it's time to target heavy drinkers. 26

QUESTIONS ON SUBJECT AND PURPOSE

1. What is "binge drinking"?
2. What is the effect of the statistics quoted in paragraph 4? How does that information function in your reading response to the essay?
3. What purpose might the essay have? Is it, for example, trying to persuade readers to do something?

QUESTIONS ON STRATEGY AND AUDIENCE

1. What are the primary sources of information in the essay?
2. What is the effect of the final paragraph?
3. The article was published in a national news magazine. What expectations would the magazine have had of its audience?

QUESTIONS ON VOCABULARY AND STYLE

1. Why might the essay begin with the example of a single student?
2. What effect is created by the final sentences in paragraphs 24 or 25?
3. Be prepared to define the following words: *panacea* (paragraph 19), *rampant* (21), *clout* (25), *rowdy* (25).

WRITING SUGGESTIONS

1. **For Your Journal.** Whether you drink or not, reflect in your journal about the role of alcohol either in your life or in the life of a close friend or classmate or family member.

2. **For a Paragraph.** In a paragraph, explore either why you drink or why you do not drink. What reasons can you give for your behavior?
3. **For an Essay.** What is your campus doing about alcohol? What are your school's policies—for underage drinking, for drinking on campus, for drinking at tail-gate parties, for drinking off-campus? What are the penalties for alcohol abuse? What educational programs are in place? How widespread a problem is alcohol on your campus? In the immediate community around the school?

   Prewriting:

   a. Contact your Dean of Students for copies of official policies concerning the use of alcohol. Also inquire to see if any educational programs are being offered on campus.

   b. Interview a substantial number of your classmates of all ages—at least two dozen—about their use of alcohol. Make notes so that you can use some of their responses in your essay.

   c. Contact your campus security office and your local police about their perceptions of student alcohol use. Is it a problem? In what ways?

   Rewriting:

   a. Look carefully at how examples and quotations are integrated into the article. Check each quotation in your paper to make sure your quotations are handled smoothly and punctuated correctly.

   b. Remember that several relevant and well-developed examples are more effective than many irrelevant or sketchy ones. Do not try to include every piece of information you found. Ask a peer reader to assess the quality of your examples.

   c. Try for an interesting title and an effective opening. Remember you want to "hook" your reader, and you want to keep your reader's attention.
4. **For Research.** Although the essay refers to some reasons why college students drink, the essay is more a description of the problem than an analysis of why the problem is there. What do studies suggest about the prevalence of drinking among college students? What explanations do researchers

offer? Is the problem confined to college students? That is, do young people who are not attending college show a similar pattern of alcohol abuse? Using published research, write a research paper in which you analyze the problem to suggest possible causes.

Website Link

Did you feel that the picture of campus drinking sketched out in this essay didn't quite match your campus or your friends? Check out a scholarly (but reader-friendly) Website that offers a somewhat different view of the situation.

TWO

Narration

When a friend asks, "What did you do last night?" you reply with a narrative: "After the chemistry midterm was over at 8:30, we went to Shakey's for pizza. Then we stopped at the bowling alley for a couple of games, and about 11 we split up and I went back to the dorm for some serious sleeping." A narrative is a story, and all stories, whether they are personal narratives, or novels, or histories, have the same essential ingredients: a series of events arranged in a chosen order and told by a narrator for some particular purpose. Your reply, for example, exhibits all four elements: a series of events (the four things you did last evening) arranged in an order (chronological) and told by a narrator ("I," a first-person narrator) for some particular purpose (to answer your friend's question).

Any type of writing can and does use narration; it is not something found only in personal experience essays or fiction. Narration can also be used to provide evidence in an argument. Bob Greene in "Cut" (Chapter 1) groups five personal narrative examples to support his assertion that being cut from an athletic team can make you a superachiever in life. Narration can also be found mixed with description in William Least Heat Moon's "Nameless, Tennessee" (Chapter 3) or underlying a persuasive essay in Richard Rodriguez's "None of This Is Fair" (Chapter 9). In fact, there are examples of narration in the readings found in every chapter of this text.

What Do You Include in a Narrative?

No one, probably not even your mother, wants to hear everything you did today. Readers, like listeners, want you to exercise selection, for some things are more important or interesting than others. Historians have to select out of a mass of data what they will include and emphasize. Bert Vallee in "Alcohol in the Western World" summarizes over 10,000 years of history in his essay. He cannot tell the whole story, for if he did, the result would be a very long book and not an essay. Moreover, the reader would get entangled in the trivia, and the significant shape and meaning of the narrative would be lost. Even in personal experiences you condense and select. Generally you need to pare away, to cut out the unnecessary and the uninteresting. What you include depends, of course, on what happened and, more important, on the purpose or meaning that you are trying to convey.

How Do You Structure a Narrative?

Time structures all narratives, although events need not always be arranged in chronological order. A narrative can begin at one point in time and then "flash back" to an earlier action or event. Langston Hughes's "Salvation" begins with a narrator looking back at an experience that occurred when he was thirteen, although the story itself is told in the order in which it happened. The most typical inversion is to begin at the end of the narrative and then to move backward in time to explain how that end was reached. More complex narratives may shift several times back and forth between incidents in the past or between the past and the present. Two cautions are obvious: first, do not switch time too frequently, especially in short papers; second, make sure that the switches are clearly marked for your reader.

Remember as well that you control where your narrative begins and ends. For example, Evans Hopkins begins "Lockdown" with his predawn visit from two prison guards in armored vests and riot helmets; he does not begin with an account of the events that led to the lockdown or with the events that led to his imprisonment. Those details Hopkins fills in later, for they are not as dramatic or central to the points that he is trying to make. In a similar way, you might want to have your narrative build to a climactic moment of insight and then end. A formal, summary conclusion added to a narrative essay sometimes just obscures the significance of the experience.

Writers frequently change or modify an actual personal experience in order to tell the story more effectively, heighten the tension, or make their purpose clearer. In her essay "On Keeping a Notebook," essayist and novelist Joan Didion remarks:

> I tell what some would call lies. "That's simply not true," the members of my family frequently tell me when they come up against my memory of a shared event. "The party was *not* for you, the spider was *not* a black widow, *it wasn't that way at all*." Very likely they are right, for not only have I always had trouble distinguishing between what happened and what merely might have happened, but I remain unconvinced that the distinction, for my purposes, matters.

Whenever you recall an experience, even if it just happened last week, you do not necessarily remember it exactly as it happened. The value of a personal narrative does not rest in accuracy to the original experience. It does not matter, for example, whether the scene with Sister Monroe in the Christian Methodist Episcopal Church occurred exactly as Maya Angelou describes it years later. What does matter is that it could have happened and that it is faithful to the purpose Angelou intends.

How Are Narratives Told?

Two things are especially important in relating your narrative. First, you need to choose a point of view from which to tell the story. Personal experience narratives, such as those by Hughes, Angelou, and Hopkins, are generally told in the first person: the narrator is an actor in the story. Historical narratives and narratives used as illustrations in a larger piece of writing are generally told in the third person. The historian, for example, is outside the narrative and provides an objective view of the actions described. Bert Vallee never interjects himself into "Alcohol and the Western World"; he remains an objective, detached historian who explains how things were. Judith Ortiz Cofer mixes first-person and third-person narration in "Marina." The essay begins with a first-person account of how she and her mother went for a walk after an argument. They encounter a distinguished older gentleman with a little girl, and that meeting leads to the "story within the story," the account or tale of Marina and Kiki, which is narrated in the third-person. Once that story is finished, the essay returns to the first person as Cofer and her mother ponder the significance of the tale. Point of view can vary in one other way. The narrator can reveal only his or her own thoughts (using what is known as the limited point of view), or the narrator can reveal what anyone else in the narrative thinks or feels (using the omniscient, or all-knowing, point of view).

Second, you need to decide whether you are going to "show" or "tell" or mix the two. You "show" in a narrative by dramatizing a scene and creating dialogue. Hughes re-creates his experience for the reader by showing what happened and by recording some of the conversation that took place the night he was "saved from sin." Telling, by contrast, is summarizing what happened. For example, the story of Marina and Kiki in Cofer's "Marina" is told to the reader by the narrator. Marina and Kiki never talk; the story within the story contains no dialogue. Showing makes a narrative more vivid, for it allows the reader to experience the scene directly. Telling allows you to include a greater number of events and details. Either way, selectivity is necessary. Even when the experience being narrated took place over a short period of time—such as Hughes's experiences one evening at church—a writer cannot dramatize everything that happened. When an experience lasts for four and a half months, like the lockdown in Hopkins's essay, a writer could never summarize events on a day-to-day basis. Each writer selects the moments that best give shape and significance to the experience.

What Do You Write About If Nothing Ever Happened to You?

It is easy to assume that the only things worth writing about are once-in-a-lifetime experiences—a heroic or death-defying act, a personal tragedy, an Olympic medal-winning performance. It is likely that few readers have been in a lockdown in a prison, and probably not many have heard a tale like that of Marina and Kiki; but a good personal-experience narrative does not need to be based on an extraordinary experience. In fact, ordinary experiences, because they are about things familiar to every reader, are the best sources for personal narratives. There is nothing extraordinary, for example, about the events related in Langston Hughes's "Salvation," even though Hughes's experience was a turning point in his life. Bob Greene in "Cut" (Chapter 1) narrates a basic story—about being "cut" from a team—that is all too familiar to most readers. In one way or another, probably everyone has experienced a similar experience and disappointment.

The secret to writing a good personal experience narrative lies in two areas. First, you must tell your story artfully. Following the advice outlined in this introduction is a good way to ensure that your narrative will be constructed as effectively as possible. Just telling what happened is not enough, though, for you must do a second, equally important thing: you must reveal a purpose in your tale. Purposes can be many. You might offer insight into human behavior or motivation; you might mark a significant moment in your life; you might reveal an awareness of what it is to be young and to have dreams; you might reflect on the precariousness of life and inevitability of change and decay; you might even use your experience to argue, as Evans Hopkins does, for a change in social attitudes. However you use your narrative, what is important is that your story have a point, a reason for being, and that you make that reason clear to your reader.

SAMPLE STUDENT ESSAY

Hope Zucker decided to write about a powerful childhood memory—a pair of red shoes that became her "ruby slippers" and the key to the Land of Oz.

EARLIER DRAFT

MY NEW SHOES

When you are four years old anything longer than five minutes feels like eternity, so when the clerk told me and my mom that it would take three to four weeks for my new shoes to arrive, I was almost in tears. Since seeing The Wizard of Oz, I had thought of little else other than owning a pair of ruby slippers. My dreams were full of spinning houses, little munchkins, flying monkeys, and talking lions. All I wanted was to be Dorothy, and the shoe store had made a promise to find me a pair of red mary-janes which would hopefully take me to Munchkin Land and Oz.

For the next three weeks I made all the preparations I could think of in order to become Dorothy. It did not matter how convincing Judy Garland was because I knew in my heart that I was the true Dorothy. I sang "Somewhere Over the Rainbow" day and night, and I played dress up with an old light blue checked dress of my mother's. I even went as far as to carry my dog in a basket, but that did not work out too well. I had my mom braid my long brown hair, and after I insisted, she tied a light blue ribbon around each braid. I skipped wherever I went, and I even went as far as coloring part of our driveway with chalk to create my very own yellow brick road.

The only thing missing to my new persona was my ruby slippers. After my mother explained to me that three weeks really was not that far off in the future, I decided to help the store in their search for my red mary-janes. For a month I called the store everyday when I got home from preschool. Mr. Rogers and Big Bird could wait because there was nothing in the whole wide world that was more important than my red patent leather shoes. By the end of the month, the nice little old ladies at the store knew me by name and thought that I was the cutest child. Lucky for them, they did not have to put up with me.

Finally, after what seemed like years, the lady on the other side of the phone said that yes, my shiny red shoes had arrived. Now I had only to plead with my mother to get her to make a special trip into the city. After a few days of delay and a great deal of futile temper tantrums, my mom took me to the store. I could hardly contain my excitement. During the ride, I practiced the one and only line that only the real Dorothy could say, "There's no place like home." And of course, I clicked my beat up boondockers three times each time I recited my part. It was all practice for the real thing.

As we pulled into the parking lot, all the little old ladies inside the store waved to me as if they had been expecting me for days. I finally got to see my shoes, and they were as perfect as I knew they'd be. I was practically jumping out of my seat when she began to remove the stiff tissue paper surrounding my shoes, so rather than wait for her to fit my little feet into my slippers, I grabbed them from her and did it myself. They were the prettiest pair of shoes any girl could have!

For the next few weeks I was Dorothy and I'd stop everyone I'd see in order to prove it by tapping my heels together and saying, "There's no place like home." But soon my feet grew too big for my ruby slippers, and as I graduated into the next larger size, I no longer wanted to be Dorothy. As I grew up, so did my dreams. Cinderella, now she was someone to be! Yet, once again that phase, like the phases I am going through now, passed fairly quickly.

Hope made enough copies of her essay so that the whole class could read and then discuss it. After reading her essay to the class, Hope asked her classmates for their reactions. Several students suggested that she tighten her narrative, eliminating details that were not essential to the story. Most of their suggestions were centered in paragraphs 4 and 5. "Why mention Mr. Rogers and Big Bird?" someone asked. "I didn't want you to have to wait several days to pick them up, and I didn't want to be reminded of your temper," commented another. When Hope came to revise her draft, she used this advice. She also eliminated a number of clichés and made a significant change in the ending of the paper. Notice how much more effective the final version is as the result of these minor revisions.

Revised Draft

THE RUBY SLIPPERS

To a four-year old, anything longer than five minutes feels like eternity, so when the clerk told me and my mom that it would take three to four weeks for my new shoes to arrive, I was almost in tears. Since seeing The Wizard of Oz, I had thought of little else other than owning a pair of ruby slippers. My dreams were full of spinning houses, little munchkins, flying monkeys, and talking lions. All I wanted was to be Dorothy, and the shoe store had made a promise to find me a pair of red mary-janes which would hopefully take me to Munchkin Land and Oz.

For the next three weeks I made all the preparations I could think of in order to become Dorothy. It did not matter how convincing Judy Garland was because I knew in my heart that I was the true Dorothy. I sang "Somewhere Over the Rainbow" day and night, and I played dress up with an old light blue checked dress of my mother's. I even went as far as to carry my dog in a basket. My mom braided my long brown hair, and after I insisted, she tied a light blue ribbon around each braid. I skipped everywhere I went and colored part of our driveway with chalk to create my very own yellow brick road.

The only thing missing was my ruby slippers. After my mother explained that three weeks really was not that far off, I decided to help the store in their search for my red mary-janes. For a month I called the store everyday when I got home from preschool. By the end of the month, the ladies at the store knew me by name.

Finally, the woman on the other end of the phone said that yes, my shiny red shoes had arrived. I could hardly contain my excitement. During the ride, I practiced the one line that only the real Dorothy could say, "There's no place like home." And of course, I clicked my beat up loafers three times each time I recited that line. It was all practice for the real thing.

As we pulled into the parking lot, all the ladies inside the store waved to me as if they had been expecting me. I finally got to see my shoes, and they were as perfect as I had imagined. I was practically jumping out of my seat when she began to remove the stiff tissue paper surrounding my shoes, so rather than wait for her to fit my little feet into my slippers, I grabbed them from her and did it myself. They were the prettiest pair of shoes any girl could have!

For the next few weeks I was Dorothy and I'd stop everyone I'd see in order to prove it by tapping my heels together and saying, "There's no place like home." But soon my feet grew too big for my ruby slippers, and as I graduated into the next larger size, I no longer wanted to be Dorothy. As I grew up, so did my dreams.

Some Things to Remember

1. Decide first why you are telling the reader *this* story. You must have a purpose clearly in mind.
2. Choose an illustration, event, or experience that can be covered adequately within the space limitations you face. Do not try to narrate the history of your life in an essay!
3. Decide on which point of view you will use. Do you want to be a part of the narrative or an objective observer? Which is more appropriate for your purpose?
4. Keeping your purpose in mind, select the details or events that seem the most important or the most revealing.
5. Arrange those details in an order—either a strict chronological one or one that employs a flashback. Remember to keep your verb tenses consistent and to signal any switches in time.
6. Remember the differences between showing and telling. Which method will be better for your narrative?

Using Narration in Your Writing for Other Courses

Various kinds of college writing assignments will require you to use narration, at least in part. Most of these will involve third-person narration rather than first-person experiential writing—although you may occasionally be asked to write about your own experiences as a means of exploring particular issues raised in a course. Here are some examples of assignments that would include narration.

- **Chemistry.** In a lab report discussing the results of an experimental procedure, in one section you would objectively recount the method used in conducting the procedure.
- **History/American Studies.** For an oral history project, you might be asked to interview a senior family member or another older person to relate that person's experiences during an important period of history.
- **Education.** For an assignment asking you to observe and report on child development during the first-grade, you might write up a final case study tracing the progress of the particular child you observed over the first three months of school.
- **Engineering.** In completing a project studying the viability of replacing a less expensive lubricant for the one currently used in particular manufacturing process, you might be assigned an interim report tracing your progress in testing and evaluating other lubricants.
- **Literature.** In studying a short story, you might be asked to write a creative response, retelling the story from the perspective of a character different from the original narrator.
- **Communications.** For an essay exam question, you might be asked to trace the development of the American broadcast industry.

Visualizing Narration

Narratives do not always involve or even require words. Visual sequences can also tell stories—remember that the earliest films were silent! Comic or cartoon strips, comic books, and graphic novels all involve narration. Here cartoonist Roz Chast has fun with a story "template" (a pattern). Think how many stories can ultimately be reduced to the pattern—"once upon a time," "suddenly," "luckily," and "happily ever after." Notice how the panel exhibits the characteristics of a narrative—a series of events arranged in a chronological order told (shown) by a narrator (artist) for some particular purpose (to entertain).

Visit the Prentice Hall Reader's Website

When you have finished reading an essay, check out the additional material available at the *Reader's* Website at www.prenhall.com/miller. For each reading, you will find a list of related readings connected with the topic or the author; additional background information; a group of relevant "hot-linked" Web resources (just click on the site you want to visit); and still more writing suggestions.

NARRATING

Have you ever visited the National Air and Space Museum in Washington, D.C.? Did you know that it is increasingly possible to "see" museum exhibits on-line? Visit one of the on-line exhibitions now available at the National Air and Space—these include "Apollo to the Moon," "The Space Race," and "Star Wars": The Magic of Myth." The site is hot-linked at the *Reader's* Website and is just a click away. Once you have seen the exhibit, practice your narration skills with the paragraph-writing assignment.

SALVATION

Langston Hughes

Born in Joplin, Missouri, Langston Hughes (1902–1967) was an important figure in the Harlem Renaissance. He is best known for his jazz- and blues-inspired poetry, though he was also a talented prose writer and playwright. Among his writings are Simple Speaks His Mind *(1950), the first of four volumes of some of his best-loved stories; and* Ask Your Mama: 12 Moods for Jazz *(1961), one of his later, angry collections of poetry, fueled by emotions surrounding the civil rights movements.*

The Big Sea: An Autobiography *(1940), published when Hughes was thirty-eight years old, is a memoir of his early years, consisting of a series of short narratives focusing on events and people. After the death of his grandmother, Hughes was raised by Auntie Reed, one of his grandmother's friends. Uncle Reed, Auntie's husband, was, as Hughes notes in* The Big Sea, *"a sinner and never went to church as long as he lived . . . but both of them were very good and kind. . . . And no doubt from them I learned to like both Christians and sinners equally well."*

On Writing: *Hughes once noted that, to him, the prime function of creative writing is "to affirm life, to yeah-say the excitement of living in relation to the vast rhythms of the universe of which we are a part, to untie the riddles of the gutter in order to closer tie the knot between man and God."*

BEFORE READING

Connecting: Was there a time in your teenage years when you were disappointed by someone or something?

Anticipating: No narrative recounts every minute of an experience. Writers must leave out far more than they include. What events connected with this experience does Hughes leave out of his narrative? Why?

1 I was saved from sin when I was going on thirteen. But not really saved. It happened like this. There was a big revival at my Auntie Reed's church. Every night for weeks there had been much preaching, singing, praying, and shouting, and some very hardened sinners had been brought to Christ, and the membership of the church had grown by leaps and bounds. Then just before the

revival ended, they held a special meeting for children, "to bring the young lambs to the fold." My aunt spoke of it for days ahead. That night I was escorted to the front row and placed on the mourners' bench with all the other young sinners, who had not yet been brought to Jesus.

My aunt told me that when you were saved you saw a light, 2
and something happened to you inside! And Jesus came into your life! And God was with you from then on! She said you could see and hear and feel Jesus in your soul. I believed her. I had heard a great many old people say the same thing and it seemed to me they ought to know. So I sat there calmly in the hot, crowded church, waiting for Jesus to come to me.

The preacher preached a wonderful rhythmical sermon, all 3
moans and shouts and lonely cries and dire pictures of hell, and then he sang a song about the ninety and nine safe in the fold, but one little lamb was left out in the cold. Then he said: "Won't you come? Won't you come to Jesus? Young lambs, won't you come?" And he held out his arms to all us young sinners there on the mourners' bench. And the little girls cried. And some of them jumped up and went to Jesus right away. But most of us just sat there.

A great many old people came and knelt around us and 4
prayed, old women with jet-black faces and braided hair, old men with work-gnarled hands. And the church sang a song about the lower lights are burning, some poor sinners to be saved. And the whole building rocked with prayer and song.

Still I kept waiting to *see* Jesus. 5

Finally all the young people had gone to the altar and were 6
saved, but one boy and me. He was a rounder's son named Westley. Westley and I were surrounded by sisters and deacons praying. It was very hot in the church, and getting late now. Finally Westley said to me in a whisper: "God damn! I'm tired o' sitting here. Let's get up and be saved." So he got up and was saved.

Then I was left all alone on the mourner's bench. My aunt 7
came and knelt at my knees and cried, while prayers and song swirled all around me in the little church. The whole congregation prayed for me alone, in a mighty wail of moans and voices. And I kept waiting serenely for Jesus, waiting, waiting—but he didn't come. I wanted to see him, but nothing happened to me. Nothing! I wanted something to happen to me, but nothing happened.

I heard the songs and the minister saying: "Why don't 8
you come? My dear child, why don't you come to Jesus? Jesus is

waiting for you. He wants you. Why don't you come? Sister Reed, what is this child's name?"

9 "Langston," my aunt sobbed.

10 "Langston, why don't you come? Why don't you come and be saved? Oh, Lamb of God! Why don't you come?"

11 Now it was really getting late. I began to be ashamed of myself, holding everything up so long. I began to wonder what God thought about Westley, who certainly hadn't seen Jesus either, but who was now sitting proudly on the platform, swinging his knickerbockered legs and grinning down at me, surrounded by deacons and old women on their knees praying. God had not struck Westley dead for taking his name in vain or for lying in the temple. So I decided that maybe to save further trouble, I'd better lie, too, and say that Jesus had come, and get up and be saved.

12 So I got up.

13 Suddenly the whole room broke into a sea of shouting, as they saw me rise. Waves of rejoicing swept the place. Women leaped in the air. My aunt threw her arms around me. The minister took me by the hand and led me to the platform.

14 When things quieted down, in a hushed silence, punctuated by a few ecstatic "Amens," all the new young lambs were blessed in the name of God. Then joyous singing filled the room.

15 That night, for the last time in my life but one—for I was a big boy twelve years old—I cried. I cried, in bed alone, and couldn't stop. I buried my head under the quilts, but my aunt heard me. She woke up and told my uncle I was crying because the Holy Ghost had come into my life, and because I had seen Jesus. But I was really crying because I couldn't bear to tell her that I had lied, that I had deceived everybody in the church, that I hadn't seen Jesus, and that now I didn't believe there was a Jesus any more, since he didn't come to help me.

QUESTIONS ON SUBJECT AND PURPOSE

1. Who narrates the story? From what point in time is it told?
2. What does the narrator expect to happen when he is to be saved? What does happen?
3. Why does the narrator cry at the end of the story?
4. What was Hughes's attitude toward his experience when it first happened? At the time he originally wrote this selection? How does the opening sentence reflect that change in attitude?

QUESTIONS ON STRATEGY AND AUDIENCE

1. Why did Hughes not tell the story in the present tense? How would doing so change the story?
2. How much dialogue is used in the narration? Why does Hughes not use more?
3. Why does Hughes blend telling with showing in the story?
4. How much time is represented by the events in the story? Where does Hughes compress the time in his narrative? Why does he do so?

QUESTIONS ON VOCABULARY AND STYLE

1. What is the effect of the short paragraphs (5, 9, and 12)? How does Hughes use paragraphing to help shape his story?
2. How much description does Hughes include in his narrative? What types of details does he single out?
3. What is the effect of the exclamation marks used in paragraph 2?
4. Try to identify or explain the following phrases: *the ninety and nine safe in the fold* (paragraph 3), *the lower lights are burning* (4), *a rounder's son* (6), *knickerbockered legs* (11).

WRITING SUGGESTIONS

1. **For Your Journal.** What can you remember from your early teenage years? In your journal, first make a list of significant moments—both high and low points—and then re-create one moment in prose.
2. **For a Paragraph.** We have all been disappointed by someone or something in our life. Single out a particular moment from your past. After spending some time remembering what happened and how you felt, narrate that experience for a general reader in a paragraph. Remember that your paragraph must reveal what the experience meant to you. Try using some dialogue.
3. **For an Essay.** Have you ever experienced anything that changed your life? It does not need to be a dramatic change—perhaps just a conviction that you will *never* do that again or that you will *always* be sure to do that again. In an essay, narrate for a reader that experience. Remember

that your narrative should illustrate or prove the experience's significance to you.

Prewriting:

a. Divide your prewriting sessions for this paper into a series of activities done on different days. On day one, concentrate just on making a list of possible vivid experiences—a near miss, a careless moment, a time you were caught, a stupid choice.

b. On day two, spend half an hour freewriting about two of the events from your list. Try to do one writing in the morning and one in the afternoon. Do not worry about writing complete, correct sentences. Do not stop during the writing.

c. On day three, spend an hour thinking about one of the two events. Jot down as much detail as you can remember.

d. On day four, write a draft of the essay, using the details gathered from the activities of the first three days.

Rewriting:

a. A successful narrative has a shape and a purpose. You do not need to include everything that happened, just those events relevant to the experience and its effect on you. Look again at the narratives included in this chapter. Notice what they include and exclude. Does your narrative show the same economy?

b. Did you use any dialogue? Sparing use will probably make your narrative more vivid—that is, it will show rather than tell.

c. Is the order of events clear to the reader? Is the story told in a strict chronological order? Did you use flashbacks? Think about other possible arrangements for your narrative.

4. **For Research.** Does Hughes seem to be serious about his experience—did he "lose" his faith as a result of what happened? Find other examples of Hughes's writing (check your college's library catalog for books by Hughes and perhaps also some of the on-line databases). Then, in an essay, analyze the significance (or insignificance) of this event in Hughes's writing. Be sure to formulate an explicit thesis about the importance of the event in Hughes's work. Be

sure to document any direct quotations or information taken from other sources.

Website Link

Did you think that the episode that Hughes narrates in the essay actually happened? Did you think it really did become a memory that Hughes never forgot? Check out the biographical background for the essay at the Website.

Sister Monroe

Maya Angelou

Maya Angelou was born Marguerita Johnson in St. Louis, Missouri, in 1928. A talented performing artist as well as a poet and autobiographer, Angelou has used much of her writing to explore the American black female identity. Among her many accomplishments, she was coordinator for the Southern Christian Leadership Conference, and she was invited by President Clinton to compose and perform a poem, "On the Pulse of Morning," for the 1993 presidential inaugural. Her most significant writings have been her five volumes of autobiography (1970–1987); among her recent books are Wouldn't Take Nothing for My Journey Now *(1993) and several collections of poems.*

The following selection is from the first of Angelou's memoirs, I Know Why the Caged Bird Sings *(1970), a work that describes her early years in Stamps, Arkansas. One critic called that work a "revealing portrait of the customs and harsh circumstances of black life in the segregated South." Here in a brilliantly comic moment, Angelou recalls how Sister Monroe "got the spirit" one Sunday morning at church.*

On Writing: *In an interview about her goals as a writer, Angelou observed: "When I'm writing, I am trying to find out who I am, who we are, what we're capable of, how we feel, how we lose and stand up. . . . But I'm also trying for the language. I'm trying to see how it can really sound. I really love language. I love it for what it does for us, how it allows us to explain the pain and the glory, the nuances and delicacies of our existence. And then it allows us to laugh. . . . We need language."*

BEFORE READING

Connecting: As a spectator, when do you find a physical mishap, such as a fight or fall, comic? What is necessary for us to laugh at "slapstick comedy" and not be concerned about the welfare of the people involved?

Anticipating: How does Angelou create humor in this narrative? What makes it funny?

1 In the Christian Methodist Episcopal Church the children's section was on the right, cater-cornered from the pew that held those ominous women called the Mothers of the Church. In the young

people's section the benches were placed close together, and when a child's legs no longer comfortably fitted in the narrow space, it was an indication to the elders that that person could now move into the intermediate area (center church). Bailey and I were allowed to sit with the other children only when there were informal meetings, church socials or the like. But on the Sundays when Reverend Thomas preached, it was ordained that we occupy the first row, called the mourners' bench. I thought we were placed in front because Momma was proud of us, but Bailey assured me that she just wanted to keep her grandchildren under her thumb and eye.

Reverend Thomas took his text from Deuteronomy. And I 2
was stretched between loathing his voice and wanting to listen to the sermon. Deuteronomy was my favorite book in the Bible. The laws were so absolute, so clearly set down, that I knew if a person truly wanted to avoid hell and brimstone, and being roasted forever in the devil's fire, all she had to do was memorize Deuteronomy and follow its teaching, word for word. I also liked the way the word rolled off the tongue.

Bailey and I sat alone on the front bench, the wooden slats 3
pressing hard on our behinds and the backs of our thighs. I would have wriggled just a bit, but each time I looked over at Momma, she seemed to threaten, "Move and I'll tear you up," so, obedient to the unvoiced command, I sat still. The church ladies were warming up behind me with a few hallelujahs and praise the Lords and Amens, and the preacher hadn't really moved into the meat of the sermon.

It was going to be a hot service. 4

On my way into church, I saw Sister Monroe, her open-faced 5
gold crown glinting when she opened her mouth to return a neighborly greeting. She lived in the country and couldn't get to church every Sunday, so she made up for her absences by shouting so hard when she did make it that she shook the whole church. As soon as she took her seat, all the ushers would move to her side of the church because it took three women and sometimes a man or two to hold her.

Once she hadn't been to church for a few months (she had 6
taken off to have a child), she got the spirit and started shouting, throwing her arms around and jerking her body, so that the ushers went over to hold her down, but she tore herself away from them and ran up to the pulpit. She stood in front of the altar, shaking like a freshly caught trout. She screamed at Reverend Taylor. "Preach it. I say, preach it." Naturally he kept on preaching as if she wasn't standing there telling him what to do. Then she

screamed an extremely fierce "I said, preach it" and stepped up on the altar. The Reverend kept on throwing out phrases like home-run balls and Sister Monroe made a quick break and grasped for him. For just a second, everything and everyone in the church except Reverend Taylor and Sister Monroe hung loose like stockings on a washline. Then she caught the minister by the sleeve of his jacket and his coattail, then she rocked him from side to side.

7 I have to say this for our minister, he never stopped giving us the lesson. The usher board made its way to the pulpit, going up both aisles with a little more haste than is customarily seen in church. Truth to tell, they fairly ran to the minister's aid. Then two of the deacons, in their shiny Sunday suits, joined the ladies in white on the pulpit, and each time they pried Sister Monroe loose from the preacher he took another deep breath and kept on preaching, and Sister Monroe grabbed him in another place, and more firmly. Reverend Taylor was helping his rescuers as much as possible by jumping around when he got a chance. His voice at one point got so low it sounded like a roll of thunder, then Sister Monroe's "Preach it" cut through the roar, and we all wondered (I did, in any case) if it would ever end. Would they go on forever, or get tired out at last like a game of blindman's bluff that lasted too long, with nobody caring who was "it"?

8 I'll never know what might have happened, because magically the pandemonium spread. The spirit infused Deacon Jackson and Sister Willson, the chairman of the usher board, at the same time. Deacon Jackson, a tall, thin, quiet man, who was also a part-time Sunday school teacher, gave a scream like a falling tree, leaned back on thin air and punched Reverend Taylor on the arm. It must have hurt as much as it caught the Reverend unawares. There was a moment's break in the rolling sounds and Reverend Taylor jerked around surprised, and hauled off and punched Deacon Jackson. In the same second Sister Willson caught his tie, looped it over her fist a few times, and pressed down on him. There wasn't time to laugh or cry before all three of them were down on the floor behind the altar. Their legs spiked out like kindling wood.

9 Sister Monroe, who had been the cause of all the excitement, walked off the dais, cool and spent, and raised her flinty voice in the hymn, "I came to Jesus, as I was, worried, wounded, and sad, I found in Him a resting place and He has made me glad."

10 The minister took advantage of already being on the floor and asked in a choky little voice if the church would kneel with him to offer a prayer of thanksgiving. He said we had been visited with a mighty spirit, and let the whole church say Amen.

On the next Sunday, he took his text from the eighteenth chapter of the Gospel according to St. Luke, and talked quietly but seriously about the Pharisees, who prayed in the streets so that the public would be impressed with their religious devotion. I doubt that anyone got the message—certainly not those to whom it was directed. The deacon board, however, did appropriate funds for him to buy a new suit. The other was a total loss. 11

QUESTIONS ON SUBJECT AND PURPOSE

1. Who is the narrator? How old does she seem to be? How do you know?
2. Why does Sister Monroe behave as she does?
3. How does the section on the narrator and Bailey act as a preface to the story of Sister Monroe? Is it relevant, for example, that the narrator's favorite book of the Bible is Deuteronomy?

QUESTIONS ON STRATEGY AND AUDIENCE

1. Part of the art of narration is knowing what events to select. Look carefully at Angelou's story of Sister Monroe (paragraphs 5–9). What events does she choose to include in her narrative?
2. How is Sister Monroe described? Make a list of all of the physical particulars we are given about her. How, other than direct description, is Sister Monroe revealed to the reader?
3. What shift occurs between paragraphs 5 and 6? Did you notice it the first time you read the selection?

QUESTIONS ON VOCABULARY AND STYLE

1. Other than a few words uttered by Sister Monroe, Angelou uses no other dialogue in the selection. How, then, is the story told? What advantage does this method have?
2. Writing humor is never easy. Having a funny situation is essential, but in addition, the story must be told in the right way. (Remember how people can ruin a good joke?) How does Angelou's language and style contribute to the humor in the selection?
3. How effective are the following images:
   a. "She stood in front of the altar, shaking like a freshly caught trout" (paragraph 6).

b. "The Reverend kept on throwing out phrases like home-run balls" (6).

c. "Everyone in the church . . . hung loose like stockings on a washline" (6).

d. "Their legs spiked out like kindling wood" (8).

WRITING SUGGESTIONS

1. **For Your Journal.** Observe people for a day. In your journal, make a list of the funny or comic moments that you notice. Select one of those moments and first describe the situation you witnessed, then analyze why it seemed funny to you.
2. **For a Paragraph.** Everyone has experienced a funny, embarrassing moment—maybe it happened to you or maybe you just witnessed it. In a paragraph, narrate that incident for your reader. Remember to keep the narrative focused.
3. **For an Essay.** Select a "first" from your experience—your first day in junior high school, your first date, your first time driving a car, your first day on a job or at college. Re-create that first for your reader. Remember to shape your narrative, and select only important contributing details. Focus your narrative around a significant aspect of that first experience, whether it was funny or serious.

   Prewriting:

   a. Several days before your essay is due, set aside an hour to comb your memories for some significant "firsts." Make a list of possibilities, jotting down whatever details you remember. Let the list rest for a day before looking at it again.

   b. Scan your list and select the most promising item. For another hour, jot down randomly whatever you remember. Focus on re-creating the event in your memory. One detail often triggers others. Do not try to write yet; just gather details.

   c. Remember that your narrative needs to hinge on a significant feature—it can be an insight (as in Hughes's "Salvation"), a serious point (as in Hopkin's "Lockdown"), or a comic pattern (as in "Sister Monroe"). Write down an explicit statement of what it is you want to reveal in your narrative. Use that statement to decide what details to include and what to exclude.

Rewriting:

a. After completing your draft, go back and look at the purpose statement you wrote in prewriting. Carefully test each detail you included to see if it relates to that intended purpose. Omit any irrelevant or inappropriate details.

b. Look at your conclusion. How did you end? Did you lead up to a climactic moment, or did you end with a flat conclusion ("And so you can see why this experience was important to me")? Compare how the writers in this chapter end their narratives.

4. **For Research.** What is an autobiography? Is it always a factual account of events in the writer's life? Is it ever "made up" or fictional? Is it ever propagandistic? What purposes do autobiographies have? Select an autobiography written by someone who interests you—check your college's library catalog for possibilities. Then analyze that work as an autobiography. Do not summarize. Instead, formulate a thesis about what you see as the writer's sense of purpose in the book. Support your argument with evidence from the text, and be sure to document your quotations.

Website Link

The Web has a number of sites with extensive information about Maya Angelou, including interviews, and even audio and video clips that you can hear and watch on your computer's screen. Visit the *Reader's* Website for the links.

MARINA

Judith Ortiz Cofer

Judith Ortiz Cofer was born in Hormigueros, Puerto Rico, in 1952. Her family settled in Paterson, New Jersey, in 1954, but because her father was in the U.S. Navy, mother and children periodically returned to Puerto Rico while his fleet was on maneuvers. She earned her M.A. in English from Florida Atlantic University in 1977. Today, she lives on a farm in rural Louisville, Georgia, and teaches English at the University of Georgia. She has published three books of poetry—one of which, Peregrina, *won a major poetry award in 1985—and a collection of essays. Her first novel,* The Line of the Sun *(1989), was nominated for the Pulitzer Prize in 1990. Her recent books include* An Island Like You: Stories of the Barrio *(1995),* Reaching for the Mainland and Selected New Poems *(1996), and* The Year of Our Revolution: New and Selected Stories and Poems *(1998), a collection focusing on Puerto Rican girls growing up in a New Jersey barrio.* "Marina" *in taken from Cofer's collection* Silent Dancing: A Partial Remembrance of a Puerto Rican Childhood *(1990).*

On Writing: *Cofer observes, "Much of my writing begins as a meditation on past events. But memory for me is the 'jumping off' point; I am not, in my poetry and fiction writing, a slave to memory. I like to believe that the poem or story contains the 'truth' of art rather than the factual, historical truth that the journalist, sociologist, scientist—most of the rest of the world—must adhere to."*

BEFORE READING

Connecting: How would you define the word *woman?* What does that word mean to you?

Anticipating: What does the story of Marina have to do with Cofer and her mother? Or is Cofer merely setting the scene in which the story of Marina is told?

1 Again it happened between my mother and me. Since her return to Puerto Rico after my father's death ten years before, she had gone totally "native," regressing into the comfortable traditions of her extended family and questioning all of my decisions. Each year

we spoke more formally to each other, and each June, at the end of my teaching year, she would invite me to visit her on the Island—so I could see for myself how much I was missing out on.

2 These yearly pilgrimages to my mother's town where I had been born also, but which I had left at an early age, were for me symbolic of the clash of cultures and generations that she and I represent. But I looked forward to arriving at this lovely place, my mother's lifetime dream of home, now endangered by encroaching "progress."

3 Located on the west coast, our pueblo is a place of contrasts: the original town remains as a tiny core of ancient houses circling the church, which sits on a hill, the very same where the woodcutter claimed to have been saved from a charging bull by a lovely dark Lady who appeared floating over a treetop. There my mother lives, at the foot of this hill; but surrounding this postcard scene there are shopping malls, a Burger King, a cinema. And where the sugar cane fields once extended like a green sea as far as the eye could see: condominiums, cement blocks in rows, all the same shape and color. My mother tries not to see this part of her world. The church bells drown the noise of traffic, and when she sits on her back porch and looks up at the old church built by the hands of generations of men whose last names she would not recognize, she feels safe—under the shelter of the past.

4 During the twenty years she spent in "exile" in the U.S. often alone with two children, waiting for my father, she dedicated her time and energy to creating a "reasonable facsimile" of a Puerto Rican home, which for my brother and me meant that we led a dual existence: speaking Spanish at home with her, acting out our parts in her traditional play, while also daily pretending assimilation in the classroom, where in the early sixties, there was no such thing as bilingual education. But, to be fair, we were not the only Puerto Rican children leading a double life, and I have always been grateful to have kept my Spanish. My trouble with Mother comes when she and I try to define and translate key words for both of us, words such as "woman" and "mother." I have a daughter too, as well as a demanding profession as a teacher and writer. My mother got married as a teenager and led a life of isolation and total devotion to her duties as mother. As a Penelope-like wife, she was always waiting, waiting, waiting, for the return of her sailor, for the return to her native land.

5 In the meantime, I grew up in the social flux of the sixties in New Jersey, and although I was kept on a steady diet of fantasies about life in the tropics, I liberated myself from her plans for me,

got a scholarship to college, married a man who supported my need to work, to create, to travel and to experience life as an individual. My mother rejoices at my successes, but is often anxious at how much time I have to spend away from home, although I keep assuring her that my husband is as good a parent as I am, and a much better cook. Her concern about my familial duties is sometimes a source of friction in our relationship, the basis for most of our arguments. But, in spite of our differences, I miss her, and as June approaches, I yearn to be with her in her tiny house filled with her vibrant presence. So I pack up and go to meet my loving adversary in her corner of the rapidly disappearing "paradise" that she waited so long to go home to.

6 It was after a heated argument one afternoon that I sought reconciliation with my mother by asking her to go with me for a walk down the main street of the pueblo. I planned to request stories about the town and its old people, something that we both enjoy for different reasons: she likes recalling the old days, and I have an insatiable curiosity about the history and the people of the Island which have become prominent features in my work.

7 We had been walking around the church when we saw a distinguished looking old man strolling hand-in-hand with a little girl. My mother touched my arm and pointed to them. I admired the pair as the old man, svelte and graceful as a ballet dancer, lifted the tiny figure dressed up in pink lace onto a stool at an outdoor cafe.

8 "Who is he?" I asked my mother, trying not to stare as we pretended to examine the menu taped on the window.

9 "You have heard his story at your grandmother's house."

10 She took my elbow and led me to a table at the far end of the cafe. "I will tell it to you again, but first I will give you a hint about who he is: he has not always been the man he is today."

11 Though her "hint" was no help, I suddenly recalled the story I had heard many years earlier as told by my grandmother, who had started the tale with similar words, "People are not always what they seem to be, that is something we have all heard, but have you heard about the one who ended up being what he was but did not appear to be?" Or something like that. Mamá could turn any story—it did not have to be as strange and fascinating as this one—into an event. I told my guess to my mother.

12 "Yes," she nodded, "he came home to retire. You know he has lived in Nueva York since before you were born. Do you remember the story?"

13 As we continued our walk, my mother recounted for me her mother's dramatic tale of a famous incident that had shaken the town in Mamá's youth. I had heard it once as a child, sitting enthralled at my grandmother's knee.

14 In the days when Mamá was a young girl, our pueblo had not yet been touched by progress. The cult of the Black Virgin had grown strong as pilgrims traveled from all over the island to visit the shrine, and the Church preached chastity and modesty as the prime virtues for the town's daughters. Adolescent girls were not allowed to go anywhere without their mothers or *dueñas*—except to a certain river that no man was allowed to approach.

15 Río Rojo, the river that ran its course around the sacred mountain where the Virgin had appeared, was reserved for the maidens of the pueblo. It was nothing but a stream, really, but crystalline, and it was bordered by thick woods where the most fragrant flowers and herbs could be found. This was a female place, a pastoral setting where no true *macho* would want to be caught swimming or fishing.

16 Nature had decorated the spot like a boudoir—royal poincianas extended their low branches for the girls to hang their clothes, and the mossy grass grew like a plush green carpet all the way down to the smooth stepping-stones where they could sun themselves like *favoritas* in a virginal harem.

17 As a "grown" girl of fifteen, Mamá had led her sisters and other girls of the pueblo to bathe there on hot summer afternoons. It was a place of secret talk and rowdy play, of freedom from mothers and chaperones, a place where they could talk about boys, and where they could luxuriate in their bodies. At the río, the young women felt free to hypothesize about the secret connection between their two concerns: their changing bodies and boys.

18 Sex was the forbidden topic in their lives, yet these were the same girls who would be given to strangers in marriage before they were scarcely out of childhood. In a sense, they were betrayed by their own protective parents who could bring themselves to explain neither the delights, nor the consequences of sex to their beloved daughters. The prevailing practice was to get them safely married as soon after puberty as possible—because nature would take its course one way or another. Scandal was to be avoided at all costs.

19 At the río, the group of girls Mamá grew up with would squeal and splash away their last few precious days as children. They would also wash each other's hair while sitting like brown

nyads upon the smooth rocks in the shallow water. They had the freedom to bathe nude, but some of them could not break through a lifetime of training in modesty and would keep their chemises and bloomers on. One of the shyest girls was Marina. She was everyone's pet.

20 Marina was a lovely young girl with her *café-con-leche* skin and green eyes. Her body was willowy and her thick black Indian hair hung down to her waist. Her voice was so soft that you had to come very close to hear what she was saying during the rare times when she did speak. Everyone treated Marina with special consideration, since she had already known much tragedy by the time she reached adolescence. It was due to the traumatic circumstances of her birth, as well as her difficult life with a reclusive mother, all the girls believed, that Marina was so withdrawn and melancholy as she ended her fifteenth year. She was surely destined for convent life, they all whispered when Marina left their company, as she often did, to go sit by herself on the bank, and to watch them with her large, wet, melancholy eyes.

21 Marina had fine hands and all the girls liked for her to braid their hair at the end of the day. They argued over the privilege of sitting between her legs while Marina ran her long fingers through their hair like a cellist playing a soothing melody. It caused much jealousy that last summer before Mamá's betrothal (which meant it was the last summer she could play at the río with her friends) when Marina chose to keep company only with Kiki, the mayor's fourteen year old daughter who had finally won permission from her strict parents to bathe with the pueblo's girls at the river.

22 Kiki would be a pale fish among the golden tadpoles in the water. She came from a Spanish family who believed in keeping the bloodlines pure, and she had spent all of her childhood in the cool shade of mansions and convent schools. She had come to the pueblo to prepare for her debut into society, her *quinceañera*, a fifteenth birthday party where she would be dressed like a princess and displayed before the Island's eligible bachelors as a potential bride.

23 Lonely for the company of girls her age, and tired of the modulated tones of afternoons on the verandah with her refined mother, Kiki had pressured her father to give her a final holiday with the other girls, whom she would see going by the mansion, singing and laughing on their way to the río. Her father began to see the wisdom of her idea when she mentioned how democratic it would seem to the girls' parents for the mayor's daughter to join them at the river. Finally, he agreed. The mother took to her bed with a sick headache when she thought of her lovely daughter

removing her clothes in front of the uncouth spawn of her husband's constituents: rough farmers and their sun-darkened wives.

Kiki removed all her clothes with glee as soon as the group arrived at the river. She ran to the water tossing lace, satin, and silk over her head. She behaved like a bird whose cage door had been opened for the first time. The girls giggled at the sight of the freckles on her shoulders, her little pink nipples, like rosebuds, her golden hair. But since she was the mayor's daughter, they dared not get too close. They acted more like her attendants than her friends. Kiki would have ended up alone again if it had not been for Marina. 24

Marina was awestruck by the exuberant Kiki; and Kiki was drawn to the quiet girl who watched the others at play with such yearning. Soon the two girls were inseparable. Marina would take Kiki's wet hair, like molten gold, into her brown hands and weave it into two perfect plaits which she would pin to the girl's head like a crown. It was fascinating to watch how the two came together wordlessly, like partners in a *pas de deux*. 25

It was an idyllic time, until one afternoon Marina and Kiki did not return to the river from an excursion into the woods where they had ostensibly gone to gather flowers. Mamá and her friends searched for them until nearly dark, but did not find them. The mayor went in person to notify Marina's mother of the situation. What he found was a woman who had fallen permanently into silence: secluded in a secret place of shadows where she wished to remain. 26

It was the events of one night long ago that had made her abandon the world. 27

Marina's mother had lost her young husband and delivered her child prematurely on the same night. The news that her man had been drowned in a fishing accident had brought on an agonizing labor. She had had a son, a tiny little boy, perfect in his parts, but sickly. The new mother, weakened in body and mind by so much pain, had decided that she preferred a daughter for company. Hysterically, she had begged the anxious midwife to keep her secret. And as soon as she was able to walk to church, she had the child dressed in a flowing gown of lace and had her christened Marina. Living the life a recluse, to which she was entitled as a widow, and attended by her loyal nurse, and later, by her quiet obedient Marina, the woman had slipped easily out of reality. 28

By the time Marina was old enough to discover the difference between her body and the bodies of her girlfriends, her mother had forgotten all about having borne a son. In fact, the poor soul 29 would have been horrified to discover a man under her roof. And so Marina kept up appearances, waiting out her body's dictates year by year. The summer that Kiki joined the bathers at the río, Marina had made up her mind to run away from home. She had been in torment until the blonde girl had appeared like an angel, bringing Marina the balm of her presence and the soothing touch of her hands.

30 The mayor found the woman sitting calmly in a rocking chair. She looked like a wax figure dressed in widow's weeds. Only her elegant hands moved as she crocheted a collar for a little girl's dress. And although she smiled deferentially at the men speaking loudly in her parlor, she remained silent. Silence was the place she had inhabited for years, and no one could draw her out now.

31 Furious, the mayor threatened to have her arrested. Finally it was the old nurse who confessed the whole sad tale—to the horror of the mayor and his men. She handed him an envelope with *Papá y Mamá* written on its face in Kiki's hand. In a last show of control, the mayor took the sealed letter home to read in the privacy of the family mansion where his wife was waiting, still under the impression that the two girls had been kidnapped for political reasons.

32 Kiki's letter explained briefly that she and *Marino* had eloped. They had fallen in love and nothing and no one could change their minds about getting married. She had sold her pearl necklace—the family heirloom given to her by her parents to wear at her quinceañera, and they were using the money for passage on the next steamship out of San Juan to New York.

33 The mayor did not finish his term in office. He and his wife, now a recluse, exiled themselves to Spain.

34 "And Marina and Kiki?" I had asked Mamá, eager for more details about Kiki and Marino. "What happened to them?"

35 "What happens to *any* married couple?" Mamá had replied, putting an end to her story. "They had several children, they worked, they got old . . . " She chuckled gently at my naiveté.

36 On our way back through town from our walk, Mother and I again saw Marino with his pretty granddaughter. This time he was lifting her to smell a white rose that grew from a vine entangled on a tree branch. The child brought the flower carefully to her nose and smelled it. Then the old man placed the child gently back on the ground and they continued their promenade, stopping to examine anything that caught the child's eye.

37 "Do you think he made a good husband?" I asked my mother.

"He would know what it takes to make a woman happy," she said as she turned to face me, and winked in camaraderie. 38

As I watched the gentle old man and the little girl, I imagined Marina sitting alone on the banks of a river, his heart breaking with pain and wild yearnings, listening to the girls asking questions he could have answered; remaining silent; learning patience, until love would give him the right to reclaim his original body and destiny. Yet he would never forget the lessons she learned at the río—or how to handle fragile things. I looked at my mother and she smiled at me; we now had a new place to begin our search for the meaning of the word *woman*. 39

QUESTIONS ON SUBJECT AND PURPOSE

1. In what way is the essay about "the clash of cultures and generations" (paragraph 2)?
2. Why does Marina not reveal his identity before?
3. Why might Cofer want to retell the story of Marina?

QUESTIONS ON STRATEGY AND AUDIENCE

1. How many narratives are there in the essay?
2. What is the effect of the riddles—"He has not always been the man he is today" (paragraph 10) and "Have you heard about the one who ended up being what he was but did not appear to be?" (11)?
3. Although it really does not matter one way or another, as you read the story of Marina and Kiki, did you think it might have actually happened?

QUESTIONS ON VOCABULARY AND STYLE

1. How is the story of Marina narrated?
2. What is the effect of the mother's reply to Cofer's question "What happened to them?" (paragraph 34)?
3. Be prepared to define the following words: *encroaching* (paragraph 2), *insatiable* (6), *svelte* (7), *boudoir* (16), *traumatic* (20), *uncouth* (23), *ostensibly* (26).

WRITING SUGGESTIONS

1. **For Your Journal.** Make a list of the characteristics that you associate with the word *woman* or the word *man*.

2. **For a Paragraph.** Use the list of characteristics that you made for your journal to write a paragraph in which you narrate an event or an action that demonstrates or reveals someone as being either a man or a woman.
3. **For an Essay.** "Clashes of cultures and generations" are inevitable. Choose a time in which you were aware that your behavior or values were in conflict with those of your parents or grandparents. Narrate the event, but at the same time explore why you did what you did and how it made you feel. Were you right, or do you now see that they were right and you were wrong?

   Prewriting:

   a. Make a list of as many times as you remember when such clashes occurred. Add to the list over a period of several days. Try to capture a mental picture of each particular experience.

   b. Try freewriting for five to ten minutes about each event. Which ones seem the most detailed and most significant?

   c. Remember that your narrative must have a beginning, a middle, and an end. Be sure to structure your account so that it has the shape necessary for a story.

   Rewriting:

   a. Look again at the draft of your narrative. Have you explored your reactions and feelings? The purpose of the narrative is more than just to retell a story.

   b. Look at the end of your narrative. Have you concluded at a climatic moment? Does the essay have a good sense of closure?

   c. Remember to catch your reader's attention in the first paragraph. Look closely at your introduction. Ask a friend to read just that paragraph. Does your friend want to continue reading?

4. **For Research.** To what extent does Cofer explore similar themes in her other work? Find other examples of her writing (see the headnote and check the catalog and databases available at your library). Another good source of information is interviews that Cofer has granted. A number of these have appeared in print, and the full text of some is available through electronic databases. Once you have gathered your information, write an essay analyzing her writing to isolate

her central concerns. Be sure to formulate a thesis about the themes that occur in her writing; do not just summarize what you have read. Be sure to document your sources.

Website Link

Several extensive interviews with Cofer are available from on-line databases and others can be found in print sources in your school's library. Check out the possibilities at the Website.

Lockdown

Evans D. Hopkins

A former inmate at Nottoway Correctional Center in Virginia and writer for the Black Panther Party, Evans Hopkins was paroled in 1997 after serving sixteen years for armed robbery. He has published essays in the Washington Post, Nerve, *and* The New Yorker, *where this essay first appeared.*

BEFORE READING

Connecting: What associations do you have with the words *prison* and *prisoner?*

Anticipating: Before you start to read, write down in a sentence or two how you feel about people sentenced to prison. For example, how should they be treated while they are in jail? Then read the essay.

1 I know something serious has happened when I wake up well before dawn to discover two guards wearing armored vests and riot helmets taking a head count. I'd gone to bed early this August evening, so that I might write in the early morning, as is my custom, before the prison clamor begins. So when I wake up I have no idea what was going down while I slept. But it's apparent that the prison is on "full lockdown status." At the minimum, we will be locked in our cells twenty-four hours a day for the next several days.

2 While lockdowns at Nottoway Correctional Center in Virginia are never announced in advance, I'm not altogether surprised by this one. The buzz among the eleven-hundred-man prison population was that a lockdown was imminent. The experienced prisoner knows to be prepared for a few weeks of complete isolation.

3 But I'm hardly prepared for the news I receive later in the day from a local TV station: two corrections officers and two nurses were taken hostage by three prisoners, following what authorities are calling "a terribly botched escape attempt" that included a fourth man. The incident was ended around 5:30 A.M. by a Department of Corrections strike-force team, with the hostages unharmed. However, according to authorities, eight of the rescuers,

including the warden, were slightly wounded when a shotgun was discharged accidentally.

Oh, God, I think. Forget a few weeks. No telling how long we'll be on lock *now.* I try to take heart by telling myself, "It's nothing you haven't seen before, might as well take the opportunity to get the old typewriter pumpin', maybe even finish your book." 4

The idea that most people have of prison life consists of images from worst-case-scenario movies, or from news footage of local jails. Visitors to prison often comment on how surprised they are to see men moving around, without apparent restraint, having believed that prisoners are kept in their cells most of the time. In modern prisons, however, there is usually lots of orderly movement, as inmates go about the activities of normal life: working, eating, education, recreation, etc. 5

In a well-run institution, long lockdowns—where all inmate movement stops—are aberrations. Yet major institutions lock down regularly, for short periods, so that the prison can be searched for weapons and other contraband. Lockdowns are also called for emergencies, as this one has been at Nottoway, or, in fact, for any reason deemed necessary for security. 6

By the second week of the lockdown, one of our hot meals has been replaced with a bag lunch—four slices of bread, two slices of either cheese or a luncheon meat, and a small piece of plain cake or, more rarely, fruit. Since counsellors or administrative personnel must do most of the cooking, the lockdown menu usually consists of meals that require minimal culinary skills. Today we have chili-mac (an ungodly concoction of macaroni and ground beef), along with three tablespoons of anemic mixed vegetables and a piece of plain cake—all served on a disposable aluminum tray the size of a hardcover book. 7

We have not yet been allowed out to shower, so I lay news paper on the concrete floor and bathe at the sink. There is a hot-water tap, in contrast to the cells at the now demolished State Penitentiary, in Richmond, where I served the first several years of my life sentence for armed robbery, and where I went through many very long lockdowns. 8

I have endured lockdowns in buildings with little or no heat; lockdowns during which authorities cut off the plumbing completely, so contraband couldn't be flushed away; and lockdowns where we weren't allowed out to shower for more than a month. I 9 have been in prison since 1981, and my attitude has had to be "I can do time on the moon," if that is what's called for. So I'm not about to let this lockdown faze me. (Besides, I am in what is known as the "honor building," where conditions are marginally better.)

10 Around one o'clock in the morning, the three guards of the "shower squad" finally get around to our building. They have full riot gear on, and a Rottweiler in tow. One by one, we are handcuffed and escorted to the shower stalls at the center of the dayroom area. As I walk past the huge dog, I turn my head to keep an eye on it. The beast suddenly lunges against the handler's leash and barks at me with such ferocity that I actually feel the force of air on my face. I walk to the shower with feigned insouciance, but my heart is pumping furiously. I can forget sleeping for a while.

11 Back in the cell, I contemplate what's happening to this place. Information about the hostage incident has been trickling in. While the show of force seems absurd to those of us here in the honor building, I have heard reports of assaults on guards in the cell houses of the main compound, where the treatment of the inmates is said to have been more severe. On the night of the original incident, some men in a section of one building refused to return to their cells, and in at least one section there was open rebellion—destruction and burning.

12 Today a memorandum from the warden is passed out, and the warden himself appears on a video broadcast on the prison's TV system. He announces that there will be no visitation until some time in October—about two months from now.

13 Other restrictions are to be imposed, he says, including immediate implementation of a new Department of Corrections guideline, stripping all prisoners of most personal property: televisions with screens larger than five and a half inches; any tape player other than a Walkman; nearly all personal clothing (jeans, nongray sweatsuits, colored underwear, etc.); and—most devastating for me—*all typewriters.*

14 I find this news disquieting, to say the least, and I decide to lie down, to try to get some sleep. This is difficult, as men are yelling back and forth from their cells, upset about this latest development. Many of them have done ten or fifteen years, like me, obeying all the rules and saving the meagre pay from prison jobs to buy a few personal items—items that we must now surrender.

15 I awaken in the night, sweating and feverish in the humid summer air. Sitting on the edge of my bed while considering my

plight, I look at photographs of my family. My eyes rest on the school portrait of my son, taken shortly before he died from heart disease ten years ago, at age twelve. Sorrow overwhelms me, and I find myself giving in to grief, then to great, mournful sobs.

The tears stop as suddenly as they began. It has been years since I've wept so, and I realize that the grief has been only a trigger—that I am, by and large, really feeling sorry for myself. This is no good, if I'm to survive with my mind and spirit intact. I can't afford to succumb to self-pity. 16

This new day begins shortly after 8 A.M., when three guards come to my cell door. One of them says, "We're here to escort you to Personal Property. You have to pack up everything in your cell, and they will sort out what you have to send out, and what you can keep, over there." 17

He looks through the long, narrow vertical slot in the steel door and—seeing all the books, magazines, journal notebooks, and piles of papers I have stacked around the cell—shakes his head in disbelief. "Looks like you're gonna need a lot of boxes," he says. I have the accumulated papers, magazines, and books of a practicing freelance writer. The only problem is that my "office" is about as big as your average bathroom—complete with toilet and sink, but with a steel cot where your bathtub would be. 18

Now the new rules say twelve books, twelve magazines, twelve audiotapes. Period. And "a reasonable number of personal and legal papers." I wonder how much of all this stuff they will say is reasonable, when sometimes even I question the sanity of holding on to so much. But who knows *when* I'll be able to get to any files, manuscripts, books, and notes that I send home? I finish packing after three hours, ending up with twelve full boxes. I sit and smoke a cigarette while waiting for the guards to return, and contemplate the stacked boxes filling the eight feet between the cot and the door. *Where are all the books, plays, and film scripts I dreamed of producing?* 19

As I walk to the property building, on the far side of the compound, the sun is bright, the sky is cloudless, and the air of the Virginia countryside is refreshing. I look away from the fortress-gray concrete buildings of the prison, and out through the twin perimeter fences and the gleaming rolls of razor wire, to note that the leaves of a distant maple have gone to orange. I realize that the season has changed since I was last out of the building. 20

I am accompanied by three guards. Two push a cart laden with my boxes, grumbling; the third, an older man I know, walks beside me, making small talk. 21

22 "Man, things are really changing here," this guard says. Lowering his voice so that the other two cannot hear him, he tells me that he considered transferring to work at another institution, but that the entire system is now going through similar changes.

23 Back in my cell, I don't have the energy to unpack the four boxes I've returned with. I am glad to have at least salvaged the part of the manuscripts I've worked on over the years.

24 I lie upon the bed like a mummy, feet crossed at the ankle and hands folded over my chest, and try to meditate. However, with my tape player gone (along with my television), I have no music to drown out the sounds coming from the cell house. A wave of defeat settles over me.

25 I think of what I've often told people who ask about my crime—that I got life for a robbery in which no one was hurt. I'll have to rephrase that from now on. If robbery can be said to be theft by force, I can't help but feel like I've just been robbed. And I've most certainly been *hurt.* Maybe that's the whole idea, I think—to injure us, eye for an eye.

26 Perhaps I should acknowledge that the lockdown—and, indeed, all these years—have damaged me more than I want to believe. But self-pity is anathema to the prisoner, and self-doubt is deadly to the writer.

27 I get up quickly, pull out a yellow pad and ballpoint from one of the boxes, and stuff spongy plugs in my ears to block out the noise. I know that if I don't go back to work immediately—on *something*—the loss of my typewriter may throw up a block that I'll never overcome.

28 Just before Christmas, the lockdown officially ends. The four and a half months have taken their toll on everyone. There have been reports of two or three suicides. Some inmates have become unhinged, and can be seen shuffling around, on Thorazine or something.

29 Things are far from being back to "normal operations." There is now the strictest control of *all* movement; attack dogs are everywhere and officers escort you wherever you go. The gym is closed, and recreation and visitation privileges have been drastically curtailed. At least the educational programs, which were once touted as among the best in the state's prison system, are to resume again in the new year.

30 On Christmas Eve, the first baked "real chicken on the bone" since summer is served. But the cafeteria-style serving line has been replaced with a wall of concrete blocks. Now the

prisoner gets a standard tray served through a small slot at the end of the wall.

As I hasten to finish my food in the allotted fifteen minutes, I look at the men from another building in the serving line. There is a drab sameness to the men, all dressed in the required ill-fitting uniform of denim jeans, blue work shirts, and prison jackets. 31

I spot a friend of more than fifteen years, whom I haven't seen in months. I can only wave and call out a greeting, for as we are seated separately, "mingling" with men from another building is nearly impossible in the chow hall. "I'm a grandfather now," he shouts to me, beaming. "I've got some pictures to show you, when we get a chance." Then he remembers the strict segregation by building now, and his smile fades. He knows that I may never get a chance to see them. 32

I notice a large number of new faces among the men in line. Most of them are black. Many are quite young, with a few appearing to be still in their teens. 33

Such young men are a primary reason for the new lockdown policies, which are calculated largely to contain the "eighty-five-per-centers"—those now entering Virginia's growing prison system, who must serve eighty-five per cent of their sentences, under new, no-parole laws. 34

Virginia, like most states and the federal government, has passed punitive sentencing laws in recent years. This has led to an unprecedented United States prison/jail population of more than a million six hundred thousand—about three times what it was when I entered prison, sixteen years ago. In the resulting expansion of the nation's prison systems, authorities have tended to dispense with much of the rehabilitative programming once prevalent in America's penal institutions. 35

When I was sent to the State Penitentiary, in 1981, I was twenty-six—the quintessential angry young black male. However, there was a very different attitude toward rehabilitation at that time, particularly as regards education. I was able to take college courses for a number of years on a Pell grant. Vocational training was available, and literacy (or at least enrollment in school) was encouraged and increased one's chances for making parole. 36

In the late seventies, there was a growing recognition that rehabilitation programs paid off in lower rates of recidivism. But things began to change a few years later. First, the highly publicized violence of the crack epidemic encouraged mandatory minimum sentencing. The throw-away-the-key fever really took off in 1988, when George Bush's Presidential campaign hit the Willie 37

Horton hot button, and sparked the tough-on-crime political climate that continues to this day. The transformation was nearly complete when President Clinton endorsed the concept of "three strikes you're out" in his 1994 State of the Union address. And when Congress outlawed Pell grants for prisoners later that year the message became clear: We really don't give a damn if you change or not.

38 Although the men are glad, after more than four months, to be out of their cells, there is little holiday spirit; it's just another day. Several watch whatever banality is on the dayroom TV screen. Most sit on the stainless-steel tables and listlessly play cards to kill time, while others wait for a place at the table. Some wait to use one of two telephones, while others, standing around in bathrobes or towels, wait for a shower stall to become available.

39 Most of the men in this section of the building are in their forties or fifties, with a few elderly. It strikes me that for most of them prison has become a life of waiting: waiting in line to eat, for a phone call, the mail, or a visit. Or just waiting for tomorrow—for parole and freedom. For the older ones, with no hope of release, I suppose that they wait for the deliverance of death.

40 As I record the day in my notebook, I find myself thinking about my aunt's grandnephew—her adopted son. He was rumored to have been dealing drugs, and he was shot dead in the doorway of her home on Thanksgiving Day, just over a month ago; my father, who is seventy-five, was called to comfort her. With violence affecting so many lives, one can understand the desire—driven by fear—to lock away young male offenders. But considering their impoverished, danger-filled lives, I wonder whether the threat of being locked up for decades can really deter them from crime.

41 I understand the philosophy behind the increased use of long sentences and harsh incarceration. The idea is to make prison a secular hell on earth—a place where the young potential felon will fear to go, where the ex-con will fear to return. But an underlying theme is that "these people" are irredeemable "predators" (i.e., "animals"), who are without worth. Why, then, provide them with the opportunity to rehabilitate—or give them any hope?

42 Still, what really bothers me is knowing that many thousands of the young men entering prison now may *never* get the "last chance to change," which I was able to put to good use—in an era that, I'm afraid, is now in the past. And more disturbing, to my mind, are the long "no hope" sentences given to so many young men now—they can be given even to people as young as thirteen

and fourteen. Although I personally remain eligible for parole—and in all likelihood will be released eventually—I can't help thinking of all the young lives that are now being thrown away. I know that if I had been born in another time I might very well have suffered the same fate.

QUESTIONS ON SUBJECT AND PURPOSE

1. How long does the lockdown last? How many specific days during that period does Hopkins write about?
2. At what point in the essay does Hopkins move away from his narrative account of the lockdown? What does Hopkins then do in the essay?
3. What objectives might Hopkins have in writing his essay?

QUESTIONS ON STRATEGY AND AUDIENCE

1. At times, Hopkins seems to talk to himself—even using quotation marks around his words, as in paragraph 4. Why? What is the effect of this strategy?
2. Hopkins uses white space to separate sections of the essay. How many divisions are there?
3. Who might Hopkins imagine as his readers? To whom is he writing? How do you know?

QUESTIONS ON VOCABULARY AND STYLE

1. When the Rottweiler lunges at him, Hopkins writes, "I walk to the shower with feigned insouciance" (paragraph 10). What is the effect of his word choice?
2. Hopkins chooses to quote a few remarks that the guards make when he is asked to pack up his possessions (paragraphs 17, 18, and 22). Why?
3. Be prepared to define the following words: *clamor* (paragraph 1), *aberrations* (6), *insouciance* (10), *anathema* (26), *punitive* (35), *quintessential* (36), *recidivism* (37), *banality* (38).

WRITING SUGGESTIONS

1. **For Your Journal.** Spend some time thinking about instances in which a personal experience that you had might be used to argue for a change in society's attitudes. For

example, were you ever discriminated against for any reason? Were you ever needlessly embarrassed or ridiculed for something? Make a list of some possible experiences.

2. **For a Paragraph.** Look at the list of personal experiences that you made for your journal. Select one of those experiences and in a paragraph narrate what happened and then reflect on the significance of that experience. Try to make your reader see the injustice that was done.
3. **For an Essay.** If you have written the paragraph in Suggestion 2, treat that as a draft for a longer, fuller narrative. Write an essay in which you narrate a personal experience for a specific purpose. If you are having trouble finding a suitable experience from your own life, you might want to narrate the experience of someone else.

   Prewriting:

   a. Complete the following sentence: "I am narrating this story so that my reader will see . . . . " Use that statement to check over your first draft.
   b. Remember that your narrative must have a beginning, a middle, and an end. You cannot tell everything, so be selective. Hopkins, for example, condenses over four months of experience into a small series of specific moments.
   c. Study Hopkins's essay or Hughes's essay as a possible structural model. Do not simply imitate, but notice instead how each writer controls his narrative.

   Rewriting:

   a. Remember to catch your reader's attention in the first paragraph. Ask a friend to read just that paragraph. Does your friend want to keep reading?
   b. Look again at the draft of your essay. Have you explored the purpose of your essay? Have you made your reasons for narrating this story clear? Remember that the purpose of your narrative is more than just to tell a story.
   c. Avoid being angry or shrill in your argument. You want your readers to see the "rightness" of your position; you want the experience to convince them.

4. **For Research.** What evidence is there to support or to refute the idea that prison can be a place for rehabilitation, can offer a "last chance to change"? Research the problem using your library's resources. Some on-line or CD-ROM

databases would also be good places to start. You might want to talk to a reference librarian for search strategy suggestions. Use your findings to argue for or against providing educational or vocational opportunities to people in prison.

Website Link

Some additional essays by Hopkins can be found in on-line e-journals and in the *Washington Post*'s newspaper archives. The links can be found at the Website, as can a number of sources about prisons. Background information for an argument on the need for or the opposition to educational programs in prisons is also available.

ALCOHOL IN THE WESTERN WORLD

Bert L. Vallee

Bert Vallee was born in Germany in 1919 and immigrated to the United States in 1938. He was educated at the University of Berne in Germany and later received a degree in medicine from New York University. He has taught at Harvard University since 1946 and is currently Edgar M. Bronfman Distinguished Senior Professor there. He also holds several honorary professorships. Vallee sits on the boards of a number of foundations, has received numerous awards for his research, and has published over 600 scientific articles, as well as nine books.

BEFORE READING

Connecting: When you turn on the water faucet to get a drink or when you open a bottle of water, what assumptions do you make about the water that you are about to drink?

Anticipating: The essay is placed in a chapter about narration. As you read the essay, think about the ways in which this essay might be an example of narration.

1 A substance, like a person, may have distinct and even contradictory aspects to its personality. Today ethyl alcohol, the drinkable species of alcohol, is a multifaceted entity; it may be social lubricant, sophisticated dining companion, cardiovascular health benefactor or agent of destruction. Throughout most of Western civilization's history, however, alcohol had a far different role. For most of the past 10 millennia, alcoholic beverages may have been the most popular and common daily drinks, indispensable sources of fluids and calories. In a world of contaminated and dangerous water supplies, alcohol truly earned the title granted it in the Middle Ages: *aqua vitae*, the "water of life."

2 Potent evidence exists to open a window into a societal relationship with alcohol that is simply unimaginable today. Consider this statement, issued in 1777 by Prussia's Frederick the Great, whose economic strategy was threatened by importation of coffee: "It is disgusting to notice the increase in the quantity of coffee

used by my subjects, and the amount of money that goes out of the country as a consequence. Everybody is using coffee; this must be prevented. His Majesty was brought up on beer, and so were both his ancestors and officers. Many battles have been fought and won by soldiers nourished on beer, and the King does not believe that coffee-drinking soldiers can be relied upon to endure hardships in case of another war."

Surely a modern leader who urged alcohol consumption over coffee, especially by the military, would have his or her mental competence questioned. But only an eyeblink ago in historical time, a powerful head of government could describe beer in terms that make it sound like mother's milk. And indeed, that nurturing role may be the one alcohol played from the infancy of the West to the advent of safe water supplies for the masses only within the past century. 3

Natural processes have no doubt produced foodstuffs containing alcohol for millions of years. Yeast, in metabolizing sugar to obtain energy, creates ethyl alcohol as a by-product of its efforts. Occasionally animals accidentally consume alcohol that came into being as fruit "spoiled" in the natural process of fermentation; inebriated birds and mammals have been reported. Humans have a gene for the enzyme alcohol dehydrogenase; the presence of this gene at least forces the conjecture that over evolutionary time animals have encountered alcohol enough to have evolved a way to metabolize it. Ingestion of alcohol, however, was unintentional or haphazard for humans until some 10,000 years ago. 4

About that time, some Later Stone Age gourmand probably tasted the contents of a jar of honey that had been left unattended longer than usual. Natural fermentation had been given the opportunity to occur, and the taster, finding the effects of mild alcohol ingestion provocative, probably replicated the natural experiment. Comrades and students of this first oenologist then codified the method for creating such mead or wines from honey or dates or sap. The technique was fairly simple: leave the sweet substance alone to ferment. 5

Beer, which relies on large amounts of starchy grain, would wait until the origin and development of agriculture. The fertile river deltas of Egypt and Mesopotamia produced large crops of wheat and barley; the diets of peasants, laborers and soldiers of these ancient civilizations were cereal-based. It might be viewed as a historical inevitability that fermented grain would be discovered. As in the instance of wine, natural experiments probably produced alcoholic substances that aroused the interest of those who sampled 6 the results. Before the third millennium B.C., Egyptians and Babylonians were drinking beers made from barley and wheat.

7 Wine, too, would get a boost from agriculture. Most fruit juice, even wild grape juice, is naturally too low in sugar to produce wine, but the selection for sweeter grapes leading to the domestication of particular grape stock eventually led to viniculture. The practice of growing grape strains suitable for wine production has been credited to people living in what is now Armenia, at about 6000 B.C., although such dating is educated guesswork at best.

8 The creation of agriculture led to food surpluses, which in turn led to even larger groups of people living in close quarters, in villages or cities. These municipalities faced a problem that still vexes, namely, how to provide inhabitants with enough clean, pure water to sustain their constant need for physiological hydration. The solution, until the 19th century, was nonexistent. The water supply of any group of people rapidly became polluted with their waste products and thereby dangerous, even fatal, to drink. How many of our progenitors died attempting to quench their thirst with water can never be known. Based on current worldwide crises of dysentery and infectious disease wrought by unclean water supplies, a safe bet is that a remarkably large portion of our ancestry succumbed to tainted water.

9 In addition, the lack of liquids safe for human consumption played a part in preventing long-range ocean voyages until relatively recently. Christopher Columbus made his voyage with wine on board, and the Pilgrims landed at Plymouth Rock only because their beer stores had run out. An early order of business was luring brewmasters to the colonies.

Alcohol versus Water

10 Negative evidence arguing against a widespread use of water for drinking can be found in perusal of the Bible and ancient Greek texts. Both the Old and New Testaments are virtually devoid of references to water as a common human beverage. Likewise, Greek writings make scant reference to water drinking, with the notable exception of positive statements regarding the quality of water from mountain springs. Hippocrates specifically cited water from springs and deep wells as safe, as was rainwater collected in cisterns. The ancients, through what must have been tragic experience, clearly understood that most of their water supply was unfit for human consumption.

11 In this context of contaminated water supply, ethyl alcohol may indeed have been mother's milk to a nascent Western civilization.

Beer and wine were free of pathogens. And the antiseptic power of alcohol, as well as the natural acidity of wine and beer, killed many pathogens when the alcoholic drinks were diluted with the sullied water supply. Dating from the taming and conscious application of the fermentation process, people of all ages in the West have therefore consumed beer and wine, not water, as their major daily thirst quenchers.

Babylonian clay tablets more than 6,000 years old give beer recipes, complete with illustrations. The Greek *akratidzomai*, which came to mean "to breakfast," literally translates as "to drink undiluted wine." Breakfast apparently could include wine as a bread dip, and "bread and beer" connoted basic necessity much as does today's expression "bread and butter." 12

The experience in the East differed greatly. For at least the past 2,000 years, the practice of boiling water, usually for tea, has created a potable supply of nonalcoholic beverages. In addition, genetics played an important role in making Asia avoid alcohol: approximately half of all Asian people lack an enzyme necessary for complete alcohol metabolism, making the experience of drinking quite unpleasant. Thus, beer and wine took their place as staples only in Western societies and remained there until the end of the last century. 13

The traditional production of beer and wine by fermentation of cereals and grapes or other fruits produced beverages with low alcohol content compared with those familiar to present-day consumers. The beverages also contained large amounts of acetic acid and other organic acids created during fermentation. Most wines of ancient times probably would turn a modern oenophile's nose; those old-style wines in new bottles would more closely resemble today's vinegar, with some hints of cider, than a prizewinning merlot. 14

As the alcohol content of daily staple drinks was low, consumers focused on issues of taste, thirst quenching, hunger satisfaction and storage rather than on intoxication. Nevertheless, the "side effects" of this constant, low-level intake must have been almost universal. Indeed, throughout Western history the normal state of mind may have been one of inebriation. 15

The caloric value of nonperishable alcoholic beverages may also have played a significant role in meeting the daily energy requirements of societies that might have faced food shortages. In addition, they provided essential micronutrients, such as vitamins and minerals. 16

Alcohol also served to distract from the fatigue and numbing boredom of daily life in most cultures, while alleviating pain for 17 which remedies were nonexistent. Today people have a plethora of handy choices against common aches and pain. But until this century, the only analgesic generally available in the West was alcohol. From the Book of Proverbs comes this prescription: "Give strong drink unto him that is ready to perish, and wine unto them that be of heavy hearts. Let him drink, and forget his poverty, and remember his misery no more." A Sumerian cuneiform tablet of a pharmacopoeia dated to about 2100 B.C. is generally cited as the oldest preserved record of medicinal alcohol, although Egyptian papyri may have preceded the tablet. Hippocrates' therapeutic system featured wines as remedies for almost all acute or chronic ailments known in his time, and the Alexandrian School of Medicine supported the medical use of alcohol.

Religion and Moderation

18 The beverages of ancient societies may have been far lower in alcohol than their current versions, but people of the time were aware of the potentially deleterious behavioral effects of drinking. The call for temperance began quite early in Hebrew, Greek and Roman cultures and was reiterated throughout history. The Old Testament frequently disapproves of drunkenness, and the prophet Ezra and his successors integrated wine into everyday Hebrew ritual, perhaps partly to moderate undisciplined drinking customs, thus creating a religiously inspired and controlled form of prohibition.

19 In the New Testament, Jesus obviously sanctioned alcohol consumption, resorting to miracle in the transformation of water to wine, an act that may acknowledge the goodness of alcohol versus the polluted nature of water. His followers concentrated on extending measures to balance the use and abuse of wine but never supported total prohibition. Saint Paul and other fathers of early Christianity carried on such moderating attitudes. Rather than castigating wine for its effects on sobriety, they considered it a gift from God, both for its medicinal qualities and the tranquilizing characteristics that offered relief from pain and the anxiety of daily life.

20 Traditionally, beer has been the drink of the common folk, whereas wine was reserved for the more affluent. Grape wine, however, became available to the average Roman after a century of vineyard expansion that ended in about 30 B.C., a boom driven by greater profits for wine grapes compared with grain. Ultimately, the increased supply drove prices down, and the common Roman

could partake in wine that was virtually free. Roman viniculture declined with the empire and was inherited by the Catholic Church and its monasteries, the only institutions with sufficient resources to maintain production.

For nearly 1,300 years the Church operated the biggest and best vineyards, to considerable profit. Throughout the Middle Ages, grain remained the basic food of peasants and beer their normal beverage, along with mead and homemade wines or ciders. The few critics of alcohol consumption were stymied by the continuing simple fact of the lack of safe alternatives. Hence, despite transitions in political systems, religions and ways of life, the West's use of and opinion toward beer and wine remained remarkably unchanged. But a technological development would alter the relationship between alcohol and humanity. 21

After perhaps 9,000 years of experience drinking relatively low alcohol mead, beer and wine, the West was faced with alcohol in a highly concentrated form, thanks to distillation. Developed in about A.D. 700 by Arab alchemists (for whom *al kohl* signified any material's basic essence), distillation brought about the first significant change in the mode and magnitude of human alcohol consumption since the beginning of Western civilization. Although yeasts produce alcohol, they can tolerate concentrations of only about 16 percent. Fermented beverages therefore had a natural maximum proof. Distillation circumvents nature's limit by taking advantage of alcohol's 78 degree Celsius (172 degree Fahrenheit) boiling point, compared with 100 degrees C for water. Boiling a water-alcohol mixture puts more of the mix's volatile alcohol than its water in the vapor. Condensing that vapor yields liquid with a much higher alcohol level than that of the starting liquid. 22

The Arab method—the custom of abstinence had not yet been adopted by Islam—spread to Europe, and distillation of wine to produce spirits commenced on the Continent in about A.D. 1100. The venue was the medical school at Salerno, Italy, an important center for the transfer of medical and chemical theory and methods from Asia Minor to the West. Joining the traditional alcoholic drinks of beer and wine, which had low alcohol concentration and positive nutritional benefit, were beverages with sufficient alcohol levels to cause the widespread problems still with us today. The era of distilled spirits had begun. 23

Knowledge of distillation gradually spread from Italy to northern Europe; the Alsatian physician Hieronymus Brunschwig described the process in 1500 in *Liber de arte distillandi*, the first printed book on distillation. By the time Brunschwig 24 was a best-selling author, distilled alcohol had earned its split personality as nourishing food, beneficent medicine and harmful drug. The widespread drinking of spirits followed closely on the heels of the 14th century's bouts with plague, notably the Black Death of 1347–1351. Though completely ineffective as a cure for plague, alcohol did make the victim who drank it at least feel more robust. No other known agent could accomplish even that much. The medieval physician's optimism related to spirits may be attributed to this ability to alleviate pain and enhance mood, effects that must have seemed quite remarkable during a medical crisis that saw perhaps two thirds of Europe's population culled in a single generation.

25 Economic recovery following the subsidence of the plague throughout Europe generated new standards of luxury and increased urbanization. This age witnessed unprecedented ostentation, gluttony, self-indulgence and inebriation. Europe, apparently relieved to have survived the pestilence of the 14th century, went on what might be described as a continentwide bender. Despite the obvious negative effects of drunkenness, and despite attempts by authorities to curtail drinking, the practice continued until the beginning of the 17th century, when nonalcoholic beverages made with boiled water became popular. Coffee, tea and cocoa thus began to break alcohol's monopoly on safety.

26 In the 18th century a growing religious antagonism toward alcohol, fueled largely by Quakers and Methodists and mostly in Great Britain, still lacked real effect or popular support. After all, the Thames River of the time was as dangerous a source of drinking water as the polluted streams of ancient cultures. Dysentery, cholera and typhoid, all using filthy water as a vehicle, were major killers and would remain so in the West as recently as the end of the 19th century, rivaling plague in mass destruction.

27 Only the realization that microorganisms caused disease and the institution of filtered and treated water supplies finally made water a safe beverage in the West. Religious antialcohol sentiment and potable water would combine with one other factor to make it finally possible for a significant percentage of the public to turn away from alcohol. That other factor was the recognition of alcohol dependence as an illness.

Diseases of Alcohol

28 Throughout the 19th century the application of scientific principles to the practice of medicine allowed clinical symptoms to be categorized into diseases that might then be understood on

a rational basis. Alcohol abuse was among the earliest medical problems to receive the attention of this approach. Two graduates of the Edinburgh College of Medicine, Thomas Trotter of Britain and Benjamin Rush of the colonies and then the U.S., made the first important contributions to the clinical recognition of alcoholism as a chronic, life-threatening disease. The influence of moralistic antialcohol Methodism may have driven their clinical research, but their findings were nonetheless sound.

In an 1813 essay on drunkenness, Trotter described alcohol 29
abuse as a disease and recognized that habitual and prolonged consumption of hard liquor causes liver disease, accompanied by jaundice, wasting and mental dysfunction, evident even when the patient is sober. Rush published similar ideas in America and to greater effect, as he was a prominent member of society and a signer of the Declaration of Independence. His personal fame, behind his correct diagnosis of a societal ill, helped to create viewpoints that eventually culminated in the American Prohibition (1919–1933).

Nineteenth-century studies detailed the clinical picture and 30
pathological basis of alcohol abuse, leading to today's appreciation of it as one of the most important health problems facing America and the rest of the world. Alcohol contributes to 100,000 deaths in this country annually, making it the third leading cause of preventable mortality in the U.S. (after smoking and conditions related to poor diet and a sedentary way of life). Although the exact number of problem drinkers is difficult to estimate accurately, America is probably home to between 14 and 20 million people whose lives are disrupted by their relationship with alcohol.

The overall alcohol problem is far broader. Perhaps 40 per- 31
cent of Americans have been intimately exposed to the effects of alcohol abuse through a family member. And every year some 12,000 children of drinking mothers are robbed of their potential, born with the physical signs and intellectual deficits associated with full-blown fetal alcohol syndrome; thousands more suffer lesser effects. Pharmaceutical treatments for alcoholism remain impractical and inadequate, with total abstinence still the only truly effective approach.

Society and science are at the threshold of new pharmaceutical 32
and behavioral strategies against alcoholism, however. As with any other disease, whether of the individual or the society, a correct diagnosis is crucial to treatment. Alcoholism, in historical terms, has only just been understood and accepted as a disease; we are still coping with the historically recent arrival of concentrated alcohol. The diagnosis having been made and acknowledged, continuing research

efforts can be counted on to produce new and more effective treatments based on the growing knowledge of the physiology of alcohol abuse and of addictive substances in general.

33 Humanity at any moment of history is inevitably caught in that time, as trapped as an insect in amber. The mores, traditions and attitudes of an era inform the individuals then living, often blinding them to the consideration of alternatives. Alcohol today is a substance primarily of relaxation, celebration and tragically, mass destruction. To consider it as having been a primary agent for the development of an entire culture may be jolting, even offensive to some. Any good physician, however, takes a history before attempting a cure.

QUESTIONS ON SUBJECT AND PURPOSE

1. What is the origin of the word "alcohol" and what did it mean in the language from which it was borrowed?
2. What aspects of alcohol does Vallee's essay examine?
3. What purpose might Vallee have in writing the essay?

QUESTIONS ON STRATEGY AND AUDIENCE

1. What is the basic organizational strategy used in the essay?
2. What is the function of the subheadings in the text (before paragraphs 10, 18, and 28)?
3. Vallee's essay originally appeared in *Scientific American*, a monthly magazine. What does its place of publication suggest about Vallee's sense of his audience?

QUESTIONS ON VOCABULARY AND STYLE

1. The essay is not written in the first-person ("I"). Why might Vallee avoid using the first-person?
2. What does Vallee's word choice suggest about his sense of audience?
3. Be prepared to define the following words: *inebriated* (paragraph 4), *gourmand* (5), *replicated* (5), *oenologist* (5), *vexes* (8), *hydration* (8), *progenitors* (8), *wrought* (8), *perusal* (10), *nascent* (11), *pathogens* (11), *potable* (13), *merlot* (14), *plethora* (17), *analgesic* (17), *deleterious* (18), *castigating* (19), *affluent* (20), *partake* (20), *stymied* (21), *volatile* (22), *venue* (23), *robust* (24), *culled* (24), *ostentation* (25), *pathological* (30), *mores* (33).

WRITING SUGGESTIONS

1. **For Your Journal.** In the process of tracing the history of alcohol in the western world, the essay provides the reader with a considerable amount of new information. Brainstorm a list of other possible subjects that might be explored in an historical narrative the same way that Vallee does. Remember that the information for this essay will have to come from research, not from your own experience. Some possibilities might include the cigarette, bottled carbonated soda, ballpoint pen, chocolate bar, any addictive drug.
2. **For a Paragraph.** Using the ideas generated in your journal (and perhaps in class discussion) develop a paragraph on your topic. Do some preliminary research in the library or on the World Wide Web and use one source for your paragraph. Be sure to document any direct quotation.
3. **For an Essay.** Extend your journal and paragraph writing into an essay. Trace the history of an object, substance, or product from its origins to the present. Remember that something that is relatively familiar to your readers is likely to be more interesting than something that is obscure and highly technical. Remember too that research will be essential to the essay and be sure, then, to document any direct quotations. Give your instructor a list of the sources you consulted.

   Prewriting:

   a. Be sure to gather sufficient information on your topic before you start to write the essay. For any topics dealing with objects or products, business periodicals might be good sources of information. Remember that you might not find books written about your subject—you might only have magazine or newspaper articles.
   b. Plan carefully your organization strategy. As a narrative, its primary order will be chronological—from its introduction to the present. Check your essay to see if that historical development is clearly outlined.
   c. Be careful about your point of view in the essay. Generally, historical narratives are told in an objective third-person—the writer does not interject herself into the essay or call attention to herself in any way. Check to see how you are narrating your story in the draft stage.

Rewriting:

a. Remember that a narrative must have a beginning, a middle, and an ending. Check your narrative to make sure that you have an interesting opening, a logically organized middle, and a compelling ending (don't just stop!).

b. Look again at your title. An informative, even catchy, title is a tremendous asset to an essay. If yours seems a little boring, try brainstorming some other possibilities.

c. Be sure to check your documentation. All direct quotations must be acknowledged, as well as paraphrases. If you are uncertain about how you have handled your sources, look at the Appendix ("Finding, Using, and Documenting Sources," pp. 604–632) and/or check with your instructor.

4. **For Research.** The popularity of bottled water is relatively new in the United States. Why are we willing to buy water in a bottle, when it's free from a fountain or a faucet? Why are we willing to drink water when it is warm, but insist that our other drinks must be ice-cold? In a research essay, explore this recent phenomenon tracing its origins and evolution.

Website Link

For one perspective on alcohol and American society, visit the online exhibit of material from the archives of the Anti-Saloon League (1893–1933). The League was a key force in bringing about Prohibition in the United States. You can also visit the American Brewery Industry Page!

THREE

DESCRIPTION

You have bought a car—your first—and understandably you can hardly wait to tell your friends. "What does it look like?" they ask and you modestly reply, "A silver-gray '94 Ford Escort with red racing stripes and gray leather seats." What you have done is provide a description; you have given your listeners enough information to allow them to form a mental picture of your new (used) car. Like narration, description is an everyday activity. You describe to a friend what cooked snails really taste like, how your favorite perfume smells, how your body feels when you have a fever, how a local rock band sounded last night. Description recreates sense impressions, ideas, and feelings by translating them into words.

That translation is not always easy. For one thing, when you have a firsthand experience, all of your senses are working at the same time: you see, taste, smell, feel, hear; you experience feelings and have thoughts about the experience. When you convey that experience to a reader or a listener, you can only record one sense impression at a time. Furthermore, sometimes it is difficult to find an adequate translation for a particular sense impression—how do you describe the smell of musk perfume or the taste of freshly squeezed orange juice? But the translation into words offers two distinct advantages: first, ideally it isolates the most important aspects of the experience, ruling out anything else that might distract your reader's attention; second, it makes those experiences more permanent. Sensory impressions decay in seconds, but written descriptions survive indefinitely.

Consider Darcy Frey's description of Russell Thomas, a star basketball player at a Brooklyn, New York, high school, as he practices on a playground in August:

> At this hour Russell usually has the court to himself; most of the other players won't come out until after dark, when the thick humid air begins to stir with night breezes and the court lights come on. But this evening is turning out to be a fine one—cool and foggy. The low, slanting sun sheds a feeble pink light over the silvery Atlantic a block away, and milky sheets of fog roll off the ocean and drift in tatters along the project walkways. The air smells of sewage and saltwater. At the far end of the court, where someone has torn a hole in the chicken wire fence, other players climb through and begin warming up.

Traditionally, descriptions are divided into two categories: objective and subjective. In objective description, you record details without making any personal evaluation or reaction. For example, Roger Angell offers this purely objective description of a baseball, recording weight, dimensions, colors, and material:

> It weighs just five ounces and measures between 2.86 and 2.94 inches in diameter. It is made of a composition-cork nucleus encased in two thin layers of rubber, one black and one red, surrounded by 121 yards of tightly wrapped blue-gray wool yarn, 45 yards of white wool yarn, 53 more yards of blue-gray wool yarn, 150 yards of fine cotton yarn, 53 more yards of blue-gray wool yarn, 150 yards of fine cotton yarn, a coat of rubber cement, and a cowhide (formerly horsehide) exterior, which is held together with 216 slightly raised red cotton stitches.

Few descriptions outside of science writing, however, are completely objective. Instead of trying to include every detail, writers choose details carefully. That process of selection is determined by the writer's purpose and by the impression that the writer wants to create. For example, when Eric Liu visits his grandmother, he washes his hands in the bathroom before eating. As he looks around, his eye is drawn to a strange assortment of details: "a frayed toothbrush in a plastic Star Trek mug I'd given her in 1979, stiff washrags and aged pantyhose hanging from a clothesline, medicine bottles and hair dye cluttered on the sinktop." Liu captures a loneliness and a sadness through those details. Not everyone looking at the room would have "seen" what Liu did.

In subjective description, you are free to interpret details for your reader; your choice of words and images can be suggestive, emotional, and value-loaded. Subjective description frequently makes use of figurative language—similes and metaphors that forge connections in the reader's mind. When Gordon Grice sees the debris that litters the ground under the spider's web, he sees "the husks of consumed insects, their antennae stiff as gargoyle horns." When Scott Russell Sanders looks at his smashed thumbnail, he sees "a crescent moon" that "month by month . . . rose across the pink sky of my thumbnail."

Descriptions serve a variety of purposes, but in every case it is important to make that purpose clear to your reader. Sometimes description is done solely to record the facts, as in Angell's description of the baseball, or to evoke an atmosphere, as in Frey's description of an August evening at a basketball court in Brooklyn. More often description is used as support for other purposes. Gordon Grice, in describing the black widow, is not trying just to describe a spider accurately. He uses description to emphasize the evil or malevolence that he sees embodied in the "flower of natural evil." The spider is more than just a physical thing; it becomes a symbol.

How Do You Describe an Object or a Place?

The first task in writing a description is to decide what you want to describe. As in every other writing task, making a good choice means that the act of writing will be easier and probably more successful. Before you begin, keep two things in mind: first, there is rarely any point in describing a common object or place—something every reader has seen—unless you do it in a fresh and perceptive way. Roger Angell describes a baseball, but he does so by dissecting it, giving a series of facts about its composition. Probably most of Frey's readers had at least seen pictures of a project playground, but after reading his description, what they are left with is a sense of vividness—this passage evokes or re-creates in our minds a mental picture of that evening.

Second, remember that your description must create a focused impression. To do that, you need to select details which contribute to your purpose. That will give you a way of deciding which details out of the many available are relevant. Details in a description must be carefully chosen and arranged; otherwise, your reader will be overwhelmed or bored by the accumulation of detail.

How Do You Describe a Person?

Before you begin to describe a person, remember an experience that everyone has had. You have read a novel and then seen a film or a made-for-television version, and the two experiences did not mesh. The characters, you are convinced, just did not look like the actors and actresses: "She was thinner and blond" or "He was all wrong—not big enough, not rugged enough." Any time you read a narrative that contains a character—either real or fictional—you form a mental picture of the person, and that picture is generally not based on any physical description that the author has provided. In fact, in many narratives, authors provide only minimal description of the people involved. For example, if you look closely at the Thurmond Watts family in William Least Heat Moon's "Nameless, Tennessee," you will find almost no physical description of the people. Thurmond, we are told, is "tall" and "thin"—those are the only adjectives used to describe him. The rest of the family—his wife, Miss Ginny; his sister-in-law, Marilyn; and his daughter, Hilda—are not physically described at all. Nevertheless, we get a vivid sense of all four as people.

Fictional characters or real people are created or revealed primarily through ways other than direct physical description. What a person does or says, for example, also reveals personality. The reader "sees" Alan in Terry Tempest Williams's "Village Watchman" in part through what he does (for example, his behavior at the bowling alley) and through what he says. The Wattses, in Least Heat Moon's narrative, are revealed by how they react, what they say, how their speech sounds, what they consider to be important. These are the key factors in re-creating Least Heat Moon's experience for the reader.

In fact, descriptions of people should not try to be verbal portraits recording physical attributes in photographic detail. Words finally are never as efficient in doing that as photographs. If the objective in describing a person is not photographic accuracy, what then is it? Go back to the advice offered earlier in this introduction: decide first what impression you want to create in your reader. Why are you describing this person? What is it about this person that is worth describing? In all likelihood the answer will be something other than physical attributes. Once you know what that something is, you can then choose the details that best reveal or display the person.

How Do You Organize a Description?

You have found a subject; you have studied it—either firsthand or in memory; you have decided on a reason for describing this particular subject; you have selected details that contribute to that reason or purpose. Now you need to organize your paragraph or essay. Descriptions, like narratives, have principles of order, although the principles vary depending on what sensory impressions are involved. When the primary descriptive emphasis is on seeing, the most obvious organization is spatial—moving from front to back, side to side, outside to inside, top to bottom, general to specific. The description moves as a camera would. Roger Angell's description of a baseball moves outward from the cork nucleus through the layers of rubber, wool yarn, and rubber cement to the cowhide exterior.

Other sensory experiences might be arranged in order of importance, from the most obvious to the least—the loudest noise at the concert, the most pervasive odor in the restaurant—or even in chronological order. Eric Liu's description of his visit to his grandmother is structured chronologically—from his arrival at her apartment building to their farewell embrace.

Does Description Mean Lots of Adjectives and Adverbs?

Remember that one-sentence description of your car: "A silver-gray '94 Ford Escort with red racing stripes and gray leather seats." Your audience would have no trouble creating a vivid mental picture from that little bit of information, because it has seen an Escort before. The noun provides the primary image. The three adjectives describe color. The point is that you can create an image without providing a mountain of adjectives and adverbs—just as you imagine what a character looks like without being told. When Terry Tempest Williams describes Alan's behavior at the bowling alley, the scene and Alan come alive for the reader: "When it was Alan's turn, it was an event. Nothing subtle. His style was Herculean. Big man. Big ball. Big roll. Big bang. Whether it was a strike or a gutter ball, he clapped his hands, spun around on the floor, clapped his thighs, and cried, 'Goddamn! Did you see that one? Send me another ball, sweet Jesus!'" One of the greatest dangers in writing a description lies in trying to describe too much, trying to qualify every noun with at least one adjective and every verb with an adverb. Precise, vivid nouns and verbs will do most of the work for you.

Sample Student Essay

Nadine Resnick chose to describe her favorite childhood toy, a stuffed doll she had named Natalie.

Earlier Draft

PRETTY IN PINK

Standing in the middle of the aisle, staring up at the world as most children in nursery school do, something pink caught my eye. Just like Rapunzel in her high tower, there was a girl inside a cardboard and plastic prison atop a high shelf that smiled down at me. I pointed to the doll and brought her home with me that same day. Somehow I knew that she was special.

She was named Natalie. I do not know why, but the name just seemed perfect, like the rest of her. Natalie was less than twelve inches tall and wore a pink outfit. Her hands and grimacing face were made of plastic while the rest of her body was stuffed with love. She had brown eyes and brown hair, just like me, which peeked through her burgundy and pink-flowered bonnet. Perhaps the most unusual feature about her was that my mom had tattooed my name on her large bottom so that if Natalie ever strayed from me at nursery school or at the supermarket, she would be able to find me.

There was some kind of magic about Natalie's face. I think it was her grin from ear to ear. Even if I had played with her until she was so dirty that most of her facial features were hidden, Natalie's never-ending smile usually shown through. When I neglected her for days to play with some new toy and then later returned, her friendly smirk was still there. When I was left home alone for a few hours, her smile assured me that I need not be afraid. Natalie's bright smile also cheered me up when I was sick or had a bad day. And she always had enough hugs for me.

As I was growing up, Natalie and her beaming face could usually be found somewhere in my room—on my bed, in her carriage, hiding under a pile of junk, and later piled in my closet with the rest of my other dolls and stuffed animals. When I got older, I foolishly decided that I no longer needed such childish toys. So I put Natalie and the rest of my stuffed animals in a large black plastic bag in a dark corner of the basement. I now realize that the basement really is not an honorable place for someone who has meant so much to me. But, I will bet that she is still smiling anyway.

Nadine had a chance to read her essay to a small group of classmates during a collaborative editing session. Everyone liked the essay and most of their suggested changes were fairly minor. For example, several people objected to her choice of the words *grimaced* and *smirk*, feeling that such words were not appropriate choices for a lovable doll. Another student, however, suggested a revision in the final paragraph. "It seems like you put her farther and farther away from you as you got older. Why don't you emphasize that distancing by having it occur in stages?" he commented. When Nadine rewrote her essay, she made a number of minor changes in the first three paragraphs and then followed her classmate's idea in the fourth paragraph.

Revised Draft

NATALIE

Standing in the store's aisle, staring up at the world as most pre-school children do, something pink caught my eye. Just like Rapunzel in her high tower, a girl trapped inside a cardboard and plastic prison atop a high shelf smiled down at me. I pointed to the doll and brought her home with me that same day. Somehow I knew that she was special.

She was named Natalie. I do not know why, but the name just seemed perfect, like the rest of her. Natalie was less than twelve inches tall and wore a pink outfit. Her hands and smiling face were made of plastic while the rest of her body was plumply stuffed. Just like me, she had brown eyes and brown hair which peeked through her burgundy and pink-flowered bonnet. Perhaps her most unusual feature was my name tattooed on her bottom so that if Natalie ever strayed from me at nursery school or at the supermarket, she would be able to find me.

Natalie's face had a certain glow, some kind of magic. I think it was her grin from ear to ear. After I had played with her, no matter how dirty her face was, Natalie's never-ending smile still beamed through. When I neglected her for days to play with some new toy and then later returned, her friendly grin was still there. Years later, when I was old enough to be left home alone for a few hours, her smile assured me that I need not be afraid. Natalie's bright smile also cheered me up when I was sick or had a bad day. And she always had enough hugs for me.

As I was growing up, Natalie and her beaming face could usually be found somewhere in my room. However, she seemed to move further away from me as I got older. Natalie no longer slept with me; she slept in her own carriage. Then she rested on a high shelf across my room. Later she made her way into my closet with the rest of the dolls and stuffed animals that I had outgrown. Eventually, I decided that I no longer needed such childish toys, so I put Natalie and my other stuffed animals in a large black plastic bag in a dark cellar corner. Even though I abandoned her, I am sure that Natalie is still smiling at me today.

Some Things to Remember

1. Choose your subject carefully, making sure that you have a specific reason or purpose in mind for whatever you describe.
2. Study or observe your subject—try to see it or experience it in a fresh way. Gather details; make a list; use all your senses.
3. Use your purpose as a way of deciding which details ought to be included and which excluded.
4. Choose a pattern of organization to focus your reader's attention.
5. Use precise, vivid nouns and verbs, as well as adjectives and adverbs, to create your descriptions.

Using Description in Your Writing for Other Courses

Description can be involved in a number of different college writing assignments. Most such descriptive writing will be objective, focusing on exact details rather than on your personal responses, but you might occasionally be asked to evaluate something you describe more aesthetically. Here are some examples of writing assignments that would involve description.

- **Art History.** An assignment asking for a detailed analysis of a painting would necessarily include a detailed description of its pictorial elements, both objectively and with an eye toward the aesthetic qualities of the work.
- **Geology.** On an exam you might be required to identify a variety of different mineral samples by describing their specific physical characteristics.
- **Anthropology.** For an anthropological field study, you might be asked for a closely observed description of the physical appearance and social interactions of the members of a clearly defined social group.
- **Anatomy.** Following your class's examination of a laboratory specimen, you might be asked to write a brief paper describing its specific anatomical structures in detail.
- **American Studies.** In a unit on American architecture, you might choose to write a paper focusing on a particular architectural style—the main features of which you would describe fully—to suggest what that style reflects about American values at a particular period in history.
- **Theater/Dramatic Literature.** On an essay exam, you might be asked to describe the physical theaters in which plays were presented at the times of the playwrights Sophocles, Shakespeare, and Ibsen.

Visualizing Description

Remember the cliche: "A picture is worth a thousand words"? Frankly, some things can't be adequately described in words alone. Imagine how difficult it would be to assemble a complex object if its set of instructions included only words and no pictures. Words might be crucial to creating an impression, focusing a reader's attention, or conveying precise information, but they are not adequate for every task. Consider the illustrator's anatomical sketch of the human back on page 155. It accompanies an article on "Low-Back Pain" aimed at a general audience. Here the illustrator reveals the complex muscle structures that surround the spine. Can you imagine trying to describe with only words the muscles found in the human back?

Visit the Prentice Hall Reader's WebSite

When you have finished reading an essay, check out the additional material available at the *Reader's* Website at www.prenhall.com/miller. For each reading, you will find a list of related readings connected with the topic or the author; additional background information; a group of relevant "hot-linked" web resources (just click your computer's mouse and automatically visit the sites listed); and still more writing suggestions.

Description

The Library of Congress in Washington, D.C., has 60 spectacular on-line exhibitions covering a broad range of topics, time frames, and geographical regions in the United States—see a fabulous collection of old baseball cards, watch Edison's films made during the Spanish American War in 1898, view over 900 photographs of the Northern Great Plains during the first decades of this century. For an overview of the exhibits and for a writing topic that invites you to describe what you saw on your virtual experience, go to the *Reader's* Website.

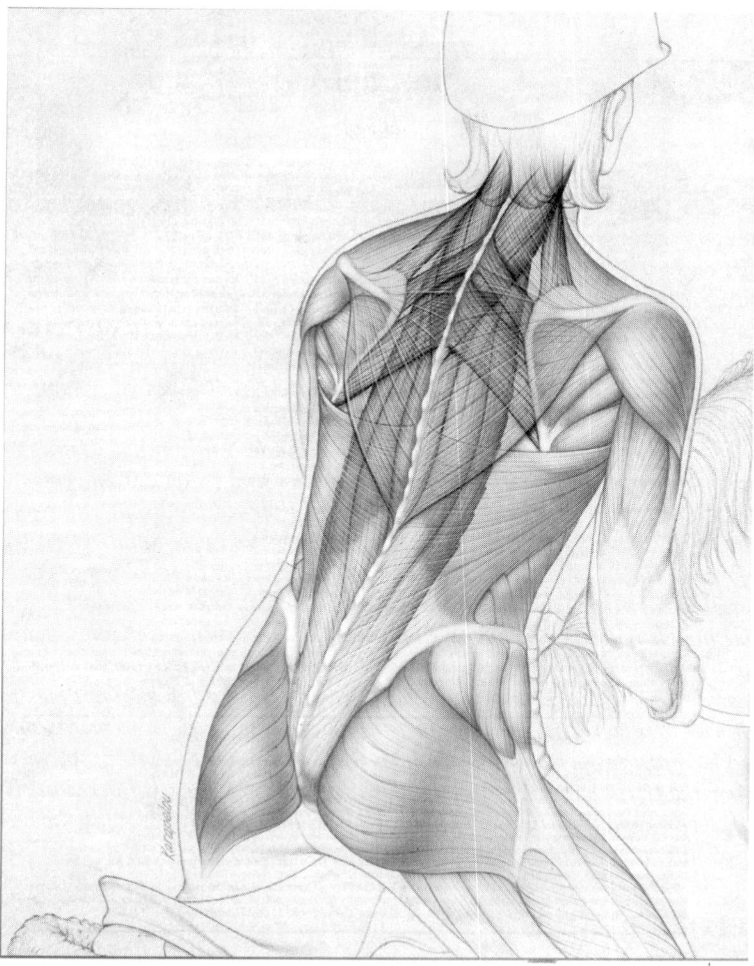

LOWER BACK consists of numerous structures, any of which may be responsible for pain. The most obvious are the powerful muscles that surround the spine. Other potential sources of pain include the strong ligaments that connect vertebrae; the disks that lie between vertebrae, providing cushioning; the face joints, which help to ensure smooth alignment and stability of the spine; the vertebral bones themselves; blood vessels; and the nerves that emerge from the spine.

Po-Po

Eric Liu

Eric Liu (1968–) graduated from Yale and in 1991 founded The Next Progressive, *a quarterly journal of Democratic Party politics and culture. In 1993, he joined President Clinton's speech-writing staff as its youngest and only Asian American member. A contributor to MSNBC,* Slate, The Washington Post, *and* USA Weekend, *Liu also edited* Next: Young American Writers on the New Generation *(1994). This essay is taken from* The Accidental Asian: Notes of a Native Speaker *(1998).*

On Writing: *In* The Accidental Asian, *Liu considers issues of personal identity—both as an Asian American and simply as an American. He longs, he says, to be grounded in a historical tradition and wonders if he should focus on "Asian American history: the trials of people before my time, whose estrangement from the mainstream years ago made possible my entry into the mainstream today." Liu goes on: "And I think here in this narrative is a source of belonging. But then I wonder: Should I stop with Asian American stories? Should I even begin there?" Then he explains that as a speechwriter for President Clinton his specialty was to compose memorial speeches for victims of tragedies such as plane crashes and for military personnel killed in battle. He discovered that his speech to honor the fiftieth anniversary of World War II's D-Day, delivered at the American cemetary in Normandy, allowed him to participate in "a* nation's *memory" and "something I, too, could claim."*

BEFORE READING

Connecting: What memories or associations come immediately to mind when you think about one of your parents or grandparents?

Anticipating: Liu is writing about his memories of his maternal grandmother. Out of the many memories that he has, why might he choose to recount his memory of a visit to her apartment? How do the included details affect our sense of Po-Po?

1 For more than two decades, my mother's mother, Po-Po, lived in a cinder-block one-bedroom apartment on the edge of New York's Chinatown. She was twenty floors up, so if you looked straight out from the main room, which faced north, one block appeared to

melt into the next, all the way to the spire of the Empire State off in the distance. This was a saving grace, the view, since her own block down below was not much to look at. Her building, one of those interchangeable towers of 1970s public housing, was on the lower east side of the Lower East Side, at the corner of South and Clinton. It was, as the realtors say, only minutes from the Brooklyn Bridge and South Street Seaport, although those landmarks, for all she cared, might as well have been in Nebraska. They weren't part of the world Po-Po inhabited, which was the world that I visited every few months during the last years of her life.

My visits followed a certain pattern. I'd get to her apartment 2
around noon, and when I knocked on the door I could hear her scurrying with excitement. When she opened the door, I'd be struck, always as if for the first time, by how tiny she was: four feet nine and shrinking. She wore loose, baggy clothes, nylons, and ill-fitting old glasses that covered her soft, wrinkled face. It was a face I recognized from my own second-grade class photo. *Eh, Po-Po, ni hao maaa?* She offered a giggle as I bent to embrace her. With an impish smile, she proclaimed my American name in her Yoda-like voice: *Areek*. She got a kick out of that. As she shuffled to the kitchen, where Li Tai Tai, her caregiver, was preparing lunch, I would head to the bathroom, trained to wash my hands upon entering Po-Po's home.

In the small bath were the accessories of her everyday life: a 3
frayed toothbrush in a plastic Star Trek mug I'd given her in 1979, stiff washrags and aged pantyhose hanging from a clothesline, medicine bottles and hair dye cluttered on the sinktop. I often paused for a moment there, looking for my reflection in the filmy, clouded mirror, taking a deep breath or two. Then I would walk back into the main room. The place was neat but basically grimy. Some of the furniture—the lumpy couch, the coffee table with old magazines and congealed candies, the lawn chair where she read her Chinese newspaper through a magnifying glass—had been there as long as I could remember. The windowsill was crammed with plants and flowers. The only thing on the thickly painted white wall was a calendar. *Your house looks so nice*, I'd say in a tender tone of Mandarin that I used only with her. On a tray beside me, also surveying the scene, was a faded black-and-white portrait of Po-Po as a beautiful young woman dressed in Chinese costume. *Lai chi ba*, Po-Po would say, inviting me to eat.

Invariably, there was a banquet's worth of food awaiting me 4
on the small kitchen table: *hongshao* stewed beef, a broiled fish with scallions and ginger, a leafy green called *jielan*, a soup with chicken

and winter melon and radishes, tofu with ground pork, stir-fried shrimp still in their salty shells. Po-Po ate sparingly, and Li Tai Tai, in her mannerly Chinese way, adamantly refused to dine with us, so it was up to me to attack this meal. I gorged myself, loosening my belt within the half hour and sitting back dazed and short of breath by the end. No matter how much I put down, Po-Po would express disappointment at my meager appetite.

5 As I ate she chattered excitedly, pouring forth a torrent of opinions about politics in China, Hong Kong pop singers, the latest developments in Taiwan. After a while, she'd move into stories about people I'd never met, distant relations, half brothers killed by the Communists, my grandfather, who had died when I was a toddler. Then she'd talk about her friends who lived down the "F" train in Flushing or on the other side of Chinatown and who were dying one by one, and she'd tell me about seeing Jesus after she'd had a cancer operation in 1988, and how this blond Jesus had materialized and said to her in Chinese, *You are a good person, too good to die now. Nobody knows how good you are. Nobody appreciates you as much as I do.* I would sit quietly then, not sure whether to smile. But just as she approached the brink she would take a sip of 7UP and swerve back to something in the news, perhaps something about her heroine, the Burmese dissident Aung San Suu Kyi. She was an incredible talker, Po-Po, using her hands and her eyes like a performer. She built up a tidal momentum, relentless, imaginative, spiteful, like a child.

6 I generally didn't have much to say in response to Po-Po's commentary, save the occasional Chinese-inflected *Oh?* and *Wah!* I took in the lilt of her Sichuan accent and relied on context to figure out what she was saying. In fact, it wasn't till I brought my girlfriend to meet Po-Po that I realized just how vague my comprehension was. *What did she say?* Carroll would ask. *Um, something about, something, I think, about the president of Taiwan.* Of course, I'm not sure Po-Po even cared whether I understood. If I interjected, she'd cut me off with a hasty *bushide—no, it's not that*—a habit I found endearing in small doses but that my mother, over a lifetime, had found maddening.

7 If there was a lull, I might ask Po-Po about her health, which would prompt her to spring up from her chair and, bracing herself on the counter, kick her leg up in the air. *I do this ten times every morning at five*, she would proudly say in Chinese. *Then this*, she'd add, and she would stretch her arms out like little wings, making circles with her fingertips. *And last week I had a headache, so I rubbed each eye like this thirty-six times.* Pretty soon I was out of my chair,

too, laughing, rubbing, kicking, as Po-Po schooled me in her system of exercises and home remedies. We did this every visit, like a ritual.

Time moved so slowly when I was at Po-Po's. After lunch, we might sit on the couch next to each other or go to her room so she could tell me things that she didn't want Li Tai Tai to hear. We would rest there, digesting, our conversation turning more mellow. I might pull out of my bag a small keepsake for her, a picture of Carroll and me, or a souvenir from a recent vacation. She would show me a bundle of poems she had written in classical Chinese, scribbled on the backs of the small cardboard rectangles that come with travel packs of Kleenex. She would recount how she'd been inspired to write this poem or that one. Then she would open a spiral notebook that she kept, stuffed with news clippings and filled with idioms and sentences she had copied out of the Chinese newspaper's daily English lesson: *Let's get a move on. I don't like the looks of this.* At my urging, she'd read the sentences aloud, tentatively. I would praise her warmly, she would chuckle, and then she might show me something else, a photo album, a book about *qigong*. 8

One day she revealed to me her own way of prayer, demonstrating how she sat on the side of her bed at night and clasped her hands, bowing as if before Buddha, repeating in fragile English, *God bless me? God bless me? God bless me?* Another time she urgently recited to me a short story that had moved her to tears, but I understood hardly a word of it. On another visit she fell asleep beside me, her glasses still on, her chin tucked into itself. And so the hours would pass, until it was time for me to go—until, that is, I had decided it was time to go, for she would have wanted me to stay forever—and I would hold her close and stroke her knotted back and tell her that I loved her and that I would miss her, and Po-Po, too modest to declare her heart so openly, would nod and press a little red envelope of money into my hand and say to me quietly in Chinese, *How I wish I had wings so I could come see you where you live.* 9

QUESTIONS ON SUBJECT AND PURPOSE

1. Liu recounts a typical visit to his grandmother's New York City apartment. How often does he visit her?
2. Why might Liu have written about his grandmother?
3. Why would a reader be interested in reading about someone else's grandmother?

QUESTIONS ON STRATEGY AND AUDIENCE

1. How does Liu structure his essay?
2. How would you describe the feelings that Liu has about Po-Po? What evidence from the essay could you cite to support your answer?
3. Why might Liu chose to end his account of a typical visit with the incidents related in paragraph 9?

QUESTIONS ON VOCABULARY AND STYLE

1. What is the effect of the final sentence of the essay?
2. Liu italicizes scraps of dialogue in the essay—for example, Po-Po's remarks and questions. What is the effect of including these little scraps of conversation?
3. Be prepared to define the following words: *scurrying* (paragraph 2), *scallions* (4), *tofu* (4), *adamantly* (4), *dissident* (5).

WRITING SUGGESTIONS

1. **For Your Journal.** How would you describe your parents' attitude toward their parents? How would you describe your attitude toward your grandparents? In your journal, explore both subjects. (If you are an older student, you could explore your and your children's attitudes toward your parents.)
2. **For a Paragraph.** In a paragraph, write a description of someone who is significantly older than you are—preferably a grandparent or someone at least a generation older. As a prewriting exercise, try to make a visit to your subject or to at least talk with the person on the telephone. Observe, listen, take notes. Try to capture your person in a paragraph.
3. **For an Essay.** Extend your paragraph into an essay. Do not just describe the person photographically. Use descriptive details—for example, about the person's behavior, environment, language, or values—to reveal character. Consider using some dialogue.

   Prewriting:

   a. Visit your subject, preferably more than once. Pretend that you are a camera panning around the room. What do you see? What descriptive details could you use in your essay?

b. Bring a tape recorder if possible (but be sure to ask permission to record) or a notebook and capture pieces of the conversation. What is said? What is revealed by what is said?

c. Do not try to describe the person photographically. Instead, select details that reveal personality and the qualities that you wish to emphasize.

Rewriting:

a. Look back at how Liu describes Po-Po. Compare his descriptive and narrative strategies to yours.

b. Look carefully at the structure of your essay. Is it strictly chronological? Would it be better to start with a flashback or to order your material in some other way? Jot down an outline for an alternate structure, even if you are basically satisfied with your own.

c. Write a single sentence that sums up the dominant impression that you want your reader to have after finishing your essay. Use that statement as a way of measuring every aspect of your essay. Do you keep your focus clear throughout? Do all the details of the essay contribute to that impression?

4. **For Research.** America is a society that worships youth and shuns old age. Old people are often not figures to be respected or honored but burdens to be cared for by hired professionals. In many other societies, however, the elderly are treated very differently. Research a society that honors its old. Do not just report on how the elderly are seen or treated in this society. Formulate a thesis that explains why this society behaves in this way. You will first need to identify those societies—a reference librarian can help you start a search through a source such as the Library of Congress Subject Headings (see the Appendix: "Finding, Using, and Documenting Sources").

Website Link

In an interview, "Asian Integration," Liu talks about race and identity in America. The text is available from an on-line bookstore. The interview is instantly accessible through the *Reader's* Website.

Caught in the Widow's Web

Gordon Grice

Gordon Grice earned his B.A. at Oklahoma State University and his M.F.A. at the University of Arkansas. Currently a faculty member at Seward County Community College in Liberal, Kansas, Grice has published essays and poems in a wide range of literary magazines. His first collection of essays was The Red Hourglass: Lives of the Predators *(1998). Grice was recipient of a Whiting Writers' Award in 1999. The following essay, originally titled "The Black Widow," first appeared in the* High Plains Literary Review. *Grice reworked it for its appearance in* Harper's *magazine and then again for* The Red Hourglass. *See Chapter 10, "Revising," for some of the draft sections of the essay.*

On Writing: *Commenting on this essay, Grice observed: "I worked on this piece for years. It was originally written in 1993, and then I put it aside for a year. One day when I was substitute-teaching in a shop class in high school and the kids were all busy, I took it out and rewrote the opening. The next journal I sent it to accepted it for publication." Widely praised for his precise and detailed attention to the "micro-world," Grice has said, "Personal observation and experience are part of my approach to writing as a whole. I like to delve into the details and give my readers the feeling of being there and having their own hands in it."*

BEFORE READING

Connecting: How do you feel about spiders? To what do you attribute your reaction?

Anticipating: In the Glossary at the back of this book, look up the word *symbol.* As you read, think about the extent to which the black widow is a symbol for Grice.

1 I hunt black widows. When I find one, I capture it. I have found them in discarded wheels and tires and under railroad ties. I have found them in house foundations and cellars, in automotive shops and toolsheds, in water meters and rock gardens, against fences and in cinder-block walls.

2 Black widows have the ugliest webs of any spider, messy-looking tangles in the corners and bends of things and under logs and debris. Often the widow's web is littered with leaves. Beneath

it lie the husks of consumed insects, their antennae stiff as gargoyle horns; on them and the surrounding ground are splashes of the spider's white urine, which looks like bird guano and smells of ammonia even at a distance of several feet.

This fetid material draws scavengers—ants, sow bugs, crickets, roaches, and so on—which become tangled in vertical strands of silk reaching from the ground up into the web. The widow climbs down and throws gummy silk onto this new prey. When the insect is seriously tangled but still struggling, the widow cautiously descends and bites it, usually on a leg joint. This is a killing bite; it pumps poison into the victim. As the creature dies, the widow delivers still more bites, injecting substances that liquefy the organs. Finally it settles down to suck the liquefied innards out of the prey, changing position two or three times to get it all. 3

Widows reportedly eat mice, toads, tarantulas—anything that wanders into that remarkable web. I have never witnessed a widow performing a gustatory act of that magnitude, but I have seen them eat scarab beetles heavy as pecans, carabid beetles strong enough to prey on wolf spiders, cockroaches more than an inch long, and hundreds of other arthropods of various sizes. 4

Many widows will eat as much as opportunity allows. One aggressive female I raised had an abdomen a little bigger than a pea. She snared a huge cockroach and spent several hours subduing it, then three days consuming it. Her abdomen swelled to the size of a largish marble, its glossy black stretching to a tight red-brown. With a different widow, I decided to see whether that appetite really was insatiable. I collected dozens of large crickets and grasshoppers and began to drop them into her web at a rate of one every three or four hours. After catching and devouring her tenth victim, this bloated widow fell from her web, landing on her back. She remained in this position for hours, making only feeble attempts to move. Then she died. 5

The first thing people ask when they hear about my fascination with the widow is why I am not afraid. The truth is that my fascination is rooted in fear. 6

I have childhood memories that partly account for this. When I was six my mother took my sister and me into the cellar of our farmhouse and told us to watch as she killed a widow. With great ceremony she produced a long stick (I am tempted to say a ten-foot pole) and, narrating her technique in exactly the hushed voice she used for discussing religion or sex, went to work. Her 7 flashlight beam found a point halfway up the cement wall where two marbles hung together—one a crisp white, the other a shiny black. My mother ran her stick through the dirty silver web around them. As it tore it sounded like the crackling of paper in fire. The black marble rose on thin legs to fight off the intruder. My mother smashed the widow onto the stick and carried it up into the light. It was still kicking its remaining legs. Mom scraped it against the floor, grinding it into a paste. Then she returned for the white marble—the widow's egg sac. This, too, came to an abrasive end.

8 My mother's stated purpose was to teach us how to recognize and deal with a dangerous creature that we would probably encounter on the farm. But, of course, we also took away the understanding that widows were actively malevolent, that they waited in dark places to ambush us, that they were worthy of ritual disposition, like an enemy whose death is not sufficient but must be followed by the murder of his children and the salting of his land and whose unclean remains must not touch our hands.

9 The odd thing is that so *many* people, some of whom presumably did not first encounter the widow in such an atmosphere of mystic reverence, hold the widow in awe. Various friends have told me that the widow's bite is always fatal to humans—in fact, it almost never is. I have heard told for truth that goods imported from the Orient are likely to be infested with widows and that women with bouffant hairdos have died of widow infestation. Any contradiction of such tales is received as if it were a proclamation of atheism.

10 We project our archetypal terrors onto the widow. It is black; it avoids the light; it is a voracious carnivore. Its red markings suggest blood. The female's habit of eating her lovers invites a strangely sexual discomfort; the widow becomes an emblem for a man's fear of extending himself into the blood and darkness of a woman, something like the legendary Eskimo vampire that takes the form of a fanged vagina.

11 The widow's venom is, of course, a sound reason for fear. The venom contains a neurotoxin that can produce sweats, vomiting, swelling, convulsions, and dozens of other symptoms. The variation in symptoms from one person to the next is remarkable. The constant is pain. A useful question for a doctor trying to diagnose an uncertain case: "Is this the worst pain you've ever felt?" A "yes" suggests a diagnosis of a black widow bite. Occasionally people die from widow bites. The very young and the very old are especially vulnerable. Some people seem to die not from the venom but from

the infection that may follow: because of its habitat, the widow carries dangerous microbes.

Researchers once hypothesized that the virulence of the venom was necessary for killing beetles of the scarabaeidae family. This family contains thousands of species, including the June beetle and the famous dung beetle that the Egyptians thought immortal. All the scarabs have thick, strong bodies and unusually tough exoskeletons, and many of them are common prey for the widow. The tough hide was supposed to require a particularly nasty venom. As it turns out, the venom is thousands of times more virulent than necessary for this purpose. 12

No one has ever offered a sufficient explanation for the dangerous venom. It provides no evolutionary advantages: all of the widow's prey would find lesser toxins fatal, and there is no particular benefit in killing or harming larger animals. A widow that bites a human being or other large animal is likely to be killed. 13

Natural selection favors the inheritance of useful characteristics that arise from random mutation and tends to extinguish disadvantageous traits. All other characteristics, the ones that neither help nor hinder survival, are preserved or extinguished at random as mutation links them with useful or harmful traits. Many people—even many scientists—assume that every animal is elegantly engineered for its ecological niche, that every bit of an animal's anatomy and behavior has a functional explanation. This assumption is false. Evolution sometimes produces flowers of natural evil—traits that are neither functional nor vestigial but utterly pointless. 14

We want the world to be an ordered room, but in a corner of that room there hangs an untidy web. Here the analytical mind finds an irreducible mystery, a motiveless evil in nature; here the scientist's vision of evil comes to match the vision of a God-fearing country woman with a ten-foot pole. No idea of the cosmos as elegant design accounts for the widow. No idea of a benevolent God is comfortable in a world with the widow. She hangs in her web, that marvel of design, and defies reason. 15

QUESTIONS ON SUBJECT AND PURPOSE

1. Why is Grice so fascinated by black widow spiders? To what does he trace his fascination?
2. What particular aspects of the black widow spider does Grice focus on?
3. What does the spider symbolize to Grice?

QUESTIONS ON STRATEGY AND AUDIENCE

1. Why does Grice begin with the simple sentence "I hunt black widows." What is the effect of that sentence?
2. Grice divides his essay into three sections through the use of additional white space (after paragraphs 5 and 10). How does that division reflect the structure of the essay?
3. What assumptions could Grice make about his audience and their attitudes toward spiders?

QUESTIONS ON VOCABULARY AND STYLE

1. In describing how his mother killed the spider, Grice writes, "With great ceremony she produced a long stick (I am tempted to say a ten-foot pole)" (paragraph 7). Why does he add the material in the parentheses?
2. What is the effect of labeling the spider a "voracious carnivore"? To what extent is that an accurate phrase?
3. Be prepared to define the following words: *fetid* (paragraph 3), *gustatory* (4), *malevolent* (8), *bouffant* (9), *voracious* (10), *carnivore* (10), *virulence* (12), *niche* (14), *vestigial* (14).

WRITING SUGGESTIONS

1. **For Your Journal.** We tend to ignore the natural details that surround us. Try looking closely, even minutely, at the things around you. For example, take a magnifying glass and carefully examine an insect or a plant leaf. Take a walk and sit down with your journal. Study the landscape around you. Make journal entries about what you are suddenly able to see.
2. **For a Paragraph.** Select one of your journal entries and expand the entry into a descriptive paragraph. Try to make your reader see with you.
3. **For an Essay.** Nature can be seen and interpreted in many ways. Look back over your journal entries, look around you, select some natural thing—a living creature, a plant or leaf, an event, or even a landscape. In an essay, describe it to your reader in such a way as to reveal a significance. You are not writing an encyclopedia article or a guide book for tourists; you are seeing a meaning.

Prewriting:

a. Develop a list of possible subjects. Try to select something that you can experience directly.

b. Next to each subject, write down what you see as "revealed" in each—for example, indifference, benevolence, or hostility toward humans.

c. Select two of the most promising subjects, and make a list of possible descriptive details to use. Remember that each detail needs to make your subject vivid to your reader; most should also be connected with the significance that you are trying to convey.

Rewriting:

a. Check to make sure that you have used vivid nouns and verbs to carry most of the descriptive burden. Do not use too many adjectives and adverbs.

b. Go through your essay and underline every descriptive detail. Are there too many? Are you trying to make the reader see too much? Compare your use of description to Grice's.

c. Have you been too heavy-handed in emphasizing the significance that you see? Remember, you are trying to reveal significance; you are not lecturing your reader.

4. **For Research.** Grice does not attempt to tell the "full" story of the black widow. Research the black widow (or any other poisonous insect or reptile) using traditional library resources. You could also explore resources on the World Wide Web and various other on-line electronic information sources. Your object is not to present an informational report—"here is everything about the subject." Rather, try to formulate a thesis about your subject. For example, you might explore the myths and symbols that have attached themselves to your subject or the role of the creature in our environment or the "lethalness" of its venom.

Website Link

How did Grice get interested in Black Widow spiders? In an online interview at one of the electronic bookstores he explains his interest in spiders, snakes, and other predatory creatures.

NAMELESS, TENNESSEE

William Least Heat Moon

William Least Heat Moon was born William Trogdon in Missouri in 1939 and earned a Ph.D. in English from the University of Missouri in 1973. Trogdon's father created his pen name in memory of their Sioux forefather. His books include Blue Highways: A Journey into America *(1992),* PrairyErth *(1991), and* River-Horse: A Voyage Across America *(1999), an account of his five-thousand mile journey across America's waterways from New York harbor to the Pacific Ocean. The following essay is from* Blue Highways, *an account of Least Heat Moon's 14,000-mile journey through American backroads in a converted van called* Ghost Dancing. *Its title refers to the blue ink used by map publisher Rand McNally to indicate smaller, or secondary, roads.*

On Writing: *Asked about his writing, Least Heat Moon observed: "Woody Allen once said the hardest thing in writing is going from nothing to something. And I think he's right. I struggle so much getting that first draft down. My writing draws so much upon every bit that I am, that I feel drained when I finish a book, and it's years before I'm ready to write again."*

BEFORE READING

Connecting: If you could get in an automobile and drive off, and time, money, and responsibilities posed no obstacles, where would you go?

Anticipating: "Nameless, Tennessee" does more than just faithfully record everything Least Heat Moon saw while visiting the Wattses. The narrative has a central focus that controls the selection of detail. What is that focus?

1 Nameless, Tennessee, was a town of maybe ninety people if you pushed it, a dozen houses along the road, a couple of barns, same number of churches, a general merchandise store selling Fire Chief gasoline, and a community center with a lighted volleyball court. Behind the center was an open-roof, rusting metal privy with PAINT ME on the door, in the hollow of a nearby oak lay a full pint of Jack Daniel's Black Label. From the houses, the odor of coal smoke.

Next to a red tobacco barn stood the general merchandise 2
with a poster of Senator Albert Gore, Jr., smiling from the window. I knocked. The door opened partway. A tall, thin man said, "Closed up. For good," and started to shut the door.

"Don't want to buy anything. Just a question for Mr. 3
Thurmond Watts."

The man peered through the slight opening. He looked me 4
over. "What question would that be?"

"If this is Nameless, Tennessee, could he tell me how it got 5
that name?"

The man turned back into the store and called out, "Miss 6
Ginny! Somebody here wants to know how Nameless come to be Nameless."

Miss Ginny edged to the door and looked me and my truck 7
over. Clearly, she didn't approve. She said, "You know as well as I do, Thurmond. Don't keep him on the stoop in the damp to tell him." Miss Ginny, I found out, was Mrs. Virginia Watts, Thurmond's wife.

I stepped in and they both began telling the story, adding a 8
detail here, the other correcting a fact there, both smiling at the foolishness of it all. It seems the hilltop settlement went for years without a name. Then one day the Post Office Department told the people if they wanted mail up on the mountain they would have to give the place a name you could properly address a letter to. The community met; there were only a handful, but they commenced debating. Some wanted patriotic names, some names from nature, one man recommended in all seriousness his own name. They couldn't agree, and they ran out of names to argue about. Finally, a fellow tired of the talk; he didn't like the mail he received anyway. "Forget the durn Post Office," he said. "This here's a nameless place if I ever seen one, so leave it be." And that's just what they did.

Watts pointed out the window. "We used to have signs on the 9
road, but the Halloween boys keep tearin' them down."

"You think Nameless is a funny name," Miss Ginny said. "I 10
see it plain in your eyes. Well, you take yourself up north a piece to Difficult or Defeated or Shake Rag. Now them are silly names."

The old store, lighted only by three fifty-watt bulbs, smelled 11
of coal oil and baking bread. In the middle of the rectangular room, where the oak floor sagged a little, stood an iron stove. To the right was a wooden table with an unfinished game of checkers and a stool made from an apple-tree stump. On shelves around

the walls sat earthen jugs with corncob stoppers, a few canned goods, and some of the two thousand old clocks and clockworks Thurmond Watts owned. Only one was ticking, the others he just looked at. I asked how long he'd been in the store.

12 "Thirty-five years, but we closed the first day of the year. We're hopin' to sell it to a churchly couple. Upright people. No athians."

13 "Did you build this store?"

14 "I built this one, but it's the third general store on the ground. I fear it'll be the last. I take no pleasure in that. Once you could come in here for a gallon of paint, a pickle, a pair of shoes, and a can of corn."

15 "Or horehound candy," Miss Ginny said. "Or corsets and salves. We had cough syrups and all that for the body. In season, we'd buy and sell blackberries and walnuts and chestnuts, before the blight got them. And outside, Thurmond milled corn and sharpened plows. Even shoed a horse sometimes."

16 "We could fix up a horse or a man or a baby," Watts said.

17 "Thurmond, tell him we had a doctor on the ridge in them days."

18 "We had a doctor on the ridge in them days. As good as any doctor alivin'. He'd cut a crooked toenail or deliver a woman. Dead these last years."

19 "I got some bad ham meat one day," Miss Ginny said, "and took to vomitin'. All day, all night. Hangin' on the drop edge of yonder. I said to Thurmond, 'Thurmond, unless you want shut of me, call the doctor.'"

20 "I studied on it," Watts said.

21 "You never did. You got him right now. He come over and put three drops of iodeen in half a glass of well water. I drank it down and the vomitin' stopped with the last swallow. Would you think iodeen could do that?"

22 "He put Miss Ginny on one teaspoon of spirits of ammonia in well water for her nerves. Ain't nothin' works better for her to this day."

23 "Calms me like the hand of the Lord."

24 Hilda, the Wattses' daughter, came out of the backroom. "I remember him," she said. "I was just a baby. Y'all were talkin' to him, and he lifted me up on the counter and gave me a stick of Juicy Fruit and a piece of cheese."

25 "Knew the old medicines," Watts said. "Only drugstore he needed was a good kitchen cabinet. None of them anteebeeotics that hit you worsen your ailment. Forgotten lore now, the old medicines, because they ain't profit in iodeen."

Miss Ginny started back to the side room where she and her sister Marilyn were taking apart a duck-down mattress to make bolsters. She stopped at the window for another look at Ghost Dancing. "How do you sleep in that thing? Ain't you all cramped and cold?" 26

"How does the clam sleep in his shell?" Watts said in my defense. 27

"Thurmond, get the boy a piece of buttermilk pie afore he goes on." 28

"Hilda, get some buttermilk pie." He looked at me. "You like good music?" I said I did. He cranked up an old Edison phonograph, the kind with the big morning-glory blossom for a speaker, and put on a wax cylinder. "This will be 'My Mother's Prayer,'" he said. 29

While I ate buttermilk pie, Watts served as disc jockey of Nameless, Tennessee. "Here's 'Mountain Rose.'" It was one of those moments that you know at the time will stay with you to the grave: the sweet pie, the gaunt man playing the old music, the coals in the stove glowing orange, the scent of kerosene and hot bread. "Here's 'Evening Rhapsody.'" The music was so heavily romantic we both laughed. I thought: It is for this I have come. 30

Feathered over and giggling, Miss Ginny stepped from the side room. She knew she was a sight. "Thurmond, give him some lunch. Still looks hungry." 31

Hilda pulled food off the woodstove in the backroom: home-butchered and canned whole-hog sausage, home-canned June apples, turnip greens, cole slaw, potatoes, stuffing, hot cornbread. All delicious. 32

Watts and Hilda sat and talked while I ate. "Wish you would join me." 33

"We've ate," Watts said. "Cain't beat a woodstove for flavorful cookin'." 34

He told me he was raised in a one-hundred-fifty-year-old cabin still standing in one of the hollows. "How many's left," he said, "that grew up in a log cabin? I ain't the last surely, but I must be climbin' on the list." 35

Hilda cleared the table. "You Watts ladies know how to cook." 36

"She's in nursin' school at Tennessee Tech. I went over for one of them football games last year there at Coevul." To say *Cookeville*, you let the word collapse in upon itself so that it comes out "Coevul." 37

"Do you like football?" I asked. 38

"Don't know. I was so high up in that stadium, I never opened my eyes." 39

40 Watts went to the back and returned with a fat spiral notebook that he set on the table. His expression had changed. "Miss Ginny's *Deathbook*."

41 The thing startled me. Was it something I was supposed to sign? He opened it but said nothing. There were scads of names written in a tidy hand over pages incised to crinkliness by a ballpoint. Chronologically, the names had piled up: Wives, grandparents, a stillborn infant, relatives, friends close and distant. Names, names. After each, the date of the unknown finally known and transcribed. The last entry bore yesterday's date.

42 "She's wrote out twenty years' worth. Ever day she listens to the hospital report on the radio and puts the names in. Folks come by to check a date. Or they just turn through the books. Read them like a scrapbook."

43 Hilda said, "Like Saint Peter at the gates inscribin' the names."

44 Watts took my arm. "Come along." He led me to the fruit cellar under the store. As we went down, he said, "Always take a newborn baby upstairs afore you take him downstairs, otherwise you'll incline him downwards."

45 The cellar was dry and full of cobwebs and jar after jar of home-canned food, the bottles organized as a shopkeeper would: sausage, pumpkin, sweet pickles, tomatoes, corn relish, blackberries, peppers, squash, jellies. He held a hand out toward the dusty bottles. "Our tomorrows."

46 Upstairs again, he said, "Hope to sell the store to the right folk. I see now, though, it'll be somebody offen the ridge. I've studied on it, and maybe it's the end of our place." He stirred the coals. "This store could give a comfortable livin', but not likely get you rich. But just gettin' by is dice rollin' to people nowadays. I never did see my day guaranteed."

47 When it was time to go, Watts said, "If you find anyone along your ways wants a good store—on the road to Cordell Hull Lake—tell them about us."

48 I said I would. Miss Ginny and Hilda and Marilyn came out to say goodbye. It was cold and drizzling again. "Weather to give a man the weary dismals," Watts grumbled. "Where you headed from here?"

49 "I don't know."

50 "Cain't get lost then."

51 Miss Ginny looked again at my rig. It had worried her from the first as it had my mother. "I hope you don't get yourself kilt in that durn thing gallivantin' around the country."

"Come back when the hills dry off," Watts said. "We'll go lookin' for some of them round rocks all sparkly inside." 52

I thought a moment. "Geodes?" 53

"Them's the ones. The country's properly full of them." 54

QUESTIONS ON SUBJECT AND PURPOSE

1. At one point in the narrative (paragraph 30), Least Heat Moon remarks, "I thought: It is for this I have come." What does he seem to be suggesting? What is the "this" that he finds in Nameless?
2. Why do "Miss Ginny's *Deathbook*" (paragraph 40) and the "fruit cellar" (44) seem appropriate details?
3. What might have attracted Least Heat Moon to this place and these people? What does he want you to sense? Is there anything in his description and narrative that suggests how he feels about Nameless?

QUESTIONS ON STRATEGY AND AUDIENCE

1. After you have read the selection, describe each member of the Watts family. Describe the exterior and interior of their store. Then carefully go through the selection and see how many specific descriptive details the author uses. List them.
2. What devices other than direct description does Least Heat Moon use to create the sense of place and personality? Make a list, and be prepared to tell how those devices work.
3. How is the narrative arranged? Is the order just spatial and chronological?
4. This selection is taken from *Blue Highways: A Journey into America*, a bestseller for nearly a year. Why would a travel narrative full of stories such as this be so appealing to an American audience?

QUESTIONS ON VOCABULARY AND STYLE

1. Least Heat Moon attempts to reproduce the pronunciation of some words—for example, *athians* (paragraph 12), *iodeen* (21), and *anteebeeotics* (25). Make a list of all such phonetic spellings. Why does Least Heat Moon do this? Do you think he captures all of the Wattses' accent or just some part of it? Is the device effective?

2. Examine how Least Heat Moon uses dialogue in his description. How are the Wattses revealed by what they say? How much of what was actually said during the visit is recorded? Can you find specific points in the story where Least Heat Moon obviously omits dialogue?
3. Try to define or explain the following words and phrases: *horehound candy* (paragraph 15), *bolsters* (26), *buttermilk pie* (28), *incised to crinkliness by a ballpoint* (41), *weary dismals* (48), *gallivantin' around* (51).

WRITING SUGGESTIONS

1. **For Your Journal.** Have you ever encountered or experienced a person, a place, or an event that seemed cut off from the modern world? In your journal, try to recall a few such experiences.
2. **For a Paragraph.** Virtually every campus has a building or a location that has acquired a strange or vivid name (for example, the cafeteria in the Student Center known as "The Scrounge"). In a paragraph, describe such a place to a friend who has never seen it. Remember to keep a central focus—you want to convey an atmosphere more than a verbal photograph.
3. **For an Essay.** Look for an unusual business in your town or city (a barber shop, a food co-op, a delicatessen or diner, a secondhand clothing store, a specialized boutique). In an essay, describe the place. Your essay will need to have a focus—a central impression or thesis—that will govern your selection of details. It will probably work best if you also include some descriptions of people and dialogue.

   Prewriting:

   a. Take a walk, and make a list of possible places.

   b. Visit one or more of these places, and take notes on what you see. Imagine yourself as a newspaper reporter. If people are present, try to write down exactly what they say.

   c. Decide on a particular quality, feeling, or idea that you want to convey about this place. Write a statement of purpose.

   d. Do not "overpeople" your description. Do not try to describe every character completely. Reveal personality through significant detail and dialogue.

Rewriting:

a. Check to make sure that you have made effective use of verbs and nouns. Do not rely on adjectives and adverbs to do the work of description.

b. Using your statement of purpose, check every detail that you included in your essay. Does it belong? Does it relate to that stated purpose?

4. **For Research.** Least Heat Moon is fascinated by unusual names and often drives considerable distances to visit towns with names such as Dime Box, Hungry Horse, Liberty Bond, Ninety-Six, and Tuba City. Choose an unusual place name (town, river, subdivision, topographical feature) from your home state and research the origin of the name. A reference librarian can show you how to locate source materials. If possible, contact your local historical society or public library for help or interview some knowledgeable local residents. Using your research, write an essay about how that name was chosen. Remember to document your sources.

WEBSITE LINK

Want to read an excerpt from Least Heat Moon's new book, *River-Horse*, an account of a 5,000-mile water voyage across America in a small boat named *Nikawa*? Is there really a Nameless, Tennessee? Visit the *Reader's* Website.

The Village Watchman

Terry Tempest Williams

Terry Tempest Williams (1955–), a fifth-generation Mormon, grew up within sight of Great Salt Lake. A former naturalist-in-residence at the Utah Museum of National History and Visiting Professor of English at the University of Utah, Williams has written and edited a number of books including the recent An Unspoken Hunger: Stories from the Field *(1994);* Desert Quartet: An Erotic Landscape *(1995); and* The New Genesis: Mormons Writing on the Environment *(1998). In 1997, she was awarded a Guggenheim Fellowship for nonfiction.* Newsweek *identified her as a person likely to have "a considerable impact on the political, economic, and environmental issues facing the western states in this decade."*

"The Village Watchman" first appeared in Between Friends *(1994), a collection of essays; it was reprinted in her collection of essays titled* An Unspoken Hunger *(1994).*

On Writing: *A writer deeply concerned about environmental issues, Williams has observed that she writes "through my biases of gender, geography, and culture, that I am a woman whose ideas have been shaped by the Colorado Plateau and the Great Basin, that these ideas are then sorted out through the prism of my culture—and my culture is Mormon. Those tenets of family and community that I see at the heart of that culture are then articulated through story."*

BEFORE READING

Connecting: In her essay, Williams writes of our attitude toward people who are "mentally disabled or challenged": "We see them for who they are not, rather than for who they are." What does that sentence mean to you?

Anticipating: Williams is writing about her memories of her uncle. Out of the many that she has, why might she select the ones that she does? How does each included detail or incident affect our sense of Alan?

1 Stories carved in cedar rise from the deep woods of Sitka. These totem poles are foreign to me, this vertical lineage of clans: Eagle,

Raven, Wolf, and Salmon. The Tlingit craftsmen create a genealogy of the earth, a reminder of mentors, a reminder that we come into this world in need of proper instruction. I sit on the soft floor of this Alaskan forest and feel the presence of Other. The totem before me is called "Wolf Pole" by locals. The Village Watchman sits on top of Wolf's head with his knees drawn to his chest, his hands holding them tight against his body. He wears a red and black striped hat. His eyes are direct, deep set, painted blue.

The expression on his face reminds me of a man I loved, a man who was born into this world feet first. "Breech," my mother told me of her brother's birth. "Alan was born feet first. As a result, his brain was denied oxygen. He is special." As a child, I was impressed by this information. I remember thinking that fish live underwater. Maybe Alan had gills, maybe he didn't need a face-first gulp of air like the rest of us. The amniotic sea he had floated in for nine months delivered him with a fluid memory. He knew something. Other. 2

There is a story of a boy who was kidnapped from his village by the Salmon People. He was taken from his family to learn the ways of water. When he returned many years later to his home, he was recognized by his own as a holy man privy to the mysteries of the unseen world. Twenty years after my uncle's death, I wonder if Alan could have been that boy. 3

But our culture tells a different story, more alien. My culture calls people of sole births retarded, handicapped, mentally disabled or challenged. We see them for who they are not, rather than for who they are. 4

My grandmother, Lettie Romney Dixon, wrote in her journal, "It wasn't until Alan was 16 months old that a busy doctor cruelly broke the news to us. Others may have suspected our son's limitations but to those of us who loved him so unquestionably, lightning struck without warning. I hugged my sorrow to myself. I felt abandoned and lost. I wouldn't accept the verdict. Then we started the trips to a multitude of doctors. Most of them were kind and explained that our child was like a car without brakes, like an electric wire without insulation. They gave us no hope for a normal life." 5

Normal. Latin: *normalis; norma*, a rule: conforming with or constituting an accepted standard, model, or pattern, especially corresponding to the median or average of a large group in type, appearance, achievement, function, or development. 6

Alan was not normal. He was unique; one and only; single; sole; unusual; extraordinary; rare. His emotions were not measured, 7 his curiosity not bridled. In a sense, he was wild like a mustang in the desert, and like most wild horses, he was eventually rounded up.

8 He was unpredictable. He created his own rules and they changed from moment to moment. Alan was 12 years old, hyperactive, mischievous, easily frustrated, and unable to learn in traditional ways. The situation was intensified by his seizures. Suddenly, without warning, he would stiffen like a rake, fall forward, and crash to the ground, hitting his head. My grandparents could not keep him home any longer. They needed professional guidance and help. In 1957, they reluctantly placed their youngest child in an institution for handicapped children called the American Fork Training School. My grandmother's heart broke for the second time.

9 Once again, from her journal: "Many a night my pillow is wet from tears of sorrow and senseless dreamings of 'if things had only been different,' or wondering if he is tucked in snug and warm, if he is well and happy, if the wind still bothers him . . . ."

10 The wind may have continued to bother Alan: certainly the conditions he was living under were less than ideal, but there was much about his private life his family never knew. What we did know was that Alan had an enormous capacity for adaptation. We had no choice but to follow him.

11 I followed him for years.

12 Alan was ten years my senior. In my mind, he was mythic. Everything I was taught not to do, Alan did. We were taught to be polite, to not express displeasure or anger in public. Alan was sheer, physical expression. Whatever was on his mind he vocalized and usually punctuated with colorful speech. We would go bowling as a family on Sundays. Each of us would take our turn, hold the black ball to our chest, take a few steps, swing our arm back, forward, glide, and release. The ball would roll down the alley, hit a few pins; we would wait for the ball to return, and then take our second run. Little emotion was shown. When it was Alan's turn, it was an event. Nothing subtle. His style was Herculean. Big man. Big ball. Big roll. Big bang. Whether it was a strike or a gutter ball, he clapped his hands, spun around on the floor, slapped his thighs, and cried, "Goddamn! Did you see that one? Send me another ball, sweet Jesus!" And the ball was always returned.

13 I could count on my uncle for a straight answer. He taught me that one of the remarkable aspects of being human was to hold opposing views in our mind at once.

14 "How are you doing?" I would ask.

"Ask me how I am feeling?" he answered. 15

"Okay, how are you feeling?" 16

"Today? Right now?" 17

"Yes." 18

"I am very happy and very sad." 19

"How can you be both at the same time?" I asked in all seri- 20
ousness, a girl of nine or ten.

"Because both require each other's company. They live in the 21
same house. Didn't you know?"

We would laugh and then go on to another topic. Talking to 22
my uncle was always like entering a maze of riddles. Ask a question. Answer with a question and see where it leads you.

My younger brother Steve and I spent a lot of time with Alan. 23
He offered us shelter from the conventionality of a Mormon family. At our home during Christmas, he would direct us in his own nativity plays. "More—" he would say to us, making wide gestures with his hands. "Give me more of yourself." He was not like anyone we knew. In a culture where we were taught to be seen and not heard. Alan was our mirror.

We could be different, too. His unquestioning belief in us as 24
children, as human beings, was in startling contrast to the way we saw the public react to him. It hurt us. We could never tell if it hurt him.

Each week, Steve and I would accompany our grandparents 25
south to visit Alan. It was an hour's drive to the school from Salt Lake City, mostly through farmlands. We would enter the grounds, pull into the parking lot to a playground filled with huge papier-mâché storybook figures (a 20-foot pied piper, a pumpkin carriage with Cinderella inside, the old woman who lived in a shoe), and nine times out of ten, Alan would be standing outside his dormitory waiting for us. We would get out of the car and he would run toward us and throw his powerful arms around us. His hugs cracked my back and at times I had to fight for my breath. My grandfather would calm him down by simply saying, "We're here, son. You can relax now."

Alan was a formidable man, now in his early twenties, stocky 26
and strong. His head was large, with a protruding forehead that bore many scars, a line-by-line history of seizures. He always had on someone else's clothes—a tweed jacket too small, brown pants too big, a striped golf shirt that didn't match. He showed us that appearances didn't matter, personality did. If you didn't know him, he could look frightening. It was an unspoken rule in our family that the character of others was gauged by how they treated Alan.

The only consistent thing about his attire was that he always wore a silver football helmet from Olympus High School, where my grandfather was coach. It was a loving, practical solution to protect Alan when he fell.

27 "Part of the team," my grandfather would say as he slapped Alan affectionaly on the back, "You're a Titan, son, and I love you."

28 The windows to the dormitory were dark, reflecting Mount Timpanogos to the east. It was hard to see inside, but I knew what the interior held. It looked like an abandoned gymnasium without bleachers, filled with hospital beds. The stained white walls and yellow-waxed floors offered no warmth. The stench was nauseating: sweat and urine trapped in the oppression of stale air. I recall the dirty sheets, the lack of privacy, and the almond-eyed children who never rose from their beds. And then I would turn around and face Alan's cheerfulness, the open and loving manner in which he would introduce me to his friends, the pride he exhibited as he showed me around his home. I kept thinking, "Doesn't he see how bad this is, how poorly they are being treated?" His words would return to me: "I am very happy and very sad."

29 For my brother and me, Alan was guide, elder. He was fearless. But neither one of us will ever be able to escape the image of Alan kissing his parents good-bye after an afternoon with family and slowly walking back to his dormitory. Before we drove away, he would turn toward us, take off his silver helmet, and wave. The look on his face haunts me still.

30 Alan liked to talk about God. Perhaps it was in these private conversations that our real friendship was forged.

31 "I know Him," he would say when all the adults were gone.

32 "You do?" I asked.

33 "I talk to Him every day."

34 "How?"

35 "I talk to Him in my prayers. I listen and then I hear His voice."

36 "What does He tell you?"

37 "He tells me to be patient. He tells me to be kind. He tells me that He loves me."

38 In Mormon culture, children are baptized as members of the Church of Jesus Christ of Latter-day Saints when they turn 8 years old. Alan had never been baptized because my grandparents believed it should be his choice, not something simply taken for granted. When he turned 22, he expressed a sincere desire to join the church. A date was set immediately.

39 The entire Dixon clan convened in the Lehi chapel, a few miles north of the group home where Alan was then living. We were there to support and witness his conversion. As we walked toward the meetinghouse where this sacred rite was to be performed, Alan had a violent seizure. My grandfather and uncle Don, Alan's elder brother, dropped down with him, holding his head and body as every muscle thrashed on the pavement like a school of netted fish brought on deck. I didn't want to look, but to walk away would have been worse. We stayed with him, all of us.

40 "Talk to God,—" I heard myself saying under my breath. "I love you, Alan."

41 "Can you hear me, darling?" It was my grandmother, holding her son's hand.

42 By now, many of us were gathered on our knees around him, our trembling hands on his rigid body.

43 Alan opened his eyes. "I want to be baptized," he said. The men helped him to his feet. The gash on his left temple was deep. Blood dripped down the side of his face. My mother had her arm around my grandmother's waist. Shaken, we all followed him inside.

44 Alan's father and brother stopped the bleeding and bandaged the pressure wound, then helped him change into the designated white garments for baptism. He entered the room with great dignity and sat on the front pew with a dozen or more 8-year-old children seated on either side. Row after row of family sat behind him.

45 "Alan Romney Dixon." His name was called by the presiding bishop. Alan rose from the pew and met his brother Don, also dressed in white, who took his hand and led him down the blue-tiled stairs into the baptismal font filled with water. They faced the congregation. Don raised his right arm to the square in the gesture of a holy oath as Alan placed his hands on his brother's left forearm. The sacred prayer was offered in the name of the Father, the Son, and the Holy Ghost, after which my uncle put his right hand behind Alan's shoulder and gently lowered him into the water for a baptism by complete immersion.

46 Alan emerged from the holy waters like an angel.

47 Six years later, I found myself sitting with my uncle at a hospital where he was being treated for a severe ear infection. I was 18. He was 28.

48 "Alan," I asked, "what is it really like to live inside your body?"

49 He crossed his legs and placed both hands on the arms of the chair. His brown eyes were piercing.

50 "I can't tell you what it's like except to say I feel pain for not being seen as the person I am."

51 A few days later, Alan died—alone, unique, one and only, single—in American Fork, Utah.

52 The Village Watchman sits on top of his totem with Wolf and Salmon. It is beginning to rain in the forest. I find it curious that this spot in southeast Alaska has brought me back into relation with my uncle, this man who came into the world feet first. He reminds me of what it means to live and love with a broken heart; how nothing is sacred, how everything is sacred. He was a weather vane, at once a storm and a clearing.

53 Shortly after his death, Alan appeared to me in a dream. We were standing in my grandmother's kitchen. He was leaning against the white stove with his arms folded.

54 "Look at me now, Terry," he said, smiling. "I'm normal—perfectly normal." And then he laughed. We both laughed.

55 He handed me his silver football helmet, which was resting on the counter, kissed me, and opened the back door.

56 "Do you recognize who I am?"

57 On this day in Sitka, I remember.

QUESTIONS ON SUBJECT AND PURPOSE

1. What associations do you have with the word *normal?* Does Williams's definition (paragraph 6) challenge those associations?
2. In two places (paragraphs 5 and 9), Williams quotes from her grandmother's journal. What is the effect of these quotations?
3. Why would a reader be interested in a tribute to her uncle? Do you find the story moving?

QUESTIONS ON STRATEGY AND AUDIENCE

1. Why does Williams begin and end with the references to the totem poles in Alaska?
2. At several places, Williams reproduces—or rather re-creates—conversations she had with Alan (for example, paragraphs 14–21, 31–37, and 48–50). Why? What is the effect of these sections?

3. What expectations might Williams have about her audience and their reaction to Alan?

QUESTIONS ON VOCABULARY AND STYLE

1. At a number of points in the essay, Williams quotes Alan. What do these quotations add to her description?
2. What is the effect of Alan's question, "Do you recognize who I am?"
3. Be prepared to define the following words: *privy* (paragraph 3) and *convened* (39).

WRITING SUGGESTIONS

1. **For Your Journal.** Select a vivid memory that involves a family member or a close friend who touched your life. In your journal, describe for yourself what you remember. Do not worry about trying to be too focused. Concentrate on recovering memories.
2. **For a Paragraph.** In a paragraph, try to "capture" that person. Remember that your description needs a central focus or purpose. Why are you writing about this person? What is important for the reader to know about this person? Select details to reveal the person to your reader rather than simply telling the reader what to think.
3. **For an Essay.** In writing about Alan, Williams achieves two purposes: she memorializes her uncle, and she comments on society's perceptions of persons who are "mentally disabled or challenged." Try for a similar effect in an essay about someone who has touched your life. Remember that your essay needs to have a duel purpose or thesis.

   Prewriting:

   a. Use your journal- or paragraph-writing exercise as a way of beginning work, of gathering possibilities. Make a list of possible people.
   b. Next to each name, jot down your associations with that person. Try freewriting or clustering ideas for the people who seem most promising as subjects.
   c. For the person you finally select, write one sentence in response to the prompt "This person touched my life in the following way."

Rewriting:

a. Ask a friend or a classmate to read your essay. After your reader has finished, give the same prompt as you used in Prewriting item c and ask for a response. Did your reader see the significance that you intended?

b. Did you reveal that significance—it could also be called a thesis—at the beginning of the essay or at the end? Try placing it in the other position. What impact does that move have on the essay?

c. Have you created a vivid sense of the person? Ask your reader, "Can you see or imagine this person?" Remember that you do not have to use physical details to achieve that effect.

4. **For Research.** Explore our society's reactions to people who are, to use Williams's words, "retarded, handicapped, mentally disabled or challenged." How does society see such people? How are they treated or portrayed? This is a large subject, so you will need to find a way to focus your research and writing. You could concentrate on changes in reaction over time (early twentieth century versus late in the century), portrayals (or their lack) in the popular media (for example, Leonardo DiCaprio in *What's Eating Gilbert Grape* and Juliette Lewis in *The Other Sister*), family attitudes versus outsiders' attitudes, or reactions to a specific disability (such as Down's syndrome). Textbooks might be one place to start. You will need to establish a list of possible subject headings and keywords before you start searching library resources, on-line databases, and the World Wide Web. Remember to document your sources, including any information that you obtain through interviews.

Website Link

A listing of sites dealing with specific genetic or birth conditions and additional writing suggestions can be found at the Website.

THE INHERITANCE OF TOOLS

Scott Russell Sanders

Born in Memphis, Tennessee, in 1945, Scott Russell Sanders received a Ph.D. from Cambridge University. Currently a professor of English at Indiana University, Sanders is a novelist, an essayist, and a science fiction writer. He has contributed fiction and essays to many journals and magazines and has published numerous books, including the recent collections of essays Writing from the Center *(1995) and* Hunting for Hope: A Father's Journeys *(1998).*

Sanders writes often about his childhood and his efforts to "ground" himself. In another of his collections of essays, Secrets of the Universe *(1991), Sanders describes growing up with an alcoholic father, noting that he "wants to drag into the light what eats at me—the fear, the guilt, the shame—so that my own children may be spared."*

On Writing: *Commenting on the development of his writing style from academic prose to creative writing and essays, Sanders observed: "I flouted the rules I learned about writing in school. I played with sound, strung images together line after line, flung out metaphors by the handful. Sin of sins, I even mixed metaphors, the way any fertile field will sprout dozens of species of grass and flower and fern. I let my feelings and opinions show. . . . I drew shamelessly on my own life. I swore off jargon and muddle and much. I wrote in the active voice."*

BEFORE READING

Connecting: Can you think of something that you learned how to do from a family member or friend?

Anticipating: In what ways is "The Inheritance of Tools" an appropriate title for the essay? What is the essay about?

At just about the hour when my father died, soon after dawn one February morning when ice coated the windows like cataracts, I banged my thumb with a hammer. Naturally I swore at the hammer, the reckless thing, and in the moment of swearing I thought of what my father would say: "If you'd try hitting the nail it would go in a whole lot faster. Don't you know your thumb's not as hard as that hammer?" We both were doing carpentry that day, but far apart. He was building cupboards at my 1 brother's place in Oklahoma; I was at home in Indiana putting up a wall in the basement to make a bedroom for my daughter. By the time my mother called with news of his death—the long distance wires whittling her voice until it seemed too thin to bear the weight of what she had to say—my thumb was swollen. A week or so later a white scar in the shape of a crescent moon began to show above the cuticle, and month by month it rose across the pink sky of my thumbnail. It took the better part of a year for the scar to disappear, and every time I noticed it I thought of my father.

2 The hammer had belonged to him, and to his father before him. The three of us have used it to build houses and barns and chicken coops, to upholster chairs and crack walnuts, to make doll furniture and book shelves and jewelry boxes. The head is scratched and pockmarked, like an old plowshare that has been working rocky fields, and it gives off the sort of dull sheen you see on fast creek water in the shade. It is a finishing hammer, about the weight of a bread loaf, too light, really, for framing walls, too heavy for cabinetwork, with a curved claw for pulling nails, a rounded head for pounding, a fluted neck for looks, and a hickory handle for strength.

3 The present handle is my third one, bought from a lumberyard in Tennessee down the road from where my brother and I were helping my father build his retirement house. I broke the previous one by trying to pull sixteen-penny nails out of floor joists—a foolish thing to do with a finishing hammer, as my father pointed out. "You ever hear of a crowbar?" he said. No telling how many handles he and my grandfather had gone through before me. My grandfather used to cut down hickory trees on his farm, saw them into slabs, cure the planks in his hayloft, and carve handles with a drawknife. The grain in hickory is crooked and knotty, and therefore rough, hard to split, like the grain in the two men who owned this hammer before me.

4 After proposing marriage to a neighbor girl, my grandfather used this hammer to build a house for his bride on a stretch of river bottom in northern Mississippi. The lumber for the place, like the hickory for the handle, was cut on his own land. By the day of the wedding he had not quite finished the house, and so right after the ceremony he took his wife home and put her to work. My grandmother had worn her Sunday dress for the wedding, with a fringe of lace tacked on around the hem in honor of the occasion. She removed this lace and folded it away before going out to help my grandfather nail siding on the house. "There she was in her good dress," he told me some fifty-odd years after that wedding day,

"holding up them long pieces of clapboard while I hammered, and together we got the place covered up before dark." As the family grew to four, six, eight, and eventually thirteen, my grandfather used this hammer to enlarge his house room by room, like a chambered nautilus expanding his shell.

By and by the hammer was passed along to my father. One 5
day he was up on the roof of our pony barn nailing shingles with it, when I stepped out the kitchen door to call him for supper. Before I could yell, something about the sight of him straddling the spine of that roof and swinging the hammer caught my eye and made me hold my tongue. I was five or six years old, and the world's commonplaces were still news to me. He would pull a nail from the pouch at his waist, bring the hammer down, and a moment later the *thunk* of the blow would reach my ears. And that is what had stopped me in my tracks and stilled my tongue, that momentary gap between seeing and hearing the blow. Instead of yelling from the kitchen door, I ran to the barn and climbed two rungs up the ladder—as far as I was allowed to go—and spoke quietly to my father. On our walk to the house he explained that sound takes time to make its way through air. Suddenly the world seemed larger, the air more dense, if sound could be held back like any ordinary traveler.

By the time I started using this hammer, at about the age 6
when I discovered the speed of sound, it already contained houses and mysteries for me. The smooth handle was one my grandfather had made. In those days I needed both hands to swing it. My father would start a nail in a scrap of wood, and I would pound away until I bent it over.

"Looks like you got ahold of some of those rubber nails," he 7
would tell me. "Here, let me see if I can find you some stiff ones." And he would rummage in a drawer until he came up with a fistful of more cooperative nails. "Look at the head," he would tell me. "Don't look at your hands, don't look at the hammer. Just look at the head of that nail and pretty soon you'll learn to hit it square."

Pretty soon I did learn. While he worked in the garage cut- 8
ting dovetail joints for a drawer or skinning a deer or tuning an engine, I would hammer nails. I made innocent blocks of wood look like porcupines. He did not talk much in the midst of his tools, but he kept up a nearly ceaseless humming, slipping in and out of a dozen tunes in an afternoon, often running back over the same stretch of melody again and again, as if searching for a way out. When the humming did cease, I knew he was faced with a task

requiring great delicacy or concentration, and I took care not to distract him.

9 He kept scraps of wood in a cardboard box—the ends of two-by-fours, slabs of shelving and plywood, odd pieces of molding—and everything in it was fair game. I nailed scraps together to fashion what I called boats or houses, but the results usually bore only faint resemblance to the visions I carried in my head. I would hold up these constructions to show my father, and he would turn them over in his hands admiringly, speculating about what they might be. My cobbled-together guitars might have been alien spaceships, my barns might have been models of Aztec temples, each wooden contraption might have been anything but what I had set out to make.

10 Now and again I would feel the need to have a chunk of wood shaped or shortened before I riddled it with nails, and I would clamp it in a vise and scrape at it with a handsaw. My father would let me lacerate the board until my arm gave out, and then he would wrap his hand around mine and help me finish the cut, showing me how to use my thumb to guide the blade, how to pull back on the saw to keep it from binding, how to let my shoulder do the work.

11 "Don't force it," he would say, "just drag it easy and give the teeth a chance to bite."

12 As the saw teeth bit down, the wood released its smell, each kind with its own fragrance, oak or walnut or cherry or pine—usually pine because it was the softest, easiest for a child to work. No matter how weathered and gray the board, no matter how warped and cracked, inside there was this smell waiting, as of something freshly baked. I gathered every smidgen of sawdust and stored it away in coffee cans, which I kept in a drawer of the workbench. When I did not feel like hammering nails I would dump my sawdust on the concrete floor of the garage and landscape it into highways and farms and towns, running miniature cars and trucks along miniature roads. Looming as huge as a colossus, my father worked over and around me, now and again bending down to inspect my work, careful not to trample my creations. It was a landscape that smelled dizzyingly of wood. Even after a bath my skin would carry the smell, and so would my father's hair, when he lifted me for a bedtime hug.

13 I tell these things not only from memory but also from recent observation, because my own son now turns blocks of wood into nailed porcupines, dumps cans full of sawdust at my feet and sculpts highways on the floor. He learns how to swing a hammer

from the elbow instead of the wrist, how to lay his thumb beside the blade to guide a saw, how to tap a chisel with a wooden mallet, how to mark a hole with an awl before starting a drill bit. My daughter did the same before him, and even now, on the brink of teenage aloofness, she will occasionally drag out my box of wood scraps and carpenter something. So I have seen my apprenticeship to wood and tools reenacted in each of my children, as my father saw his own apprenticeship renewed in me.

The saw I use belonged to him, as did my level and both of my squares, and all four tools had belonged to his father. The blade of the saw is the bluish color of gun barrels, and the maple handle, dark from the sweat of hands, is inscribed with curving leaf designs. The level is a shaft of walnut two feet long, edged with brass and pierced by three round windows in which air bubbles float in oil-filled tubes of glass. The middle window serves for testing if a surface is horizontal, the others for testing if a surface is plumb or vertical. My grandfather used to carry this level on the gun-rack behind the seat in his pickup, and when I rode with him I would turn around to watch the bubbles dance. The larger of the two squares is called a framing square, a flat steel elbow, so beat up and tarnished you can barely make out the rows of numbers that show how to figure the cuts on rafters. The smaller one is called a try square, for marking right angles, with a blued steel blade for the shank and a brass-faced block of cherry for the head. 14

I was taught early on that a saw is not to be used apart from a square: "If you're going to cut a piece of wood," my father insisted, "you owe it to the tree to cut it straight." 15

Long before studying geometry, I learned there is a mystical virtue in right angles. There is an unspoken morality in seeking the level and the plumb. A house will stand, a table will bear weight, the sides of a box will hold together only if the joints are square and the members upright. When the bubble is lined up between two marks etched in the glass tube of a level, you have aligned yourself with the forces that hold the universe together. When you miter the corners of a picture frame, each angle must be exactly forty-five degrees, as they are in the perfect triangles of Pythagoras, not a degree more or less. Otherwise the frame will hang crookedly, as if ashamed of itself and of its maker. No matter if the joints you are cutting do not show. Even if you are butting two pieces of wood together inside a cabinet, where not one except a wrecking crew will ever see them, you must take pains to insure that the ends are square and the studs are plumb. 16

17 I took pains over the wall I was building on the day my father died. Not long after that wall was finished—paneled with tongue-and-groove boards of yellow pine, the nail holes filled with putty and the wood all stained and sealed—I came close to wrecking it one afternoon when my daughter ran howling up the stairs to announce that her gerbils had escaped from their cage and were hiding in my brand new wall. She could hear them scratching and squeaking behind her bed. Impossible! I said. How on earth could they get inside my drum-tight wall? Through the heating vent, she answered. I went downstairs, pressed my ear to the honey-colored wood, and heard the *scritch scritch* of tiny feet.

18 "What can we do?" my daughter wailed. "They'll starve to death, they'll die of thirst, they'll suffocate."

19 "Hold on," I shouted, "I'll think of something."

20 While I thought and she fretted, the radio on her bedside table delivered us the headlines. Several thousand people had died in a city in India from a poisonous cloud that had leaked overnight from a chemical plant. A nuclear-powered submarine had been launched. Rioting continued in South Africa. An airplane had been hijacked in the Mediterranean. Authorities calculated that several thousand homeless people slept on the streets within sight of the Washington Monument. I felt my usual helplessness in face of all these calamities. But here was my daughter weeping because her gerbils were holed up in a wall. This calamity I could handle.

21 "Don't worry," I told her. "We'll set food and water by the heating vent and lure them out. And if that doesn't do the trick, I'll tear the wall apart until we find them."

22 She stopped crying and gazed as me. "You'd really tear it apart? Just for my gerbils? The *wall?*" Astonishment slowed her down only for a second, however, before she ran to the workbench and began tugging at drawers, saying, "Let's see, what'll we need? Crowbar. Hammer. Chisels. I hope we don't have to use them—but just in case."

23 We didn't need the wrecking tools. I never had to assault my handsome wall, because the gerbils eventually came out to nibble at a dish of popcorn. But for several hours I studied the tongue-and-groove skin I had nailed up on the day of my father's death, considering where to begin prying. There were no gaps in that wall, no crooked joints.

24 I had botched a great many pieces of wood before I mastered the right angle with a saw, botched even more before I learned to miter a joint. The knowledge of these things resides in my hands and eyes and the webwork of muscles, not in the tools. There are

machines for sale—powered miter boxes and radial-arm saws, for instance—that will enable any casual soul to cut proper angles in boards. The skill is invested in the gadget instead of the person who uses it, and this is what distinguishes a machine from a tool. If I had to earn my keep by making furniture or building houses, I suppose I would buy powered saws and pneumatic nailers; the need for speed would drive me to it. But since I carpenter only for my own pleasure or to help neighbors or to remake the house around the ears of my family, I stick with hand tools. Most of the ones I own were given to me by my father, who also taught me how to wield them. The tools in my work-bench are a double inheritance, for each hammer and level and saw is wrapped in a cloud of knowing.

All of these tools are a pleasure to look at and to hold. Merchants would never paste NEW NEW NEW! signs on them in stores. Their designs are old because they work, because they serve their purpose well. Like folksongs and aphorisms and the grainy bits of language, these tools have been pared down to essentials. I look at my claw hammer, the distillation of a hundred generations of carpenters, and consider that it holds up well beside those other classics—Greek vases, Gregorian chants, *Don Quixote*, barbed fish hooks, candles, spoons. Knowledge of hammering stretches back to the earliest humans who squatted beside fires chipping flints. Anthropologists have a lovely name for those unworked rocks that served as the earliest hammers. *Dawn stones*, they are called. Their only qualification for the work, aside from hardness, is that they fit the hand. Our ancestors used them for grinding corn, tapping awls, smashing bones. From dawn stones to this claw hammer is a great leap in time, but no great distance in design or imagination. 25

On that iced-over February morning when I smashed my thumb with the hammer, I was down in the basement framing the wall that my daughter's gerbils would later hide in. I was thinking of my father, as I always did whenever I built anything, thinking how he would have gone about the work, hearing in memory what he would have said about the wisdom of hitting the nail instead of my thumb. I had the studs and plates nailed together all square and trim, and was lifting the wall into place when the phone rang upstairs. My wife answered, and in a moment she came to the basement door and called down softly to me. The stillness in her voice made me drop the framed wall and hurry upstairs. She told me my father was dead. Then I heard the details over the phone from my mother. Building a set of cupboards for my brother in Oklahoma, he had 26 knocked off work early the previous afternoon because of cramps in his stomach. Early this morning, on his way into the kitchen of my brother's trailer, maybe going for a glass of water, so early that no one else was awake, he slumped down on the linoleum and his heart quit.

27 For several hours I paced around inside my house, upstairs and down, in and out of every room, looking for the right door to open and knowing there was no such door. My wife and children followed me and wrapped me in arms and backed away again, circling and staring as if I were on fire. Where was the door, the door, the door? I kept wondering. My smashed thumb turned purple and throbbed, making me furious. I wanted to cut it off and rush outside and scrape away the snow and hack a hole in the frozen earth and bury the shameful thing.

28 I went down into the basement, opened a drawer in my workbench, and stared at the ranks of chisels and knives. Oiled and sharp, as my father would have kept them, they gleamed at me like teeth. I took up a clasp knife, pried out the longest blade and tested the edge on the hair of my forearm. A tuft came away cleanly, and I saw my father testing the sharpness of tools on his own skin, the blades of axes and knives and gouges and hoes, saw the red hair shaved off in patches from his arms and the backs of his hands. "That will cut bear," he would say. He never cut a bear with his blades, now my blades, but he cut deer, dirt, wood. I closed the knife and put it away. Then I took up the hammer and went back to work on my daughter's wall, snugging the bottom plate against a chalkline on the floor, shimming the top plate against the joists overhead, plumbing the studs with my level, making sure before I drove the first nail that every line was square and true.

QUESTIONS ON SUBJECT AND PURPOSE

1. What is the subject of Sanders's essay? Is it tools? His father's death?
2. Is Sanders's father or grandfather (or his children) ever described in the story? How are they revealed to the reader?
3. What "door" (paragraph 27) is Sanders searching for?
4. What exactly has Sanders inherited from his father?

QUESTIONS ON STRATEGY AND AUDIENCE

1. How does Sanders use time to structure his essay? Is the story told in chronological order?

2. What is the function of each of the following episodes or events in the essay?
   a. The sore thumb
   b. "A mystical virtue in right angles" (paragraph 16)
   c. The wall he was building
3. What expectations does Sanders seem to have about his audience?

QUESTIONS ON VOCABULARY AND STYLE

1. How much dialogue does Sanders use in the story? What does the dialogue contribute?
2. Throughout the essay, Sanders makes use of many effective similes and metaphors. Make a list of six such devices. What does each contribute to the essay? How fresh and arresting are these images?
3. Be able to define each of the following words or phrases: *plowshare* (paragraph 2), *sixteen-penny nails* (3), *chambered nautilus* (4), *rummage* (7), *lacerate* (10), *smidgen* (12), *plumb* (14), *miter* (24), *aphorisms* (25), *shimming* (28).

WRITING SUGGESTIONS

1. **For Your Journal.** The word *inheritance* may suggest money or property that is bequeathed to a descendent. But you can "inherit" many things that are far less tangible. In your journal, explore what you might have inherited from someone in your family—perhaps a talent, an interest, an ability, or an obsession.
2. **For a Paragraph.** Study the childhood scenes or episodes that Sanders includes in his essay—for example, calling his father to supper (paragraph 5), hammering nails (6–9), landscaping with sawdust (12). Notice how Sanders re-creates sensory experiences. Then in a paragraph, re-create a similar experience from your childhood. Remember to evoke sensory impressions for your reader—sight, sound, smell, touch.
3. **For an Essay.** Think about a skill, talent, or habit that you have learned from or share with a family member. In addition to the ability or trait, what else have you "inherited"? How does it affect your life? In an essay, describe the inheritance and its effect on you.

Prewriting:

a. Divide a piece of paper into two columns. In the left-hand column, make a list of possible subjects. Work on the list over a period of several days. In the right-hand column, jot down the significance that you see in such an inheritance.

b. Select one of the items from your list and freewrite for fifteen minutes. Concentrate on the significance of this ability or trait in your life. How has it shaped or altered your life or your perceptions? Reread what you have just written. Then freewrite for another fifteen minutes.

c. Like Sanders, you will be dealing with two "times" in the essay—your childhood and your present. Notice how Sanders manipulates time in his essay. He does not narrate the story in a strict chronological sequence. Experiment with time as an organizational strategy in your essay. Outline two or more structures for the essay.

Rewriting:

a. Check your essay to see if you have used vivid verbs and concrete nouns. Watch that you do not overwork adjectives and adverbs.

b. Did you include dialogue in your essay? If not, try adding some. Remember, though, that dialogue slows the pace of a story. Do not overuse it.

c. Look carefully at your conclusion. You want to end forcefully; you want to emphasize the significance of your inheritance. Reread your essay several times, and then try freewriting a new conclusion. Try for a completely new ending. If you are using a peer reader, ask that reader to judge both conclusions.

4. **For Research.** The passing on of traditional crafts or skills is an important part of cultural tradition. Choose a society that interests you, and find a particular craft that is preserved from one generation to another. It might also be something that has been preserved in your family's religious or ethnic heritage. In a research paper, document the nature of the craft and the methods by which the culture ensures its transmission. What is important about this craft? What does it represent to that society? Why bother to preserve it?

Website Link

Another view of Sanders' relationship with his father can be found in his essay "Under the Influence" which can be read on-line. The hot-link is available at the Website.

FOUR

Division and Classification

Division and classification are closely related methods of analysis, but you can remember the difference by asking yourself whether you are analyzing a single thing or analyzing two or more things. Division occurs when a single subject is subdivided into its parts. To list the ingredients in a can of soup or a box of cereal is to perform a division. The key is that you begin with a single thing.

In the following excerpt from a "chemistry primer" for people interested in cooking, Harold McGee uses division twice—first to subdivide the atom into its smaller constituent particles and second to subdivide the "space" within the atom into two areas (nucleus and shell):

> An atom is the smallest particle into which an element can be subdivided without losing its characteristic properties. The atom too is divisible into smaller particles, *electrons*, *protons*, and *neutrons*, but these are the building blocks of all atoms, no matter of what element. The different properties of the elements are due to the varying combinations of subatomic particles contained in their atoms. The Periodic Table arranges the elements in order of the number of protons contained in one atom of each element. That number is called the atomic number.
>
> The atom is divided into two regions: the nucleus, or center in which the protons and neutrons are located, and a surrounding "orbit," or more accurately a "cloud" or "shell," in which the electrons move continuously. Both protons and neutrons weigh about 2000 times as much as electrons, so practically all of an atom's mass is concentrated in the nucleus.

Similarly, David Bodanis in an essay in this chapter uses division to structure a discussion of toothpaste; he analyzes its composition, offering some surprising insights into the "ingredients" we brush with every morning. Barbara Ehrenreich in "In Defense of Talk Shows" also uses division when she analyzes the distinctive features that a number of different television talk shows exhibit. She treats the shows—hosted by people such as Montel Williams, Sally Jessy Raphael, and Geraldo Rivera—as a single subject that can then be divided or analyzed into its component parts. Ehrenreich does not classify television talk shows; rather, she analyzes the common characteristics that such shows share.

Division, then, is used to show the components of a larger subject; it helps the reader understand a complex whole by considering it in smaller units.

Classification, instead of starting with a single subject and then subdividing it into smaller units, begins with two or more items that are then grouped or classified into categories. Newspapers, for example, contain "classified" sections in which advertisements for the same type of goods or services are grouped or classified together. A classification must have at least two categories. Depending on how many items you start with and how different they are, you can end up with quite a few categories. You probably remember, in at least rough form, the taxonomic classification you learned in high school biology. It begins by setting up five kingdoms (animals, plants, monera, fungi, and protista) and then moves downward to increasingly narrower categories (phylum or division, class, order, family, genus, species).

Most classifications outside of the sciences are not as precisely and hierarchically defined. For example, E. B. White uses classification to discuss the three different groups of people who make up New York City:

> There are roughly three New Yorks. There is, first, the New York of the man or woman who was born here, who takes the city for granted and accepts its size and its turbulence as natural and inevitable. Second, there is the New York of the commuter—the city that is devoured by locusts each day and spat out each night. Third, there is the New York of the person who was born somewhere else and came to New York in quest of something. Of these three trembling cities the greatest is the last—the city of final destination, the city that is a goal.

In this chapter, Bernard R. Berelson's classification of the reasons people want children is precisely and logically ordered—

something we would expect in an essay that is titled "The Value of Children: A Taxonomical Essay" and that uses headings to display its organizational pattern clearly. More informally, in "Cinematypes" Susan Allen Toth classifies boyfriends by the kinds of movies they want to see.

How Do You Choose a Subject?

In choosing your subject for either division or classification, be sure to avoid the obvious approach to the obvious subject. Every teacher has read at some point a classification essay placing teachers into three groups based solely on the grade level at which they teach: elementary school teachers teach in elementary school, middle school teachers teach in middle school, and high school teachers teach in high school. Although the classification is complete and accurate, such a subject and approach are likely to lead you into writing that is boring and simply not worth your time or your reader's. No subject is inherently bad, but if you choose to write about something common, you need to find an interesting angle from which to approach it. Before you begin to write, answer two questions: first, what is your purpose? and second, will your reader learn something or be entertained by what you plan to write?

How Do You Divide or Classify a Subject?

Since both division and classification involve separation into parts—either dividing a whole into pieces or sorting many things into related groups or categories—you have to find ways in which to divide or group. Those ways can be objective and formal, such as the classification schemes used by biologists, or subjective and informal, like Susan Allen Toth's scheme in "Cinematypes." Either way, several things are particularly important.

First, you subdivide or categorize for a reason or a purpose, and your division or classification should be made with that end in mind. Bernard R. Berelson in the "The Value of Children: A Taxonomical Essay" places people's reasons for wanting children into six categories: biological, cultural, political, economic, familial, and personal. His purpose is to explain the various factors that motivate people to *want* children, and these six categories represent the spectrum of reasons why adults *want* children. Berelson does not include, for example, a category labeled "accidental," for such a heading would be irrelevant to his stated purpose.

Second, your division or classification must be complete—you cannot omit pieces or leave items unclassified. How complete your classification needs to be depends on your purpose. Given the limited purpose that Toth has, it is sufficient to offer just three types of dates. They do not represent all possible dates, but in the comic context of Toth's essay, the three are enough to establish her point. Berelson, by contrast, sets out to be exhaustive, to isolate all of the reasons people at any time or in any place have wanted children. As a result, he has to include some categories that are essentially irrelevant for most Americans. For example, probably few Americans ever want children for political reasons, that is, because their government encourages them or forbids them to have children. But in some societies at certain times political reasons have been important. Therefore, Berelson must include that category as well.

Third, the categories or subdivisions you establish need to be parallel in form. In mathematical terms, the categories should share a lowest common denominator. A simple and fairly effective test for parallelism is to see whether your categories are all phrased in similar grammatical terms. Berelson, for example, defines his categories (the reasons for wanting children) in exactly parallel form:

- Biological
- Cultural
- Political
- Economic
- Familial
- Personal
    - Personal power
    - Personal competence
    - Personal status
    - Personal extension
    - Personal experience
    - Personal pleasure

For this reason, you should not establish a catch-all category that you label something like "Other." When Berelson is finished with his classification scheme, no reasons for wanting children are left unaccounted for; everything fits into one of the six subdivisions.

Finally, your categories or subdivisions should be mutually exclusive; that is, items should belong in only one category. Toth's "cinematypes" cannot be mistaken for one another.

How Do You Structure a Division or Classification Essay?

The body of a division or classification essay will have as many parts as you have subdivisions or categories. Each subdivision or category will probably be treated in a single paragraph or in a group of related paragraphs. Toth, for example, uses a very symmetrical form in her essay: she organizes "Cinematypes" around the three different men with whom she has gone to the movies, treating each date in three paragraphs. Not every essay will be so evenly and perfectly divided. Judith Ortiz Cofer's essay "The Myth of the Latin Woman" uses narrative examples to establish and explore the common stereotypes of the "Latin woman" that she has encountered. Though the essay has a clear, chronological structure, Cofer analyzes the myth in sections of varying length.

Once you have decided how many subdivisions or categories you will have and how long each one will be, you have to decide in what order to arrange those parts or categories. Sometimes you must devise your own order. Toth, for example, could have arranged her "cinematypes" in any order. Nothing in the material itself determines the sequence. However, not all divisions or classifications have the same flexibility in their arrangement. Some invite, or imply, or even demand a particular order. For example, if you were classifying films using the ratings established by the motion picture industry, you would essentially have to follow the G, PG, PG-13, R, and NC-17 sequence; you could begin at either end, but it would not make sense to begin with one of the middle categories. In his essay "The Virus Wars," Robert Buderi classifies computer viruses chronologically. As computer systems have become more complicated, different types of viruses, attacking and multiplying in different ways, have been created. Here a classification based on chronology makes perfect sense.

Having an order underlying your division or classification can be a great help for both you and your reader. It allows you to know where to place each section, dictating the order you will follow. It gives your reader a clear sense of direction. Berelson, for example, in "The Value of Children: A Taxonomical Essay," arranges his reasons why people have children in an order that "starts with chemistry and proceeds to spirit." That is, he deals first with the biological reasons for wanting children and moves finally to the most spiritual of reasons, love.

Sample Student Essay

Evan James had chosen to write his term paper for his introductory American studies course on the hobo in America. He had read widely in the library about the phenomenon, so he had plenty of information, but he was having trouble getting started and getting organized. He took his draft to the Writing Center.

Earlier Draft

HOBOS

Among the many social problems that the United States faced at the turn of this past century was that of the "hobo." My interest in hobos came about because of the book The Ways of the Hobo that we read. The term hobo, the dictionary says, was probably derived from the greeting "Ho! Beau!" commonly used by vagrants to greet each other, although other possibilities have been suggested as well. The number of hobos in the United States at the turn of the century was large because of soldiers returning from the Civil War and because increasing mechanization had reduced the number of jobs in factories and businesses. In fact, the unemployment rate in the late 1800s ran as high as 40% of the workforce. We think that unemployment rates of 6% are unacceptable today!

Actually hobos were careful about how they referred to themselves. Today, for example, we might use the words hobo, tramp, and bum interchangeably. I was surprised to learn that among the hobos themselves, the distinctions were clear. A hobo was a migrant worker, a tramp was a migrant nonworker, and a bum was a nonmigrant nonworker.

When the tutor asked about the problems Evan saw in his essay, Evan listed a couple: he thought the introduction was flat and boring and the essay didn't move smoothly from sentence to sentence ("I think I just jump around from idea to idea"). The tutor and Evan collaborated on a list of the qualities that make a good introduction. They also discussed how writers can group information and make transitions. In the process of revising, Evan found a stronger, more interesting way to begin, and he reparagraphed and developed his opening paragraphs to reflect an analysis both by division and by cause and effect.

Revised Draft

RIDING THE RAILS: THE AMERICAN HOBO

Although homelessness and vagrancy might seem to be a distinctively modern phenomenon, the problem is probably less acute today (in terms of percentage of our total population) than it was at the turn of the twentieth century. At that time, a series of factors combined to create a large migratory population comprised almost exclusively of young males.

The Civil War was an uprooting experience for thousands of young men. Many left home in their teenage years, had acquired no job skills during their military service, and had grown accustomed to the nomadic life of the soldier—always on the move, living off the land, sleeping in the open. As the armies disbanded, many young men chose not to return home but to continue wandering the countryside.

Even if these former soldiers had wanted to work, few jobs were available to absorb the thousands of men who were mustered out. Increasingly, mechanization in the last decades of the 1800s brought the loss of jobs. In a world before unemployment benefits and social welfare, unemployment encouraged migration. The problem worsened in the 1870s when the country spiraled into a depression. Businesses failed, construction sagged, and the unemployment rate soared to an estimated 40%. Men, looking for work, took to the road.

Such men were called by a variety of names. One was hobo. The origin of that word is unknown. It has been suggested that hobo might be a shortened form of the Latin phrase homo bonus ("good man") or derived from the greeting "Ho! Beau!" commonly used among vagrants (dictionaries favor this suggestion). Other possibilities include a shortened form of the phrase "homeward bound" or "hoe boy," a term used in the eighteenth century for migrant farm workers.

Strictly speaking, not everyone who took to the road should be called a hobo. "Real" hobos were quick to insist on a series of distinctions. The words hobo, tramp, and bum were not interchangeable. By definition within the hobo community, the term hobo referred to a migrant worker, tramp to a migrant nonworker, and bum to a nonmigrant nonworker.

Obviously, the motives of the men traveling the road varied widely. Some were in search of work—migrant agricultural workers were an accepted fact by the turn of the century. Others were fleeing from the law, from family responsibilities, from themselves. Many were alcoholics; some were mentally impaired. All, though, were responding to a version of the American myth—the hope that a better future lay somewhere (geographically) ahead and that, meanwhile, the open road was the place to be.

Some Things to Remember

1. In choosing a subject for division or classification, ask yourself, first, what is my purpose? and second, will my reader learn something or be entertained by my paper?
2. Remember that your subdivision or classification should reflect your purpose—that is, the number of categories or parts is related to what you are trying to do.
3. Make sure that your division or classification is complete. Do not omit any pieces or items. Everything should be accounted for.
4. Take care that the parts or categories are phrased in parallel form.
5. Avoid a category labeled something such as "Other" or "Miscellaneous."
6. Remember to make your categories or subdivisions mutually exclusive.
7. Once you have established your subdivisions, check to see whether there is an order implied or demanded by your subject.
8. As you move from one subdivision to another, provide markers for the reader so that the parts are clearly labeled.

Using Division and Classification in Writing for Your Other Courses

Many kinds of college writing assignments will call for analysis—dividing a theory, event, cultural movement, historical period, literary style, or other broad subject into its component elements and examining how each contributes to the whole. Others will require classifying subjects—artistic works, kinds of behavior, individual thinkers and writers, natural phenomena, biological organisms—into established categories based on characteristic they share with others in that category—historical periods, groupings established by expert opinion or specific theories, artistic movements, and the like. Here are some examples of writing assignments that would require division (analysis) or classification.

- **Economics.** For an independent research paper in a contemporary economics course, you might be asked to read the work of a contemporary economist and analyze the theories presented in terms of labor, markets, and the distribution of wealth.
- **Art History or Introduction to Music.** For an exam, you might be asked to look at or listen to a number of works, classify each according to the period during which it was probably created, and write a paragraph or two explaining your reasoning in each case.
- **Sociology or Psychology.** As part of a case study of a particular group of your choice, you might be asked to classify the behaviors you observe according to the kinds of patterns you've learned about in the course.
- **Communications.** For a writing assignment asking you to examine bias in the media, you might observe and read a number of news reports focusing on the same subject or issue and then write a paper classifying each according to the level of bias it seemed to exhibit—for example, highly biased, somewhat biased, essentially neutral—based on criteria you establish prior to your research.
- **Physics.** On an exam, you might be asked to judge the conductivity of various solids based on an analysis of their atomic structure.

Visualizing Division and Classification

Did you ever think about how many trees it took to provide your Sunday newspaper? J. B. Handelsman's cartoon is a reminder of the relationship between a newspaper and the trees it takes to produce it. The cartoon visually depends on division. The tree about to be harvested for newsprint is playfully subdivided into the newspaper's sections. Division occurs when a single subject (a tree, a Sunday newspaper) is subdivided into its parts. At least one section of a newspaper—the classifieds—shows, as its name suggests, classification at work. Advertisements for the same types of goods (real estate, houses, pets) or services or employment opportunities are grouped or classified together. Consider the number of these small

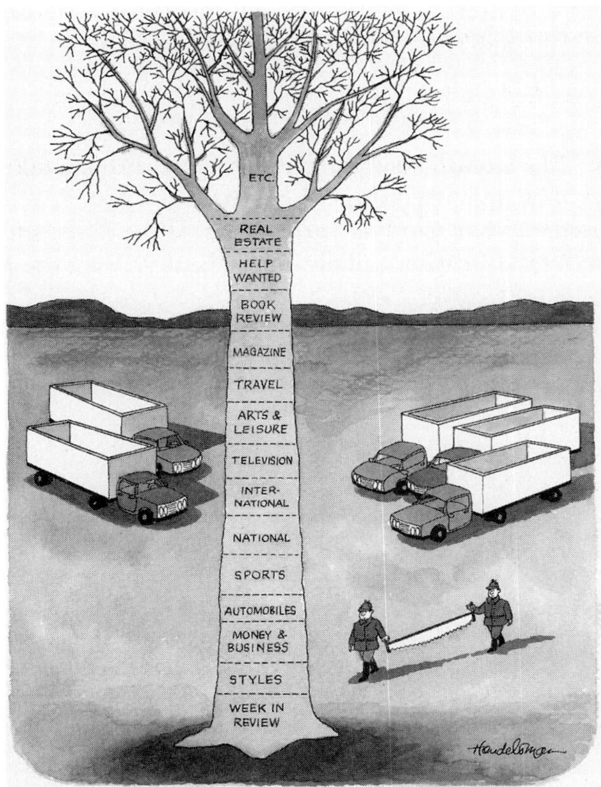

advertisements in your Sunday newspaper. The only way that you can find what you are looking for is if the advertisements are grouped together (or classified) under headings. Without such a classification scheme, the Sunday reader would be faced with hundreds of small advertisements arranged in a random order.

Visit the Prentice Hall Reader's WebSite

When you have finished reading an essay, check out the additional material available at the *Reader's* Website at www.prenhall.com/miller. For each reading, you will find a list of related readings connected with the topic or the author; additional background information; a group of relevant "hot-linked" Web resources (just click your computer's mouse and automatically visit the sites listed); and still more writing suggestions.

Dividing and Classifying

Visit the "Electronic" Newsstand and browse through 900 different magazines organized into 25 categories. Then write a paragraph based on your "surfing" experience. Want to see additional examples of classification and division schemes? Visit the *Reader's* Website.

WHAT'S IN YOUR TOOTHPASTE

David Bodanis

Raised in Chicago, David Bodanis earned a degree in mathematics from the University of Chicago and did postgraduate work in theoretical biology and population genetics. He traveled to London and then to Paris, where he began his journalism career as a copyboy at the International Herald Tribune. *Bodanis has a special talent for explaining complex concepts in simple, yet entertaining, language. His books include* The Body Book: A Fantastic Voyage to the World Within *(1984);* The Secret House *(1986);* The Secret Garden: Dawn to Dusk in the Astonishing Hidden World of the Garden *(1992);* The Secret Family: Twenty-Four Hours Inside the Mysterious World of Our Minds and Bodies *(1997); and* $E=Mc^2$ *(2000).*

This essay is excerpted from The Secret House. *One reviewer noted: "The book explores the gee-whiz science that sits unnoticed under every homeowner's nose." If you are appalled to discover what is in your toothpaste, you ought to read Bodanis's account of some mass-produced ice cream that contains "leftover cattle parts that no one else wants."*

BEFORE READING

Connecting: Most of us are well aware of the toxic nature of some common products, but there are many others that we assume are safe and maybe even good for us. Think about the things that you use, eat, or drink every day. Which ones have you never worried about?

Anticipating: Is Bodanis being fair and objective in his essay? How can you judge?

Into the bathroom goes our male resident, and after the most pressing need is satisfied it's time to brush the teeth. The tube of toothpaste is squeezed, its pinched metal seams are splayed, pressure waves are generated inside, and the paste begins to flow. But what's in this toothpaste, so carefully being extruded out? 1

Water mostly, 30 to 45 percent in most brands: ordinary, everyday simple tap water. It's there because people like to have a big gob of toothpaste to spread on the brush, and water is the cheapest stuff there is when it comes to making big gobs. Dripping 2 a bit from the tap onto your brush would cost virtually nothing; whipped in with the rest of the toothpaste the manufacturers can sell it at a neat and accountant-pleasing $2 per pound equivalent. Toothpaste manufacture is a very lucrative occupation.

3 Second to water in quantity is chalk: exactly the same material that schoolteachers use to write on blackboards. It is collected from the crushed remains of long-dead ocean creatures. In the Cretaceous seas chalk particles served as part of the wickedly sharp outer skeleton that these creatures had to wrap around themselves to keep from getting chomped by all the slightly larger other ocean creatures they met. Their massed graves are our present chalk deposits.

4 The individual chalk particles—the size of the smallest mud particles in your garden—have kept their toughness over the aeons, and now on the toothbrush they'll need it. The enamel outer coating of the tooth they'll have to face is the hardest substance in the body—tougher than skull, or bone, or nail. Only the chalk particles in toothpaste can successfully grind into the teeth during brushing, ripping off the surface layers like an abrading wheel grinding down a boulder in a quarry.

5 The craters, slashes, and channels that the chalk tears into the teeth will also remove a certain amount of build-up yellow in the carnage, and it is for that polishing function that it's there. A certain amount of unduly enlarged extra-abrasive chalk fragments tear such cavernous pits into the teeth that future decay bacteria will be able to bunker down there and thrive; the quality control people find it almost impossible to screen out these errant super-chalk pieces, and government regulations allow them to stay in.

6 In case even the gouging doesn't get all the yellow off, another substance is worked into the toothpaste cream. This is titanium dioxide. It comes in tiny spheres, and it's the stuff bobbing around in white wall paint to make it come out white. Splashed around onto your teeth during the brushing it coats much of the yellow that remains. Being water soluble it leaks off in the next few hours and is swallowed, but at least for the quick glance up in the mirror after finishing it will make the user think his teeth are truly white. Some manufacturers add optical whitening dyes—the stuff more commonly found in washing machine bleach—to make extra sure that that glance in the mirror shows reassuring white.

7 These ingredients alone would not make a very attractive concoction. They would stick in the tube like a sloppy white plastic

lump, hard to squeeze out as well as revolting to the touch. Few consumers would savor rubbing in a mixture of water, ground-up blackboard chalk, and the whitener from latex paint first thing in the morning. To get around that finicky distaste the manufacturers have mixed in a host of other goodies.

To keep the glop from drying out, a mixture including glycerine glycol—related to the most common car antifreeze ingredient—is whipped in with the chalk and water, and to give *that* concoction a bit of substance (all we really have so far is wet colored chalk) a large helping is added of gummy molecules from the seaweed *Chondrus Crispus*. This seaweed ooze spreads in among the chalk, paint, and antifreeze, then stretches itself in all directions to hold the whole mass together. A bit of paraffin oil (the fuel that flickers in camping lamps) is pumped in with it to help the moss ooze keep the whole substance smooth. 8

With the glycol, ooze, and paraffin we're almost there. Only two major chemicals are left to make the refreshing, cleansing substance we know as toothpaste. The ingredients so far are fine for cleaning, but they wouldn't make much of the satisfying foam we have come to expect in the morning brushing. 9

To remedy that every toothpaste on the market has a big dollop of detergent added too. You've seen the suds detergent will make in a washing machine. The same substance added here will duplicate that inside the mouth. It's not particularly necessary, but it sells. 10

The only problem is that by itself this ingredient tastes, well, too like detergent. It's horribly bitter and harsh. The chalk put in toothpaste is pretty foul-tasting too for that matter. It's to get around that gustatory discomfort that the manufacturers put in the ingredient they tout perhaps the most of all. This is the flavoring, and it has to be strong. Double rectified peppermint oil is used—a flavorer so powerful that chemists know better than to sniff it in the raw state in the laboratory. Menthol crystals and saccharin or other sugar simulators are added to complete the camouflage operation. 11

Is that it? Chalk, water, paint, seaweed, antifreeze, paraffin oil, detergent, and peppermint? Not quite. A mix like that would be irresistible to the hundreds of thousands of individual bacteria lying on the surface of even an immaculately cleaned bathroom sink. They would get in, float in the water bubbles, ingest the ooze and paraffin, maybe even spray out enzymes to break down the chalk. The result would be an uninviting mess. The way manufacturers avoid that final obstacle is by putting something in to kill 12 the bacteria. Something good and strong is needed, something that will zap any accidentally intrudant bacteria into oblivion. And that something is formaldehyde—the disinfectant used in anatomy labs.

13 So it's chalk, water, paint, seaweed, antifreeze, paraffin oil, detergent, peppermint, formaldehyde, and fluoride (which can go some way towards preserving children's teeth)—that's the usual mixture raised to the mouth on the toothbrush for a fresh morning's clean. If it sounds too unfortunate, take heart. Studies show that thorough brushing with just plain water will often do as good a job.

QUESTIONS ON SUBJECT AND PURPOSE

1. Bodanis explains to the reader what toothpaste is composed of. Is his description objective? Could it appear, for example, in an encyclopedia?
2. After reading the essay, you might feel that Bodanis avoids certain crucial issues about the composition of toothpaste. Does he raise for you any questions that he does not answer?
3. What might Bodanis's purpose be? Is he arguing for something? Is he attacking something?

QUESTIONS ON STRATEGY AND AUDIENCE

1. How does Bodanis seem to arrange or order his division?
2. Bodanis gives the most space (three paragraphs) to chalk. Why? What is his focus in the section?
3. What could Bodanis expect about his audience?

QUESTIONS ON VOCABULARY AND STYLE

1. How would you characterize the tone of the essay?
2. Bodanis links most of the ingredients to their use in another product. Find these links, and be prepared to comment on the effect that these linkages have on the reader.
3. Be prepared to define the following words: *splayed* (paragraph 1), *extruded* (1), *lucrative* (2), *aeons* (4), *abrading* (4), *carnage* (5), *errant* (5), *finicky* (7), *dollop* (10), *gustatory* (11), *tout* (11), *intrudant* (12).

WRITING SUGGESTIONS

1. **For Your Journal.** Over a period of several days, keep a list of every product that you use or consume—everything from a lip balm to cosmetics to after-shave or cologne to mouthwash to chewing gum. When you really think about it, which ones would you like to know more about?
2. **For a Paragraph.** Select a common food or beverage, and subdivide it into its constituent parts. Use the contents label on the package as a place to start. You could use either the list of ingredients or the nutrition information. Present your division in a paragraph. Do not just describe what you find; rather, develop an attitude or thesis toward those findings. Bodanis, for example, certainly expresses (or implies) how he feels about what he finds in toothpaste.
3. **For an Essay.** Americans exhibit widely differing attitudes toward the food they eat, in large part because they have the greatest choice of any people in the world. In an essay, classify the American eater. You can approach your subject from a serious or a comic point of view. Do not just describe types; your essay should either state or imply your feelings or judgments about your findings. Try to establish four to six categories.

   Prewriting:

   a. Establish, through observation, a series of types. Visit a supermarket, a health food co-op, a fast-food restaurant, a sandwich shop, a vegetarian restaurant. Consult the Yellow Pages for a listing of food suppliers and restaurants. Jot down your observations on the diversity of food and eaters around you.

   b. Interview several people who have strong feelings about food or whose food habits are strikingly different from your own.

   c. Plan out a strategy for organizing your categories—look, for example, at the organizational plan used by Berelson.

   Rewriting:

   a. Check to see if your categories are stated in parallel form. On a separate sheet of paper, jot down the key word or phrase for each one. Are they in parallel grammatical form?

b. Are there adequate links or transitions from one category to another in your essay? Compare your links to those used by Berelson.

c. Find a peer reader, and ask for an honest reaction to your paper and its organization.

4. **For Research.** Americans have become increasingly concerned about the additives that are put into food. Research the nature of food additives. How many are there? In general, what do they do? Develop a classification scheme to explain the largest groups or subdivisions. Be sure to adopt a stand or thesis about the use of such additives; also be sure to document your sources.

Website Link

Shocked to find out what's in your tube of toothpaste? That's nothing compared to the ingredients in a jar of baby food! Read a description from Bodanis' *The Secret Family* at the *Reader's* Website.

CINEMATYPES

Susan Allen Toth

*Born in Ames, Iowa, in 1940, Susan Allen Toth graduated from Smith College and Berkeley and received a Ph.D. from the University of Minnesota in 1969. She taught English at San Francisco State College and now teaches at Macalester College in Minnesota. Toth has contributed articles and stories to a wide range of magazines and newspapers. She has written two memoirs—*Blooming: A Small Town Girlhood *(1981) and* Ivy Days: Making My Way Out East *(1984). She has also written a series of books on England, including* My Love Affair with England *(1992),* England as You Like It *(1995),* England for All Seasons *(1997), and* Victoria, the Heart of England: A Journal of Discovery *(1999).*

On Writing: *Toth's essay, originally published in* Harper's, *grows out of personal experience. In commenting about the evolution of the essay, she observed that it grew out of frustration after dating three such "types." The ending of the essay was actually rewritten several times, and this more positive note was originally the suggestion of the magazine's editor.*

BEFORE READING

Connecting: Think about the people who are or have been significant in your life. What characteristics do they share? Are you drawn to the same type of person? To radically different types of people?

Anticipating: The core of Toth's essay describes her experiences going to the movies with three different men. Why should the reader care? Does Toth have a reason for relating these experiences—a larger purpose or thesis?

Aaron takes me only to art films. That's what I call them, anyway: strange movies with vague poetic images I don't always understand. Long dreamy movies about a distant Technicolor past, even longer black-and-white movies about the general meaninglessness of life. We do not go unless at least one reputable critic has found the cinematography superb. We went to the *The Devil's Eye*, 1 and Aaron turned to me in the middle and said, "My God, this is *funny.*" I do not think he was pleased.

2 When Aaron and I go to the movies, we drive our cars separately and meet by the box office. Inside the theater he sits tentatively in his seat, ready to move if he can't see well, poised to leave if the film is disappointing. He leans away from me, careful not to touch the bare flesh of his arm against the bare flesh of mine. Sometimes he leans so far I am afraid he may be touching the woman on his other side. If the movie is very good, he leans forward, too, peering between the heads of the couple in front of us. The light from the screen bounces off his glasses; he gleams with intensity, sitting there on the edge of his seat, watching the screen. Once I tapped him on the arm so I could whisper a comment in his ear. He jumped.

3 After *Belle de Jour* Aaron said he wanted to ask me if he could stay overnight. "But I can't," he shook his head mournfully before I had a chance to answer, "because I know I never sleep well in strange beds." Then he apologized for asking. "It's just that after a film like that," he said, "I feel the need to assert myself."

4 Pete takes me only to movies that he thinks have redeeming social value. He doesn't call them "films." They tend to be about poverty, war, injustice, political corruption, struggling unions in the 1930s, and the military-industrial complex. Pete doesn't like propaganda movies, though, and he doesn't like to be too depressed, either. We stayed away from *The Sorrow and the Pity;* it would be, he said, just too much. Besides, he assured me, things are never that hopeless. So most of the movies we see are made in Hollywood. Because they are always topical, these movies offer what Pete calls "food for thought." When we saw *Coming Home,* Pete's jaw set so firmly with the first half-hour that I knew we would end up at Poppin' Fresh Pies afterward.

5 When Pete and I go to the movies, we take turns driving so no one owes anyone else anything. We leave the car far from the theater so we don't have to pay for parking space. If it's raining or snowing, Pete offers to let me off at the door, but I can tell he'll feel better if I go with him while he finds a spot, so we share the walk too. Inside the theater Pete will hold my hand when I get scared if I ask him. He puts my hand firmly on his knee and covers it completely with his own hand. His knee never twitches. After a while, when the scary part is past, he loosens his hand slightly and I know that is a signal to take mine away. He sits companionably close, letting his jacket just touch my sweater, but

he does not infringe. He thinks I ought to know he is there if I need him.

One night, after *The China Syndrome*, I asked Pete if he wouldn't like to stay for a second drink, even though it was past midnight. He thought a while about that, considering my offer from all possible angles, but finally he said no. Relationships today, he said, have a tendency to move too quickly. 6

Sam likes movies that are entertaining. By that he means movies that Will Jones in the *Minneapolis Tribune* loved and either *Time* or *Newsweek* rather liked; also movies that do not have sappy love stories, are not musicals, do not have subtitles, and will not force him to think. He does not go to movies to think. He liked *California Suite* and *The Seduction of Joe Tynan*, though the plots, he said, could have been zippier. He saw it all coming too far in advance, and that took the fun out. He doesn't like to know what is going to happen. "I just want my brain to be tickled," he says. It is very hard for me to pick out movies for Sam. 7

When Sam takes me to the movies, he pays for everything. He thinks that's what a man ought to do. But I buy my own popcorn, because he doesn't approve of it; the grease might smear his flannel slacks. Inside the theater, Sam makes himself comfortable. He takes off his jacket, puts one arm around me, and all during the movie he plays with my hand, stroking my palm, beating a small tattoo on my wrist. Although he watches the movie intently, his body operates on instinct. Once I inclined my head and kissed him lightly just behind his ear. He beat a faster tattoo on my wrist, quick and musical, but he didn't look away from the screen. 8

When Sam takes me home from the movies, he stands outside my door and kisses me long and hard. He would like to come in, he says regretfully, but his steady girlfriend in Duluth wouldn't like it. When the *Tribune* gives a movie four stars, he has to save it to see with her. Otherwise her feelings might be hurt. 9

I go to some movies by myself. On rainy Sunday afternoons I often sneak into a revival house or a college auditorium for old Technicolor musicals, *Kiss Me Kate, Seven Brides for Seven Brothers, Calamity Jane*, even once, *The Sound of Music.* Wearing saggy jeans so I can prop my feet on the seat in front, I sit toward the rear where no one can see me. I eat large handfuls of popcorn with double butter. Once the movie starts, I feel completely at home. Howard Keel and I are old friends; I grin back at him on the screen. I know the sound 10 tracks by heart. Sometimes when I get really carried away I hum along with Kathryn Grayson, remembering how I once thought I would fill out a formal like that. I am rather glad now I never did. Skirts whirl, feet tap, acrobatic young men perform impossible feats, and then the camera dissolves into a dream sequence I know I can comfortably follow. It is not, thank God, Bergman.

11 If I can't find an old musical, I settle for Hepburn and Tracy, vintage Grant or Gable, on adventurous days Claudette Colbert or James Stewart. Before I buy my ticket I make sure it will all end happily. If necessary, I ask the girl at the box office. I have never seen *Stella Dallas* or *Intermezzo.* Over the years I have developed other peccadilloes: I will, for example, see anything that is redeemed by Thelma Ritter. At the end of *Daddy Long Legs* I wait happily for the scene when Fred Clark, no longer angry, at last pours Thelma a convivial drink. They smile at each other, I smile at them, I feel they are smiling at me. In the movies I go to by myself, the men and women always like each other.

QUESTIONS ON SUBJECT AND PURPOSE

1. Characterize each of Toth's cinematypes. How is each type revealed?
2. What types of movies does Toth go to alone? What common characteristics do they have?
3. Why does Toth end with the remark: "In the movies I go to by myself, the men and women always like each other"?

QUESTIONS ON STRATEGY AND AUDIENCE

1. Why does Toth begin as she does? Why not give an introductory paragraph? What would be the effect of such a paragraph?
2. Why does Toth end each of the three narrative "types" with a comment on the male-female relationship?
3. Does Toth's essay capture your interest? It is, after all, one person's experiences with three types of moviegoers. Why should we as readers be interested in the essay?

QUESTIONS ON VOCABULARY AND STYLE

1. How does Toth use parallel structures in her essay? How many different types of parallelism can you find? How does each function?

2. How would you characterize the tone of Toth's essay? How is it achieved? Be able to point to at least three different devices or techniques.
3. Be able to define the following words: *tattoo* (paragraph 8), *peccadilloes* (11), *convivial* (11).

WRITING SUGGESTIONS

1. **For Your Journal.** In your journal, make a list of the people who have been significant in your life. You can either confine yourself to one category (for example, "significant others," "role models and mentors," or "friends"), or you can mix categories. After each name, try to capture in a sentence or two what was most significant or important about that person.
2. **For a Paragraph.** Using the journal entries as a prewriting exercise, see if you can establish a classification scheme for the people to whom you are attracted. In a paragraph, classify the characteristics of those people. Try to find a coherent thesis to explain what you discover. Does this scheme reveal, for example, anything about your needs or values?
3. **For an Essay.** Make a list of two dozen or more recent films (from the last six months). Check your list against newspaper and magazine listings to make sure that it is fairly representative of what has been released, and not just movies you have seen. Then, using the list, devise a scheme of classification for these films. In addition to being descriptive, try to explain as well what such a classification reveals about our society and our tastes. Other possible subjects might include video or computer games, bestselling books, television shows, and musical groups.

   Prewriting:
   - **a.** Check a metropolitan newspaper. If necessary, do so in your campus library. Most Friday, Saturday, or Sunday editions include brief reviews of new films. That will help you construct your scheme.
   - **b.** Talk to relatives and friends about recent films as well. That will give you an additional body of information.
   - **c.** Write the relevant pieces of information about each film on index cards. Sort the cards into as many categories as seem appropriate. Remember, however, that you do not

want twelve categories, each containing a single example. Try to create a scheme that has three to six categories.

Rewriting:

a. Look again at how you organized your classification scheme. Why begin with that category? Why end with that one? Complete the following: "The ordering principle in my essay is ______."

b. Since your reader will not have seen every one of these films, you will have to summarize each in a sentence or two. But your essay should not consist just of summaries of the films. Make a copy of your paper, and highlight in colored pen all of the sentences that summarize plot. Then look at what remains. Have you defined and analyzed the categories as well?

c. Find a peer reader, and ask for some honest criticism. Did the reader find the essay interesting? Is the scheme too obvious? Are there enough examples to explain your categories?

4. **For Research.** What is "hot" and why? Select a range of popular items—for example, clothing styles, films, activities or sports, music, books, lifestyles—that seem particularly important or popular right now. Collectively, what do these things say about our society and our values? In a research paper, classify what those items seem to have in common. Taken as a whole, how do they help define American society today? Be sure to document your sources wherever appropriate.

Website Link

The World Wide Web has an astonishing collection of sites devoted to film. Find your favorite film, a "filmography" for your favorite star, listings of award-winning films. Good places to start can be found at the Website.

In Defense of Talk Shows

Barbara Ehrenreich

Born in Butte, Montana, in 1941, Barbara Ehrenreich earned her Ph.D. in biology at Rockefeller University. After a period of university teaching, Ehrenreich turned to writing full time. A prolific writer, Ehrenreich has recently published two collections of essays, The Worst Years of Our Lives *(1990) and* The Snarling Citizen *(1995). Her most recent book is* Blood Rites: Origins and History of the Passions of War *(1997).*

On Writing: *Ehrenreich writes regularly for* The Progressive *and a wide range of other magazines, including* Time, *where "In Defense of Talk Shows" first appeared. Commenting on writing essays for magazines, she observed: "I don't see myself as writing polemics where I'm just trying to beat something into people's heads. An essay is like a little story, a short story, and I will obsess about what is the real point, what are the real connections, a long time before I ever put finger to keyboard."*

BEFORE READING

Connecting: Do you ever watch talk shows such as the ones that Ehrenreich mentions? What attracts you to them?

Anticipating: To what extent is the essay a "defense" of talk shows?

Up until now, the targets of Bill *(The Book of Virtues)* Bennett's 1
crusades have at least been plausible sources of evil. But the latest victim of his wrath—TV talk shows of the Sally Jessy Raphael variety—are in a whole different category from drugs and gangsta rap. As anyone who actually watches them knows, the talk shows are one of the most excruciatingly moralistic forums the culture has to offer. Disturbing and sometimes disgusting, yes, but their very business is to preach the middle-class virtues of responsibility, reason and self-control.

Take the case of Susan, recently featured on *Montel Williams* 2
as an example of a woman being stalked by her ex-boyfriend. Turns out Susan is also stalking the boyfriend and—here's the sexual frisson—has slept with him only days ago. In fact Susan is neck deep in trouble without any help from the boyfriend: She's serving a yearlong stretch of home incarceration for assaulting

another woman, and home is the tiny trailer she shares with her nine-year-old daughter.

3 But no one is applauding this life spun out of control. Montel scolds Susan roundly for neglecting her daughter and failing to confront her role in the mutual stalking. A therapist lectures her about this unhealthy "obsessive kind of love." The studio audience jeers at her every evasion. By the end Susan has lost her cocky charm and dissolved into tears of shame.

4 The plot is always the same. People with problems—"husband says she looks like a cow," "pressured to lose her virginity or else," "mate wants more sex than I do"—are introduced to rational methods of problem solving. People with moral failings—"boy crazy," "dresses like a tramp," "a hundred sex partners"—are introduced to external standards of morality. The preaching—delivered alternately by the studio audience, the host and the ever present guest therapist—is relentless. "This is wrong to do this," Sally Jessy tells a cheating husband. "Feel bad?" Geraldo asks the girl who stole her best friend's boyfriend. "Any sense of remorse?" The expectation is that the sinner, so hectored, will see her way to reform. And indeed, a Sally Jessy update found "boy crazy," who'd been a guest only weeks ago, now dressed in schoolgirlish plaid and claiming her "attitude {had} changed"—thanks to the rough-and-ready therapy dispensed on the show.

5 All right, the subjects are often lurid and even bizarre. But there's no part of the entertainment spectacle, from *Hard Copy* to *Jade*, that doesn't trade in the lurid and bizarre. At least in the talk shows, the moral is always loud and clear: Respect yourself, listen to others, stop beating on your wife. In fact it's hard to see how *The Bill Bennett Show*, if there were to be such a thing, could deliver a more pointed sermon. Or would he prefer to see the feckless Susan, for example, tarred and feathered by the studio audience instead of being merely booed and shamed?

6 There is something morally repulsive about the talks, but it's not anything Bennett or his co-crusader Senator Joseph Lieberman has seen fit to mention. Watch for a few hours, and you get the claustrophobic sense of lives that have never seen the light of some external judgment, of people who have never before been listened to, and certainly never been taken seriously if they were. "What kind of people would let themselves be humiliated like this?" is often asked, sniffily, by the shows' detractors. And the answer, for the most part, is people who are so needy—of social support, of education, of material resources and self-esteem—that they mistake being the center of attention for being actually loved and respected.

What the talks are about, in large part, is poverty and the distortions it visits on the human spirit. You'll never find investment bankers bickering on *Rolonda*, or the host of *Gabrielle* recommending therapy to sobbing professors. With few exceptions the guests are drawn from trailer parks and tenements, from bleak streets and narrow, crowded rooms. Listen long enough, and you hear references to unpaid bills, to welfare, to twelve-hour workdays and double shifts. And this is the real shame of the talks: that they take lives bent out of shape by poverty and hold them up as entertaining exhibits. An announcement appearing between segments of *Montel* says it all: The show is looking for "pregnant women who sell their bodies to make ends meet." 7

This is class exploitation, pure and simple. What next—"homeless people so hungry they eat their own scabs"? Or would the next step be to pay people outright to submit to public humiliation? For $50 would you confess to adultery in your wife's presence? For $500 would you reveal your thirteen-year-old's girlish secrets on *Ricki Lake?* If you were poor enough, you might. 8

It is easy enough for those who can afford spacious homes and private therapy to sneer at their financial inferiors and label their pathetic moments of stardom vulgar. But if I had a talk show, it would feature a whole different cast of characters and category of crimes than you'll ever find on the talks: "CEOs who rake in millions while their employees get downsized" would be an obvious theme, along with "Senators who voted for welfare and Medicaid cuts"—and, if he'll agree to appear, "well-fed Republicans who dithered about talk shows while trailer-park residents slipped into madness and despair." 9

QUESTIONS ON SUBJECT AND PURPOSE

1. Write a thesis statement—or find one—for the essay.
2. According to Ehrenreich, why would people agree to appear on these talk shows?
3. What makes such shows "morally repulsive" (paragraph 6)?

QUESTIONS ON STRATEGY AND AUDIENCE

1. How does Ehrenreich divide or analyze the distinctive common features of the talk shows?
2. Why are such shows popular?
3. What expectations does Ehrenreich seem to have about her audience?

QUESTIONS ON VOCABULARY AND STYLE

1. In paragraphs 4 and 5, Ehrenreich uses an extended metaphor to explain the pattern that the shows follow. What is that metaphor? (Check the Glossary for a definition of *metaphor.*)
2. How would you characterize the tone of the rhetorical questions that Ehrenreich asks in paragraph 8? (Check the Glossary for a definition of *tone.*)
3. Be prepared to define the following words: *excruciatingly* (paragraph 1), *frisson* (2), *hectored* (4), *lurid* (5), *feckless* (5), *dithered* (9).

WRITING SUGGESTIONS

1. **For Your Journal.** All forms of media—compact discs, software programs, magazines, books, television or radio shows, even Websites—try to mimic whatever has been successful. For example, if one television show about "friends" or a new primetime game show is popular, expect next season to see several other imitators. Select one medium, and make notes in your journal about the similarities that you see among the items that belong in that category.
2. **For a Paragraph.** Expand your observations from your journal into a paragraph. Try for the same type of analysis or division that Ehrenreich achieves. Focus your paragraph around a single shared element.
3. **For an Essay.** Expand your paragraph analysis or division into a full essay. You are analyzing the elements that a series of similar media products share—for example, the common elements of television cooking shows or of magazines intended for teenage girls. Remember that the choice of medium is yours—software programs, magazines, advertisements, Websites. You will probably want to analyze three or four shared elements. How do these shared elements work together? To what purpose or goal do all of these things contribute?

   Prewriting:

   a. Gather examples of the media products that you want to analyze. For example, get a stack of magazines intended for the same type of audience or videotape several cooking shows.

b. Analyze what you see. To what extent are these products similar? If you were going to start a new product that imitated these, what would be its essential features? What must it have?

c. Suggest significance. Ehrenreich does not just describe; she analyzes. What accounts for the popularity of this product? Does it fill a need that its audience has? Does it reflect a certain set of values?

Rewriting:

a. Look carefully at the organizational principle that you used in the body of your essay. Have you clearly called out or marked the divisions?

b. Underline your thesis statement. Check the introductory section "How to Write an Essay" to see if your thesis meets the test provided there.

c. Look at your introduction. Have you tried to catch your reader's interest? Or have you written a standard thesis introduction? How would *Time* or *Newsweek* begin a story on this topic?

4. **For Research.** Test your analysis by checking research done on the subject. Using the resources of your library, and perhaps of on-line databases and the World Wide Web, see what other writers have said. Remember that information will appear in communication journals, marketing and business journals, trade papers for that particular medium, and scholarly and general journals and magazines. A keyword search might be a good place to begin. If you are having trouble gathering information, ask a reference librarian.

Website Link

Did you know that most of the television talk shows have their own Websites, complete with additional photographs, backstage "live" minicams, and other special features? Find out where to go.

The Myth of the Latin Woman: I Just Met a Girl Named Maria

Judith Ortiz Cofer

Judith Ortiz Cofer's "Marina" is one of the readings in Chapter 2, and biographical information about her can be found in that headnote.

On Writing: *Cofer comments about living in and writing about two cultures: "The very term 'bilingual' tells you I have two worlds. At least now, they're very strictly separated, but when I was growing up it was a constant shift back and forth. I think my brain developed a sense of my world and my reality as being composed of two halves. But I'm not divided in them. I accept them, and I think they have basically been the difference that has allowed me to write things that are not like anybody else's."*

BEFORE READING

Connecting: Have you ever been treated as a stereotype? Have people ever expected certain things of you (good or bad) because of how you were classified in their eyes?

Anticipating: What expectations would you have of a "Latin woman"? Or a "Latin man"? Do those expectations coincide with those about which Cofer writes?

1 On a bus trip to London from Oxford University where I was earning some graduate credits one summer, a young man, obviously fresh from a pub, spotted me and as if struck by inspiration went down on his knees in the aisle. With both hands over his heart he broke into an Irish tenor's rendition of "Maria" from *West Side Story.* My politely amused fellow passengers gave his lovely voice the round of gentle applause it deserved. Though I was not quite as amused, I managed my version of an English smile: no show of teeth, no extreme contortions of the facial muscles—I was at this time of my life practicing reserve and cool. Oh, that British control, how I coveted it. But "Maria" had followed me to London, reminding me of a prime fact of my life: you can leave the island, master the English language, and travel as far as you can, but if you are a Latina, especially one like me who so

obviously belongs to Rita Moreno's gene pool, the island travels with you.

This is sometimes a very good thing—it may win you that extra minute of someone's attention. But with some people, the same things can make *you* an island—not a tropical paradise but an Alcatraz, a place nobody wants to visit. As a Puerto Rican girl living in the United States and wanting like most children to "belong," I resented the stereotype that my Hispanic appearance called forth from many people I met. 2

Growing up in a large urban center in New Jersey during the 1960s, I suffered from what I think of as "cultural schizophrenia." Our life was designed by my parents as a microcosm of their *casas* on the island. We spoke in Spanish, ate Puerto Rican food bought at the *bodega*, and practiced strict Catholicism at a church that allotted us a one-hour slot each week for mass, performed in Spanish by a Chinese priest trained as a missionary for Latin America. 3

As a girl I was kept under strict surveillance by my parents, since my virtue and modesty were, by their cultural equation, the same as their honor. As a teenager I was lectured constantly on how to behave as a proper *señorita*. But it was a conflicting message I received, since the Puerto Rican mothers also encouraged their daughters to look and act like women and to dress in clothes our Anglo friends and their mothers found too "mature" and flashy. The difference was, and is, cultural; yet I often felt humiliated when I appeared at an American friend's party wearing a dress more suitable to a semi-formal than to a playroom birthday celebration. At Puerto Rican festivities, neither the music nor the colors we wore could be too loud. 4

I remember Career Day in our high school, when teachers told us to come dressed as if for a job interview. It quickly became obvious that to the Puerto Rican girls "dressing up" meant wearing their mother's ornate jewelry and clothing, more appropriate (by mainstream standards) for the company Christmas party than as daily office attire. That morning I had agonized in front of my closet, trying to figure out what a "career girl" would wear. I knew how to dress for school (at the Catholic school I attended, we all wore uniforms), I knew how to dress for Sunday mass, and I knew what dresses to wear for parties at my relatives' homes. Though I do not recall the precise details of my Career Day outfit, it must have been a composite of these choices. But I remember a comment my friend (an Italian American) made in later years that coalesced my impressions of that day. She said that at the business school she was attending, the Puerto Rican girls always stood out for wearing 5 "everything at once." She meant, of course, too much jewelry, too many accessories. On that day at school we were simply made the negative models by the nuns, who were themselves not credible fashion experts to any of us. But it was painfully obvious to me that to the others, in their tailored skirts and silk blouses, we must have seemed "hopeless" and "vulgar." Though I now know that most adolescents feel out of step much of the time, I also know that for the Puerto Rican girls of my generation that sense was intensified. The way our teachers and classmates looked at us that day in school was just a taste of the cultural clash that awaited us in the real world, where prospective employers and men on the street would often misinterpret our tight skirts and jingling bracelets as a "come-on."

6 Mixed cultural signals have perpetuated certain stereotypes—for example, that of the Hispanic woman as the "hot tamale" or sexual firebrand. It is a one-dimensional view that the media have found easy to promote. In their special vocabulary, advertisers have designated "sizzling" and "smoldering" as the adjectives of choice for describing not only the foods but also the women of Latin America. From conversations in my house I recall hearing about the harassment that Puerto Rican women endured in factories where the "boss-men" talked to them as if sexual innuendo was all they understood, and worse, often gave them the choice of submitting to their advances or being fired.

7 It is custom, however, not chromosomes, that leads us to choose scarlet over pale pink. As young girls, it was our mothers who influenced our decisions about clothes and colors—mothers who had grown up on a tropical island where the natural environment was a riot of primary colors, where showing your skin was one way to keep cool as well as to look sexy. Most important of all, on the island, women perhaps felt freer to dress and move more provocatively since, in most cases, they were protected by the traditions, mores, and laws of a Spanish/Catholic system of morality and machismo whose main rule was: *You may look at my sister, but if you touch her I will kill you.* The extended family and church structure could provide a young woman with a circle of safety in her small pueblo on the island; if a man "wronged" a girl, everyone would close in to save her family honor.

8 My mother has told me about dressing in her best party clothes on Saturday nights and going to the town's plaza to promenade with her girlfriends in front of the boys they liked. The males were thus given an opportunity to admire the women and to express their admiration in the form of *piropos:* erotically charged

street poems they composed on the spot. (I have myself been subjected to a few *piropos* while visiting the island, and they can be outrageous, although custom dictates that they must never cross into obscenity.) This ritual, as I understand it, also entails a show of studied indifference on the woman's part; if she is "decent," she must not acknowledge the man's impassioned words. So I do understand how things can be lost in translation. When a Puerto Rican girl dressed in her idea of what is attractive meets a man from the mainstream culture who has been trained to react to certain types of clothing as a sexual signal, a clash is likely to take place. I remember the boy who took me to my first formal dance leaning over to plant a sloppy, over-eager kiss painfully on my mouth; when I didn't respond with sufficient passion, he remarked resentfully: "I thought you Latin girls were supposed to mature early," as if I were expected to *ripen* like a fruit or vegetable, not just grow into womanhood like other girls.

It is surprising to my professional friends that even today 9 some people, including those who should know better, still put others "in their place." It happened to me most recently during a stay at a classy metropolitan hotel favored by young professional couples for weddings. Late one evening after the theater, as I walked toward my room with a colleague (a woman with whom I was coordinating an arts program), a middle-aged man in a tuxedo, with a young girl in satin and lace on his arm, stepped directly into our path. With his champagne glass extended toward me, he exclaimed "Evita!"

Our way blocked, my companion and I listened as the man 10 half-recited, half-bellowed "Don't Cry for Me, Argentina," When he finished, the young girl said: "How about a round of applause for my daddy?" We complied, hoping this would bring the silly spectacle to a close. I was becoming aware that our little group was attracting the attention of the other guests. "Daddy" must have perceived this too, and he once more barred the way as we tried to walk past him. He began to shout-sing a ditty to the tune of "La Bamba"—except the lyrics were about a girl named Maria whose exploits rhymed with her name and gonorrhea. The girl kept saying "Oh, Daddy" and looking at me with pleading eyes. She wanted me to laugh along with the others. My companion and I stood silently waiting for the man to end his offensive song. When he finished, I looked not at him but at his daughter. I advised her calmly never to ask her father what he had done in the army. Then I walked between them and to my room. My friend complimented me on my cool handling of the situation, but I confessed that I had really wanted to push the jerk into the swimming pool. This same man—probably a corporate executive, well-educated, even worldly by most standards—would not have been likely to regale an Anglo woman with a dirty song in public. He might have checked his impulse by assuming that she could be somebody's wife or mother, or at least *somebody* who might take offense. But, to him, I was just an Evita or a Maria: merely a character in his cartoon-populated universe.

11 Another facet of the myth of the Latin woman in the United States is the menial, the domestic—Maria the housemaid or countergirl. It's true that work as domestics, as waitresses, and in factories is all that's available to women with little English and few skills. But the myth of the Hispanic menial—the funny maid, mispronouncing words and cooking up a spicy storm in a shiny California kitchen—has been perpetuated by the media in the same way that "Mammy" from *Gone with the Wind* became America's idea of the black woman for generations. Since I do not wear my diplomas around my neck for all to see, I have on occasion been sent to that "kitchen" where some think I obviously belong.

12 One incident has stayed with me, though I recognize it as a minor offense. My first public poetry reading took place in Miami, at a restaurant where a luncheon was being held before the event. I was nervous and excited as I walked in with notebook in hand. An older woman motioned me to her table, and thinking (foolish me) that she wanted me to autograph a copy of my newly published slender volume of verse, I went over. She ordered a cup of coffee from me, assuming I was the waitress. (Easy enough to mistake my poems for menus, I suppose.) I know it wasn't an intentional act of cruelty. Yet of all the good things that happened later, I remember that scene most clearly, because it reminded me of what I had to overcome before anyone would take me seriously. In retrospect I understand that my anger gave my reading fire. In fact, I have almost always taken any doubt in my abilities as a challenge, the result most often being the satisfaction of winning a convert, of seeing the cold, appraising eyes warm to my words, the body language change, the smile that indicates I have opened some avenue for communication. So that day as I read, I looked directly at that woman. Her lowered eyes told me she was embarrassed at her faux pas, and when I willed her to look up at me, she graciously allowed me to punish her with my full attention. We shook hands at the end of the reading and I never saw her again. She has probably forgotten the entire incident, but maybe not.

Yet I am one of the lucky ones. There are thousands of Latinas without the privilege of an education or the entrees into society that I have. For them life is a constant struggle against the misconceptions perpetuated by the myth of the Latina. My goal is to try to replace the old stereotypes with a much more interesting set of realities. Every time I give a reading, I hope the stories I tell, the dreams and fears I examine in my work, can achieve some universal truth that will get my audience past the particulars of my skin color, my accent, or my clothes. 13

I once wrote a poem in which I called all Latinas "God's brown daughters." This poem is really a prayer of sorts, offered upward, but also, through the human-to-human channel of art, outward. It is a prayer for communication and for respect. In it, Latin women pray "in Spanish to an Anglo God / with a Jewish heritage," and they are "fervently hoping / that if not omnipotent, / at least He be bilingual." 14

QUESTIONS ON SUBJECT AND PURPOSE

1. What exactly is a stereotype? Where does the word *stereotype* come from?
2. What are the stereotypes or "myths" of the Latin woman that Cofer has experienced?
3. What is Cofer's announced goal in writing?

QUESTIONS ON STRATEGY AND AUDIENCE

1. At what point in time does the essay begin? Why does Cofer start with this example?
2. How does Cofer use time or chronology as a structural device in her essay?
3. Who does Cofer imagine as her reader? How can you tell?

QUESTIONS ON VOCABULARY AND STYLE

1. What does Cofer mean when she writes, "It is custom, however, not chromosomes, that leads us to choose scarlet over pale pink"?
2. What does *machismo* (paragraph 7) mean?
3. Be prepared to define the following words: *coveted* (paragraph 1), *microcosm* (3), *coalesced* (5), *innuendo* (6), *mores* (7), *regale* (10), *menial* (11), *faux pas* (12).

WRITING SUGGESTIONS

1. **For Your Journal.** Probably most people have in one way or another been stereotyped by someone else. Stereotyping is not reserved only for individuals from particular races or cultures. Think about the wide range of other stereotypes that exists in our culture, based on gender, age, physical appearance, hair or clothing styles, language dialects, or geography. In your journal, make a list of such stereotypes, focusing on either those that have been applied to you or those that you have consciously or unconsciously applied to others.
2. **For a Paragraph.** Using your journal writing as a prewriting exercise, take one of the stereotypes and in a paragraph develop one aspect of that stereotype and how it is evidenced by others or by yourself.
3. **For an Essay.** Expand your paragraph into an essay. Remember now that you are fully exploring a stereotype that you yourself have encountered or that you apply to others. Stereotypes are everywhere—they are not encountered solely by people from different cultures, races, or religions. For example, has anyone ever considered you a "dumb blonde" or a "nerd" or a "jock"? What aspects of personality do people expect when they see you as a stereotype (or do you expect when you see someone else as a stereotype)? Classify these reactions.

   Prewriting:

   a. Remember that you will probably want to have about three categories (of myths or expectations) in your essay. Keep developing a list over time.
   b. If you are having trouble in coming up with a subject or with a number of aspects of a stereotype, look at Suzanne Britt Jordan's essay "That Lean and Hungry Look" in Chapter 5. Jordan explores society's stereotypes of fat and thin people.
   c. Make sure that you develop each aspect of your selected stereotype. Notice that Cofer basically does so by using specific examples that demonstrate the points that she is trying to make. That is a good writing strategy for this assignment.

   Rewriting:

   a. Have you made clear statements that signal the sections of your essay? Notice how Cofer uses such signals (for example, "Another facet of the myth of the Latin woman in the United States . . ." in paragraph 11).

b. Make sure that you have phrased your categories in parallel grammatical form. Check the introduction of this chapter for guidelines.

c. Remember to catch your reader's attention in the first paragraph. Look closely at your introduction. Ask a friend to read just that paragraph. Does your friend want to continue reading?

4. **For Research.** Think about the stereotypes that Americans commonly hold about people from another culture. Cultural differences sometimes produce a great deal of misunderstanding. Select a culture (or some aspect of that culture) that seems to be widely misunderstood by most Americans. Research the cultural differences, and present your findings in an essay. One excellent source of information would be interviews with students from other countries and cultures. Where do they see those misunderstandings occurring most frequently? Your library, on-line databases, and the World Wide Web can also be good sources of information when you are able to narrow your search with appropriate specific subjects and keywords. Be sure to document all of your sources and to ask permission of any interviewees.

Website Link

A range of on-line and print interviews with Cofer can be found at the Website.

THE VALUE OF CHILDREN: A TAXONOMICAL ESSAY

Bernard R. Berelson

Bernard R. Berelson (1912–1979) was born in Spokane, Washington, and received a Ph.D. from the University of Chicago. He divided his time between the academic world and the world of international development assistance. In 1962, he joined the Population Council, eventually serving as its president until his retirement in 1974. Berelson published extensively on population policy and the prospects for fertility declines in developing countries.

Berelson's concern with population policy is obvious in this essay reprinted from the Annual Report *of the Population Council. Using a clear scheme of classification, Berelson analyzes the reasons why people want children.*

BEFORE READING

Connecting: The phrase "the value of children" might seem a little unusual. What, for example, was your "value" to your parents? If you have children, in what sense do they have "value" to you?

Anticipating: Despite the many reasons for having or wanting children, people in many societies today consciously choose to limit the number of children that they have. How might Berelson explain this phenomenon?

1 Why do people want children? It is a simple question to ask, perhaps an impossible one to answer.

2 Throughout most of human history, the question never seemed to need a reply. These years, however, the question has a new tone. It is being asked in a nonrhetorical way because of three revolutions in thought and behavior that characterize the latter decades of the twentieth century: the vital revolution in which lower death rates have given rise to the population problem and raise new issues about human fertility; the sexual revolution from reproduction; and the women's revolution, in which childbearing and -rearing no longer are being accepted as the only or even the primary roles of half the human race. Accordingly, for about the

first time, the question of why people want children now can be asked, so to speak, with a straight face.

"Why" questions of this kind, with simple surfaces but profound depths, are not answered or settled; they are ventilated, explicated, clarified. Anything as complex as the motives for having children can be classified in various ways, and any such taxonomy has an arbitrary character to it. This one starts with chemistry and proceeds to spirit. 3

The Biological

Do people innately want children for some built-in reason of physiology? Is there anything to maternal instinct, or parental instinct? Or is biology satisfied with the sex instinct as the way to assure continuity? 4

In psychoanalytic thought there is talk of the "child-wish," the "instinctual drive of physiological cause," "the innate femaleness of the girl direct(ing) her development toward motherhood," and the wanting of children as "the essence of her self-realization," indicating normality. From the experimental literature, there is some evidence that man, like other animals, is innately attracted to the quality of "babyishness." 5

> If the young and adults of several species are compared for differences in bodily and facial features, it will be seen readily that the nature of the difference is apparently the same almost throughout the phylogenetic scale. Limbs are shorter and much heavier in proportion to the torso in babies than in adults. Also, the head is proportionately much larger in relation to the body than is the case with adults. On the face itself, the forehead is more prominent and bulbous; the eyes large and perhaps located as far down as below the middle of the face, because of the large forehead. In addition, the cheeks may be round and protruding. In many species there is also a greater degree of overall fatness in contrast to normal adult bodies. . . . In man, as in other animals, social prescriptions and customs are not the sole or even primary factors that guarantee the rearing and protection of babies. This seems to indicate that the biologically rooted releaser of babyishness may have promoted infant care in primitive man before societies ever were formed, just as it appears to do in many animal species. Thus this releaser may have a high survival value for the species of man.* 6

*Eckhard H. Hess, "Ethology and Developmental Psychology," in Paul H. Musser, ed., *Carmichael's Manual of Child Psychology*, Vol. 1 (New York: Wiley, 1970), pp. 20–21.

7 In the human species the question of social and personal motivation distinctively arises, but that does not necessarily mean that the biology is completely obliterated. In animals the instinct to reproduce appears to be all; in humans is it something?

THE CULTURAL

8 Whatever the biological answer, people do not want all the children they physically can have—no society, hardly any woman. Everywhere social traditions and social pressures enforce a certain conformity to the approved childbearing pattern, whether large numbers of children in Africa or small numbers in Eastern Europe. People want children because that is "the thing to do"—culturally sanctioned and institutionally supported, hence about as natural as any social behavior can be.

9 Such social expectations, expressed by everyone toward everyone, are extremely strong in influencing behavior even on such an important element in life as childbearing and on whether the outcome is two children or six. In most human societies, the thing to do gets done, for social rewards and punishments are among the most powerful. Whether they produce lots of children or few and whether the matter is fully conscious or not, the cultural norms are all the more effective if, as often, they are rationalized as the will of God or the hand of fate.

THE POLITICAL

10 The cultural shades off into political considerations: reproduction for the purposes of a higher authority. In a way, the human responsibility to perpetuate the species is the grandest such expression—the human family pitted politically against fauna and flora—and there always might be people who partly rationalize their own childbearing as a contribution to that lofty end. Beneath that, however, there are political units for whom collective childbearing is or has been explicitly encouraged as a demographic duty—countries concerned with national glory or competitive political position; governments concerned with the supply of workers and soldiers; churches concerned with propagation of the faith or their relative strength; ethnic minorities concerned with their political power; linguistic communities competing for position; clans and tribes concerned over their relative status within a larger setting. In ancient Rome, according to the Oxford English Dictionary, the proletariat—from the root *proles*, for progeny—were "the

lowest class of the community, regarded as contributing nothing to the state but offspring": and a proletaire was "one who served the state not with his property but only with his offspring." The world has changed since then, but not all the way.

The Economic

As the "new home economics" is reminding us in its current atten- 11
tion to the microeconomics of fertility, children are economically valuable. Not that that would come as a surprise to the poor peasant who consciously acts on the premise, but it is clear that some people want children or not for economic reasons.

Start with the obvious case of economic returns from chil- 12
dren that appears to be characteristic of the rural poor. To some extent, that accounts for their generally higher fertility than that of their urban and wealthier counterparts: labor in the fields; hunting, fishing, animal care; help in the home and with the younger children; dowry and "bride-wealth"; support in later life (the individualized system of social security).

The economics of the case carries through on the negative 13
side as well. It is not publicly comfortable to think of children as another consumer durable, but sometimes that is precisely the way parents do think of them, before conception: another child or a trip to Europe; a birth deferred in favor of a new car, the *n*th child requiring more expenditure on education or housing. But observe the special characteristics of children viewed as consumer durables: they come only in whole units; they are not rentable or returnable or exchangeable or available on trial; they cannot be evaluated quickly; they do not come in several competing brands or products; their quality cannot be pretested before delivery; they usually are not available for appraisal in large numbers in one's personal experience; they themselves participate actively in the household's decisions. And in the broad view, both societies and families tend to choose standard of living over number of children when the opportunity presents itself.

The Familial

In some societies people want children for what might be called 14
familial reasons: to extend the family line or the family name; to propitiate the ancestors; to enable the proper functioning of religious rituals involving the family (e.g., the Hindu son needed to light the father's funeral pyre, the Jewish son needed to say

Kaddish for the dead father). Such reasons may seem thin in the modern, secularized society but they have been and are powerful indeed in other places.

15 In addition, one class of family reasons shares a border with the following category, namely, having children in order to maintain or improve a marriage: to hold the husband or occupy the wife; to repair or rejuvenate their marriage; to increase the number of children on the assumption that family happiness lies that way. The point is underlined by its converse: in some societies the failure to bear children (or males) is a threat to the marriage and a ready cause for divorce.

16 Beyond all that is the profound significance of children to the very institution of the family itself. To many people, husband and wife alone do not seem a proper family—they need children to enrich the circle, to validate its family character, to gather the redemptive influence of offspring. Children need the family, but the family seems also to need children, as the social institution uniquely available, at least in principle, for security, comfort, assurance, and direction in a changing, often hostile, world. To most people, such a home base, in the literal sense, needs more than one person for sustenance and in generational extension.

The Personal

17 Up to here the reasons for wanting children primarily refer to instrumental benefits. Now we come to a variety of reasons for wanting children that are supposed to bring direct personal benefits.

18 *Personal Power.* As noted, having children sometimes gives one parent power over the other. More than that, it gives the parents power over the child(ren)—in many cases, perhaps most, about as much effective power as they ever will have the opportunity of exercising on an individual basis. They are looked up to by the child(ren), literally and figuratively, and rarely does that happen otherwise. Beyond that, having children is involved in a wider circle of power:

> 19 In most simple societies the lines of kinship are the lines of political power, social prestige and economic aggrandizement. The more children a man has, the more successful marriage alliances he can arrange, increasing his own power and influence by linking himself to men of greater power or to men who will be his supporters. . . . In primitive and peasant societies, the man with

few children is the man of minor influence and the childless man is virtually a social nonentity.*

20 *Personal Competence.* Becoming a parent demonstrates competence in an essential human role. Men and women who are closed off from other demonstrations of competence, through lack of talent or educational opportunity or social status, still have this central one. For males, parenthood is thought to show virility, potency, *machismo.* For females it demonstrates fecundity, itself so critical to an acceptable life in many societies.

21 *Personal Status.* Everywhere parenthood confers status. It is an accomplishment open to all, or virtually all, and realized by the overwhelming majority of adult humankind. Indeed, achieving parenthood surely must be one of the two most significant events in one's life—that and being born in the first place. In many societies, then and only then is one considered a real man or a real woman.

22 Childbearing is one of the few ways in which the poor can compete with the rich. Life cannot make the poor man prosperous in material goods and services but it easily can make him rich with children. He cannot have as much of anything else worth having, except sex, which itself typically means children in such societies. Even so, the poor still are deprived by the arithmetic; they have only two or three times as many children as the rich whereas the rich have at least forty times the income of the poor.

23 *Personal Extension.* Beyond the family line, wanting children is a way to reach for personal immortality—for most people, the only way available. It is a way to extend oneself indefinitely into the future. And short of that, there is simply the physical and psychological extension of oneself in the children, here and now—a kind of narcissism: there they are and they are mine (or like me).

24 *Look in thy glass and tell the face thou viewest,*
Now is the time that face should form another;
But if thou live, remember'd not to be,
Die single, and thine image dies with thee.
—Shakespeare's Sonnets, III

25 *Personal Experience.* Among all the activities of life, parenthood is a unique experience. It is a part of life, or personal growth,

*Burton Benedict, "Population Regulation in Primitive Societies," in Anthony Ellison, *Population Control* (London: Penguin, 1970), pp. 176–77.

that simply cannot be experienced in any other way and hence is literally an indispensable element of the full life. The experience has many profound facets: the deep curiosity as to how the child will turn out; the renewal of self in the second chance; the reliving of one's own childhood; the redemptive opportunity; the challenge to shape another human being; the sheer creativity and self-realization involved. For a large proportion of the world's women, there was and probably still is nothing else for the grown female to do with her time and energy, as society defines her role. And for many women, it might be the most emotional and spiritual experience they ever have and perhaps the most gratifying as well.

26 *Personal Pleasure.* Last, but one hopes not least, in the list of reasons for wanting children is the altruistic pleasure of having them, caring for them, watching them grow, shaping them, being with them, enjoying them. This reason comes last on the list but it is typically the first one mentioned in the casual inquiry: "because I like children." Even this reason has its dark side, as with parents who live through their children, often to the latter's distaste and disadvantage. But that should not obscure a fundamental reason for wanting children: love.

27 There are, in short, many reasons for wanting children. Taken together, they must be among the most compelling motivations in human behavior: culturally imposed, institutionally reinforced, psychologically welcome.

QUESTIONS ON SUBJECT AND PURPOSE

1. What is "the value of children"? How many different values does Berelson cite?
2. Berelson gives positive, negative, and neutral reasons for wanting children. Is the overall effect of the essay positive, negative, or neutral?
3. Which of Berelson's reasons seem most relevant in American society today? Which seem least relevant?

QUESTIONS ON STRATEGY AND AUDIENCE

1. How does Berelson organize his classification? Can you find an explicit statement of organization?
2. Could the classification have been organized in a different way? Would that have changed the essay in any way?

3. How effective is Berelson's introduction? His conclusion? Suggest other ways in which the essay could have begun or ended.

QUESTIONS ON VOCABULARY AND STYLE

1. Berelson asks a number of rhetorical questions (see the Glossary). Why does he ask them? Does he answer them? Does he "ventilate," "explicate," and "clarify" them (paragraph 3)?
2. Describe the tone of Berelson's essay—what does he sound like? Be prepared to support your statement with some specific illustrations from the text.
3. Be able to define the following words: *taxonomy* (paragraph 3), *physiology* (4), *phylogenetic* (6), *bulbous* (6), *sanctioned* (8), *fauna and flora* (10), *demographic* (10), *consumer durable* (13), *propitiate* (14), *sustenance* (16), *aggrandizement* (19), *nonentity* (19), *machismo* (20), *fecundity* (20), *narcissism* (23).

WRITING SUGGESTIONS

1. **For Your Journal.** In your journal, explore the reasons why you do or do not want to have children. Would you choose to limit the number of children that you have? Why or why not?
2. **For a Paragraph.** Using your journal writing as a starting point, in a paragraph classify the reasons for your decision. Focus on two or three reasons at most, and be sure to have some logical order to your arrangement.
3. **For an Essay.** Few issues are so charged in American society today as abortion. In an essay, classify the reasons why people are either pro-choice or pro-life. Despite your personal feelings on the topic, try in your essay to be as objective as possible. Do not write an argument for or against abortion or a piece of propaganda.

   Prewriting:

   a. Interview twenty fellow students, asking their feelings about the subject. Try to get a broad spectrum of ages, religions, and socioeconomic backgrounds, as well as a balance in terms of gender.
   b. Analyze your own feelings on the subject.

c. If your instructor approves the use of outside sources, you can search for additional information from the many organizations on both sides of the issue. Your campus's health service will probably also have information.

Rewriting:

a. Look carefully at the organizational principle you have used in the body of your essay. How did you decide which reasons to put first? Which last? Try reordering the body of your paper.

b. Have you avoided emotionally charged language? Remember, you are not trying to defend a position or to prove that the other side is wrong; you are trying to classify the reasons people feel as they do, whether you agree with them or not.

c. Ask several peers to read your essay and to provide honest reactions to what you have written. Are they in agreement? Consider their reactions when revising your paper.

4. **For Research.** Studies have shown that as countries become increasingly industrialized, their population growth approaches zero. For example, India's fertility rate has declined from six infants per female reproductive lifetime to four. In China, the rate is now 2.3 (zero growth is 2.1). In a research paper, explore how increasingly industrialized societies—such as India, China, Costa Rica, or Sri Lanka—have changed their views of the "value" of children. Be sure to document your sources wherever appropriate.

Website Link

Is the world still facing a population explosion? Have birth rates stabilized? Declined? What type of population growth will the world see in the next millennium? For variety of Web resources, visit www.prenhall.com/miller.

THE VIRUS WARS

Robert Buderi

Robert Buderi, a former technology editor at Business Week, *is the author of* The Invention That Changed the World: How a Small Group of Radar Pioneers Won the Second World War and Launched a Technological Revolution *(1996) and* Engines of Tomorrow: How the World's Best Companies Are Using Research Labs to Win the Future *(2000).*

On Writing: *Commenting on his writing process, Buderi said: "My mode of operation is to do voluminous reading, taking notes into my computer, sometimes as I'm reading, but usually marking up books as I go and then entering notes. When I actually begin writing, I like to work as early as possible in the morning. . . . I always write directly on the computer, but once a chapter draft, or even a section draft gets fairly honed, I print it out and edit on paper."*

BEFORE READING

Connection: In working with computers either at home, school, or work, have you encountered a computer "virus"?

Anticipating: As you read the essay, think about how Buderi uses other writing strategies to organize the essay. Can you find examples of narration? Of comparison and contrast? Of process? Of definition?

In December of 1987 an electronic message named "CHRISTMA EXEC" arrived at IBM's flagship Thomas J. Watson Research Laboratory, in Yorktown Heights, New York. Steve R. White, a theoretical physicist, was working on an unrelated computer-security problem when the communiqué first unfolded on a colleague's screen, slowly tapping out keyboard characters in the shape of a pine tree and then signing off with the salutation "Merry Christmas." 1

Any enchantment, though, turned to worry as the visitor accessed the colleague's electronic address book and sent a copy of itself—ostensibly from the colleague—to the 1,500 or so entries in the database. A magician doing a disappearing act, CHRISTMA EXEC then erased itself. People were stunned. Loudspeakers blared 2 a warning not to run the rogue program, but it was too late. The holiday message was a Scroogelike virus that replicated itself hundreds of thousands of times, clogging up the company's internal E-mail system for nearly a day. Long before all the damage reports were in, however, White had dropped what he was doing to concentrate on the invader. "You realize as soon as this happens that it's something bad," he recalls. "I said, 'That's it, I'm not working today. I'm going to watch this happen, because this is a seminal event in history.' "

3 This was an early battle in the Virus Wars, a struggle between good and evil that affects a million computer users every year and threatens to intensify in the age of Internet communications and commerce, when viruses can be passed rapidly around the globe. With huge bets placed on the future of E-business, and with virtually every virus aimed at IBM computers and compatibles (such machines running Microsoft's DOS and Windows operating systems today account for some 90 percent of all personal computers), few companies take the threat as seriously as IBM does. In 1987 perhaps three digital viruses existed. Today, every day, six to ten PC viruses stream into the Anti-Virus Center at IBM's Hawthorne Laboratory, an extension of the Watson lab a few miles down the road from its parent. So far the IBM group has battled about 20,000 separate invaders.

4 And that's not even the half of it. Until recently the enemy at least seemed contained: once IBM's investigators or their counterparts in a few other organizations turn their attention to a virus, it typically takes less than twenty-four hours to decipher the code and divine a cure. But with millions of people swapping files and conducting Internet business around the clock, once-sluggish mutant codes can go global in well under a day.

5 On a recent visit to the Hawthorne Lab, White took me to a two-room suite a couple of floors above the Anti-Virus Center. Here, sealed off from the outside world by computer firewalls and other defenses against hackers, resides a prototype of what IBM thinks might be the savior of the Net. It's called the Digital Immune System. The idea is to create digital white blood cells—much as human beings develop antibodies to biological agents—that will be permanently available on-line. In theory, automatic virus-scouting programs will transmit suspect codes directly to the immune center, where they will be analyzed and debugged and the cure beamed back before mere mortals even know there's a problem. "If the Internet is going to survive," White says, "we're going to need an automated response on this rapid time scale."

A computer virus is a bit of software code that gets into a machine—typically through a disk or an electronic message—and coopts its host's resources, making copies of itself and ordering up aberrant behavior ranging from posting an innocuous message to wiping out hard drives. Although the theory behind viruses goes back at least to the 1970s, they did not emerge in the "wild" until the late 1980s. They speedily became an everyday menace. Annual sales of anti-virus software are expected to surpass $1 billion next year. 6

Nearly as soon as viruses came into existence, myths emerged about virus writers. In TV shows and movies they are brilliant iconoclasts who run circles around hapless corporations. No such romanticism affects IBM's twenty-five-person anti-virus team, however. Viral codes are rife with bugs—and none of their writers would land a job with IBM. "The writers might think that they're showing off their programming prowess," says Jeffrey O. Kephart, an instrumental figure in IBM's anti-virus fight. "But in most cases they're displaying their ineptitude to the world." Though few good studies of virus writers exist, the available evidence indicates that they're almost always male, usually in their teens or early twenties, and have an attitude. A pair of file cabinets inside the Anti-Virus Center hold boxes of diskettes bearing copies of every virus the lab has tackled. A few samples from this morgue illustrate the point. 7

One is Wazzu, which in its heyday, in 1997, infected Microsoft Word files by randomly shuffling words and inserting its name into text, as in "Now is wazzu the country to come to the aid of your time." Form, another demon, caused keyboards to make an annoying clicking sound on the twenty-fourth of each month. Inside his errant code, where only debuggers would see it, Form's creator left this message: "Virus sends greetings to everyone who's reading this text. Form doesn't destroy data! don't panic. F---ings go to corinne." 8

These creations may seem like harmless pranks, but anti-virus researchers warn that there's no such thing as a benign virus. Take Wazzu. "You might think it's a funny virus unless you're writing the Israeli-Palestinian peace treaty," White says. Even Form is far from harmless, since a virus's very presence means that a computer's standard operations have been disrupted, increasing the risk of crashes and tainted files. And without naming names, White tells horror stories of corporate mergers in which one company infected another because viruses got into the spreadsheets they exchanged. 9

10 Which explains why IBM opened the Anti-Virus Center in early 1989, barely a year after CHRISTMA EXEC hit. Working initially with IBM corporate customers, and later expanding into the consumer sector with its IBM AntiVirus software package, the center's team has not only assembled a collection of viruses but also classified each according to what it attacks—files, the operating system, and so forth—and tracked its incidence rate. Setting the stage for the coming showdown in cyberspace, White identifies five epochs in the war against viruses.

11 *Cambrian Explosion* (1982–1988). The real Cambrian Period saw an explosion of multicellular invertebrate life. Viruses are not quite the same but close enough. By the mid-1980s the personal computer had evolved from an oddity into a productive tool—and long-theorized viruses became a reality. Toward the end of the period CHRISTMA EXEC arrived at IBM.

12 *Age of Dinosaurs* (1988–1992). Invertebrates were joined by great beasts. Some were file infectors, so named because they infected individual files, or applications. An early arrival was the Jerusalem virus, which on every Friday the thirteenth put black rectangles on screens and erased any files executed that day. A programming error allowed the virus to invade files multiple times, adding 1,813 bytes of data with every re-infection: programs infected repeatedly would no longer fit in memory.

13 Around the same time, boot infectors arose. They were activated when users started up, or "booted," their computers with a floppy diskette. From 1990 to 1992 the Stoned virus was the world's most prevalent. The only consequence of the virus was that one out of every eight times a user booted up from a floppy disk, it flashed the message "Your PC is now Stoned!"

14 *Asteroids Hit Earth* (1992–1995). File infectors were the first casualty. Their decline coincided with Microsoft's segue out of DOS and the growing popularity of its Windows 3.1 operating system, which wouldn't work with infected files. Thus the file infectors' environment was made unlivable, just as asteroids or comets striking Earth may have made it unlivable for the dinosaurs.

15 Boot infectors, however, co-existed perfectly with Windows. Early in 1992 viruses were elevated to national prominence by the discovery of Michelangelo, set to be activated on March 6—the artist's birthday. The widely publicized virus—even *Nightline* did a segment on it—raised the specter of computer Armageddon, because it promised to erase hard disks on a specific day. Lines ran around the block outside some stores selling antivirus software.

Michelangelo proved largely a dud. Anxious scanning of disks for signs of the virus turned up scores of other boot infectors—but these viruses mounted a comeback that lasted nearly three years. Then Windows 95 had its debut. Thanks to a design quirk, it refused to spread boot viruses—making the environment uninhabitable for these agents, much as Windows 3.1 had for the file infectors. Boot infectors, too, went the way of the dinosaurs. 16

Mammals on the Rise (1995–1999). A new predator evolved: the macro virus. Far more nimble than the file- and boot-osaurs, it hid inside "macros," the little programs inside Microsoft Word documents and Excel spreadsheets that busy themselves with formatting and other subtasks. These viruses, including Wazzu and contemporaries dubbed Npad and Paix, thrived with the widespread sharing of files by way of E-mail—where such exchanges take place far more readily than they do through disks. For the first time, the tools of executives were affected. A CEO might dash off an electronic memo to all employees and contaminate every computer in the company. 17

The first macro virus, Concept, arrived just as boot infectors suffered their mortal blow, late in 1995. Its one overt act was to put up a message box containing the number 1. A message in the macro code, at the spot that could have included instructions for more-damaging action, read, "This should be enough to show the concept." 18

The period 1996 through 1998 was a brief golden time for anti-virus forces. Even the stealthiest new beasts rarely lasted longer than twelve months. The telling factor seemed to be anti-virus software, as IBM and others grew increasingly adept at putting out timely updates, and people seemed more willing to use them. 19

Monster From the Cyber Lagoon (1999–?). But then the Internet blossomed. As long as viruses replicated chiefly through disk exchanges, it could take a year for one to spread around the world. That left plenty of time to install anti-virus updates. In the age of E-mail and macro viruses, infections could become global in a month—still a reasonable amount of time to fortify defenses. But now viruses can travel worldwide in twenty-four hours. "The compression of the time scales from a year to a month to a day changes everything," White says. "Basically, the way the anti-virus industry is trying to solve the problem right now just breaks down." 20

In 1990, when the Anti-Virus Center was only a year old, White discussed the need to automate virus hunting with Jeffrey 21

Kephart, who was then a newly arrived expert in nonlinear dynamics. This concern ultimately persuaded Kephart to join the Virus Wars.

22 "Patterns and connections have always thrilled me," Kephart told me recently. "For the past decade or so I've had lots of fun exploring analogies between large, decentralized computer systems and things like ecosystems, biological systems, and economies." Almost as soon as White started talking to him on that day nine years ago, the analogy bells started ringing for Kephart. He began musing about how human beings ward off biological bugs by building up antibodies, and wondering whether a similar system could be contrived to fight digital viruses—especially ones that had yet to be seen.

23 The first step was to understand viruses better. The lab began compiling its elaborate database of attacks on IBM's corporate customers. Armed with the location and date of each incident, the number of infected PCs, and the type of virus involved, researchers employed techniques from mathematical epidemiology to figure out how viruses replicated and spread. In addition to watching for alterations in key parts of memory and other hallmarks of virus activity, most scanning programs today roam hard drives or disks looking for specific pieces of known viral code. These codes typically run a few dozen bytes in length. Drawing on pattern-matching techniques from computational biology, the IBM group was eventually able to spot known viruses from snippets as small as three to five bytes—speeding up detection. Identifying unknown agents was tougher. But the fact that a single signature often characterizes whole virus "families" proved crucial: since these set code patterns are directly linked to function, a wide variety of viruses could be recognized—and cured—even though they had never been seen before.

24 In the end, it took nine patents and seven years for what came to be called the Digital Immune System to materialize in the two-room suite at Hawthorne. The inner sanctum holds a series of computers and components stacked floor to ceiling. In the outer room, equipped with a large sofa, a kickboxing bag, and more computers, a small research group monitors the system and labors to perfect it.

25 The basic concept is that anti-virus clients will be networked directly to the prototype's central computer. Monitoring programs on clients' PCs will beam a copy of any suspicious program to the system's analysis engine, which will make a quick guess as to what kind of virus might be arriving. From there the sample will be

passed to what the team describes as a series of digital petri dishes—a separate collection of computers fitted with decoy, or "goat," programs that simulate the kinds of environments viruses like to invade. Goats can be run in different languages, and since certain dates—Friday the 13th, for example—might trigger certain viruses, it's even possible to rapidly simulate all the days of the year, and also different hours of each day. Because the starting condition of each goat is known, the system can track the exact path of any infection, determine the invader's traits, develop rules for removing the virus—and, with luck, undo any damage it has done. The immune system will then copy the virus and test its assumptions to make sure its cure works. The resulting "antibodies" will be transmitted back to the infected client and to any other machines on the network, and will become a permanent part of their memories. Eventually every customer will receive a copy through regular updates.

IBM publicly demonstrated the Digital Immune System in October of 1997, at the International Virus Bulletin Conference, a gathering of the world's top virus fighters and their customers, held that year in San Francisco. Kephart and a few colleagues brought a virus-plagued PC onstage, and the delighted audience watched as errant code was transmitted to Hawthorne, a cure derived, and the solution beamed back—in just over three minutes. Since then, field trials have been scheduled, with a commercial rollout planned for later this year. Last year the company announced a deal to give Symantec Corporation, the California-based maker of the market-leading Norton AntiVirus, rights to its anti-virus work—thereby fusing Norton's strong market position with IBM's technology. 26

Without an immune-system-like defense, White says, viruses threaten to "stop the forward progress of computing." But that's not to say he thinks the days of the computer virus are numbered. Even as the Digital Immune System was being readied for field trials, a renegade program for automating macro-virus production was circulating in the virus-writing community. It also appears that today's rapid-fire file exchanges, which often involve passing data among various applications, can cause viruses to mutate and take on properties more damaging than even their creators intended. 27

In short, just as there is no end to the human battle against biological bugs, the campaign against their digital counterparts endures. White says, "This is going to be a problem that stays with humanity as long as we use computers." 28

QUESTIONS ON SUBJECT AND PURPOSE

1. What does the title "The Virus Wars" suggest? In what way is this a "war"? Does the military metaphor seem appropriate? (Check the Glossary for a definition of "metaphor.")
2. What is the significance of the "CHRISTMA EXEC" virus?
3. What purpose does Buderi appear to have in writing the essay? For example, is he entertaining, informing, arguing?

QUESTIONS ON STRATEGY AND AUDIENCE

1. What strategy does Buderi use in the opening paragraphs of the essay?
2. When Buderi classifies the computer viruses (paragraphs 11–20), he uses a series of subheadings to group them over time. From where do those subheadings come? To what do they refer?
3. What expectations does Buderi seem to have about his audience? For example, do you have to have an extensive background in computers to understand the article?

QUESTIONS ON VOCABULARY AND STYLE

1. Write a one-sentence definition of the phrase "computer virus," or find such a definition in Buderi's essay.
2. If war is one metaphor that is used in the title, what is the other one?
3. Be prepared to define the following words: *ostensibly* (paragraph 2), *replicated* (2), *seminal* (2), *divine* (4), *aberrant* (6), *innocuous* (6), *iconoclasts* (7), *rife* (7), *errant* (8), *benign* (9), *segue* (14), *specter* (15), *Armageddon* (15), *stealthiest* (19), *epidemiology* (23), *renegade* (27).

WRITING SUGGESTIONS

1. **For Your Journal.** Think about the other subjects that you are studying this semester. How might division or classification be used to present some idea central to the subject matter of those courses? The suggestions presented in "Using Division and Classification in Writing for Your Other Courses" (p. 204) might give you some ideas. In your journal make a list of possible subjects or ideas.

2. **For a Paragraph.** Using your journal as a starting point, select one idea or concept and in a paragraph using either division or classification, present that idea to a general reader.

3. **For an Essay.** Expand your paragraph writing into an essay. Remember that you are writing to a general audience and make sure that you avoid highly technical language, that you define unfamiliar terms, that you find analogies that might help your reader.

   Prewriting:

   a. Look back to the list of ideas that you made for your journal. You might want to ask a classmate or friend to review your list. Which ideas seem particularly interesting to a general reader?

   b. Make a list of any technical terms that are common in the discipline from which your subject is taken. Will you use any of these in your essay? If so, will you need to provide a definition for these terms? If you are uncertain about a general reader's knowledge, quiz some friends about the terms. Can they define them?

   c. Would analogies help explain the idea? Remember that the idea behind an analogy is to use a familiar thing to explain an unfamiliar one—for example, a hard drive on a computer is like a filing cabinet.

   Rewriting:

   a. Look carefully at your introduction. Do you attempt to catch your reader's attention? Reread the body of your paper several times. Now try freewriting a new introduction to your paper. Imagine that your essay will appear in a magazine, so work to grab and hold your reader's attention.

   b. Is your division or classification clearly organized? Is this the best order in which to structure the middle of the essay? What principle of order did you use? In a sentence, explain and justify the use of that organizational principle.

   c. Look again at your title. Is it interesting? Descriptive? Provocative? Or just flat and boring? An effective title is a vital part of your essay—brainstorm some other possibilities.

4. **For Research.** How do you stay in touch with family and friends? What are the possible ways in which you could communicate with them? In an essay using classification, examine the current methods we have for interpersonal communication. Don't limit yourself to what you already do (for example, telephone calls, letters). Expand your possibilities by investigating other types of communication. You will need to do some research; that research might involve interviewing people who are selling various types of electronic communication.

Website Link

Want the latest information about a new computer virus? Whom do you call? Find out at the Website.

FIVE

COMPARISON AND CONTRAST

Whenever you decide between two alternatives, you engage in comparison and contrast. Which portable CD player is the best value or has the most attractive set of features? Which professor's section of introductory sociology should you register for in the spring semester? In both cases, you make the decision by comparing alternatives on a series of relevant points and then deciding which has the greatest advantages.

In comparison and contrast, subjects are set in opposition in order to reveal their similarities and differences. Comparison involves finding similarities between two or more things, people, or ideas; contrast involves finding differences. Comparison and contrast writing tasks can involve, then, three activities: emphasizing similarities, emphasizing differences, or emphasizing both.

John Fischer uses comparison in this paragraph to emphasize the similarities between Ukrainians and Texans:

> The Ukrainians are the Texans of Russia. They believe they can fight, drink, ride, sing, and make love better than anybody else in the world, and if pressed will admit it. Their country, too, was a borderland—that's what Ukraine means—and like Texas it was originally settled by outlaws, horse thieves, land-hungry farmers, and people who hadn't made a go of it somewhere else. Some of these hard cases banded together, long ago, to raise hell and livestock. They called themselves Cossacks, and they would have felt right at home in any Western movie. Even today the Ukrainians cherish a wistful tradition of horsemanship, although most of them would feel as uncomfortable in a saddle as any Dallas

> banker. They still like to wear knee-high boots and big, furry hats, made of gray or Persian lamb, which are the local equivalent of the Stetson.

Fischer emphasizes only similarities. He tries to help his readers understand a foreign country by likening it to a place far more familiar to most Americans.

Henry Petroski, in his essay "The Gleaming Silver Bird and the Rusty Iron Horse," contrasts air travel and train travel, emphasizing their differences.

> The airplane lets us fly and forget. We are as gods, even in coach class, attended by young, smiling stewards and stewardesses who bring us food, drink, and entertainment. From the window of the airplane we marvel at the cities far beneath us, at the great land formations and waterways, and at the clouds. Political boundaries are forgotten, and the world is one. Everything is possible.
>
> Nothing is forgotten on the train, however. The right of way is strewn with the detritus of technology, and technology's disruptiveness is everywhere apparent. Outside the once-clean picture window of the train, which has probably slowed down to pass over a deteriorating roadbed under repair, one sees not heaven in the clouds but the graveyards of people and machines. One cannot help but notice how technology has changed the land and the lives of those who live beside the rails. The factory abandoned is a blight not easily removed; the neglected homes of myriad factory (and railroad?) workers are not easily restored.

Like every writing task, comparison and contrast is done to achieve a particular purpose. In practical situations, you use it to help make a decision. You compare CD players or professors in order to make an intelligent choice. In academic situations, comparison and contrast allows you to compare two or more subjects carefully and thoroughly, on a point-by-point basis.

How Do You Choose a Subject?

Many times, especially on examinations in other academic courses, the subject for comparison and contrast is already chosen for you. On an economics examination you are asked, "What are the main differences between the public and private sectors?" In political science you are to "compare the political platforms of the Republican and Democratic parties in the last presidential election." At other times, however, you must choose the subject for comparison and contrast yourself.

The choice of subject is crucial. It is best to limit your paragraph or essay to subjects that have obvious similarities or differences. William Zinsser compares his writing process to Dr. Brock's; Mary Pipher contrasts the educational experiences and encouragements given to adolescent girls and boys; Suzanne Britt Jordan explores the stereotypes we have for thin and fat people; Bruce Catton pairs the two Civil War generals, Grant and Lee; Meghan Daum is shocked to find that her "virtual love" Pete is much better than the "real" Pete; and finally Susan Faludi contrasts the evolving nature and role of the football fan.

Two other cautions are also important. First, be sure that you have a reason for making the comparison or contrast, that it will reveal something new or important and so give your comparison or contrast an interesting thesis. Meghan Daum begins a "virtual," that is, an electronic, on-line relationship with an admirer named Pete. The romance flourishes until she meets the "real" Pete. Although the two have an electronic, but "old-fashioned kind of courtship," although neither had lied or pretended to be someone else, although the two "real" people are the same as the two "virtual" people, the romance instantly dies when they meet each other in person. Daum uses comparison/contrast to make a point not just about this one relationship, but about our needs and our frustrations in trying to establish lasting relationships in society today. She comments, "our need to worship somehow fuses with our need to be worshipped."

Second, limit your comparison and contrast to important points; do not try to cover everything. Mary Pipher, for example, focuses on how our educational system treats adolescent girls and boys differently. She does not write about parental expectations, for example.

Do You Always Find Both Similarities and Differences?

You can compare and contrast only if there is some basic similarity between the two subjects: John Fischer compares two *groups of people*—Ukrainians and Texans; Henry Petroski compares two *modes of transportation*—the airplane and the railroad. There is no point in comparing two totally unrelated subjects; for example, the mind could be compared to a computer since both process information, but there would be no reason to compare a computer to an airplane. Remember, too, that some similarities will be obvious and hence not worth writing about. It would be pointless for William Zinsser to observe that both he and Dr. Brock write on word processors, use dictionaries, or work best in a quiet study. This does not mean that similarities are not important or should not be mentioned. Bruce Catton, after spending most of his essay pointing out differences between Grant and Lee, ends with their similarities.

Once you have chosen your subject, make a list of the possible points of comparison and contrast. Be sure that those points are shared. Zinsser, for example, organizes his comparison and contrast around six questions. To each of the six, Zinsser gives first Dr. Brock's response and then his own. The contrast depends on the two responses to each of the six questions. If Brock had answered one group of three and Zinsser a different group of three, the contrast would not have worked.

How Do You Use Analogy, Metaphor, and Simile?

Writing a comparison often involves constructing an analogy, an extended comparison in which something complex or unfamiliar is likened to something simple or familiar. The reason for making the analogy is to help your reader understand or visualize the more complex or unfamiliar more easily. For example, if you are trying to explain how the hard disk on your computer is organized, you might use the analogy of a file cabinet. The hard disk, you write, is the file cabinet, which is partitioned off into directories (the file drawers), each of which contains subdirectories (the hanging folders), which in turn contain the individual files (the manila folders in which documents are stored).

Analogies are also used to provide a new way of seeing something. J. Anthony Lukas, for example, explains his attraction to the game of pinball by an analogy:

> Pinball is a metaphor for life, pitting man's skill, nerve, persistence, and luck against the perverse machinery of human existence. The playfield is rich with rewards: targets that bring huge scores, bright lights, chiming bells, free balls, and extra games. But is it replete with perils, too: culs-de-sac, traps, gutters, and gobble holes down which the ball may disappear forever.

Lukas's analogy does not seek to explain the unfamiliar. Probably every reader has seen a pinball game. Rather, the analogy invites the reader to see the game in a fresh way. The suggested similarity might help the reader understand why arcade games such as pinball have a particular significance or attraction.

Two common forms of analogy in writing are *metaphor* and *simile.* A metaphor directly identifies one thing with another. When Henry Petroski contrasts air travel and train travel (see p. 252), he uses metaphors—the airplane is a "silver bird" and the train is an "iron horse."

A simile, as its name suggests, is also a comparison based on a point or points of similarity. A simile differs from a metaphor by using the word *like* or *as* to link the two things being compared. In this sense, a simile suggests, rather than directly establishes, the comparison. On that February morning when his father died, Scott Russell Sanders saw that the ice "coated the windows like cataracts." Seventeenth-century poet Robert Herrick found a witty similarity: "Fain would I kiss my Julia's dainty leg, / Which is as white and hairless as an egg."

Be careful when you create analogies, similes, and metaphors. Do not try to be too clever, or your point will seem forced. But do not avoid such devices altogether. Used sparingly, these compressed comparisons can be evocative and effective.

How Do You Structure a Comparison and Contrast?

Comparison and contrast is not only an intellectual process but also a structural pattern that can be used to organize paragraphs and essays. In comparing and contrasting two subjects, three organizational models are available.

- *Subject by Subject*—you treat all of subject A and then all of subject B (A123, B123).
- *Point by Point*—you organize by the points of comparison: point 1 in A, then point 1 in B (A1/B1, A2/B2, A3/B3).
- *Mixed Sequence*—you mix the two patterns together.

All three alternatives can be seen in the essays appearing in this chapter.

Subject by Subject

Bruce Catton's comparison of Robert E. Lee and Ulysses S. Grant uses the subject-by-subject pattern. Paragraphs 5 and 6 of that essay are devoted to Lee; paragraphs 7, 8, and 9 to Grant; paragraph 10 to Lee; paragraph 11 to Grant. As Catton's example suggests, the subject-by-subject pattern for comparison and contrast works in paragraph units. If your comparison paper is fairly short, you could treat all of subject A in a paragraph or group of paragraphs and then all of subject B in a paragraph or group of paragraphs. If your paper is fairly long and the comparisons are fairly complicated, you might want to use either the point-by-point or mixed pattern.

Point by Point

William Zinsser's comparison of his writing process with that of Dr. Brock uses a point-by-point pattern of contrast. The two authors take turns responding to a series of six questions asked by students. The essay then follows a pattern that can be described as A1B1, A2B2, A3B3, A4B4, A5B5, A6B6. In replying to the fourth question, for example, about whether or not feeling "depressed or unhappy" will affect their writing, Brock and Zinsser reply:

[A4] "Probably it will," Dr. Brock replied. "Go fishing. Take a walk."

[B4] "Probably it won't," I said. "If your job is to write every day, you learn to do it like any other job."

The point-by-point, or alternating, pattern emphasizes the individual points of comparison or contrast rather than the subject as a whole. In college writing, this pattern most frequently devotes a sentence, a group of sentences, or a paragraph to each point, alternating between subject A and subject B. If you use the alternating pattern, you must decide how to order your points—for instance, by beginning or by ending with the strongest or most significant.

Mixed Sequence

In longer pieces of writing, writers typically mix the subject-by-subject and point-by-point patterns. Such an arrangement provides variety for the reader. Suzanne Britt Jordan in her comparison of thin and fat people uses a mixed pattern, so mixed, in fact, that at times it is not easy to see the underlying structure. The essay begins with a subject-by-subject pattern. It is not until the end of her second paragraph, for example, that she even mentions fat people. At other points, as in paragraph 5, she will start with an explicit point-by-point contrast: "Thin people believe in logic. Fat people see all sides."

Sample Student Essay

As part of the library research paper unit in Freshman English, Alicia Gray's class had been talking about searching their school's on-line library catalog for relevant books. The instructor had mentioned a number of times that card catalogs could be searched for both subjects and keywords since the software program allowed for both. To give the students practice in both kinds of searches, Meghan, their instructor, gave them a worksheet to do for homework. On the way out of class, Alicia stopped and remarked to her instructor, "I always just do a keyword search," she said, "and it always seems like I find plenty of material." She added, "Since we have the capability to do a keyword search, isn't doing a subject search just unnecessary and even old-fashioned?" "Do the worksheet," Meghan replied. "Maybe," she added, "you could compare and contrast the two methods for your essay which is due next week." A week later, Alicia brought to class the following rough draft of her essay comparing keyword and subject searches.

Earlier Draft

SUBJECT VS. KEYWORD SEARCHES

When it is time to start gathering information for your research paper in Freshman English, you will need to consult our Library's on-line catalog. The card catalog is a listing of the books that our library holds. Those books are catalogued, or listed, by author, title, subject, and keyword. Since normally we start by looking for books about our intended topic—rather than for specific titles by specific authors—we must start with either subject searches or keyword searches. What exactly is the difference between these two types of searches and how do you know when to use each?

When librarians refer to a "subject" search, they mean something quite specific and different from a "keyword." The term subject in library catalogs refers to a large listing of subject headings that are used by the Library of Congress to catalog a book. In fact, if you want to do a subject search in a library catalog, you don't start with the catalog itself. Instead you go to a multivolume series of books entitled the Library of Congress Subject Headings. Those books list alphabetically the various headings under which the Library of Congress files books. That listing is complete with cross-references, that is, with references to broader terms and to narrower, more specific terms. When catalogers at the Library of Congress look at new books, they do not just randomly assign a heading or a group of headings to the book, nor do they take the heading from a word in the book's title. Instead, they choose a heading or headings from the published list.

The principle behind the subject headings is to group related books under one heading. So instead of filing books about "the death penalty," capital punishment," "death by lethal injection" under three separate subject headings, the Library of Congress uses a single subject heading ("capital punishment") and then provides cross references from any other synonymous terms. The subject heading can also be followed by a whole series of other headings (for example, capital punishment—history). These other, more specific headings are very important because the Library of Congress always tries to assign the most specific subject heading to a book that it can. You never want to look under a large general heading if a more specific one is used. And how do you know if a more specific heading exists? You need to check the printed collection of headings currently in use. Subject headings impose a control on the vocabulary words used for headings.

In contrast, keyword searches look for words that are present somewhere in the book's record—typically in its title or subtitle, its author, its publisher. A keyword search retrieves information only when that word or group of words that you have entered appear in a record. That means there is no attempt at controlling the vocabulary. A book that had the phrase "the death penalty" somewhere in the title could be retrieved only if you typed in the keywords "death" and "penalty." A book on the same subject that used "capital punishment" would never appear—and keyword searches do not suggest related synonyms to you. Moreover, the presence of the key words would not necessarily mean that the book would be about the "death penalty" in the sense of "capital punishment." The words could appear in the title of novel or a collection of poems; they could refer to vastly different and unrelated circumstances—"the death penalty in ancient Rome." And, if you don't indicate the relationship (for example, immediately next to each other) that the two (or more) terms are to have, you'll end up retrieving a mountain of records that have the terms "death" and "penalty" somewhere in the record (for example, "The Penalty of Life: The Death of John Sayce."

Keyword searches have an advantage in that they can be used to find the very specific words for which you might be looking. Maybe those words haven't yet been added to the subject headings. Since subject headings depend on printed lists, subject headings are slow to react to new fields of study or new technologies.

Alicia shared the opening paragraphs of her rough draft with a classmate during in-class peer editing. The instructor had asked the students to concentrate on the organizational pattern used in the body of the essay and on the introduction. After reading Alicia's paper, her partner Sara LaBarca offered some advice on revising the draft. "You have lots of information," she said, "but your main pattern of development is subject-by-subject except for the fifth paragraph where you switch to point-by-point. Maybe you should try doing more with the point-to-point, otherwise by the time your readers come to the second half of your essay they might forget the contrasts you established in the first half." "I also think you need a strong introduction," she added. "You have a good thesis statement, but, well, frankly, I found the opening paragraph a little boring." Alicia tried to take Sara's advice and revised the opening of her essay and re-organized the body.

REVISED DRAFT

MINIMIZING THE GUESSWORK
IN A LIBRARY SEARCH

The Cecil County Community College Library has twenty books dealing with the death penalty, but unless you pay attention to the next couple of pages, you will never find most of them. Why? Because no single search strategy will lead you to all twenty books.

Looking for book sources is more complicated than you might think. A successful search will require two different types of searches—a subject and a keyword search. They are very different kinds of searches with different rules and results. But to maximize your sources for a quality research paper, you will need to know how to do both.

In both subject and keyword searches, you are looking for single words or phrases that will lead you to the books you need. Those subject or keyword terms come from two different places. The term subject in library catalogs refers to a large alphabetized listing of subject headings that are assigned by the Library of Congress when cataloging a book. You find an appropriate heading not by guessing as you stand at a computer terminal, but by looking in a multivolume series of books entitled Library of Congress Subject Headings. When catalogers at the Library of Congress look at new books, they do not just randomly assign a heading or a group of headings to the book, nor do they necessarily take the heading from a word in the book's title. Instead, they choose a heading or headings from the published list. A keyword, on the other hand, is a significant word, generally a noun, that is typically in a book's title or subtitle. Unlike a subject search where the categories are "controlled" (that is, someone has predetermined what subject headings will be used), a keyword search is, in one sense, guesswork. You think of an important word or phrase that might describe the topic about which you want information and you try that. Just like any time you guess, though, there are risks. A keyword search retrieves information only when that word or group of words that you have entered appears in a record.

"If I have the choice of having to look things up in a set of books or of just guessing, I'll guess," you might reply. But before you reject subject searches, consider the problem of synonyms—that is, words or phrases that mean roughly the same thing. A controlled subject search groups related books under one heading. So instead of filing books about "the death penalty," "capital punishment," and "death by lethal injection" under three separate subject headings, the Library of Congress uses a single subject heading ("capital punishment") and then provides cross references from any other synonymous terms. In contrast, you can only retrieve a book in a keyword search if it has those specific words somewhere in its record. A book that had the phrase "the death penalty" somewhere in the title could be retrieved only if you typed in the keywords "death" and "penalty." A book on the same subject that used "capital punishment" would never appear, and keyword searches do not suggest related synonyms to you. Moreover, the presence of the key words would not necessarily mean that the book would be about the "death penalty" in the sense of "capital punishment." The words could appear in the title of novel or a collection of poems; they could refer to vastly different and unrelated circumstances—"the death penalty in ancient Rome." And, if you don't indicate the relationship (for example, immediately next to each other) that the two (or more) terms are to have, you'll end up retrieving a mountain of records that have the terms "death" and "penalty" somewhere in the record (for example, "The Penalty of Life: The Death of John Sayce").

Keyword searches have a some distinct advantages, however. Since subject searches are controlled, the Library of Congress tries to find existing appropriate terms under which to file books—even if they end up having to use more general terms. Although new subject headings are regularly added to the lists, emerging fields and technologies are rarely represented adequately in the subject headings. On the other hand, since keywords do not depend on any pre-existing published categories and since no one has tried to classify those keywords into categories, keywords can be the best way to look for books on new and emerging subjects. In that sense, a keyword can be far more precise (if you guess the right one!) than a subject heading.

Some Things to Remember

1. Limit your comparison and contrast to subjects that can be adequately developed in a paragraph or an essay.
2. Make sure that the subjects you are comparing and contrasting have some basic similarities. Make a list of similarities and differences before you begin to write.
3. Decide why the comparison or contrast is important. What does it reveal? Remember to make the reason clear to the reader.
4. Decide what points of comparison or contrast are the most important or the most revealing. In general, omit any points of comparison that would be obvious to anybody.
5. Decide which of the three patterns of comparison and contrast best fits your purpose: subject by subject, point by point, or mixed.
6. Remember to make clear to your reader when you are switching from one subject to another or from one point of comparison to another.

Using Comparison and Contrast in Writing for Your Other Courses

Writing assignments and essay test questions that require comparison and contrast are common throughout the college curriculum. Instructors will often ask that you consider two subjects in depth, pointing out similarities and differences between them in order to demonstrate your familiarity with both subjects as well as to show how well you can apply the analytical concepts and skills being taught in the course. Here are some examples of writing assignments that would require comparison and contrast.

- **Literature.** For a five- to six-page paper, you might be asked to compare two works by the same author, one written early and one from later in his or her career, in order to analyze the development of the writer's style and the central themes explored in the works. Similarly, you might be asked to look at two works by different authors with similar themes in order to discuss similarities and differences in the development of these themes.
- **Life Sciences.** An exam question might ask that you compare and contrast two theories of evolutionary change—for example, natural selection and punctuated equilibrium.
- **Political Science.** For a research assignment to evaluate the role government plays in a particular aspect of a nation's economy, you might compare the United States' policies toward industrial planning with those of another major world power, such as Japan.
- **Theater History.** On an essay exam, you might be asked to compare the physical structure of the theaters where ancient Greek plays were performed with the kinds of theaters Shakespeare's plays were originally performed in two thousand years later.
- **Business Management.** For a research paper, you might be asked to compare how two different companies responded to a public relations challenge—for example, an outbreak of salmonella poisoning at a fast-food chain or accusations that a restaurant chain discriminated against minority customers—and then to explain which response you find the more effective and the more ethical.

Visualizing Comparison and Contrast

This advertisement uses comparison and contrast to make a point about racial stereotyping. The same man appears in both photographs. In one, however, his skin color is darkened—that is the only difference between the two photographs. The advertisement asks you to make a quick judgment by comparing and contrasting the two photographs and answering the question, "Which man looks guilty?" Although comparison and contrast is an important way by which we know things (What is this similar to? How is this different from that?), the advertisement also suggests that we can react uncritically on the basis of a simple comparison.

DeVito, Verdi Advertising Agency

Which man looks guilty? If you picked the man on the right, you're wrong. Wrong for judging people based on the color of their skin. Because if you look closely, you'll see they're the same man. Unfortunately, racial stereotyping like this happens every day. On America's highways, police stop drivers based on their skin color rather than for the way they are driving. For example, in Florida 80% of those stopped and searched were black and Hispanic, while they constituted only 5% of all drivers. These humiliating and illegal searches are violations of the Constitution and must be fought. Help us defend your rights. Support the ACLU. www.aclu.org **american civil liberties union**

VISIT THE PRENTICE HALL READER'S WEBSITE

When you have finished reading an essay, check out the additional material available at the *Reader's* Website at www.prenhall.com/miller. For each reading, you will find a list of related readings connected with the topic or the author; additional background information; a group of relevant "hot-linked" Web resources (just click your computer's mouse and automatically visit the sites listed); and still more writing suggestions.

COMPARING AND CONTRASTING

Most of us are familiar with the "supermarket tabloids," those newspapers with the sensational headlines and photographs sold in the check-out lanes of supermarkets. Are they an accurate source of information? How do they compare with a regular newspaper? Visit the *National Enquirer* on-line and compare it with a newspaper such as *The Christian Science Monitor*. Comparison is easy with hot-links at the *Reader's* Website.

The Transaction: Two Writing Processes

William Zinsser

William Zinsser was born in New York in 1922 and received a B.A. from Princeton in 1944. For thirteen years he was an editor, critic, and editorial writer with the New York Herald Tribune. *He left in 1959 to become a freelance writer and has since written regularly for leading magazines, including* The New Yorker, The Atlantic, *and* Life. *During the 1970s he taught nonfiction writing and humor writing and was master of Branford College at Yale University. Currently, Zinsser teaches at the New School for Social Research and serves as a consultant on the art of writing, working with colleges, newspapers, and corporations. He is the author of fifteen books, including* On Writing Well: An Informal Guide to Writing Nonfiction *(now in its sixth edition), a textbook classic of which* The New York Times *wrote: "It belongs on any shelf of serious reference works for writers."*

On Writing: *As someone who earns his living as a writer, Zinsser sees writing as hard work. "The only way to learn to write," he has observed, "is to force yourself to produce a certain number of words on a regular basis." In an interview, he once remarked: "I don't think writing is an art. I think sometimes it's raised to an art, but basically it's a craft, like cabinet making or carpentry."*

BEFORE READING

Connecting: If you had to describe your writing process to a group of younger students, what would you say?

Anticipating: Why should writing seem so easy to Brock and so difficult to Zinsser? If he finds it so difficult, why does Zinsser continue to write?

1 A school in Connecticut once held "a day devoted to the arts," and I was asked if I would come and talk about writing as a vocation. When I arrived I found that a second speaker had been invited—Dr. Brock (as I'll call him), a surgeon who had recently begun to write and had sold some stories to magazines. He was going to talk about writing as an avocation. That made us a panel, and we sat

down to face a crowd of students and teachers and parents, all eager to learn the secrets of our glamorous work.

Dr. Brock was dressed in a bright red jacket, looking vaguely bohemian, as authors are supposed to look, and the first question went to him. What was it like to be a writer? 2

He said it was tremendous fun. Coming home from an arduous day at the hospital, he would go straight to his yellow pad and write his tensions away. The words just flowed. It was easy. I then said that writing wasn't easy and wasn't fun. It was hard and lonely, and the words seldom just flowed. 3

Next Dr. Brock was asked if it was important to rewrite. Absolutely not, he said. "Let it all hang out," he told us and whatever form the sentences take will reflect the writer at his most natural. I then said that rewriting is the essence of writing. I pointed out that professional writers rewrite their sentences repeatedly over and over and then rewrite what they have rewritten. 4

"What do you do on days when it isn't going well?" Dr. Brock was asked. He said he just stopped writing and put the work aside for a day when it would go better. I then said that the professional writer must establish a daily schedule and stick to it. I said that writing is a craft, not an art, and that the man who runs away from his craft because he lacks inspiration is fooling himself. He is also going broke. 5

"What if you're feeling depressed or unhappy?" a student asked. "Won't that affect your writing?" 6

Probably it will, Dr. Brock replied. Go fishing. Take a walk. Probably it won't, I said. If your job is to write every day, you learn to do it like any other job. 7

A student asked if we found it useful to circulate in the literary world. Dr. Brock said he was greatly enjoying his new life as a man of letters, and he told several stories of being taken to lunch by his publisher and his agent at Manhattan restaurants where writers and editors gather. I said that professional writers are solitary drudges who seldom see other writers. 8

"Do you put symbolism in your writing?" a student asked me. 9

"Not if I can help it," I replied. I have an unbroken record of missing the deeper meaning in any story, play or movie, and as for dance and mime, I have never had any idea of what is being conveyed. 10

"I *love* symbols!" Dr. Brock exclaimed, and he described with gusto the joys of weaving them through his work. 11

So the morning went, and it was a revelation to all of us. At the end Dr. Brock told me he was enormously interested in my 12 answers—it had never occurred to him that writing could be hard. I told him I was just as interested in *his* answers—it had never occurred to me that writing could be easy. Maybe I should take up surgery on the side.

13 As for the students, anyone might think we left them bewildered. But in fact we probably gave them a broader glimpse of the writing process than if only one of us had talked. For there isn't any "right" way to do such personal work. There are all kinds of writers and all kinds of methods, and any method that helps you to say what you want to say is the right method for you. . . .

QUESTIONS ON SUBJECT AND PURPOSE

1. Zinsser uses contrast to make a point about how people write. What is that point?
2. How effective is the beginning? Would the effect have been lost if Zinsser had opened with a statement similar to his final sentence?
3. What process do you use when you write? Does it help in any way to know what other people do? Why? Why not?

QUESTIONS ON STRATEGY AND AUDIENCE

1. Which method of development does Zinsser use for his example? How many points of contrast does he make?
2. Would it have made any difference if he had used another pattern of development? Why?
3. How effective are the short paragraphs? Should they be longer?

QUESTIONS ON VOCABULARY AND STYLE

1. What makes Zinsser's story humorous? Try to isolate several aspects of humor.
2. Zinsser uses a number of parallel structures in his narrative. Make a list of them, and be prepared to show how they contribute to the narrative's effectiveness.
3. Be able to explain or define the following: *avocation* (paragraph 1), *bohemian* (2), *arduous* (3), *mime* (10), *gusto* (11), *drone* (12).

WRITING SUGGESTIONS

1. **For Your Journal.** How do you feel about writing? How do you feel about having other people read your writing? Is writing a source of great anxiety? Of pleasure? In your journal, explore those feelings.
2. **For a Paragraph.** Using the details provided by Zinsser, rewrite the narrative using a subject-by-subject pattern. Choose either writer, and put together his advice in a single paragraph. Be sure to formulate a topic sentence that will control the paragraph.
3. **For an Essay.** Let's be honest—writing instructors and textbooks offer one view of the writing process, but the practice of most writers can differ sharply. Prewriting and revising get squeezed out when a paper is due and only one night is available. In an essay, compare and contrast your typical behavior as a writer with the process outlined in this text. Do not be afraid to be truthful.

   Prewriting:

   a. For fifteen minutes, freewrite on the topic. Do not stop to edit or check spelling. Just write without stopping about how you write your papers—or how you wrote them before you took this course. Take a short break and then write for another fifteen minutes.

   b. Based on what you have learned so far in the course, make a list of some steps involved in the writing process. Be sure to include some details or examples under each step.

   c. On a separate sheet of paper, divided into halves, list the stages of the ideal writing process on the left-hand side and the stages of your typical (or former) writing process on the right-hand side.

   d. Before you begin, weigh the three possible structures for your paper—point by point, subject by subject, or the mixed sequence. Consider all the alternatives.

   Rewriting:

   a. Look carefully at the points of comparison or contrast that you have chosen. Are they the most important? The most revealing?

   b. Have you adequately developed each point? Have you included appropriate details and examples? Check to make sure that your body paragraphs are more than two or three sentences in length.

c. Copy your introduction onto a separate sheet of paper. Show it to some friends and ask them to be honest—do they want to keep reading? Or is this just another boring English essay?

4. **For Research.** Compare the creative processes of two or more artists. You can choose painters, musicians, dancers, writers, actors—anyone involved in the creative arts. Check your library's catalog and the various periodical indexes and electronic databases for books and articles about the creative work of each person. Try to find interviews or statements in which the artists talk about how they work. If you are having trouble finding information, ask a reference librarian to help you. Be sure to document your sources.

Website Link

Interested in some on-line help for your writing? A list of sites is available at www.prenhall.com/miller.

Academic Selves

Mary Pipher

Mary Pipher earned her B.A. in cultural anthropology from the University of California at Berkeley and a Ph.D. in psychology from the University of Nebraska. A clinical psychologist in private practice in Lincoln, Nebraska, she is the author of Reviving Ophelia: Saving the Selves of Adolescent Girls *(1994), which was on* The New York Times *best-seller list for 149 weeks, and* Another Country: Navigating the Emotional Terrain of Our Elders *(1999). This selection is taken from* Reviving Ophelia.

BEFORE READING

Connecting: In the years that you were in middle or high school, did you ever feel as if boys and girls were treated differently?

Anticipating: As you read Pipher's essay, try to decide which of the three patterns for comparison and contrast (point-by-point, subject-by-subject, or mixed) she uses.

Schools have always treated girls and boys differently. What is new in the nineties is that we have much more documentation of this phenomenon. Public awareness of the discrimination is increasing. This is due in part to the American Association of University Women (AAUW), which released a study in 1992 entitled "How Schools Shortchange Girls." 1

In classes, boys are twice as likely to be seen as role models, five times as likely to receive teachers' attention and twelve times as likely to speak up in class. In textbooks, one-seventh of all illustrations of children are of girls. Teachers chose many more classroom activities that appeal to boys than to girls. Girls are exposed to almost three times as many boy-centered stories as girl-centered stories. Boys tend to be portrayed as clever, brave, creative, and resourceful, while girls are depicted as kind, dependent and docile. Girls read six times as many biographies of males as of females. Even in animal stories, the animals are twice as likely to be males. (I know of one teacher who, when she reads to her classes, routinely changes the sex of the characters in the stories so that girls will have stronger role models.) 2

3 Analysis of classroom videos shows that boys receive more classroom attention and detailed instruction than girls. They are called on more often than girls and are asked more abstract, open-ended and complex questions. Boys are more likely to be praised for academics and intellectual work, while girls are more likely to be praised for their clothing, behaving properly and obeying rules. Boys are likely to be criticized for their behavior, while girls are criticized for intellectual inadequacy. The message to boys tends to be: "You're smart, if you would just settle down and get to work." The message to girls is often: "Perhaps you're just not good at this. You've followed the rules and haven't succeeded."

4 Because with boys failure is attributed to external factors and success is attributed to ability, they keep their confidence, even with failure. With girls it's just the opposite. Because their success is attributed to good luck or hard work and failure to lack of ability, with every failure, girls' confidence is eroded. All this works in subtle ways to stop girls from wanting to be astronauts and brain surgeons. Girls can't say why they ditch their dreams, they just "mysteriously" lose interest.

5 Some girls do well in math and continue to like it, but many who were once good at math complain that they are stupid in math. Girl after girl tells me, "I'm not good in math." My observations suggest that girls have trouble with math because math requires exactly the qualities that many junior-high girls lack—confidence, trust in one's own judgment and the ability to tolerate frustration without becoming overwhelmed. Anxiety interferes with problem solving in math. A vicious circle develops—girls get anxious, which interferes with problem solving, and so they fail and are even more anxious and prone to self-doubt the next time around.

6 When boys have trouble with a math problem, they are more likely to think the problem is hard but stay with it. When girls have trouble, they think they are stupid and tend to give up. This difference in attribution speaks to girls' precipitous decline in math. Girls need to be encouraged to persevere in the face of difficulty, to calm down and believe in themselves. They need permission to take their time and to make many mistakes before solving the problem. They need to learn relaxation skills to deal with the math anxiety so many experience.

7 The AAUW study found that as children go through school, boys do better and feel better about themselves and girls' self-esteem, opinions of their sex and scores on standardized achievement tests all decline. Girls are more likely than boys to say that they are not smart enough for their dream careers. They emerge

from adolescence with a diminished sense of their worth as individuals.

Gifted girls seem to suffer particularly with adolescence. 8
Lois Murphy found that they lose IQ points as they become feminized. In the 1920s Psychologist Louis Terman studied gifted children in California. Among the children, the seven best writers were girls and all the best artists were girls, but by adulthood all the eminent artists and writers were men.

Junior high is when girls begin to fade academically. Partly 9
this comes from the very structure of the schools, which tend to be large and impersonal. Girls, who tend to do better in relationship-based, cooperative learning situations, get lost academically in these settings. Partly it comes from a shift girls make at this time from a focus on achievement to a focus on affiliation. In junior high girls feel enormous pressure to be popular. They learn that good grades can even interfere with popularity. Lori learned to keep quiet about grades. She said, "Either way I lose. If I make a good grade, they are mad. If I make a bad grade, they spread it around that even I can screw up." Another girl said, "When I started junior high I figured out that I'd have more friends if I focused on sports. Smart girls were nerds." Another, who almost flunked seventh grade, told me, "All I care about is my friends. Grades don't matter to me."

I saw a seventh-grader who was failing everything. I asked her 10
why and she said, "My friends and I decided that making good grades wasn't cool." Her story has a happy ending, not because of my work, but because the next year, in eighth grade, she and her friends had another meeting and decided that it was now "cool" to make good grades. My client's academic situation improved enormously.

This tendency for girls to hide their academic accomplish- 11
ments is an old one. Once on a date I was particularly untrue to myself. Denny and I went to the A&W Root Beer Drive-In on Highway 81, and he asked me what I would like. Even though I was famished I ordered only a small Coke. (Nice girls didn't eat too much.) Then he asked about my six-week grades. I had made As, but I said I had two Cs and was worried my parents would be mad. I can still remember his look of visible relief.

QUESTIONS ON SUBJECT AND PURPOSE

1. According to Pipher why do young girls "fade academically"?

2. Although Pipher cites a study done by the American Association of University Women (paragraph 1), she does not quote from the study or specifically document the "facts" that she provides. Does that affect your reading experience of the essay? Do you, for example, doubt anything that she says?
3. What purpose might Pipher have in her essay? Notice the title and subtitle of the book from which this is taken in the headnote above.

QUESTIONS ON STRATEGY AND AUDIENCE

1. In paragraphs 9 and 10, Pipher introduces examples of young girls reacting to peer pressure. How do these examples work in the essay?
2. In the final paragraph, Pipher relates a personal experience. What is the effect of telling that story about her own life?
3. To whom is Pipher writing? Would the imagined or intended audience be adolescent girls? Someone else?

QUESTIONS ON VOCABULARY AND STYLE

1. What effect does Pipher gain by quoting—rather than summarizing—the remarks of the girls in paragraphs 9 and 10?
2. Reread paragraph 11. Does it seem unusual that Pipher is able to recall such detailed information from her own past? Does it really matter whether or not each detail is accurate and truthful?
3. Be prepared to define the following words: *docile* (paragraph 2), *precipitous* (6), *persevere* (6).

WRITING SUGGESTIONS

1. **For Your Journal.** Pipher is writing about the educational and peer experiences that adolescent girls have. Do similar discrimination and pressure extend into the college years? Think about male and female students at your school. Do they behave differently in class? Do males talk more? Do professors call on males more often? Is peer pressure a factor in academic success or failure? For several days, just listen and watch what is going on in your classes and elsewhere on campus. Take notes in your journal.

2. **For a Paragraph.** Use your journal to provide the examples for a paragraph in which you explore gender differences in your college's classrooms.
3. **For an Essay.** Expand your paragraph writing into an essay. What differences do you see between male and female students, in the classroom, in the laboratory, in their expectations, in their assumptions?

   Prewriting:

   a. Be sure to gather a sufficient number of specific examples. Your own observations are important, but you will probably want to interview other students of both sexes. Remember to look for patterns in the data rather than trying to impose patterns on the data.

   b. Formulate a thesis on the basis of the evidence that you have gathered. Use that thesis as a way of selecting the most relevant examples.

   c. Make a trial outline. Rearrange the body of the essay in several ways. Try both a point-by-point and a subject-by-subject arrangement to see which works best.

   Rewriting:

   a. Remember that the quality of your examples and your analysis are more important than the quantity of your evidence. Look carefully at each example, and discard any that seem weak.

   b. Ask your classmates and friends to read your essay. Be sure to enlist both male and female readers. Do they feel that you have demonstrated the "truth" of your thesis?

   c. Look back over your essay. Have you not only compared and contrasted, but also attempted to analyze the significance of any differences that you have seen? Have you attributed those differences to particular reasons?

4. **For Research.** Your essay dealt with your own experience and observation and the experiences and observations of fellow students. Does the body of scholarly research see any difference between how men and women are treated in college classrooms? Is there any perceived difference in peer pressure? In expectations? Is it suddenly acceptable to be a "brilliant" student in college if you are a woman? In an essay that includes research in printed or on-line sources, compare and contrast the educational experience

for men and women in college. Be sure to document your sources.

Website Link

A number of interviews with Pipher are available on-line. A good place to start is with the listing at the Website.

That Lean and Hungry Look

Suzanne Britt Jordan

Suzanne Britt Jordan was born in Winston-Salem, North Carolina, and attended Salem College and Washington University. She has been a columnist for the Raleigh News and Observer *and* Stars and Stripes, *European edition, and has written for other newspapers and newsmagazines. Jordan's books include a collection of essays,* Show and Tell *(1982);* Skinny People Are Dull and Crunchy like Carrots *(1982), an expansion of her essay "That Lean and Hungry Look"; and* A Writer's Rhetoric *(1988), a college textbook. This essay originally appeared in the "My Turn" column of* Newsweek *magazine.*

BEFORE READING

Connecting: Despite that fact that many Americans are overweight, our society associates fatness with many negative images. What are some immediate stereotypes that fat people bring to mind?

Anticipating: Should thin people be offended by the way they are ridiculed in Jordan's essay?

1 Caesar was right. Thin people need watching. I've been watching them for most of my adult life, and I don't like what I see. When these narrow fellows spring at me, I quiver to my toes. Thin people come in all personalities, most of them menacing. You've got your "together" thin person, your mechanical thin person, your condescending thin person, your tsk-tsk thin person, your efficiency-expert thin person. All of them are dangerous.

2 In the first place, thin people aren't fun. They don't know how to goof off, at least in the best, fat sense of the word. They've always got to be adoing. Give them a coffee break, and they'll jog around the block. Supply them with a quiet evening at home, and they'll fix the screen door and lick S&H green stamps. They say things like "there aren't enough hours in the day." Fat people never say that. Fat people think the day is too damn long already.

3 Thin people make me tired. They've got speedy little metabolisms that cause them to bustle briskly. They're forever rubbing their bony hands together and eyeing new problems to "tackle." I

like to surround myself with sluggish, inert, easy-going fat people, the kind who believe that if you clean it up today, it'll just get dirty again tomorrow.

4 Some people say the business about the jolly fat person is a myth, that all of us chubbies are neurotic, sick, sad people. I disagree. Fat people may not be chortling all day long, but they're a hell of a lot *nicer* than the wizened and shriveled. Thin people turn surly, mean, and hard at a young age because they never learn the value of a hot-fudge sundae for easing tension. Thin people don't like gooey soft things because they themselves are neither gooey nor soft. They are crunchy and dull, like carrots. They go straight to the heart of the matter while fat people let things stay all blurry and hazy and vague, the way things actually are. Thin people want to face the truth. Fat people know there is no truth. One of my thin friends is always staring at complex, unsolvable problems and saying, "The key thing is . . . ." Fat people never say that. They know there isn't any such thing as the key thing about anything.

5 Thin people believe in logic. Fat people see all sides. The sides fat people see are rounded blobs, usually gray, always nebulous and truly not worth worrying about. But the thin person persists. "If you consume more calories than you burn," says one of my thin friends, "you will gain weight. It's that simple." Fat people always grin when they hear statements like that. They know better.

6 Fat people realize that life is illogical and unfair. They know very well that God is not in his heaven and all is not right with the world. If God was up there, fat people could have two doughnuts and a big orange drink anytime they wanted it.

7 Thin people have a long list of logical things they are always spouting off to me. They hold up one finger at a time as they reel off these things, so I won't lose track. They speak slowly as if to a young child. The list is long and full of holes. It contains tidbits like "get a grip on yourself," "cigarettes kill," "cholesterol clogs," "fit as a fiddle," "ducks in a row," "organize," and "sound fiscal management." Phrases like that.

8 They think these 2,000-point plans lead to happiness. Fat people know happiness is elusive at best and even if they could get the kind thin people talk about, they wouldn't want it. Wisely, fat people see that such programs are too dull, too hard, too off the mark. They are never better than a whole cheesecake.

9 Fat people know all about the mystery of life. They are the ones acquainted with the night, with luck, with fate, with playing it by ear. One thin person I know once suggested that we arrange all

the parts of a jigsaw puzzle into groups according to size, shape, and color. He figured this would cut the time needed to complete the puzzle by at least 50 percent. I said I wouldn't do it. One, I like to muddle through. Two, what good would it do to finish early? Three, the jigsaw puzzle isn't the important thing. The important thing is the fun of four people (one thin person included) sitting around a card table, working a jigsaw puzzle. My thin friend had no use for my list. Instead of joining us, he went outside and mulched the boxwoods. The three remaining fat people finished the puzzle and made chocolate, double-fudged brownies to celebrate.

The main problem with thin people is they oppress. Their good intentions, bony torsos, tight ships, neat corners, cerebral machinations, and pat solutions loom like dark clouds over the loose, comfortable, spread-out, soft world of the fat. Long after fat people have removed their coats and shoes and put their feet up on the coffee table, thin people are still sitting on the edge of the sofa, looking neat as a pin, discussing rutabagas. Fat people are heavily into fits of laughter, slapping their thighs and whooping it up, while thin people are still politely waiting for the punch line. 10

Thin people are downers. They like math and morality and reasoned evaluation of the limitations of human beings. They have their skinny little acts together. They expound, prognose, probe, and prick. 11

Fat people are convivial. They will like you even if you're irregular and have acne. They will come up with a good reason why you never wrote the great American novel. They will cry in your beer with you. They will put your name in the pot. They will let you off the hook. Fat people will gab, giggle, guffaw, gallumph, gyrate, and gossip. They are generous, giving, and gallant. They are gluttonous and goodly and great. What you want when you're down is soft and jiggly, not muscled and stable. Fat people know this. Fat people have plenty of room. Fat people will take you in. 12

QUESTIONS ON SUBJECT AND PURPOSE

1. What is the subject of Jordan's essay? What expectations does she think that her audience might have about that subject?
2. What major points of contrast between thin and fat people does Jordan isolate?
3. Is there anything serious about Jordan's essay, or is she just trying to make us laugh?

QUESTIONS ON STRATEGY AND AUDIENCE

1. Does Jordan use the point-by-point or the subject-by-subject pattern for her essay?
2. Would it make any difference if Jordan's essay were written from the other point of view—that is, a thin person making fun of fat people? Why or why not?
3. The essay originally appeared in the "My Turn" column of *Newsweek* magazine. In identifying the author, presumably quoting from something that Jordan wrote about herself, *Newsweek* offered this descriptive sentence: "Stately, plump Jordan teaches English at North Carolina State University." Why?

QUESTIONS ON VOCABULARY AND STYLE

1. Characterize the tone of Jordan's essay. What types of sentence structure does she use most frequently? Does she ever write sentence fragments? What types of words does she use?
2. Why might Jordan use so much alliteration in the final paragraph?
3. Be prepared to define the following words: *condescending* (paragraph 1), *inert* (3), *chortling* (4), *wizened* (4), *surly* (4), *nebulous* (5), *machinations* (10), and *rutabagas* (10).

WRITING SUGGESTIONS

1. **For Your Journal.** It is a rare person who has not at some point in his or her life been the subject of ridicule. Perhaps it had to do with a physical trait (wearing eyeglasses or being very tall), a habit, a lack of coordination, a stupid nickname—whatever. In your journal, explore such a memory. If you wanted to turn that prejudice around, as Jordan does, what would have been your opposite?
2. **For a Paragraph.** Using a tone similar to Jordan's, write a paragraph in which you take one side of a traditional pairing such as:
   - **a.** Short people and tall people
   - **b.** Early risers and late sleepers
   - **c.** Tidy people and sloppy people
   - **d.** Savers and spenders

3. **For an Essay.** Society has many stereotypes, often even conflicting ones. In a serious essay, contrast a pairing such as the ones listed below. Be sure to explore the cultural stereotype(s) that we have constructed.
   - **a.** Smokers and nonsmokers
   - **b.** Drinkers and nondrinkers
   - **c.** Suntanned people and untanned people
   - **d.** Tall people and short people

   Prewriting:
   - **a.** Jot down some possible subjects on a sheet of paper. For each one, describe the stereotype that society has created. What associations immediately come to mind?
   - **b.** Look for public manifestations of that stereotype. For example, how is such a person portrayed on television or in commercials or advertisements? Are there clichés associated with the stereotype?
   - **c.** Free-associate with a group of friends. "When I say ______, what do you think of?" Take notes on their reactions.

   Rewriting:
   - **a.** Look again at how you have arranged your points of contrast. Have you used a subject-by-subject approach or a point-by-point one? Justify your choice of strategy in a sentence or two.
   - **b.** Check each body paragraph. Does each have a single focal point? Does each contain enough detail? Remember that paragraphs should contain more than a couple of sentences but should not go on for a page or more.
   - **c.** Ask two friends or classmates to read your essay and then describe to you what they liked best and least. Listen to them. Do not let them just say that it is good—you want constructive criticism.

4. **For Research.** Select a stereotype that has changed in recent decades, for example, people who smoke cigarettes (or cigars), who have tattoos or body piercings, who ride motorcycles. Research those changing views. One good source of information about earlier attitudes—especially visual examples—would be old issues of popular magazines. Check as well in both general and specialized periodical indexes and databases for shifting public or scholarly attitudes

toward your subject. Be sure to document your sources wherever appropriate.

Website Link

Jordan's essay is about the stereotypes we associate with thin and fat people. Additional information about gender, racial, and ethnic stereotypes—among others—can be found at a number of Websites conveniently listed for you.

Grant and Lee: A Study in Contrasts

Bruce Catton

Born in Petoskey, Michigan, the son of a Congregationalist minister, Bruce Catton (1899–1978) attended Oberlin College in 1916 but left to serve in World War I. After the war, Catton became a journalist, writing for the Cleveland News, *the* Cleveland Plain Dealer, *and the* Boston American, *as well as editing* American Heritage *magazine. Catton won the Pulitzer Prize and the National Book Award for* A Stillness at Appomattox *(1953). This, along with such works as* Mr. Lincoln's Army *(1951) and* This Hallowed Ground *(1956), rank him as one of the country's major Civil War historians, although he never took a college history course. As this essay demonstrates, Catton's approach to history emphasized the personalities of the people who made it. Catton's classic essay was first a radio address, part of a series of broadcasts made by American historians, which he later revised for printed publication.*

On Writing: *In an address to the Society of American Historians, Catton had this to say about writing history: "Any man who undertakes to talk about history as literature ought to begin by expressing his deep conviction that when it becomes literature, history does not cease to be history. . . . If our work has any final value, that value must depend very largely on . . . performing with not only the historian's competence but also with the skill, the insight, and the demanding conscience of the literary artist. If we succeed, the history we write takes its place as literature. Good history is literature."*

BEFORE READING

Connecting: What associations do you already make regarding these two Civil War generals? What do you recall about them?

Anticipating: What is it about Grant and Lee that interests Catton? What do they symbolize for him?

When Ulysses S. Grant and Robert E. Lee met in the parlor of a modest house at Appomattox Court House, Virginia, on April 9, 1865, to work out the terms for the surrender of Lee's Army of 1

Northern Virginia, a great chapter in American life came to a close, and a great new chapter began.

2 These men were bringing the Civil War to its virtual finish. To be sure, other armies had yet to surrender, and for a few days the fugitive Confederate government would struggle desperately and vainly, trying to find some way to go on living now that its chief support was gone. But in effect it was all over when Grant and Lee signed the papers. And the little room where they wrote out the terms was the scene of one of the poignant, dramatic contrasts in American history.

3 They were two strong men, these oddly different generals, and they represented the strengths of two conflicting currents that, through them, had come into final collision.

4 Back of Robert E. Lee was the notion that the old aristocratic concept might somehow survive and be dominant in American life.

5 Lee was tidewater Virginia, and in his background were family, culture, and tradition . . . the age of chivalry transplanted to a New World which was making its own legends and its own myths. He embodied a way of life that had come down through the age of knighthood and the English country squire. America was a land that was beginning all over again, dedicated to nothing much more complicated than the rather hazy belief that all men had equal rights, and should have an equal chance in the world. In such a land Lee stood for the feeling that it was somehow of advantage to human society to have a pronounced inequality in the social structure. There should be a leisure class, backed by ownership of land; in turn, society itself should be keyed to the land as the chief source of wealth and influence. It would bring forth (according to this ideal) a class of men with a strong sense of obligation to the community; men who lived not to gain advantage for themselves, but to meet the solemn obligations which had been laid on them by the very fact that they were privileged. From them the country would get its leadership; to them it could look for the higher values—of thought, of conduct, of personal deportment—to give it strength and virtue.

6 Lee embodied the noblest elements of this aristocratic ideal. Through him, the landed nobility justified itself. For four years, the Southern states had fought a desperate war to uphold the ideals for which Lee stood. In the end, it almost seemed as if the Confederacy fought for Lee; as if he himself was the Confederacy . . . the best thing that the way of life for which the Confederacy stood could ever have to offer. He had passed into legend before

Appomattox. Thousands of tired, underfed, poorly clothed Confederate soldiers, long since past the simple enthusiasm of the early days of the struggle, somehow considered Lee the symbol of everything for which they had been willing to die. But they could not quite put this feeling into words. If the Lost Cause, sanctified by so much heroism and so many deaths, had a living justification, its justification was General Lee.

Grant, the son of a tanner on the Western frontier, was everything Lee was not. He had come up the hard way, and embodied nothing in particular except the eternal toughness and sinewy fiber of the men who grew up beyond the mountains. He was one of a body of men who owed reverence and obeisance to no one, who were self-reliant to a fault, who cared hardly anything for the past but who had a sharp eye for the future. 7

These frontier men were the precise opposites of the tidewater aristocrats. Back of them, in the great surge that had taken people over the Alleghenies and into the opening Western country, there was a deep implicit dissatisfaction with a past that had settled into grooves. They stood for democracy, not from any reasoned conclusion about the proper ordering of human society, but simply because they had grown up in the middle of democracy and knew how it worked. Their society might have privileges, but they would be privileges each man had won for himself. Forms and patterns meant nothing. No man was born to anything, except perhaps to a chance to show how far he could rise. Life was competition. 8

Yet along with this feeling had come a deep sense of belonging to a national community. The Westerner who developed a farm, opened a shop or set up in business as a trader, could hope to prosper only as his own community prospered—and his community ran from the Atlantic to the Pacific and from Canada down to Mexico. If the land was settled, with towns and highways and accessible markets, he could better himself. He saw his fate in terms of the nation's own destiny. As its horizons expanded, so did his. He had, in other words, an acute dollars-and-cents stake in the continued growth and development of his country. 9

And that, perhaps, is where the contrast between Grant and Lee becomes most striking. The Virginia aristocrat, inevitably, saw himself in relation to his own region. He lived in a static society which could endure almost anything except change. Instinctively, his first loyalty would go to the locality in which that society existed. He would fight to the limit of endurance to defend it, because 10 in defending it he was defending everything that gave his own life its deepest meaning.

11 The Westerner, on the other hand, would fight with an equal tenacity for the broader concept of society. He fought so because everything he lived by was tied to growth, expansion, and a constantly widening horizon. What he lived by would survive or fall with the nation itself. He could not possibly stand by unmoved in the face of an attempt to destroy the Union. He would combat it with everything he had, because he could only see it as an effort to cut the ground out from under his feet.

12 So Grant and Lee were in complete contrast, representing two diametrically opposed elements in American life. Grant was the modern man emerging; beyond him, ready to come on the stage, was the great age of steel and machinery, of crowded cities and a restless, burgeoning vitality. Lee might have ridden down from the old age of chivalry, lance in hand, silken banner fluttering over his head. Each man was the perfect champion of his cause, drawing both his strengths and his weaknesses from the people he led.

13 Yet it was not all contrast, after all. Different as they were—in background, in personality, in underlying aspiration—these two great soldiers had much in common. Under everything else, they were marvelous fighters. Furthermore, their fighting qualities were really very much alike.

14 Each man had, to begin with, the great virtue of utter tenacity and fidelity. Grant fought his way down the Mississippi Valley in spite of acute personal discouragement and profound military handicaps. Lee hung on in the trenches at Petersburg after hope itself had died. In each man there was an indomitable quality . . . the born fighter's refusal to give up as long as he can still remain on his feet and lift his two fists.

15 Daring and resourcefulness they had, too; the ability to think faster and move faster than the enemy. These were the qualities which gave Lee the dazzling campaigns of Second Manassas and Chancellorsville and won Vicksburg for Grant.

16 Lastly, and perhaps greatest of all, there was the ability, at the end, to turn quickly from war to peace once the fighting was over. Out of the way these two men behaved at Appomattox came the possibility of a peace of reconciliation. It was a possibility not wholly realized, in the years to come, but which did, in the end, help the two sections to become one nation again . . . after a war whose bitterness might have seemed to make such a reunion wholly

impossible. No part of either man's life became him more than the part he played in their brief meeting in the McLean house at Appomattox. Their behavior there put all succeeding generations of Americans in their debt. Two great Americans, Grant and Lee—very different, yet under everything very much alike. Their encounter at Appomattox was one of the great moments of American history.

QUESTIONS ON SUBJECT AND PURPOSE

1. According to Catton, what were the differences between Grant and Lee? What were the similarities?
2. How were both men representative of America?
3. Why does Catton use contrast to make his main point? What is that point?

QUESTIONS ON STRATEGY AND AUDIENCE

1. How does Catton structure his essay? Does he use the subject-by-subject pattern or the point-by-point pattern?
2. How does the structure of the last four paragraphs differ from that of the first part of the essay?
3. Catton devotes most of the essay to contrasting Grant and Lee. How then does he manage to emphasize finally the similarities between the two? Why does he do so?
4. Catton was a very popular historian of the American Civil War. What would be the range of audiences to whom Catton's essay might appeal? What does Catton expect of his audience?

QUESTIONS ON VOCABULARY AND STYLE

1. How does Catton use paragraphing in his essay to make his argument clearer?
2. Does Catton show any bias in his comparison? Is there any point in the essay when it appears that he favors one man over the other?
3. Be able to define the following words: *poignant* (paragraph 2), *sinewy* (7), *obeisance* (7), *tenacity* (11), *diametrically* (12), *burgeoning* (12), *indomitable* (14).

WRITING SUGGESTIONS

1. **For Your Journal.** If you had to select someone who represented or symbolized something in American society in the late 1990s, who would you choose and why? In your journal, jot down a series of possibilities. To the side of each name, indicate what this particular person seems to represent about our society.
2. **For a Paragraph.** Start with your journal entry for suggestion 1. Who would represent an opposing figure to this person? In a paragraph, pair off the two figures. Be sure to indicate what each represents and why. Given that you are working with just a paragraph, you might want to try the subject-by-subject pattern as an organizational model.
3. **For an Essay.** In an essay, contrast two aspects or segments of American society. Your contrast might be based on geography (the East versus the West), population (rural versus urban), sex (women versus men), age (young versus old), political viewpoint (liberal versus conservative), or a similar opposition. Be careful to avoid stereotypes. Remember as well to have a thesis that explains the significance or reason for making the contrast.

   Prewriting:

   a. Make a list of possible oppositions. Try for at least ten possible topics. Work on your list over a two-day period.

   b. Select two of the most promising and interesting oppositions, and freewrite for twenty minutes about each member of the pair. Do not worry about proofreading what you write; just try to explore your ideas.

   c. Write an explicit and precise thesis statement that explains the significance you see in the opposition.

   Rewriting:

   a. Look at how you organized your essay. Did you use a subject-by-subject, point-by-point, or mixed sequence? Would it be possible to use an arrangement other than the one you chose for the draft? Experiment using photocopies, scissors, and tape or the cut-and-paste function of your word processor.

   b. Find two readers. Once they have finished reading your draft, ask them to answer each of the following questions. First, what is the paper's thesis? Second, which points of contrast seem the most important and which the least? Compare their answers. Do they parallel your own answers to those questions?

c. Honestly evaluate your conclusion. Did you have trouble ending? Put your paper away, and then try freewriting a new ending. Force it to be different from your original conclusion.

4. **For Research.** Choose two figures from history or two people of some current notoriety (for example, politicians, world leaders, entertainers, artists, musicians, athletes, scientists). Research your two subjects. (This will probably be easier to do if your subjects are historical or are controversial.) Then contrast the two in a paper. Remember that there must be some basis or reason—a thesis—that makes it clear why you are contrasting these two people. Be sure to document your sources wherever appropriate.

Website Link

Large, detailed Websites are available for both Ulysses S. Grant and Robert E. Lee. See if historians still agree with Catton's assessment of these two leaders.

VIRTUAL LOVE

Meghan Daum

Meghan Daum graduated from Vassar College and earned an M.F.A. at Columbia University. Her essays and articles have appeared in The New Yorker, The New York Times Book Review, GQ, Vogue *and* Self, *among others. She has contributed to National Public Radio's* This American Life *and currently lives in Lincoln, Nebraska. She is a contributing writer for* Harper's Bazaar. *"Virtual Love" first appeared in* The New Yorker.

On Writing: *Asked about her writing, Daum commented: "The subjects that I find most fascinating concern ideas or events that have not only affected me personally but seem to resonate with the culture at large. Though I am often called a 'confessional' writer, I am less interested in 'confessing' than in using specific experiences as a tool for looking at more general or abstract phenomena in the world. The key to writing about yourself without falling into solipsism is to explore issues that transcend the merely personal and shed a new light on the experiences that many of us share. It also helps to have a sense of humor and respect for the absurdity of life by not taking yourself too seriously."*

BEFORE READING

Connecting: Do you think that it is possible to "fall in love" with someone that you have never met face-to-face?

Anticipating: What is it about this "virtual" relationship that attracts Daum?

1 It was last November; fall was drifting away into an intolerable chill. I was at the end of my twenty-sixth year, and was living in New York City, trying to support myself as a writer, and taking part in the kind of urban life that might be construed as glamorous were it to appear in a memoir in the distant future. At the time, however, my days felt more like a grind than like an adventure: hours of work strung between the motions of waking up, getting the mail, watching TV with my roommates, and going to bed. One morning, I logged on to my America Online account to find a message under the heading "is this the real meghan daum?" It came from someone with the screen name PFSlider. The body of the

message consisted of five sentences, written entirely in lower-case letters, of perfectly turned flattery: something about PFSlider's admiration of some newspaper and magazine articles I had published over the last year and a half, something about his resulting infatuation with me, and something about his being a sportswriter in California.

I was engaged for the thirty seconds that it took me to read the message and fashion a reply. Though it felt strange to be in the position of confirming that I was indeed "the real meghan daum," I managed to say, "Yes, it's me. Thank you for writing." I clicked the "Send Now" icon, shot my words into the void, and forgot about PFSlider until the next day, when I received another message, this one headed "eureka." 2

"wow, it is you," he wrote, still in lower case. He chronicled the various conditions under which he'd read my few-and-far-between articles—a boardwalk in Laguna Beach, the spring-training pressroom for a baseball team that he covered for a Los Angeles newspaper. He confessed to having a crush on me. He referred to me as "princess daum." He said he wanted to have lunch with me during one of his two annual trips to New York. 3

The letter was outrageous and endearingly pathetic, possibly the practical joke of a friend trying to rouse me out of a temporary writer's block. But the kindness pouring forth from my computer screen was bizarrely exhilarating, and I logged off and thought about it for a few hours before writing back to express how flattered and "touched"—this was probably the first time I had ever used that word in earnest—I was by his message. 4

I am not what most people would call a computer person. I have no interest in chat rooms, newsgroups, or most Websites. I derive a palpable thrill from sticking a letter in the United States mail. But I have a constant low-grade fear of the telephone, and I often call people with the intention of getting their answering machines. There is something about the live voice that I have come to find unnervingly organic, as volatile as live television. E-mail provides a useful antidote for my particular communication anxieties. Though I generally send and receive only a few messages a week, I take comfort in their silence and their boundaries. 5

PFSlider and I tossed a few innocuous, smart-assed notes back and forth over the week following his first message. Let's say his name was Pete. He was twenty-nine, and single. I revealed very little about myself, relying instead on the ironic commentary and forced witticisms that are the conceit of so many E-mail messages. 6

But I quickly developed an oblique affection for PFSlider. I was excited when there was a message from him, mildly depressed when there wasn't. After a few weeks, he gave me his phone number. I did not give him mine, but he looked it up and called me one Friday night. I was home. I picked up the phone. His voice was jarring, yet not unpleasant. He held up more than his end of the conversation for an hour, and when he asked permission to call me again I granted it, as though we were of an earlier era.

7 Pete—I could never wrap my mind around his name, privately thinking of him as PFSlider, "E-mail guy," or even "baseball boy"—began phoning me two or three times a week. He asked if he could meet me, and I said that that would be O.K. Christmas was a few weeks away, and he told me that he would be coming back East to see his family. From there, he would take a short flight to New York and have lunch with me.

8 "It is my off-season mission to meet you," he said.

9 "There will probably be a snowstorm," I said.

10 "I'll take a team of sled dogs," he answered.

11 We talked about our work and our families, about baseball and Bill Clinton and Howard Stern and sex, about his hatred for Los Angeles and how much he wanted a new job. Sometimes we'd find each other logged on simultaneously and type back and forth for hours.

12 I had previously considered cyber-communication an oxymoron, a fast road to the breakdown of humanity. But, curiously, the Internet—at least in the limited form in which I was using it—felt anything but dehumanizing. My interaction with PFSlider seemed more authentic than much of what I experienced in the daylight realm of living beings. I was certainly putting more energy into the relationship than I had put into many others. I also was giving Pete attention that was by definition undivided, and relishing the safety of the distance between us by opting to be truthful instead of doling out the white lies that have become the staple of real life. The outside world—the place where I walked around avoiding people I didn't want to deal with, peppering my casual conversations with half-truths, and applying my motto "Let the machine take it" to almost any scenario—was sliding into the periphery of my mind.

13 For me, the time on-line with Pete was far superior to the phone. There were no background noises, no interruptions from "call waiting," no long-distance charges. Through typos and misspellings, he flirted maniacally. "I have an absurd crush on you," he said. "If I like you in person, you must promise to marry me." I

was coy and conceited, telling him to get a life, baiting him into complimenting me further, teasing him in a way I would never have dared to do in person, or even on the phone. I would stay up until 3 A.M. typing with him, smiling at the screen, getting so giddy that when I quit I couldn't fall asleep. I was having difficulty recalling what I used to do at night. It was as if he and I lived together in our own quiet space—a space made all the more intimate because of our conscious decision to block everyone else out. My phone was tied up for hours at a time. No one in the real world could reach me, and I didn't really care.

Since my last serious relationship, I'd had the requisite number of false starts and five-night stands, dates that I wasn't sure were dates, and emphatically casual affairs that buckled under their own inertia. With PFSlider, on the other hand, I may not have known my suitor, but, for the first time in my life, I knew the deal: I was a desired person, the object of a blind man's gaze. He called not only when he said he would call but unexpectedly, just to say hello. He was protected by the shield of the Internet; his guard was not merely down but nonexistent. He let his phone bill grow to towering proportions. He told me that he thought about me all the time, though we both knew that the "me" in his mind consisted largely of himself. He talked about me to his friends, and admitted it. He arranged his holiday schedule around our impending date. He managed to charm me with sports analogies. He didn't hesitate. He was unblinking and unapologetic, all nerviness and balls to the wall. 14

And so PFSlider became my everyday life. All the tangible stuff fell away. My body did not exist. I had no skin, no hair, no bones. All desire had converted itself into a cerebral current that reached nothing but my frontal lobe. There was no outdoors, no social life, no weather. There was only the computer screen and the phone, my chair, and maybe a glass of water. Most mornings, I would wake up to find a message from PFSlider, composed in Pacific time while I slept in the wee hours. "I had a date last night," he wrote. "And I am not ashamed to say it was doomed from the start because I couldn't stop thinking about you." 15

I fired back a message slapping his hand. "We must be careful where we tread," I said. This was true but not sincere. I wanted it, all of it. I wanted unfettered affection, soul-mating, true romance. In the weeks that had elapsed since I picked up "is this the real meghan daum?" the real me had undergone some kind of meltdown—a systemic rejection of all the savvy and independence I had worn for years, like a grownup Girl Scout badge. 16

17 Pete knew nothing of my scattered, juvenile self, and I did my best to keep it that way. Even though I was heading into my late twenties, I was still a child, ignorant of dance steps and health insurance, a prisoner of credit-card debt and student loans and the nagging feeling that I didn't want anyone to find me until I had pulled myself into some semblance of an adult. The fact that Pete had literally seemed to discover me, as if by turning over a rock, lent us an aura of fate which I actually took half-seriously. Though skepticism seemed like the obvious choice in this strange situation, I discarded it precisely because it was the obvious choice, because I wanted a more interesting narrative than cynicism would ever allow. I was a true believer in the urban dream: the dream of years of struggle, of getting a break, of making it. Like most of my friends, I wanted someone to love me, but I wasn't supposed to need it. To admit to loneliness was to smack the face of progress, to betray the times in which we lived. But PFSlider derailed me. He gave me all of what I'd never even realized I wanted.

18 My addiction to PFSlider's messages indicated a monstrous narcissism, but it also revealed a subtler desire, which I didn't fully understand at that time. My need to experience an old-fashioned kind of courtship was stronger than I had ever imagined. And the fact that technology was providing an avenue for such archaic discourse was a paradox that both fascinated and repelled me. Our relationship had an epistolary quality that put our communication closer to the eighteenth century than to the impending millennium. Thanks to the computer, I was involved in a well-defined courtship, a neat little space in which he and I were both safe to express the panic and the fascination of our mutual affection. Our interaction was refreshingly orderly, noble in its vigor, dignified despite its shamelessness. It was far removed from the randomness of real-life relationships. We had an intimacy that seemed custom-made for our strange, lonely times. I seemed custom-made for me.

19 The day of our date, a week before Christmas, was frigid and sunny. Pete was sitting at the bar of the restaurant when I arrived. We shook hands. For a split second, he leaned toward me with his chin, as if to kiss me. He was shorter than I had pictured, though he was not short. He struck me as clean-cut. He had very nice hands. He wore a very nice shirt. We were seated at a very nice table. I scanned the restaurant for people I knew, saw none, and couldn't decide how I felt about that.

20 He talked, and I heard nothing he said. I stared at his profile and tried to figure out whether I liked him. He seemed to be

saying nothing in particular, but he went on forever. Later, we went to the Museum of Natural History and watched a science film about storm chasers. We walked around looking for the dinosaurs, and he talked so much that I wanted to cry. Outside, walking along Central Park West at dusk, through the leaves, past the yellow cabs and the splendid lights of Manhattan at Christmas, he grabbed my hand to kiss me and I didn't let him. I felt as if my brain had been stuffed with cotton. Then, for some reason, I invited him back to my apartment. I gave him a few beers and finally let him kiss me on the lumpy futon in my bedroom. The radiator clanked. The phone rang and the machine picked up. A car alarm blared outside. A key turned in the door as one of my roommates came home. I had no sensation at all—only a clear conviction that I wanted Pete out of my apartment. I wanted to hand him his coat, close the door behind him, and fight the ensuing emptiness by turning on the computer and taking comfort in PFSlider.

When Pete finally did leave, I berated myself from every 21
angle: for not kissing him on Central Part West, for letting him kiss me at all, for not liking him, for wanting to like him more than I had wanted anything in such a long time. I was horrified by the realization that I had invested so heavily in a made-up character—a character in whose creation I'd had a greater hand than even Pete himself. How could I, a person so self-congratulatingly reasonable, have been sucked into a scenario that was more akin to a television talk show than to the relatively full and sophisticated life I was so convinced I led? How could I have received a fan letter and allowed it to go this far?

The next day, a huge bouquet of FTD flowers arrived from 22
him. No one had ever sent me flowers before. I forgave him. As human beings with actual flesh and hand gestures and Gap clothing, Pete and I were utterly incompatible, but I decided to pretend otherwise. He returned home and we fell back into the computer and the phone, and I continued to keep the real world safely away from the desk that held them. Instead of blaming him for my disappointment, I blamed the earth itself, the invasion of roommates and ringing phones into the immaculate communication that PFSlider and I had created.

When I pictured him in the weeks that followed, I saw the 23
image of a plane lifting off over an overcast city. PFSlider was otherworldly, more a concept than a person. His romance lay in the notion of flight, the physics of gravity defiance. So when he offered to send me a plane ticket to spend the weekend with him in

Los Angeles I took it as an extension of our blissful remoteness, a three-dimensional E-mail message lasting an entire weekend.

24 The temperature of the runway at J.F.K. was seven degrees Fahrenheit. Our DC-10 sat for three hours waiting for deicing. Finally, it took off over the frozen city, and the ground below shrank into a drawing of itself. Phone calls were made, laptop computers were plopped onto tray tables. The recirculating air dried out my contact lenses. I watched movies without the sound and told myself that they were probably better that way. Something about the plastic interior of the fuselage and the plastic forks and the din of the air and the engines was soothing and strangely sexy.

25 Then we descended into LAX. We hit the tarmac, and the seat-belt signs blinked off. I hadn't moved my body in eight hours, and now I was walking through the tunnel to the gate, my clothes wrinkled, my hair matted, my hands shaking. When I saw Pete in the terminal, his face seemed to me just as blank and easy to miss as it had the first time I'd met him. He kissed me chastely. On the way out to the parking lot, he told me that he was being seriously considered for a job in New York. He was flying back there next week. If he got the job, he'd be moving within the month. I looked at him in astonishment. Something silent and invisible seemed to fall on us. Outside, the wind was warm, and the Avis and Hertz buses ambled alongside the curb of Terminal 5. The palm trees shook, and the air seemed as heavy and palpable as Pete's hand, which held mine for a few seconds before dropping it to get his car keys out of his pocket. He stood before me, all flesh and preoccupation, and for this I could not forgive him.

26 Gone were the computer, the erotic darkness of the telephone, the clean, single dimension of Pete's voice at 1 A.M. It was nighttime, yet the combination of sight and sound was blinding. It scared me. It turned me off. We went to a restaurant and ate outside on the sidewalk. We strained for conversation, and I tried not to care that we had to. We drove to his apartment and stood under the ceiling light not really looking at each other. Something was happening that we needed to snap out of. Any moment now, I thought. Any moment and we'll be all right. These moments were crowded with elements, with carpet fibres and automobiles and the smells of everything that had a smell. It was all wrong. The physical world had invaded our space.

27 For three days, we crawled along the ground and tried to pull ourselves up. We talked about things that I can no longer remember. We read the Los Angeles *Times* over breakfast. We drove north past Santa Barbara to tour the wine country. I felt

like an object that could not be lifted, something that secretly weighed more than the world itself. Everything and everyone around us seemed imbued with a California lightness. I stomped around the countryside, an idiot New Yorker in my clunky shoes and black leather jacket. Not until I studied myself in the bathroom mirror of a highway rest stop did I fully realize the preposterousness of my uniform. I was dressed for war. I was dressed for my regular life.

That night, in a tiny town called Solvang, we ate an expensive dinner. We checked into a Marriott and watched television. Pete talked at me and through me and past me. I tried to listen. I tried to talk. But I bored myself and irritated him. Our conversation was a needle that could not be threaded. Still, we played nice. We tried to care, and pretended to keep trying long after we had given up. In the car on the way home, he told me that I was cynical, and I didn't have the presence of mind to ask him just how many cynics he had met who would travel three thousand miles to see someone they barely knew. 28

Pete drove me to the airport at 7 A.M. so I could make my eight-o'clock flight home. He kissed me goodbye—another chaste peck that I recognized from countless dinner parties and dud dates. He said that he'd call me in a few days when he got to New York for his job interview, which we had discussed only in passing and with no reference to the fact that New York was where I happened to live. I returned home to frozen January. A few days later, he came to New York, and we didn't see each other. He called me from the plane taking him back to Los Angeles to tell me, through the static, that he had got the job. He was moving to my city. 29

PFSlider was dead. There would be no meeting him in distant hotel lobbies during the baseball season. There would be no more phone calls or E-mail messages. In a single moment, Pete had completed his journey out of our mating dance and officially stepped into the regular world—the world that gnawed at me daily, the world that fostered those five-night stands, the world where romance could not be sustained, because so many of us simply did not know how to do it. Instead, we were all chitchat and leather jackets, bold proclaimers of all that we did not need. But what struck me most about this affair was the unpredictable nature of our demise. Unlike most cyber-romances, which seem to come fully equipped with the inevitable set of misrepresentations and false expectations, PFSlider and I had played it fairly straight. Neither of us had lied. We'd done the best we could. Our affair had died from natural causes rather than virtual ones. 30

31 Within a two-week period after I returned from Los Angeles, at least seven people confessed to me the vagaries of their own E-mail affairs. This topic arose, unprompted, in the course of normal conversation. I heard most of these stories in the close confines of smoky bars and crowded restaurants, and we all shook our heads in bewilderment as we told our tales, our eyes focussed on some point in the distance. Four of these people had met their correspondents, by travelling from New Haven to Baltimore, from New York to Montana, from Texas to Virginia, and from New York to Johannesburg. These were normal people, writers and lawyers and scientists. They were all smart, attractive, and more than a little sheepish about admitting just how deeply they had been sucked in. Mostly, it was the courtship ritual that had seduced us. E-mail had become an electronic epistle, a yearned-for rule book. It allowed us to do what was necessary to experience love. The Internet was not responsible for our remote, fragmented lives. The problem was life itself.

32 The story of PFSlider still makes me sad, not so much because we no longer have anything to do with each other but because it forces me to see the limits and the perils of daily life with more clarity than I used to. After I realized that our relationship would never transcend the screen and the phone—that, in fact, our face-to-face knowledge of each other had permanently contaminated the screen and the phone—I hit the pavement again, went through the motions of everyday life, said hello and goodbye to people in the regular way. If Pete and I had met at a party, we probably wouldn't have spoken to each other for more than ten minutes, and that would have made life easier but also less interesting. At the same time, it terrifies me to admit to a firsthand understanding of the way the heart and the ego are snarled and entwined like diseased trees that have folded in on each other. Our need to worship somehow fuses with our need to be worshipped. It upsets me still further to see how inaccessibility can make this entanglement so much more intoxicating. But I'm also thankful that I was forced to unpack the raw truth of my need and stare at it for a while. It was a dare I wouldn't have taken in three dimensions.

33 The last time I saw Pete, he was in New York, three thousand miles away from what had been his home, and a million miles away from PFSlider. In a final gesture of decency, in what I later realized was the most ordinary kind of closure, he took me out to dinner. As the few remaining traces of affection turned into embarrassed regret, we talked about nothing. He paid the bill. He

drove me home in a rental car that felt as arbitrary and impersonal as what we now were to each other.

Pete had know how to get me where I lived until he came to where I lived: then he became as unmysterious as anyone next door. The world had proved to be too cluttered and too fast for us, too polluted to allow the thing we'd attempted through technology ever to grow in the earth. PFSlider and I had joined the angry and exhausted living. Even if we met on the street, we wouldn't recognize each other, our particular version of intimacy now obscured by the branches and bodies and falling debris that make up the physical world. 34

QUESTIONS ON SUBJECT AND PURPOSE

1. What is a "virtual" love?
2. In paragraph 18, Daum writes, "My need to experience an old-fashioned kind of courtship was stronger than I had ever imagined." How could an Internet romance be old-fashioned?
3. What is Daum saying or implying about "real" relationships in our society?

QUESTIONS ON STRATEGY AND AUDIENCE

1. What is the central contrast in Daum's essay?
2. The essay can be roughly divided into half. Where does the second half of the essay begin? What is the event that begins the second half?
3. Realistically, how large is Daum's audience? That is, to whom is she writing? How did you react to her essay?

QUESTIONS ON VOCABULARY AND STYLE

1. In paragraph 12, Daum writes: "I had previously considered cyber-communication an *oxymoron.*" What is an "oxymoron"? What does she mean by that sentence?
2. Pete accuses Daum of being "cynical" (paragraph 28). What does that mean?
3. Be prepared to define the following words: *construed* (paragraph 1), *palpable* (5), *volatile* (5), *innocuous* (6), *conceit* (6), *periphery* (12), *unfettered* (16), *archaic* (18), *epistolary* (18), *berated* (21), *imbued* (27), *demise* (30), *vagaries* (31).

WRITING SUGGESTIONS

1. **For Your Journal.** Think about the times in your relationships—with a family member, a close friend, someone you were dating, someone to whom you might have been engaged or even married—when you suddenly realized something about the other person that really changed the way in which you "saw" that person. It could be a change for the better or for the worse. What you are looking for basically is a contrast—a before and an after. In your journal, first, make a list of possible subjects and, second, write two sentences for each about the before/after experience.
2. **For a Paragraph.** Using your journal as a prewriting exercise, explore one of these before/after situations in a paragraph.
3. **For an Essay..** Expand your paragraph writing into an essay. Look back at the guidelines for the assignment above. Remember that you are basically working on a contrast—what you had thought or assumed before and the reality that you discovered after.

   Prewriting:

   a. Take a sheet of paper and divide it down the middle. At the top of one column write "before" and at the top of the other "after." Work for a day simply exploring mentally the contrasts and take notes on the sheet of paper.

   b. Look at your sheet of notes—do you see parallel items in both columns? Try arranging these items so that they also fall into a parallel pattern in the body paragraphs of your essay. The parallelism will make it easier for your reader.

   c. Make a trial outline. Daum uses a chronological pattern. She could also have used a flashback. You could also begin with the moment of realization that the other person was not who you thought he or she was. Explore alternate arrangements.

   Rewriting:

   a. Have you used any dialogue? Daum uses just a little. Although dialogue slows down a narrative, it does help to make the characters seem a bit more convincing. See if you might work a little dialogue into your paper. Don't overdo it though.

b. Look critically at your title. Is it really effective, or is it just plain and uninspiring? On another sheet of paper or on your computer screen, write ten different titles. Be silly if necessary; be creative; push yourself to expand your possibilities.
c. Remember that the primary focus in your contrast essay is the realization that you came to—have you made it clear to the reader why you felt as you did in the before stage and in the after stage? Part of the success of Daum's essay is that she reflects on and analyzes why she felt as she did—both before and after.

4. **For Research.** The remarkable thing about Daum's "virtual" relationship was that it was honest—neither person pretended to be different from whom they were; neither "doled out white lies." Why do people often change their identities or their personalities in cyberspace? Research the problem. What you are exploring are the contrasts that occur between people's real life identities and personalities and the virtual identities and personalities that they assume. What do we know about these contrasts? Why do they occur? You might find that databases of articles are better sources for information than your school's on-line library catalog. Check with a reference librarian for search strategy suggestions. Be sure to document any direct quotations, paraphrases, or ideas that you take from your sources.

Website Link

Other essays by Daum are available on-line. Links are available at the *Reader's* Website. Web search engines also turn up a wide variety of sources about on-line courtships.

Sold Out: From Team Booster to TV Backdrop

Susan Faludi

Susan Faludi graduated from Harvard in 1981 as a history and literature major. She was managing editor of the Harvard Crimson, *the student newspaper. Currently a contributing editor to* Newsweek, *she previously wrote for* The Wall Street Journal *and won a Pulitzer Prize in 1991 for labor reporting. Her essays have appeared in magazines such as* The New Yorker, Esquire, *and* The Nation, *and she is the author of* Backlash: The Undeclared War against American Women *(1992), which won the National Book Critics Circle Award for Nonfiction, and* Stiffed: The Betrayal of the American Man *(1999), from which this essay is taken.*

On Writing: *Asked about whether she sees herself as a journalist or as a gender activist, Faludi replied: "I try to throw these ideas out there and pray that others are thinking about them too. My role is as a writer, because that's where I enter public life. For me, being a writer is the best way to be an activist."*

BEFORE READING

Connecting: If you are a "fan" of any sport, how do you see your role? What does a "fan" do? If you have no interest in sports, how do you see those who are "fans"? How would you characterize them?

Anticipating: As you read, ask yourself, what is the central contrast that Faludi is trying to make?

1 On the evening of December 17, 1995, Big Dawg staggered through the door, past his wife, Mary, and collapsed on the couch in their tiny living room. An hour earlier, Mary had seen him on television. Now, she described how the cameras moved in for close-ups when he started crying. He shrugged. "I don't mind it," he said, his voice a monotone.

2 All day long, the reporters had been on him. They had "mugged" him in the parking lot and followed him into the bleachers. "There were so many out-of-town reporters," he said. "Gary

Myers from HBO, and the *Daily News, The New York Times*, the top guys from ESPN. It took me an hour to get a hundred yards." In the stands, three reporters sat with him the entire game, monitoring his every emotion, and wherever he looked, he found himself staring down the barrel of a camera lens. When they asked for his feelings on this, the final day, he stuck with an appropriately updated version of his trusty reply: "Today, it all ended and my best friend died." This was how Big Dawg, aka John Thompson, described the final game that his beloved Cleveland Browns were ever going to play in Municipal Stadium.

The football team's owner, Art Modell, was moving the languishing 50-year-old franchise to Baltimore, where he had struck a sugar plum deal dripping with juicy perks, tax breaks, and government subsidies that guaranteed him an income of $30 million a year regardless of the team's performance or the size of the crowds. The "employees"—the players—would come with him. But he was leaving the fans behind. 3

Big Dawg was not just any Browns fan. He was the self-avowed leader of the Dawg Pound, a rabid pack of men who had turned the decrepit bleachers by the stadium's east end zone into a barking kennel, a howling Greek chorus accompanying the action on the field. "I like to think that the Dawg Pounders are the 12th man," Big Dawg liked to say. *Big* referred to his weight, which hovered around 385 pounds, setting him apart from D. Dawg and Junkyard Dawg, Jam Dawg, Sick Dawg, and Ugly Dawg. For years, most of these men (they were almost all men) had presided over every home game in dog masks and floppy, fake-fur dog ears, greeting every play with a brandishing of foam and rawhide bones, raining dog biscuits onto the field, and offering up a perpetual cacophony of woofs and yelps. Displaying "how they felt." you might say, was their raison d'être. And this had been their last performance. 4

"We won the game." Big Dawg recalled later, "but I sat around after like we had lost." He was hard-pressed to put a name to the nature of his particular loss, although he knew that it was irrevocable and, in some strange way, the source of unspeakable personal shame. He was certain of only one thing. "I want to win," he said, and he looked up at the ceiling wringing his hands as if imploring some deity on high. "I want to win so bad." 5

Football has been a part of American male ritual since the 1890s. It was first embraced on the college gridiron during the great imperial and masculine anxieties of the turn of the century. Its founding father, Walter Camp, was a clock company executive for whom the new sport represented, according to historian 6

Michael Oriard, "the ideal training ground for a managerial elite" who would run a new business world of trusts and combines.

7 But in those prewar days, football had another face as well, one more familiar on the factory floor than in the company boardroom. Pro football, as opposed to college football, was the sport of the steelworker, the ironworker, and the miner, whose faces, long before they were helmeted and smeared with anti-reflective face paint, had been covered with the soot and sweat of manual labor. This version of the game emerged on the soggy, snowbound fields of America's heavy-industrial belt, in gritty contests between underfunded teams with names like the Ironton Tanks and the Providence Steam Roller. In the imaginations of their fans, the players on these gridirons were right out of WPA murals, monumental stone-faced workers come to life and playing out a gruntlike drama on a muddy swath of land under the frosted skies of smokestack America.

8 Conventional wisdom said that spectators flocked to football stadiums precisely because the drama therein celebrated an ascendant American power and authority that they identified with. They were reveling in their nation's empire building, and the more they saw, the more it whetted their appetites. But the fans' relationship to the game was never that conveniently straightforward. For the working-class spectator, "supporting" his team was also a way of fighting against marginalization, a way of clinging to the idea that national destiny was still something played out by common men on a muddy field, even in an era dominated by skyboxes, television, and Astroturf.

9 "One of the great mistakes of superficial observers is to believe that players do all the work while fans merely sit passive and 'vicariously' have things done for them," philosopher and sports devotee Michael Novak has written, describing his own experience watching football as "an ordeal, an exercise, a struggle lived through." Football was a workingman's way of resisting being sidelined, even as he sat in the stands. Here he might still believe himself a central "player" in one of his culture's central dramas. He would be ill-prepared for his ultimate marginalization when the transformation of a sport pumped up by TV and ad revenues, and geared largely to America's sports bars and living rooms, revealed just how passive and insignificant a force he was to his team's fortunes.

10 The Cleveland Browns were hardly the first team to pull up stakes, but their fans had especially good reasons to dread "The End," as Big Dawg called it. The Browns represented a pro football

tradition grounded in loyalty, stoicism, and industry, and conceived in the rivalry of two steelworker communities 50 miles south of Cleveland. The American Professional Football Association, the direct forerunner of the National Football League, was organized in a garage in Canton, Ohio, now home to the Pro Football Hall of Fame. Paul Brown, the founding coach of the Browns, was raised in neighboring Massillon, his father a dispatcher on the railroads that hauled the fruits of industrial labor out of town. At Massillon's Washington High School, in the depths of the Depression, coach Brown created a brand of play that would earn him the title "father of modern pro football." He also created something else at Massillon: the modern football fan.

The meaning of that creation was made clear to me by a 62- 11
year-old Massillonian named Phil Glick. A 1951 Washington High School graduate, Glick had been a lifelong parts sizer at Timken Roller Bearing Company in Canton until 1992, when he opted for early retirement over the risk of being laid off. He was also a fan extraordinaire whose devotion to his high school football team, the Massillon Tigers, led to his election as president of the Massillon Tigers Football Booster Club.

His vintage boosterism had less to do with spectatorship or 12
expropriation of the players' fame than with community service—being know for doing something useful and supportive. The Massillon boosters weren't "fans" as we now understand the word; they were care providers, and the recipients of their care were young athletes. "It's sort of like Big Brothers, except with a player," Glick explained of the Sideliners, the first Massillon booster club he helped guide. Each Sideliner "adopts" a player, becoming a surrogate father who is responsible for the boy's needs and there to help him when he is in trouble. Some Sideliners help with homework; some make sure their players are properly clothed and provided for; others offer postgraduation advice.

Sports fans as paternal providers was Paul Brown's notion. 13
Once the town fathers were invested in the young men's welfare, Brown calculated, they would also be invested in the team's future, and he was right. Brown had given the men of Massillon a special paternal stake in the game. Every Monday night, he would show the Boosters Club films of the previous game and ruminate with them about the upcoming contest. At one point, interest was so great that 2,500 fans showed up for an outdoor briefing.

The team repaid fan devotion with a legendary record that 14
elevated Massillon to "the capital of high school football in the nation." In the nine years Paul Brown coached them, the Tigers won

80 games and lost only 8. Six times the Tigers prevailed in the Ohio state championships and twice they were named national champions. When Brown finally left in 1940 for a coaching job at Ohio State, it was on the wings of a 33-game winning streak.

15 While the townsmen reclaimed their breadwinning roles with the Depression's end, supporting the team gave them something assembly-line jobs at the steel mills didn't: a sense that they were more than cogs in a corporate machine. To the Tigers Boosters, the team belonged to them—its triumphs were legitimately theirs. It put their small town on the map at a time when national manufacturers, national brands, and national entertainment were beginning to erase small-town identities. "The proprietors in town explain it this way," a local accountant commented: "Some poor guy might work eight hours a day down the street at the steel mill and be a nobody, but for 10 weeks every fall, he's a king because he's from Massillon."

16 For a man to have a hand in the making of a team's fortunes, at a time when the making of everything else was fast slipping out of his grasp, was the root of what it meant to be a "fan." He could, in the common parlance, help "build a winner." The field became an artisan's workshop where products could still be made locally and custom crafted.

17 In 1946, Brown took his winning formula to Cleveland, and fans there would prove as intensely devoted and ecstatically loyal as those he left in Massillon. But as the years passed, a painful role reversal would take place. It was evident in a large photograph framed and hanging behind the desk of Robert Gries Jr., who was, like his father before him, a minority owner of the Browns. A passionate Clevelander whose family's philanthropic and civic commitment to the city spans five generations, Gries divested himself of his holdings in the team rather than profit from the move to Baltimore. While we spoke in his office one afternoon, Gries rose and turned to study a photograph on the wall—a black-and-white shot from a 1953 game at Municipal Stadium. "This was the first time the stadium was full for a football game. And look at it. What do you see? There's something here that's very different."

18 The hats? I ventured. Because every man—and the stands were virtually all male—was wearing a fedora, along with a suit and tie.

19 "Yes. It's the hats," Gries said, eyes still fixed on the photo. "Hats and suits. And this was in the end zone." The very seats to which the Dawg Pounders would eventually lay claim.

Gries' father was part of the original group of men who first 20
organized in 1936 to bring football to Cleveland. His father's motives, Gries Jr. recalled, were "civic, totally civic. My father was not a 'fan.'" Nor were his motives fiscal. "There wasn't money in football in those days. . . . It was the idea of bringing something to Cleveland."

Much later, a crucial difference between those fedoras and 21
the bill caps of today would strike me. The fedora was the haberdashery of a man in a position to give, an adult man with some sense of his value and purpose in a civic society into which he blended seamlessly. The cap was the garb of a boy, a man-child still waiting for his inheritance, still hoping to be ushered in by the male authorities and given a sign, a badge, perhaps a fedora, to indicate his induction into adult society. The Massillon boosters had backed their team with such enthusiasm because it was a way literally to give a boost, a leg up, to the next generation; they had embraced their role as supporters because it allowed them to father a team. A generation later, fans like Big Dawg were seeking exactly the opposite; they were looking for a team to father them. For these new-era fans, the hope was that the team would be their boosters.

The members of the original Browns team had entered 22
football older, many of them already experienced in the world of work, not to mention the cauldron of war. They weren't depending on football to be their masculine crucible. But a younger generation joining the Browns in the late '50s and early '60s had come of age under the shadow of the postwar corporation, and they had a more vulnerable, more uneasy relationship to a "master organizer" like Paul Brown. They didn't feel like good soldiers, they felt like impotent yes-men. They came directly from school, not war, and resented Brown's acting *in loco parentis*. Most of them had arrived at training camp expecting that inside its gates lay the key to adult recognition, which the coach would deliver.

So the players rebelled against and eventually overthrew Paul 23
Brown, and adopted a big brother in his place: Art Modell, who bought the Browns in 1961 for the then unheard-of price of $4 million. He was only 35, and his claim to fame heretofore had been producing, in 1949, New York's first daytime television show, *Melodies*, which played on TV sets installed in supermarkets to whet the consumer appetites of female shoppers.

Modell was thrilled to be in the presence of these young 24
American centurions, and unlike Paul Brown, he was accessible

and adoring, more like one of the boys than a father figure. He acted at first like a boy with an autograph book—"a goggle-eyed fan," as Bernie Parrish put it, "overly impressed with us as players."

25 As a TV producer, Modell understood that the future of football lay in the medium that would eventually command every team owner's loyalties. Modell would become a key player in brokering the ascendance of football as a televised sport; he chaired the National Football League's television committee for 31 years. He helped create *Monday Night Football.* He was in on the breakthrough $14 million sale of TV rights to CBS in 1964, and helped to negotiate a four-year $656 million deal with the networks in 1977—the first time the league earned more from television than from ticket sales.

26 The new media culture changed the way the game was played and the relationship not only between the sport and its players but also between the sport and its fans. In the new relationship, the players would be the superstars and fans their wide-eyed idolizers. The players were to become the fly-boys, the astronauts, and all that was left for the average fan to do, it seemed, was watch from his living room couch.

27 In the process, the players—not just in football but in baseball and basketball as well—would gain much. No longer could owners keep them for their short careers in a state of near peonage, controlling their every move. Now, players found themselves in a lively labor market where they could bargain and negotiate.

28 Television and ad money had decoupled them from servitude, but also from the very idea of "the team," from any concept of loyalty to anything except perhaps their own agents, their own careers, their own images. But the freer many of them became, the less independent they often felt. To market themselves, after all, they were forced to market images of themselves in a culture where sports was increasingly just that—a series of images played and replayed between all the car and beer ads in the living rooms of America. It was no mistake that the new sports "stars" like Browns fullback Jim Brown would sometimes go on to act in Hollywood movies or would become TV sports announcers and personalities introducing the next generation of stars—and their media-wise quirks—to the public.

29 Much has been written about how televised football sliced the game into consumable bits sandwiched between commercials, forced the use of injurious Astroturf because it was prettier to look at, turned the sport into a big-stakes money machine, and so forth. But what did it do to the fans?

At first, the only "fans" who seemed to have a visible role were the cheerleaders. It was no coincidence that at the same time football began to be televised, the male "yell captains" of college football were replaced with pom-pom girls. By the late '70s, most pro football teams had a corps of cheerleaders, none so extravagantly unclothed as the Dallas Cowboys', who became a business institution in their own right, complete with a line of costume jewelry and trading cards. The yell captains had connected the fans with the action on the field, but the pom-pom girls became an entertainment concession at the service of the cameras. Meanwhile, the new male fans, the ones the advertisers salivated over, were increasingly not in the stands. By the '80s many of them would be huddled at sports bars, gazing up like so many worshippers at the TV pulpit posted over their heads, framed by Bud Lite signs. The boosters were long gone. Reshaped in Modell's own image would be the "goggle-eyed fan." Which is to say that, in the end, the fans would be betrayed by one of their own. 30

The stadiums would increasingly become the preserves of an upper crust as ticket prices rose out of the range of the average working-class salary. The men pro football had originally promised to speak for and glorify—the hardworking factory workers of what was now becoming the rust belt—were the ones most shut out and turned off in the transition to an electronic age. Football's television viewers were more white-collar, middle-management, and suburban—more likely to have the wherewithal to buy the high-ticket items being advertised on-screen than the traditional working-class ethnic audience. Paul Brown had started out seeking to elevate pro football into a "high-class" realm. From the beginning in Massillon, class transformation had been a tacit part of the program of the boosters who were football's founding fans. But instead of pulling up the working-class community that football represented, the Modells of the sport left those who belonged to that world behind. 31

This betrayal of the sports boosters did not, however, come without a fight—especially in Cleveland, where the fans were unwilling to relinquish a long-standing relationship. But, as the team entered the '90s, the fans who had donned dog faces and hard hats found themselves face to face with a truth they had been desperately trying to dodge. The battle now was for the camera's attention. The show of hard hats, of dog suits, of toughing it out in the rain and the snow, in the end became exactly that—a show, a beauty contest of sorts, where the object was to attract the camera with bizarre caricatures of working stiffs. They, too, had become 32 just more entertaining images for the real fans of this new age, the consumers watching TV.

QUESTIONS ON SUBJECT AND PURPOSE

1. Another subheading for the essay in its magazine appearance was "the demise of the true fan." What does that subheading mean or suggest to you?
2. According to Faludi, what happened to change the role of the fan?
3. In the final paragraph, what is Faludi implying about the men who made up the "dog pound"?

QUESTIONS ON STRATEGY AND AUDIENCE

1. The story of Big Dawg's reaction to the final game takes five paragraphs. What is the effect of such a long example? Did you find that it caught your attention?
2. At the end of paragraph 5, Big Dawg says: "I want to win. . . . I want to win so bad." What does Big Dawg mean by that observation, and how does it tie into Faludi's essay?
3. Who did Faludi imagine her audience to be? Is it men like Big Dawg? What evidence could you cite to support your answer?

QUESTIONS ON VOCABULARY AND STYLE

1. In paragraph 16, Faludi writes, "The field became an artisan's workshop where products could still be made locally and custom crafted." What figure of speech is she using?
2. What is a "fedora"? Can you guess by the context in which it is used (paragraph 18)? Check the word in a dictionary and write down the formal definition and the word's origin.
3. Be prepared to define the following words: *languishing* (3), *cacophony* (4), *raison d'être* (4), *irrevocable* (5), *vicariously* (9), *expropriation* (12), *ruminate* (13), *parlance* (16), *peonage* (27), *tacit* (31).

WRITING SUGGESTIONS

1. **For Your Journal.** How would you characterize the "fans" at athletic events at your school? Visit a game—in any

sport—and make some notes. Are the students "into" the game? In what ways? Is their behavior in any way unusual? Just concentrate on recording what you see.

2. **For a Paragraph.** In a paragraph develop a contrast between two different types of fans, perhaps between "fans" of different sports (football versus tennis), between male and female fans, between fans of men's teams versus those of women's teams.
3. **For an Essay.** Expand your paragraph writing into a comparison and contrast essay. Remember that like Faludi you are, first, listing significant contrasts (not everything you can think of) and, second, offering some analysis for or explanation of what you observe.

Prewriting:

a. Remember that your primary sources of information are observations and interviews. Be sure to plan ahead so that you can visit several games and talk with fans. This is not an essay that you will be able to write the night before it is due unless you have gathered information ahead of time.

b. Are you contrasting point-by-point or subject-by-subject? Make an outline for your working plan to make sure that you have maintained parallelism in the points that you are making throughout the essay.

c. Draft a thesis statement for your paper, making sure that it is precise. Your paper needs to make a definite point about the differences that you see.

Rewriting:

a. Look over your paper carefully. Have you focused on the significant contrasts—those that seem especially important or significant?

b. Do you have an effective introduction? Have you used a "hook" or a "thesis" introduction? Either one will work, but remember that to be effective an introduction has to pull the reader into an essay. Make a copy of your introduction and try it out on some classmates or friends.

c. Make a copy of the list of "Some Things to Remember" at the end of the introduction to this chapter. Give a copy of that checksheet and a copy of your paper to a classmate to read. Ask your reader to use the checklist to critique what you have written.

4. **For Research.** Have other sports seen the same changes that football has? Choose a professional or collegiate sport, and in a research paper compare and contrast what has happened to that sport during the twentieth century. Have the players changed in any way? Have the rules of the sport? Have the conditions under which it was played? Is the sport more corrupt? More professional? More indifferent to its fans? Focus on a single sport, looking at it from two or more time periods. Be sure to document your sources.

Website Link

Listen to a twenty-five-minute interview with Susan Faludi online and read several interviews about her latest book, *Stiffed*, from which this essay is taken.

Process

What do a recipe in a cookbook, a discussion of how the body converts food into energy and fat, a description of how igneous rocks are formed, and three sentences from your college's registration office on how to drop or add a course have in common? Each is a process analysis—either a set of directions for how to do something (make lasagna or drop a course) or a description of how something happens or is done (food is converted or rocks are formed). These two different types of process writing have two different purposes.

The function of a set of directions is to allow the reader to duplicate the process. For example, *The Amy Vanderbilt Complete Book of Etiquette* offers the following step-by-step advice to the young executive woman about how to handle paying for a business lunch or dinner.

> No one likes a man who is known never to pick up a check. In today's world, people are going to feel the same about a woman who is known never to pick up a tab. The woman executive is going to have to learn how to pay gracefully when it's her turn.
>
> In order to save embarrassment all around, who will pay for the next business lunch should be decided without question in advance. If it's a woman's turn, she should make it very clear over the telephone or face to face when the appointment is made that she will be paying. She has only to say with a smile that it really *is* her turn. She should name the time and the place, call the restaurant, and make the reservation in her name.
>
> At the end of lunch she should unobtrusively ask for the bill, add the waiter's tip to the total without an agonizing exercise in mathematics, and then use her credit card or sign her name and her company's address to the back of the check (if she

> has a charge account there). If she does this quietly, no one around them need be aware of her actions.

Several readings in this chapter similarly offer advice or instructions. Lars Eighner in "My Daily Dives in the Dumpster" describes both how to "dive" into dumpsters and what the process eventually taught him about life and human acquisitiveness. Diane Cole offers the reader suggestions on how to respond to distasteful and bigoted remarks. Charlie Drozdyk offers advice to soon-to-graduate college students on how to "get the job you want after graduation."

As noted in the opening of this chapter, not every example of process is a set of directions about how to do something. Process can also be used to tell the reader how something happens or is made. Harold McGee, for example, explains to his readers how chewing gum, the quintessential American product, is made. McGee's paragraph is not a recipe. Instead, its function is to provide a general view of the manufacturing process.

> Today, chewing gum is made mostly of synthetic polymers, especially styrene-butadiene rubber and polyvinyl acetate, though 10 to 20% of some brands is still accounted for by chicle or jelutong, a latex from the Far East. The crude gum base is first filtered, dried, and then cooked in water until syrupy. Powdered sugar and corn syrup are mixed in, then flavorings and softeners—vegetable oil derivatives that make the gum easier to chew—and the material is cooked, kneaded to an even, smooth texture, cut, rolled thin, and cut again into strips, and packaged. The final product is about 60% sugar, 20% corn syrup, and 20% gum materials.

Diane Ackerman tells us "Why Leaves Turn Color in the Fall." Judith Viorst in "How Books Helped Shape My Life" and Lynne Sharon Schwartz in "The Page Turner" both describe a process, but not one meant to be performed or imitated by the reader. Viorst describes her own process of maturing by looking at the books that shaped the various stages of her life; Schwartz describes the process of watching a concert from the viewpoint of an audience member who, in turn, focuses on the process followed by the pianist's page turner.

How Do You Choose a Subject to Write About?

Choosing a subject is not a problem if you have been given a specific assignment—to describe how a congressional bill becomes a law, how a chemistry experiment was performed, how to write an A paper for your English course. Often, however, you have to choose your own subject. Several considerations are crucial in making that decision.

First, choose a subject that can be adequately described or analyzed in the space you have available. When Judith Viorst in "How Books Helped Shape My Life" catalogs the heroines with whom she identified on her "journey into young womanhood," she isolates six examples, one from each stage of her own development. She does not try to identify every influential heroine or every possible influence; she confines her analysis to these six examples.

Second, in a process analysis, as in any other writing assignment, identify the audience to whom you are writing. What does that audience already know about your subject? Are you writing to a general audience, an audience of your fellow classmates, or a specialized audience? You do not want to bore your reader with the obvious, nor do you want to lose your reader in a tangle of unfamiliar terms and concepts. Your choice of subject and certainly your approach to it should be determined by your audience. Charlie Drozdyk's essay on job-seeking strategies for young college students appeared in *Rolling Stone* magazine; to appeal to readers of this publication, he focused on interviewing people who held relatively "glamorous" positions in publishing, on Wall Street, in advertising, in fashion design, in interior design, and in television. Judith Viorst's essay originally appeared in *Redbook*, a magazine that targets its audience as "women 18–34 years old," a group of readers who would identify with Viorst's experience. Identifying your audience—what they might be interested in, what they already know—will help in both selecting a subject and deciding on how or what to write about it. Subjects can generally be approached from a number of points of view. A process essay on how to apply eye makeup reaches a large but still limited audience (women who wear eye makeup), but an essay explaining the process of developing, testing, and marketing a new brand of eye makeup would have, potentially, a much broader audience.

How Do You Structure a Process Paper?

If you have ever tried to assemble something from a set of directions, you know how important it is that each step or stage in the process be clearly defined and properly placed in the sequence. Because process always involves a series of events or steps that must be done or must occur in proper order, the fundamental structure for a process paragraph or essay will be chronological.

Since proper order is essential, begin your planning by making a list of the various steps in the process. Once your list seems complete, arrange the items in the order in which they are performed or in which they occur. Check to make sure that nothing has been omitted or misplaced. If your process is a description of how to do or make something, you should check your arranged list by performing the process according to the directions you have assembled so far. This ordered list will serve as the outline for your process paper.

Converting your list or outline into a paragraph or an essay is the next step. Be sure that all of the phrases on your outline have been turned into complete sentences and that any technical terms have been carefully explained for your reader. You will need some way of signaling to your reader each step or stage in the process. On your list, you simply numbered the steps, but in your paragraph or essay you generally cannot use such a device. More commonly, process papers employ various types of step or time markers to indicate order. Step markers like *first*, *second*, and *third* can be used at the beginning of sentences or paragraphs devoted to each individual stage. Time markers like *begin*, *next*, *in three minutes*, or *while this is being done* remind the reader of the proper chronological sequence. Diane Ackerman in "Why Leaves Turn Color in the Fall" carefully uses time markers to indicate stages in the sequence ("When the days begin to shorten," "by the end of autumn," "at first," "then").

Sample Student Essay

As part of her student-teaching assignment, Julie Anne Halbfish was asked by her cooperating teacher to write out a set of directions on how to play dreidel, a game associated with the Jewish holiday Hanukkah. Most of the students in the seventh-grade class in which Julie was student-teaching had never played the game.

EARLIER DRAFT

HOW TO PLAY DREIDEL

A dreidel is a small top with four sides. On each side is a Hebrew letter. The letters correspond to the first letters in each word of the Hebrew phrase "*Nes gadol haya sham*," which means "A great miracle happened there." That phrase refers to the military victory of the Maccabees over the Greeks and the story of the small jug of olive oil that burned for eight days. The corresponding Hebrew letters on the dreidel are called *nun* [נ], *gimel* [ג], *hay* [ה], and *shin* [ש].

Many people have heard the Hanukkah song "Dreidel," but most are unfamiliar with how to play the traditional children's game of the same name. The rules are actually quite simple.

To start the game, every player receives ten pieces of "money" (usually peanuts, candies, pennies, or anything else the players choose to play for) and a dreidel. Each player puts two pieces of money into the "pot" and then spins the dreidel. When the dreidel stops spinning, the letter that is on the side facing up determines how many pieces the player takes from or adds to the pot. If the dreidel lands on *nun*, the player takes nothing. If it lands on *gimel*, the player takes all of the pot. If the dreidel lands on *hay*, the player receives half of the pot. Finally, if the dreidel lands on *shin*, the player must put two additional pieces into the pot. After as many rounds of play as the players want, the game ends, and whoever has the most goodies is declared the winner. However, the reason so many people love this game is that everyone ends up with treats to enjoy, so nobody loses.

After Julie had finished a draft of her essay, she showed her paper to Adam Helenic, a fellow classmate. At first, Adam simply praised the draft—"It's good; it's clear; it's fine, Julie." But Julie would not settle for simple approval. When pushed, Adam made several suggestions. Since many students have heard the dreidel song, he urged her somehow to work at least part of the song into the essay—maybe as an attention-getting introduction. He also suggested that she reorder paragraphs 1 and 2 and that she tighten up her prose in a number of places. When Julie revised her set of directions, she tried to incorporate all of the changes that Adam had suggested. Interestingly, when Julie set out to check her "facts" about the song and the game, she used the World Wide Web. She found a computerized dreidel game that you might like to try (you can play at *http://www.jcn18.com/spinner.htm*).

REVISED DRAFT

HOW TO PLAY DREIDEL

I have a little dreidel,
I made it out of clay.
And when it's dry and ready,
Oh, dreidel I shall play!

• • • • • •

It has a lovely body,
With legs so short and thin.
And when it gets all tired,
It drops and then I win.

During Hanukkah, we often hear the "Dreidel" song, but most people have never actually played the traditional children's game to which the song refers. The game is quite simple, and since every player is sure to win something, dreidel is a popular Hanukkah game.

A dreidel is a small, four-sided top, traditionally made out of clay. On each side is a Hebrew letter. The letters correspond to the first letters in each word of the Hebrew phrase "Nes gadol haya sham," which means "A great miracle happened there." That phrase refers to the military victory of the Maccabees over the Greeks and the story of the small jug of olive oil that miraculously burned for eight days. The corresponding Hebrew letters on the dreidel are called nun [נ], gimel [ג], hay [ה], and shin [ש].

To start the game, every player receives ten pieces of "money" (usually peanuts, candies, pennies, or anything else the players choose to play for) and a dreidel. Each player puts two pieces of money into the "pot" and then spins the dreidel. When the dreidel is spinning, the players are encouraged to sing a Hanukkah song or to shout "Gimel!" When the dreidel stops spinning, the letter that is on the side facing up determines how many pieces the player takes from or adds to the pot. If the dreidel lands on nun, the player takes nothing. If it lands on gimel, the player takes all of the pot. If the dreidel lands on hay, the player receives half of the pot. Finally, if the dreidel lands on shin, the player must put two additional pieces into the pot.

After as many rounds of play as the players want, the game ends, and whoever has the most goodies is declared the winner. Whether you win or not, no one really loses since everyone ends up with treats to enjoy.

Some Things to Remember

1. Choose a subject that can be analyzed and described within the space you have available.
2. Remember that process takes one of two forms, reflecting its purpose: either to tell the reader how to do something or to tell the reader how something happens. Make sure that you have a purpose clearly in mind before you start your paper.
3. Identify your audience and write to that audience. Ask yourself, "Will my audience be interested in what I am writing about?" and "How much does my audience know about this subject?"
4. Make a list of the steps or stages in the process.
5. Order or arrange a list, checking to make sure nothing is omitted or misplaced.
6. Convert the list into paragraphs using complete sentences. Remember to define any unfamiliar terms or concepts.
7. Use step or time markers to indicate the proper sequence in the process.
8. Check your process one final time to make sure that nothing has been omitted. If you are describing how to do something, use your paper as a guide to the process. If you are describing how something happens, ask a friend to read your process analysis to see whether it is clear.

Using Process in Writing for Your Other Courses

Writing that explains processes is common in the sciences, where you may often be asked to demonstrate your understanding of natural biological or physical processes by tracing them in detail. Although less common in the humanities, writing assignments requiring this pattern do turn up with some frequency in courses that deal with contemporary institutions and culture, courses that focus on any aspect of human development, and courses for which writing instructions might be part of the curriculum. Here are some examples of writing assignments that would require you to use the process pattern.

- **Life Sciences.** On an exam, you might be asked to trace the life cycle of a particular organism.
- **Communications.** For a research project on the telecommunications industry, you might write a paper recounting the stages involved in the development of a new television series.
- **Computer Science.** As part of a team developing an original software program, you might be asked to write a user's manual documenting how to use the program.
- **American Government.** On an essay exam, you might be asked to examine in detail the procedure by which a bill is introduced in Congress and ultimately enacted into law.
- **Physical Education.** As part of teacher training, you might be asked to write out instructions for a particular game or exercise.
- **Psychology.** For a short paper on learning disabilities, you might trace the cognitive process that results in the reversal of letters that troubles many dyslexic readers.

Visualizing Process

Any set of illustrated instructions is a perfect example of process at work: First, attach piece A to piece B with fastener C. As anyone who has ever assembled anything knows, illustrated, step-by-step instructions are vitally important. Mere words aren't enough; illustrations must accompany the text. Not every process narrative, however, tells us how to do something. Process can also be used to explain to us how something is done or how it works. This short, illustrated article on the Zamboni ice-resurfacing machine is an

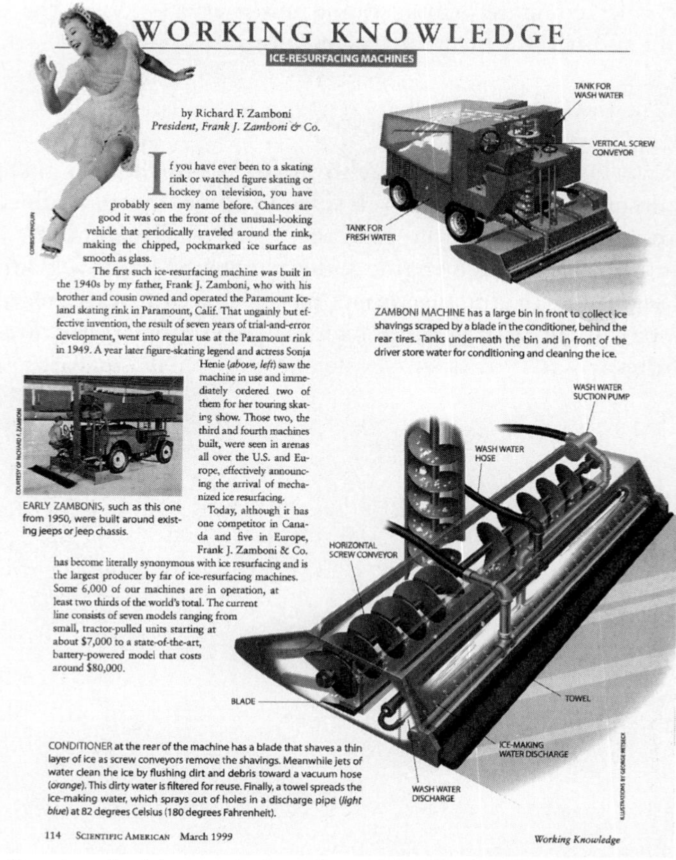

WORKING KNOWLEDGE

ICE-RESURFACING MACHINES

by Richard F. Zamboni
President, Frank J. Zamboni & Co.

If you have ever been to a skating rink or watched figure skating or hockey on television, you have probably seen my name before. Chances are good it was on the front of the unusual-looking vehicle that periodically traveled around the rink, making the chipped, pockmarked ice surface as smooth as glass.

The first such ice-resurfacing machine was built in the 1940s by my father, Frank J. Zamboni, who with his brother and cousin owned and operated the Paramount Iceland skating rink in Paramount, Calif. That ungainly but effective invention, the result of seven years of trial-and-error development, went into regular use at the Paramount rink in 1949. A year later figure-skating legend and actress Sonja Henie (*above, left*) saw the machine in use and immediately ordered two of them for her touring skating show. Those two, the third and fourth machines built, were seen in arenas all over the U.S. and Europe, effectively announcing the arrival of mechanized ice resurfacing.

Today, although it has one competitor in Canada and five in Europe, Frank J. Zamboni & Co. has become literally synonymous with ice resurfacing and is the largest producer by far of ice-resurfacing machines. Some 6,000 of our machines are in operation, at least two thirds of the world's total. The current line consists of seven models ranging from small, tractor-pulled units starting at about $7,000 to a state-of-the-art, battery-powered model that costs around $80,000.

CORBIS/PENGUIN

COURTESY OF RICHARD F. ZAMBONI

EARLY ZAMBONIS, such as this one from 1950, were built around existing jeeps or jeep chassis.

ZAMBONI MACHINE has a large bin in front to collect ice shavings scraped by a blade in the conditioner, behind the rear tires. Tanks underneath the bin and in front of the driver store water for conditioning and cleaning the ice.

CONDITIONER at the rear of the machine has a blade that shaves a thin layer of ice as screw conveyors remove the shavings. Meanwhile jets of water clean the ice by flushing dirt and debris toward a vacuum hose (*orange*). This dirty water is filtered for reuse. Finally, a towel spreads the ice-making water, which sprays out of holes in a discharge pipe (*light blue*) at 82 degrees Celsius (180 degrees Fahrenheit).

ILLUSTRATIONS BY GEORGE RETSECK

114 Scientific American March 1999 *Working Knowledge*

example of a visualized process. The illustrations that accompany the text allow us to understand how an ice resurfacing machine works.

Visit the Prentice Hall Reader's Website

When you have finished reading an essay, check out the additional material available at the *Reader's* Website at www.prenhall.com/ miller. For each reading, you will find a list of related readings connected with the topic or the author; additional background information; a group of relevant "hot-linked" web resources (just click your computer's mouse and automatically visit the sites listed); and still more writing suggestions.

Describing a Process

The World Wide Web is home to thousands of "how to . . ." process descriptions. Using a Web search engine, locate a subject of interest to you. Better yet, read the "help with searching" notes on your favorite search engine and learn how to improve your online searching techniques. Some possible sites to explore, along with paragraph writing assignments, can be found at the *Reader's* Website.

Why Leaves Turn Color in the Fall

Diane Ackerman

Diane Ackerman, a poet and nature writer, was born in Waukegan, Illinois, in 1948. During her twenties, she published three books of poetry while earning an M.F.A. and a Ph.D. in English from Cornell University. Widely regarded as a gifted lyric poet, she incorporates a surprising amount of scientific fact into her work, breaking through the traditional barrier between poetry and science. Ackerman has also published books of nonfiction that exhibit the same unquenchable curiosity and precise metaphor that characterize her poetry. A prolific writer and editor, Ackerman's most recent book of poems is I Praise My Destroyer *(1998).*

"Why Leaves Turn Color in the Fall" is from A Natural History of the Senses *(1990), a bestselling book that has been called an "encyclopedia of the senses" and "an intriguing assortment of history, biology, anthropology, cultural fact, and folklore, woven together with poetic inspiration to celebrate the faculties of human perception."*

On Writing: *Both poet and prose writer, Ackerman commented: "When I write prose, I don't fret about the prose rhythm of the whole chapter. I don't think in large structures like that, although I know fiction writers who do. I understand the general architecture of the book—I outline the book so I do know what I'm going to be writing. But, I write it tiny piece by tiny piece and worry about how each word will fit. I think that my structures are smaller."*

BEFORE READING

Connecting: For understandable reasons, we rarely think about the wonders of the natural processes that surround us. Think about something that is happening in the natural world around you right now—the blue sky, the wind, clouds, snow, blooming flowers. Can you explain how that something is happening?

Anticipating: In what ways does Ackerman's account of the coloring of leaves seem different from what you might expect to read in a science textbook?

1 The stealth of autumn catches one unaware. Was that a goldfinch perching in the early September woods, or just the first turning leaf? A red-winged blackbird or a sugar maple closing up shop for the winter? Keen-eyed as leopards, we stand still and squint hard, looking for signs of movement. Early-morning frost sits heavily on the grass, and turns barbed wire into a string of stars. On a distant hill, a small square of yellow appears to be a lighted stage. At last the truth dawns on us: Fall is staggering in, right on schedule, with its baggage of chilly nights, macabre holidays, and spectacular, heart-stoppingly beautiful leaves. Soon the leaves will start cringing on the trees, and roll up in clenched fists before they actually fall off. Dry seedpods will rattle like tiny gourds. But first there will be weeks of gushing color so bright, so pastel, so confettilike, that people will travel up and down the East Coast just to stare at it—a whole season of leaves.

2 Where do the colors come from? Sunlight rules most living things with its golden edicts. When the days begin to shorten, soon after the summer solstice on June 21, a tree reconsiders its leaves. All summer it feeds them so they can process sunlight, but in the dog days of summer the tree begins pulling nutrients back into its trunk and roots, pares down, and gradually chokes off its leaves. A corky layer of cells forms at the leaves' slender petioles, then scars over. Undernourished, the leaves stop producing the pigment chlorophyll, and photosynthesis ceases. Animals can migrate, hibernate, or store food to prepare for winter. But where can a tree go? It survives by dropping its leaves, and by the end of autumn only a few fragile threads of fluid-carrying xylem hold leaves to their stems.

3 A turning leaf stays partly green at first, then reveals splotches of yellow and red as the chlorophyll gradually breaks down. Dark green seems to stay longest in the veins, outlining and defining them. During the summer, chlorophyll dissolves in the heat and light, but it is also being steadily replaced. In the fall, on the other hand, no new pigment is produced, and so we notice the other colors that were always there, right in the leaf, although chlorophyll's shocking green hid them from view. With their camouflage gone, we see these colors for the first time all year, and marvel, but they were always there, hidden like a vivid secret beneath the hot glowing greens of summer.

4 The most spectacular range of fall foliage occurs in the northeastern United States and in eastern China, where the leaves are robustly colored, thanks in part to a rich climate. European maples don't achieve the same flaming reds as their American

relatives, which thrive on cold nights and sunny days. In Europe, the warm, humid weather turns the leaves brown or mildly yellow. Anthocyanin, the pigment that gives apples their red and turns leaves red or red-violet, is produced by sugars that remain in the leaf after the supply of nutrients dwindles. Unlike the carotenoids, which color carrots, squash, and corn, and turn leaves orange and yellow, anthocyanin varies from year to year, depending on the temperature and amount of sunlight. The fiercest colors occur in years when the fall sunlight is strongest and the nights are cool and dry (a state of grace scientists find vexing to forecast). This is also why leaves appear dizzyingly bright and clear on a sunny fall day: The anthocyanin flashes like a marquee.

Not all leaves turn the same colors. Elms, weeping willows, and the ancient ginkgo all grow radiant yellow, along with hickories, aspens, bottlebrush buckeyes, cottonweeds, and tall, keening poplars. Basswood turns bronze, birches bright gold. Water-loving maples put on a symphonic display of scarlets. Sumacs turn red, too, as do flowering dogwoods, black gums, and sweet gums. Though some oaks yellow, most turn a pinkish brown. The farmlands also change color, as tepees of cornstalks and bales of shredded-wheat-textured hay stand drying in the fields. In some spots, one slope of a hill may be green and the other already in bright color, because the hillside facing south gets more sun and heat than the northern one. 5

An odd feature of the colors is that they don't seem to have any special purpose. We are predisposed to respond to their beauty, of course. They shimmer with the colors of sunset, spring flowers, the tawny buff of a colt's pretty rump, the shuddering pink of a blush. Animals and flowers color for a reason—adaptation to their environment—but there is no adaptive reason for leaves to color so beautifully in the fall any more than there is for the sky or ocean to be blue. It's just one of the haphazard marvels the planet bestows every year. We find the sizzling colors thrilling, and in a sense they dupe us. Colored like living things, they signal death and disintegration. In time, they will become fragile and, like the body, return to dust. They are as we hope our own fate will be when we die: Not to vanish, just to sublime from one beautiful state into another. Though leaves lose their green life, they bloom with urgent colors, as the woods grow mummified day by day, and Nature becomes more carnal, mute, and radiant. 6

We call the season "fall," from the Old English *feallan*, to fall, which leads back through time to the Indo-European *phol*, which also means to fall. So the word and the idea are both 7 extremely ancient, and haven't really changed since the first of our kind needed a name for fall's leafy abundance. As we say the word, we're reminded of that other Fall, in the garden of Eden, when fig leaves never withered and scales fell from our eyes. Fall is the time when leaves fall from the trees, just as spring is when flowers spring up, summer is when we simmer, and winter is when we whine from the cold.

8 Children love to play in piles of leaves, hurling them into the air like confetti, leaping into soft unruly mattresses of them. For children, leaf fall is just one of the odder figments of Nature, like hailstones or snowflakes. Walk down a lane overhung with trees in the never-never land of autumn, and you will forget about time and death, lost in the sheer delicious spill of color. Adam and Eve concealed their nakedness with leaves, remember? Leaves have always hidden our awkward secrets.

9 But how do the colored leaves fall? As a leaf ages, the growth hormone, auxin, fades, and cells at the base of the petiole divide. Two or three rows of small cells, lying at right angles to the axis of the petiole, react with water, then come apart, leaving the petioles hanging on by only a few threads of xylem. A light breeze, and the leaves are airborne. They glide and swoop, rocking in invisible cradles. They are all wing and may flutter from yard to yard on small whirlwinds or updrafts, swiveling as they go. Firmly tethered to earth, we love to see things rise up and fly—soap bubbles, balloons, birds, fall leaves. They remind us that the end of a season is capricious, as is the end of life. We especially like the way leaves rock, careen, and swoop as they fall. Everyone knows the motion. Pilots sometimes do a maneuver called a "falling leaf," in which the plane loses altitude quickly and on purpose, by slipping first to the right, then to the left. The machine weighs a ton or more, but in one pilot's mind it is a weightless thing, a falling leaf. She has seen the motion before, in the Vermont woods where she played as a child. Below her the trees radiate gold, copper, and red. Leaves are falling, although she can't see them fall, as she falls, swooping down for a closer view.

10 At last the leaves leave. But first they turn color and thrill us for weeks on end. Then they crunch and crackle underfoot. They *shush*, as children drag their small feet through leaves heaped along the curb. Dark, slimy mats of leaves cling to one's heels after a rain. A damp, stuccolike mortar of semidecayed leaves protects the tender shoots with a roof until spring, and makes a rich humus. An occasional bulge or ripple in the leafy mounds signals a shrew or a field mouse tunneling out of sight. Sometimes one finds in fossil stones the imprint of a leaf, long since disintegrated,

whose outlines remind us how detailed, vibrant, and alive are the things of this earth that perish.

QUESTIONS ON SUBJECT AND PURPOSE

1. According to Ackerman, why do leaves turn color?
2. From the point of view of a naturalist, what is surprising about the fact that fall leaves offer such a vivid show of color?
3. Obviously, Ackerman is not writing a textbook explanation of why leaves turn color and fall. What then does she seem to be doing?

QUESTIONS ON STRATEGY AND AUDIENCE

1. How does Ackerman use process in her essay?
2. In paragraph 7, Ackerman digresses to discuss the significance of the word *fall.* How is this material related to the point she is trying to make in the essay?
3. What assumptions does Ackerman make about her audience?

QUESTIONS ON VOCABULARY AND STYLE

1. How effective is Ackerman's introductory paragraph? What is she trying to do?
2. What figure of speech is Ackerman using in each of the following examples:
   - **a.** "Keen-eyed as leopards . . ." (paragraph 1)
   - **b.** "Early-morning frost sits heavily on the grass . . ." (1)
   - **c.** "The anthocyanin flashes like a marquee." (4)
   - **d.** "Children love to play in piles of leaves, hurling them into the air like confetti, leaping into soft unruly mattresses of them." (8)
3. Be prepared to define the following words: *stealth* (paragraph 1), *edicts* (2), *petioles* (2), *xylem* (2), *vexing* (4), *dupe* (6), *carnal* (6), *tethered* (9), *capricious* (9), *careen* (9).

WRITING SUGGESTIONS

1. **For Your Journal.** Observe the physical world around you. Select a natural phenomenon that is occurring, one that you would like to have explained. Brainstorm a list of promising

topics. Do not worry about trying to explain each; just try to find phenomena that seem promising subjects.

2. **For a Paragraph.** In an interview, Ackerman once observed that she tries to be "open," to be "completely available to experience every second." In contrast, probably most of the time we are "closed"—we ignore the sea of sense impressions that surround us. Select an experience and try to be open. Record the experience as it happens using a process strategy. You do not need to explain how something happens scientifically; instead, explain how you perceive and experience it.
3. **For an Essay.** Using the paragraph-writing strategy outlined in item 2, write an essay in which you record how and what you perceive in a sensory experience—a sound, a sight, a taste, a touch. Focus this time on what the experience reveals either about yourself or about the world. Do not just record; record for a reason, developing a thesis that controls your essay.

   Prewriting:

   a. Gather experiences for at least two days. Try out or pay attention to a variety of sensory experiences. Remember, you are not looking for the bizarre or the shocking. You want to see the extraordinary in the ordinary.

   b. Select two of the most promising experiences, and freewrite for fifteen minutes about each. At the end, try to sum up in each case your central observations.

   c. Select an organizational order. What options do you have in arranging the middle of the essay? Experiment with at least two different patterns.

   Rewriting:

   a. Look again at your thesis statement. Is it precise? Are you making an assertion about this experience and what it reveals?

   b. Ask a peer reader or a classmate to read over your essay. Then show your reader your thesis statement. Does the essay reflect that statement?

   c. Never underestimate the power of a good title. Try to write at least six different titles for your paper. Ask some friends to comment on each.

4. **For Research.** Go back to your journal writing in item 1, and choose one of the topics that you put on your list.

Research the phenomenon. Reference books in your college's library might be a good place to start. On-line databases and the World Wide Web might also provide good information. In a research paper, explain how the phenomenon works. Try, as Ackerman does, to provoke a little mystery or wonder. Be sure to acknowledge all of your sources wherever appropriate.

Website Link

You can read a pair of interviews with Diane Ackerman and, if you are interested in nature, check out the Websites for a number of nature magazines.

My Daily Dives in the Dumpster

Lars Eighner

Born in 1948, Lars Eighner grew up in Houston, Texas. He attended the University of Texas at Austin but dropped out before graduation to do social work. In the mid-1980s, he lost his job as an attendant at a mental institution, which launched him on a three-year nightmare as a homeless person, with his dog, Lizbeth, as his companion. After publishing short stories in a variety of periodicals aimed at gay audiences, Eighner began to attract mainstream attention with the publication of short essays about homelessness in the Threepenny Review, *the* Utne Reader, *and* Harper's *in the late 1980s. He later reworked these as a book,* Travels with Lizbeth *(1993), the final manuscript of which was written on a personal computer that Eighner found in a dumpster.*

On Writing: *Advice from Eighner's Website: "The best thing you can do for your writing is to learn to revise effectively. Sure, some natural geniuses may never have to revise a word, but the number of writers who consider themselves geniuses must outnumber the true geniuses by a factor of a thousand. And yes, some writers who practice revision for a long time eventually learn to avoid most mistakes so that their first drafts do not need much revision. But everyone else needs to* revise and revise and revise. *Putting a work through a spelling checker or a grammar checker is not revision. . . . Revision means changing words and phrases and sometimes changing whole sentences and paragraphs. Almost everyone's writing needs this kind of revision."*

BEFORE READING

Connecting: If you came across someone "diving" into a dumpster, what assumptions would you be likely to make about that person?

Anticipating: One would hope that few of Eighner's readers will ever have to dive into dumpsters to survive. What then can readers learn from his essay?

1 I began Dumpster diving about a year before I became homeless.

I prefer the term "scavenging" and use the word "scrounging" when I mean to be obscure. I have heard people, evidently meaning to be polite, use the word "foraging," but I prefer to reserve that word for gathering nuts and berries and such, which I do also, according to the season and opportunity. 2

I like the frankness of the word "scavenging." I live from the refuse of others. I am a scavenger. I think it a sound and honorable niche, although if I could I would naturally prefer to live the comfortable consumer life, perhaps—and only perhaps—as a slightly less wasteful consumer owing to what I have learned as a scavenger. 3

Except for jeans, all my clothes come from Dumpsters. Boom boxes, candles, bedding, toilet paper, medicine, books, a typewriter, a virgin male love doll, change sometimes amounting to many dollars: All came from Dumpsters. And, yes, I eat from Dumpsters too. 4

There are a predictable series of stages that a person goes through in learning to scavenge. At first the new scavenger is filled with disgust and self-loathing. He is ashamed of being seen and may lurk around trying to duck behind things, or he may try to dive at night. (In fact, this is unnecessary, since most people instinctively look away from scavengers.) 5

Every grain of rice seems to be a maggot. Everything seems to stink. The scavenger can wipe the egg yolk off the found can, but he cannot erase the stigma of eating garbage from his mind. 6

This stage passes with experience. The scavenger finds a pair of running shoes that fit and look and smell brand-new. He finds a pocket calculator in perfect working order. He finds pristine ice cream, still frozen, more than he can eat or keep. He begins to understand: People do throw away perfectly good stuff, a lot of perfectly good stuff. 7

At this stage he may become lost and never recover. All the Dumpster divers I have known come to the point of trying to acquire everything they touch. Why not take it, they reason, it is all free. This is, of course, hopeless, and most divers come to realize that they must restrict themselves to items of relatively immediate utility. 8

The finding of objects is becoming something of an urban art. Even respectable, employed people will sometimes find something tempting sticking out of a Dumpster or standing beside one. Quite a number of people, not all of them of the bohemian 9 type, are willing to brag that they found this or that piece in the trash.

10 But eating from Dumpsters is the thing that separates the dilettanti from the professionals. Eating safely involves three principles: using the senses and common sense to evaluate the condition of the found materials; knowing the Dumpsters of a given area and checking them regularly; and seeking always to answer the question, Why was this discarded?

11 Perhaps everyone who has a kitchen and a regular supply of groceries has, at one time or another, eaten half a sandwich before discovering mold on the bread, or has gotten a mouthful of milk before realizing the milk had turned. Nothing of the sort is likely to happen to a Dumpster diver because he is constantly reminded that most food is discarded for a reason.

12 Yet perfectly good food can be found in Dumpsters. Canned goods, for example, turn up fairly often in the Dumpsters I frequent. All except the most phobic people would be willing to eat from a can even if it came from a Dumpster. I have few qualms about dry foods such as crackers, cookies, cereal, chips, and pasta if they are free of visible contaminates and still dry and crisp. Raw fruits and vegetables with intact skins seem perfectly safe to me, excluding, of course, the obviously rotten. Many are discarded for minor imperfections that can be pared away. Chocolate is often discarded only because it has become discolored as the cocoa butter de-emulsified.

13 I began scavenging by pulling pizzas out of the Dumpster behind a pizza delivery shop. In general, prepared food requires caution, but in this case I knew what time the shop closed and went to the Dumpster as soon as the last of the help left.

14 Because the workers at these places are usually inexperienced, pizzas are often made with the wrong topping, baked incorrectly, or refused on delivery for being cold. The products to be discarded are boxed up because inventory is kept by counting boxes: A boxed pizza can be written off; an unboxed pizza does not exist. So I had a steady supply of fresh, sometimes warm pizza.

15 The area I frequent is inhabited by many affluent college students. I am not here by chance; the Dumpsters are very rich. Students throw out many good things, including food, particularly at the end of the semester and before and after breaks. I find it advantageous to keep an eye on the academic calendar.

16 A typical discard is a half jar of peanut butter—though nonorganic peanut butter does not require refrigeration and is unlikely

to spoil in any reasonable time. Occasionally I find a cheese with a spot of mold, which, of course, I just pare off, and because it is obvious why the cheese was discarded, I treat it with less suspicion than an apparently perfect cheese found in similar circumstances. One of my favorite finds is yogurt—often discarded, still sealed, when the expiration date has passed—because it will keep for several days, even in warm weather.

I avoid ethnic foods I am unfamiliar with. If I do not know what it is supposed to look or smell like when it is good, I cannot be certain I will be able to tell if it is bad. 17

No matter how careful I am I still get dysentery at least once a month, oftener in warm weather. I do not want to paint too romantic a picture. Dumpster diving has serious drawbacks as a way of life. 18

Though I have a proprietary feeling about my Dumpsters, I don't mind my direct competitors, other scavengers, as much as I hate the sodacan scroungers. 19

I have tried scrounging aluminum cans with an able-bodied companion, and afoot we could make no more than a few dollars a day. I can extract the necessities of life from the Dumpsters directly with far less effort than would be required to accumulate the equivalent value in aluminum. Can scroungers, then, are people who *must* have small amounts of cash—mostly drug addicts and winos. 20

I do not begrudge them the cans, but can scroungers tend to tear up the Dumpsters, littering the area and mixing the contents. There are precious few courtesies among scavengers, but it is a common practice to set aside surplus items: pairs of shoes, clothing, canned goods, and such. A true scavenger hates to see good stuff go to waste, and what he cannot use he leaves in good condition in plain sight. Can scroungers lay waste to everything in their path and will stir one of a pair of good shoes to the bottom of a Dumpster to be lost or ruined in the muck. They become so specialized that they can see only cans and earn my contempt by passing up change, canned goods, and readily hockable items. 21

Can scroungers will even go through individual garbage cans, something I have never seen a scavenger do. Going through individual garbage cans without spreading litter is almost impossible, and litter is likely to reduce the public's tolerance of scavenging. But my strongest reservation about going through individual garbage cans is that this seems to me a very personal kind of invasion, one to which I would object if I were a homeowner. 22

Though Dumpsters seem somehow less personal than garbage cans, they still contain bank statements, bills, correspondence, pill 23 bottles, and other sensitive information. I avoid trying to draw conclusions about the people who dump in the Dumpsters I frequent. I think it would be unethical to do so, although I know many people will find the idea of scavenger ethics too funny for words.

24 Occasionally a find tells a story. I once found a small paper bag containing some unused condoms, several partial tubes of flavored sexual lubricant, a partially used compact of birth control pills, and the torn pieces of a picture of a young man. Clearly, the woman was through with him and planning to give up sex altogether.

25 Dumpster things are often sad—abandoned teddy bears, shredded wedding albums, despaired-of sales kits. I find diaries and journals. College students also discard their papers; I am horrified to discover the kind of paper that now merits an A in an undergraduate course.

26 Dumpster diving is outdoor work, often surprisingly pleasant. It is not entirely predictable; things of interest turn up every day, and some days there are finds of great value. I am always very pleased when I can turn up exactly the thing I most wanted to find. Yet in spite of the element of chance, scavenging, more than most other pursuits, tends to yield returns in some proportion to the effort and intelligence brought to bear.

27 I think of scavenging as a modern form of self-reliance. After ten years of government service, where everything is geared to the lowest common denominator, I find work that rewards initiative and effort refreshing. Certainly I would be happy to have a sinecure again, but I am not heart-broken to be without one.

28 I find from the experience of scavenging two rather deep lessons. The first is to take what I can use and let the rest go. I have come to think that there is no value in the abstract. A thing I cannot use or make useful, perhaps by trading, has no value, however fine or rare it may be. (I mean useful in the broad sense—some art, for example, I would think valuable.)

29 The second lesson is the transience of material being. I do not suppose that ideas are immortal, but certainly they are longer-lived than material objects.

30 The things I find in Dumpsters, the love letters and rag dolls of so many lives, remind me of this lesson. Many times in my travels I have lost everything but the clothes on my back. Now I hardly pick up a thing without envisioning the time I will cast it away. This, I think, is a healthy state of mind. Almost everything I have now has already been cast out at least once, proving that what I own is valueless to someone.

I find that my desire to grab for the gaudy bauble has been largely sated. I think this is an attitude I share with the very wealthy—we both know there is plenty more where whatever we have came from. Between us are the rat-race millions who have confounded their selves with the objects they grasp and who nightly scavenge the cable channels looking for they know not what. 31

I am sorry for them. 32

QUESTIONS ON SUBJECT AND PURPOSE

1. Is the subject of Eighner's essay simply how to "dive" into a dumpster? What other points does he make?
2. A substantial part of the essay deals with scavenging for food. Why does Eighner devote so much space to this?
3. What larger or more general lesson or truth does Eighner see in his experiences? For example, for whom does Eighner say he feels sorry at the end of the essay?

QUESTIONS ON STRATEGY AND AUDIENCE

1. In what ways does the essay use process as a writing strategy?
2. What are the "predictable stages" that a scavenger goes through?
3. What assumptions does Eighner make about his audience?

QUESTIONS ON VOCABULARY AND STYLE

1. Why does Eighner prefer the term *scavenging* to a more ambiguous or better-sounding term?
2. In what way is Eighner's final sentence ironic? Why might he choose to make it a separate paragraph?
3. Be prepared to define the following words: *niche* (paragraph 3), *stigma* (6), *pristine* (7), *bohemian* (9), *dilettanti* (10), *phobic* (12), *qualms* (12), *de-emulsified* (12), *affluent* (15), *proprietary* (19), *sinecure* (27), *transience* (29), *gaudy* (31), *bauble* (31), *sated* (31).

WRITING SUGGESTIONS

1. **For Your Journal.** Suppose that suddenly you found yourself without a full-time job or financial support from your family. What would you do? Using an ordered sequence,

plan out the steps that you would take in trying to deal with the situation.

2. **For a Paragraph.** In a world in which many Americans can find only low-paying jobs with no benefits, what advice could you offer to a young high school student today? In a paragraph organized according to a process structure, address that audience. Be sure to have a specific point or thesis to your paragraph. Try to avoid clichéd answers; just saying "go to college," for example, is not particularly good advice since many college students are not able to find well-paying, full-time jobs.
3. **For an Essay.** Where are you going in your life, and how do you plan to get there? What are your objectives, goals, or aspirations? Where do you hope to be in ten years? In twenty years? What are you doing now to try to achieve those goals? What should you be doing? In an essay, honestly examine your directions and your actions.

   Prewriting:

   a. Brainstorm a list of objectives, goals, or aspirations. Be as specific as possible. Try to think ten years into the future.

   b. Beside each item on your list, make another list of the steps that you are now taking that will help you reach that goal. If you find that you are having trouble with either list, you will need to spend some time trying to connect your goals with your current actions.

   c. Establish an order for your actions—what is most important and least important? Begin to establish the order you will use to present points as you develop the body of your essay.

   Rewriting:

   a. Check to see if your process sequence—"here is what I am doing to achieve my goals"—is clearly structured. Outline the middle of your essay as a way of checking that structure.

   b. Have you tried to confront the question honestly? Have you relied on clichéd answers? Ask a friend to read your essay and to respond to those two questions.

   c. Look again at both your introduction and your conclusion. Do you catch the reader's interest in your introduction? Do you have a clear statement of your thesis?

Does your conclusion simply repeat what you said in your introduction? Or do you end, as Eighner does, on a thought-provoking note?

4. **For Research.** With corporate and business "downsizing," many Americans have suddenly found themselves out of work. As advice for those trapped in such a situation, write a guide to the resources available to the newly unemployed. Use a process strategy as a way of providing step-by-step advice to your audience. Contact local and state agencies to see what help is available and how one goes about making an application. Be sure to document your sources—including interviews—wherever appropriate.

Website Link

Eighner has a home page on the Web that includes a wide range of information about his books, his other publications, and a bibliography of articles about him and his work. Check the Website.

Don't Just Stand There

Diane Cole

Diane Cole was born in Baltimore, Maryland, in 1952. Educated at Radcliffe College (B.A.) and Johns Hopkins University (M.A.), she is a freelance journalist well versed in psychological issues, such as the "fear of finishing," and women's career issues, such as networking and professional ladder climbing. Her most recent book, co-authored with Scott Wetzler, is Is It You or Is It Me?: How We Turn Our Emotions Inside Out and Blame Each Other *(1998). "Don't Just Stand There" originally appeared as part of a national campaign against bigotry in a special supplement to* The New York Times *titled "A World of Difference" (April 16, 1989), sponsored by the Anti-Defamation League of B'nai B'rith.*

On Writing: *In an article about her life as a writer, Cole wrote: "I've been scribbling things down for as long as I can remember. . . . And when [my fourth-grade teacher] encouraged me to keep on writing I thought: Maybe it's possible, maybe I can become a writer one day. And there was also the desire—maybe the need—to leave my mark, by writing something that would somehow be of use to others, whether it entertained, gave solace, provided practical information, or simply made another person smile."*

BEFORE READING

Connecting: Can you remember a time when you were told a joke that maligned your national or ethnic origin, race, religion, gender, sexual orientation, or age? How did you respond?

Anticipating: According to Cole and the experts that she cites, what are improper responses to such distasteful or bigoted remarks?

1 It was my office farewell party, and colleagues at the job I was about to leave were wishing me well. My mood was one of ebullience tinged with regret, and it was in this spirit that I spoke to the office neighbor to whom I had waved hello every morning for the past two years. He smiled broadly as he launched into a long, rambling story, pausing only after he delivered the punch line. It was a very long pause because, although he laughed, I did not: This joke was unmistakably anti-Semitic.

I froze. Everyone in the office knew I was Jewish; what could he have possibly meant? Shaken and hurt, not knowing what else to do, I turned in stunned silence to the next well-wisher. Later, still angry, I wondered, what else should I—could I—have done? 2

Prejudice can make its presence felt in any setting, but hearing its nasty voice in this way can be particularly unnerving. We do not know what to do and often we feel another form of paralysis as well: We think, "Nothing I say or do will change this person's attitude, so why bother?" 3

But left unchecked, racial slurs and offensive ethnic jokes "can poison the atmosphere," says Michael McQuillan, adviser for racial/ethnic affairs for the Brooklyn borough president's office. "Hearing these remarks conditions us to accept them; and if we accept these, we can become accepting of other acts." 4

Speaking up may not magically change a biased attitude, but it can change a person's behavior by putting a strong message across. And the more messages there are, the more likely a person is to change that behavior, says Arnold Kahn, professor of psychology at James Madison University, Harrisonburg, Va., who makes this analogy: "You can't keep people from smoking in *their* house, but you can ask them not to smoke in *your* house." 5

At the same time, "Even if the other party ignores or discounts what you say, people always reflect on how others perceive them. Speaking up always counts," says LeNorman Strong, director of campus life at George Washington University, Washington, D.C. 6

Finally, learning to respond effectively also helps people feel better about themselves, asserts Cherie Brown, executive director of the National Coalition Building Institute, a Boston-based training organization. "We've found that, when people felt they could at least in this small way make a difference, that made them more eager to take on other activities on a larger scale," she says. Although there is no "cookbook approach" to confronting such remarks—every situation is different, experts stress—these are some effective strategies. 7

When the "joke" turns on who you are—as a member of an ethnic or religious group, a person of color, a woman, a gay or lesbian, an elderly person, or someone with a physical handicap—shocked paralysis is often the first response. Then, wounded and vulnerable, on some level you want to strike back. 8

Lashing out or responding in kind is seldom the most effective response, however. "That can give you momentary satisfaction, but you also feel as if you've lowered yourself to that other 9 person's level," Mr. McQuillan explains. Such a response may further label you in the speaker's mind as thin-skinned, someone not to be taken seriously. Or it may up the ante, making the speaker, and then you, reach for new insults—or physical blows.

10 "If you don't laugh at the joke, or fight, or respond in kind to the slur," says Mr. McQuillan, "that will take the person by surprise, and that can give you more control over the situation." Therefore, in situations like the one in which I found myself—a private conversation in which I knew the person making the remark—he suggests voicing your anger calmly but pointedly: "I don't know if you realize what that sounded like to me. If that's what you meant, it really hurt me."

11 State how *you* feel, rather than making an abstract statement like, "Not everyone who hears that joke might find it funny." Counsels Mr. Strong: "Personalize the sense of 'this is how I feel when you say this.' That makes it very concrete"—and harder to dismiss.

12 Make sure you heard the words and their intent correctly by repeating or rephrasing the statement: "This is what I heard you say. Is that what you meant?" It's important to give the other person the benefit of the doubt because, in fact, he may *not* have realized that the comment was offensive and, if you had not spoken up, would have had no idea of its impact on you.

13 For instance, Professor Kahn relates that he used to include in his exams multiple-choice questions that occasionally contained "incorrect funny answers." After one exam, a student came up to him in private and said, "I don't think you intended this, but I found a number of those jokes offensive to me as a woman." She explained why. "What she said made immediate sense to me," he says. "I apologized at the next class, and I never did it again."

14 But what if the speaker dismisses your objection, saying, "Oh, you're just being sensitive. Can't you take a joke?" In that case, you might say, "I'm not so sure about that, let's talk about that a little more." The key, Mr. Strong says, is to continue the dialogue, hear the other person's concerns, and point out your own. "There are times when you're just going to have to admit defeat and end it," he adds, "but I have to feel that I did the best I could."

15 When the offending remark is made in the presence of others—at a staff meeting, for example—it can be even more distressing than an insult made privately.

16 "You have two options," says William Newlin, director of field services for the Community Relations division of the New York City Commission on Human Rights. "You can respond

immediately at the meeting, or you can delay your response until afterward in private. But a response has to come."

Some remarks or actions may be so outrageous that they cannot go unnoted at the moment, regardless of the speaker or the setting. But in general, psychologists say, shaming a person in public may have the opposite effect of the one you want: The speaker will deny his offense all the more strongly in order to save face. Further, few people enjoy being put on the spot, and if the remark really was not intended to be offensive, publicly embarrassing the person who made it may cause an unnecessary rift or further misunderstanding. Finally, most people just don't react as well or thoughtfully under a public spotlight as they would in private. 17

Keeping that in mind, an excellent alternative is to take the offender aside afterward: "Could we talk for a minute in private?" Then use the strategies suggested above for calmly stating how you feel, giving the speaker the benefit of the doubt, and proceeding from there. 18

At a large meeting or public talk, you might consider passing the speaker a note, says David Wertheimer, executive director of the New York City Gay and Lesbian Anti-Violence Project: You could write, "You may not realize it, but your remarks were offensive because . . ." 19

"Think of your role as that of an educator," suggests James M. Jones, Ph.D., executive director for public interest at the American Psychological Association. "You have to be controlled." 20

Regardless of the setting or situation, speaking up always raises the risk of rocking the boat. If the person who made the offending remark is your boss, there may be an even bigger risk to consider: How will this affect my job? Several things can help minimize the risk, however. First, know what other resources you may have at work, suggests Caryl Stern, director of the A World of Difference–New York City campaign: Does your personnel office handle discrimination complaints? Are other grievance procedures in place? 21

You won't necessarily need to use any of these procedures, Ms. Stern stresses. In fact, she advises, "It's usually better to try a one-on-one approach first." But simply knowing a formal system exists can make you feel secure enough to set up that meeting. 22

You can also raise the issue with other colleagues who heard the remark: Did they feel the same way you did? The more support you have, the less alone you will feel. Your point will also carry more validity and be more difficult to shrug off. Finally, give your boss credit—and the benefit of the doubt: "I know you've worked 23 hard for the company's affirmative action programs, so I'm sure you didn't realize what those remarks sounded like to me as well as the others at the meeting last week. . . ."

24 If, even after this discussion, the problem persists, go back for another meeting, Ms. Stern advises. And if that, too, fails, you'll know what other options are available to you.

25 *It's a spirited dinner party, and everyone's having a good time, until one guest starts reciting a racist joke. Everyone at the table is white, including you. The others are still laughing, as you wonder what to say or do.*

26 No one likes being seen as a party-pooper, but before deciding that you'd prefer not to take on this role, you might remember that the person who told the offensive joke has already ruined your good time.

27 If it's a group that you feel comfortable in—a family gathering, for instance—you will feel freer to speak up. Still, shaming the person by shouting "You're wrong!" or "That's not funny!" probably won't get your point across as effectively as other strategies. "If you interrupt people to condemn them, it just makes it harder," says Cherie Brown. She suggests trying instead to get at the resentments that lie beneath the joke by asking open-ended questions: "Grandpa, I know you always treat everyone with such respect. Why do people in our family talk that way about black people?" The key, Ms. Brown says, "is to listen to them first, so they will be more likely to listen to you."

28 If you don't know your fellow guests well, before speaking up you could turn discreetly to your neighbors (or excuse yourself to help the host or hostess in the kitchen) to get a reading on how they felt, and whether or not you'll find support for speaking up. The less alone you feel, the more comfortable you'll be speaking up: "I know you probably didn't mean anything by that joke, Jim, but it really offended me. . . ." It's important to say that *you* were offended—not state how the group that is the butt of the joke would feel. "Otherwise," LeNorman Strong says, "you risk coming off as a goody two-shoes."

29 If you yourself are the host, you can exercise more control; you are, after all, the one who sets the rules and the tone of behavior in your home. Once, when Professor Kahn's party guests began singing offensive, racist songs, for instance, he kicked them all out, saying, "You don't sing songs like that in my house!" And, he adds, "they never did again."

30 *At school one day, a friend comes over and says, "Who do you think you are, hanging out with Joe? If you can be friends with those people, I'm through with you!"*

Peer pressure can weigh heavily on kids. They feel vulnerable and, because they are kids, they aren't as able to control the urge to fight. "But if you learn to handle these situations as kids, you'll be better able to handle them as an adult," William Newlin points out. 31

Begin by redefining to yourself what a friend is and examining what friendship means, advises Amy Lee, a human relations specialist at Panel of Americans, an intergroup-relations training and educational organization. If that person from a different group fits your requirement for a friend, ask, "Why shouldn't I be friends with Joe? We have a lot in common." Try to get more information about whatever stereotypes or resentments lie beneath your friend's statement. Ms. Lee suggests: "What makes you think they're so different from us? Where did you get that information?" She explains: "People are learning these stereotypes from somewhere, and they cannot be blamed for that. So examine where these ideas came from." Then talk about how your own experience rebuts them. 32

Kids, like adults, should also be aware of other resources to back them up: Does the school offer special programs for fighting prejudice? How supportive will the principal, the teachers, or other students be? If the school atmosphere is volatile, experts warn, make sure that taking a stand at that moment won't put you in physical danger. If that is the case, it's better to look for other alternatives. 33

These can include programs or organizations that bring kids from different backgrounds together. "When kids work together across race lines, that is how you break down the barriers and see that the stereotypes are not true," says Laurie Meadoff, president of CityKids Foundation, a nonprofit group whose programs attempt to do just that. Such programs can also provide what Cherie Brown calls a "safe place" to express the anger and pain that slurs and other offenses cause, whether the bigotry is directed against you or others. 34

In learning to speak up, everyone will develop a different style and a slightly different message to get across, experts agree. But it would be hard to do better than these two messages suggested by teenagers at CityKids: "Everyone on the face of the earth has the same intestines," said one. Another added, "Cross over the bridge. There's a lot of love on the streets." 35

QUESTIONS ON SUBJECT AND PURPOSE

1. According to Cole, why should we object to "racial slurs and offensive ethnic jokes"?

2. The body of Cole's essay (paragraphs 8–34) offers strategies to use when confronting offensive remarks or jokes. How does Cole divide or organize this part of her subject?
3. What purposes might Cole have had in writing the essay?

QUESTIONS ON STRATEGY AND AUDIENCE

1. Why does Cole begin the essay with a personal example (paragraphs 1 and 2)?
2. Cole quotes a number of authorities in her essay. Why? What do the quotations and the authorities contribute to the article?
3. Why might Cole include the final section—the advice to children about handling such situations among friends? What does this section suggest about her intended audience?

QUESTIONS ON VOCABULARY AND STYLE

1. Throughout the essay, Cole uses first- or second-person pronouns such as *I*, *you*, and *we*. Why? How would the essay differ if she used *one* or *he or she?*
2. At several points (in paragraph 23, for instance), Cole suggests a possible response to a situation, enclosing that remark within quotation marks. Why might she create these imagined sentences for her reader?
3. Be prepared to define the following words: *ebullience* (paragraph 1), *tinged* (1), *rift* (17), *volatile* (33).

WRITING SUGGESTIONS

1. **For Your Journal.** Would you honestly say that after reading Cole's essay you will respond as she suggests when you hear offensive remarks? Does it matter if they are directed at a group to which you belong or at another group? Start with a typical offensive remark that you have often heard, and plan a response to it. If you feel that you would still "just stand there," explain for yourself why you would choose not to react.
2. **For a Paragraph.** Studies from colleges and universities across the United States suggest that many students have

cheated at some point during their college years. Typically, these students either plagiarized someone else's work in a paper or a laboratory report or copied answers on a quiz or an exam. Suppose that a friend asks to borrow your research paper or laboratory report, explaining that he or she wants to submit it as his or her own work, or that a friend tries to copy answers from your paper. How can you handle such a situation? In a process paragraph, explain a procedure for replying to that person.

3. **For an Essay.** Cole's essay describes a process—what to do when you encounter prejudice. Select another occasion when we might need advice on how to handle a similarly awkward situation, and write an essay offering advice on what to do.

   Prewriting:

   a. Brainstorm about possible difficult situations—dealing with roommates, friends, or coworkers; observing a classmate cheating on a test or causing distractions in class; and so forth. Jot down as many uncomfortable situations as possible.
   b. Ask some friends about similar experiences they might have had. How did they react? Try out your ideas on them.
   c. Select what seems to be the most promising possibility and try freewriting for twenty minutes. Do not worry about your grammar; concentrate on getting some ideas from which to begin writing. If you are not pleased with the result, switch to another topic and try freewriting on it.

   Rewriting:

   a. Look carefully at the organizational strategy you have used. Are the steps in the process in a logical order? Could you, for example, construct a flow chart outlining those steps?
   b. Try writing imaginary responses to the situation as Cole does. Put these sentences within quotation marks. Does that strategy seem effective?
   c. Reread your introduction. Does it re-create the situation for the reader? Does it catch a reader's interest? Compare your introductory strategy with that used by Cole.

4. **For Research.** Many colleges and universities have established policies for dealing with sexual harassment and discrimination. Research your own institution's position on these issues. See if, for example, a policy statement is available. You might also wish to interview members of the administration and faculty. Then, using your research, write an essay in which you explain to students how to handle a case of sexual harassment or discrimination.

Website Link

The Web has wonderful resources for dealing with discrimination—check out the sites maintained by the Anti-Defamation League of B'nai B'rith, the National Organization for Women, and the National Association for Colored People.

How Books Helped Shape My Life

Judith Viorst

Judith Viorst was born in Newark, New Jersey, and educated at Rutgers University and the Washington Psychoanalytic Institute. She is a poet, essayist, journalist, book reviewer, and author of numerous children's books, including the popular "Alexander" series. She has worked as contributing editor for Redbook *magazine, and her poems and essays have appeared in major national publications. Viorst's many books fall into three broad categories—books for children, collections of humorous verse, and popular nonfiction books on psychology and self-help. Her first novel for adults was* Murdering Mr. Monti *(1994) and her most recent nonfiction book is* Imperfect Control: Our Lifelife Struggles with Power and Surrender *(1998). "How Books Helped Shape My life" was first published in* Redbook, *a consideration that obviously influenced her choice of subject and approach.*

On Writing: *In an interview, Viorst described her concentration as a writer: "If I'm working on an article, I'll write longhand in the airport and in the airplane, and it doesn't matter what kind of noise is going on. I'm very disciplined about that." Of her goals as a writer, she remarked: "I guess what you try to do is find your own authentic voice that doesn't sound like anybody else. I loved it when my son Alexander read [her 1986 nonfiction work]* Necessary Losses, *and said, 'It sounds just like you, Mom.'" In another interview she discussed her central themes: "Everything I write is in one piece: What's going on inside us and issues within our relationships with people. Whether I am writing for children or grown-ups, that is what I am writing about."*

BEFORE READING

Connecting: At the start of the essay, Viorst talks about "searching for heroines who could serve as ideals, as models, as possibilities." Can you remember ever "searching" for a heroine or a hero? Is it something that only children do?

Anticipating: Viorst discusses six fictional heroines. How does she arrange her six examples? What is the central thread that provides the organization for her essay?

1 In books I've read since I was young I've searched for heroines who could serve as ideals, as models, as possibilities—some reflecting the secret self that dwelled inside me, others pointing to whole new ways that a woman (if only she dared!) might try to be. The person that I am today was shaped by Nancy Drew; by Jo March, Jane Eyre and Heathcliff's soul mate Cathy; and by other fictional females whose attractiveness or character or audacity for a time were the standards by which I measured myself.

2 I return to some of these books to see if I still understand the powerful hold that these heroines once had on me. I still understand.

3 Consider teen-aged Nancy Drew—beautiful, blond-haired, blue-eyed girl detective—who had the most terrific life that I as a ten-year-old could ever imagine. Motherless (in other words, quite free of maternal controls), she lived with her handsome indulgent lawyer father in a large brick house set back from the street with a winding tree-lined driveway on the outside and a faithful, nonintrusive housekeeper Hannah cooking yummy meals on the inside. She also had a boy friend, a convertible, nice clothes and two close girl friends—not as perfect as she, but then it seemed to me that no one could possibly be as perfect as Nancy Drew, who in dozens and dozens of books *(The Hidden Staircase, The Whispering Statue, The Clue in the Diary, The Clue of the Tapping Heels)* was resourceful and brave and intelligent as she went around solving mysteries left and right, while remaining kind to the elderly and invariably polite and absolutely completely delightfully feminine.

4 I mean, what else *was* there?

5 I soon found out what else when I encountered the four March sisters of *Little Women*, a sentimental, old-fashioned book about girls growing up in Civil War time in New England. About spoiled, vain, pretty Amy. And sickly, saintly Beth. And womanly, decent Meg. And about—most important of all—gawky, bookworm Jo. Dear Jo, who wasn't as flawless as the golden Nancy Drew but who showed me that girls like her—like *us*—could be heroines. Even if we weren't much to look at. Even if we were clumsy and socially gauche. And even if the transition into young womanhood often appeared to our dubious eye to be difficult and scary and even unwelcome.

6 Jo got stains on her dress and laughed when she shouldn't and lost her temper and didn't display tact or patience or restraint. Jo brought a touch of irreverence to the cultural constraints of the world she lived in. And yet her instincts were good and her heart

was pure and her headstrong ways led always to virtue. And furthermore Jo—as I yearned to be—was a writer!

7 In the book the years go by, Beth dies, Meg and Amy marry and Jo—her fierce heart somewhat tamed—is alone. "An old maid, that's what I'm to be. A literary spinster, with a pen for a spouse, a family of stories for children, and twenty years hence a morsel of fame, perhaps!" . . . Jo sighed, as if the prospect was not inviting.

8 This worried young reader concurred—not inviting at all!

9 And so I was happy to read of Jo's nice suitor. Mr. Bhaer, not handsome or rich or young or important or witty, but possessed of kindness and dignity and enough intelligence to understand that even a girl who wasn't especially pretty, who had no dazzling charms and who wanted to write might make a wonderful wife. And a wonderful mother. And live happily ever after.

10 What a relief!

11 What Jo and Nancy shared was active participation in life—they went out and *did;* they weren't simply done to—and they taught and promised me (at a time when mommies stayed home and there was no Women's Movement) that a girl could go out and do and still get a man. Jo added the notion that brusque, ungainly girls could go out and do and still get a man. And Jane of *Jane Eyre,* whose author once said, "I will show you a heroine as small and as plain as myself," added the further idea that such women were able to "feel just as men feel" and were capable of being just as passionate.

12 Orphaned Jane, a governess at stately Thornfield Hall, was a no-nonsense lady, cool and self-contained, whose lonely, painful childhood had ingrained in her an impressive firmness of character, an unwillingness to charm or curry favor and a sense of herself as the equal of any man. Said Jane to Mr. Rochester, the brooding, haughty, haunted master of Thornfield: "Do you think I am an automaton?—a machine without feelings? Do you think, because I am poor, obscure, plain, and little, I am soulless and heartless? You think wrong!—I have as much soul as you, and full as much heart!"

13 I loved it that such hot fires burned inside so plain a Jane. I loved her for her unabashed intensity. And I loved her for being so pure that when she learned of Mr. Rochester's lunatic wife, she sacrificed romance for honor and left him immediately.

14 For I think it's important to note that Nancy and Jo and Jane, despite their independence, were basically as good as girls can be: honest, generous, kind, sincere, reliable, respectable, possessed of absolute integrity. They didn't defy convention. They

didn't challenge the rules. They did what was right, although it might cause them pain. And their virtue was always rewarded—look at Jane, rich and married at last to her Mr. Rochester. Oh, how I identified with Jane!

15 But then I read *Wuthering Heights*, a novel of soul-consuming love on the Yorkshire moors, and Catherine Earnshaw totally captured me. And she captured me, not in spite of her dangerous, dark and violent spirit, but *because* of it.

16 Cathy was as wild as the moors. She lied and connived and deceived. She was insolent, selfish, manipulative and cruel. And by marrying meek, weak Edgar instead of Heathcliff, her destiny, she betrayed a love she described in throbbing, forgettable prose as . . . elemental:

17 "My love for Heathcliff resembles the eternal rocks beneath—a source of little visible delight, but necessary. Nelly, I *am* Heathcliff—he's always, always in my mind—not as a pleasure, any more than I am always a pleasure to myself—but as my own being. . . ."

18 Now who, at the age of 16, could resist such quivering intensity? Who would settle for less than elemental? Must we untamed creatures of passion—I'd muse as I lay awake in my red flannel nightie—submit ourselves to conventional morality? Or could I actually choose not to be a good girl?

19 Cathy Earnshaw told me that I could. And so did lost Lady Brett, of *The Sun Also Rises*.

20 Brett Ashley was to me, at 18, free, modern, woman incarnate, and she dangled alluring new concepts before my eyes:

21 The value of style: "She wore a slipover jersey sweater and a tweed skirt, and her hair was brushed back like a boy's. She started all that."

22 The glamour of having a dark and tortured past: "Finally, when he got really bad, he used to tell her he'd kill her. . . . She hasn't had an absolutely happy life."

23 The excitement of nonconformity: "I've always done just what I wanted."

24 The importance of (understated) grace under pressure: "Brett was rather good. She's always rather good."

25 And the thrill of unrepressed sexuality: "Brett's had affairs with men before. She tells me all about everything."

26 Brett married lovelessly and drank too much and drifted too much and had an irresponsible fling with a bullfighter. But she also had class—and her own morality. She set her bullfighter free—"I'd have lived with him if I hadn't seen it was bad for him." And

even though she was broke, she lied and "told him I had scads of it. . . . I couldn't take his money, you know."

Brett's wasn't the kind of morality that my mother was teaching me in suburban New Jersey. But maybe I wasn't meant for suburban life. Maybe—I would muse as I carefully lined my eyes with blue liner—maybe I'm meant for something more . . . emancipated. 27

I carried Brett's image with me when, after college, I lived for a while in Greenwich Village, in New York. But I couldn't achieve her desperate gallantry. And it struck me that Brett was too lonely and sad, and that Cathy had died too young (and that Scarlett O'Hara got Tara but lost her Rhett), and that maybe I ought to forget about unconventionality if the price was going to be so painfully high. Although I enjoyed my Village fling, I had no wish to live anguishedly ever after. I needed a heroine who, like me, wanted just a small taste of the wild before settling down into happy domesticity. 28

I found her in *War and Peace*. Her name was Natasha. 29

Natasha, the leading lady of this epic of Russian society during Napoleon's time, was "poetic . . . charming . . . overflowing with life," an enchanting girl whose sweet eagerness and passionate impulsivity were tempered by historic and private tragedies. Betrothed to the handsome and excellent Prince Andrew, she fell in love with a heel named Anatole, and when she was warned that this foolish and dangerous passion would lead to her ruin, "I'll go to my ruin . . . ," she said, "as soon as possible." 30

It ended badly with Anatole. Natasha tried suicide. Prince Andrew died. Natasha turned pale, thin, subdued. But unlike Brett and Cathy, her breach with convention was mended and, at long last, she married Pierre—a decent, substantial, loving man, the kind of man all our mothers want us to marry. 31

In marriage Natasha grew stouter and "the old fire very rarely kindled in her face now." She became an exemplary mother, an ideal wife. "She felt that her unity with her husband was maintained not by the poetic feelings that had attracted him to her but by something else—indefinite but firm as the bond between her own body and soul." 32

It sounded—if not elemental and doomed—awfully nice. 33

I identified with Natasha when, the following year, I married and left Greenwich Village. I too was ready for domesticity. And yet . . . her husband and children became "the subject which wholly engrossed Natasha's attention." She had lost herself—and I didn't want to lose me. What I needed next was a heroine who could reconcile all the warring wants of my nature—for fire and quiet, 34 independence and oneness, ambition and love, and marriage and family.

35 But such reconciling heroines, in novels and real life, may not yet exist.

36 Nevertheless Natasha and Jane and Jo, Cathy, Nancy and Brett—each spoke to my heart and stirred me powerfully. On my journey to young womanhood I was fortunate to have them as my companions. They were, they will always remain, a part of me.

QUESTIONS ON SUBJECT AND PURPOSE

1. How many heroines does Viorst treat? What does she see in each? How are those qualities related to her own maturation?
2. When you were a child, did any hero or heroine seem a particularly attractive model? Was he or she a character in a novel? Has television or film replaced novels as a source of models? Were any of these real-life models?
3. Why would any reader be interested in an essay explaining how something shaped your life? Did you find anything of interest here? If so, why? If not, why not?

QUESTIONS ON STRATEGY AND AUDIENCE

1. How does Viorst structure her essay? What progression is there? What controls the arrangement of the heroines?
2. Viorst switches the way she handles her examples when she reaches Lady Brett in *The Sun Also Rises.* Why the change?
3. For whom is Viorst writing? What expectations does she have of her audience? Can you find specific evidence to support your assumptions?

QUESTIONS ON VOCABULARY AND STYLE

1. Viorst frequently uses dashes in her sentences. What is the effect of their use?
2. Viorst seems to delight in breaking the rules we might expect writing to obey. Consider the following categories of examples and be able to show how and why each works in the essay:
   a. Informal, even casual words ("yummy," "a heel")
   b. Clichés ("solving mysteries left and right," "live happily ever after")

   c. Sentence fragments
   d. Extremely short paragraphs
3. Be able to define the following words: *gawky* (paragraph 5), *gauche* (5), *brusque* (11), *curry favor* (12), *unabashed* (13), *incarnate* (20).

WRITING SUGGESTIONS

1. **For Your Journal.** Who served as your models when you were between the ages of ten and fifteen? Your list can include real people and characters from films, television, or books. Next to each name, try to jot down the reasons why you admired this person or character. If you find it difficult to isolate figures from that time in your life, try another age. If you can think of no such figures, speculate on why models were not attractive to you.
2. **For a Paragraph.** Select one of the figures you wrote about in your journal, and write a paragraph in which you explain why that particular model was important to you at that particular stage in your life. Remember that your goal is not just to narrate a story; you should explain what that figure meant to you—how that figure reflected your life and values at that moment.
3. **For an Essay.** "How X Helped Shape My Life." Using Viorst's essay as a structural model, write a process analysis showing how a series of events, situations, or people helped you grow up. Subjects might include teachers, friends, or supervisors; jobs or hobbies; books or movies; or places you've lived.

   Prewriting:
   a. A workable subject must meet two criteria. First, the items in the series must be parallel in form. (Viorst's are all characters from books.) Second, each item must have played a role in your life at a particular time. (Viorst's reflect her reading from age ten to her mid-twenties.) With those criteria in mind, brainstorm a list of possible subjects.
   b. Narrow your list to the two best possibilities. Then decide how many time periods you could represent. Viorst includes six. That is probably too many for your essay, but be sure to have at least three. For both subjects, list in outline form the time periods you could include with

an example representing each. Finally, narrow your focus to the most promising subject.

c. Develop each example for this subject clearly. Ask friends who are the same age what they remember about their growing up. Ask them to evaluate the examples you plan to use. That might help add important details.

Rewriting:

a. For each of the examples that you include, complete the statement "What this example meant to me was . . . ." Write your answers on a separate sheet of paper.

b. Look back at Viorst's essay. Not every reader has read these books, so Viorst is careful to explain exactly what was appealing or influential about each one. Have you made your essay accessible to readers?

c. The appeal of Viorst's essay is its universality. Because we all grow up and because we go through certain common stages in that process, we are interested in her analysis. Can you say the same thing about your essay? Have you made it universal enough? Will the reader want to keep reading? Find a peer reader, and check your essay's appeal. If your reader is bored, ask why.

4. **For Research.** To what extent does Viorst's description of her own maturation process coincide with the maturation process in other children? Are these, for example, "predictable" stages? What does research tell us about the maturation process from the preteen years to the early twenties? Your reference librarian will be able to point you to the appropriate indexes and databases to research the question. Be sure to document your sources wherever appropriate.

WEBSITE LINK

The Web offers a number of links to Viorst's work. You can listen to an interview with her and you can hear her read from her book *Imperfect Control.*

INTO THE LOOP: HOW TO GET THE JOB YOU WANT AFTER GRADUATION

Charlie Drozdyk

Charlie Drozdyk has had a wide range of job experiences. He has worked for the Big Apple Circus and the Brooklyn Academy of Music. He has also been theater manager at the Criterion Center on Broadway, a researcher at CBS, a director of development for a film production company, a producer of videos, and a talent agent. He is the author of Hot Jobs Handbook *(1994) and* Jobs That Don't Suck *(1998). This essay originally appeared in* Rolling Stone *magazine.*

BEFORE READING

Connecting: At this point, what expectations do you have about your first job after college?

Anticipating: What seems like the most surprising piece of information or advice in the essay?

When Benjamin Braddock, Dustin Hoffman's bewildered twentysomething hero in *The Graduate*, finished college, he was hit with a mind-numbing barrage of good wishes from well-meaning friends. Who can forget that single depressing word of advice that sent Benjamin into catatonic shock—*plastics?* It was no wonder he wound up sleeping with his girlfriend's mother and hanging out all summer at the bottom of his parents' swimming pool. 1

In 1995, 1.38 million college graduates will find themselves in Benjamin's shoes. They might not share *all* of his summer adventures, but with the flip of a tassel, they will soon find themselves at the bottom of the employment pool. Whom are they going to listen to? 2

The truth is, Benjamin had it pretty good back in 1967. Not only were jobs being created as fast as the labor force would grow, but once a job seeker got a foot in the door at an IBM or a Grey Advertising, he or she could expect to stroll the halls for some 40 years while waiting for the gold watch. Unfortunately, the Fortune 3

500 companies that 20 years ago employed one in five of all Americans now employ fewer than one in 10.

4 It's called corporate downsizing, and it's not over yet. In 1994 the largest U.S. companies dropped around 700,000 employees. But in spite of that, unemployment numbers are actually shrinking. The big guys may be busy handing out pink slips, but small employers are even busier signing up new hires.

5 But beware of *under*employment. Among the 30 fastest-growing occupations, 21 require no college degree. In fact, the 10 occupations that will pour the greatest number of jobs into the economy, in order, are salespeople (retail), registered nurses, cashiers, general office clerks, truck drivers, waiters/waitresses, nursing aides, janitors/cleaners, food-preparation workers and systems analysts. It is the service industry that will contribute the bulk—approximately two-thirds—of all new jobs.

6 So the question is, How can the class of 1995 put to use the $140 billion it spent on higher education last year? The graduates didn't spend five years—the average amount of time it now takes to get a B.A.—to land a job that doesn't require a college degree. Or did they? Well, the sad truth is that 25 percent of the class of 1995 will be working at jobs that don't require a college diploma.

7 They could always stay on campus. If you're planning on getting a master's degree, the odds of not using your education in a career will drop to 10 percent. For Ph.D.s the odds drop to a 4 percent chance. As you can see, the burger-flipping probability decreases with degrees earned. For those who are thinking about postponing the inevitable job thing, that's good news.

8 For anyone else eager to get on with a career, including Benjamin, if you're still looking, I've talked to plenty of people who have advice. And they're not talking plastics.

9 But before diving into how to get a job, there's one thing to keep in mind, and it's this: Bosses hate hiring people; in fact, they loathe and generally resent the entire process. Put yourself in a boss' shoes. The person they hired two years, or maybe just six months ago, has quit, and now they have to dig through the résumés on their desks and meet with a bunch of random strangers all over again. Or not. What they usually do is toss those résumés in the old circular file and call their friends and business associates, asking them if they know of anyone who's looking for a job.

10 This is exactly how Lauren Marino, a book editor at Hyperion (a trade-book publishing company owned by Disney), hired her assistant. She called the literary agencies she works with on a

daily basis and asked her contacts if they knew anyone who was looking for a job. "Not only do they know the business already," she says, "but if someone I know recommends them, then it's not going to be a complete waste of time meeting with them."

So how do you get to be the person who is recommended? Get in the loop. You will never even hear of most of the job openings out there if you're not in the loop. Once you get your first job, however, you're automatically in the loop. In many companies, workers are paid to talk to people at different companies all day. And it will instantly start to make sense how the average worker manages to change jobs 7.5 times between the ages of 18 and 30. As obnoxious as the word sounds, it's all about *networking*. 11

For recent graduates without the benefits of business contacts and associates, instant entry into the loop is through a connection. For a lot of people, the word *connection* is as loathsome as that other word. Friends will snivel, "Hey, man, he only got that job because he knows somebody." Absolutely. It's how the game works. So don't discount anyone as a connection—your neighbor, your parents' friends, your baby sitter from 10 years ago. Ask them if they know anyone—or know anyone who knows anyone—who works in the industry into which you want to get. Meet with as many people as you can for a five-minute informational interview, and then go in there and pick their brains: Are they hiring? Do they know anyone who is? (But let them think you're there to simply learn what they do. They know why you're really there.) 12

Don't worry that you'll be bugging them. As Bill Wright-Swadel, director of career services at Dartmouth College, says, "Most people who have an expertise love to talk about the things that they're knowledgeable about." Contacts aren't just about getting an interview, though. Once you've interviewed somewhere, find out if any alumni from your college work there—or any friend of a friend. Call that person, say you've just interviewed and ask him to make a call on your behalf. Basically, it's just someone giving testament that you're *one of them.* It's standard networking procedure—but something often ignored. 13

"People don't know how to network," says David McNulty, a recruiter for Smith Barney. "If you want to get hired by a Wall Street firm, you should find out who went to your school and who works in the firm and call them." 14

Melissa Statmore, human-resources manager at J. Walter Thompson advertising, agrees. "Use any connections you have," she says. "We love referrals. They're taken very seriously." 15

Recruiting Roulette

16 Say, however, that you've got no connections. You've just crawled out from under the rock of your undergraduate studies, your parents live in Tibet, and you have no friends. There's always recruiting, right? Yes and no. Finding a job by interviewing with firms that show up on your campus is like getting a job through the want ads—it's a passive take-what's-being-thrown-in-front-of-you-approach. And considering that employers will visit an average of 7.4 fewer campuses in 1995 than they did in 1994, it's also a somewhat dying approach.

17 If you're at one of the Ivy League schools, the University of Virginia, Stanford, Michigan or about a dozen select others, and if you want to work for Smith Barney, you're lucky—the company will visit your school. And if you want to work for J. Walter Thompson, and if you're at Amherst, Yale, Colby or Bates, to name a random few, you're also in luck. My senior year at school—not among the chosen few—I remember seeing recruiters from a railroad, a pharmaceutical firm and a company that had something to do with socks and underwear.

18 Even though it's March, and you haven't scored a job via recruiting with some company you never really wanted to work for in the first place, don't worry about it—you're probably better off. Remember Lauren Marino, the editor who was looking for an assistant? When Marino was about to graduate, she interviewed on campus with a printing company based in Tennessee and was offered a job. The company then had to rescind the offer because of a hiring freeze, and Marino was forced to continue searching. If the offer hadn't been rescinded, instead of loving her life as a book editor (at only 27) in New York, she would be destined, as she puts it, to be "living in Kingsport, Tenn., a member of the Junior League and would have 10 kids."

Intern into the Loop

19 So don't fret that you blew off that recruiter. Truth is, if you're about to graduate, it may not be you they're after. The new trend in recruiting is lassoing sophomores and juniors as interns, giving them a summer or semester of experience and then hiring them as soon as they're done with school. This gives the company a chance to see if they fit in and saves time and money in training.

20 But just because you're about to graduate doesn't mean you can't still intern. In fact, you probably should. In a survey by the College Placement Council, employers say that three out of 10 new

hires will be former interns. Christian Breheney is part of that 30 percent. Right before she was about to graduate a semester early from Johns Hopkins and armed with her Spanish major, she saw a flier on a bulletin board and ripped it off the wall. After she was offered the nonpaying internship at *Late Night with David Letterman*, she put the flier back up.

Some of her friends thought that Breheney's decision to work for free was questionable. After all, she was about to be a college graduate. Her plan worked, though. After four months of commuting from New Jersey five days a week, working from 10 A.M. to 7 P.M., she got her break. A receptionist quit, and Breheney got the job. How? "If you're well liked and make a good impression, you can get hired right off of your internship," she says. Which is something that happens quite often, apparently, as she lists about a dozen full timers who started as interns. 21

Two years later and now the assistant to the head writer at the *Late Show with David Letterman*, Breheney has yet to send out a single résumé. It's just been a matter of "moving up that ladder," she says gleefully. 22

Temp into the Loop

The cost-effective benefits in hiring interns—pretrained, proven commodities—are the same reason that temps (temporary employees who are hired to fill in when needed) are landing full-time jobs at the companies where they're assigned. Thirty-eight percent of all temporary workers are offered full-time employment while on an assignment. 23

Temping has become a recruiting technique in itself, not just a means of replacing somebody when he or she is out sick. It's becoming known as "temping to perm." As Jules Young, president of Friedman Personnel Agency, in West Hollywood, Calif., says: "Temping is like living with someone before you marry them. A lot of placement is based on chemistry between the people you're going to work with. That's why a temp is a good way to go—because it gives the employer a chance to check out whether the chemistry matches." 24

At many large companies like Nike or Paramount Pictures—as well as most of the faster-growing small companies (200 employees or fewer) that by the year 2000 will employ 85 percent of all Americans—a great way in, and a fairly common one, is through temping. The best way to go is to call the company you want to work for and ask which temp agency they use. Then call 25 that agency, go in and pass its typing test and boom! You're in the door. Get familiar with some of the more popular computer programs (WordPerfect, Microsoft Word, Excel and Lotus 1-2-3)—the agencies are going to be looking for them.

The Personnel Myth

26 We're practically programmed to do it. We make a list of the companies we want to work for, write a standard cover letter (changing the name of the company and the person to whom we're sending it, of course) and drop that and a résumé in the mailbox. A hundred letters sent to 100 personnel departments. Probability alone suggests that at least one or two interviews will come out of it, right? Not likely. You know how many résumés Nike got in 1994? More than 23,000. It hired 511 people. Smith Barney hired around 80 people last year from a pool of applicants that numbered about 10,000. Do the math: The odds aren't good.

27 When Lauren Marino decided to go into publishing, she sent résumés to every publishing house in New York. You know how many interviews she got? Zero. As she realizes now, "That was a huge waste of my time. Personnel departments don't hire anybody. The only way to get an editorial job in publishing is by knowing somebody or by sending a letter directly to the editor."

28 Although it's not a rule to live by, most people don't use their company's personnel departments for a job search. If you want to work at a company, pinpoint which department you want to work in and then find the person who can make a hiring decision. Approach that person directly.

29 If you don't know anybody who knows anybody who knows anybody who knows the person with whom you want to work—or under—at a specific company, then you're going to have to be a little resourceful. The first tactic is obvious. Cold-call them. Pick up the phone and try to get the person on the line. Tell him truthfully how you would really love to work for his company and would love to meet with him for five minutes. Chances are you're not going to get past this person's assistant, however.

30 This is exactly what happened to Michael Landau when he called the national sales manager (he got her name from a friend) at Nicole Miller, a New York fashion-design company. The first four times he called, he got an assistant on the phone who was nice enough but wouldn't put her boss on the phone. This is what assistants are for.

Figuring that the assistant probably left at around 6 p.m., Landau called at 6:30, thinking the boss might still be there—and if so, would pick up her own phone. She was, and she did. She was nice to him but said there wasn't anything available. Standard stuff, but Landau was persistent, and as such would have it, the CEO of the company walked into the sales manager's office. "Talk to this guy, he sounds good," the sales manager said to her colleague. The exec repeated that the company wasn't hiring but that it was, however, always interested in meeting good people. 31

At that moment, Landau decided to fly to New York, a trip he told them he just happened to be taking. Landau started out in sales and is now happily employed in the public-relations department at Nicole Miller. 32

Say Yes

This is the first thing you should know about interviewing: If someone asks you in an interview if you know a certain computer program (which you don't) or if you know how to drive a car (and you never have), just say yes. As Sheryl Vandermolen, a junior designer at Robert Metzger Interiors, says: "It's all about selling yourself and believing in yourself. Don't say you think you can, say you can—even if you don't know if you can." 33

Research

"Please do your research," says Cheryl Nickerson, director of employment for Nike. "Be able to ask intelligent questions about the company and what's going on in the industry. [As an employer] you're making a judgment about that person's curiosity, their willingness to learn and grow." And where do you find information about the company? Start by reading the firm's annual report. Not doing this is a "cardinal sin," says David McNulty of Smith Barney. Just call up the company and ask that a report be mailed to you. You don't even have to leave your couch. 34

Get Psyched

Employers want someone who's going to come in and kick ass. Interviews are about convincing the employer that you're that person. As Brian Johnson, co-owner of the Dogwater Cafe, a fast-growing restaurant chain in Florida, says, "When I'm interviewing, 35

I'm looking for someone with a lot of energy who wants this job more than anything. I want them to basically beg me not to interview anybody else—that this is their job."

Follow Up

36 When I was in Jules Young's office at the Friedman agency, a young woman who had just had an interview with someone at the William Morris Agency called to report back that it had gone well. Without pausing, Young said, "Drop a note off to her in the morning thanking her and saying you really want the job. Drop it off in person to the reception desk."

37 "I don't think people [write thank-you notes] as much as they think they should anymore," says Nike's Cheryl Nickerson. "If you're in the running, that special touch of following up to say thank you may be the edge that you need." Sometimes, however, a thank-you letter isn't enough to push you over that edge. You need to do more. You need to . . .

Be Persistent

38 When Tracy Grandstaff interviewed for her first job, at MTV, she was told that they would let her know quickly since they needed someone right away. "It took three months of me hounding this woman to get that job," she says. "I called her constantly. She couldn't make a decision." Finally, the woman told Grandstaff that it was between her and someone else and that she just couldn't decide. To which Grandstaff said, "Flat out: What do I have to say to you to give me the edge? What do you want to hear, and I'll say it. What do you want me to do? I'll do it." Apparently these questions were what the MTV executive wanted to hear. Grandstaff got the job.

Be Nice to the Interviewer's Secretary

39 A survey of executives at the country's largest companies found that nearly two-thirds of the interviewers consider the opinion of their administrative assistants with regard to the interviewee who walks past them on their way in and out of their bosses' offices. So be smart and just say, "I just had some water, I'm fine, thank you," when they ask you if you would like anything to drink. Asking for a coffee, light, one sugar, isn't going to score you points.

There's no formula to any of this. Some applicants get really lucky and land something quickly. Most, however, collect a few horror stories to tell. And that's the reality: At best, getting a job has always been an elusive and difficult task. So whatever you do, don't get sucked into that slacker pity party presently taking place on couches and in bars everywhere, the one that goes like this: "Man, there's no jobs available. The baby boomers took them all." 40

As Greg Drebin, vice president of programming at MTV, says, "When people say, 'Well, now is a really hard time for the industry,' and all that . . . well, it's always a hard time. There's no such thing as 'Oh, it's hiring season; we've got all these jobs that just became available.' You know what? There's always jobs, and there's never jobs." 41

QUESTIONS ON SUBJECT AND PURPOSE

1. Drozdyk's opening example is drawn from a film, *The Graduate,* made in 1967. How effective is that example? Why might he use it?
2. Are there ever times in Drozdyk's essay when you disagree or feel uncomfortable with the advice that he is giving?
3. What assumptions does Drozdyk make about the reasons why people attend college? Do you agree with those assumptions?

QUESTIONS ON STRATEGY AND AUDIENCE

1. Why might Drozdyk title the essay "Into the Loop"?
2. Drozdyk quotes from a number of people throughout the essay. Why might he do so, and how effective is the strategy?
3. To whom is Drozdyk writing? How specifically can you define that audience?

QUESTIONS ON VOCABULARY AND STYLE

1. How would you characterize the tone of Drozdyk's essay? (See the Glossary for a definition of *tone.*)
2. Find examples of words or expressions that Drozdyk uses to connect with an audience of late teenagers and "twentysomethings."

3. Be prepared to define the following words and phrases: *barrage* (paragraph 1), *catatonic* (1), *snivel* (12), *rescind* (18), *proven commodities* (23), *cold-call* (29), *cardinal sin* (34).

WRITING SUGGESTIONS

1. **For Your Journal.** Jot down in your journal a list of possible internships or volunteer positions for which you might apply. Remember that such positions might not involve specific job skills but rather particular "people" skills that are transferable to many jobs. Visit your college's placement office for possible suggestions as well. Your major department might also be a source of information.
2. **For a Paragraph.** Using your list, the advice in Drozdyk's essay, and any advice that you can get from your college's placement office, write a paragraph in which you describe the process by which you (or anyone else) would apply for a specific internship or volunteer position.
3. **For an Essay.** Write an essay in which you offer advice on how an undergraduate at your college can locate and apply for internships and volunteer positions. With your instructor's approval, you might consider writing the essay for your school's student newspaper or as a brochure that could be handed out by the placement office.

   Prewriting:

   a. Remember that your essay will be readable and valuable to the extent to which you are able to give specific information and details. Make sure you spend enough time gathering examples before you sit down to write.
   b. Brainstorm about your particular audience. Who reads the student newspaper? What is the composition of the undergraduate class? Are many of the students returning adults? Do most of your classmates work while attending school?
   c. Interview a number of students. See what they know and don't know about internships. What are their attitudes toward volunteering their time and skills? What do their attitudes tell you about your writing task?

   Rewriting:

   a. Make sure that the steps or stages in the process of identifying and applying are clearly marked and called out.

b. It is always good to rethink your organizational strategy. Make a copy of your essay, cut the body paragraphs apart, and rearrange them in an alternative order. Force yourself to experiment with this change. Is the new order any better? Even if it isn't, the process will make you look in a new way at the sequence you have used.
c. Ask a friend or classmate to read through your essay. Did your reader find your essay interesting? Helpful? Are there specific things that could be improved? Prod your reader for some constructive criticism.

4. **For Research.** In what ways is electronic communication changing the nature of a job search? For example, increasing numbers of individuals are mounting personal Web pages that advertise their talents and skills in ways somewhat similar to the old printed résumé. How are the new technologies influencing job search strategies? Research the problem and the future directions. Remember that source information will have to be current, so look for very recent books and articles. You might want to use the World Wide Web to find examples, as well, or interview people. In a researched essay, bring Drozdyk's advice up to date for the early 2000s.

Website Link

Can the Web help you find a job? What Web resources are available for job seekers? If you post your resume on the Web, will you find a job? The Website links you to some good advice.

The Page Turner

Lynne Sharon Schwartz

Lynne Sharon Schwartz (1939–) is the author of a number of books including novels, collections of essays, and a children's book. Some of her shorter work has been collected in A Lynne Sharon Schwartz Reader: Selected Prose and Poetry *(1992). She has been awarded grants from the Guggenheim Foundation and the National Endowment for the Arts and has been a frequent teacher of fiction writing in a number of graduate programs. Her most recent book is* Face to Face: A Reader in the World *(2000).*

On Writing: *In* Ruined by Reading *Schwartz writes about what she admires in other writers: "The good writer offers a new language, the silent language of the inner voice. . . . From Faulkner to Gertrude Stein to Virginia Woolf, the writers who claim our attention do so by voice and idiom, which are the audible manifestations of the mind. This is how it sounds inside, they declare. Listen, hear the shape within me. . . . [T]he only new thing under the sun is the sound of another voice."*

BEFORE READING

Connecting: If you have been to a piano concert—or seen one on television—have you ever noticed the page turner? Do you think that you, as a member of the audience, should notice a page turner?

Anticipating: What is it about the page turner that so captures Schwartz's attention?

1 The page turner appears from the wings and walks onstage, into the light, a few seconds after the pianist and the cellist, just as the welcoming applause begins to wane. By her precise timing the page turner acknowledges, not so much humbly as serenely, lucidly, that the applause is not meant for her: she has no intention of appropriating any part of the welcome. She is onstage merely to serve a purpose, a worthy purpose even if a bit absurd—a concession, amid the coming glories, to the limitations of matter and of spirit. Precision of timing, it goes without saying, is the most important attribute of a page turner. Also important is unobtrusiveness.

2 But strive though she may to be unobtrusive, to dim or diminish her radiance in ways known only to herself, the page turner

cannot render herself invisible, and so her sudden appearance onstage is as exciting as the appearance of the musicians; it gives the audience an unanticipated stab of pleasure. The page turner is golden-tressed—yes, "tresses" is the word for the mass of hair rippling down her back, hair that emits light like a shower of fine sparkles diffusing into the glow of the stage lights. She is young and tall, younger and taller than either of the musicians, who are squarish, unprepossessing middle-aged men. She wears black, a suitable choice for one who should be unobtrusive. Yet the arresting manner in which her black clothes shelter her flesh, flesh that seems molded like clay and yields to the fabric with a certain playful, even droll resistance, defies unobtrusiveness. Her black long-sleeved knit shirt reaches just below her waist, and the fabric of her perfectly fitting black slacks stirs gently around her narrow hips and thighs. Beyond the hem of her slacks can be glimpsed her shiny, but not too conspicuously shiny, black boots with a thick two-inch heel. Her face is heart-shaped, like the illustrations of princesses in fairy tales. The skin of her face and neck and hands, the only visible skin, is pale, an off-white like heavy cream or the best butter. Her lips are painted magenta.

Of course she is not a princess or even a professional beauty 3
hired to enhance the decor but most likely, offstage, a music student, selected as a reward for achievement or for having demonstrated an ability to sit still and turn the pages at the proper moment. Or else she has volunteered for any number of practical reasons: to help pay for her studies, to gain experience of being onstage. Perhaps she should have been disqualified because of her appearance, which might distract from the music. But given the principles of fair play and equal opportunity, beauty can no more disqualify than plainness. For the moment, though, life offstage and whatever the page turner's place in it might be are far removed from the audience, transported as they are by the hair combed back from her high forehead and cascading in a loose, lacy mass that covers her back like a cloak.

In the waiting hush, the page turner lowers her body onto a 4
chair to the left and slightly behind the pianist's seat, the fabric of her slacks adjusting around her recalcitrant hips, the hem rising a trifle to reveal more of her boots. She folds her white hands patiently in her lap like lilies resting on the surface of a dark pond and fixes her eyes on the sheets of music on the rack, her body calm but alert for the moment when she must perform her task.

After the musicians' usual tics and fussing, the pianist's last- 5
minute swipes at face and hair, the cellist's slow and fastidious

tuning of his instrument, his nervous flicking of his jacket away from his body as if to let his torso breathe, the music begins. The page turner, utterly still, waits. Very soon, she rises soundlessly and leans forward—and at this instant, with the right side of her upper body leaning over the pianist, the audience inevitably imagines him, feels him, inhaling the fragrance of her breast and arm, of her cascading hair; they imagine she exudes a delicate scent, lightly alluring but not so alluring as to distract the pianist, not more alluring than the music he plays.

6 She stays poised briefly in that leaning position until with a swift movement, almost a surprise yet unsurprising, she reaches her hand over to the right-hand page. The upper corner of the page is already turned down, suggesting that the page turner has prepared the music in advance, has, in her patient, able manner (more like a lady in waiting, really, than an idle fairy-tale princess), folded down all the necessary corners so that she need not fumble when the moment arrives. At the pianist's barely perceptible nod, she propels the page in the blink of an eye through its small leftward arc and smooths it flat, then seats herself, her body drifting lightly yet firmly, purposefully, down to the chair. Once again the edge of her short shirt sinks into her waist and the folds of her slacks reassemble beguilingly over her hips; the hem of her slacks rises to reveal more of her shiny boots. With her back straight, her seated body making a slender black L shape, once again she waits with hands folded, and very soon rises, quite silently, to perform the same set of movements. Soon this becomes a ritual, expected and hypnotic, changeless and evocative.

7 The page turner listens attentively but appears, fittingly, unmoved by the music itself; her body is focused entirely on her task, which is a demanding one, not simply turning the pages at the proper moments but dimming her presence, suppressing everything of herself except her attentiveness. But as able as she proves to be at turning pages—never a split second late, never fumbling with the corners or making an excessive gesture—she cannot, in her helpless radiance, keep from absorbing all the visual energy in the concert hall. The performance taking place in the hall is a gift to the ear, and while all ears are fully occupied, satiated—the musicians being excellent, more than excellent, capable of seraphic sounds—the listeners' eyes are idle. The musicians are only moderately interesting to look at. The eyes crave occupation too. Offered a pleasure to match that of the ears, naturally the eyes accept the offering. They fix on the page turner—pale skin, black clothes, and gold tresses—*who surely knows she is being watched, who cannot*

deflect the gaze of the audience, only absorb it into the deep well of her stillness, her own intent yet detached absorption in the music.

The very banality of her task lends her a dignity, adds a rich- 8
ness to her already rich presence, since it illustrates a crucial truth: banality is necessary in the making of splendid music, or splendid anything for that matter, much like the pianist's probable clipping of his fingernails or the cellist's rosining of his bow, though such banalities are performed in private, which is just as well.

And then little by little, while the listeners' eyes yearn to- 9
ward the page turner, it comes to appear that her purpose is not so banal after all, nor is she anything so common as a distraction. Instead it appears that she has an unusual and intimate connection with the music. She is not a physical expression of it, a living symbol; that would be too facile. More subtly, she might be an emanation of the music, a phantom conjured into being by the sounds, but her physical reality—her stylish clothes and shiny boots—contradicts this possibility, and besides, the audience has seen her enter minutes before the music began and can attest to her independent life. No, the connection must be this: though the pianist is clearly striking the keys and the cellist drawing the bow over the strings (with, incidentally, many unfortunate contortions of his face), it comes to seem, through the force of the audience's gaze, that the music is issuing from the page turner, effortlessly, or through some supernatural, indescribable effort, as she sits in her golden radiance and stillness. So that as the concert proceeds, the audience gazes ever more raptly at the page turner. By virtue of her beauty and their gaze, she has become an ineffable instrument—no longer a distraction but rather the very source of the music.

Though the concert is long, very long, the air in the hall re- 10
mains charged with vitality, the seraphic sounds yielding an ecstasy for which the entranced listeners silently bless the page turner. But perhaps because the concert is long and the page turner is only human, not even a princess, she cannot maintain her aloof pose forever. Though not flagging in her task, without any lapse of efficiency, she begins to show her pleasure in the music as any ordinary person might: her eyelids tremble at a finely executed turn, her lips hint at a smile for a satisfying chord resolution. Her breathing is visible, her upper body rising and sinking with the undulations of the sounds swirling about her. She leans into the music, once or twice even swaying her body a bit. While undeniably pretty to watch, this relaxation of discipline is a sad portent. It suggests the concert has gone on almost long enough, that beauty cannot be endlessly sustained, and that we, too, cannot remain

absorbed indefinitely in radiant stillness: we have our limits, even for ecstasy. Banality beckons us back to its leaden, relieving embrace. The ordinary, appreciative movements of the page turner are a signal that the concert will soon end. We feel an anticipatory nostalgia for the notes we are hearing, even for the notes we have not yet heard, have yet to hear, which will be the closing notes. The early notes of a concert lead us into a safe and luxuriant green meadow of sound, a kind of Eden of the ear, but there comes a point, the climax in the music's arc, when we grasp that the notes are curving back and leading us out of the meadow, back into silent and harsher weather.

11 And this impression of being led regrettably back to dailiness grows still stronger when now and then the pianist glances over at the page turner with a half-smile, a tacit acknowledgment related to some passage in the music, maybe to a little problem of page turning successfully overcome, a private performance within the public performance, which will remain forever unfathomed by the audience and for those instants makes us feel excluded. With their work almost over the performers can afford such small indulgences—a foretaste of the inevitable melancholy moment when audience and performers, alike excluded, will file out into their lives, stripped of this glory, relieved of its burden.

12 When the music ends, as it must, the page turner remains composed and still: unlike the musicians, she does not relax into triumphant relief. As they take their bows, they show intimate glimpses of themselves in the ardor of achievement, as well as a happy camaraderie—their arms around each other's shoulders—in which the page turner cannot share, just as she cannot share in the applause or show intimate glimpses of herself. She stands patiently beside her chair near the piano and then, with the same precise timing as at the start, leaves the stage a few seconds after the musicians, deftly gathering up the music from the rack to carry off with her, tidying up like a good lady in waiting.

13 The musicians reappear for more bows. The page turner does not reappear. Her service is completed. We understand her absence yet we miss her, as though an essential part of the lingering pleasure is being withheld, as though the essential instrument through which the music reached us has vanished along with the sounds themselves. We do not wish to think of what ordinary gestures she might now be performing off in the wings, putting the music away or lifting her hair off her neck with long staved-off weariness, released from the burden of being looked at. We cannot deny her her life, her future, yet we wish her to be only as she was onstage, in

the beginning. We will forget how the musicians looked, but ever after when we revisit the music we will see the page turner—black clothes, golden hair, regal carriage—radiant and still, emitting the sounds that too briefly enraptured us.

QUESTIONS ON SUBJECT AND PURPOSE

1. In what way is this essay an example of a process narrative?
2. What does Schwartz leave out of her essay? That is, what doesn't she tell us about the concert?
3. How does the role of the page turner change in paragraph 9?

QUESTIONS ON STRATEGY AND AUDIENCE

1. Schwartz insists in paragraphs 1 and 2 that an important attribute of a page turner is that the person be "unobtrusive." What is ironic about that comment?
2. How is the essay told or narrated?
3. Does the essay describe only Schwartz's reaction? Does she ever imply that others saw and felt what she did?

QUESTIONS ON VOCABULARY AND STYLE

1. Schwartz uses a number of similes in her description of the page turner. Check the Glossary first to make sure you know what a simile is, and then locate the similes in the essay.
2. Would you say that Schwartz's essay is a vivid description? What makes an essay descriptive?
3. Be prepared to define the following words: *wane* (paragraph 1), *droll* (2), *recalcitrant* (4), *tics* (5), *fastidious* (5), *beguilingly* (6), *evocative* (6), *satiated* (7), *seraphic* (7), *banality* (8), *facile* (9), *emanation* (9), *raptly* (9), *ineffable* (9), *portent* (10), *camaraderie* (12).

WRITING SUGGESTIONS

1. **For Your Journal.** A live concert, regardless of the nature of the music it features—rock, ska, hip-hop, country, classical—is a performance, an experience that involves all the senses. Think about your experiences at a live concert. If possible, attend one at your school. Take notes, jot down

your memories in your journal about what is happening or happened to you as a member of the audience during the entire performance.

2. **For a Paragraph.** Use your journal experiences as a basis for a paragraph. Remember that you are not "reviewing" the music. Schwartz, for example, never tells us what pieces the musicians played; she never comments on their specific execution of that music. Rather, she focuses on the visual perceptions and observations of an audience member—and by implication all audience members—during the performance. In your paragraph, focus on a single detail.
3. **For an Essay.** Expand your paragraph into an essay. You might want to follow your experience from beginning to end—that is, use a chronological pattern for your process narrative.

Prewriting:

a. Try to use a relatively "fresh" concert experience, ideally, a concert that you attended with the intention of writing about it. In that way, you are more likely to be attentive to the process of listening and watching.

b. Try to compare your notes/experiences with those of others who attended the concert. Remember you are looking for your involvement in the experience. What were your eyes drawn to? What role did the audience play in enhancing your experience? How were your other senses involved?

c. Remember that your experience needs to be controlled or shaped—that, in a sense, your experience has a thesis. Don't just jot down unrelated observations; try for a central thread that holds the entire experience together.

Rewriting:

a. Look for your thesis statement—or write a one- or two-sentence thesis statement for your paper. Use that statement as a way of carefully examining every detail that you have included in your paper. If a detail is not related, eliminate it.

b. Have you kept your focus on your experience of the concert as a audience member? Remember that you are not reviewing or critiquing the performance. Don't, for example, list the songs/pieces that were included in the concert.

c. Have you brought closure to the experience? Remember that your essay shouldn't just abruptly stop, and it shouldn't just mechanically sum up the point(s) you have been making. Look at Schwartz's conclusion as a possible model or strategy that might work for you.

4. **For Research.** Tours by major recording artists today are generally complicated, elaborately staged, corporately sponsored affairs. Sometimes the tours even have names. Choose your favorite big-name artist or group and research the process by which they mount such elaborate productions. What is involved? How does the tour develop and what does it involve? What type of planning and strategy lies behind the production?

WEBSITE LINK

According to a story on the Web, an MIT inventor recently built an inexpensive automatic page turner, created at the request of musicians. How would that have changed Schwartz's essay!

SEVEN

Cause and Effect

It is a rainy morning and you are late for class. Driving to campus in an automobile with faulty brakes, you have an accident. Considering the circumstances, the accident might be attributable to a variety of causes:

- You were driving too fast.
- The visibility was poor.
- The roads were slippery.
- The brakes did not work properly.

The accident, in turn, could produce a series of consequences or effects:

- You miss class.
- You get a ticket.
- Your license is suspended.
- You injure yourself or someone else.

As this suggests, cause and effect analyses can frequently go in either direction—an examination of the reasons why something occurred or of the effects or consequences that follow from a particular event or situation.

Susan Strasser, for example, uses a cause and effect strategy when she suggests that part of the popularity of fast-food restaurants lies in the appeal of "stylized, repetitive, stereotyped events." Notice how Strasser structures the following paragraph to show how this ritualization is one "cause" for such restaurants' popularity:

> People arrive at McDonald's—and to a lesser extent at the other chains—knowing what they will eat, what they will pay, what to

> say to the counter person and how she or he will respond, what the restaurant will look like—in short, knowing exactly what to expect and how to behave; children learn these expectations and behaviors early in life. For some, the ritual constitutes an attraction of these restaurants; they neither wish to cook nor to chat with a waitress as she intones and delivers the daily specials. The fast-food ritual requires no responsibility other than ordering (with as few words as possible) and paying; nobody has to set or clear the table, wash the dishes, or compliment the cook on her cuisine, the traditional responsibilities of husbands and children at the family dinner.*

Strasser turns her analysis of fast-food restaurants in the other direction—toward effects—when she discusses how "fast food eating" has affected mealtime rituals at home:

> Fast foods have changed eating habits far beyond the food itself; they have invaded the mealtime ritual even at home. The chief executive officer of Kraft, Inc., maintained that eating out accustomed people to "portion control" and therefore to accepting a processor's statement that a package of macaroni and cheese serves four. "Generally speaking," one writer claimed in *Advertising Age*, "the homemaker no longer sets the table with dishes of food from which the family fills their plates—the individual plates are filled and placed before the family, no second helpings." Eating out even accustoms diners at the same table to eating different food, putting home meals of different prepared foods within the realm of possibility and altering the nature of parental discipline; freed from the "shut up—you'll eat what we're eating" rule, children experience the pleasures and also the isolation of individual free choice at earlier ages.*

Causes and effects can be either *immediate* or *remote* with reference to time. The lists regarding the hypothetical car accident suggest only immediate causes and effects, things that could be most directly linked in time to the accident. Another pair of lists of more remote causes and effects could be compiled—for example, your brakes were faulty because you did not have the money to fix them, or because of your accident, your insurance rates will go up.

Causes and effects can be either *primary* or *secondary* with reference to their significance or importance. If you had not been in a hurry and driving too fast, it might not have mattered that the visibility was poor, the roads were slippery, or your brakes were

* Susan Strasser, *Never Done: A History of American Housework* (New York: Random House, 1982), pp. 296–297.

faulty. Similarly, if you or someone else had been injured, the other consequences would have seemed insignificant in comparison.

In some instances, causes and effects are linked in a *causal chain*: if you were driving too fast and tried to stop on slippery roads with inadequate brakes, each of those causes is interlinked in the inevitable accident. Likewise, the accident means that you will get a ticket, that ticket carries points against your license, your license could as a result be suspended, and either way your insurance rates will certainly climb.

Why Do You Write a Cause and Effect Analysis?

Cause and effect analyses are intended to reveal the reasons why something happened or the consequences of a particular occurrence. E. M. Forster in "My Wood" examines the consequences of owning property. Elizabeth Larsen in "Buying Time" suggests the reasons why certain "fantasies" created to sell products appeal to consumers. Joan Jacobs Brumberg in "The Origins of Anorexia Nervosa" examines some of the causes of anorexia nervosa, tracing the disease back to its origins in middle-class families in the nineteenth century. Jonathan Kellerman in "The Scapegoat We Love to Hate" looks at and then rejects the often-suggested causal link between media violence and violent children. He offers instead other causes for remorseless criminality in children. Fox Butterfield in "Why They Excel" explores some of the reasons why Asian and Asian American students do so well in academic studies. Finally, Kyle Pope in "Network and Cable TV" traces the downfall of the network news broadcast and forecasts the effects that he anticipates from the coming of digital television and the merging of the television with the World Wide Web.

Cause and effect analyses can also be used to persuade readers to do or believe something. Butterfield's analysis of the cultural roots of Asian academic excellence is obviously meant to encourage readers to reevaluate their own approach toward their children's education. Kellerman believes that politicians use the media "as a whipping boy" to explain why some children commit horrendous crimes, wasting both money and time in searching for "causes and fixes" that simply cannot be found. If we, as a society, really want to address the issue of child criminality, then we have to look closely for another set of causes.

How Do You Choose a Subject?

In picking a subject to analyze, first remember the limits of your assignment. The larger the subject, the more difficult it will be to do justice to. Trying to analyze the causes of the Vietnam War or the effects of technology in five hundred words is an invitation to disaster. Second, make sure that the relationships you see between causes and effects are genuine. The fact that a particular event preceded another does not necessarily mean that the first *caused* the second. In logic this error is labeled *post hoc, ergo propter hoc* ("after this, therefore because of this").

How Do You Isolate and Evaluate Causes and Effects?

Before you begin to write, take time to analyze and, if necessary, research your subject thoroughly. It is important that your analysis consider all of the major factors involved in the relationship. Relatively few things are the result of a single cause, and rarely does a cause have a single effect. Owning a piece of property—even if it's something that cannot possibly be stolen—can have a number of effects on you, as E.M. Forster discovers. He becomes far more preoccupied by his property than he ever thought possible. Or, as Kyle Pope shows, the decision by network television executives to cover a football playoff game and not the impeachment vote in Congress was not simply a matter of hoping for higher audience ratings—it signaled a significant change in the network's role of news broadcasting.

Depending on your subject, your analysis could be based on personal experience, thoughtful reflection and examination, or research. E. M. Forster's analysis of the effects of owning property is derived completely from studying his own reactions. Elizabeth Larsen's analysis of mail-order marketing strategies is a thoughtful reflection on American culture and values at the turn of the millennium. Kyle Pope, a reporter who covered television for *The Wall Street Journal*, draws on his knowledge from years of reporting to analyze the changing future of network news and of television itself. Jonathan Kellerman, a clinical child psychologist and researcher, uses both his own insights and a published body of research to explain why some children become so violent. Fox Butterfield relies on interviews and on statistical evidence gathered from library or database searches. Joan Jacobs Brumberg's essay is also built on extensive research, especially in printed sources in history, literature, medicine, and psychology. As these selections show, sometimes causes and effects are certain and unquestionable. At other times, the relationships are only probable or even speculative.

Once you have gathered a list of possible causes or effects, the next step is to evaluate each item. Any phenomenon can have many causes or many effects, so you will have to select the explanations that seem the most relevant or most convincing. Rarely should you list every cause or every effect you can find. Generally, you choose the causes or effects that are immediate and primary, although the choice is always determined by your purpose. Moreover, as Jonathan Kellerman points out, a correlation and a cause or effect are two quite different things. Media violence might attract or stimulate an "already psychopathic boy," but that is not to say that media violence "caused" the child to become a psychopath.

How Do You Structure a Cause and Effect Analysis?

By definition, causes precede effects, so a cause and effect analysis involves a linear or chronological order. Most commonly, you structure your analysis to reflect that sequence. If you are analyzing causes, typically you begin by identifying the subject that you are trying to explain and then move to analyze its causes. Elizabeth Larsen begins by describing the marketing strategies that she sees in two mail-order catalogs. Both companies display their clothes in a "fantasy" world, a world that is simpler, more rural, less time-driven. Apparently, such images sell clothes; Larsen explores why. Why do such images appeal to us? If you are analyzing effects, typically you begin by identifying the subject that produced the effects and then move to enumerate or explain what those effects were. E. M. Forster begins by describing how he came to purchase his "wood" and then describes four distinct effects that ownership had on him.

Kyle Pope begins by recounting what he sees as an "end-of-an-era" media decision—CBS choosing to broadcast a playoff football game between the Buffalo Bills and the New York Jets rather than cover Congress's vote to impeach President Clinton.

He explains the causes that led to that decision and to the steady decline in network news. But Pope also moves forward, looking then at the effects that he sees coming from the emergence of digital television and the World Wide Web.

Within these patterns, you face one other choice: If you are listing multiple causes or effects, how do you decide in what order to treat them? That arrangement depends on whether or not the reasons or consequences are linked in a chain. If they happen in a definite sequence, you would arrange them in an order to reflect that sequence—normally a chronological order (this happened, then this, and finally this). This linear arrangement is very similar to what you do in a process narrative except that your purpose is to answer the question why rather than how. In a cause and effect essay that appears in Chapter 10, "Black Men and Public Space," Brent Staples follows a chronological pattern of development. He begins with his first experience as a night walker in Chicago and ends with his most recent experiences in Brooklyn. The essay includes a brief flashback as well, to his childhood days in Chester, Pennsylvania. As he is narrating his experiences, Staples explores the reasons why people react as they do when they encounter him at night on a city street. At the same time, Staples analyzes the impact or effects that their reactions have had on him.

But multiple causes and effects are not always linked. Brumberg's causes do not occur in any inevitable chronological order, nor do Forster's effects. If the causes or effects that you have isolated are not linked in a chain, you must find another way in which to order them. They could be arranged from immediate to remote, for example. When the degree of significance or importance varies, the most obvious structural choice would be to move from the primary to the secondary or from the secondary to the primary. Before you set any sequence, study your list of causes or effects to see whether any principle of order is evident—chronological, spatial, immediate to remote, primary to secondary. If you see a logical order, follow it.

Sample Student Essay

For a cause and effect analysis, Cathy Ferguson chose to examine the effects that television's depiction of violence has on young children.

EARLIER DRAFT

TV AGGRESSION AND CHILDREN

Let's face it. Television producers are out to make money. Their main concern is with what sells. What does sell? Sensationalism. People like shocking stories. In the effort to sell, the limit of the outrageous on TV has been pushed far beyond what it was, say, ten years ago. Television aggression is one aspect of sensationalism that has been exploited to please a thrill-seeking audience. Television is not showing a greater number of aggressive scenes, but the scenes portray more violent and hostile acts. Psychologists, prompted by concerned parents, have been studying the effects of children viewing increased aggression, since the average program for kids contains twenty acts of violence per hour, while the overall average is only seven acts of violence per hour. Research reveals three outstanding consequences of viewing greater TV hostility. First of all, TV aggression numbs children to real-world violence. One experiment showed that even a brief exposure to a fairly violent show made kids indifferent to the same aggression in real life. Preschoolers are especially affected by TV violence because they are usually unable to distinguish between reality and fantasy. If they see a hostile act, they are liable to believe that it is reality and accept it as the norm.

This leads to the second effect of viewing TV aggression: a distorted perception of the world. Most TV shows do not present real-world consequences of violence; thus children are getting a false picture of their world. Some kids are led to believe that acts of hostility are normal, common, expected even, and may lead a fearfully restricted life. In general, however, most children learn not how to be afraid of violence but how to be violent, which is the third and most drastic effect of viewing television aggression. Almost all studies show that kids are more aggressive after they watch an aggressive show, like "Batman" or "Power Rangers," than after watching a pro-social show like "Barney and Friends" or a neutral show. So although sensationalism, especially violent sensationalism, is making money for TV producers, it is also creating a generation that is numb to real violence, has a distorted picture of the environment, and is itself more hostile. These effects are so palpable, it is now realized that the single best predictor of how aggressive an 18-year-old will be is how much aggressive television he watched when he was 8 years old.

After Cathy handed in her first draft, she had a conference with her instructor. The instructor commented on her effective use of examples. Because the essay contains specific evidence, the cause and effect analysis seems much more convincing.

Her instructor offered some specific advice about revisions in word choice, sentence structure, and paragraph division. He noted that the essay repeated the phrase "television aggression" or a related variant seven times. Since condensed forms can be confusing, he recommended that she indicate that what she was writing about was aggression, violence, or hostility depicted on television shows. Noting that her first draft begins with five very short sentences and a single-word sentence fragment, he urged her to combine the sentences to reduce the choppy effect. Finally, he recommended that she use paragraph divisions to separate the three effects that she discusses. That division would make it easier for her reader to see the structure of the paper.

Cathy's revision addressed each of the problems that had been discussed in conference. In addition, she made a number of minor changes to tighten the prose and make it clearer.

Revised Draft

THE INFLUENCE OF TELEVISED VIOLENCE ON CHILDREN

Let's face it. Television producers are in business to make money. Their main concern is what sells, and nothing sells better than sensationalism. In an effort to gain a larger share of the audience, television producers now treat subject matter that would never have been acceptable ten years ago. The depiction of violence on television is one aspect of that sensationalism, exploited to please a thrill-seeking audience. The number of aggressive scenes shown on television has not increased, but those scenes now portray more violent and hostile acts. This is especially true on shows aimed at children.

Psychologists, prompted by concerned parents, have begun studying the effects on children of viewing this increased aggression. The average program for children contains twenty acts of violence per hour, compared to an overall average of seven acts of violence per hour. Research reveals three significant consequences of viewing violence on television.

First, aggressive acts on television numb children to real-world violence. One study showed that even a brief exposure to a fairly violent show made children indifferent to the same aggression in real life. Preschoolers are especially affected by television because they are usually unable to distinguish between reality and fantasy. If they see an aggressive act, they are likely to believe that it is real and so accept it as normal.

This potential confusion leads to the second effect of watching violence on television: a distorted perception of the world. Some children are led to believe that acts of hostility are normal, common, and even expected. As a result, these children may lead a restricted life, afraid of the violence that they imagine lurks everywhere.

In general, however, most children learn not to be afraid of violence but how to be violent—the third and most drastic effect of viewing aggression on television. Almost all studies show that children are more aggressive after they watch a show that includes violence than after watching a show that excludes it.

All three effects are so palpable that it is now realized the single best predictor of how aggressive an 18-year-old will be is how much violence he watched on television when he was 8 years old.

Some Things to Remember

1. Choose a topic that can be analyzed thoroughly within the limits of the assignment.
2. Decide on a purpose: are you trying to explain or to persuade?

3. Determine an audience. For whom are you writing? What does your audience already know about your subject?
4. Analyze and research your subject. Remember to provide factual support wherever necessary. Not every cause and effect analysis can rely on unsupported opinion.
5. Be certain that the relationships you see between causes and effects are genuine.
6. Concentrate your efforts on immediate and primary causes or effects rather than on remote or secondary ones. Do not try to list every cause or every effect that you can.
7. Begin with the cause and then move to effects, or begin with an effect and then move to its causes.
8. Look for a principle of order to organize your list of causes or effects. It might be chronological or spatial, for example, or it might move from immediate to remote or from primary to secondary.
9. Remember that you are explaining why something happens or what will happen. You are not just describing how.

Using Cause and Effect in Writing for Your Other Courses

Writing to analyze causes and effects is common in many of the social sciences, in which research and study often involve an attempt to explain why people behave in certain ways or what the results of particular behaviors may be. Causal analysis is also common in the sciences, in which explaining the causes or effects of natural phenomena is a fundamental concern. Examples of assignments that would require analysis of causes or effects include the following.

- **Sociology or Communication.** For a research paper on the effects of racial or gender balance on group decision making, you might read about a number of jury decisions, considering closely the makeup of the juries in terms of race or gender, and write a paper explaining whether or not the makeup of each jury seemed to affect the eventual verdict.
- **Chemistry.** For an exam, you might be asked to trace the causal chain that leads to a specific chemical reaction.
- **History.** On an essay exam, you might be asked to explain the causes of the Great Depression (or another decisive period of history, such as the French Revolution or the collapse of the Soviet Union). Alternatively, you might be asked to discuss the effects of such a period.
- **Environmental Studies.** As part of an ongoing research assignment, you might be asked to draft an environmental impact statement, researching the short-term and long-term effects of a proposed development in your community.
- **Theater.** For a short interpretive paper, you might analyze one of Shakespeare's plays in terms of how its structure and characters were influenced by the physical conditions of English Renaissance theaters and the companies that acted the play.
- **Geology.** On an exam, you might be asked to explain the causes or effects (or both) of a phenomenon such as continental drift.
- **Education.** For a research paper on the effects of a controversial educational policy, you might research bilingual education to report on how successfully or unsuccessfully it seems to prepare students for English-language proficiency.

Visualizing Cause and Effect

At the core of every murder mystery is the search for causes, or motives—a reason for committing the crime. George Booth's cartoon depends on our awareness of cause and effect. We know the effect of the falling potted begonia—Mr. Goodrich is dead. Mrs. Burlington Wells suggests a cause (which clearly rules out any possibility of her having a motive)—the plant "went off by accident." A likely story, we might reply!

"This is Mrs. Burlington Wells. One of my begonias went off by accident and killed Mr. Goodrich."

Visit the Prentice Hall Reader's Website

When you have finished reading an essay, check out the additional material available at the *Reader's* Website at www.prenhall.com/miller. For each reading, you will find a list of related readings connected with the topic or the author; additional background information; a group of relevant "hot-linked" Web resources (just click your computer's mouse and automatically visit the sites listed); and still more writing suggestions.

Tracing Causes and Effects

What do you know about Alzheimer's disease? Visit the Alzheimer's Association Website and read about the causes and effects of the disease. Write a paragraph on this or another disease. A collection of links can be found at the *Reader's* Website.

My Wood

E. M. Forster

Edward Morgan Forster (1879–1970) was born in London, England, and earned two undergraduate degrees and a master's degree from King's College, Cambridge University. He is best known as a novelist, but he also wrote short stories, literary criticism, biographies, histories, and essays. His novels, many of which have recently been made into popular films, include A Room with a View *(1908),* Howard's End *(1910), and* A Passage to India *(1924). He published two collections of essays,* Abinger Harvest *(1936) and* Two Cheers for Democracy *(1951).*

On Writing: *Once, after having broken his right arm in a fall, Forster contemplated writing with his left hand: "The attempt to write with the left hand raises new hopes in the human heart. For how many years have our thoughts been transmitted by the nerves and muscles of the right hand. How much of their essence might not have been absorbed in the passage. Now when new organs are brought into play new thoughts or new parts of thoughts may find their way on to the page, how many old ones can be absent and fail to reach it. A physiological outcry may be raised at this. But at all events the thought that it may occur is new. . . . [T]he thoughts that have so long struggled for expression may at last find it."*

BEFORE READING

Connecting: What would you regard as the most important "thing" that you own? Why is it most important to you?

Anticipating: Forster observes that owning the wood made him feel "heavy." In what sense does it make him feel "heavy"?

A few years ago I wrote a book which dealt in part with the difficulties of the English in India. Feeling that they would have had no difficulties in India themselves, the Americans read the book freely. The more they read it the better it made them feel, and a cheque to the author was the result. I bought a wood with the cheque. It is not a large wood—it contains scarcely any trees, and it is intersected, blast it, by a public footpath. Still, it is the first property that I have owned, so it is right that other people should participate in my shame, and should ask themselves, in accents that will vary in horror, this very important question: What is the 1 effect of property upon the character? Don't let's touch economics; the effect of private ownership upon the community as a whole is another question—a more important question, perhaps, but another one. Let's keep to psychology. If you own things, what's their effect on you? What's the effect on me of my wood?

2 In the first place, it makes me feel heavy. Property does have this effect. Property produces men of weight, and it was a man of weight who failed to get into the Kingdom of Heaven. He was not wicked, that unfortunate millionaire in the parable, he was only stout; he stuck out in front, not to mention behind, and as he wedged himself this way and that in the crystalline entrance and bruised his well-fed flanks, he saw beneath him a comparatively slim camel passing through the eye of a needle and being woven into the robe of God. The Gospels all through couple stoutness and slowness. They point out what is perfectly obvious, yet seldom realized: that if you have a lot of things you cannot move about a lot, that furniture requires dusting, dusters require servants, servants require insurance stamps, and the whole tangle of them makes you think twice before you accept an invitation to dinner or go for a bathe in the Jordan. Sometimes the Gospels proceed further and say with Tolstoy that property is sinful; they approach the difficult ground of asceticism here, where I cannot follow them. But as to the immediate effects of property on people, they just show straightforward logic. It produces men of weight. Men of weight cannot, by definition, move like the lightning from the East unto the West, and the ascent of a fourteen-stone bishop into a pulpit is thus the exact antithesis of the coming of the Son of Man. My wood makes me feel heavy.

3 In the second place, it makes me feel it ought to be larger.

4 The other day I heard a twig snap in it. I was annoyed at first, for I thought that someone was blackberrying, and depreciating the value of the undergrowth. On coming nearer, I saw it was not a man who had trodden on the twig and snapped it, but a bird, and I felt pleased. My bird. The bird was not equally pleased. Ignoring the relation between us, it took fright as soon as it saw the shape of my face, and flew straight over the boundary hedge into a field, the property of Mrs. Henessy, where it sat down with a loud squawk. It had become Mrs. Henessy's bird. Something seemed grossly amiss here, something that would not have occurred had the wood been larger. I could not afford to buy Mrs. Henessy out, I dared not murder her, and limitations of this sort beset me on every side. Ahab did not want that vineyard—he only needed it to round off his property, preparatory to plotting a new curve—and all the land

around my wood has become necessary to me in order to round off the wood. A boundary protects. But—poor little thing—the boundary ought in its turn to be protected. Noises on the edge of it. Children throw stones. A little more, and then a little more, until we reach the sea. Happy Canute! Happier Alexander! And after all, why should even the world be the limit of possession? A rocket containing a Union Jack, will, it is hoped, be shortly fired at the moon. Mars. Sirius. Beyond which . . . But these immensities ended by saddening me. I could not suppose that my wood was the destined nucleus of universal dominion—it is so very small and contains no mineral wealth beyond the blackberries. Nor was I comforted when Mrs. Henessy's bird took alarm for the second time and flew clean away from us all, under the belief that it belonged to itself.

In the third place, property makes its owner feel that he 5
ought to do something to it. Yet he isn't sure what. A restlessness comes over him, a vague sense that he has a personality to express—the same sense which, without any vagueness, leads the artist to an act of creation. Sometimes I think I will cut down such trees as remain in the wood, at other times I want to fill up the gaps between them with new trees. But impulses are pretentious and empty. They are not honest movements towards moneymaking or beauty. They spring from a foolish desire to express myself and from an inability to enjoy what I have got. Creation, property, enjoyment form a sinister trinity in the human mind. Creation and enjoyment are both very, very good, yet they are often unattainable without a material basis, and at such moments property pushes itself in as a substitute, saying, "Accept me instead—I'm good enough for all three." It is not enough. It is, as Shakespeare said of lust, "the expense of spirit in a waste of shame": it is "Before, a joy proposed; behind, a dream." Yet we don't know how to shun it. It is forced on us by our economic system as the alternative to starvation. It is forced on us by an internal defect in the soul, by the feeling that in property may lie the germs of self-development and of exquisite or heroic deeds. Our life on earth is, and ought to be, material and carnal. But we have not learned to manage our materialism and carnality properly; they are still entangled with the desire for ownership, where (in the words of Dante) "Possession is one with loss."

And this brings us to our fourth and final point: the 6
blackberries.

Blackberries are not plentiful in the meagre grove, but they 7
are easily seen from the public footpath which traverses it, and all

too easily gathered. Foxgloves, too—people will pull up the foxgloves, and ladies of an educational tendency even grub for toadstools to show them on the Monday in class. Other ladies, less educated, roll down the bracken in the arms of their gentlemen friends. There is paper, there are tins. Pray, does my wood belong to me or doesn't it? And, if it does, should I not own it best by allowing no one else to walk there? There is a wood near Lyme Regis, also cursed by a public footpath, where the owner has not hesitated on this point. He has built high stone walls on each side of the path, and has spanned it by bridges, so that the public circulate like termites while he gorges on the blackberries unseen. He really does own his wood, this able chap. Dives in Hell did pretty well, but the gulf dividing him from Lazarus could be traversed by vision, and nothing traverses it here. And perhaps I shall come to this in time. I shall wall in and fence out until I really taste the sweets of property. Enormously stout, endlessly avaricious, pseudocreative, intensely selfish, I shall weave upon my forehead the quadruple crown of possession until those nasty Bolshies come and take it off again and thrust me aside into the outer darkness.

QUESTIONS ON SUBJECT AND PURPOSE

1. According to Forster, what are the consequences of owning property?
2. Is there any irony in buying property from the royalties earned from a book about England's problems in India?
3. What purpose or purposes might Forster have had in writing the essay?

QUESTIONS ON STRATEGY AND AUDIENCE

1. In what way is this a cause and effect essay?
2. Look at the conclusion of the essay. Why does Forster end in this way? Why not add a more conventional conclusion?
3. What expectations does Forster seem to have about his audience? How do you know?

QUESTIONS ON VOCABULARY AND STYLE

1. Characterize the tone of Forster's essay. Is it formal? Informal? How is that tone achieved?
2. Forster makes extensive use of allusion in the essay. Some of the names are easily recognizable; others are less so. Identify

the following allusions (all but c are to biblical stories). How does each fit into the context of the essay?

a. The wealthy man in the parable (paragraph 2)

b. Ahab and the vineyard (4)

c. Canute and Alexander (4)

d. Dives and Lazarus (7)

3. Be able to define the following words: *asceticism* (paragraph 2), *stone* (2), *depreciating* (4), *pretentious* (5), *carnal* (5), *foxgloves* (7), *bracken* (7), *avaricious* (7), *Bolshies* (7).

WRITING SUGGESTIONS

1. **For Your Journal.** Commenting on the second effect of owning property, Forster observes: "it makes me feel it ought to be larger" (paragraph 3). To what extent does something you own make you want to own something more? Concentrate on the possession you value most highly. Does owning it ever make you want to own more? Explore the idea.
2. **For a Paragraph.** Select something you own that is important to you—a house, a car, a stereo system, a pet, something you use for recreation. In a paragraph, describe the consequences of owning it. How has it changed your life and behavior? Are there negative as well as positive consequences?
3. **For an Essay.** Extend your paragraph into an essay. Explore each of the consequences you described in a separate paragraph.

   Prewriting:

   a. Make a list of possible subjects. For each item, try to list at least four possible effects of owning it. Do not commit to a specific subject until you have considered the range of possibilities.

   b. Once you have selected an item, try freewriting for fifteen minutes on each consequence of ownership. You are still gathering ideas for your essay; this material will not necessarily become part of your first draft.

   c. The consequences will surely vary in terms of their significance and order of importance. Plan out an organizational strategy. Which effect should come first? Try writing each paragraph on a separate sheet of paper so that you can shuffle their order easily. Consider the alternatives.

Rewriting:

a. Make a brief outline of Forster's essay. It can be used as a model. Try to consider the author's strategy—that is, how did Forster solve the problems that this type of essay poses? Do not just imitate his form.

b. The biggest problem might come in the conclusion. Look at what you have written. Have you avoided an ending that starts, "In conclusion, there are four consequences that result from owning a . . ."?

c. Do you have an interesting title? Do not title your paper "My X." Remember that titles figure significantly in arousing a reader's curiosity. Brainstorm for some possibilities. Imagine yourself as a copywriter in an advertising agency trying to sell a product.

4. **For Research.** Property ownership has frequently been used throughout history as a precondition for full participation in the affairs of government (voting, for example). A number of states in this country applied such a restriction until the practice was declared unconstitutional. Using outside sources, write a research essay that explains and analyzes either the reasons for such practices or their negative consequence. Be sure to document your sources.

Website Link

An "unofficial" Website devoted to E. M. Forster includes a wide range of links to related topics such as hypertext versions of some of Forster's novels and Merchant/Ivory Productions, the film company responsible for making, among others, the film versions of Forster's novels *Howards End* and *A Room with a View.*

BUYING TIME

Elizabeth Larsen

Elizabeth Larsen graduated from Barnard College with a B.A. in English. Her first publishing job was with Sassy *magazine. She has been contributing editor and Web-site editor at* Utne Reader; *an editor and content coordinator of* PioneerPlanet, *the online service of the St. Paul* Pioneer Press; *and a producer at* Twincities.sidewalk, *an online arts and entertainment guide sponsored by Microsoft. She is currently a graduate student at the University of Minnesota where she teaches creative writing. She is also working on a memoir.*

On Writing: *Commenting on this essay, Larsen said, "I think that I find my best topics when I allow myself to write about issues that I have a complex relationship to. Like many Americans who have a decent amount of disposable income, I struggle with my materialism. Writing this essay was a good way for me to take a deeper look at the forces at play behind my shopping urges. . . . I wrote many, many drafts of this piece. I'm a big believer in revision as I think that it is during the revising process that you sink deeper into your thoughts and discover what it is that you really want to say."*

BEFORE READING

Connecting: Can you think of a time recently when you purchased something or chose a particular brand of something because of the associations that you had with that particular product?

Anticipating: How does Larsen feel about marketing strategies that sell a fantasy of life?

It seems like the only people with any free time these days are models in mail-order catalogs who lounge around in sunny breakfast nooks or picturesque farmyards wearing clothes they're trying to sell us. 1

It used to be that most middle-class people had enough free time to watch TV on weeknights *and* spend their weekends driving around in boat-size cars. But since the early '70s, when Americans' real wages started contracting and women began to enter 2 the workforce en masse, leisure time has had to be scheduled between sorting the laundry, paying the bills, and changing the cat litter.

3 Of course, there are more and more people who would do just about anything to fill the free time that is the emblem of their unemployment. But among those lucky enough to have jobs that pay a decent wage, is it any wonder that images of the simple life have become so attractive? Just look at the popularity of Amish and Shaker aesthetics—captured in a burgeoning cottage industry of furniture, books, cookbooks, and movies—that sell the fantasy of a life where there's enough time to can fruit, build barns, and drive around in buggies.

4 But what about those of us who know that a life of such noble austerity would be too much work? What do we do to get simplicity—and the freedom from everyday drudgery that it implies? We buy it, gathering souvenirs of other cultures and hoping that through osmosis, a high-backed chair or a Navajo rug will bring us a more thoughtful, less complicated existence.

5 As advertisements for appliances from the '40s and '50s—which show high-heeled women smiling at their families as they fill aspic molds—make clear, leisure-class aspirants have been purchasing little pieces of their imaginary movie sets for some time. In the '60s and early '70s, people who wanted a slice of the counterculture eschewed consumerism but still bought drugs that altered their sense of time, making them feel like they had all day to just sit around and experience the universe. When those fantasies got boring (and the American economy was pumped up by Reaganomics), the coke rodeo moved into high gear: Relaxing was passé; nightclubbing and German kitchen appliances that were rarely used became the insignias for people who thought that time was something that needed to be filled—and then managed in the pages of a Filofax.

6 Now, like the guy who cringes under the covers when he remembers groping the boss's wife at a party the night before, those of us attracted to simple chic are also nursing a hangover. But instead of doing it with Bloody Marys, we've turned to chamomile tea and dreams of a house in the country.

7 No one understands our yearning for a simple, unhurried life—and our desire to get it through shopping—better than those mail-order catalogs that picture groups of (tastefully dressed) friends in an unending string of weekend getaways. Take J. Crew, that paragon of WASP chic that's getting more popular as Gap stores move into almost all non-working-class neighborhoods. In

an oh-so-Shaker (and oh-so-*not*-Sears) style, J. Crew has started to display their inventory like museum pieces: Flannel shirts, baseball caps, thermal underwear, and jeans (plain, stonewashed, or "broken in") are placed one or two to a page against stark white backgrounds. Every item is a masterpiece of artful rumpling. Even a $218 cashmere sweater looks as comfy and casual as an old college sweatshirt.

When the items are worn by actual people (including light-skinned black women, whose presence assures the customer that this country club is hip to the times), the models strike casual poses on the hood of a Jeep or a Cape Cod porch. You see, the prospect of a weekend without errands or chores is the heartstring that J. Crew tugs at: Couples with no kids (and certainly none of their messy accessories) laze around on Oriental rugs, sipping coffee and reading the paper until it's time to make brunch. Then, still in their flannels, they stage a flirtatious boxing match that leads to sex on unbleached cotton sheets before they finish the Sunday crossword. It's a less tarty version of the same fantasy that's made Victoria's Secret into a gold mine. 8

Whereas J. Crew sticks to the endless preppy weekend, Tweeds concentrates on a funkier Euro-world. Like its competitor, Tweeds plies its customers with seductive images of leisure, but in Mediterranean village settings full of horse-drawn wagons and old men on bikes with baskets of baguettes. While much of the stuff Tweeds peddles can be worn to work, you'd never guess that by the look on the models' faces. Square-jawed men and women with Pre-Raphaelite curls slouch against stone farmhouses and haystacks, their lips lifted in three-glasses-of-wine smiles. (A friend of mine said that the Tweeds catalog looks like an advertisement for chronic fatigue syndrome.) All this nostalgia makes for good business. After all, which would you choose?—a dress modeled by a babe riding a rickety old bike through a meadow, or the same dress worn by a harried secretary standing against a gray cubicle wall? 9

Even as I was scrutinizing these catalogs to see how they hoodwink the poor, naive consumer, I picked up the phone, dialed J. Crew's 800 number, and ordered some of their pajamas. This made me think that maybe leisure time is something I can't handle any way other than as an unrealized desire. Like the people who think that going to a bed and breakfast for a weekend is the equivalent of getting away from it all, I get nervous about too much unstructured time. 10

Last summer, after waiting months for my week of vacation in Puget Sound, I got so stir-crazy listening to the birds and 11 watching for sea lions that I compulsively started to read anything I could get my hands on to fill what seemed like an endless amount of free time. By night number four, I was in such a panic that I drove clear to the other side of the island to see *Free Willy.*

12 Maybe this is what the demise of the American dream has brought many of us to: a life in which we have to work so hard that we're more comfortable watching someone have free time on TV than actually experiencing it, a life of marginal discontent in which we're more than happy to complain, but not unhappy enough to actually change the way we live.

13 While this kind of existence is certainly uncomfortable, it's also not that bad. Selling the car and the answering machine (and ditching the kids) to move to a charming white clapboard house in Iowa is at its core a denial of American existence in the last years of the 20th century. If we isolate ourselves from the strung-out, fragmented dilemma that is modern life, we're probably not going to be motivated to look for the political and social solutions to the problems that underlie the frenzy and the fatigue.

The key lies in being able to consciously understand our de- 14
sires. After all, yearning for enough free time to nurture ourselves and others is a good, even noble, ideal. The challenge is not to drop out of life entirely but to find ways to incorporate small pieces of our dreams into our routine. J. Crew and Tweeds know this, and in their own way they remind us of the gentle, leisurely days that for the past 40 years have been our utopias—utopias we nourish every time we consume these images.

What they don't count on is that any of us will ever actually 15
downscale our *spending habits.* The only way to really get more free time is to stop buying all of these things that sell our fantasies back to us. Whether it's a picnic basket or clothes available in colors like java, lagoon, and yam, it all takes money. And the way that most of us get money is not by planting vegetables or baking pies, but by getting up each and every morning and going to work.

QUESTIONS ON SUBJECT AND PURPOSE

1. Larsen is writing about how products are marketed through mail-order catalogs. How does that type of marketing differ from simply selling clothing or goods in a store?
2. Why might Larsen have titled the essay "Buying Time"?
3. In the final paragraph, Larsen suggests that many people are caught in a "spending" dilemma. What is that problem?

QUESTIONS ON STRATEGY AND AUDIENCE

1. What assumption underlines Larsen's comments in paragraph 13?
2. Why might Larsen include the detail, "Even as I was scrutinizing these catalogs to see how they hoodwink the poor, naive consumer, I picked up the phone, dialed J. Crew's 800 number, and ordered some of their pajamas"?
3. What assumptions does Larsen make about her audience?

QUESTIONS ON VOCABULARY AND STYLE

1. Look at the vocabulary words listed in Question 3. What does that list of words suggest about Larsen's essay and her audience?
2. How would you describe Larsen's tone in the essay? What sets that tone? How formal or informal is her language?
3. Be prepared to define the following words and phrases: *en masse* (paragraph 2), *burgeoning* (3), *cottage industry* (3), *austerity* (4), *osmosis* (4), *aspic* (5), *eschewed* (5), *passé* (5), *chic* (6), *paragon* (7), *plies* (9), *baguettes* (9), *harried* (9), *demise* (12), *nurture* (14).

WRITING SUGGESTIONS

1. **For Your Journal.** Advertisers frequently sell products by associating them with certain attractive lifestyles. In your journal, jot down examples of this strategy that you see in print, on television, on the World Wide Web, and on billboards.
2. **For a Paragraph.** Select one of the examples from your journal, and in a paragraph, first describe the fantasy lifestyle being created and then suggest what it is about ourselves and our society that makes such a fantasy attractive. Concentrate on a single cause for this effect (the fantasy).
3. **For an Essay.** Expand your description and analysis of a marketing strategy into an essay. What factors in our lives, our values, and our environment account for the attractiveness of this fantasy?

Prewriting:

a. Narrow your possible subjects down to three, and then brainstorm about each, listing all of the specific aspects of that fantasy that you notice. If you have print advertisements, study them carefully. If you have electronic media examples, concentrate on how the image is created and what is included in that image. Create thorough lists.

b. Once you have developed several possibilities, choose the one that seems the richest in detail and in analysis. Make a list of the significant features in that fantasy; then, next to each item, speculate on why this detail might be included.

c. Plan out an organizational strategy. Do you want to describe the fantasy first and then suggest reasons (or causes)? Do you want to mix the description and the analysis together, working through a series of points? Experiment with organization.

Rewriting:

a. Make a list of the potential problems that you see in your essay—these may be grammatical or mechanical things, or they may be structural. Take your list to your school's Writing Center and ask a tutor for help, or take your list to your instructor—perhaps during office hours—and ask for help.

b. Find at least one peer reader. Ask your reader if your essay seems like an adequate (or insightful) explanation. Does your analysis make sense? Have you omitted any other explanations?

c. Look carefully at your introduction. Does it catch your reader's attention? Does it "introduce" what is to follow?

4. **For Research.** Select a particular magazine, one that you read regularly or occasionally, that is targeted at people of a particular age group, gender, or socioeconomic class. Obtain a number of issues of the magazine, and carefully analyze it—its editorial content, its advertisements, its cover designs, its layout. (Some magazines also have home pages on the World Wide Web.) Then analyze the image of the audience that the magazine is projecting. Why is that image attractive to its readers? In addition to your primary sources, your instructor might want you to do a search for

scholarly analyses, especially through journals specializing in marketing and advertising.

Website Link

E-commerce has exploded within the last year. Check out the companies whose catalogs Larsen mentions—do they have Websites? Are the same marketing strategies used there? Why or why not?

The Origins of Anorexia Nervosa

Joan Jacobs Brumberg

Born in 1944 in Mount Vernon, New York, Joan Jacobs Brumberg earned a Ph.D. in American history at the University of Virginia. She is the Stephen H. Weiss Presidential Fellow and Professor at Cornell University. She has written many articles and several books, including Fasting Girls: The Emergence of Anorexia Nervosa *(1988), which studies the disease from historical, social, and familial perspectives, attempting to explain why anorexia has become so prominent in recent decades. Her most recent book is* The Body Project: An Intimate History of American Girls *(1997). Her research for that book entailed studying more than one hundred diaries of American adolescent girls from the past 150 years. The following selection is from* Fasting Girls *and was published in* Harper's *magazine.*

On Writing: *In her preface to* The Body Project, *Brumberg praised an editor for helping her achieve "accessibility" and "shed the girdle of acadamese that shapes so many historical accounts of the past."*

BEFORE READING

Connecting: What attitudes toward food and toward mealtime do the members of your family share? Do you have "family" meals? Are there any rituals connected with mealtime?

Anticipating: Brumberg defines a certain environment in which anorexia nervosa emerged. What are the essential conditions of that environment?

1 Contrary to the popular assumption that anorexia nervosa is a peculiarly modern disorder, the malady first emerged in the Victorian era—long before the pervasive cultural imperative for a thin female body. The first clinical descriptions of the disorder appeared in England and France almost simultaneously in 1873. They were written by two well-known physicians: Sir William Withey Gull and Charles Lasègue. Lasègue, more than any other nineteenth-century doctor, captured the rhythm of repeated

offerings and refusals that signaled the breakdown of reciprocity between parents and their anorexic daughter. By returning to its origins, we can see anorexia nervosa for what it is: a dysfunction in the bourgeois family system.

Family meals assumed enormous importance in the bourgeois milieu, in the United States as well as in England and France. Middle-class parents prided themselves on providing ample food for their children. The abundance of food and the care in its preparation became expressions of social status. The ambience of the meal symbolized the values of the family. A popular domestic manual advised, "Simple, healthy food, exquisitely prepared, and served upon shining dishes and brilliant silverware . . . a gentle blessing, and cheerful conversation, embrace the sweetest communions and the happiest moments of life." Among the middle class it seems that eating correctly was emerging as a new morality, one that set its members apart from the working class. 2

At the same time, food was used to express love in the nineteenth-century bourgeois household. Offering attractive and abundant meals was the particular responsibility and pleasure of middle-class wives and mothers. In America the feeding of middle-class children, from infancy on, had become a maternal concern no longer deemed appropriate to delegate to wet nurses, domestics, or governesses. Family meals were expected to be a time of instructive and engaging conversation. Participation was expected on both a verbal and gustatory level. In this context, refusing to eat was an unabashedly antisocial act. Anorexic behavior was antithetical to the ideal of bourgeois eating. One advice book, *Common Sense for Maid, Wife, and Mother*, stated: "Heated discussion and quarrels, fretfulness and sullen taciturnity while eating, are as unwholesome as they are unchristian." 3

Why would a daughter affront her parents by refusing to eat? Lasègue's 1873 description of anorexia nervosa, along with other nineteenth-century medical reports, suggests that pressure to marry may have precipitated the illness. 4

Ambitious parents surely understood that by marrying well, at an appropriate moment, a daughter, even though she did not carry the family name, could help advance a family's social status—particularly in a burgeoning middle-class society. As a result, the issue of marriage loomed large in the life of a dutiful middle-class daughter. Although marriage did not generally occur until the girl's early twenties, it was an event for which she was continually prepared, and a desirable outcome for all depended on the 5 ability of the parents and the child to work together—that is, to state clearly what each wanted or to read each other's heart and mind. In the context of marital expectations, a daughter's refusal to eat was a provocative rejection of both the family's social aspirations and their goodwill toward her. All of the parents' plans for her future (and their own) could be stymied by her peculiar and unpleasant alimentary nihilism.

6 Beyond the specific anxieties generated by marital pressure, the Victorian family milieu in America and in Western Europe harbored a mélange of other tensions and problems that provided the emotional preconditions for the emergence of anorexia nervosa. As love replaced authority as the cement of family relations, it began to generate its own set of emotional disorders.

7 Possessiveness, for example, became an acute problem in Victorian family life. Where love between parents and children was the prevailing ethic, there was always the risk of excess. When love became suffocating or manipulative, individuation and separation from the family could become extremely painful, if not impossible. In the context of increased intimacy, adolescent privacy was especially problematic: For parents and their sexually maturing daughters, what constituted an appropriate degree of privacy? Middle-class girls, for example, almost always had their own rooms or shared them with sisters, but they had greater difficulty establishing autonomous psychic space. The well-known penchant of adolescent girls for novel-reading was an expression of their need for imaginative freedom. Some parents, recognizing that their daughters needed channels for expressing emotions, encouraged diary-keeping. But some of the same parents who gave lovely marbled journals as gifts also monitored their content. Since emotional freedom was not an acknowledged prerogative of the Victorian adolescent girl, it seems likely that she would have expressed unhappiness in non-verbal forms of behavior. One such behavior was refusal of food.

8 When an adolescent daughter became sullen and chronically refused to eat, her parents felt threatened and confused. The daughter was perceived as willfully manipulating her appetite the way a younger child might. Because parents did not want to encourage this behavior, they often refused at first to indulge the favorite tastes or caprices of their daughter. As emaciation became visible and the girl looked ill, many violated the contemporary canon of prudent child-rearing and put aside their moral objections to pampering the appetite. Eventually they would beg their

daughter to eat whatever she liked—and eat she must, "as a sovereign proof of affection" for them. From the parents' perspective, a return to eating was a confirmation of filial love.

The significance of food refusal as an emotional tactic within the family depended on food's being plentiful, pleasing, and connected to love. Where food was eaten simply to assuage hunger, where it had only minimal aesthetic and symbolic messages, or where the girl had to provide her own nourishment, refusal of food was not particularly noteworthy or defiant. In contrast, the anorexic girl was surrounded by a provident, if not indulgent, family that was bound to be distressed by her rejection of its largess. 9

Anorexia nervosa was an intense form of discourse that honored the emotional guidelines that governed the middle-class Victorian family. Refusing to eat was not as confrontational as yelling, having a tantrum, or throwing things; refusing to eat expressed emotional hostility without being flamboyant. And refusing to eat had the advantage of being ambiguous. If a girl repeatedly claimed lack of appetite she might indeed be ill and therefore entitled to special treatment and favors. 10

In her own way, the anorexic was respectful of what historian Peter Gay called "the great bourgeois compromise between the need for reserve and the capacity for emotion." The rejection of food, while an emotionally charged behavior, was also discreet, quiet, and ladylike. The unhappy adolescent who was in all other ways a dutiful daughter chose food refusal from within the symptom repertoire available to her. Precisely because she was not a lunatic, she selected a behavior that she knew would have some efficacy within her own family. 11

QUESTIONS ON SUBJECT AND PURPOSE

1. According to Brumberg, when did anorexia nervosa emerge as a definable disease? Why did it emerge in that particular time period?
2. On the basis of what Brumberg writes here, who is the most likely candidate for anorexia nervosa?
3. What purpose might Brumberg have in writing about anorexia nervosa?

QUESTIONS ON STRATEGY AND AUDIENCE

1. Why does Brumberg begin by referring to "the popular assumption that anorexia nervosa is a peculiarly modern disorder"?
2. To what extent does isolating the origins of anorexia nervosa help us understand the disorder in young people today?
3. Brumberg uses quite a few words that might be unfamiliar to many readers. What do her vocabulary choices imply about her sense of audience?

QUESTIONS ON VOCABULARY AND STYLE

1. In paragraphs 2 and 3, Brumberg quotes from two popular domestic manuals of the nineteenth century. What do the quotations contribute to her essay?
2. In paragraph 5, Brumberg uses the phrase "alimentary nihilism" with reference to anorexics. What does the phrase mean?
3. Be prepared to define the following words: *malady* (paragraph 1), *imperative* (1), *reciprocity* (1), *dysfunction* (1), *bourgeois* (1), *milieu* (2), *ambience* (2), *wet nurses* (3), *gustatory* (3), *unabashedly* (3), *antithetical* (3), *taciturnity* (3), *burgeoning* (5), *stymied* (5), *alimentary* (5), *nihilism* (5), *mélange* (6), *individuation* (7), *autonomous* (7), *penchant* (7), *prerogative* (7), *caprices* (8), *emaciation* (8), *assuage* (9), *largess* (9), *flamboyant* (10), *efficacy* (11).

WRITING SUGGESTIONS

1. **For Your Journal.** How would you characterize your mealtimes? Do you care about the circumstances in which you eat? Do you have to eat with someone else? Can you just grab something on the run? Explore your attitudes toward mealtime. Do not just accept what you are doing without thinking about it. What do you expect of meals? Why?
2. **For a Paragraph.** Define your "ideal" body. Then in a second paragraph speculate on the reasons why that body type or shape seems "ideal."
3. **For an Essay.** Cultural historians have observed that American society is "obesophobic" (excessively or

irrationally fearful of fat and being fat). Certainly weight consciousness permeates American society and the weight-loss industries are multimillion dollar businesses. Why?

Prewriting:

a. For a single day, keep a record of every reference that you encounter to being overweight—advertisements in the media, references made by friends, remarks that you overhear. These examples will provide detail in your essay.

b. Think about the "ideal" body types in our society. What does the ideal male or female body look like? Freewrite about that ideal as it relates to you and your friends.

c. Construct a list of possible causes that have contributed to this "fear of fat." Try to come up with at least six possible causes. Discuss possible reasons with some classmates or friends.

Rewriting:

a. Look again at your list of causes and your essay. Is there any order that seems most appropriate? Which cause ought to come first? Which last? Construct several possible outlines, or, if you are writing on a word processor, construct several different bodies for your essay. Which arrangement seems to work best?

b. Have you provided enough examples and details to support your analysis and to make your essay interesting to read? Look back over that one-day record. Have you used your best examples?

c. Think about how an article in *Time* or *Newsweek* might introduce such an essay. Does your introduction grab your reader's attention?

4. **For Research.** Anorexia nervosa is only one of a number of diseases that are common today but were previously unknown or undiagnosed. Other examples include Alzheimer's disease, osteoporosis, premenstrual syndrome, and chronic fatigue syndrome. Select a "new" disease or disorder, and research its history. When was it first defined? What might account for its emergence during the past decade or two? If you are using information from electronic sources, such as the World Wide Web, make sure

that the information is authoritative. Be sure to document all of your sources, including electronic ones, wherever appropriate.

Website Link

The Web has extensive resources for dealing with anorexia nervosa and other related eating disorders. A listing of key sites is available at the *Reader's* Website.

The Scapegoat We Love to Hate

Jonathan Kellerman

Jonathan Kellerman is clinical professor of pediatrics at the University of Southern California School of Medicine and clinical professor of psychology at the University of Southern California. He was founding director of the Psychosocial Program at Children's Hospital of Los Angeles. In addition, he is the author of, among others, three books on psychology, two children's books, and a series of bestselling suspense novels starring psychologist-sleuth Dr. Alex Delaware. The following essay is from Kellerman's 1999 nonfiction work, Savage Spawn: Reflections on Violent Children.

On Writing: *In an essay about research for writing mysteries, Kellerman (along with his wife, Faye) gave the following advice, equally applicable to nonfiction writing: "Rewriting is especially useful. . . . You may find yourself larding your manuscript with nuggets of esoterica that seem fascinating upon first reading and lose luster in the cold light of an editorial morning-after. Like a sculpture, the [work] often takes form gradually. Don't be afraid to chip away until what remains is really important."*

BEFORE READING

Connecting: Have you ever been attracted to "gory" movies? To "gory" Halloween performances?

Anticipating: For Kellerman, what are the causes of violent, murderous behavior by children?

Social problems may require long-term solutions, but that shouldn't deter us from seeking efficient, short-term solutions to severe juvenile crime. If increased public safety is our goal, efficiency also dictates that we cease pouring money into research and clinical activities that have little direct impact upon rates of child criminality. A prime example of such diminished returns is the flood of studies conducted on the factor most often blamed for childhood criminality: *media violence.* 1

2 Each time another "senseless" crime involving a young criminal hits the news, one reaction is certain: a spate of editorials blaming the outrage—and the downfall of society in general—on rising levels of violence portrayed on television, motion pictures, and video games.

3 This is nothing new. During the pioneering days of radio, panic calls were sounded about the deleterious effects of radio crime shows upon American youth (1). And there is no doubt that children do have the opportunity to avail themselves of more vicarious violence than in previous generations (though it might be argued that boys drafted into the wars that preoccupied America during the previous two and half centuries were exposed to a good deal more *real* violence than are today's virtual warriors).

4 Numerous studies have produced correlations and other statistical associations between media violence and aggression in children (2). Explanations include (a) *sanitization and desensitization*—after repeated exposure to violence, kids get used to witnessing cruelty and mayhem and grow less loath to use it; (b) *identification*—kids imitate whatever they see on-screen; (c) *arousal*—kids are unhealthily stimulated by media violence and perceive it as thrilling and something to be tried; and (d) *positive reinforcement*—kids learn from TV and the movies that violence is rewarded.

5 Though some statistical support has been obtained for all four suppositions, *not a single causal link between media violence and criminality has ever been produced.*

6 Part of the reason for the failure to establish causation may be methodological: Television and motion picture viewing are ubiquitous—virtually every child in America and other Western cultures watches oodles on TV, so it is difficult to come up with control groups and to otherwise tease out specific effects of media violence. For that reason, most prospective media studies have taken place in laboratory settings where children are exposed to media images and then tested, using paper-and-pencil questionnaires or interviews, on their attitudes about violence and aggressiveness.

7 The problem with this approach is one that plagues social science research in general: laboratory experiments and field ("real-life") studies have proven notoriously inconsistent. In fact, in certain areas of psychological inquiry, such as attitude change, results from lab research are often the *opposite* of those obtained by field studies, with the former concluding that attitudes are

comparatively easy to modify while the latter find them resistant to change.

Lab/field discrepancies may be due to the artificial nature of the experimental setting: The experimenter overly controls the situation by projecting an air of authority that leads the subject to respond in a certain manner. In addition, the attitudes and behaviors measured in the lab are often constructed to be experimentally "clean"—unrelated to prior prejudices and relatively value-free. Unfortunately, this also means they have little or no relevance to the experimental subjects. It is fairly easy to change one's opinion about some trivial construct created by Professor Gadget, and quite another matter to modify one's deeply ingrained views on race and religion. 8

Another problem with media violence research involves applicability. Do the results of a questionnaire about some theoretical situation involving risk taking or aggressive problem solving filled out by a child who's just watched a violent cartoon have anything to do with real-life aggressiveness, let alone psychopathy or criminality? 9

Further clouding the issue are contradictory data, such as a lack of evidence of rising crime rates in comparatively nonviolent societies, such as Japan, following the introduction of TV, and the fact that the highest rates of recorded violence in today's world are found in regions, such as Latin America and Africa, where television viewing is *lower* than it is in the United States. 10

Yet other findings bring us back to the old correlation/causation snafu: Both degree of exposure and reactions to the violent images portrayed by TV and film appear to *interact* with the traits and characteristics that the child brings into the viewing situation. 11

For example, it has been found that highly aggressive boys watch more TV than nonaggressive boys and that they are affected more by what they see (3). This may be due to their lack of creativity and subsequent need for "canned" stimulation. It is also consistent with biological notions of psychopaths as chronically, physiologically understimulated emotional paupers who lack rich mental imagery and chase sensation. 12

Another reason high-risk boys may be the ones mostly attracted to the easy, passive stimulation provided by the visual media may be *parental incompetence.* We know that many violent kids are more likely to grow up in chaotic, neglectful, and abusive households, and to be exposed to drug and alcohol abuse. Perhaps the poorly raised boy, allowed to play hooky and to veg out at 13 home, stoned or drunk, simply has more time available to sit glued to the tube.

14 Yet another potential complication is the possibility that children who grow up in the rotten households that practice and glamorize violence may be more likely to regard the violent imagery they see on the screen as comfortingly familiar. If so, the media are playing a reinforcing role rather than a generative one. While this is certainly harmful, it is the chaotic family that we should be addressing, rather than the media.

15 The importance of considering temperament, traits, and personality characteristics as they interact with media violence cannot be overemphasized. Let me offer a totally unscientific, but I believe instructive, example from my personal experience.

16 I have four children, three of whom are old enough to have viewed many popular violent movies, including numerous horror films. My eldest daughter, in particular, displayed an early attraction to motion pictures full of images I found disgusting and shocking. My wife and I were reluctant to let her watch these bloody flicks, but my daughter insisted they wouldn't harm her. Since she'd always been a delightful girl, we relented . . . and watched for problems. None followed. My eldest daughter passed through the splatter-flick phase and moved on to new fare. Never did she exhibit a trace of violence or antisocial behavior as a consequence of what she saw. Never did I observe *any* side effect of viewing, and this shrink dad was *looking* for symptoms. Years later, my eldest daughter remains an honor student and one of the sweetest, least violent people I've ever met.

17 My son and my second daughter never developed any idiosyncratic interest in violent films, but simply by being teenagers in contemporary America, they too were exposed to violence and gore at a level much more explicit than what I grew up with.

18 I recall viewing the classic Hitchcock film *Psycho* in my late teens and leaving the theater absolutely petrified. At its initial release, *Psycho* was considered a revolutionary film primarily because it ratcheted screen violence up several notches. Adults were terrified by the images Hitchcock purveyed, especially the famous shower stabbing scene. Some viewers were even reported to have experienced heart attacks.

19 When my three oldest watched *Psycho*—as *early* adolescents—the film barely raised their eyebrows, so mild did they find it compared to *Nightmare on Elm Street*, *Friday the 13th*, *Halloween*, and others.

Personal anecdotes are not scientific. But the absolute lack of effect upon my progeny of violent media images remains in stark contrast to all the warnings promulgated by would-be media-blamers. Yes, desensitization definitely occurred in my kids—lowering their anxiety about screen violence but not real-life violence—and I suspect the same is true of tens of millions of other kids, because while nearly all American children watch violent movies and TV, only a very minute percentage becomes criminal. 20

This is not to say media violence is harmless. To the extent that gory junk attracts high-risk youngsters, it's anything but. Is it possible that an already psychopathic boy with a head full of violent impulses that have festered since early childhood, sitting around the house sucking on a joint or sniffing glue while he watches *Scream*, can be spurred to imitate what he sees on the screen? Absolutely. 21

The same is true of printed violence—serial killers often collect violent pornography and true-crime magazines in order to heighten sexual arousal. But for these psychopaths, print images are used to stimulate associations between sexuality and violence that are already well developed. The overwhelming majority of people who read pornography and true-crime magazines are not serial killers, nor do they become serial killers because of what they encounter between the covers of *Shocking Detective*. 22

Given no bloody books, no Freddy Krueger on video, no thrash metal or gangsta rap, would Billy Rotten of bullying, cat-mutilating proclivities have picked up a knife and stabbed his mother anyway? No way to know for sure, but I'd bet yes. And the likelihood of Billy's engaging in serious violence somewhere along the line would remain extremely high no matter what he read or viewed, because the variables that strongly influence violent behavior are likely to be a lot more personal than those elicited by wielding the remote control. 23

Even granting that media violence affects some kids negatively, what can be done to fix the problem? 24

The best solution is obviously to have parents exercise good judgment and restrict access to nasty material in the case of a child who shows tendencies toward violence. But failure to limit TV is way at the bottom of the list of parental inadequacies experienced by high-risk kids. 25

We are certainly unlikely to put in place the large-scale solution that might partially handle the problem—widespread 26 censorship foisted upon 99.9 percent of the population in order to shield a tiny minority—because that type of group punishment is antagonistic to our democratic norms, not to mention unconstitutional. And I emphasize *partially*, because any kind of blanket prohibition of violent films and shows will inevitably result in a black market of forbidden images, with those we are trying to shield most likely to get their hands on illegal goods.

27 A thorough and well-thought-out review of media violence and children summed it up wisely: "Aggression as a problem solving behavior is learned early in life, is usually learned well, and is resistant to change. Individual variation in the level of aggressive behavior and violence in children, adolescents and adults depends on many interacting factors of which media influences are likely to be less important than constitutional, parental, educational and other environmental influences. Contributing factors include being the victims of violence and bullying and witnessing violence perpetrated against others, especially at home. The emphasis on establishing whether television violence and actual violence are related has resulted in the neglect of these other, more important influences on the development of aggressive behaviors" (4).

28 Nevertheless, railing against the media is likely to continue as the knee-jerk response to child criminality because it is the type of facile, glib "explanation" that is perfectly in sync with today's short-attention-span journalism, and because it offends no constituency other than a small group of network executives and moguls. Using the media as a whipping boy is also extremely attractive to that most superficial and insincere group of "experts"—politicians—because it lends itself to sound bites and generates funding for the scores of do-nothing legislative commissions that pass for problem-solving units in a bureaucracy.

29 Though essentially a dead-end topic, media violence is likely to endure as a fruitful source of research grants for social scientists, producing much more heat than light about the causes and fixes of criminal violence.

Notes

1. Dennis, P.M. Chills and thrills: Does radio harm our children? The controversy over program violence during the age of radio. *J. Hist. Behav. Sci.*, Winter 1998, 33–50.
2. Heath, L., et al. Effects of media violence on children: A review of the literature. *Arch. Gen. Psychiat.*, June 1990, 595–96.

3. Bushman, B.J. Moderating role of trait aggressiveness in the effects of violent media on aggression. *J. Person. Soc. Psychol.*, November 1995, 950–60.
4. Black, D., and Newman, M. Television violence and children. *Brit. Med. J.*, February 1995, 273–74.

QUESTIONS ON SUBJECT AND PURPOSE

1. What is a "scapegoat"?
2. How or what is the scapegoat in this case and why do we "love to hate" it?
3. What purpose does Kellerman seem to have in this essay?

QUESTIONS ON STRATEGY AND AUDIENCE

1. In what way is Kellerman's essay an example of a cause-and-effect analysis?
2. In paragraphs 15 through 20, Kellerman offers the reactions of his own children as examples to support his contention. He acknowledges that "personal anecdotes are not scientific" (paragraph 20). Do you find the personal examples in any way convincing or appropriate?
3. What could Kellerman assume about his audience?

QUESTIONS ON VOCABULARY AND STYLE

1. Kellerman's essay appears in his book *Savage Spawn*. What does the title imply?
2. How does Kellerman use typographical devices (that is, print devices) to help draw attention to paragraph 5?
3. Be prepared to define the following words: *spate* (paragraph 2), *deleterious* (3), *vicarious* (3), *ubiquitous* (6), *notoriously* (7), *psychopathy* (9), *ratcheted* (18), *progeny* (20), *promulgated* (20), *proclivities* (23), *foisted* (26), *facile* (28), *glib* (28), *moguls* (28).

WRITING SUGGESTIONS

1. **For Your Journal.** Think back to your days in middle and high school. Do you remember examples of peer violence? Maybe not criminal acts, but acts that might have been physical, social, or verbal abuse? In your journal jot down

some memories. Try to make each memory as vivid and specific as possible.

2. **For a Paragraph.** In a paragraph explore a memory of peer violence that occurred during your middle or high school years. In your paragraph, offer either some possible causes for such behavior or some possible effects.
3. **For an Essay.** Although public schools increasingly have metal detectors, police patrolling the hallways, and various kinds of dress codes that prohibit certain types of clothing (trench coats, for example), colleges and universities seem to be immune to problems of peer violence. Why? In an essay, explore what you see as the possible reasons why institutions of higher learning don't seem to face similar problems.

Prewriting:

a. Try brainstorming with a group of friends or classmates about the question. Would they agree that college seems "safer" than high school? What could cause a college environment to be safer?

b. Ask friends or classmates to reflect on the journal writing topic above. What causes could they imagine for the examples of peer violence that they encountered earlier in school. What are the differences between an adolescent and a young adult in terms of peer pressure and response?

c. Outline briefly the reasons that you see as explaining the differences in behavior. How will you organize those reasons? Which one makes the most sense as the first point? Which as the last? Experiment with some different orders.

Rewriting:

a. When you have finished a draft, outline it. Does it fall into a coherent pattern? Have you clearly signaled when you are moving from one reason to another? Have you made adequate transitions?

b. Convert the list of things to remember at the end of this chapter's introduction into a series of questions. Then answer each question honestly. Try to look at your paper as if someone else wrote it.

c. Look critically at your introduction. Does it stimulate reader interest? Test your introduction on several peer readers. Do they want to keep reading?

4. **For Research.** Unfortunately, in the past several years we have had a number of examples of children who kill—generally their classmates—without remorse. In the period of the time that has elapsed, have we gained any additional knowledge that might help explain the reasons why such violence occurred? Choose a specific example (for example, the shootings at Columbine High School) and research what we know now about the child-killers involved. Be sure to document your sources.

Website Link

The Web contains a variety of sites dealing with the topic of violent children and the possible connections between media violence and criminal behavior in children.

Why They Excel

Fox Butterfield

Born in 1939 in Lancaster, Pennsylvania, Fox Butterfield earned a B.A. and an M.A. at Harvard University. He made his mark on American journalism as a member of The New York Times *reporting team that edited* The Pentagon Papers *(1971). That book, which earned the team a 1972 Pulitzer Prize for meritorious public service, revealed the scope of U.S. involvement in the Vietnam War. In 1979, he was granted permission by the Chinese government to live in Peking as a reporter for* The New York Times. *His book* China: Alive in the Bitter Sea *(1982), which won an American Book Award, is about his perceptions of Chinese life. His most recent book is* All God's Children: The Bosket Family and the American Tradition of Violence *(1995). He is currently a national correspondent for* The New York Times, *writing about crime and violence. "Why They Excel" originally appeared in* Parade, *a Sunday newspaper magazine supplement.*

On Writing: *Of the job of a reporter Butterfield has said: "I was trained to think you've got to write what you find, warts and all, if you believe it to be accurate." An inveterate researcher, he describes his office as full of "lots of file cabinets and the floor littered with piles of paper that I could never put away."*

BEFORE READING

Connecting: What expectations do your parents have for you? How do those expectations influence you?

Anticipating: According to Butterfield, what are the main reasons that Asian and Asian American students excel? Would or do these reasons motivate you?

1 Kim-Chi Trinh was just 9 in Vietnam when her father used his savings to buy a passage for her on a fishing boat. It was a costly and risky sacrifice for the family, placing Kim-Chi on the small boat, among strangers, in hopes she would eventually reach the United States, where she would get a good education and enjoy a better life. Before the boat reached safety in Malaysia, the supply of food and water ran out.

Still alone, Kim-Chi made it to the United States, coping with a succession of three foster families. But when she graduated from San Diego's Patrick Henry High School in 1988, she had a straight-A average and scholarship offers from Stanford and Cornell universities. 2

"I have to do well—it's not even a question," said the diminutive 19-year-old, now a sophomore at Cornell. "I owe it to my parents in Vietnam." 3

Kim-Chi is part of a tidal wave of bright, highly motivated Asian-Americans who are suddenly surging into our best colleges. Although Asian-Americans make up only 2.4 percent of the nation's population, they constitute 17.1 percent of the undergraduates at Harvard, 18 percent at the Massachusetts Institute of Technology and 27.3 percent at the University of California at Berkeley. 4

With Asians being the fastest-growing ethnic group in the country—two out of five immigrants are now Asian—these figures will increase. At the University of California at Irvine, a staggering 35.1 percent of the undergraduates are Asian-American, but the proportion in the freshman class is even higher: 41 percent. 5

Why are the Asian-Americans doing so well? Are they grinds, as some stereotypes suggest? Do they have higher IQs? Or are they actually teaching the rest of us a lesson about values we have long treasured but may have misplaced—like hard work, the family and education? 6

Not all Asians are doing equally well. Poorly educated Cambodian and Hmong refugee youngsters need special help. And Asian-Americans resent being labeled a "model minority," feeling that is just another form of prejudice by white Americans, an ironic reversal of the discriminatory laws that excluded most Asian immigration to America until 1965. 7

But the academic success of many Asian-Americans has prompted growing concern among educators, parents and other students. Some universities have what look like unofficial quotas, much as Ivy League colleges did against Jews in the 1920s and '30s. Berkeley Chancellor Ira Heyman apologized last spring for an admissions policy that, he said, had "a disproportionately negative impact on Asian-Americans." 8

I have wondered about the reason for the Asians' success since I was a fledgling journalist on Taiwan in 1969. That year, a team of boys from a poor, isolated mountain village on Taiwan won the annual Little League World Series at Williamsport, Pa. Their victory was totally unexpected. At the time, baseball was a largely 9 unknown sport on Taiwan, and the boys had learned to play with bamboo sticks for bats and rocks for balls. But since then, teams from Taiwan, Japan or South Korea have won the Little League championship in 16 out of the 21 years. How could these Asian boys beat us at our own game?

10 Fortunately, the young Asians' achievements have led to a series of intriguing studies. "There is something going on here that we as Americans need to understand," said Sanford M. Dornbusch, a professor of sociology at Stanford. Dornbusch, in surveys of 7000 students in six San Francisco-area high schools, found that Asian-Americans consistently get better grades than any other group of students, regardless of their parents' level of education or their families' social and economic status, the usual predictors of success. In fact, those in homes where English is spoken often, or whose families have lived longer in the United States, do slightly less well.

11 "We used to talk about the American melting pot as an advantage," Dornbusch said. "But the sad fact is that it has become a melting pot with low standards."

12 Other studies have shown similar results. Perhaps the most disturbing have come in a series of studies by a University of Michigan psychologist, Harold W. Stevenson, who has compared more than 7000 students in kindergarten, first grade, third grade and fifth grade in Chicago and Minneapolis with counterparts in Beijing; Sendai, Japan; and Taipei, Taiwan. On a battery of math tests, the Americans did worst at all grade levels.

13 Stevenson found no differences in IQ. But if the differences in performance are showing up in kindergarten, it suggests something is happening in the family, even before the children get to school.

14 It is here that the various studies converge: Asian parents are able to instill more motivation in their children. "My bottom line is, Asian kids work hard," said Professor Dornbusch.

15 In his survey of San Francisco–area high schools, for example, he reported that Asian-Americans do an average of 7.03 hours of homework a week. Non-Hispanic whites average 6.12 hours, blacks 4.23 hours and Hispanics 3.98 hours. Asians also score highest on a series of other measures of effort, such as fewer class cuts and paying more attention to the teacher.

16 Don Lee, 20, is a junior at Berkeley. His parents immigrated to Torrance, Calif., from South Korea when he was 5, so he could get a better education. Lee said his father would warn him about the danger of wasting time at high school dances or football games.

"Instead," he added, "for fun on weekends, my friends and I would go to the town library to study."

The real question, then, is how do Asian parents imbue their offspring with this kind of motivation? Stevenson's study suggests a critical answer. When the Asian parents were asked why they think their children do well, they most often said "hard work." By contrast, American parents said "talent." 17

"From what I can see," said Stevenson, "we've lost our belief in the Horatio Alger myth that anyone can get ahead in life through pluck and hard work. Instead, Americans now believe that some kids have it and some don't, so we begin dividing up classes into fast learners and slow learners, where the Chinese and Japanese believe all children can learn from the same curriculum." 18

The Asians' belief in hard work also springs from their common heritage of Confucianism, the philosophy of the 5th-century B.C. Chinese sage who taught that man can be perfected through practice. "Confucius is not just some character out of the past—he is an everyday reality to these people," said William Liu, a sociologist who directs the Pacific Asian-American Mental Health Research Center at the University of Illinois in Chicago. 19

Confucianism provides another important ingredient in the Asians' success. "In the Confucian ethic," Liu continued, "there is a centripetal family, an orientation that makes people work for the honor of the family, not just for themselves." Liu came to the United States from China in 1948. "You can never repay your parents, and there is a strong sense of guilt," he said. "It is a strong force, like the Protestant Ethic in the West." 20

Liu has found this in his own family. When his son and two daughters were young, he told them to become doctors or lawyers—jobs with the best guaranteed income, he felt. Sure enough, his daughters have gone into law, and his son is a medical student at UCLA, though he really wanted to be an investment banker. Liu asked his son why he picked medicine. The reply: "Ever since I was a little kid, I always heard you tell your friends their kids were a success if they got into med school. So I felt guilty. I didn't have a choice." 21

Underlying this bond between Asian parents and their children is yet another factor I noticed during 15 years of living in China, Japan, Taiwan and Vietnam. It is simply that Asian parents establish a closer physical tie to their infants than do most parents in the United States. When I let my baby son and daughter crawl on the floor, for example, my Chinese friends were horrified and rushed to pick them up. We think this constant attention is 22 overindulgence and old-fashioned, but for Asians, who still live through the lives of their children, it is highly effective.

23 Yuen Huo, 22, a senior at Berkeley, recalled growing up in an apartment above the Chinese restaurant her immigrant parents owned and operated in Millbrae, Calif. "They used to tell us how they came from Taiwan to the United States for us, how they sacrificed for us, so I had a strong sense of indebtedness," Huo said. When she did not get all A's her first semester at Berkeley, she recalled, "I felt guilty and worked harder."

24 Here too is a vital clue about the Asians' success: Asian parents expect a high level of academic performance. In the Stanford study comparing white and Asian students in San Francisco high schools, 82 percent of the Asian parents said they would accept only an A or a B from their children, while just 59 percent of white parents set such a standard. By comparison, only 17 percent of Asian parents were willing to accept a C, against 40 percent of white parents. On the average, parents of black and Hispanic students also had lower expectations for their children's grades than Asian parents.

25 Can we learn anything from the Asians? "I'm not naïve enough to think everything in Asia can be transplanted," said Harold Stevenson, the University of Michigan psychologist. But he offered three recommendations.

26 "To start with," he said, "we need to set higher standards for our kids. We wouldn't expect them to become professional athletes without practicing hard."

27 Second, American parents need to become more committed to their children's education, he declared. "Being understanding when a child doesn't do well isn't enough." Stevenson found that Asian parents spend many more hours really helping their children with homework or writing to their teachers. At Berkeley, the mothers of some Korean-American students move into their sons' apartments for months before graduate school entrance tests to help by cooking and cleaning for them, giving the students more time to study.

28 And, third, schools could be reorganized to become more effective—without added costs, said Stevenson. One of his most surprising findings is that Asian students, contrary to popular myth, are not just rote learners subjected to intense pressure. Instead, nearly 90 percent of Chinese youngsters said they actually enjoy school, and 60 percent can't wait for school vacations to end. These are vastly higher figures for such attitudes than are

found in the United States. One reason may be that students in China and Japan typically have a recess after each class, helping them to relax and to increase their attention spans. Moreover, where American teachers spend almost their entire day in front of classes, their Chinese and Japanese counterparts may teach as little as three hours a day, giving them more time to relax and prepare imaginative lessons.

Another study, prepared for the U.S. Department of Education, compared the math and science achievements of 24,000 13-year-olds in the United States and five other countries (four provinces of Canada, plus South Korea, Ireland, Great Britain and Spain). One of the findings was that the more time students spent watching television, the poorer their performance. The American students watched the most television. They also got the worst scores in math. Only the Irish students and some of the Canadians scored lower in science. 29

"I don't think Asians are any smarter," said Don Lee, the Korean-American at Berkeley. "There are brilliant Americans in my chemistry class. But the Asian students work harder. I see a lot of wasted potential among the Americans." 30

QUESTIONS ON SUBJECT AND PURPOSE

1. According to Butterfield, what are the "causes" of the success of Asian-American students?
2. Why do American students not excel to the same extent as Asian and Asian-American students?
3. In addition to providing an explanation for the high achievement of Asian students, what other purpose does Butterfield seem to have? What might his American readers take from his essay?

QUESTIONS ON STRATEGY AND AUDIENCE

1. Why might Butterfield have begun with the example of Kim-Chi Trinh? Why not begin, for example, with a thesis paragraph?
2. Why might Butterfield choose to end the essay the way he does?
3. What assumptions does Butterfield seem to make about his readers? How do you know?

QUESTIONS ON VOCABULARY AND STYLE

1. What aspects of the essay suggest that Butterfield is writing for a popular rather than a scholarly audience?
2. What types of sources does Butterfield use in his essay?
3. Be prepared to define the following words: *imbue* (paragraph 17), *pluck* (18), *centripetal* (20), *rote learners* (28).

WRITING SUGGESTIONS

1. **For Your Journal.** Are you "driven to excel"? In academics? In sports? In an artistic pursuit? In your career? Explore your motivations. Make a list of the ways you have sought to excel and the reasons why. Conversely, if the phrase frightens you or seems contrary to your thinking, explore the reasons you react that way.
2. **For a Paragraph.** Butterfield basically attributes the motivation of Asian and Asian-American students to their desire to please their parents. In a paragraph, explore the typical motivations of students from another cultural group—your own or one to which friends of yours belong. (If you are Asian or Asian-American, or have many Asian-American friends, you might prefer to critique Butterfield's analysis.)
3. **For an Essay.** Expand your paragraph into an essay. Using a cause and effect analysis, either explain what motivates a particular group of students or compare what motivates Asian or Asian-American students to what motivates students from another cultural group. Try to define a specific audience—for example, readers of your college's newspaper.

   Prewriting:

   a. Before you begin, think about your possible audience—their characteristics, their concerns. How will that audience influence both what you say and how you say it?
   b. Brainstorm a list of possible motivations. Also brainstorm a list of reasons why people might *not* be motivated to excel. Consider both sides of the subject before choosing your approach.
   c. Spend ten to fifteen minutes freewriting about each item on both lists. Use these freewriting exercises to help define your subject and to analyze the possible significance or importance of each item.

Rewriting:

a. Look again at how you have arranged or ordered the middle of your essay. Did you move from the most important to the least important cause or in the opposite direction? Try another order to see what happens.

b. Check how you made the transitions from one reason to another. Have you used transitional devices? Do you provide the reader with a clear, logical pattern?

c. Examine your introduction and conclusion. Put your essay aside, and without looking at what you have already done, freewrite a new beginning and a new ending. Experiment with the strategies that Butterfield uses.

4. **For Research.** In paragraph 28, Butterfield describes some differences between Asian schools and American schools. Research the nature and methods of high school education in China, Japan, or another Pacific Rim country. Then explain in an essay how that educational system prepares and motivates students. Be sure to acknowledge your sources wherever appropriate.

WEBSITE LINK

A pair of Websites offer an extensive assortment of links devoted to Asian-American resources and students. You can also find a link that ties Butterfield's most recent book to a point that Kellerman is making in his essay.

Network and Cable TV

Kyle Pope

Kyle Pope graduated from the University of Texas at Austin in 1986 with a degree in political science, serving also as the news editor of the campus newspaper. He worked for a series of newspapers—the American-Statesman *in Austin (where he covered technology); the Houston* Chronicle *(oil);* The Wall Street Journal, *first, in Dallas (technology), then London, and finally New York (television). He is currently involved in launching an on-line magazine aimed at the media and entertainment industry. With his wife Tara Parker-Pope, he writes a column for* The Wall Street Sunday Journal *titled "A Balanced Life."*

"Network and Cable TV" originally appeared in the Media Studies Journal, *a publication intended as a "forum for scholars, journalists and informed commentators to discuss topical themes of enduring importance to the news media and the public."*

On Writing: *Commenting on this essay and reporting, Pope said: "In terms of the process, this piece, like all major features I do, was written in two waves. First, I just sit down and write everything I know, without looking at a slip of paper. I find this keeps me from spending hours flipping through notes and frees me up to think about what the story really should say. I focus on themes, people, major points I need to make. I then go back through, with my reporting at hand. Some stuff is scratched, much of it is revised. The point, though, is that all of the big-picture issues are already down on the page. The broader lesson here is a simple one, I think: The more you know about a subject, the more reporting and learning you do, the easier it is to write."*

BEFORE READING

Connecting: Do you have access to cable television? If so, how has cable TV influenced your television viewing habits?

Anticipating: If you wanted to check the day's news, how would you do so? In a newspaper, on the radio, on a network news show, on a cable news station, on the Internet?

1 In the end, it was the twin American passions of sex and football that marked the last gasp of the network news business.

Saturday, December 19, 1998. In Washington, Congress is 2
voting on the impeachment of a president for only the second time in history. In New York, the Buffalo Bills and the New York Jets are locked in a bitter play-off battle for a shot at football's Super Bowl.

And at CBS News, once the most respected news organiza- 3
tion in the world, anchorman Dan Rather is watching helplessly as CBS chooses football.

The contrast on the tube was, at times, surreal. As CBS's 4
competitors broadcast the roll call of members of Congress impeaching President Clinton for his dalliance with an intern, the most-watched network on TV was forced to update its viewers between quarters and during time-outs. At one point, CBS even used the ultimate sports-television gimmick—the split screen—showing the action on the field on one side and Rather's grim-faced vote count on the other.

While CBS executives defended their decision the next 5
day—after all, CBS only months earlier had ponied up $4 billion to steal the rights to professional football away from rival NBC—the episode nevertheless carried with it a distinctive end-of-an-era feel.

In case anybody had any doubt about it before, it was clear on 6
that Saturday that the network news business had finally run its course. Viewership of the evening news is at a record low. News operations at the networks are bleeding money, as are the companies themselves. And for the first time in our TV generation, at least two of the Big Three networks have actively talked about farming out a chunk of their news-gathering operations to CNN, once a bitter rival. We are watching—or most likely, not watching—as one of the most powerful news vehicles of our time fades away.

Emerging in its place is a made-to-order TV news landscape 7
spun out of the Internet and digital cable television. News, like much of the rest of pop culture in America, is becoming a niche game. Just as *Wired* and *Outside* magazines have become print stars by catering to people's individualized interests, TV news itself is becoming a newsstand of options, with the broad, mass-market properties increasingly getting shoved onto the back shelf. Why settle for a minute and a half of Wall Street action on "World News Tonight" when you can watch a CNBC reporter counting down the ticks of the Dow Jones Industrial Average, or log onto The Street.com and see your individualized portfolio grow as the market soars past 10,000. Want foreign news? Click over to a new

digital channel provided by the BBC. Local news? For a subscription fee, there's a regional channel for you as well.

8 You can mourn if you want the end of our idea of a "broadcast"—a place where the entire country can sit down together and get its information. Truth is, our individual communities have simply become too small, our shared activities too few. The dinner hour is over.

9 After a half-century of dominance, the big networks themselves are in rapid decline. CBS, NBC and ABC have lost tens of millions of dollars over the past year, forcing them to shed hundreds of employees. NBC—the prime-time ratings champ for most of the past decade—has lost nearly a quarter of its viewers this season alone. Of the four big networks, two of them, CBS and NBC, are seen by Wall Street as being on the sale block.

10 While some of this is the result of the intense competition from cable, which last year surpassed the networks in viewership for the first time ever, network bungling has sped up the decline: first, they paid too much for programming in a last-ditch effort to bring the viewers back. NBC last year shelled out $13 million an episode for "ER," just as many critics were saying that the drama was losing its zip and viewers were getting bored. Result? "ER's" ratings are down sharply this year, and its biggest weekly draw, the actor George Clooney, has bailed out.

11 Second, the networks have relied on too shallow a talent pool for their ideas, resulting in shows that are derivative, at best. When "ER" executive producer John Wells proposed yet another show about a hard-luck Irish family last year, NBC—which has already invested so much in his medical drama—could hardly afford to say no. The result was "Trinity," a show panned by the critics and, ultimately, canceled by NBC.

12 In this climate of failure and fear, news stands out as a luxury the networks simply can't afford. The image boost that a news division once provided to the networks is no longer worth the $400 million a year it takes to keep one of these operations afloat. As a result, CBS has held serious talks with CNN about selling off part of its news-gathering operations, as has ABC. The idea is to let cable cover the breaking news, while leaving the networks to focus on newsmagazines and the morning shows, the only two news genres now that consistently make money.

13 Dan Rather, meantime, has been agitating inside CBS to can the 6:30 P.M. "Evening News" and shift it to a prime-time slot where more people may watch. But, even Rather concedes that may ultimately be too small a step. "Could a network bow out of the

news business entirely?" Rather asked me rhetorically, in a conversation in his office just off the "Evening News" set. "I don't think I could argue with you if you said it was probable."

The end of the network news comes precisely a half-century after the genre was born, in a 15-minute NBC program hosted by John Cameron Swayze called "The Camel News Caravan." As part of the sponsorship deal, a Camel cigarette had to be burning on the set, and Swayze himself had to take a puff at some point during the broadcast. CBS jumped in later the same year, with a similar show hosted by Douglas Edwards. 14

Throughout the 1940s and 1950s, TV news was no big deal. When President Eisenhower briefed the nation on military moves off the coast of China, the networks duly taped the bulletin, then ran it after prime time was over. Richard Nixon's "Checkers" speech of 1952 reached the public only because the Republican National Committee bought airtime to run it. 15

It was the quiz-show scandal of the late 1950s that changed the game. That controversy prompted the Federal Communications Commission to force the networks to air much more "public service" broadcasting as an absolution for their quiz-show sins. To their credit, the mandate was embraced by network chiefs, who saw news as a prestige product that could polish the image of their companies. 16

By the mid 1960s, Walter Cronkite was hailed by *Time* magazine as the most trusted man in America, adopted as a father figure at a tumultuous time in America, through the civil-rights battles and the Vietnam War, and the resignation of Nixon after Watergate. The bond forged during the Cronkite era between the network news and the viewers who watched it would come to define the next three decades of television, and wouldn't be broken until CNN arrived as a force in the 1980s. 17

The all-news cable network is, perhaps more than any other single force, responsible for the undoing of the network news business in America. It is more profitable than the three network news divisions combined and, arguably, the most influential. And, it has done all of this despite the fact that hardly anybody watches: on an average day, fewer than 1 percent of Americans tune in to CNN. 18

But it is the ubiquity of CNN and its half-dozen copycats that have killed the network news business. With more than 75 percent of the country now plugged into cable, it's difficult to argue that America is missing a big news event if it's not on ABC, CBS or NBC. Indeed, Leslie Moonves, the one-time actor who runs CBS Television in Hollywood, cites this fact in defending his 19 decision to show football on the network rather than Congress' impeachment vote. If you want a constant rehashing on the vote, he says, tune in to CNN.

20 Similar explanations were given by other network news chiefs last year, in defending their decisions not to go live with the resignation of former House Speaker Newt Gingrich, for instance, or with the results of the mid-term Senate elections. The danger, of course, is that viewers begin to assume that the networks won't be there when news breaks, which is precisely what has happened. On the day that CBS made its football decision, CNN received its highest rating of the year. And at several points during the day, more people were watching the cable network than either ABC or NBC, which stuck to the political coverage.

21 Yet in looking ahead at the future of TV journalism, it's not enough to simply say that the big networks will continue to decline and that cable will continue to grow. Not only is that old news, but it's somehow predictable, given that the three network news divisions now compete against a dozen cable channels offering essentially the same information. A fracturing of the news market is inevitable.

22 Beyond the decline of broadcast network news as we have known it, a much more revolutionary change is unfolding. For today's big broadcast and cable networks, the arrival of digital TV represents a brutal leveling of the playing field. Distribution is no longer key. Over the next decade, what once was a shortage of space on cable systems and in the airwaves will become a glut, thanks to the shrunken data size of digital video. Being one of the few players rich or established enough to send out a signal will no longer be enough; indeed, being a behemoth will quickly become a disadvantage, as the TV news business transforms itself from a passive medium, where viewers are told what's important, to a participatory one, where they decide for themselves.

23 For the future of news, instead of evening dinner around the kitchen table think of Sunday lunch at a suburban cafeteria: you will be able to watch—and pay for—only what you're interested in; if you're bored with foreign news, for instance, you needn't be bothered. Already, cable's Fox News is testing the notion of regional sports and news networks, meaning that newscast viewers in the Bronx will soon be able to see a different program than the one beamed to Manhattan's Upper West Side. Imagine the prickly social and racial questions involved in picking different stories for different neighborhoods. It is a quandary that has already been faced by Kraft Foods, which last year began testing a plan to use

cable TV to target its commercials at different neighborhoods. Ads for fat-free salad dressing, for instance, might be beamed to an upscale, suburban neighborhood, while an urban neighborhood nearby would get ads for Cheez Whiz and Kool-Aid. If companies aren't careful, say Madison Avenue experts, they could find themselves catering more to stereotypes than to actual consumer tastes.

CNN is working on a plan for news-on-demand, meaning viewers will be able to call up essentially any story, by topic, regardless of what time they tune in. Producers, once the gatekeepers of news and information, are on their way to becoming moviehouse ticket-takers, passing on news and entertainment that viewers say they're interested in paying for. 24

Driving all of this is the shift to digital television, already under way in most big cities in America. Because digital data is so much more compact than the analog streams that now go into your television, broadcasters and cable networks soon will be able to quadruple the amount of information they can send out, without buying more channel space. While Congress intended that TV networks use this extra space to offer super-clear high-definition television, few networks are headed in that direction. Instead, they plan to vastly expand the number of choices on offer, even if it's simply several versions of the same signal. 25

The possibilities in entertainment are endless. ABC, for instance, has been testing the idea of using one of its new channels to replay its soap operas at night, for viewers who work during the day. MTV plans to offer several different versions of its flagship service, each catering to a different genre of music. And PBS, which sees the arrival of digital television as a long-awaited opportunity to reinvent itself, hopes to use the new technology to vastly beef up its educational programming. Brace yourself for Barney in Spanish. 26

In news, the arrival of digital TV offers a way around the networks' primary conundrum: The fact that fewer and fewer Americans are home at 6:30 to see the evening news. All three networks are toying with the idea of replaying their newscasts later in the evening on a digital channel, and perhaps teaming up with a cable news provider to fill the time the rest of the day. 27

But even the coming explosion in choices offered by digital TV doesn't capture what's about to happen to TV news. The real revolution, less than a decade away, is in merging those digital TV bits with the World Wide Web. It is that move, thanks to improvements in Internet video, that will ultimately decide the fate of the network news divisions. 28

29 Recent moves by NBC and CBS show how seriously executives at the networks view the transition. NBC in recent months has made no fewer than 15 major investments in Internet content companies, many of them related to news. It has taken financial stakes in the Snap Internet portal service and in the iVillage news and information site for women. And it has revamped the Website for CNBC, more closely melding the information provided on the Internet with what appears on the screen. CBS, meantime, has hooked up with Internet giant America Online. Under that deal, CBS News provides content to AOL and mentions the service at the end of Rather's "Evening News." In exchange, CBS gets much-needed cash and a chance to align with the younger, hipper users of AOL.

30 The flurry of deal-making reflects where news is moving. For the next few years, the action will be in combining what you see on television with data pumped down digital cable lines. Though only a handful of people in the country see it now, NBC already is offering enhanced data along with many of its newscasts. Watch a story on Kosovo and pull up a short history of the crisis. The latest settlement in the tobacco legal wars? Available, on demand, via your television screen.

31 Soon, though, the entire game will migrate to the Web. Using remote control devices linked to set-top boxes already in production, viewers will be able to call up the programs they want when they want them. Ultimately, once the melding of the TV and the PC is complete, you will be able to "bookmark" news like many people now electronically dog-ear the Internet sites they most watch: stories about the weather, plane crashes and Belgium will be all you have to see, if that's your fancy.

32 Lost, of course, is the wonderful serendipity of stumbling across news you didn't know you needed, or cared about. And, shifting some of the editorial process to the viewers will only add to our information stress: now, it will be our job to decide what's important, to prioritize the news. In a sense, we are all about to climb inside our television sets, changing the future of news forever.

QUESTIONS ON SUBJECT AND PURPOSE

1. Does Pope expect that the television networks will continue to broadcast news in the same way in the future as they do today? Why or why not?
2. Has network television always had "evening" or "11 O'Clock News" shows?
3. What purpose or purposes do you sense in Pope's essay?

QUESTIONS ON STRATEGY AND AUDIENCE

1. Why might Pope begin his essay with the extended example that occupies paragraphs 1–5?
2. Why doesn't Pope's essay end with the increasing domination of cable news channels (paragraph 20)? Why does the essay continue?
3. In the final paragraph, Pope's choice of pronouns is "our" and "we." To whom is he referring?

QUESTIONS ON VOCABULARY AND STYLE

1. When the essay appeared in the *Media Studies Journal*, it carried the subtitle, "From Electronic Hearth to TV News on Demand." What does the phrase "electronic hearth" imply?
2. Twice in the essay, Pope uses the metaphor of the "dinner hour" (paragraphs 8 and 23) in referring to the old concept of network news. What is Pope suggesting?
3. Be prepared to define the following words: *dalliance* (paragraph 4), *niche* (7), *absolution* (16), *tumultuous* (17), *ubiquity* (19), *behemoth* (22), *quandary* (23), *conundrum* (27), *serendipity* (32).

WRITING SUGGESTIONS

1. **For Your Journal.** Given the choice of print media (newspapers, magazines, e-mail), an audio medium (radio), a visual media (television and the World Wide Web), which are you likely to choose for information or entertainment? Why? In your journal jot down your responses and try at the same time to suggest a reason for your choice in each instance—what is the cause for your preference?
2. **For a Paragraph.** Although it might be just a stereotype, many college students report that during their college years they pay little attention to the news—delivered in any format. Is that true of you? Of your friends? Why? If so, what are the effects of ignoring what is going on in the world around you? Or of being actively aware? In a paragraph, explore your own involvement or lack of involvement in the news. Concentrate either on the causes for your lack of interest (or your interest) or on the effects of this lack of knowledge (or abundance of knowledge).

3. **For an Essay.** Expand your paragraph writing into an essay. Remember that you are concentrating either on causes (what explains your behavior with regard to the news) or on effects (what are the results of your decision).

   Prewriting:

   a. Spend a couple of days thinking about the topic. Try to take notes on what you do and why you do it. Make a list of possible causes or possible effects. Just concentrate on getting ideas.
   b. Decide which direction your essay will go. Will you analyze the reasons why you do what you do? Will you analyze the effects of what you do? Remember that your essay should probably concentrate on one or the other, rather than trying to go in both directions at the same time.
   c. Construct a rough outline for your paper. Get it down at least a day before your complete draft is due. Allow some time to look at the outline objectively.

   Rewriting:

   a. Look again at your paragraphing in the essay. Probably the most typical arrangement would be to place each cause or each effect in a separate paragraph. Have you done so? Have you then adequately developed the idea so that each paragraph contains more than a single sentence?
   b. Reread your introduction and conclusion. Did you try to engage your reader at the outset? Did you write a thesis introduction? What type of conclusion did you write? Did you just repeat your crucial points in the essay? Ask a friend or a classmate to comment on just the opening and closing of your paper.
   c. Check your title. You have a title, right? Every paper needs a title and not something like "Essay." A title is an important part of catching your readers' attention, of signaling what the paper will be about.

4. **For Research.** What is happening with radio in an age that is increasingly Web-based? The interaction between the Web and radio has been a topic about which much has been written lately. Research the problem and discuss the interaction either from the point of view of causes or effects.

What has brought about Web delivery of radio signals? What are the effects of such a delivery mechanism? Be sure to document any information that you take from sources.

Website Link

Interested in reading more about the future of media? The entire issue of *Media Studies*, in which Pope's essay first appeared, is available on-line. Check it out at the Website.

EIGHT

DEFINITION

On the midterm examination in your introductory economics class, only the essay question remains to be answered: "What is capitalism?" You are tempted to write the one-sentence definition you memorized from the glossary of your textbook and dash from the room. But it is unlikely that your professor will react positively or even charitably to such a skimpy (rote) response. Instead, you realize that what is needed is an extended definition, one that explains what factors were necessary before capitalism could emerge, what elements are most characteristic of a capitalistic economy, how capitalism differs from other economic systems, how a capitalistic economy works, how capitalism is linked to technology and politics. What you need is a narrative, a division, a comparison and contrast, a process, and a cause and effect analysis all working together to give you a full definition of what is finally a very complex term.

When you are asked to define a word, you generally do two things: first, you provide a dictionarylike definition, normally a single sentence; and second, if the occasion demands, you provide a longer, extended definition, analyzing the subject, giving examples or details. If you use technical or specialized words that may be unfamiliar to your reader, you include a parenthetical definition: "Macroeconomics, the portion of economics concerned with large-scale movements such as inflation and deflation, is particularly interested in changes in the GDP, or gross domestic product."

Definitions can be denotative, connotative, or a mixture of the two. Dictionary definitions are denotative; that is, they offer a literal and explicit definition of a word. A dictionary, for example, defines the word *prejudice* as "a judgment or opinion formed before the facts are known; preconceived idea." In most cases, however, a single sentence is not enough to give a reader a clear understanding of the word or concept.

Many words have more than just literal meanings; they also carry connotations, either positive or negative, and these connotations may make up part of an extended definition. For example, in 1944, when the United States was at war on two fronts, E. B. White was asked to write about the "meaning of democracy" for the Writers' War Board. White's one-paragraph response goes beyond a literal definition to explore the connotations and associations that surround the word *democracy*:

> Surely the Board knows what democracy is. It is the line that forms on the right. It is the don't in Don't Shove. It is the hole in the stuffed shirt through which the sawdust trickles; it is the dent in the high hat. Democracy is the recurrent suspicion that more than half of the people are right more than half of the time. It is the feeling of privacy in the voting booths, the feeling of communion in the libraries, the feeling of vitality everywhere. Democracy is the score at the beginning of the ninth. It is an idea which hasn't been disproved yet, a song the words of which have not gone bad. It's the mustard on the hot dog and the cream in the rationed coffee. Democracy is a request from a War Board, in the middle of a morning in the middle of a war, wanting to know what democracy is.

Democracy was, to White, not simply a form of government, but a whole way of life.

Most writing situations, especially those you encounter in college, require extended definitions. The selections in this chapter define a variety of subjects, and they suggest how differently extended definitions can be handled. Bob Greene's definition of the phrase "adults only" is drawn from a description of the content and the language found in products—films, music, television shows—so labeled. Judging from the products, Greene ironically concludes that adult behavior is violent and deviant and that adult language consists mostly of four-letter words. Judy Brady defines the word *wife* through the many associations that people have with that word. Gloria Naylor explains how the meaning of a word depends upon who uses it when she confronts the label *nigger.* Amy Tan explores a definition of *mother tongue* based on her own mother's Chinese-inflected English. John Hollander describes the *mess* in his office, offering both a history of the word's meaning and examples of how artists have represented "messes." Finally

Margaret Atwood uses multiple examples to define that "capacious" topic, the *female body.*

How Much Do You Include in a Definition?

Every word, whether it refers to a specific physical object or to the most theoretical concept, has a dictionary definition. Whether that one-sentence definition is sufficient depends on why you are defining the word. Complex words and words with many nuances and connotations generally require a fuller definition than a single sentence can provide. Moreover, one-sentence definitions often contain other words and phrases that also need to be defined.

For example, if you were asked, "What is a wife?" you could reply, "A woman married to a man." Although that definition is accurate, it does not convey any sense of what such a relationship might involve. Judy Brady's "I Want a Wife" defines the word by showing what men (or some men) expect in a wife. Brady divides and lists a wife's many responsibilities—things expected of her by an actual or potential husband. Brady's essay, comically overstated as it is, offers a far more meaningful definition of the term *wife* than any one-sentence dictionary entry. Her intention surely was to reveal inequality in marriage, and she makes her point by listing a stereotypical set of male expectations.

Writing a definition is a fairly common activity in college work. In your literature course, you are asked to define the romantic movement; in art history, the baroque period; in psychology, abnormal behavior. Since a single-sentence definition can never do justice to such complicated terms, an extended definition is necessary. In each case, the breadth and depth of your knowledge is being tested; your professor expects you to formulate a definition that accounts for the major subdivisions and characteristics of the subject. Your purpose is to convince your professor that you have read and mastered the assigned materials and can select and organize them, often adding some special insight of your own, into a logical and coherent response.

How Do You Structure a Definition?

Sentence definitions are relatively easy to write. You first place the word in a general class ("A wife is a *woman*") and then add any distinguishing features that set it apart from other members of the class ("married to a man"). But the types of definitions you are asked to write for college are generally more detailed than dictionary entries. How, then, do you get from a single sentence to a paragraph or an essay?

Extended definitions do not have a structure peculiar to themselves. That is, when you write a definition, you do not have a predetermined structural pattern as you do with comparison and contrast, division and classification, process, or cause and effect. Instead, definitions are constructed using all of the various strategies in this book. Bob Greene is not interested in how a dictionary might define the term "adults only," nor does he acknowledge the legal "signal" that lies behind the phrase. Instead, he focuses on the nature of the content and the language typically found in anything labeled "adults only." Judy Brady's definition of a wife uses division to organize the many types of responsibilities demanded of a wife. Gloria Naylor and Amy Tan uses narration as a vital part of their definitions. John Hollander uses description and comparison and contrast. Margaret Atwood gathers a wide range of examples to suggest the complexity involved in the phrase "the female body," ending with an imaginative contrast between the brain of a man and that of a woman.

Once you have chosen a subject for definition, think first about its essential characteristics, steps, or parts. What examples would best define it? Then plan your organization by seeing how those details can be presented most effectively to your reader. If your definition involves breaking a subject into its parts, use division or possibly even process. If you are defining by comparing your subject to another, use a comparison and contrast structure. If your subject is defined as the result of some causal connection, use a cause and effect structure. Definitions can also involve narration, description, and even persuasion. The longer the extended definition, the greater the likelihood that your paper will involve a series of structures.

Sample Student Essay

Sherry Heck's essay started from a simple set of directions: "Write an extended definition of a word of your choice." Sherry's approach to the assignment, however, was very different from everyone else's in the class. In her purpose statement, Sherry wrote, "I wanted to inform a general audience in an amusing way of the connotations and associations that accrue to the word *fall.* I got the idea while thumbing through a dictionary looking for words!" Her first draft reads as follows.

EARLIER DRAFT

FALLING

When you were four years old, covered in scrapes and bruises, the word fall was probably too familiar. Perhaps you went exploring, discovering the creek in the woods, and following it to its falls. Summers would end too quickly and fall would arrive, and Mom would send you off to school.

You mastered the art of walking, yet it remained all too easy to fall over yourself in front of your peers. The popular kids would laugh, sending you to fall into the wrong crowd. As you sprayed graffiti triumphantly, you fell into agreement with your friends that this was the best way to slander the principal.

Then one day, you are sitting in school and you feel someone's glance fall on you. You fall silent and stare back. Soon you find yourself falling for that special someone, and you fall in love. Eventually, you have a huge falling out with that person. Your friends have long abandoned you, leaving you no one to fall back on. Your spirits fall, and you feel like the fall guy around your old peers.

Eventually, out of school, you fall into a good job, and you are able to fall out of your trance. Determined not to fall short of your career goals, you fall into line with society. Events seem to fall into place. The pace of the job speeds up, and several people fall out of the rat race. Their jobs fall to you, tripling your workload. It is difficult not to avoid falling from power, and your life's plans begin to fall through.

Alone, rejected, and jobless, you begin to blame your misfortunes on the root of all evil, the fall of Adam and Eve. Life continues, and you ponder this thought until your friends begin to fall off. Your face falls at the thought of your own fall. Your bones are weak, and falling means more than a scraped knee. Your blood pressure falls more easily. These physical worries all disappear when one day, after feeling a free-fall sensation, you fall asleep, peacefully, forever.

Sherry met with her instructor, Nathan Andrews, to go over her preliminary draft. He encouraged her to watch that she not repeat phrases—for example, in the fourth paragraph, Sherry had repeated *fall out* twice. After they had brainstormed some additional *fall* phrases, he encouraged her to search for more in the dictionaries in her school's library. He also suggested that she italicize each *fall* phrase so that the reader could more easily see the word play. In her revised essay, Sherry was able to add a number of new examples.

Revised Draft

INFALLIBLE

When you were four years old, covered in scrapes and bruises, the word fall was probably too familiar. Perhaps you went exploring, discovering the creek in the woods, and following it to its falls. Summers would end too quickly and fall would arrive, and Mom would send you off to school.

You mastered the art of walking, yet it remained all too easy to fall all over yourself in front of your peers. The popular kids would laugh, sending you to fall in with the wrong crowd. As you sprayed the graffiti triumphantly, you fell in agreement with your friends that this was the best way to slander the principal. Your behavior was leading you to fall afoul of the law.

Then one day, you are sitting in school and you feel someone's glance fall on you. You fall silent and stare back. Soon you find yourself falling for that special someone, and you fall in love. Eventually, you have a huge falling out with that person. The relationship falls apart. Your friends have long abandoned you, leaving you no one to fall back on. Your cries for help fall on deaf ears. Your spirits fall, and you feel like the fall guy around your old peers.

Eventually, out of school, you fall over backwards to get a good job, and you are able to fall out of your trance. Your love life has fallen by the wayside. Determined not to fall short of your career goals, you fall into line with society. Events seem to fall into place. The pace of the job speeds up, and several people fall on their faces. Their jobs fall to you, tripling your workload. You fall behind in your work. It is difficult not to avoid falling from power, and your life's plans begin to fall through.

Alone, rejected and jobless, you begin to blame your misfortunes on the root of all evil, the Fall of Adam and Eve. Life continues, and you ponder this thought until your friends begin to fall off. Your face falls at the thought of your own fall. Your bones are weak, and falling means more than a scraped knee. Your blood pressure falls more easily. These physical worries all disappear when one day, after feeling a free-fall sensation, you fall asleep, peacefully, forever.

Some Things to Remember

1. Choose a subject that can be reasonably and fully defined within the limits of your paper. That is, make sure it is neither too limited nor too large.
2. Determine a purpose for your definition.
3. Spend time analyzing your subject to see what its essential characteristics, steps, or parts are.
4. Write a dictionary-type definition for your subject. Do this even if you are writing an extended definition. The features that set your subject apart from others in its general class reveal what must be included in your definition.
5. Choose examples that are clear and appropriate.
6. Decide which of the organizational patterns will best convey the information you have gathered.
7. Be careful about beginning with a direct dictionary definition. There are usually more effective and interesting ways to announce your subject.

Using Definition in Writing for Your Other Courses

In college writing, definition assignments are especially common on essay exams. You may also write extended definitions for certain kinds of research papers. Examples of assignments requiring definition include the following.

- **Marketing.** For a course in retail management, you might research and write a paper defining the concept of customer value management and its relation to a particular marketing plan using examples, process, and cause and effect.
- **Criminology.** For a course in juvenile justice, you might write an essay exam defining the characteristics of juvenile offenders using description, examples, and cause and effect.
- **Political Science.** For an American presidency course, you might research and write a paper examining changing conceptions of the presidency over the past two hundred years using examples, comparison, and cause and effect.
- **Communication.** For a course in persuasion, you might write an essay exam defining psychological resistance using example, narration, and cause and effect.
- **Environmental Studies.** For a course in environmental economics, you might research and write a paper defining public and private property rights in terms of pollution control using examples, description, and comparison and contrast.
- **Geography.** For a geography of the city course, you might research and write a paper about urban renewal using examples, description, comparison and contrast, and cause and effect.

VISUALIZING DEFINITION

Central to our understanding of everything expressed in words—either spoken or written—is an understanding of what those words mean—we must know what the words refer to or how they are defined. The need to define is especially acute in college courses. As we move from one academic discipline to another, we constantly learn the meaning of new words and new concepts. Dictionaries and even textbooks, such as this one, provide us with lists or "glossaries" of new or unfamiliar terms, but often a subject is complex or

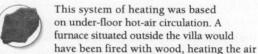

HYPOCAUST HEATING

This system of heating was based on under-floor hot-air circulation. A furnace situated outside the villa would have been fired with wood, heating the air that was fed into the flue pipes. The hot air would have circulated underneath the villa floor, which was supported on stone or ceramic pillars. It would then be fed through the walls in a series of pipes or flues made out of box tiles. The hot air and smoke would then escape through a series of chimneys or apertures. Only some rooms would have been heated, as the hypocaust would have required large quantities of wood and labor. This exposed hypocaust system was found at the Roman site of Chedworth in England.

The Atlas of Archaeology by M. Aston and T. Taylor (Dorling Kindersley ©1998). Photograph provided by the National Trust Photo Library/Ian Shaw.

unfamiliar enough that we need more than a one-sentence definition. Longer, extended definitions provide us with details, examples, explanations, even pictures and diagrams. Let's compare two definitions of the terms "hypocaust" and "hypocaust heating," used in archeology to refer to a type of under-the-floor hot-air heating found in ancient Roman buildings. A standard college dictionary offers this definition of the term "hypocaust": "A space below the floor in some ancient Roman buildings, into which hot air was piped to warm the rooms." In contract, an illustrated book on archeology offers this extended example with two visuals to help us understand this heating concept more fully. Which of the two—the dictionary or the extended visual definition—is more helpful?

Visit the Prentice Hall Reader's Website

When you have finished reading an essay, check out the additional material available at the *Reader's* Website at www.prenhall.com/miller. For each reading, you will find a list of related readings connected with the topic or the author; additional background information; a group of relevant "hot-linked" Web resources (just click your computer's mouse and automatically visit the sites listed); and still more writing suggestions.

Defining

Are you frustrated when you see or hear words connected with computers that you don't understand? Can you define the "Internet," "the WWW," "RAM"? When you hear the verb "surfing" do you think of an ocean? Answer all your questions on a Website devoted to definitions of computer-related terms and then try a paragraph-writing exercise in which you show off your new knowledge.

ADULTS ONLY

Bob Greene

Bob Greene's essay "Cut" is one of the readings in Chapter 1, and biographical information about Greene can be found in that headnote.

BEFORE READING

Connecting: When you see the label "adults only" (maybe with reference to a video, show, film, or CD), what do you expect? What associations do you have with that phrase?

Anticipating: What is it about the label "adults only" that Greene is objecting to?

1 It's one of the great untruths of our times, and it is so common that it passes without notice.

2 You see it—or some variation of it—on television screens, in movie advertisements, on the labels of recorded music. The wording goes something like this:

3 "Adult content." Or: "Contains adult language."

4 Few people ever stop to think about what this means. What, exactly, is adult content? What words constitute adult language?

5 In our contemporary culture, adult content usually means that people are shown attacking each other with guns, hatchets and blowtorches; that half-naked people are assaulting other people, ripping their clothes off, treating humans like garbage; that people are detonating other people's cars and houses, setting fire to property, bludgeoning and disemboweling and pumping holes in one another. That's adult content; that's how adults behave.

6 Adult language? Adult language, by our current definition, consists of the foulest synonyms for excrement, for sexual activity, for deviant conduct. Adult language usually consists of four letters; adult language is the kind of language that civilized people are never supposed to use.

7 It makes you wonder what lesson we are sending—not only to children, but to ourselves. If a TV show or a motion picture concerned itself with responsible adults treating each other and the people around them with kindness, with consideration, with

thoughtfulness, that TV show or movie would never be labeled as containing adult content. If a TV show or movie dealt quietly and responsibly with the many choices of conscience and generosity that adults face every day in the world, it would not warrant an "adult content" rating.

Similarly, if a movie featured adults talking with each other civilly, never resorting to gutter language or obscenities, choosing their words with care and precision, no one would ever think to describe the dialogue as "adult." A cable TV show or a music CD in which every word spoken or sung was selected to convey a thought or emotion without resorting to cheap and offensive vulgarities—that TV show or that CD would never be labeled as containing adult language. 8

We seem to be so sheepish about what our culture has become—so reluctant to concede the debasement of society—that we have decided to declare that darkness is light, that down is up, that wrong is right. We are sending a clear signal to young people: The things in our world that are violent, that are crude, that are dull and mean-spirited are the things that are considered "adult." The words that children are taught not to say because they are ugly and foul are "adult language." As if they are something to strive for, to grow into. 9

What is the solution? Truth in packaging might be a good idea, although it will never happen. No movie studio that has hired a top-money action star to headline in a film that consists of explosions, bloodshed and gore would ever agree to describe the movie truthfully. The lie of "adult content" is acceptable to Hollywood; the true label of "pathetic, moronic content, suitable for imbeciles" will never see the light of day. 10

Language? The movie studios, cable channels and record labels can live with the inaccurate euphemism of "adult language." To phrase it honestly—"infantile, ignorant, pitiful language"—would remove a certain sheen from a big-budget entertainment project. 11

Ours is becoming a society in which the best ideals of childhood—innocence, kindness, lack of spitefulness, rejection of violence—are qualities toward which adults ought to strive. A paradoxical society in which the things labeled "adult"—lack of restraint, conscienceless mayhem, vulgarity, raw and cynical carnality—are the things that children should be warned against growing up to embrace. 12

So perhaps we should learn to read the current "adult" warning labels in a different way. "Adult content" on a movie or television 13 show should be read as a warning against becoming the kind of adult who welcomes such things into his or her life. The "adult language" label on a TV show or CD should be read as a genuine kind of warning, a warning to children against becoming the sort of adult who chooses to speak that way.

14 Then there is "For Mature Audiences Only," but that will have to wait for another day. . . .

QUESTIONS ON SUBJECT AND PURPOSE

1. Why is the phrase "adults only" (or some variation) used to label potentially offensive or objectionable content or language?
2. What does Greene mean by his first sentence? What is "one of the great untruths of our times"? What is an "untruth"?
3. How does Greene feel about material that is labeled "adults only"?

QUESTIONS ON STRATEGY AND AUDIENCE

1. Why might Greene paragraph so frequently? What does the paragraphing suggest about where the essay was originally published?
2. Greene implies that a phrase like "adult content" (paragraph 13) could be defined in several ways. How many definitions could you give after reading Greene's essay?
3. How do you as a reader react to what Greene is saying? Does he win your agreement? Do you feel that he is being unfair?

QUESTIONS ON VOCABULARY AND STYLE

1. How does your dictionary define "adult"? What connotations does the word have for you?
2. Greene ends his essay with a series of spaced periods. What is this mark of punctuation called? Why does he use it here?
3. Be prepared to define the following words: *bludgeoning* (paragraph 5), *deviant* (6), *warrant* (7), *debasement* (9), *moronic* (10), *imbeciles* (10), *euphemism* (11), *sheen* (11), *mayhem* (12).

WRITING SUGGESTIONS

1. **For Your Journal.** What does the term "free speech" mean to you? In your journal, jot down your thoughts and reactions to that phrase. Are there, for example, any limits to "free" speech? Any restrictions?
2. **For a Paragraph.** Use your journal reactions as the basis for a paragraph definition of the term "free speech." Be sure to give several examples of what you think might be covered or protected by this First Amendment guarantee.
3. **For an Essay.** Expand your paragraph writing into an essay-length extended definition of the term "free speech." Remember that the concept has been used to refer to not only sexually explicit material, but also material that advocates racial, ethnic, and religious hatred and material that promotes or describes dangerous or even terroristic activities (for example, how to build a bomb). Try to define the term as precisely as you can, making use of examples.

   Prewriting:

   a. Begin by looking back to the First Amendment of the Constitution. What does it actually say?

   b. Remember the differences between denotation and connotation (see the Glossary). In your essay, you are writing an extended denotative definition.

   c. Look back at the section titled "How Do You Structure a Definition" (pp. 436–437). Review the advice given there and see how it might help you plan a structure for your essay.

   Rewriting

   a. Look again at your introduction. Have you avoided beginning with a direct dictionary-type definition? Could you open with a particularly arresting example, for instance?

   b. Remember that your purpose in the essay is to define "free speech," not to argue for or against free speech. Look carefully at your paper. Have you been objective? Have you avoided arguing for or against the concept of free speech?

   c. Coming up with an effective, interesting title is not always an easy matter. Moreover, it does not always seem important when you are worried about finishing the paper. Look back at your title and try to critique it honestly. Brainstorm some other possibilities.

4. **For Research.** In an attempt to protect children from online pornography, Congress passed the Communications Decency Act as a part of the Telecommunications Deregulation and Reform Act in 1996. The CDA allowed fines of up to $250,000 and prison terms of up to two years for anyone who transmitted "indecent" or "patently offensive" material over the Internet. In 1997, the Supreme Court unanimously declared the law unconstitutional. Part of the problem with the CDA was how to define the terms "indecent" or "patently offensive." In a research paper, explore what "indecent" means in our culture. Is it possible to write an extended definition of that term? How would you characterize "indecent" material? You might use the extensive materials available on the CDA as a way of researching the term and the problems associated with it.

Website Link

What do you know about the Supreme Court's recent decision to declare the Communications Decency Act of 1996 unconstitutional? What is involved in trying to define the term "indecent"? Check out a group of hot-linked sites at the *Reader's* Website.

I Want a Wife

Judy Brady

Judy Brady was born in 1937 in San Francisco, California, and received a B.F.A. in painting from the University of Iowa. As a freelance writer, Brady has written essays on topics such as union organizing, abortion, and the role of women in society. Currently an activist focusing on issues related to cancer and the environment, she has edited two books on the subject, including One in Three: Women with Cancer Confront an Epidemic *(1991).*

Brady's most frequently reprinted essay is "I Want a Wife," which originally appeared in Ms. *magazine in 1971. After examining the stereotypical male demands in marriage, Brady concludes, "Who* wouldn't *want a wife?"*

BEFORE READING

Connecting: In a relationship, what separates reasonable needs or desires from unreasonable or selfish ones?

Anticipating: What is the effect of the repetition of the phrase "I want a . . ." in the essay?

I belong to that classification of people known as wives. I am A Wife. And, not altogether incidentally, I am a mother. 1

Not too long ago a male friend of mine appeared on the scene fresh from a recent divorce. He had one child, who is, of course, with his ex-wife. He is obviously looking for another wife. As I thought about him while I was ironing one evening, it suddenly occurred to me that I, too, would like to have a wife. Why do I want a wife? 2

I would like to go back to school so that I can become economically independent, support myself, and, if need be, support those dependent upon me. I want a wife who will work and send me to school. And while I am going to school I want a wife to take care of my children. I want a wife to keep track of the children's doctor and dentist appointments. And to keep track of mine, too. I want a wife to make sure my children eat properly and are kept clean. I want a wife who will wash the children's clothes and keep them mended. I want a wife who is a good nurturant attendant to my 3 children, who arranges for their schooling, makes sure that they have an adequate social life with their peers, takes them to the park, the zoo, etc. I want a wife who takes care of the children when they are sick, a wife who arranges to be around when the children need special care, because, of course, I cannot miss classes at school. My wife must arrange to lose time at work, and not lose the job. It may mean a small cut in my wife's income from time to time, but I guess I can tolerate that. Needless to say, my wife will arrange and pay for the care of the children while my wife is working.

4 I want a wife who will take care of my physical needs. I want a wife who will keep my house clean. A wife who will pick up after me. I want a wife who will keep my clothes clean, ironed, mended, replaced when need be, and who will see to it that my personal things are kept in their proper place so that I can find what I need the minute I need it. I want a wife who cooks the meals, a wife who is a good cook. I want a wife who will plan the meals, do the necessary grocery shopping, prepare the meals, serve them pleasantly, and then do the cleaning up while I do my studying. I want a wife who will care for me when I am sick and sympathize with my pain and loss of time from school. I want a wife to go along when our family takes a vacation so that someone can continue to care for me and my children when I need a rest and change of scene.

5 I want a wife who will not bother me with rambling complaints about a wife's duties. But I want a wife who will listen to me when I feel the need to explain a rather difficult point I have come across in my course of studies. And I want a wife who will type my papers for me when I have written them.

6 I want a wife who will take care of the details of my social life. When my wife and I are invited out by my friends, I want a wife who will take care of the babysitting arrangements. When I meet people at school that I like and want to entertain, I want a wife who will have the house clean, will prepare a special meal, serve it to me and my friends, and not interrupt when I talk about the things that interest me and my friends. I want a wife who will have arranged that the children are fed and ready for bed before my guests arrive so that the children do not bother us. I want a wife who takes care of the needs of my guests so that they feel comfortable, who makes sure that they have an ashtray, that they are passed the hors d'oeuvres, that they are offered a second helping of the food, that their wine glasses are replenished when necessary, that their coffee is served to them as they like it. And

I want a wife who knows that sometimes I need a night out by myself.

I want a wife who is sensitive to my sexual needs, a wife who makes love passionately and eagerly when I feel like it, a wife who makes sure that I am satisfied. And, of course, I want a wife who will not demand sexual attention when I am not in the mood for it. I want a wife who assumes the complete responsibility for birth control, because I do not want more children. I want a wife who will remain sexually faithful to me so that I do not have to clutter up my intellectual life with jealousies. And I want a wife who understands that *my* sexual needs may entail more than strict adherence to monogamy. I must, after all, be able to relate to people as fully as possible. 7

If, by chance, I find another person more suitable as a wife than the wife I already have, I want the liberty to replace my present wife with another one. Naturally I will expect a fresh, new life; my wife will take the children and be solely responsible for them so that I am left free. 8

When I am through with school and have a job, I want my wife to quit working and remain at home so that my wife can more fully and completely take care of a wife's duties. 9

My God, who *wouldn't* want a wife? 10

QUESTIONS ON SUBJECT AND PURPOSE

1. In what way is this a definition of a wife? Why does Brady avoid a more conventional definition?
2. Is Brady being fair? Is there anything that she leaves out of her definition that you would have included?
3. What purpose might Brady have been trying to achieve?

QUESTIONS ON STRATEGY AND AUDIENCE

1. How does Brady structure her essay? What is the order of the development? Could the essay have been arranged in any other way?
2. Why does Brady identify herself by her roles—wife and mother—at the beginning of the essay? Is that information relevant in any way?
3. What assumptions does Brady have about her audience (readers of *Ms.* magazine in the early 1970s)? How do you know?

QUESTIONS ON VOCABULARY AND STYLE

1. How does Brady use repetition in the essay? Why? Does it work? What effect does it create?
2. How effective is Brady's final rhetorical question? Where else in the essay does she use a rhetorical question?
3. Be able to define the following words: *nurturant* (paragraph 3), *hors d'oeuvres* (6), *replenished* (6), *monogamy* (7).

WRITING SUGGESTIONS

1. **For Your Journal.** What do you look for in a possible spouse or "significant other"? Make a list of what you expect or want from a relationship with another person. Once you have brainstormed the list, rank each item in order of importance—which is most important, and which is least important? If you are in a relationship right now, try evaluating that relationship in light of your own priorities.
2. **For a Paragraph.** Using the material that you generated in your journal entry, write a paragraph definition of the kind of person you seek for a committed relationship. Be serious. Do not try to imitate Brady's style.
3. **For an Essay.** Define a word naming a central human relationship role, such as *husband*, *lover*, *friend*, *mother*, *father*, *child*, *sister*, *brother*, or *grandparent*. Define the term indirectly by showing what such a person does or should do.

   Prewriting:

   a. Select a word as a possible subject. Then write down a dictionary definition. The inadequacies of such a short definition (for example, *wife*: "a female partner in a marriage") will be obvious. What expectations do you have about the role or function of the person in this position? Make a list.
   b. Try freewriting about the items on the list you have just made. Treat each expectation as the subject for a separate freewrite. You might not use any of the prose that you produce here; you are just trying to generate ideas.
   c. Plan an organizational strategy. Look carefully at how Brady puts her essay together. How does she structure the middle of her essay? Can you use a similar structure?

Rewriting:

a. Characterize the tone of what you have written. For example, are you serious or satirical? Is it formal or informal? Does your tone complement your purpose? Look back through your essay and imagine how it would sound to a reader.

b. Check each paragraph in your essay. Is there a consistent, unified subject for each? That unity might be expressed in an explicit topic sentence, or it might just be implicit.

c. Look again at your introduction and conclusion. Avoid imitating Brady's strategies—especially her conclusion. Look at the advice on introductions and conclusions in the Glossary. Be honest about what you have written. Could either be stronger, clearer, more interesting?

4. **For Research.** What does it mean to be a wife in another culture? Choose at least two other cultures, and research those societies' expectations of a wife. Try to find cultures that show significant differences. Remember that interviews might be a good source of information—even e-mail interviews with wives in other cultures. Using your research, write an essay offering a comparative definition of *wife.* Assume that your audience is American. Be certain to document your sources, including any interviews or e-mail conversations.

Website Link

Visit a group of Websites devoted to marriage and marital contracts—the WWW offers a range of resources from the most conservative to the most liberal. Some places to start can be found at www.prenhall.com/miller.

A Word's Meaning Can Often Depend on Who Says It

Gloria Naylor

Gloria Naylor was born in 1950 in New York City. When Martin Luther King was assassinated, Naylor became determined to make the world a better place, and she worked as a missionary for Jehovah's Witnesses for seven years before deciding to pursue her writing interests. She graduated from Brooklyn College of the City University of New York in 1981 and then earned her M.A. in Afro-American Studies at Yale University in 1983. Naylor has written what she calls her "novel quartet," four novels that explore the black experience: The Women of Brewster Place *(1982)*, Linden Hills *(1985)*, Mama Day *(1988), and* Bailey's Cafe *(1992). Her most recent book is* The Men of Brewster Place *(1998). The following essay was first published in* The New York Times.

On Writing: *On the task of becoming a writer, Naylor commented: "I wrote because I had no choice, but that was a long road from gathering the authority within myself to believe that I could be a writer. The writers I had been taught to love were either male or white." Asked about writer's block in an on-line chat sponsored by barnesandnoble.com, Naylor replied, "Writer's block is just difficult . . . but for the most part I will play music and go about my life thinking 'I am not blocked,' and something slowly does happen. It's a terrifying feeling to have writer's block."*

BEFORE READING

Connecting: Have you ever been called a "name," a derogatory label that signaled someone's prejudice toward you? How did that act make you feel?

Anticipating: Why do people call others "names"? What are the implications of labeling people in such ways?

1 Language is the subject. It is the written form with which I've managed to keep the wolf away from the door and, in diaries, to keep my sanity. In spite of this, I consider the written word inferior to the spoken, and much of the frustration experienced by

novelists is the awareness that whatever we manage to capture in even the most transcendent passages falls far short of the richness of life. Dialogue achieves its power in the dynamics of a fleeting moment of sight, sound, smell, and touch.

I'm not going to enter the debate here about whether it is language that shapes reality or vice versa. That battle is doomed to be waged whenever we seek intermittent reprieve from the chicken and egg dispute. I will simply take the position that the spoken word, like the written word, amounts to a nonsensical arrangement of sounds or letters without a consensus that assigns "meaning." And building from the meanings of what we hear, we order reality. Words themselves are innocuous; it is the consensus that gives them true power. 2

I remember the first time I heard the word *nigger*. In my third-grade class, our math tests were being passed down the rows, and as I handed the papers to a little boy in back of me, I remarked that once again he had received a much lower mark than I did. He snatched his test from me and spit out that word. Had he called me a nymphomaniac or a necrophiliac, I couldn't have been more puzzled. I didn't know what a nigger was, but I knew whatever it meant, it was something he shouldn't have called me. This was verified when I raised my hand, and in a loud voice repeated what he had said and watched the teacher scold him for using a "bad" word. I was later to go home and ask the inevitable question that every black parent must face—"Mommy, what does *nigger* mean?" 3

And what exactly did it mean? Thinking back, I realize that this could not have been the first time the word was used in my presence. I was part of a large extended family that had migrated from the rural South after World War II and formed a close-knit network that gravitated around my maternal grandparents. Their ground-floor apartment in one of the buildings they owned in Harlem was a weekend mecca for my immediate family, along with countless aunts, uncles, and cousins who brought along assorted friends. It was a bustling and open house with assorted neighbors and tenants popping in and out to exchange bits of gossip, pick up an old quarrel, or referee the ongoing checkers game in which my grandmother cheated shamelessly. They were all there to let down their hair and put up their feet after a week of labor in the factories, laundries, and shipyards of New York. 4

Amid the clamor, which could reach deafening proportions—two or three conversations going on simultaneously, punctuated by the sound of a baby's crying somewhere in the back rooms or 5 out on the street—there was still a rigid set of rules about what was said and how. Older children were sent out of the living room when it was time to get into the juicy details about "you-know-who" up on the third floor who had gone and gotten herself "p-r-e-g-n-a-n-t!" But my parents, knowing that I could spell well beyond my years, always demanded that I follow the others out to play. Beyond sexual misconduct and death, everything else was considered harmless for our young ears. And so among the anecdotes of the triumphs and disappointments in the various workings of their lives, the word *nigger* was used in my presence, but it was set within contexts and inflections that caused it to register in my mind as something else.

6 In the singular, the word was always applied to a man who had distinguished himself in some situation that brought their approval for his strength, intelligence, or drive:

7 "Did Johnny *really* do that?"

8 "I'm telling you, that nigger pulled in $6,000 of overtime last year. Said he got enough for a down payment on a house."

9 When used with a possessive adjective by a woman—"my nigger"—it became a term of endearment for her husband or boyfriend. But it could be more than just a term applied to a man. In their mouths it became the pure essence of manhood—a disembodied force that channeled their past history of struggle and present survival against the odds into a victorious statement of being: "Yeah, that old foreman found out quick enough—you don't mess with a nigger."

10 In the plural, it became a description of some group within the community that had overstepped the bounds of decency as my family defined it. Parents who neglected their children, a drunken couple who fought in public, people who simply refused to look for work, those with excessively dirty mouths or unkempt households were all "trifling niggers." This particular circle could forgive hard times, unemployment, the occasional bout of depression—they had gone through all of that themselves—but the unforgivable sin was a lack of self-respect.

11 A woman could never be a "nigger" in the singular, with its connotation of confirming worth. The noun *girl* was its closest equivalent in that sense, but only when used in direct address and regardless of the gender doing the addressing. *Girl* was a token of respect for a woman. The one-syllable word was drawn out to sound like three in recognition of the extra ounce of wit, nerve, or daring that the woman had shown in the situation under discussion.

"G-i-r-l, stop. You mean you said that to his face?" 12

But if the word was used in a third-person reference or shortened so that it almost snapped out of the mouth, it always involved some element of communal disapproval. And age became an important factor in these exchanges. It was only between individuals of the same generation, or from any older person to a younger (but never the other way around), that *girl* would be considered a compliment. 13

I don't agree with the argument that use of the word *nigger* at this social stratum of the black community was an internalization of racism. The dynamics were the exact opposite: the people in my grandmother's living room took a word that whites used to signify worthlessness or degradation and rendered it impotent. Gathering there together, they transformed *nigger* to signify the varied and complex human beings they knew themselves to be. If the word was to disappear totally from the mouths of even the most liberal of white society, no one in that room was naive enough to believe it would disappear from white minds. Meeting the word head-on, they proved it had absolutely nothing to do with the way they were determined to live their lives. 14

So there must have been dozens of times that *nigger* was spoken in front of me before I reached the third grade. But I didn't "hear" it until it was said by a small pair of lips that had already learned it could be a way to humiliate me. That was the word I went home and asked my mother about. And since she knew that I had to grow up in America, she took me in her lap and explained. 15

QUESTIONS ON SUBJECT AND PURPOSE

1. Are the definitions that Naylor offers denotative or connotative? See the Glossary for definitions of those two terms.
2. In what ways did Naylor's family use the word "nigger"? How does their use differ from the way in which the third-grader used the word?
3. What purpose or purposes does Naylor appear to have in the essay?

QUESTIONS ON STRATEGY AND AUDIENCE

1. Why does Naylor preface her essay with the two introductory paragraphs? Why not begin with paragraph 3?

2. In paragraphs 11–13, Naylor defines the term "girl." How does that definition fit into the essay? Why include it?
3. Naylor's essay originally appeared in *The New York Times.* What influence might the place of publication have had on the nature of the essay?

QUESTIONS ON VOCABULARY AND STYLE

1. What does Naylor seem to mean when she observes: "words themselves are innocuous; it is the consensus that gives them true power" (paragraph 2)?
2. What is the effect of the following clichés: "to keep the wolf away from the door" (paragraph 1), "the chicken and egg dispute" (2), "let down their hair" (5), "meeting the word head-on" (14).
3. Be prepared to define the following words: *innocuous* (paragraph 2), *necrophiliac* (3), *mecca* (4), *clamor* (5), *anecdotes* (5), *unkempt* (10), *trifling* (10), *connotation* (11), *stratum* (14).

WRITING SUGGESTIONS

1. **For Your Journal.** Listen carefully to yourself and to those around you for at least a day. Jot down in your journal every name or label that you use or that you hear others use. What groups seem to be singled out the most often? Why?
2. **For a Paragraph.** Select a common word that has a range of connotations or associations. In a paragraph define that word by including examples of how the word might be used.
3. **For an Essay.** Write an extended definition of a word that carries a range of connotations. Remember to get your instructor's approval of your word.

   Prewriting:

   a. Make a list of at least six possibilities. Choose words that are used frequently and have a variety of meanings. Ask your friends for suggestions as well.
   b. Go to the reference room of your school's library and using a range of dictionaries, including dictionaries of slang, see how many different meanings and associations you can find.
   c. Look back over the details that you plan to include in your extended definition. What organizational strategy

seems appropriate? Are you dividing the subject into parts? Are you defining through comparison? Sketch out a possible framework that organizes the examples and details you plan to use.

Rewriting:

a. Check your introduction. Copy it onto a separate sheet of paper and reread it. Do you think a reader would want to continue reading? Does your introduction stimulate interest?

b. Check each individual paragraph. Is there a unified idea that controls each one? Make a copy of your essay, and highlight the topic sentence or key idea of each paragraph with a colored pen.

c. Evaluate the conclusion that you have written. Do you conclude or just stop? Do you just repeat in slightly altered words what you wrote in the introduction? Check the advice about introductions and conclusions offered in the Glossary. If your conclusion seems weak, try freewriting at least one alternative ending.

4. **For Research.** Research the history of one "hate" word. Where did it originate? Why? What connotations does the word have? Have those connotations changed over the years? The many dictionaries in the reference department of your college's library will be a good place in which to start your research. Be sure to document your sources wherever appropriate.

WEBSITE LINK

Extensive resources about the life and work of Gloria Naylor can be found on the Web. A group of important sites are hot-linked for you.

MOTHER TONGUE

Amy Tan

Born in Oakland, California, in 1952 to Chinese immigrants, Amy Tan graduated from San Jose State University with a double major in English and linguistics and an M.A. in linguistics. Though her writing has been praised for its vivid language and characters, Tan did not write fiction until 1985, when she began the stories that would become her first and very successful novel, The Joy Luck Club *(1989), also a popular film. That book and her second novel,* The Kitchen God's Wife *(1991), portray the mother-daughter relationship in the Chinese-American and Chinese cultures. Tan's children's book* The Chinese Siamese Cat *(1994) is the basis for a new daily animated television series,* Sagwa, The Chinese Siamese Cat, *that will premiere on PBS KIDS channel in the fall of 2001.*

On Writing: *Asked about her writing, Tan responded: "I welcome criticism when I'm writing my books. I want to become better and better as a writer. I go to a writer's group every week. We read our work aloud." In another interview she commented, "I still think of myself, in many ways, as a beginning writer. I'm still learning my craft, learning what makes for a good story, what's an honest voice."*

BEFORE READING

Connecting: How sensitive are you to the language that you use or your family uses? Are you ever conscious of that language? Are you ever embarrassed by it? Are you proud of it?

Anticipating: In what ways does the language of Tan and her mother "define" them in the eyes of others?

1 I am not a scholar of English or literature. I cannot give you much more than personal opinions on the English language and its variations in this country or others.

2 I am a writer. And by that definition, I am someone who has always loved language. I am fascinated by language in daily life. I spend a great deal of my time thinking about the power of language—the way it can evoke an emotion, a visual image, a complex idea, or a simple truth. Language is the tool of my trade. And I use them all—all the Englishes I grew up with.

Recently, I was made keenly aware of the different Englishes I do use. I was giving a talk to a large group of people, the same talk I had already given to half a dozen other groups. The nature of the talk was about my writing, my life, and my book, *The Joy Luck Club*. The talk was going along well enough, until I remembered one major difference that made the whole talk sound wrong. My mother was in the room. And it was perhaps the first time she had heard me give a lengthy speech, using the kind of English I have never used with her. I was saying things like, "The intersection of memory upon imagination" and "There is an aspect of my fiction that relates to thus-and-thus"—a speech filled with carefully wrought grammatical phrases, burdened, it suddenly seemed to me, with nominalized forms, past perfect tenses, conditional phrases, all the forms of standard English that I had learned in school and through books, the forms of English I did not use at home with my mother. 3

Just last week, I was walking down the street with my mother, and I again found myself conscious of the English I was using, the English I do use with her. We were talking about the price of new and used furniture and I heard myself saying this: "Not waste money that way." My husband was with us as well, and he didn't notice any switch in my English. And then I realized why. It's because over the twenty years we've been together I've often used that same kind of English with him, and sometimes he even uses it with me. It has become our language of intimacy, a different sort of English that relates to family talk, the language I grew up with. 4

So you'll have some idea of what this family talk I heard sounds like, I'll quote what my mother said during a recent conversation which I videotaped and then transcribed. During this conversation, my mother was talking about a political gangster in Shanghai who had the same last name as her family's, Du, and how the gangster in his early years wanted to be adopted by her family, which was rich by comparison. Later, the gangster became more powerful, far richer than my mother's family, and one day showed up at my mother's wedding to pay his respects. Here's what she said in part: 5

"Du Yusong having business like fruit stand. Like off the street kind. He is Du like Du Zong—but not Tsung-ming Island people. The local people call putong, the river east side, he belong to that side local people. That man want to ask Du Zong father take him in like become own family. Du Zong father wasn't look down on him, but didn't take seriously, until that man big like become a mafia. Now important person, very hard to inviting him. 6

Chinese way, came only to show respect, don't stay for dinner. Respect for making big celebration, he shows up. Mean gives lots of respect. Chinese custom. Chinese social life that way. If too important won't have to stay too long. He come to my wedding. I didn't see, I heard it. I gone to boy's side, they have YMCA dinner. Chinese age I was nineteen."

7 You should know that my mother's expressive command of English belies how much she actually understands. She reads the *Forbes* report, listens to *Wall Street Week*, converses daily with her stockbroker, reads all of Shirley MacLaine's books with ease—all kinds of things I can't begin to understand. Yet some of my friends tell me they understand 50 percent of what my mother says. Some say they understand 80 to 90 percent. Some say they understand none of it, as if she were speaking pure Chinese. But to me, my mother's English is perfectly clear, perfectly natural. It's my mother tongue. Her language, as I hear it, is vivid, direct, full of observation and imagery. That was the language that helped shape the way I saw things, expressed things, made sense of the world.

8 Lately, I've been giving more thought to the kind of English my mother speaks. Like others, I have described it to people as "broken" or "fractured" English. But I wince when I say that. It has always bothered me that I can think of no way to describe it other than "broken," as if it were damaged and needed to be fixed, as if it lacked a certain wholeness and soundness. I've heard other terms used, "limited English," for example. But they seem just as bad, as if everything is limited, including people's perceptions of the limited English speaker.

9 I know this for a fact, because when I was growing up, my mother's "limited" English limited *my* perception of her. I was ashamed of her English. I believed that her English reflected the quality of what she had to say. That is, because she expressed them imperfectly her thoughts were imperfect. And I had plenty of empirical evidence to support me: the fact that people in department stores, at banks, and at restaurants did not take her seriously, did not give her good service, pretended not to understand her, or even acted as if they did not hear her.

10 My mother has long realized the limitations of her English as well. When I was fifteen, she used to have me call people on the phone to pretend I was she. In this guise, I was forced to ask for information or even to complain and yell at people who had been rude to her. One time it was a call to her stockbroker in New York.

She had cashed out her small portfolio and it just so happened we were going to go to New York the next week, our very first trip outside California. I had to get on the phone and say in an adolescent voice that was not very convincing, "This is Mrs. Tan."

And my mother was standing in the back whispering loudly, "Why he don't send me check, already two weeks late. So mad he lie to me, losing me money." 11

And then I said in perfect English, "Yes, I'm getting rather concerned. You had agreed to send the check two weeks ago, but it hasn't arrived." 12

Then she began to talk more loudly. "What he want, I come to New York tell him front of his boss, you cheating me?" And I was trying to calm her down, make her be quiet, while telling the stockbroker, "I can't tolerate any more excuses. If I don't receive the check immediately, I am going to have to speak to your manager when I'm in New York next week." And sure enough, the following week there we were in front of this astonished stockbroker, and I was sitting there red-faced and quiet, and my mother, the real Mrs. Tan, was shouting at his boss in her impeccable broken English. 13

We used a similar routine just five days ago, for a situation that was far less humorous. My mother had gone to the hospital for an appointment, to find out about a benign brain tumor a CAT scan had revealed a month ago. She said she had spoken very good English, her best English, no mistakes. Still, she said, the hospital did not apologize when they said they had lost the CAT scan and she had come for nothing. She said they did not seem to have any sympathy when she told them she was anxious to know the exact diagnosis, since her husband and son had both died of brain tumors. She said they would not give her any more information until the next time and she would have to make another appointment for that. So she said she would not leave until the doctor called her daughter. She wouldn't budge. And when the doctor finally called her daughter, me, who spoke in perfect English—lo and behind—we had assurances the CAT scan would be found, promises that a conference call on Monday would be held, and apologies for any suffering my mother had gone through for a most regrettable mistake. 14

I think my mother's English almost had an effect on limiting my possibilities in life as well. Sociologists and linguists probably will tell you that a person's developing language skills are more influenced by peers. But I do think that the language spoken in the family, especially in immigrant families which are 15 more insular, plays a large role in shaping the language of the child. And I believe that it affected my results on achievement tests, IQ tests, and the SAT. While my English skills were never judged as poor, compared to math, English could not be considered my strong suit. In grade school I did moderately well, getting perhaps B's, sometimes B-pluses, in English and scoring perhaps in the sixtieth or seventieth percentile on achievement tests. But those scores were not good enough to override the opinion that my true abilities lay in math and science, because in those areas I achieved A's and scored in the ninetieth percentile or higher.

16 This was understandable. Math is precise; there is only one correct answer. Whereas, for me at least, the answers on English tests were always a judgment call, a matter of opinion and personal experience. Those tests were constructed around items like fill-in-the-blank sentence completion, such as, "Even though Tom was __________, Mary thought he was __________." And the correct answer always seemed to be the most bland combinations of thoughts, for example, "Even though Tom was shy, Mary thought he was charming," with the grammatical structure "even though" limiting the correct answer to some sort of semantic opposites, so you wouldn't get answers like, "Even though Tom was foolish, Mary thought he was ridiculous." Well, according to my mother, there were very few limitations as to what Tom could have been and what Mary might have thought of him. So I never did well on tests like that.

17 The same was true with word analogies, pairs of words in which you were supposed to find some sort of logical, semantic relationship—for example, "*Sunset* is to *nightfall* as __________ is to __________." And here you would be presented with a list of four possible pairs, one of which showed the same kind of relationship: *red* is to *stoplight*, *bus* is to *arrival*, *chills* is to *fever*, *yawn* is to *boring*. Well, I could never think that way. I knew what the tests were asking, but I could not block out of my mind the images already created by the first pair, "*sunset* is to *nightfall*"—and I would see a burst of colors against a darkening sky, the moon rising, the lowering of a curtain of stars. And all the other pairs of words—*red*, *bus*, *stoplight*, *boring*—just threw up a mass of confusing images, making it impossible for me to sort out something as logical as saying: "A sunset precedes nightfall" is the same as "a chill precedes a fever." The only way I would have gotten that answer right would have been to imagine an associative situation, for example, my being disobedient and staying out past sunset,

catching a chill at night, which turns into feverish pneumonia as punishment, which indeed did happen to me.

18 I have been thinking about all this lately, about my mother's English, about achievement tests. Because lately I've been asked, as a writer, why there are not more Asian-Americans represented in American literature. Why are there few Asian Americans enrolled in creative writing programs? Why do so many Chinese students go into engineering? Well, these are broad sociological questions I can't begin to answer. But I have noticed in surveys—in fact, just last week—that Asian students, as a whole, always do significantly better on math achievement tests than in English. And this makes me think that there are other Asian-American students whose English spoken in the home might also be described as "broken" or "limited." And perhaps they also have teachers who are steering them away from writing and into math and science, which is what happened to me.

19 Fortunately, I happen to be rebellious in nature and enjoy the challenge of disproving assumptions made about me. I became an English major my first year in college, after being enrolled as pre-med. I started writing nonfiction as a freelancer the week after I was told by my former boss that writing was my worst skill and I should hone my talents toward account management.

20 But it wasn't until 1985 that I finally began to write fiction. And at first I wrote using what I thought to be wittily crafted sentences, sentences that would finally prove I had mastery over the English language. Here's an example from the first draft of a story that later made its way into *The Joy Luck Club*, but without this line: "That was my mental quandary in its nascent state." A terrible line, which I can barely pronounce.

21 Fortunately, for reasons I won't get into today, I later decided I should envision a reader for the stories I would write. And the reader I decided upon was my mother, because these were stories about mothers. So with this reader in mind—and in fact she did read my early drafts—I began to write stories using all the Englishes I grew up with: the English I spoke to my mother, which for lack of a better term might be described as "simple"; the English she used with me, which for lack of a better term might be described as "broken"; my translation of her Chinese, which could certainly be described as "watered down"; and what I imagined to be her translation of her Chinese if she could speak in perfect English, her internal language, and for that I sought to preserve the essence, but neither an English nor a Chinese structure. I wanted

to capture what language ability tests can never reveal: her intent, her passion, her imagery, the rhythms of her speech and the nature of her thoughts.

22 Apart from what any critic had to say about my writing, I knew I had succeeded where it counted when my mother finished reading my book and gave me her verdict: "So easy to read."

QUESTIONS ON SUBJECT AND PURPOSE

1. What does the title "Mother Tongue" suggest?
2. How many subjects does Tan explore in the essay?
3. How does Tan feel about her mother's "tongue"?

QUESTIONS ON STRATEGY AND AUDIENCE

1. In paragraph 6, Tan quotes part of one of her mother's conversations. Why?
2. After paragraphs 7 and 17, Tan uses additional space to indicate divisions in her essay. Why does she divide the essay into three parts?
3. Tan notes in paragraph 21 that she thinks of her mother as her audience when she writes stories. Why?

QUESTIONS ON VOCABULARY AND STYLE

1. How would you characterize Tan's tone (see the Glossary for a definition) in the essay?
2. In paragraph 20, Tan quotes a "terrible line" she once wrote: "That was my mental quandary in its nascent state." What is so terrible about that line?
3. Be prepared to define the following words: *belies* (7), *empirical* (9), *benign* (14), *insular* (15), *semantic* (16), *hone* (19), *quandary* (20), *nascent* (20).

WRITING SUGGESTIONS

1. **For Your Journal.** What makes up your "mother tongue"? To what extent is your language (such things as word choice, pronunciation, dialect, and second-language skills) influenced by your parents, your education, the part of the country in which you grew up, and your peers? Make a series of notes exploring those influences.

2. **For a Paragraph.** Using the information that you gathered for your journal entry, write a paragraph in which you define your "mother tongue." Try to define the influences that have shaped both how and what you say.
3. **For an Essay.** Tan suggests that a certain type or dialect of English is a language of power, that if you speak and write that English, people in authority will listen to you and respect you. How might that public, powerful English (sometimes referred to as "edited American English") be defined?

   Prewriting:

   a. Think of your own language habits. Do you speak in a different way when you address a teacher, a boss, a member of the clergy? How do you change your language?
   b. Browse through the writing textbook that you use in your freshman English course. What types of advice does the text offer about subjects such as usage and diction? Does it also define the term *dialect?*
   c. Use your examples—drawn from your own experiences, from the experiences of others, from your textbook—as the basis from which to formulate a definition of the features of this public or "edited American English."

   Rewriting:

   a. Have you provided enough examples to support your generalizations? Go through a photocopy of your essay, underlining generalizations in one color and examples in another. Is there a good balance between the two?
   b. Check each individual paragraph. Is there a unified idea that controls each one? Highlight the topic sentence or key idea of each paragraph with a colored pen. If any paragraph seems less than unified, look for ways to improve it.
   c. Once you have a complete draft, jot down on a separate sheet of paper what troubles you the most about the essay. What could be better? Allow a day to pass; then try to solve that problem. If your school has a Writing Center or a peer-tutoring program, take your specific problem there.

4. **For Research.** Linguists have defined a wide range of dialects in the United States. Choose one of the dialects that interests you—a reference librarian or your instructor can

help you find a list. You might choose one based on the geographical area in which you live or one defined by your heritage. Using the resources of your library, write a definition of that dialect. What are its distinctive features? Where did those features come from? Where is this dialect spoken in the United States? What are some particularly colorful examples? Be sure to document your sources wherever appropriate.

Website Link

Read on-line interviews with Tan, watch video clips of her talking about her books, listen to audio excerpts from her works. Hotlinked sites on Tan can be found at the *Reader's* Website.

MESS

John Hollander

Born in 1929, John Hollander is a distinguished and widely published poet and critic. He is Sterling Professor of English at Yale University and the author of seventeen books of poetry. His most recent books are The Work of Poetry *(1997), a collection of essays, and* Figurehead: And Other Poems *(1999). "Mess" was originally published in the* Yale Review *in 1995.*

On Writing: *Commenting on this essay, Hollander observed: "This brief essay was generated more from within, like a poem, than most other prose of mine—nobody asked me to write it, but I felt impelled to observe something about one aspect of life that tends to get swept under the rug, as it were."*

BEFORE READING

Connecting: Are you "messy"? How do you feel about the messes that you make or about the messes of others?

Anticipating: In the final paragraph, Hollander refers to his essay as a "meditation on mess." What does the word *meditation* suggest to you? In what ways is the essay a meditation?

Mess is a state of mind. Or rather, messiness is a particular relation between the state of arrangement of a collection of things and a state of mind that contemplates it in its containing space. For example, X's mess may be Y's delight—sheer profusion, uncompromised by any apparent structure even in the representation of it. Or there may be some inner order or logic to A's mess that B cannot possibly perceive. Consider: someone—Alpha—rearranges all the books on Beta's library shelf, which have been piled or stacked, sometimes properly, sometimes not, but all in relevant sequence (by author and, within that, by date of publication), and rearranges them neatly, by size and color. Beta surveys the result, and can only feel, if not blurt out, "WHAT A MESS!" This situation often occurs with respect to messes of the workplace generally. 1

2 For there are many kinds of mess, both within walls and outside them: neglected gardens and the aftermath of tropical storms, and the indoor kinds of disorder peculiar to specific areas of our life with, and in and among, *things*. There are messes of one's own making, messes not even of one's own person, places, or things. There are personal states of mind about common areas of messiness—those of the kitchen, the bedroom, the bathroom, the salon (of whatever sort, from half of a bed-sitter to some grand public parlor), or those of personal appearance (clothes, hair, etc.). Then, for all those who are in any way self-employed or whose avocations are practiced in some private space—a workshop, a darkroom, a study or a studio—there is the mess of the workplace. It's not the most common kind of mess, but it's exemplary: the eye surveying it is sickened by the roller-coaster of scanning the scene. And, alas, it's the one I'm most afflicted with.

3 I know that things are really in a mess when—as about ninety seconds ago—I reach for the mouse on my Macintosh and find instead a thick layer of old envelopes, manuscript notes consulted three weeks ago, favorite pens and inoperative ones, folders used hastily and not replaced, and so forth. In order to start working, I brush these accumulated impedimenta aside, thus creating a new mess. But this is, worse yet, absorbed by the general condition of my study: piles of thin books and thick books, green volumes of the Loeb Classical Library and slimy paperbacks of ephemeral spy-thrillers, mostly used notepads, bills paid and unpaid, immortal letters from beloved friends, unopened and untrashed folders stuffed with things that should be in various other folders, book-mailing envelopes, unanswered mail whose cries for help and attention are muffled by three months' worth of bank statements enshrouding them in the gloom of continued neglect. Even this fairly orderly inventory seems to simplify the confusion: in actuality, searching for a letter or a page of manuscript in this state of things involves crouching down with my head on one side and searching vertically along the outside of a teetering pile for what may be a thin, hidden layer of it.

4 Displacement, and lack of design, are obscured in the origins of our very word *mess*. The famous biblical "mess of red pottage" (lentil mush or dal) for which Esau sold his birthright wasn't "messy" in our sense (unless, of course, in the not very interesting case of Esau having dribbled it on his clothing). The word meant a serving of food, or a course in a meal: something *placed* in front of you (from the Latin *missus*, put or placed), hence "messmates" (dining companions) and ultimately "officers' mess" and the like.

It also came to mean a dish of prepared mixed food—like an *olla podrida* or a minestrone—then by extension (but only from the early nineteenth century on) any hodge-podge: inedible, and outside the neat confines of a bowl or pot, and thus unpleasant, confusing, and agitating or depressing to contemplate. But for us, the association with food perhaps remains only in how much the state of mind of being messy is like that of being fat: for example, X says, "God I'm getting gross! I'll have to diet!" Y, *really* fat, cringes on hearing this, and feels that for the slender X to talk that way is an obscenity. Similarly, X: "God, this place is a pigsty!" Y: (ditto). For a person prone to messiness, Cyril Connolly's celebrated observation about fat people is projected onto the world itself: inside every neat arrangement is a mess struggling to break out, like some kind of statue of chaos lying implicit in the marble of apparent organization.

In Paradise, there was no such thing as messiness. This was 5
partly because unfallen, ideal life needed no supplemental *things*—objects of use and artifice, elements of any sort of technology. Thus there was nothing to leave lying around, messily or even neatly, by Adam and Eve—according to Milton—"at their savory dinner set / Of herbs and other country messes." But it was also because order, hence orderliness, was itself so natural that whatever bit of nature Adam and Eve might have been occupied with, or even using in a momentary tool-like way, flew or leapt or crept into place in some sort of reasonable arrangement, even as in our unparadised state things *fall* under the joyless tug of gravity. But messiness may seem to be an inevitable state of the condition of having so many *things*, precious or disposable, in one's life.

As I observed before, even to describe a mess is to impose 6
order on it. The ancient Greek vision of primal chaos, even, was not *messy* in that it was pre-messy: there weren't any categories by which to define order, so that there could be no disorder—no nextness or betweenness, no above, below, here, there, and so forth. "*Let there be light*" meant "Let there be perception of something," and it was then that order became possible, and mess possibly implied. Now, a list or inventory is in itself an orderly literary form, and even incoherent assemblages of items fall too easily into some other kind of order: in *Through the Looking-Glass,* the Walrus's "Of shoes, and ships, and sealing-wax, / Of cabbages, and kings," is given a harmonious structure by the pairs of alliterating words, and even by the half-punning association of "ships, [sailing] sealing-wax." The wonderful catalogue in *Tom Sawyer* of the elements of what must have been, pocketed or piled on the ground, a

mess of splendid proportions, is a poem of its own. The objects of barter for a stint of fence whitewashing (Tom, it will be remembered, turns *having* to do a chore into *getting* to do it by sheer con-man's insouciance) comprise

> twelve marbles, part of a jewsharp, a piece of blue bottle-glass to look through, a spool cannon, a key that wouldn't unlock anything, a fragment of chalk, a glass stopper of a decanter, a tin soldier, a couple of tadpoles, six fire-crackers, a kitten with only one eye, a brass door-knob, a dog collar—but no dog—the handle of a knife, four pieces of orange peel, and a dilapidated old window sash.

7 Thus such representations of disorder as lists, paintings, photos, etc., all compromise the purity of true messiness by the verbal or visual order they impose on the confusion. To get at the mess in my study, for example, a movie might serve best, alternately mixing mid-shot and zoom on a particular portion of the disaster, which would, in an almost fractal way, seem to be a mini-disaster of its own. There are even neatly conventionalized emblems of messiness that are, after all, all too neat; thus, whenever a movie wants to show an apartment or office that has been ransacked by Baddies (cop Baddies or baddy Baddies or whatever) in search of the Thing They Want, the designer is always careful to show at least one picture on the wall hanging carefully askew. All this could possibly tell us about a degree of messiness is that the searchers were so messy (at another level of application of the term) in their technique that they violated their search agenda to run over to the wall and tilt the picture (very messy procedure indeed), or that, hastily leaving the scene to avoid detection, they nonetheless took a final revenge against the Occupant for not having the Thing on his or her premises, and tilted the picture in a fit of pique. And yet a tilted picture gives good cueing mileage: it can present a good bit of disorder at the expense of a minimum of misalignment, after all.

8 A meditation on mess could be endless. As I struggle to conclude this one, one of my cats regards me from her nest in and among one of the disaster areas that all surfaces in my study soon become. Cats disdain messes in several ways. First, they are proverbially neat about their shit and about the condition of their fur. Second, they pick their way so elegantly among my piles of books, papers, and ancillary objects (dishes of paper clips, scissors, functional and dried-out pens, crumpled envelopes, outmoded postage stamps, boxes of slides and disks, staplers, glue bottles, tape dispensers—*you* know) that they cannot even be said to acknowledge

the mess's existence. The gray familiar creature currently making her own order out of a region of mess on my desk—carefully disposing herself around and over and among piles and bunches and stacks and crazily oblique layers and thereby reinterpreting it as natural landscape—makes me further despair until I realize that what she does with her body, I must do with my perception of this inevitable disorder—shaping its forms to the disorder and thereby shaping the disorder to its forms. She has taught me resignation.

QUESTIONS ON SUBJECT AND PURPOSE

1. In what sense is a mess "a state of mind"?
2. What role do "things" play in creating a mess?
3. Having contemplated the "mess" in which he works, Hollander reaches what conclusion?

QUESTIONS ON STRATEGY AND AUDIENCE

1. In what way does describing a mess "impose order on it" (paragraph 6)?
2. Toward the end of the essay, Hollander notes that he "struggles" to conclude. Why is it a struggle?
3. Hollander makes reference throughout the essay to other writers and works of literature. What do these allusions suggest about Hollander and his sense of his audience?

QUESTIONS ON VOCABULARY AND STYLE

1. Hollander is a poet. Does he ever sound like a poet in the essay? Can you find examples of phrasing or language that sounds like something you would imagine a poet would write?
2. Find the two shortest sentences in the essay (not counting the exchange between X and Y in paragraph 4).
3. Make a list of words in the essay whose meanings are uncertain to you. Bring your list to class.

WRITING SUGGESTIONS

1. **For Your Journal.** In your journal, brainstorm a list of words that you might define. Try for a list of words that are somehow related to or associated with you. They might be

words that describe your behavior (for example, *orderly*, *outgoing*, *shy*, *ambitious*), your physical self *(short*, *tall*, *athletic)*, or your attitudes toward life or events *(optimistic*, *cynical)*. Try for a substantial list.

2. **For a Paragraph.** In a paragraph, define one of the words. Do not write a dictionary definition; write an extended definition that includes examples, details, connotations.
3. **For an Essay.** Select one of the words from your journal, and write an essay definition of the word. Remember to get your instructor's approval of the word.

   Prewriting:
   a. Go to the reference area of your school's library, and using the range of dictionaries there, gather a range of denotative definitions.
   b. Brainstorm, perhaps with some peers, a range of connotations for the word—what associations do you have with the word?
   c. Look back over the details that you plan to include in your extended definition. What organizational strategy seems appropriate? Are you dividing your subject into parts? Are you defining through comparison? Sketch out a possible framework that organizes the examples and details you plan to include.

   Rewriting:
   a. Check your introduction. Copy it onto a separate sheet of paper and reread it. Do you think a reader would want to continue reading? Does your introduction stimulate interest? Ask a friend to evaluate it as well.
   b. Check each individual paragraph. Is there a unified idea that controls each one? Make a copy of your essay, and highlight the topic sentence or key idea of each paragraph with a colored pen.
   c. Evaluate your conclusion. Do you conclude or just stop? Do you just repeat in a slightly altered form what you wrote in the introduction? Check the advice about introductions and conclusions offered in the Glossary. If your conclusion seems weak, try freewriting at least one alternative ending.

4. **For Research.** To judge from the number of books, videos, and products that are marketed to American consumers, messiness is clearly something that people would like to

avoid. Whether it is how to clean up the clutter on your desk or in your closets at home or how to organize your every moment through elaborate daily planners and software programs, we seem to want desperately to be "neat." In a researched essay, define the word *neat*. You can draw examples from advertisements as well as from books, articles, and the electronic media. You will also want to research the history of the word (using, for example, some of the historical dictionaries in your school's library). Be sure to document all of your sources.

Website Link

A number of Hollander's poems can be found on the Web, as well as an audio file in which you can hear him read.

The Female Body

Margaret Atwood

Margaret Atwood was born in Ottawa, Canada, in 1939. She received a B.A. from the University of Toronto in 1961 and earned an M.A. at Radcliffe College in 1962. A poet, essayist, short story writer, and novelist, Atwood has enjoyed critical and popular acclaim throughout her writing career, winning numerous awards and honorary degrees. Her work has explored broad themes of feminism, dystopia, and the opposition of art and nature, but always through the eyes of an individual. Her best known novel is The Handmaid's Tale *(1986), in which a totalitarian state assigns roles to women according to their reproductive abilities.*

On Writing: *At a meeting of the Toronto Council of Teachers of English, Atwood was asked about the importance of punctuation in good writing. She commented on her own use of punctuation: "I've recently taken up a new device, which is the set of dashes. Some people overuse this quite a lot—everything is a set of dashes—but in prose I'm tending to prefer it to parentheses. In prose fiction a lot is associative, one idea suggests another which can lead to an interposition in the middle of a sentence. The question is, how do you set that off? Sometimes you can do it with parenthesis, but sets of dashes are often quite useful."*

BEFORE READING

Connecting: What image is suggested to you by the phrase "the female body"?

Anticipating: Does Atwood's essay fulfill your expectations of an essay on the "female body"? Why or why not?

> . . . entirely devoted to the subject of "The Female Body." Knowing how well you have written on this topic . . . this capacious topic . . .
>
> Letter from *Michigan Quarterly Review*

1

1 I agree, it's a hot topic. But only one? Look around, there's a wide range. Take my own, for instance.

2 I get up in the morning. My topic feels like hell. I sprinkle it with water, brush parts of it, rub it with towels, powder it, add

lubricant. I dump in the fuel and away goes my topic, my topical topic, my controversial topic, my capacious topic, my limping topic, my nearsighted topic, my topic with back problems, my badly behaved topic, my vulgar topic, my outrageous topic, my aging topic, my topic that is out of the question and anyway still can't spell, in its oversized coat and worn winter boots, scuttling along the sidewalk as if it were flesh and blood, hunting for what's out there, an avocado, an alderman, an adjective, hungry as ever.

2

The basic Female Body comes with the following accessories: 3 garter belt, panti-girdle, crinoline, camisole, bustle, brassiere, stomacher, chemise, virgin zone, spike heels, nose ring, veil, kid gloves, fishnet stockings, fichu, bandeau, Merry Widow, weepers, chokers, barrettes, bangles, beads, lorgnette, feather boa, basic black, compact, Lycra stretch one-piece with modesty panel, designer peignoir, flannel nightie, lace teddy, bed, head.

3

The Female Body is made of transparent plastic and lights up when 4 you plug it in. You press a button to illuminate the different systems. The circulatory system is red, for the heart and arteries, purple for the veins; the respiratory system is blue; the lymphatic system is yellow; the digestive system is green, with liver and kidneys in aqua. The nerves are done in orange and the brain is pink. The skeleton, as you might expect, is white.

The reproductive system is optional, and can be removed. It 5 comes with or without a miniature embryo. Parental judgment can thereby be exercised. We do not wish to frighten or offend.

4

He said, I won't have one of those things in the house. It gives a 6 young girl a false notion of beauty, not to mention anatomy. If a real woman was built like that she'd fall on her face.

She said, If we don't let her have one like all the other girls 7 she'll feel singled out. It'll become an issue. She'll long for one and she'll long to turn into one. Repression breeds sublimation. You know that.

He said, It's not just the pointy plastic tits, it's the 8 wardrobes. The wardrobes and that stupid male doll, what's his name, the one with the underwear glued on.

9 She said, Better to get it over with when she's young. He said, All right, but don't let me see it.

10 She came whizzing down the stairs, thrown like a dart. She was stark naked. Her hair had been chopped off, her head was turned back to front, she was missing some toes and she'd been tattooed all over her body with purple ink in a scrollwork design. She hit the potted azalea, trembled there for a moment like a botched angel, and fell.

11 He said, I guess we're safe.

5

12 The Female Body has many uses. It's been used as a door knocker, a bottle opener, as a clock with a ticking belly, as something to hold up lampshades, as a nutcracker, just squeeze the brass legs together and out comes your nut. It bears torches, lifts victorious wreaths, grows copper wings and raises aloft a ring of neon stars; whole buildings rest on its marble heads.

13 It sells cars, beer, shaving lotion, cigarettes, hard liquor; it sells diet plans and diamonds, and desire in tiny crystal bottles. Is this the face that launched a thousand products? You bet it is, but don't get any funny big ideas, honey, that smile is a dime a dozen.

14 It does not merely sell, it is sold. Money flows into this country or that country, flies in, practically crawls in, suitful after suitful, lured by all those hairless pre-teen legs. Listen, you want to reduce the national debt, don't you? Aren't you patriotic? That's the spirit. That's my girl.

15 She's a natural resource, a renewable one luckily, because those things wear out so quickly. They don't make 'em like they used to. Shoddy goods.

6

16 One and one equals another one. Pleasure in the female is not a requirement. Pair-bonding is stronger in geese. We're not talking about love, we're talking about biology. That's how we all got here, daughter.

17 Snails do it differently. They're hermaphrodites, and work in threes.

7

18 Each Female Body contains a female brain. Handy. Makes things work. Stick pins in it and you get amazing results. Old popular songs. Short circuits. Bad dreams.

Anyway: each of these brains has two halves. They're joined together by a thick cord; neural pathways flow from one to the other, sparkles of electric information washing to and fro. Like light on waves. Like a conversation. How does a woman know? She listens. She listens in. 19

The male brain, now, that's a different matter. Only a thin connection. Space over here, time over there, music and arithmetic in their own sealed compartments. The right brain doesn't know what the left brain is doing. Good for aiming through, for hitting the target when you pull the trigger. What's the target? Who's the target? Who cares? What matters is hitting it. That's the male brain for you. Objective. 20

This is why men are so sad, why they feel so cut off, why they think of themselves as orphans cast adrift, footloose and stringless in the deep void. What void? she asks. What are you talking about? The void of the universe, he says, and she says Oh and looks out the window and tries to get a handle on it, but it's no use, there's too much going on, too many rustlings in the leaves, too many voices, so she says, Would you like a cheese sandwich, a piece of cake, a cup of tea? And he grinds his teeth because she doesn't understand, and wanders off, not just alone but Alone, lost in the dark, lost in the skull, searching for the other half, the twin who could complete him. 21

Then it comes to him: he's lost the Female Body! Look, it shines in the gloom, far ahead, a vision of wholeness, ripeness, like a giant melon, like an apple, like a metaphor for "breast" in a bad sex novel; it shines like a balloon, like a foggy noon, a watery moon, shimmering in its egg of light. 22

Catch it. Put it in a pumpkin, in a high tower, in a compound, in a chamber, in a house, in a room. Quick, stick a leash on it, a lock, a chain, some pain, settle it down, so it can never get away from you again. 23

QUESTIONS ON SUBJECT AND PURPOSE

1. What appears to be the occasion for Atwood's essay?
2. In what ways might this be considered a definition of the "female body"?
3. Is it true, as Atwood notes in section 7, that the structure of the brain varies with gender?

QUESTIONS ON STRATEGY AND AUDIENCE

1. Why might Atwood have chosen to divide the essay as she does?

2. Why doesn't Atwood write transitions to bridge from one section of the essay to another instead of dividing it into sections?
3. The letter from the magazine refers to the topic as "capacious." What does that word mean? In what way does that word suggest the shape and nature of Atwood's response?

QUESTIONS ON VOCABULARY AND STYLE

1. How would you characterize Atwood's tone in the essay? (See the Glossary for a definition of *tone*.)
2. In what context might you expect to find section 3 of the essay? What does it sound like?
3. Be prepared to define the words *alderman* (paragraph 2) and *sublimation* (7).

WRITING SUGGESTIONS

1. **For Your Journal.** Suppose you had been invited to write something (an essay, a poem, a story) about either the male or the female body. What would you say? In your journal, jot down some possible ideas for your response.
2. **For a Paragraph.** Select one of the ideas that you came up with in your journal writing, and expand that into a developed paragraph. Remember to use example—either a variety of different ones or a single, extended one—to develop your definition.
3. **For an Essay.** In section 5, Atwood makes numerous references to the ways in which the female body has been used to sell products. Similarily, advertisers today also use male bodies. Judging just from the images of women or of men presented in advertisements, write an essay about how the female or male body is defined in our culture.

   Prewriting:

   a. Gather a range of magazines, and look in them for advertisements in which women or men are used to sell particular products. If you are using magazines in your college's library, you might want to photocopy the advertisements.
   b. Make a list of what you observe in that group of ads. In what ways are images of women and men used? What do the images look like? Are they of a particular physical

type? Is there any relationship between the image and the product?

c. Remember to consider as well what is *not* pictured or represented in the images. What types of images never appear?

Rewriting:

a. Have you provided enough examples—either by referring briefly to many or by developing a representative few in detail—to justify your definition? Check back through your draft to make sure.

b. Try outlining your draft. Do you see a clear, logical organization? Are there adequate transitions from section to section? Make a list of any problems you discover in the organization, and then devote some time to trying to solve just those problems. If your college has a Writing Center, ask for help there.

c. Look carefully at your conclusion. You want to end forcefully; you do not just want to repeat the same ideas and words used in your introduction. Reread your essay several times, and then try freewriting a new conclusion. Aim for a completely different ending than the one you originally wrote.

4. **For Research.** How have society's definitions of *masculinity* and *femininity* changed over time? Choose one of the two terms, and research its shifting definitions over the past two hundred years. What did society expect of a man or a women in 1800? In 1900? In the early 2000s? What is considered masculine or feminine? Remember that no single reference source will provide you with the answers you need. You may need to infer the definitions from the roles that society forced on men and women and the images that represented those roles. Be sure to acknowledge your sources wherever appropriate.

Website Link

Atwood maintains an extensive personal home page on the Web. Dozens of Websites contain a wide range of information about Atwood and her work, including the texts of a number of her short stories. Start at the *Reader's* Website.

NINE

ARGUMENT AND PERSUASION

We live in a world of persuasive messages—billboards, advertisements in newspapers and magazines, commercials on television and radio, electronic advertisements on the Internet and the World Wide Web, signs on stores, bumper stickers, T-shirts and caps with messages, and manufacturers' logos prominently displayed on clothing. Advertisements demonstrate a wide range of persuasive strategies. Sometimes they appeal to logic and reason—they ask you to compare the features and price of one car stereo system with those of any competitor and judge for yourself. More often, though, they appeal to your emotions and feelings—you will not be stylish unless you wear this particular style and brand of athletic shoe; you are not a "real man" unless you smoke this brand of cigarette; you have not signaled your success in the world unless you drive this particular German automobile.

In the following paragraph, for example, William Junius Wilson appeals to logic when he argues that the "school-to-work transition" confronts many young Americans by citing specific factual evidence to establish the magnitude of the problem:

> The problem of school-to-work transition confronts young people of all ethnic and racial backgrounds, but it is especially serious for black youths. According to a recent report by the U.S. Bureau of Labor Statistics, only 42 percent of black youths who had not enrolled in college had jobs in October after graduating from high school a few months earlier in June, compared with 69 percent of their white counterparts. The figures for black youngsters in inner-city ghetto neighborhoods are obviously even lower. The inadequate system of school-to-work transition has also contributed significantly to the growing wage gap between those with high school diplomas and those with college training.

> In the 1950s and 1960s, when school-to-work transition was compatible with the mass production system, the average earnings of college graduates was only about 20 percent higher than those of high school graduates. By 1979, it had increased to 49 percent, and then rapidly grew to 83 percent by 1992.
>
> Thus, the school-to-work transition is a major problem in the United States, and it has reached crisis proportions in the inner-city ghetto.

In the face of such evidence, few readers would dispute the need to attack this problem. Later in this chapter you will find the editorial writer for *The New Yorker* in "Help for Sex Offenders" using a similar logical appeal to convince an audience of the truth of argument's claim.

As an example of an argument appealing to readers' emotions, notice how the writer of this editorial from the magazine *The Disability Rag* persuasively argues against the substitution of the phrase "physically challenged" for "physically disabled":

> "Physically challenged" attempts to conceal a crucial fact: that the reason we can't do lots of things is not because we're lazy or because we won't accept a "challenge," but because many things are simply beyond our control—like barriers. Like discrimination. People who favor "physically challenged" are making a statement: Barriers, discrimination, are not *problems* for us, but *challenges*. We want those barriers, we almost seem to be saying—because by overcoming them we'll become better persons! Stronger. More courageous. After all, isn't that what challenges are for?
>
> Until you've made it your responsibility to get downtown, and discovered that there are no buses with lifts running on that route, you may not fully comprehend that it isn't a personal "challenge" you're up against, but a system resistant to change.

Similarly, later in this chapter Martin Luther King Jr., in his famous "I Have a Dream" speech, will appeal to his listeners' (and readers') emotions. Despite the differences in strategy, though, the objective in both argument and persuasion is the same: to convince readers to believe or act in a certain way.

Whether you realize it or not, you have already had extensive experience in constructing arguments and in persuading an audience. Every time you try to convince someone to do or to believe something, you have to argue. Consider a hypothetical example. You are concerned about your father's health. He smokes cigarettes, avoids exercise, is overweight, and works long hours in a stressful job. Even though you are worried, he is completely unconcerned and has always resisted your family's efforts to change his ways. Your task is to persuade him to change or modify his lifestyle, and doing so involves making its dangers clear, offering convincing reasons for change, and urging specific action.

Establishing the dangers is the first step, and you have a wide range of medical evidence from which to draw. That evidence involves statistics, testimony or advice from doctors, and case histories of men who have suffered the consequences of years of abusing or ignoring their health. From that body of material, you select the items that are most likely to get through to your obstinate father. He might not be moved by cold statistics citing life-expectancy tables for smokers and nonexercisers, but he might be touched by the story of a friend his age who suffered a heart attack or stroke. The evidence you gather and use becomes a part of the convincing reasons for change that you offer in your argument. If your father persists in ignoring his health, he is likely to suffer some consequences. You might at this point include emotional appeals in your strategy. If he is not concerned about what will happen to him, what about his family? What will they do if he dies?

Having gotten your father to realize and acknowledge the dangers inherent in his lifestyle and to understand the reasons why he should make changes, it remains to urge specific action. In framing a plan for that action, you again need to consider your audience. If you urge your father to stop smoking immediately, join a daily exercise class at the local YMCA or health club, go on a thousand-calorie-a-day diet, and find a new job, chances are that he will think your proposal too drastic even to try. Instead, you might urge a more moderate plan, phasing in changes over a period of time or offering compromises (for example, that he work fewer hours).

How Do You Analyze Your Audience?

Argument or persuasion, unlike the other types of writing included in this text, has a special purpose—to persuade its audience. Because you want your reader to agree with your position or act as you urge, you need to analyze your audience carefully before you start to write. Try to answer each of the following questions:

- Who are my readers?
- What do they already know about this subject?

- How interested are they likely to be?
- How impartial or prejudiced are they going to be?
- What values do my readers share?
- Is my argument going to challenge any of my readers' beliefs or values?
- What types of evidence are most likely to be effective?
- Is my plan for requested action reasonable?

Your argumentative strategy should always reflect an awareness of your audience. Even in the hypothetical case of the unhealthy father, it is obvious that some types of evidence would be more effective than others and that some solutions or plans for action would be more reasonable and therefore more acceptable than others.

The second important consideration in any argument is to anticipate your audience's objections and be ready to answer them. Debaters study both sides of an argument so that they can effectively counter any opposition. In arguing the abortion issue, the right-to-life speaker has to be prepared to deal with subjects such as abnormal fetuses or pregnancy resulting from rape or incest. The pro-choice speaker must face questions about when life begins and when the rights of the unborn might take precedence over the mother's rights.

WHAT DOES IT TAKE TO PERSUADE YOUR READER?

In some cases, nothing will persuade your reader. For example, if you are arguing for legalized abortion, you will never convince a reader who believes that an embryo is a human being from the moment of conception. Abortion to that reader will always be murder. It is extremely difficult to argue any position that is counter to your audience's moral or ethical values. It is also difficult to argue a position that is counter to your audience's normal patterns of behavior. For example, you could reasonably argue that your readers ought to stop at all stop signs and to obey the speed limit. However, the likelihood of persuading your audience to do these two things—even though not doing so breaks the law—is slim.

These cautions are not meant to imply that you should argue only "safe" subjects or that winning is everything. Choose a subject about which you feel strongly; present a fair, logical argument; express honest emotion; but avoid distorted evidence or inflammatory language. Even if no one is finally persuaded, at least you have offered a clear, intelligent explanation of your position.

In most arguments, you have two possible types of support: you can supply factual evidence, and you can appeal to your reader's values. Suppose you are arguing that professional boxing should be prohibited because it is dangerous. The reader may or may not accept your premise but at the very least would expect some support for your assertion. Your first task would be to gather evidence. The strongest evidence is factual—statistics dealing with the number of fighters each year who are fatally injured or mentally impaired. You might quote appropriate authorities—physicians, scientists, former boxers—on the risks connected with professional boxing. You might relate several instances or even a single example of a particular fighter who was killed or permanently injured while boxing. You might describe in detail how blows affect the body or head; you might trace the process by which a series of punches can cause brain damage. You might catalog the effects that years of physical punishment can produce in the human body. In your argument you might use some or all of this factual evidence. Your job as a writer is to gather the best—the most accurate and the most effective—evidence and present it in a clear and orderly way for your reader.

You can also appeal to your reader's values. You could argue that a sport in which a participant can be killed or permanently injured is not a sport at all. You could argue that the objective of a boxing match—to render one's opponent unconscious or too impaired to continue—is different in kind from any other sport and not one that we, as human beings, should condone, let alone encourage. Appeals to values can be extremely effective.

Effective argumentation generally involves appealing to both reason and emotion. It is often easier to catch your reader's attention by using an emotional appeal. Demonstrators against vivisection, the dissecting of animals for laboratory research, display photographs of the torments suffered by these animals. Organizations that fight famine throughout the world use photographs of starving children. Advertisers use a wide range of persuasive tactics to touch our fears, our anxieties, our desires. But the types of argumentative writing that you are asked to do in college or in your job rarely allow for only emotional evidence.

One final thing is crucially important in persuading your reader. You must sound (and be) fair, reasonable, and credible in order to win the respect and possibly the approval of your reader.

Readers distrust arguments that use unfair or inflammatory language, faulty logic, and biased or distorted evidence.

How Do You Make Sure That Your Argument Is Logical?

Because logic or reason is so crucial to effective argumentation, you will want to avoid logical fallacies or errors. When you construct your argument, make sure that you have avoided the following common mistakes:

- **Ad hominem argument** (literally to argue "to the person"): criticizing a person's position by criticizing his or her personal character. If an underworld figure asserts that boxing is the manly art of self-defense, you do not counter his *argument* by claiming that he makes money by betting on the fights.
- **Ad populum argument** (literally to argue "to the people"): appealing to the prejudices of your audience instead of offering facts or reasons. You do not defend boxing by asserting that it is part of the American way of life and that anyone who criticizes it is a communist who seeks to undermine our society.
- **Appeal to an unqualified authority:** using testimony from someone who is unqualified to give it. In arguing against boxing, your relevant authorities would be physicians or scientists or former boxers—people who have had some direct experience. You do not quote a professional football player or your dermatologist.
- **Begging the question:** assuming the truth of whatever you are trying to prove. "Boxing is dangerous, and because it is dangerous, it ought to be outlawed." The first statement ("boxing is dangerous") is the premise you set out to prove, but the second statement uses that unproved premise as a basis for drawing a conclusion.
- **Either-or:** stating or implying that there are only two possibilities. Do not assert that the two choices are either to ban boxing or to allow this brutality to continue. Perhaps other changes might make the sport safer and hence less objectionable.
- **Faulty analogy:** using an inappropriate or superficially similar analogy as evidence. "Allowing a fighter to kill

another man with his fists is like giving him a gun and permission to shoot to kill." The analogy might be vivid, but the two acts are much more different than they are similar.

- **Hasty generalization:** basing a conclusion on evidence that is atypical or unrepresentative. Do not assert that *every* boxer has suffered brain damage just because you can cite a few well-known cases.
- **Non sequitur** (literally "it does not follow"): arriving at a conclusion not justified by the premises or evidence. "My father has watched many fights on television; therefore, he is an authority on the physical hazards that boxers face."
- **Oversimplification:** suggesting a simple solution to a complex problem. "If professional boxers were made aware of the risks they take, they would stop boxing."

How Do You Structure an Argument?

If you are constructing an argument based on a formal, logical progression, you can use either *inductive* or *deductive* reasoning. An *inductive* argument begins with specific evidence and then moves to a generalized conclusion that accounts for the evidence. The writer assumes the role of detective, piecing together the evidence in an investigation and only then arriving at a conclusion. An inductive structure is often effective because it can arouse the reader's interest or even anger by focusing on examples. Gregg Easterbrook in "Watch and Learn" uses detailed examples of violence depicted in the media to catch our attention. He subtly builds the link for which he is arguing—watching simulated violence in films and television can make children become violent. Barbara Katz Rothman in "The Potential Cost of the Best Genes That Money Can Buy" uses a similar pattern. She begins with an observation on how eggs are priced in a supermarket—brown eggs cost more than white, extra large are more expensive than small. We are five paragraphs into the essay before the analogy and Rothman's point become clear—the selling of human eggs makes us "confront the question of what makes for 'worth' in human beings."

A deductive argument moves in the opposite direction: It starts with a general truth or assumption and moves to a provide evidence or support. Here the detective announces who the murderer is and then proceeds to show us how she arrived at that conclusion. Aline D. Wolf in "Advertising and Children" opens her essay with her thesis: "Corporate America is dictating interests, choices, and values to our children." In the rest of her essay, Wolf provides the support that leads to her conclusion. Since a deductive pattern immediately announces its thesis, it can run the risk of instantly alienating a reader, especially if it is arguing for something about which many of its readers might disagree. David Gelernter in "What Do Murderers Deserve?" is careful not to announce his point—murderers ought to be executed—until he has invited his readers to think about why we hesitate to exercise this "moral responsibility."

The simplest form of a deductive argument is the *syllogism*, a three-step argument involving a major premise, a minor premise, and a conclusion. Few essays—either those you write or those you read—can be reduced to a syllogism. Our thought patterns are rarely so logical; our reasoning is rarely so precise. Although few essays state a syllogism explicitly, syllogisms do play a role in shaping an argument. For example, a number of essays in this reader begin with the same syllogism, even though it is not directly stated:

Major premise: All people should have equal opportunities.
Minor premise: Minorities are people.
Conclusion: Minorities should have equal opportunities.

Despite the fact that a syllogism is a precise structural form, you should not assume that a written argument will imitate it—that the first paragraph or group of paragraphs will contain a major premise; the next, a minor premise; and the final, a conclusion. Syllogisms can be basic to an argument without being the framework on which it is constructed.

No matter how you structure your argument, one final consideration is important. Since the purpose of argumentation is to get a reader to agree with your position or to act in a particular way, it is always essential to end your paper decisively. Effective endings or conclusions to arguments can take a variety of forms. You might end with a call to action. For example, Martin Luther King's speech rises to an eloquent, rhythmical exhortation to his audience to continue to fight until they are "free at last." After several closing paragraphs in which she offers specific suggestions for parents and caretakers who wish to limit "the commercialism invading our children's lives," Aline Wolf directly states the goal of these actions: "As adults one of our most important challenges is to protect and nurture" the special, unique qualities of each individual child.

You might end with a thought-provoking question directed at your audience. *The New Yorker* editorial writer in "Help for Sex Offenders" challenges readers' attitudes toward sex offenders: "If castration helps, why not let them have what they want?" Richard Rodriguez, aware of the poor and the silent who are generally bypassed by opportunity despite affirmative action programs, chooses to end his essay with an arresting image: "They are distant, faraway figures like the boys I have seen peering down from freeway overpasses in some other part of town."

If you have used personal experience as evidence in your argument or injected yourself into the argument in some way, you might end as Barbara Katz Rothman does in "The Potential Cost of the Best Genes Money Can Buy." Rothman describes her own experience at a panel discussion on the issue of egg donation. Rothman is urging her fellow faculty to take a stand on the issue with their students. Maybe by speaking she didn't change anyone's mind, she notes, but it did "help [the young women] make a more informed and thoughtful decision." Or you might end by reaffirming the point that your argument has been making, as David Gelernter does in "What Do Murderers Deserve?": "In executing murderers, we declare that deliberate murder is absolutely evil and absolutely intolerable."

Sample Student Essay

Beth Jaffe decided to tackle a subject on the minds of many career-minded, dollar-conscious college students: why do you have to take so many courses outside of your major? Beth's argument is sure to arouse the attention of every advocate of a liberal arts education, and you might consider exploring the subject in an argument of your own.

EARLIER DRAFT

REDUCING COLLEGE REQUIREMENTS

With the high costs of college still on the rise, it is not fair to make college students pay for courses labeled "requirements" which are not part of their major. Although many students want a well-rounded college education, many cannot afford to pay for one. By eliminating all of the requirements that do not pertain to a student's major, college costs could be cut tremendously. At the University of Delaware, for example, a student in the College of Arts and Science is required to take twelve credits of arts and humanities, twelve of culture and institutions of time, twelve of human beings and their environment, and thirteen of natural phenomena or science which include at least one lab. Although some of their major courses may fit into these categories, many others do not. Frequently students do not like and are not interested in the courses which fit into the four categories and feel they are wasting their money by paying for courses they do not enjoy, do not put much work into, and usually do not get much out of. It should be an option to the student to take these extra courses. Why should a humanities or social studies major have to take biology or chemistry? Many of these students thought their struggle with science was over after high school only to come to college and find yet more "requirements" in the sciences. Students are getting degrees in one area of concentration. They should be able to take only courses in their field of study and not have to waste their money on courses they have no desire to take.

Beth's essay, with her permission, was duplicated and discussed in class. Not surprisingly, it provoked a lively reaction. One student asked Beth whether she was serious and exactly what it was that she was proposing. Beth admitted that she did not advocate turning a college education into career training but that she had a number of friends who were deeply in debt because of their four-year education. "Why not just cut some requirements?" Beth asked. Several other students then suggested that since she did not really advocate an extreme position, maybe she could find a compromise proposal. Her instructor added that she might find a way of rewording her remarks about science classes. Few people, after all, are sympathetic to a position that seems to say, "I don't want to do that. It's too hard. It's too boring."

When Beth revised her paper, she tried to follow the advice the class had offered. In addition, she made the problem vivid by using her roommate as an example and by pointing out what specifically might be saved by her proposal.

REVISED DRAFT

LOWERING THE COST OF A COLLEGE EDUCATION

When my roommate graduates in June, she will be $20,000 in debt. The debt did not come from spring breaks in Fort Lauderdale or a new car. It came from four years of college expenses, expenses that were not covered by the money she earned as a part-time waitress or by the small scholarship she was awarded annually. So now in June at age 21, with her first full-time job (assuming she gets one), Alison can start repaying her student loans.

Alison's case is certainly not unusual. In fact, because she attends a state-assisted university, her debt is less than it might be. We cannot expect education to get cheaper. We cannot expect government scholarship programs to get larger. We cannot ask that students go deeper and deeper into debt. We need a new way of combating this cost problem. We need the Jaffe proposal.

If colleges would eliminate some of the general education course requirements, college costs could be substantially lowered. At the University of Delaware, for example, a student at the College of Arts and Science is required to take twelve credits of arts and humanities, twelve of culture and the institutions of time, twelve of human beings and their environment, and thirteen of natural phenomena or science, including at least one laboratory course. Approximately half of these requirements are fulfilled by courses which are required for particular majors. The others are not, and these are likely to be courses that students are not interested in and so get little out of.

If some of these requirements were eliminated, a student would need approximately twenty-five fewer credits for a bachelor's degree. A student who took a heavier load or went to summer school could graduate either one or two semesters earlier. The result would cut college costs by anywhere from one-eighth to one-fourth.

The Jaffe proposal does decrease the likelihood that a college graduate will receive a well-rounded education. On the other hand, it allows students to concentrate their efforts in courses which they feel are relevant. Perhaps most important, it helps reduce the burden that escalating college costs have placed on all of us.

Some Things to Remember

1. Choose a subject that allows for the possibility of persuading your reader. Avoid emotionally charged subjects that resist logical examination.
2. Analyze your audience. Who are your readers? What do they already know about your subject? How are they likely to feel about it? How impartial or prejudiced are they going to be?
3. Make a list of the evidence or reasons you will use in your argument. Analyze each piece of evidence to see how effective it might be in achieving your end.
4. Honest emotion is fair, but avoid anything that is distorted, inaccurate, or inflammatory. Argue with solid, reasonable, fair, and relevant evidence.
5. Avoid the common logical fallacies listed in this introduction.
6. Make a list of all the possible counterarguments or objections your audience might have. Think of ways in which you can respond to those objections.
7. Decide how to structure your essay. You can begin with a position and then provide evidence, or you can begin with the evidence and end with a conclusion. Which structure seems to fit your subject and evidence better?
8. End forcefully. Conclusions are what listeners and readers are most likely to remember. Repeat or restate your position. Drive home the importance of your argument.

Using Argument and Persuasion in Writing for Your Other Courses

A good deal of the writing you do for college courses is implicitly persuasive: you want to persuade an instructor that your mastery of a subject or area of inquiry is such that you deserve a good grade.

You do this by presenting information accurately and in sufficient detail without oversimplification, by avoiding unnecessary repetition and padding, by achieving clarity through your organization and use of a thesis statement and topic sentences, by observing conventions of the particular discipline in terms of documenting sources and other matters, by the following standard English grammar and usage rules, and by adhering to the terms of the specific assignment. This is the case even when you are not arguing for a particular position.

Sometimes, however, your purpose in writing may be more explicitly argumentative—that is, to present your own position on a subject about which there is some controversy or disagreement or to try to convince your reader that an accepted conclusion or interpretation should be modified in some way. Keep in mind that academic argument should rely exclusively on logical rather than on emotional appeals. The following is a sampling of assignments involving argumentation.

- **Literature.** In writing about a particular literary work, you might argue against a prevailing interpretation of the work, presenting evidence from the text itself and perhaps the circumstances of its creation to support your own interpretation.
- **Environmental Studies.** For a research paper on global warming, you might weigh the differing scientific evidence on the extent of the phenomenon and its causes and then argue your own position based on your interpretation of that evidence.
- **Communication.** For a paper focusing on media analysis, you might closely analyze a broadcast news report to argue that it was put together in such a way as to promote a particular political or social viewpoint.
- **Philosophy.** For an ethics course, you might write a paper analyzing the competing values surrounding a particular ethical issue, such as assisted suicide or animal testing, and in so doing argue for your own position on the issue.
- **Marketing or Business Management.** For a marketing strategies course or technical writing requirement, you might be asked to draft a proposal for increasing the profits of a local small business with the ultimate purpose of convincing the owner of the effectiveness and ease of implementing your suggestions.

VISUALIZING ARGUMENT AND PERSUASION

We are surrounded each day by hundreds of examples of visual argumentation and persuasion—advertisements. Sometimes advertisements appeal to reason, citing specific facts, figures, and statistics to buttress their claims. "Look at how our mutual fund has performed over the past year, over the past five years. Check our line charts and tables." Other times, we are assaulted by subtle persuasive appeals—if we wore this cologne or perfume, we would be irresistible; if we drove this automobile, we would be a hardy adventurer or an important professional. Probably we like to think that we "see through" the claims of advertisers, that we are not susceptible to their appeals. The truth, however, is that we do respond to these visual appeals—otherwise, companies would stop advertising their goods and services. So powerful are advertisements that they can even sell products that don't exist! Graphic artist Fiona Jack designed a billboard campaign in New Zealand to sell "Nothing™." The poster appeared on 27 billboards around the Auckland area, and what happened? People telephoned the billboard company to find out where they could buy "Nothing™." Jack commented, "You can market anything if there's enough money behind it."

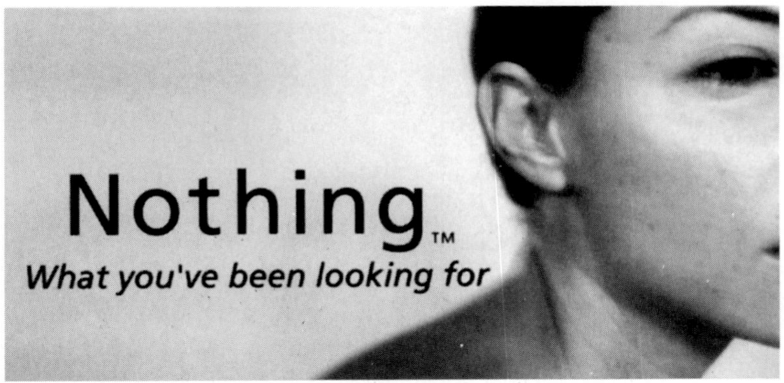

Copyright ©1998 by Fiona Jack.

VISIT THE PRENTICE HALL READER'S WEBSITE

When you have finished reading an essay, check out the additional material available at the *Reader's* Website at www.prenhall.com/miller. For each reading, you will find a list of related readings connected with the topic or the author; additional background information; a group of relevant hot-linked Web resources (just click your computer's mouse and automatically visit the sites listed); and still more writing suggestions.

Persuading and Arguing

High school and college students have generally had extensive experiences with minimum wage jobs. But what if you faced a future of minimum wage jobs? Arguments for and against minimum wage hikes occur annually in Congress. The WWW can provide extensive information supporting both sides of the debate. Visit a site supporting such hikes and another in opposition to them and do a paragraph writing assignment at the *Reader's* Website.

I HAVE A DREAM

Martin Luther King Jr.

Martin Luther King Jr. (1929–1968) was born in Atlanta, the son of a Baptist minister. Ordained in his father's church in 1947, King received a doctorate in theology from Boston University in 1955. That same year he achieved national prominence by leading a boycott protesting the segregation of the Montgomery, Alabama, city bus system, based on ideas of nonviolent civil resistance derived from Thoreau and Gandhi. A central figure in the civil rights movement, King was awarded the Nobel Peace Prize in 1964. He was assassinated in Memphis in 1968. His birthday, January 15, is celebrated as a national holiday.

King's "I Have a Dream" speech was delivered at the Lincoln Memorial to an audience of 250,000 people who assembled in Washington, D.C., on August 28, 1963. That march, commemorating in part the hundredth anniversary of Lincoln's Emancipation Proclamation, was intended as an act of "creative lobbying" to win the support of Congress and the president for pending civil rights legislation. King's speech is one of the most memorable and moving examples of American oratory.

BEFORE READING

Connecting: Probably every American has heard at least a small portion of King's speech. Before you begin to read, jot down what you know about the speech or the phrases that you remember from recordings and television clips.

Anticipating: King's speech is marked by the extensive use of images. As you read, make a note of the most powerful and recurrent images that he uses.

Five score years ago, a great American, in whose symbolic shadow we stand, signed the Emancipation Proclamation. This momentous decree came as a great beacon light of hope to millions of Negro slaves who had been seared in the flames of withering injustice. It came as a joyous daybreak to end the long night of captivity. 1

But one hundred years later, we must face the tragic fact that the Negro is still not free. One hundred years later, the life of the Negro is still sadly crippled by the manacles of segregation and the 2 chains of discrimination. One hundred years later, the Negro lives on a lonely island of poverty in the midst of a vast ocean of material prosperity. One hundred years later, the Negro is still languishing in the corners of American society and finds himself an exile in his own land. So we have come here today to dramatize an appalling condition.

3 In a sense we have come to our nation's capital to cash a check. When the architects of our republic wrote the magnificent words of the Constitution and the Declaration of Independence, they were signing a promissory note to which every American was to fall heir. This note was a promise that all men would be guaranteed the unalienable rights of life, liberty, and the pursuit of happiness.

4 It is obvious today that America has defaulted on this promissory note insofar as her citizens of color are concerned. Instead of honoring this sacred obligation, America has given the Negro people a bad check; a check which has come back marked "insufficient funds." But we refuse to believe that the bank of justice is bankrupt. We refuse to believe that there are insufficient funds in the great vaults of opportunity of this nation. So we have come to cash this check—a check that will give us upon demand the riches of freedom and the security of justice. We have also come to this hallowed spot to remind America of the fierce urgency of *now*. This is no time to engage in the luxury of cooling off or to take the tranquilizing drugs of gradualism. *Now* is the time to make real the promises of Democracy. *Now* is the time to rise from the dark and desolate valley of segregation to the sunlit path of racial justice. *Now* is the time to open the doors of opportunity to all of God's children. *Now* is the time to lift our nation from the quicksands of racial injustice to the solid rock of brotherhood.

5 It would be fatal for the nation to overlook the urgency of the moment and to underestimate the determination of the Negro. This sweltering summer of the Negro's legitimate discontent will not pass until there is an invigorating autumn of freedom and equality. 1963 is not an end, but a beginning. Those who hope that the Negro needed to blow off steam and will now be content will have a rude awakening if the nation returns to business as usual. There will be neither rest nor tranquility in America until the Negro is granted his citizenship rights. The whirlwinds of revolt will continue to shake the foundations of our nation until the bright day of justice emerges.

6 But there is something that I must say to my people who stand on the warm threshold which leads into the palace of justice.

In the process of gaining our rightful place we must not be guilty of wrongful deeds. Let us not seek to satisfy our thirst for freedom by drinking from the cup of bitterness and hatred. We must forever conduct our struggle on the high plane of dignity and discipline. We must not allow our creative protest to degenerate into physical violence. Again and again we must rise to the majestic heights of meeting physical force with soul force. The marvelous new militancy which has engulfed the Negro community must not lead us to a distrust of all white people, for many of our white brothers, as evidenced by their presence here today, have come to realize that their destiny is tied up with our destiny and their freedom is inextricably bound to our freedom. We cannot walk alone.

And as we walk, we must make the pledge that we shall march 7 ahead. We cannot turn back. There are those who are asking the devotees of civil rights, "When will you be satisfied?" We can never be satisfied as long as the Negro is the victim of the unspeakable horrors of police brutality. We can never be satisfied as long as our bodies, heavy with the fatigue of travel, cannot gain lodging in the motels of the highways and the hotels of the cities. We cannot be satisfied as long as the Negro's basic mobility is from a smaller ghetto to a larger one. We can never be satisfied as long as a Negro in Mississippi cannot vote and a Negro in New York believes he has nothing for which to vote. No, no, we are not satisfied, and we will not be satisfied until justice rolls down like waters and righteousness like a mighty stream.

I am not unmindful that some of you have come here out of 8 great trials and tribulations. Some of you have come fresh from narrow jail cells. Some of you have come from areas where your quest for freedom left you battered by the storms of persecution and staggered by the winds of police brutality. You have been the veterans of creative suffering. Continue to work with the faith that unearned suffering is redemptive.

Go back to Mississippi, go back to Alabama, go back to South 9 Carolina, go back to Georgia, go back to Louisiana, go back to the slums and ghettos of our northern cities, knowing that somehow this situation can and will be changed. Let us not wallow in the valley of despair.

I say to you today, my friends, that in spite of the difficulties 10 and frustrations of the moment I still have a dream. It is a dream deeply rooted in the American dream.

I have a dream that one day this nation will rise up and live 11 out the true meaning of its creed: "We hold these truths to be self-evident: that all men are created equal."

12 I have a dream that one day on the red hills of Georgia the sons of former slaves and the sons of former slave owners will be able to sit down together at the table of brotherhood.

13 I have a dream that one day even the state of Mississippi, a desert state sweltering with the heat of injustice and oppression, will be transformed into an oasis of freedom and justice.

14 I have a dream that my four little children will one day live in a nation where they will not be judged by the color of their skin but by the content of their character.

15 I have a dream today.

16 I have a dream that one day the state of Alabama, whose governor's lips are presently dripping with the words of interposition and nullification, will be transformed into a situation where little black boys and black girls will be able to join hands with little white boys and white girls and walk together as sisters and brothers.

17 I have a dream today.

18 I have a dream that one day every valley shall be exalted, every hill and mountain shall be made low, the rough places will be made plain, and the crooked places will be made straight, and the glory of the Lord shall be revealed, and all flesh shall see it together.

19 This is our hope. This is the faith with which I return to the South. With this faith we will be able to hew out of the mountain of despair a stone of hope. With this faith we will be able to transform the jangling discords of our nation into a beautiful symphony of brotherhood. With this faith we will be able to work together, to pray together, to struggle together, to go to jail together, to stand up for freedom together, knowing that we will be free one day.

20 This will be the day when all of God's children will be able to sing with new meaning

> My country, 'tis of thee,
> Sweet land of liberty,
>   Of thee I sing:
> Land where my fathers died,
> Land of the pilgrims' pride,
> From every mountain-side
>   Let freedom ring.

21 And if America is to be a great nation this must become true. So let freedom ring from the prodigious hilltops of New Hampshire. Let freedom ring from the mighty mountains of New York. Let freedom ring from the heightening Alleghenies of Pennsylvania!

Let freedom ring from the snowcapped Rockies of Colorado! 22

Let freedom ring from the curvaceous peaks of California! 23

But not only that; let freedom ring from Stone Mountain of Georgia! 24

Let freedom ring from Lookout Mountain of Tennessee! 25

Let freedom ring from every hill and molehill of Mississippi. From every mountainside, let freedom ring. 26

When we let freedom ring, when we let it ring from every village and every hamlet, from every state and every city, we will be able to speed up that day when all of God's children, black men and white men, Jews and Gentiles, Protestants and Catholics, will be able to join hands and sing in the words of the old Negro spiritual, "Free at last! free at last! thank God almighty, we are free at last!" 27

QUESTIONS ON SUBJECT AND PURPOSE

1. What is King's dream?
2. King's essay was a speech delivered before thousands of marchers and millions of television viewers. How are its oral origins revealed in the written version?
3. In what way is King's speech an attempt at persuasion? Whom was he trying to persuade to do what?

QUESTIONS ON STRATEGY AND AUDIENCE

1. Why does King begin with the words "Five score years ago"? Why does he say at the end of paragraph 6, "We cannot walk alone"? What do such words have to do with the context of King's speech?
2. How does King structure his speech? Is there an inevitable order or movement? How effective is his conclusion?
3. What expectations does King have of his audience? How do you know that?

QUESTIONS ON VOCABULARY AND STYLE

1. How many examples of figurative speech (images, metaphors, similes) can you find in the speech? What effect does such figurative language have?
2. The speech is full of parallel structures. See how many you can find. Why does King use so many?

3. Be able to define the following words: *seared* (paragraph 1), *manacles* (2), *languishing* (2), *promissory note* (3), *unalienable* (3), *invigorating* (5), *inextricably* (6), *tribulations* (8), *nullification* (16), *prodigious* (21).

WRITING SUGGESTIONS

1. **For Your Journal.** It is impossible for most people to read or hear King's speech without being moved. What is it about the speech that makes it so emotionally powerful? In your journal, speculate on the reasons the speech has such an impact. What does it suggest about the power of language?
2. **For a Paragraph.** In a paragraph, argue for equality for a minority group of serious concern on your campus (the disabled; a sexual, racial, or religious minority; returning adults, commuters).
3. **For an Essay.** Expand the argument you explored in Suggestion 2 to essay length.

   Prewriting:
   a. To write convincingly about such a problem, you will need specific information drawn from your own experience or the experiences of others. Interview several members of the minority group about whom you are writing. Take notes on index cards.
   b. Organize your cards by sorting them into groups according to topic. Make a list of those topics, and then convert the list into a working outline.
   c. What objections or reservations might your audience have? Try to imagine a critic's objections to your essay.

   Rewriting:
   a. Highlight all the specific evidence in your essay. Remember that details make an argument effective. Have you included enough? Each body paragraph needs details and examples.
   b. Check each paragraph for a unified idea. Is there a single focused idea controlling the paragraph? Jot down a key word or phrase for each paragraph.
   c. Find someone to read your essay. Does your reader find your argument fair? Convincing? If the reader disagrees, ask for specific reasons why.

4. **For Research.** According to the U.S. Census Bureau, 43 million Americans have some type of physical or mental disability. Like members of other minorities, the disabled regularly confront discrimination ranging from prejudice to physical barriers that deny them equal access to facilities. The federal government, with the passage of Title V of the Rehabilitation Act in 1973 and the Americans with Disabilities Act of 1990, has attempted to address these problems. Research the problem on your college's campus. What has been done to eliminate discrimination against the disabled? What remains to be done? Argue for the importance of such changes. Alternatively, you might argue that the regulations are burdensome and should be abandoned. Be sure to document your sources wherever appropriate.

Website Link

Extensive on-line resources are available for King including texts of speeches, video and audio clips, texts of sermons, and photographs. Some key sites, all with extensive additional Internet links, are available.

What Do Murderers Deserve?

David Gelernter

David Gelernter earned his B.A. at Yale and his Ph.D. at the State University of New York at Stony Brook. He joined the Yale faculty in 1982 where he is a professor of computer science and chief scientist at Mirror Worlds Technologies in New Haven. Gelernter is regarded as "a leading figure in the third generation of artificial intelligence scientists" and developed, with Nicholas Carriero, the coordination language "Linda" that is widely used for parallel programming. Gelernter's many books include a semi-novel, 1939: The Lost World of the Fair *(1995) and his recent* Machine Beauty: Elegance and Technology *(1998). An artist as well, Gelernter serves as art critic for* The Weekly Standard. *In 1993, Gelernter was a victim of Theodore Kaczynski, the so-called Unabomber, who mailed out anonymous packages containing explosives to a number of people involved in technological research. The injuries he suffered required ten operations.*

On Writing: *Of his book about the Unabomber attack,* Drawing Life: Surviving the Unabomber *(1998), Gelernter has said: "An author writes because he has to, and it's a kind of compulsion, it's a personality type. . . . One of my first conscious thoughts coming to in the hospital is how soon I could get to a word processor and start writing. . . . The project changed in scope a little. When I actually set down to tell the story, I found that I was struggling with questions that I really didn't have any particular desire to examine or to ask, but they were so urgent I couldn't avoid them."*

BEFORE READING

Connecting: How do you feel about the death penalty? If you had to vote in a referendum on legalizing or outlawing the death penalty in your state, how would you vote?

Anticipating: What does Gelernter mean by suggesting that society needs to assume "moral responsibility"?

1 A Texas woman, Karla Faye Tucker, murdered two people with a pickax, was said to have repented in prison, and was put to death. A Montana man, Theodore Kaczynski, murdered three people

with mail bombs, did not repent, and struck a bargain with the Justice Department: He pleaded guilty and will not be executed. (He also attempted to murder others and succeeded in wounding some, myself included.) Why did we execute the penitent and spare the impenitent? However we answer this question, we surely have a duty to ask it.

And we ask it—I do, anyway—with a sinking feeling, because in modern America, moral upside-downness is a specialty of the house. To eliminate race prejudice we discriminate by race. We promote the cultural assimilation of immigrant children by denying them schooling in English. We throw honest citizens in jail for child abuse, relying on testimony so phony any child could see through it. We make a point of admiring manly women and womanly men. None of which has anything to do with capital punishment directly, but it all obliges us to approach any question about morality in modern America in the larger context of this country's desperate confusion about elementary distinctions. 2

Why execute murderers? To deter? To avenge? Supporters of the death penalty often give the first answer, opponents the second. But neither can be the whole truth. If our main goal were deterring crime, we would insist on public executions—which are not on the political agenda, and not an item that many Americans are interested in promoting. If our main goal were vengeance, we would allow the grieving parties to decide the murderer's fate; if the victim had no family or friends to feel vengeful on his behalf, we would call the whole thing off. 3

In fact, we execute murderers in order to make a communal proclamation: that murder is intolerable. A deliberate murderer embodies evil so terrible that it defiles the community. Thus the late social philosopher Robert Nisbet wrote: "Until a catharsis has been effected through trial, through the finding of guilt and then punishment, the community is anxious, fearful, apprehensive, and, above all, contaminated." 4

When a murder takes place, the community is obliged to clear its throat and step up to the microphone. Every murder demands a communal response. Among possible responses, the death penalty is uniquely powerful because it is permanent. An execution forces the community to assume forever the burden of moral certainty; it is a form of absolute speech that allows no waffling or equivocation. 5

Of course, we could make the same point less emphatically, by locking up murderers for life. The question then becomes: Is the death penalty overdoing it? 6

7 The answer might be yes if we were a community in which murder was a shocking anomaly. But we are not. "One can guesstimate," writes the criminologist and political scientist John J. DiIulio Jr., "that we are nearing or may already have passed the day when 500,000 murderers, convicted and undetected, are living in American society."

8 DiIulio's statistics show an approach to murder so casual as to be depraved. Our natural bent in the face of murder is not to avenge the crime but to shrug it off, except in those rare cases when our own near and dear are involved.

9 This is an old story. Cain murders Abel, and is brought in for questioning: "Where is Abel, your brother?" The suspect's response: "What am I, my brother's keeper?" It is one of the first human statements in the Bible; voiced here by a deeply interested party, it nonetheless expresses a powerful and universal inclination. Why mess in other people's problems?

10 Murder in primitive societies called for a private settling of scores. The community as a whole stayed out of it. For murder to count, as it does in the Bible, as a crime not merely against one man but against the whole community and against God is a moral triumph still basic to our integrity, and it should never be taken for granted. By executing murderers, the community reaffirms this moral understanding and restates the truth that absolute evil exists and must be punished.

11 On the whole, we are doing a disgracefully bad job of administering the death penalty. We are divided and confused: The community at large strongly favors capital punishment; the cultural elite is strongly against it. Consequently, our attempts to speak with assurance as a community sound like a man fighting off a chokehold as he talks. But a community as cavalier about murder as we are has no right to back down. The fact that we are botching things does not entitle us to give up.

12 Opponents of capital punishment describe it as a surrender to emotions—to grief, rage, fear, blood lust. For most supporters of the death penalty, this is false. Even when we resolve in principle to go ahead, we have to steel ourselves. Many of us would find it hard to kill a dog, much less a man. Endorsing capital punishment means not that we yield to our emotions but that we overcome them. If we favor executing murderers, it is not because we want to but because, however much we do not want to, we consider ourselves obliged to.

13 Many Americans no longer feel that obligation; we have urged one another to switch off our moral faculties: "Don't be

judgmental!" Many of us are no longer sure evil even exists. The cultural elite oppose executions not (I think) because they abhor killing more than others do, but because the death penalty represents moral certainty, and doubt is the black-lung disease of the intelligentsia—an occupational hazard now inflicted on the whole culture.

Returning then to the penitent woman and the impenitent man: The Karla Faye Tucker case is the harder of the two. We are told that she repented. If that is true, we would still have had no business forgiving her, or forgiving any murderer. As theologian Dennis Prager has written apropos this case, only the victim is entitled to forgive, and the victim is silent. But showing mercy to penitents is part of our religious tradition, and I cannot imagine renouncing it categorically. 14

I would consider myself morally obligated to think long and hard before executing a penitent. But a true penitent would have to have renounced (as Karla Faye Tucker did) all legal attempts to overturn the original conviction. If every legal avenue has been tried and has failed, the penitence window is closed. 15

As for Kaczynski, the prosecutors say they got the best outcome they could, under the circumstances, and I believe them. But I also regard this failure to execute a cold-blooded, impenitent terrorist and murderer as a tragic abdication of moral responsibility. The community was called on to speak unambiguously. It flubbed its lines, shrugged its shoulders, and walked away. 16

In executing murderers, we declare that deliberate murder is absolutely evil and absolutely intolerable. This is a painfully difficult proclamation for a self-doubting community to make. But we dare not stop trying. Communities in which capital punishment is no longer the necessary response to deliberate murder may exist. America today is not one of them. 17

QUESTIONS ON SUBJECT AND PURPOSE

1. How does Gelernter feel about the death penalty? Would there ever be circumstances that might affect his attitude?
2. In the first paragraph Gelernter mentions that he was one of the many victims of Theodore Kaczynski (the Unabomber). Does knowing that have any impact on your reading of the essay?
3. What might Gelernter's purpose be in writing?

QUESTIONS ON STRATEGY AND AUDIENCE

1. In paragraph 2, Gelernter cites a number of examples of what he regards as the "moral upside-downness" of American society. Does this strategy strengthen or weaken his argument for you?
2. What expectations does Gelernter's title create in your mind? Can you anticipate his position from his title?
3. Gelernter criticizes the "cultural elite" in this country in part because they lack "moral certainty." Who do you think those "cultural elite" might be? Could you define the characteristics of such a group?

QUESTIONS ON VOCABULARY AND STYLE

1. What does it mean to be "penitent"? "Impenitent"?
2. How would you characterize the tone of Gelernter's essay? (See the Glossary for a definition of *tone.*)
3. Be prepared to define the following words: *assimilation* (paragraph 2), *catharsis* (4), *equivocation* (5), *anomaly* (7), *cavalier* (11), *abhor* (13), *apropos* (14), *abdication* (16).

WRITING SUGGESTIONS

1. **For Your Journal.** How do you feel about the death penalty? In your journal, brainstorm about your feelings.
2. **For a Paragraph.** Extend your journal writing into a paragraph. Given the space restrictions, focus on what you regard as your strongest argument about the issue.
3. **For an Essay.** Extend the paragraph writing into an essay. Your essay could be argumentative or persuasive or contain elements of both. That means that you might want to use specific examples, facts, and statistics to buttress your position. If you are going to take a qualified position (under certain circumstances), make sure that you make those circumstances clear.

   Prewriting:

   a. Make a list of the reasons why you feel the way you do. Next to each one, try to write a response or a counterargument.

b. Brainstorm an organizational strategy for your essay. Do you want to start with what you regard as your strongest point or to conclude with it? Experiment with different orders.

c. Look at what you gathered so far. Interesting, effective writing depends on appropriate detail. Do you have a body of information to support your points?

Rewriting:

a. Make a list of the problems that you see in your first draft—mechanical, grammatical, and organizational. If your school has a Writing Center or a peer-tutoring service, ask for help, or visit your instructor during office hours and ask for some help then.

b. Ask a peer to read your paper—try to find someone who has the opposite opinion on this issue. How does this person respond to your argument? Try to use that response in revising your essay.

c. Look back at your introduction and your conclusion. Both parts are crucial in effective writing. Have you aroused your reader's interest? Have you left your reader with a forceful conclusion that makes your position (and any response that you hope to get from the reader) clear?

4. **For Research.** Thirty-eight of the fifty states enforce the death penalty. Does your state (either the state in which you live or the state in which you go to school)? To what extent should states be allowed to decide independently whether or not murder should be punished by execution? Why should such a decision rest with the states? In an essay, argue either for or against uniform penalties for murder in all fifty states. Be sure to document all of your sources including information you gathered from the World Wide Web.

Website Link

The Death Penalty Information Center is the place to begin your research. The WWW also has an on-line interview with Gelernter who was a victim of the Unabomber.

Help for Sex Offenders

The New Yorker

The New Yorker, *a weekly magazine famous for its high-caliber writing and witty cartoons, was founded by Harold Ross and first published in February 1925. Originally focused on life and amusements in New York City, the magazine gradually broadened its scope to appeal to a wide audience of sophisticated and well-educated readers. "Help for Sex Offenders" appeared in a section labeled "Comment," which is reserved for editorial opinions. Until recently, the "comments" were never signed. These essays were sometimes written by members of the magazine's staff and sometimes by outside contributors.*

BEFORE READING

Connecting: How should our legal system handle persons who have committed sex crimes?

Anticipating: Why as a society should we be concerned about how our legal system handles sex offenders?

1 Recently, a debate has arisen in this country over requests by sex criminals that they be permitted to undergo the surgical operation known as orchiectomy—more plainly, castration. The argument began in 1992, when Steve Allen Butler, a previously convicted child rapist, asked Judge Michael McSpadden, of the 209th Criminal District Court, in Houston, to let him be castrated rather than go to prison. McSpadden acceded to this request, setting off a hubbub that raged through the talk shows. Local black leaders contended that the bargain was racist, because the offender in the case was black. The director of the Rape Crisis Program at the Houston Area Women's Center opposed castration on principle, even when it was voluntary. She asserted that rape is a crime of violence, not of sex, and therefore the operation would not affect Butler's tendency to offend. The general counsel of the American Civil Liberties Union in Houston was already on record as opposing castration, having raised the spectre of Nazi sterilization programs. In the face of the controversy, doctors who had volunteered to perform the operation backed out, leaving the judge with no option but to send Butler to prison.

Since then, however, other sex offenders have come forward with similar requests. They draw attention to the failure of our present approaches to dealing with sex criminals. A comprehensive study of the effectiveness of various therapies which appeared in the *Psychological Bulletin* in 1989 concluded that "the recidivism rate for treated offenders is not lower than that for untreated offenders; if anything, it tends to be higher." Other studies have reported equally dismal findings. Sex criminals reoffend at high rates no matter what the treatment. 2

The State of Florida, once a pioneer in the humane treatment of sex offenders, has thrown up its hands and retreated to long prison sentences. Washington State recently enacted a "sexual predator" law, which provides indefinite terms of confinement for habitual offenders. Governor Pete Wilson, of California, now running for reelection, has proposed life sentences for some *first-time* sex offenders. Other states have continued to explore therapeutic approaches ranging from role-playing to olfactory aversion therapy. According to Dr. William Pithers, the psychologist who directs Vermont's program, "the most successful candidates for treatment are men who have no other criminal record, have an established network of family and friends, and are not so preoccupied by their fantasies that they think of them hours a day." Few offenders meet such standards. 3

One out of six prisoners in the federal and state systems is a sex offender. The offenses include everything from exhibitionism to pedophilia and rape. Given the compulsive nature of the behavior of sex criminals, their share of the prison population is bound to rise with the passage of the "three strikes and you're out" proposals now sweeping through Congress and the legislatures. Although there are differences between men who fondle and men who rape, most sex criminals actually commit a variety of offenses as well as an appalling number of them. An eight-year study by Emory University researchers of five hundred and sixty-one male offenders who had voluntarily sought treatment reported a total of 291,737 specific acts committed against 195,407 victims. The average offender had been arrested in about one out of thirty crimes he committed; some had never been arrested at all. 4

Can a sex offender be cured of his need to offend? Of course he can, given the will to change, given the opportunity, given the proper care and treatment. Unfortunately, these elements rarely meet in the case of the chronic offender, and, even when they do, the struggle toward reform is likely to be lengthy and marked by failure. Anyone who has gone through the torment of giving up 5 smoking or drinking or of following a prolonged diet can testify to the difficulty of changing a compulsive behavior. And yet, when the urge to eat or smoke becomes overwhelming, the consequences are merely personal. When sex offenders fail, other lives are destroyed.

6 Why, then, resist the demands of men who are willing to risk sacrificing sexual activity in order to be free of their damaging impulses? Most of the arguments against voluntary castration are based on misconceptions, such as the common belief that it is a barbaric practice that has been used only in Third World countries. The fact is that it has been effectively and humanely used as treatment in Denmark, Czechoslovakia, Holland, Switzerland, Norway, Iceland, Sweden, and Finland. A 1973 Swiss study of a hundred twenty-one castrated offenders found that the rate of reoffending dropped to 4.1 per cent, compared with 76.9 per cent before the operation. A Danish study in the sixties which followed as many as nine hundred castrated sex offenders, found that recidivism rates dropped to 2.2 per cent.

7 Many European countries have turned to so-called chemical castration, which involves injections of female hormones, and this treatment is also common in the United States and Canada. But, while chemical castration effectively blunts the male sex drive, it may place the subject at risk for certain medical problems, including gallstones and diabetes. Moreover, such programs, both here and abroad, are plagued by dropouts; and as soon as the injections cease the sexual drive returns to its previous level.

8 That surgical castration is permanent and irreversible is a source of alarm to its opponents and of security to its advocates. An orchiectomy is not a Bobbitt-like mutilation. It involves removing the testicles from the scrotum and replacing them with silicone prostheses that make the procedure virtually undetectable. The operation is far less invasive than a hysterectomy, for instance, or many forms of cosmetic surgery. Nor is it necessarily a "sexual death sentence," as some opponents have called it. A 1991 Czech study of eighty-four castrated sexual delinquents found that eighteen per cent were capable of occasional intercourse and that twenty-one per cent lived in a stable heterosexual partnership. Only three men committed another sexual offense after castration, and those offenses were not of an aggressive character. Similarly, in the Danish study none of the rapists were found to rape again.

9 Some opponents of the castration option, while conceding its effectiveness, attack it on moral grounds. Here an odd double

standard comes into play. A woman who suffers from excessive premenstrual tension may choose to have her uterus removed. A woman who is carrying a baby she doesn't want (and many such women are rape victims) may elect to have an abortion. But a man who molests children or brutalizes women can't ask to have his testicles removed, because that would be barbarous.

10 Our society is so squeamish when it comes to discussing sexual deviance that we tend to demonize sex offenders, forgetting that in many cases they themselves are victims, not only of sexual abuse in their own childhood but also of their overwhelming sexual impulses. Most of them, every time they exercise their sexual preference, break the law. It amounts to fraud when we offer these men treatment that doesn't work. If castration helps, why not let them have what they want?

QUESTIONS ON SUBJECT AND PURPOSE

1. Specifically, what does the essay argue for?
2. Why types of sexual activities are included under the rubric "sexual crimes"?
3. Why should the public be concerned about the treatment that sexual offenders receive?

QUESTIONS ON STRATEGY AND AUDIENCE

1. What strategy does the author use in beginning the essay?
2. What objections do people have to voluntary castration?
3. What might the author be able to assume about his or her audience?

QUESTIONS ON VOCABULARY AND STYLE

1. What does *recidivism* mean?
2. What does the title, "Help for Sex Offenders," suggest?
3. Be prepared to define the following words: *acceded* (paragraph 1), *spectre* (1), *habitual* (3), *therapeutic* (3), *chronic* (5), *prostheses* (8), *squeamish* (10).

WRITING SUGGESTIONS

1. **For Your Journal.** The Internet and the World Wide Web contain material that many people find offensive—sexually

explicit material, calls to hatred and violence, directions for building bombs, pages promoting the use of drugs. Should such information be policed or censored? By the government? By parents? By the companies that provide Websites? In your journal, freewrite about the need for censoring or the importance of not censoring the dissemination of information through electronic means.

2. **For a Paragraph.** In a paragraph, focus on one aspect of the argument that you began in your journal. If your instructor approves, you could concentrate on either logical argument or emotional appeal.
3. **For an Essay.** Extend your paragraph into an essay. Again you can argue either for or against such censorship. Remember that in part you will need to define the nature of such offensive documents and images.

Prewriting:

a. Brainstorm a list of reasons, in your opinion, for or against censorship. Look over your list, and determine which reasons seem most important to you. Make a short list of your strong arguments.
b. Using your short list, brainstorm possible objections to each argument or reason. Anticipate the reactions of readers who will not agree with you.
c. Arrange your reasons in an order, deciding which reasons should come first, which next, and so forth. Make these decisions carefully. For example, do you want to begin or to end with what you feel is your strongest point?

Rewriting:

a. Check to make sure that you have adequately defined what you are writing about—for example, what constitutes "hate speech" or what is "sexually explicit"?
b. Go through your draft, underlining any emotionally charged words or phrases. Look at each carefully. Are they likely to alienate your audience?
c. Ask a friend to read your essay, preferably someone who has not also written on the same topic. Ask your reader for reactions. Did the reader agree with you? Why or why not? Consider that reaction when you revise your draft.

4. **For Research.** What should be done about sex offenders once they have been released back into their communities? Should they be required to register with the police? Should neighbors be informed of their presence in neighborhoods? Should their houses or apartments or even their persons be labeled in some way? Do any of these actions seem unreasonable? Unconstitutional? Research the problems and suggested solutions for dealing with sex offenders who are returning to society. Argue for or against specific measures. Don't rely on just your own opinions. Research what is happening, how effective such measures are, and what objections have been raised. Be sure to document your sources.

Website Link

As more states are considering chemical castration as a punishment for sexual offenders, the debate over such practices has been growing. Some good places to start gathering information are hotlinked at the *Reader's* Website.

The Potential Cost of the Best Genes Money Can Buy

Barbara Katz Rothman

Barbara Katz Rothman (1948–) is a Professor of Sociology at the City University of New York. She earned her B.A. and M.A. at Brooklyn College of the City University of New York and her Ph.D. from New York University. The author and editor of many articles and books, Rothman's research has centered around reproductive health and childbirth. Her most recent book is Genetic Maps and Human Imaginations: The Limits of Science in Understanding Who We Are *(1998). Part of Rothman's argument in that book, one reviewer observed, is that "genetic engineering will turn beauty and intelligence into market commodities."*

On Writing: *Speaking generally of her work, Rothman has said: "The basic question in my work has been how do we know what we know, and who controls that knowledge? I am a feminist and a sociologist, a sociologist and a feminist; my work and my life reflect the interplay of those two perspectives."*

BEFORE READING

Connecting: Would you sell your sperm or eggs? Why or why not? Do you think that such a practice ought to be made illegal?

Anticipating: As you read, think about how Rothman defines her audience. To whom is she writing and how does that influence what she says in the essay?

1 Brown eggs cost more than white at my supermarket. From large through extra-large to jumbo, there's an orderly progression of prices, with a premium for color.

2 There is a market in human eggs, too, although we judge them by different criteria.

3 The latest story about human eggs comes from early March, when a couple advertised in newspapers on the campuses of such universities as Harvard, Princeton, and Stanford, offering to pay \$50,000 for the eggs of a woman who is 5′10″ or taller and who had scored at least 1,400 on her SATS. It's the height thing that pulled

the story forward. The money isn't out of line, actually: $35,000 to $50,000 has been the going rate for Ivy League eggs for months now. But people have been wondering, "Why so tall?" Not, I notice, "Why so smart?"

Adoption, too, operates like a market, but the hierarchy for human children is the opposite of that for hen's eggs. With children, the younger (smaller) and lighter are more expensive than the older and darker. Big enough or dark enough, and you can't give the kids away: Our foster-care system is overflowing with unplaced children, too dark or too long on the shelf. 4

The market has long affected sperm banks, too, with ads for sperm donors aimed at medical students through the 1970s, but shifting to business students in the 1980s. Surely that change reflected the increasing status of business executives in our culture. 5

In a system of "donating" gametes in which banking is the dominant metaphor, sperm and eggs naturally are sorted by "worth." That forces us to confront the question of what makes for "worth" in human beings. We don't like to speak of eugenics anymore, but it is hard not to think of eugenics when people are actively seeking the very best genes money can buy. 6

Class and commerce are not new issues in procreation. Members of elites have purchased the reproductive services of poor women from time immemorial: Pharaoh's daughter not only took the baby from the water, but also hired his mother as a wet nurse. And, at various historical moments, questions have arisen about what qualities a child was imbibing along with its milk. The fluids of human life—blood, semen, and milk—are never just the proteins of which they are composed. Every culture and every time have invested them with meaning. 7

Today, we think of the sperm and eggs that we trade in as—at one and the same time—purchasable commodities and the roots of human life, both commercial and mystical in their power. We believe that the core of human identity lies in the tangled strands of DNA. That is arguably the most determinist belief system the world has ever seen. Even in the eugenics era of *Brave New World*, people saw each individual as the product of an interplay between genes and environment: Alphas were differentiated from Betas and Gammas by the material in the incubating fluid. But we increasingly push the role of the environment to the background, while focusing on genes. We think of the environment—from the cytoplasm surrounding the nucleus of the egg, to the pregnant mother's body, to the child-rearing practices of a culture—as 8 merely permitting or failing to permit the child to develop to its full genetic potential.

9 That is the context in which "quality" eggs have come to command such a high price. But people are not just chromosomes grown big. People whose used sperm from the once highly controversial "genius sperm bank" could have had kids who inherited the genius's nose, not his brain. Tall, smart women do not always have tall, smart children. Even people who understand that intellectually, however, still may try to get the child they want—especially if they can afford to pay for the genius's sperm or the tall, smart woman's eggs.

10 Most countries do not permit the sale of eggs, sperm, or embryos, nor do they allow women to offer pregnancy as a service for hire. The United States would probably never enact such bans. If someone is willing to sell and someone else is ready to buy, then interfering in the process seems downright un-American. It is not surprising that, during the 1960s, more Americans were outraged by the fact that an African American with a dollar in his hand could not buy a slice of pie at a lunch counter than by the fact that most African Americans in the South didn't have the dollar. The right to buy is almost holy in America, and legislating against it isn't likely to work.

11 If we are going to permit the sale of sperm and eggs, should we set any limits on what characteristics parents can order? What if it turns out that the couple who advertised for a tall, smart woman's eggs aren't all that smart themselves? If the woman who is going to be pregnant with and give birth to this potential child has an SAT score of 1,100, has she forfeited her right to buy eggs from someone with a score of 1,400? What if she's not all that tall, either, but just thought height was an asset?

12 And what if she's not white, but thought being black in the United States was too much of a burden and wanted to purchase white privilege for her child? If white privilege is for sale—as it appears to be when "white" eggs and sperm are in the marketplace and so marked to allow donors and recipients to be matched by race—do only white folks have the right to purchase it? What about a black woman married to a white man: Must that couple purchase only "black" eggs?

13 Although an ad for human eggs in a college newspaper cannot say "whites only," a woman with an African-American grandparent would not be chosen as a donor. Nor would a woman with a schizophrenic mother, a gay brother, or an alcoholic aunt, or a woman who is fat. No matter what the scientific evidence, many people feel that those characteristics are determined by genes.

The market is very good at forcing us to confront our values. Translated into dollars, the incomparable becomes comparable. The cost of a batch of Ivy League eggs is approximately that of a German sports car. Or, in very practical terms, two bouts of egg selling equal a college education. Eggs from say, a typical student in my class at the City University of New York—a white woman who had emigrated from Eastern Europe—would fetch enough to pay for half of her college education; a Yale or Harvard woman's eggs would pay for half of hers. Symmetry, yes, but fairness? And my students of African descent don't even have the option of financing their education that way. Not only you, those students are told, but—like your slave forebears—even your descendants are not worth very much on the open market. 14

If we cannot ban the sale of human eggs and sperm, what can we do? When we discuss the implications of new reproductive technologies, we usually focus on ways to protect the children who result. However, we must not ignore what the technologies mean for potential mothers and fathers, and for the way we define family. Children are not consumer goods, and parenting is more about nurturing relationships than about biology and genetics. 15

Nor must we forget the third parties. It is college women who are being targeted in college-newspaper ads for egg donors. They are our students. In the days of the eugenics movement, elite college women were told to go home and breed, to prevent the "elite stock" from dying out. Eugenics courses are not longer, as they once were, a regular and respectable part of the college curriculum. But does it absolve us of responsibility if the class session that a woman misses for her appointment at the egg-donation clinic is in bioethics, instead of eugenics? 16

An overly simplistic genetic determinism is creeping into our thinking, and colleges and universities are not exempt. We must maintain the skeptical, critical stance that we pride ourselves on as academics. We must help keep the boundaries clear between the rigorous science of genetics and the value system of eugenics. 17

Some time ago, when ads for egg donors first started to appear in newspapers at Columbia University, I was invited by the Barnard College women's-studies program to speak on a panel exploring the issue. Some of the women who attended had been thinking about selling their eggs. I don't know if what they heard—from me, from one of the doctors whose clinic brokers the sales, or from others on the panel—changed any minds. But it did, 18 at the very least, help them make a more informed and thoughtful decision.

QUESTIONS ON SUBJECT AND PURPOSE

1. What is Rothman suggesting by her title?
2. In paragraph 8, Rothman comments that "we believe that the core of human identity lies in the tangled strands of DNA." She then writes, "That is arguably the most determinist belief system the world has ever seen." What does that last sentence mean?
3. Why is Rothman writing? What reaction/action might she wish to elicit from her readers?

QUESTIONS ON STRATEGY AND AUDIENCE

1. Why does Rothman begin by writing about the cost of chicken eggs in the supermarket? How does she tie this to the points that she is trying make?
2. The procedure through which eggs are "harvested" is complicated, requiring extensive testing, weeks of hormone therapy, and invasive surgery. In short, it's a risky and potentially dangerous procedure. Why doesn't Rothman use this information in her essay?
3. To whom is Rothman writing? How can you tell who her imagined audience is?

QUESTIONS ON VOCABULARY AND STYLE

1. At several points in the essay, Rothman mentions "eugenics." What does the term mean?
2. Egg donation forces us, Rothman writes, "to confront the questions of what makes for 'worth' in human beings." What does she mean by that statement?
3. Be prepared to define the following words: *procreation* (paragraph 7), *imbibing* (7), *absolve* (16).

WRITING SUGGESTIONS

1. **For Your Journal.** Suppose such an advertisement such as Rothman describes appeared in your college's newspaper. As a member of the paper's editorial staff, you are asked to

write an editorial about the advertisement. In your journal, jot down ideas for your response. Will you condemn such a practice? Endorse it? On what grounds will you argue?

2. **For a Paragraph.** Expand your journal writing into a paragraph in which you take your stand. Develop one argument for or against such a practice.
3. **For an Essay.** Expand your paragraph into an essay. You will need to have an effective introduction, to develop a number of points in your body paragraphs, and to conclude by urging your readers to agree with your position and, perhaps, to react or act in a certain way.

   Prewriting:

   a. Brainstorm on both sides of the argument regardless of the position you intend to take. Remember that the quality of your argument is always improved when you understand the issues from various points of view.

   b. Write a specific statement of the action or reaction that you want to elicit from your audience. As you write, use that statement as a way of checking your developing argument.

   c. Pay particular attention to how your essay concludes. What would you like your readers to do? How do you want them to feel? Remember that persuasive essays ought to end forcefully.

   Rewriting:

   a. Make a copy of your essay, and highlight in colored ink all emotionally charged words and phrases. Look carefully at those highlighted sections. How will your audience react to them? Have you avoided distorted or inflammatory statements?

   b. An effective title is important to an essay. It should not only represent the essay, but also attract a reader's attention. Write several possible titles for your essay. Ask a friend or classmate to comment on each.

   c. Look carefully at how you have structured your essay. Did you begin with a position and then provide evidence? Did you begin with specific examples and then draw your conclusion? Is the structure the right one for your essay?

4. **For Research.** As Rothman notes in the essay, the concept of purchasing "quality" sperm or eggs reflects an assumption that genes are more important than environment. However, there is no guarantee that what will be genetically passed on will be brilliance or athletic ability or whatever made the genes so valuable to begin with. What do we know about the transmission of "valuable traits" from one generation to another? Do great athletes have children who are also athletically gifted? Do geniuses have offspring who are geniuses? Are children of gifted artists or musicians more likely to have artistic talent? Choose one area, research the issue, and then use your research to argue for or against the assumption that genes are the crucial determiner. Be sure to document your sources.

Website Link

The WWW is a rich source for information about the sale or donation of eggs and sperm and about the moral, ethical, and legal problems that can arise. For some tips on key words and phrases for your search, visit the *Reader's* Website.

ADVERTISING AND CHILDREN

Aline D. Wolf

Aline Wolf earned her B.A. from Marywood College and has an honorary Doctorate of Pedagogy from St. Francis College. The author of sixteen books, she is regarded as the spokesperson for Maria Montessori's philosophy and methods of childhood education. She and her husband, Gerald, founded Pennsylvania's first Montessori school in 1961. Wolf's A Parent's Guide to the Montessori Classroom *is regarded as a classic. Her most recent book is* Nurturing the Spirit: In Non-Sectarian Classrooms *(1996).*

BEFORE READING

Connecting: Can you remember ever desperately wanting a toy or a fast food product because of the commercials you saw on television?

Anticipating: Does Wolf convince you that "corporate America" is a threat to childhood? If so, why? If not, why not?

Corporate America is dictating interests, choices and values to our children. Disney and McDonald's have more power to shape consciousness and promote a cultural curriculum than do elementary schools, according to Joseph Kincheloe and Shirley Steinberg, the editors of *Kinderculture—the Corporate Construction of Childhood.* 1

The executives who create this cultural curriculum are not educational specialists interested in shaping responsible, creative, well-informed adults. They are marketing specialists whose goal is to develop long-term customers who will insure corporate profits for years to come. These companies employ psychologists, not to help children cope with problems, but to hook them and their parents into spending on whatever product they are promoting. Their appeal to the emotions is extremely clever. Children have no idea how to resist it. And not many parents have the guts or energy to oppose these commercial forces dominating our culture. 2

What parent has not been pestered to buy toys representing Barney or the Power Rangers, to buy Nike sneakers even when other brands are more affordable, to go to McDonald's when there is better food at home and to take a child to yet another 3 questionable Disney movie advertised incessantly on television as family entertainment?

4 A few years ago a young mother of two Montessori students called to see if I could find a Power Ranger Halloween costume for her son. She had exhausted all the retail outlets in their area and wanted me to look in the stores where I live. How old was her son? Three-and-a-half. "He won't wear anything else," she told me. His parents responded to Power Ranger promotions exactly as the marketing executives had planned. The child pestered and demanded. The mother never realized how cleverly she had been hooked.

5 According to Consumer Reports, businesses and trade associations aim no fewer than 30,000 commercial messages at children every day through television, radio and billboards. Many thousands more are emblazoned on school buses, posters, study sheets, workbooks, audio-visuals and clothing. Corporations regularly pay school districts to let them advertise. In our local school district, at junior and senior high school entrances there are big signs announcing "Pepsi" along with schedules of sports and special events. In allowing this, the school district closed its eyes to the large amounts of sugar and caffeine in that drink that addict young people to a lifelong craving for these unhealthy substances.

6 Today's elementary-age children have tremendous spending power. They spend $11 billion per year on a variety of products from food, beverages and clothes to toys and games. In addition, they influence another $160 billion of spending controlled by their parents. One Madison Avenue advertising agency blatantly brags it can put its client's product in kindergarten lesson plans and can help develop product loyalty by distributing samples to elementary students. They recently released documents from the R.J. Reynolds Tobacco Company showed how well corporations know the value of starting product loyalty early. Their corporate papers reveal that they had aimed their cigarette ads at 14-year-olds.

7 How does corporate advertising "hook" our children?

8 First, they make the audience believe this product will make them happy. Kids in commercials all smile broadly as they consume a particular hamburger, candy bar or soft drink.

9 Second, they strongly suggest all other children have seen this hit movie or wear that brand of jeans or sneakers. This ploy gives a feeling of inferiority to any child without these alleged advantages.

10 Third, they flood every avenue of communication with visual images that reinforce the popularity of their products. This is particularly true of Disney, one of four or five multinational

corporations that now control nearly all our media. Disney constantly intensifies its images by repeating them in movies, videos, television programs and commercials, books, clothing, toys and other products that children use. Its media monopoly is so extensive that when you come across a rave review for a Disney movie in a newspaper, magazine, on television or radio you should be aware that that particular medium may be promoting its own product.

Fourth, to increase sales, corporate specialists promote the idea of "collecting"—or getting the next one in the series. The mother who buys one expensive American Girl doll for her daughter is soon asked to buy another. The infinite variety of Beanie Babies and Barbies are designed to make children want as many as possible. The back cover of every book in the Goosebumps series gives children a "chilling preview" of the next in the series. Even though these books feature unsavory monsters, terrorizing zombies and disgusting images such as pimples on gangrene, they consistently represent three of the top four best sellers in the Publisher's Weekly list of children's trade books. Collecting as a hobby can be both interesting and productive for children. But would it not be better for them to collect something corresponding to their own natural interests instead of what multinational companies are foisting upon them? 11

As parents and caretakers of children we must be aware of these corporate strategies. Children are infinitely impressionable. Maria Montessori, the great educator (1870–1952) described the mind of the child between birth and seven years as "absorbent," like a sponge, that effortlessly soaks up whatever is in the environment. We have a responsibility to monitor the quality of what our children absorb and look carefully at the characteristics of the corporate pap so pervasive in our school and homes. What are these characteristics? 12

First there is violence. There are 16 acts of violence per hour of children's television programming with very few peaceful solutions to conflicts. Video games go a step further by requiring the player to participate physically in what takes place onscreen. To win, the child must commit violent acts. Even though these acts are on a screen and not in real life, they still promote violence as the way to get ahead. 13

Presently video games are found in over one-third of U.S. homes, a $35 billion industry. But the video company Sega recently joined Time Warner Entertainment and Telecommunications to start delivering video games by cable. This represents the beginning of a new interactive television cable industry that will probably be 14 extremely violent. According to corporate plans, the largest single target audience will be children and teenagers.

15 The second characteristic is stereotyping. Racist stereotyping, for example, is rampant in the Disney movie "Aladdin." The opening song, "Arabian Nights," begins its depiction of Arab culture with: "Oh I come from a Land/From a faraway place/Where the caravan camels roam/Where they cut off your ear/If they don't like your face/It's barbaric, but hey, it's home."

16 In response to protests, these lyrics were changed in the video. But the producers did not correct the racist representations of supporting characters portraying Arabs as grotesque, violent and cruel. This film subtly teaches children to fear or even hate Arabs at a time when world peace depends on children learning to understand and respect cultures other than our own.

17 Negative stereotypes of women appear in "The Little Mermaid." Mermaid Ariel, modeled after a slightly anorexic Barbie doll, trades her voice for a pair of legs so she can pursue the handsome Prince Eric, thus suggesting to children that real empowerment comes from catching a handsome man. Ursula tells Ariel that taking away her voice is not so bad because men don't like women who talk.

18 The third characteristic is mediocrity that often includes misinformation. By taking stories from history ("Pocahontas"), literature ("The Hunchback of Notre Dame") and myth ("Hercules") and retelling them in cartoon format with only casual attention to the original details. Disney has reduced them to insipid entertainments. For example, history is quite distorted in the film "Pocahontas." Captain John Smith, known historically for his murderous pursuit of Native Americans, is changed in the movie to a morally uplifted character, a Mr. Right for the ill-fated Pocahontas.

19 The quality of such movies and videos is at best mediocre. There are times when all of us can relax with mediocrity, but a constant diet of it limits our children, leaving no room for poetry or for the classic stories that reveal human nature and illustrate the real lessons of life.

20 Perhaps more serious than these negative characteristics is the consequence of children watching long hours of television. The ready-made images of the television world blunt children's imagination, one of the most precious gifts they have. Imagination is largely responsible for many of the great advances in our civilization—scientific discoveries, art masterpieces, symphonies, operas, literature, dance and drama. A child's imagination is strongest during the first seven years, years when it must have many opportunities

to be exercised and expressed. When free from corporate influences, children of this age have imaginary playmates; they make a ship from a board and a piece of cloth, or a tent in the mountains from a sheet draped over a living-room chair. Telling children a story stimulates their imagination because it invites them to create mentally their own images of characters and scenes. But television offers children ready-made images; nothing is left to their creative imagination. The child is given an image created by someone else's imagination, one that can be easily recreated for more corporate profit in books, toys, T-shirts and games.

Joseph Chilton Pearce, an expert on human intelligence and 21
creativity and author of *The Magical Child and Evolution's End*, believes that "the major damage of television has little to do with content; its greatest damage is neurological." He says: "Television floods the infant-child brain with images at the very time his or her brain is supposed to make images from within. This imaging is the foundation of future symbolic thought, mathematics, science and philosophy. Children who constantly watch TV gradually weaken this vital ability." The inadequacy begins to show on the playground. Instead of pretending or making up games, many children at playtime simply mimic scenes they have seen on television.

The average American at 20 years of age has seen one million 22
television commercials. Not only is this a great waste of time for the young; it has filled their minds with useless details and questionable values. Advertising, with its resultant consumerism, favors manufactured products over the gifts of nature. It frequently disregards environmental issues. It promotes selfishness and accumulation rather than sharing and kindness. It values passive entertainment rather than self-directed, creative activities.

Although consumerism and materialism boost our national 23
economy and enrich huge corporations, they ultimately produce failure in our personal lives. Accumulating material goods can never satisfy the human spirit that yearns for a more meaningful way of life. People obsessed with buying always want one more thing to make them happy. In reality, the more things one has, the less free one is, because things take time and space from our lives.

Passive entertainment also fails the human spirit. This is 24
not to say one should never watch television. But we have to be selective and use our power to turn television off when the selected program is over. Watching a good television program can be enlightening or relaxing. But indiscriminate watching, hour after hour, nearly always leaves one with an empty feeling. The human spirit that yearns for expression in creativity, in challenges, in

communing with nature or in serving others is left unnourished by inferior fare.

25 What are we, as parents and caregivers, to do about all the commercialism invading our children's lives if we wish to foster values that will lead children to become compassionate, peaceful and loving adults who value their particular role in life?

26 *Kinderculture* tells us it is our parental, civic and professional responsibility to study the corporate curriculum and become aware of its effects on our children. Simply throwing out the television is not realistic, but we can refrain from using it as a baby sitter. We can carefully select what young children watch. (I know one responsible mother who carefully taped good television programs for her children, eliminating all the commercials.) We can tell our children stories or read them quality books. We can refuse to buy reading material, toys and games that reinforce television images. We can give our children many more experiences of nature. We can encourage children to make their own designs for T-shirts so they can show what is important to them rather than displaying what is important to a multinational corporation. At P.T.A. or church meetings we can remind other parents to resist the corporate curriculum.

27 Perhaps most importantly we can teach children in elementary school how to resist advertising. Without such help our children are victims of marketing psychologists who know how to hook them.

28 To encourage such resistance, we can bring tapes of ads into the classroom and ask questions to help students analyze the commercial messages. "Do you think that if you drink this soft drink you will be able to do a spectacular ski jump like the Olympic athlete who just drank the same drink?" "Do you really think that using this shampoo will make your hair look like the model in the commercial—a model who is under special lights to make her hair shine and surrounded by special fans to make it blow gently in the wind?" "Do these ads appeal to your emotions or to your good judgment?" We have to enable our children to say confidently: "I am aware of all the deceptions in advertising. I know that Michael Jordan wears Nike sneakers, not because they are the best on the market, but because he is paid *more* to wear them than all the people in the third world countries are paid to make them. I know that wearing a shirt, a cap or sneakers with the Nike mark on them will not make me a better athlete or even a cool kid. It will only make me an easy mark for companies that want me to give them free advertising."

If we can help a generation of young people to analyze in this way, to be savvy and discerning, we can break the hold corporations have on their lives. As adults we can give children more of our time. We can give human encounter priority over the media. We can play with our children, laugh with them, hug them, challenge them, listen to their concerns and help them realize that their value lies within themselves and not in their possessions. 29

One of our greatest gifts as human beings is our uniqueness. Individual uniqueness is now threatened by corporate pedagogy that prompts all children to see the same movies, read the same books, have the same toys, collect the same products and play the same games—all chosen, not by the children, but by marketing executives. 30

Each human being has a unique vocation in life, a special gift to contribute to society. As adults, one of our most important challenges is to protect and nurture this special quality within each child so that the child will not be swayed by mass media, but will follow an inner direction to an authentic vocation that will give satisfaction and meaning to each one's life. 31

QUESTIONS ON SUBJECT AND PURPOSE

1. Why does Wolf focus on the impact of advertising on the very young? Doesn't advertising have similar effects even on adults?
2. How does Wolf feel about consumerism and materialism?
3. What would Wolf like her audience to do? What is her "call to action"?

QUESTIONS ON STRATEGY AND AUDIENCE

1. What is the effect of the examples Wolf uses in paragraphs 3 and 4? How are these examples connected to her intended audience?
2. How do the criticisms that Wolf makes in paragraphs 13–20 fit into her argument?
3. To whom is Wolf writing? Can you find a point in the essay when she identifies her audience?

QUESTIONS ON VOCABULARY AND STYLE

1. How do you react to the phrase "corporate America"? What connotations do you associate with it?

2. How would you characterize Wolf's tone in the essay? How does that tone affect her argument?
3. Be prepared to define the following words: *blatantly* (paragraph 6), *ploy* (9), *foisting* (11), *pap* (12), *rampant* (15), *mediocrity* (18), *insipid* (18).

WRITING SUGGESTIONS

1. **For Your Journal.** Increasingly schools (high schools, colleges, and universities) have signed contracts with companies that allow the exclusive sale of a product on the campus (for example, the vending machines and the food services carry soft drinks bottled by only one company) or that endorse a product through some form of advertisement (for example, a particular product symbol or logo is displayed in the cafeteria or gymnasium). In your journal speculate on such arrangements. Assuming that the school is receiving revenue through such an arrangement, do you think such deals are good or bad? Would knowing how the money generated in this way is used change your opinion?
2. **For a Paragraph.** Expand your journal writing into a paragraph. Because of the space limitations, focus your argument (either for or against) on a single point.
3. **For an Essay.** Expand your paragraph writing into an essay. It would be best to begin by knowing whether or not your current school (or your former school) has any such arrangements. If there are revenues received from such endorsements, for what are those revenues used? In your essay, you will have space to develop your argument through several points and to provide examples as well.

   Prewriting:

   a. Research the problem first. What endorsements or exclusive contracts seem to exist at your school? Do such arrangements generate revenue? How is it used? For example, do they help fund scholarships?
   b. Speculate whether such arrangements seem to have any impact on student choices. Student life? Values? Should they be expanded?
   c. Once you have formulated your ideas, find a classmate or peer who disagrees. Try to persuade each other. What appear to be the strongest, most effective arguments?

Rewriting:

a. Once you have completed a draft, outline your essay. Are some points of the argument developed in great detail and others in little detail? Use the outline to help identify any structural problems.

b. Avoid the trivial. Remember that your audience will respond best to thoughtful, significant observations. For example, don't complain about an arrangement because you personally must drink one brand of cola rather than another.

c. Remember that conclusions are important. Plan a specific, forceful concluding strategy. Are you recommending a certain course of action?

4. **For Research.** Expensive designer clothes frequently display their brand name or logo, often in very conspicuous ways. Many of the T-shirts and caps that people wear today advertise a product or represent a symbol of consumer culture. Essentially we have been turned into walking advertisements. Not only have we been "recruited" to serve as advertisements, we have even paid (by buying the clothing) for the privilege of acting in this way. How did such commercialism in fashion come about? How should we feel about apparel as advertisement? Are we simply conveying a sense of style and defining a group with which we identify, or are we being manipulated? Research the practice of commercialism in fashion and in an essay argue either for or against these practices. Assume that your audience is a group of fellow students (recognizing that this represents a very diverse group of people).

WEBSITE LINK

1. You can read an interview with the authors of *Kinderculture*, the collection of essays that Wolf cites, and check out what the toy industry has to say about "Advertising to Children" at the *Reader's* Website.

None of This Is Fair

Richard Rodriguez

Born in 1944 in San Francisco to Spanish-speaking Mexican-American parents, Richard Rodriguez first learned English in grade school. Educated in English literature at Stanford, Columbia, and the University of California at Berkeley, Rodriguez is best known for his conservative opinions on bilingual education and affirmative action, and in "None of This Is Fair," he uses his personal experience to argue that affirmative action programs are ineffective in reaching the seriously disadvantaged. Yet he also suggests in his two autobiographical works, Hunger of Memory: The Education of Richard Rodriguez *(1982) and* Days of Obligation: An Argument with My Mexican Father *(1992), that he harbors deep regret at losing his own Hispanic heritage when he became assimilated into the English-speaking world.*

Basically, the phrase "affirmative action" refers to policies and programs that try to redress past discrimination by increasing opportunities for underrepresented or minority groups. In the United States, the major classifications affected by affirmative action are defined by age, race, religion, national origin, and sex. The phrase was coined in 1965 in an executive order issued by President Lyndon Johnson that required any contractor dealing with the federal government to "take affirmative action to ensure that applicants are employed . . . without regard to their race, creed, color, or national origin." In the decades following, affirmative action, in the form of weighted admissions policies, became a potent tool for colleges and universities seeking increased enrollments of previously underrepresented students. Controversy has always surrounded such policies, and in recent years a number of states have enacted legislation banning race-based admissions selection.

On Writing: *In an interview, Rodriguez noted: "It takes me a very long time to write. What I try to do when I write is break down the line separating the prosaic world from the poetic world. I try to write about everyday concerns—an educational issue, say, or the problems of the unemployed—but to write about them as powerfully, as richly, as well as I can.*

BEFORE READING

Connecting: To what extent has your education—in elementary and secondary schools—provided you with opportunities that others have not had?

Anticipating: Why did it trouble Rodriguez to be labeled as a "minority student"?

My plan to become a professor of English—my ambition during long years in college at Stanford, then in graduate school at Columbia and Berkeley—was complicated by feelings of embarrassment and guilt. So many times I would see other Mexican-Americans and know we were alike only in race. And yet, simply because our race was the same, I was, during the last years of my schooling, the beneficiary of their situation. Affirmative Action programs had made it all possible. The disadvantages of others permitted my promotion; the absence of many Mexican-Americans from academic life allowed my designation as a "minority student." 1

For me opportunities had been extravagant. There were fellowships, summer research grants, and teaching assistantships. After only two years in graduate school, I was offered teaching jobs by several colleges. Invitations to Washington conferences arrived and I had the chance to travel abroad as a "Mexican-American representative." The benefits were often, however, too gaudy to please. In three published essays, in conversations with teachers, in letters to politicians and at conferences, I worried the issue of Affirmative Action. Often I proposed contradictory opinions. Though consistent was the admission that—because of an early, excellent education—I was no longer a principal victim of racism or any other social oppression. I said that but still I continued to indicate on applications for financial aid that I was a Hispanic-American. It didn't really occur to me to say anything else, or to leave the question unanswered. 2

Thus I complied with and encouraged the odd bureaucratic logic of Affirmative Action. I let government officials treat the disadvantaged condition of many Mexican-Americans with my advancement. Each fall my presence was noted by Health, Education, and Welfare department statisticians. As I pursued advanced literary studies and learned the skill of reading Spenser and Wordsworth and Empson, I would hear myself numbered among the culturally disadvantaged. Still, silent, I didn't object. 3

But the irony cut deep. And guilt would not be evaded by averting my glance when I confronted a face like my own in a crowd. By late 1975, nearing the completion of my graduate studies at Berkeley, I was so wary of the benefits of Affirmative Action that I feared my inevitable success as an applicant for a teaching position. The months of fall—traditionally that time of academic job-searching—passed without my applying to a single school. 4

When one of my professors chanced to learn this in late November, he was astonished, then furious. He yelled at me: Did I think that because I was a minority student jobs would just come looking for me? What was I thinking? Did I realize that he and several other faculty members had already written letters on my behalf? Was I going to start acting like some other minority students he had known? They struggled for success and then when it was almost within reach, grew strangely afraid and let it pass. Was that it? Was I determined to fail?

5 I did not respond to his questions. I didn't want to admit to him, and thus to myself, the reason I delayed.

6 I merely agreed to write to several schools. (In my letter I wrote: "I cannot claim to represent disadvantaged Mexican-Americans. The very fact that I am in a position to apply for this job should make that clear.") After two or three days, there were telegrams and phone calls, invitations to interviews, then airplane trips. A blur of faces and the murmur of their soft questions. And, over someone's shoulder, the sight of campus buildings shadowing pictures I had seen years before when I leafed through Ivy League catalogues with great expectations. At the end of each visit, interviewers would smile and wonder if I had any questions. A few times I quietly wondered what advantage my race had given me over other applicants. But that was an impossible question for them to answer without embarrassing me. Quickly, several persons insisted that my ethnic identity had given me no more than a "foot inside the door"; at most, I had a "slight edge" over other applicants. "We just looked at your dossier with extra care and we liked what we saw. There was never any question of having to alter our standards. You can be certain of that."

7 In the early part of January, offers arrived on stiffly elegant stationery. Most schools promised terms appropriate for any new assistant professor. A few made matters worse—and almost more tempting—by offering more: the use of university housing; an unusually large starting salary; a reduced teaching schedule. As the stack of letters mounted, my hesitation increased. I started calling department chairmen to ask for another week, then 10 more days—"more time to reach a decision"—to avoid the decision I would need to make.

8 At school, meantime, some students hadn't received a single job offer. One man, probably the best student in the department, did not even get a request for his dossier. He and I met outside a classroom one day and he asked about my opportunities. He seemed happy for me. Faculty members beamed. They said they

had expected it. "After all, not many schools are going to pass up getting a Chicano with a Ph.D. in Renaissance literature," somebody said, laughing. Friends wanted to know which of the offers I was going to accept. But I couldn't make up my mind. February came and I was running out of time and excuses. (One chairman guessed my delay was a bargaining ploy and increased his offer with each of my calls.) I had to promise a decision by the 10th; the 12th at the very latest.

On the 18th of February, late in the afternoon, I was in the office I shared with several other teaching assistants. Another graduate student was sitting across the room at his desk. When I got up to leave, he looked over to say in an uneventful voice that he had some big news. He had finally decided to accept a position at a faraway university. It was not a job he especially wanted, he admitted. But he had to take it because there hadn't been any other offers. He felt trapped, and depressed, since his job would separate him from his young daughter. 9

I tried to encourage him by remarking that he was lucky at least to have found a job. So many others hadn't been able to get anything. But before I finished speaking I realized that I had said the wrong thing. And I anticipated his next question. 10

"What are your plans?" he wanted to know. "Is it true you've gotten an offer from Yale?" 11

I said that it was. "Only, I still haven't made up my mind." 12

He stared at me as I put on my jacket. And smiling, then unsmiling, he asked if I knew that he too had written to Yale. In his case, however, no one had bothered to acknowledge his letter with even a postcard. What did I think of that? 13

He gave me no time to answer. 14

"Damn!" he said sharply and his chair rasped the floor as he pushed himself back. Suddenly, it was to *me* that he was complaining. "It's just not right, Richard. None of this is fair. You've done some good work, but so have I. I'll bet our records are just about equal. But when we look for jobs this year, it's a different story. You get all of the breaks." 15

To evade his criticism, I wanted to side with him. I was about to admit the injustice of Affirmative Action. But he went on, his voice hard with accusation. "It's all very simple this year. You're a Chicano. And I am a Jew. That's the only real difference between us." 16

His words stung me: there was nothing he was telling me that I didn't know. I had admitted everything already. But to hear someone else say these things, and in such an accusing tone, was 17 suddenly hard to take. In a deceptively calm voice, I responded that he had simplified the whole issue. The phrases came like bubbles to the tip of my tongue: "new blood"; "the importance of cultural diversity"; "the goal of racial integration." These were all the arguments I had proposed several years ago—and had long since abandoned. Of course the offers were unjustifiable. I knew that. All I was saying amounted to a frantic self-defense. I tried to find an end to a sentence. My voice faltered to a stop.

18 "Yeah, sure," he said. "I've heard all that before. Nothing you say really changes the fact that Affirmative Action is unfair. You see that, don't you? There isn't any way for me to compete with you. Once there were quotas to keep my parents out of certain schools; now there are quotas to get you in and the effect on me is the same as it was for them."

19 I listened to every word he spoke. But my mind was really on something else. I knew at that moment that I would reject all of the offers. I stood there silently surprised by what an easy conclusion it was. Having prepared for so many years to teach, having trained myself to do nothing else, I had hesitated out of practical fear. But now that it was made, the decision came with relief. I immediately knew I had made the right choice.

20 My colleague continued talking and I realized that he was simply right. Affirmative Action programs *are* unfair to white students. But as I listened to him assert his rights, I thought of the seriously disadvantaged. How different they were from white, middle-class students who come armed with the testimony of their grades and aptitude scores and self-confidence to complain about the unequal treatment they now receive. I listen to them. I do not want to be careless about what they say. Their rights are important to protect. But inevitably when I hear them or their lawyers, I think about the most seriously disadvantaged, not simply Mexican-Americans, but of all those who do not ever imagine themselves going to college or becoming doctors: white, black, brown. Always poor. Silent. They are not plaintiffs before the court or against the misdirection of Affirmative Action. They lack the confidence (my confidence!) to assume their right to a good education. They lack the confidence and skills a good primary and secondary education provides and which are prerequisites for informed public life. They remain silent.

21 The debate drones on and surrounds them in stillness. They are distant, faraway figures like the boys I have seen peering down from freeway overpasses in some other part of town.

QUESTIONS ON SUBJECT AND PURPOSE

1. In paragraph 4, Rodriguez makes reference to the "irony" of the situation. In what ways was it ironic?
2. Why does Rodriguez decide to reject all of the offers?
3. Is Rodriguez criticizing affirmative action policies? How could such policies reach or change the lives of those who are really seriously disadvantaged?

QUESTIONS ON STRATEGY AND AUDIENCE

1. To what extent does Rodriguez present a formal argument based on an appeal to reason? To what extent does he attempt to persuade through an appeal to emotion? Which element is stronger in the piece?
2. What is the difference between objectively stating an opinion and narrating a personal experience? Do we as readers react any differently to Rodriguez's story as a result?
3. What expectations does Rodriguez have of his audience? How do you know that?

QUESTIONS ON VOCABULARY AND STYLE

1. In paragraphs 11–18, Rodriguez dramatizes a scene with a fellow student. He could have just summarized what was said without using dialogue. What advantage is gained by developing the scene?
2. Be prepared to discuss the significance of the following sentences:
   - **a.** "For me opportunities had been extravagant" (paragraph 2).
   - **b.** "The benefits were often, however, too gaudy to please" (2).
   - **c.** "The phrases came like bubbles to the tip of my tongue" (17).
   - **d.** "Always poor. Silent" (20).
3. What is the effect of the simile ("like the boys I have seen . . .") Rodriguez uses in the final line?

WRITING SUGGESTIONS

1. **For Your Journal.** What made you pursue your education? What are the important motivating factors? Explore the questions in your journal.
2. **For a Paragraph.** Describe a time when you encountered an obstacle because of your age, gender, race, religion, physical ability, physical appearance, or socioeconomic status. Describe the experience briefly, and then argue against the unfairness of such discrimination.
3. **For an Essay.** Are minorities and women fairly represented on the faculty of your college or university? Check the proportion of white males to minority and women faculty members, looking not only at raw numbers but also at rank, tenure, and so forth. Then, in an essay, argue for or against the need to achieve a better balance.

   Prewriting:

   a. Before you begin writing, you will need accurate information. The Affirmative Action Office at your school can provide those statistics. Check a campus telephone directory to locate that office.

   b. Statistics about the undergraduate population of your college will also help. The admissions office or the dean of students should be able to provide a breakdown of the student body.

   c. On the basis of your evidence and your own feelings, decide on a position. Make a list of the evidence and the reasons you will use. Then try to anticipate the objections that your audience will have to your position.

   Rewriting:

   a. Find a classmate or roommate to read your essay. Ask that reader to evaluate your position. Does your reader agree with you? Why or why not? Listen carefully to your reader's reaction and try to use that response in revising your paper.

   b. Is your essay structured inductively or deductively? Briefly outline a new strategy. Which of the two arrangements seems more effective?

   c. Look at your conclusion. Arguments—either emotional or logical—need to end forcefully. Freewrite a totally different ending to your essay. Ask your reader to evaluate both.

4. **For Research.** Rodriguez feels that as a result of "an early, excellent education" (paragraph 2), he was no longer "a principal victim of racism or any other social oppression." If the key to helping the "seriously disadvantaged" lies in improving the quality of elementary and secondary education, how successful have American schools been? Has the quality of education for the disadvantaged improved in the past twenty years? Research the problem, and then write an essay in which you evaluate some existing programs and make recommendations about continuing, expanding, modifying, or dropping them. Be sure to document your sources wherever appropriate.

Website Link

In 1997 Rodriguez won the George Foster Peabody Award for his essays on the PBS *NewsHour*. Many of these essays are available online.

WATCH AND LEARN

Gregg Easterbrook

Gregg Easterbrook (1953–) earned his B.A. at Colorado College and a M.S.J. at Northwestern University. Easterbrook has been a contributing editor to Washington Monthly *and* Newsweek. *He is currently a Senior Editor at the* New Republic *and a Contributing Editor at* Atlantic Monthly. *An award-winning journalist, his books include a novel,* This Magic Moment *(1987), and his most recent collection of essays,* Beside Still Waters: Searching for Meaning in an Age of Doubt *(1998).*

BEFORE READING

Connecting: What impact has viewing violence depicted in the media had on your life? Have you ever been troubled by the violence portrayed in films?

Anticipating: What evidence does Easterbrook provide to convince you that there is a link between the violence depicted in media and the actual violence committed in society?

1 Millions of teens have seen the 1996 movie *Scream*, a box-office and home-rental hit. Critics adored the film. *The Washington Post* declared that it "deftly mixes irony, self-reference, and social wry commentary." The *Los Angeles Times* hailed it as "a bravura, provocative send-up." *Scream* opens with a scene in which a teenage girl is forced to watch her jock boyfriend tortured and then disemboweled by two fellow students who, it will eventually be learned, want revenge on anyone from high school who crossed them. After jock boy's stomach is shown cut open and he dies screaming, the killers tab and torture the girl, then cut her throat and hang her body from a tree so that Mom can discover it when she drives up. A dozen students and teachers are graphically butchered in the film, while the characters make running jokes about murder. At one point, a boy tells a big-breasted friend she'd better be careful because the stacked girls always get it in horror films; in the next scene, she's grabbed, stabbed through the breasts, and murdered. Some provocative send-up, huh? The movie

builds to a finale in which one of the killers announces that he and his accomplice started off by murdering strangers but then realized it was a lot more fun to kill their friends.

Now that two Colorado high schoolers have murdered twelve classmates and a teacher—often, it appears, first taunting their pleading victims, just like celebrity stars do in the movies!—some commentators have dismissed the role of violence in the images shown to the young, pointing out that horrific acts by children existed before celluloid or the phosphor screen. That is true—the Leopold-Loeb murder of 1924, for example. But mass murders by the young, once phenomenally rare, are suddenly on the increase. Can it be coincidence that this increase is happening at the same time that Hollywood has begun to market the notion that mass murder is fun? 2

For, in cinema's never-ending quest to up the ante on violence, murder as sport is the latest frontier. Slasher flicks began this trend; most portray carnage from the killer's point of view, showing the victim cowering, begging, screaming as the blade goes in, treating each death as a moment of festivity for the killer. (Many killers seek feelings of power over their victims, criminology finds; by reveling in the pleas of victims, slasher movies promote this base emotion.) The 1994 movie *Natural Born Killers* depicted slaying the helpless not only as a way to have a grand time but also as a way to become a celebrity; several dozen onscreen murders are shown in that film, along with a discussion of how great it makes you feel to just pick people out at random and kill them. The 1994 movie *Pulp Fiction* presented hit men as glamour figures having loads of interesting fun; the actors were mainstream stars like John Travolta. The 1995 movie *Seven*, starring Brad Pitt, portrayed a sort of contest to murder in unusually grotesque ways. (Screenwriters now actually discuss, and critics comment on, which film's killings are most amusing.) The 1995 movie *The Basketball Diaries* contains an extended dream sequence in which the title character, played by teen heartthrob Leonardo DiCaprio, methodically guns down whimpering, pleading classmates at his high school. A rock soundtrack pulses, and the character smiles as he kills. 3

The new Hollywood tack of portraying random murder as a form of recreation does not come from schlock-houses. Disney's Miramax division, the same mainstream studio that produced *Shakespeare in Love*, is responsible for *Scream* and *Pulp Fiction*. Time-Warner is to blame for *Natural Born Killers* and actually ran television ads promoting this film as "delirious, daredevil fun." 4

(After it was criticized for calling murder "fun," Time-Warner tried to justify *Killers* as social commentary; if you believe that, you believe *Godzilla* was really about biodiversity protection.) Praise and publicity for gratuitously violent movies come from the big media conglomerates, including the newspapers and networks that profit from advertising for films that glorify murder. Disney, now one of the leading promoters of violent images in American culture, even feels that what little kids need is more violence. Its Christmas 1998 children's movie *Mighty Joe Young* begins with an eight-year-old girl watching her mother being murdered. By the movie's end, it is 20 years later, and the killer has returned to stalk the grown daughter, pointing a gun in her face and announcing, "Now join your mother in hell." A Disney movie.

5 One reason Hollywood keeps reaching for ever-more-obscene levels of killing is that it must compete with television, which today routinely airs the kind of violence once considered shocking in theaters. According to studies conducted at Temple University, prime-time network (non-news) shows now average up to five violent acts per hour. In February, NBC ran in prime time the movie *Eraser*, not editing out an extremely graphic scene in which a killer pulls a gun on a bystander and blasts away. The latest TV movie based on *The Rockford Files*, which aired on CBS the night of the Colorado murders, opened with a scene of an eleven-year-old girl in short-shorts being stalked by a man in a black hood, grabbed, and dragged off, screaming. *The Rockford Files* is a *comedy*. Combining television and movies, the typical American boy or girl, studies find, will observe a stunning 40,000 dramatizations of killing by age 18.

6 In the days after the Colorado slaughter, discussion of violent images in American culture was dominated by the canned positions of the anti-Hollywood right and the mammon-is-our-God film lobby. The debate missed three vital points: the distinction between what adults should be allowed to see (anything) and what the inchoate minds of children and adolescents should see; the way in which important liberal battles to win free expression in art and literature have been perverted into an excuse for antisocial video brutality produced by cynical capitalists; and the difference between censorship and voluntary acts of responsibility.

7 The day after the Colorado shooting, Mike De Luca, an executive of New Line Cinema, maker of *The Basketball Diaries*, told *USA Today* that, when kids kill, "bad home life, bad parenting, having guns in the home" are "more of a factor than what we put out there for entertainment." Setting aside the disclosure that

Hollywood now categorizes scenes of movie stars gunning down the innocent as "entertainment," De Luca is correct: studies do show that upbringing is more determinant of violent behavior than any other factor. But research also clearly shows that the viewing of violence can cause aggression and crime. So the question is, in a society already plagued by poor parenting and unlimited gun sales, why does the entertainment industry feel privileged to make violence even more prevalent?

Even when researchers factor out other influences such as parental attention, many peer-reviewed studies have found causal links between viewing phony violence and engaging in actual violence. A 1971 surgeon general's report asserted a broad relationship between the two. Studies by Brandon Centerwall, an epidemiologist at the University of Wisconsin, have shown that the postwar murder rise in the United States began roughly a decade after TV viewing became common. Centerwall also found that, in South Africa, where television was not generally available until 1975, national murder rates started rising about a decade later. Violent computer games have not existed long enough to be the subject of many controlled studies, but experts expect it will be shown that playing such games in youth also correlates with destructive behavior. There's an eerie likelihood that violent movies and violent games amplify one another, the film and television images placing thoughts of carnage into the psyche while the games condition the trigger finger to act on those impulses. 8

Leonard Eron, a psychologist at the University of Michigan, has been tracking video violence and actual violence for almost four decades. His initial studies, in 1960, found that even the occasional violence depicted in 1950s television—to which every parent would gladly return today—caused increased aggression among eight-year-olds. By the adult years, Eron's studies find, those who watched the most TV and movies in childhood were much more likely to have been arrested for, or convicted of, violent felonies. Eron believes that ten percent of U.S. violent crime is caused by exposure to images of violence, meaning that 90 percent is not but that a ten percent national reduction in violence might be achieved merely by moderating the content of television and movies. "Kids learn by observation," Eron says. "If what they observe is violent, that's what they learn." To cite a minor but telling example, the introduction of vulgar language into American public discourse traces, Eron thinks, largely to the point at which stars like Clark Gable began to swear onscreen, and kids then imitated swearing as normative. 9

10 Defenders of bloodshed in film, television, and writing often argue that depictions of killing don't incite real violence because no one is really affected by what they see or read; it's all just water off a duck's back. At heart, this is an argument against free expression. The whole reason to have a First Amendment is that people *are* influenced by what they see and hear: words and images do change minds, so there must be free competition among them. If what we say, write, or show has no consequences, why bother to have free speech?

11 Defenders of Hollywood bloodshed also employ the argument that, since millions of people watch screen mayhem and shrug, feigned violence has no causal relation to actual violence. After a horrific 1992 case in which a British gang acted out a scene from the slasher movie *Child's Play 3*, torturing a girl to death as the movie had shown, the novelist Martin Amis wrote dismissively in *The New Yorker* that he had rented *Child's Play 3* and watched the film, and it hadn't made him want to kill anyone, so what was the problem? But Amis isn't homicidal or unbalanced. For those on the psychological borderline, the calculus is different. There have, for example, been at least two instances of real-world shootings in which the guilty imitated scenes in *Natural Born Killers*.

12 Most telling, Amis wasn't affected by watching a slasher movie because Amis is not young. Except for the unbalanced, exposure to violence in video "is not so important for adults; adults can watch anything they want," Eron says. Younger minds are a different story. Children who don't yet understand the difference between illusion and reality may be highly affected by video violence. Between the ages of two and eight, hours of viewing violent TV programs and movies correlates closely to felonies later in life; the child comes to see hitting, stabbing, and shooting as normative acts. The link between watching violence and engaging in violence continues up to about the age of 19, Eron finds, after which most people's characters have been formed, and video mayhem no longer correlates to destructive behavior.

13 Trends in gun availability do not appear to explain the murder rise that has coincided with television and violent films. Research by John Lott Jr., of the University of Chicago Law School, shows that the percentage of homes with guns has changed little throughout the postwar era. What appears to have changed is the willingness of people to fire their guns at one another. Are adolescents now willing to use guns because violent images make killing seem acceptable or even cool? Following the Colorado slaughter, *The New York Times* ran a recounting of other postwar mass murders staged by the young, such as the 1966 Texas tower killings, and noted that

they all happened before the advent of the Internet or shock rock, which seemed to the *Times* to absolve the modern media. But all the mass killings by the young occurred after 1950—after it became common to watch violence on television.

When horrific murders occur, the film and television industries routinely attempt to transfer criticism to the weapons used. Just after the Colorado shootings, for instance, TV talk-show host Rosie O'Donnell called for a constitutional amendment banning all firearms. How strange that O'Donnell didn't call instead for a boycott of Sony or its production company, Columbia Tristar—a film studio from which she has received generous paychecks and whose current offerings include *8MM*, which glamorizes the sexual murder of young women, and *The Replacement Killers*, whose hero is a hit man and which depicts dozens of gun murders. Handguns should be licensed, but that hardly excuses the convenient sanctimony of blaming the crime on the weapon, rather than on what resides in the human mind. 14

And, when it comes to promoting adoration of guns, Hollywood might as well be the NRA's marketing arm. An ever-increasing share of film and television depicts the firearm as something the virile must have and use, if not an outright sexual aid. Check the theater section of any newspaper, and you will find an ever-higher percentage of movie ads in which the stars are prominently holding guns. Keanu Reeves, Uma Thurman, Laurence Fishburne, Geena Davis, Woody Harrelson, and Mark Wahlberg are just a few of the hip stars who have posed with guns for movie advertising. Hollywood endlessly congratulates itself for reducing the depiction of cigarettes in movies and movie ads. Cigarettes had to go, the film industry admitted, because glamorizing them gives the wrong idea to kids. But the glamorization of firearms, which is far more dangerous, continues. Today, even female stars who otherwise consider themselves politically aware will model in sexualized poses with guns. Ads for the new movie *Goodbye Lover* show star Patricia Arquette nearly nude, with very little between her and the viewer but her handgun. 15

But doesn't video violence merely depict a stark reality against which the young need be warned? American society is far too violent, yet the forms of brutality highlighted in the movies and on television—prominently "thrill" killings and serial murders—are pure distortion. Nearly 99 percent of real murders result from robberies, drug deals, and domestic disputes; figures from research affiliated with the FBI's behavioral sciences division show an average of only about 30 serial or "thrill" murders nationally per year. 16

Thirty is plenty horrifying enough, but, at this point, each of the major networks and movie studios alone depicts more "thrill" and serial murders annually than that. By endlessly exploiting the notion of the "thrill" murder, Hollywood and television present to the young an entirely imaginary image of a society in which killing for pleasure is a common event. The publishing industry, including some TNR advertisers, also distorts for profit the frequency of "thrill" murders.

17 The profitability of violent cinema is broadly dependent on the "down-rating" of films—movies containing extreme violence being rated only R instead of NC-17 (the new name for X)—and the lax enforcement of age restrictions regarding movies. Teens are the best market segment for Hollywood; when moviemakers claim their violent movies are not meant to appeal to teens, they are simply lying. The millionaire status of actors, directors, and studio heads—and the returns of the mutual funds that invest in movie companies—depends on not restricting teen access to theaters or film rentals. Studios in effect control the movie ratings board and endlessly lobby it not to label extreme violence with an NC-17, the only form of rating that is actually enforced. *Natural Born Killers*, for example received an R following Time-Warner lobbying, despite its repeated close-up murders and one charming scene in which the stars kidnap a high school girl and argue about whether it would be more fun to kill her before or after raping her. Since its inception, the movie ratings board has put its most restrictive rating on any realistic representation of lovemaking, while sanctioning ever-more-graphic depictions of murder and torture. In economic terms, the board's pro-violence bias gives studios an incentive to present more death and mayhem, confident that ratings officials will smile with approval.

18 When R-and-X battles were first fought, intellectual sentiment regarded the ratings system as a way of blocking the young from seeing films with political content, such as *Easy Rider*, or discouraging depictions of sexuality; ratings were perceived as the rubes' counterattack against cinematic sophistication. But, in the 1960s, murder after murder after murder was not standard cinema fare. The most controversial violent film of that era, *A Clockwork Orange*, depicted a total of one killing, which was heard but not on-camera. (*Clockwork Orange* also had genuine political content, unlike most of today's big-studio movies.) In an era of runaway screen violence, the '60s ideal that the young should be allowed to see what they want has been corrupted. In this, trends in video mirror the misuse of liberal ideals generally.

Anti-censorship battles of this century were fought on firm ground, advocating the right of films to tackle social and sexual issues (the 1930s Hays office forbid among other things cinematic mention of cohabitation) and free access to works of literature such as *Ulysses*, *Story of O*, and the original version of Norman Mailer's *The Naked and the Dead.* Struggles against censors established that suppression of film or writing is wrong. 19

But to say that nothing should be censored is very different from saying that everything should be shown. Today, Hollywood and television have twisted the First Amendment concept that occasional repulsive or worthless expression must be protected, so as to guarantee freedom for works of genuine political content or artistic merit, into a new standard in which constitutional freedoms are employed mainly to safeguard works that make no pretense of merit. In the new standard, the bulk of what's being protected is repulsive or worthless, with the meritorious work the rare exception. 20

Not only is there profit for the performers, producers, management, and shareholders of firms that glorify violence, so, too, is there profit for politicians. Many conservative or Republican politicians who denounce Hollywood eagerly accept its lucre. Bob Dole's 1995 anti-Hollywood speech was not followed up by any anti-Hollywood legislation or campaign-funds strategy. After the Colorado murders, President Clinton declared, "Parents should take this moment to ask what else they can do to shield children from violent images and experiences that warp young perceptions." But Clinton was careful to avoid criticizing Hollywood, one of the top sources of public backing and campaign contributions for him and his would-be successor, Vice President Al Gore. The president had nothing specific to propose on film violence—only that parents should try to figure out what to do. 21

When television producers say it is the parents' obligation to keep children away from the tube, they reach the self-satire point of warning that their own product is unsuitable for consumption. The situation will improve somewhat beginning in 2000, by which time all new TVs must be sold with the "V chip"—supported by Clinton and Gore—which will allow parents to block violent shows. But it will be at least a decade before the majority of the nation's sets include the chip, and who knows how adept young minds will prove at defeating it? Rather than relying on a technical fix that will take many years to achieve an effect, TV producers could simply stop churning out the gratuitous violence. Television could dramatically reduce its output of scenes of killing and still depict 22 violence in news broadcasts, documentaries, and the occasional show in which the horrible is genuinely relevant. Reduction in violence is not censorship; it is placing social responsibility before profit.

23 The movie industry could practice the same kind of restraint without sacrificing profitability. In this regard, the big Hollywood studios, including Disney, look craven and exploitative compared to, of all things, the porn-video industry. Repulsive material occurs in underground porn, but, in the products sold by the mainstream triple-X distributors such as Vivid Video (the MGM of the erotica business), violence is never, ever, ever depicted—because that would be irresponsible. Women and men perform every conceivable explicit act in today's mainstream porn, but what is shown is always consensual and almost sunnily friendly. Scenes of rape or sexual menace never occur, and scenes of sexual murder are an absolute taboo.

24 It is beyond irony that today Sony and Time-Warner eagerly market explicit depictions of women being raped, sexually assaulted, and sexually murdered, while the mainstream porn industry would never dream of doing so. But, if money is all that matters, the point here is that mainstream porn is violence-free and yet risqué and highly profitable. Surely this shows that Hollywood could voluntarily step back from the abyss of glorifying violence and still retain its edge and its income.

25 Following the Colorado massacre, Republican presidential candidate Gary Bauer declared to a campaign audience, "In the America I want, all of these producers and directors, they would not be able to show their faces in public" because fingers "would be pointing at them and saying, 'Shame, shame.'" The statement sent chills through anyone fearing right-wing thought-control. But Bauer's final clause is correct—Hollywood and television do need to hear the words "shame, shame." The cause of the shame should be removed voluntarily, not to stave off censorship, but because it is the responsible thing to do.

26 Put it this way. The day after a teenager guns down the sons and daughters of studio executives in a high school in Bel Air or Westwood, Disney and Time-Warner will stop glamorizing murder. Do we have to wait until that day?

QUESTIONS ON SUBJECT AND PURPOSE

1. For Easterbrook, what is the principle reason for the depiction of violence in our media?

2. How does Easterbrook feel about the introduction of the V-chip?
3. For what is Easterbrook arguing? Does he want censorship? If not, why not? If so, who would be the judging body? The industry? The government?

QUESTIONS ON STRATEGY AND AUDIENCE

1. What is the effect of placing the detail of paragraph 2 immediately after the detail of paragraph 1?
2. Easterbrook cites so many examples of offending films and television shows, often developing the examples at great length. Why?
3. To whom is Easterbrook writing? Does he seem to make any assumptions about his audience?

QUESTIONS ON VOCABULARY AND STYLE

1. What is "ironic" about the situation that Easterbrook cites in the first sentence of paragraph 24?
2. On several occasions, Easterbrook will use an expression such as "up the ante" (paragraph 3) or "it's all just water off a duck's back" (paragraph 10). What are such expressions called and why might Easterbrook use them?
3. Be prepared to define the following words: *bravura* (paragraph 1), *schlock* (4), *gratuitously* (4), *inchoate* (6), *prevalent* (7), *carnage* (8), *normative* (9), *mayhem* (11), *feigned* (11), *sanctimony* (14), *rubes* (18), *craven* (23).

WRITING SUGGESTIONS

1. **For Your Journal.** The impact of violence in television and film has been widely written about and debated. What about violence-based video, computer, or Internet games? Lyrics in contemporary music? Violence in professional sports or in entertainment events such as professional wrestling? In your journal, speculate about the violence that surrounds us in one other media. Concentrate on recording some particular examples.
2. **For a Paragraph.** In a paragraph, argue for or against some form of censorship as it relates to a specific type of activity in which violence, either real or simulated, occurs.

3. **For an Essay.** Expand your paragraph into an essay. Remember that it is probably best to focus on a single subject or two very closely related subjects (for example, violent video and computer games). Remember that you can argue either for or against the idea of censorship or self-monitoring.

   Prewriting:

   a. Make a list of the reasons why you think censorship is necessary or wrong. Freewrite on each reason for fifteen minutes. Do not stop; do not edit. Just allow your mind to explore your reasons.

   b. Brainstorm a list of possible examples that you can use. Remember that specific examples or details work best. If you are arguing for First Amendment protection, be sure that you know what the First Amendment says and how it has been interpreted.

   c. In preparing your argument, always think about the points and objections that your opponents might have. You need to anticipate your opposition and be able to counter it.

   Rewriting:

   a. Find a classmate or peer to read your essay. Ask that reader to evaluate your position. Does the reader agree? Why or why not? Listen carefully to your reader's reaction.

   b. Once you have completed a draft of your essay, make an outline of what you have written. Does the essay outline easily? Are some points of your argument developed in great detail and some in little detail? Use the outline to locate any major structural problems.

   c. Look at your conclusion again. Arguments—either emotional or logical—need to end forcefully. Freewrite a totally different ending to your essay. Ask a classmate to evaluate both.

4. **For Research.** If you have not already done so, read Jonathan Kellerman's "The Scapegoat We Love to Hate" (Chapter 4). Basically, Kellerman's essay is a counterargument to the points that Easterbrook is making. Research the impact of media violence on children yourself. Remember that you need to find published research that points to connections or the lack of connections—it is not enough to

rely on personal experience or anecdotal evidence. Be sure to document your sources.

Website Link

The impact of media violence on children is widely debated, and a number of Websites are devoted to information about the subject. Additional articles, Web links, and even classroom activities are accessible through www.prenhall.com/miller.

TEN

REVISING

Not even the best professional writers produce only perfect sentences and paragraphs. Good writing almost always results from rewriting or revising. Although the terms *rewriting* and *revising* are interchangeable, *revising* suggests some important aspects of this vital stage of your writing process: a "re-vision" is a reseeing of what you have written. In its broadest sense, this reseeing can be a complete rethinking of a paper from idea through execution. As such, revising a paper is quite different from proofreading it for mechanical and grammatical errors. When you proofread, you are mostly looking for small things—misspellings or typographical errors, incorrect punctuation, awkwardly constructed sentences. When you *revise,* however, you look for larger concerns as well—such things as a clear thesis, an effective structure, or adequate and relevant details.

Revising does not occur only after you have written a complete draft of a paper. In fact, many writers revise as they draft. They may write a sentence, then stop to change its structure, even erase it and start over; they may shift the positions of sentences and paragraphs or delete them altogether. In this search for the right words, the graceful sentence, the clear structure, writers revise constantly.

But rewriting does not end with the first draft. For one thing, revision while writing usually focuses on the sentence or paragraph being composed. When you are struggling to find the right word or the right sentence structure, you're probably not thinking much about the larger whole.

Consequently, allowing some time to elapse between drafts of your paper is important. You need to put the draft aside for a while if you are to get a perspective on what you have written and read your paper objectively. For this reason, it is important to finish a complete draft at least one day before you have to hand in the paper. If circumstances prevent you from finishing a paper until an hour or two before class, you will not have a chance to revise. You will have time only to proofread.

Analyzing Your Own Writing

The key to improving your writing is self-awareness. You have to look carefully and critically at what you have written, focus on areas that caused you the most problems, and then work to correct them. Most writers are, in fact, able to identify the key problems they faced in a particular paper or in writing in general, even though they might not know how to solve those problems. Knowing what causes you problems is the essential first step toward solving them.

When you analyze the first draft of a paper, begin by asking a series of specific questions, starting with the larger issues and working toward the smaller ones. Ideally, you should write out your answers—doing so will force you to have a specific response. Here are some questions you might consider:

1. What were you asked to do in this paper? Look again at the assignment. Circle the key action words, verbs such as *analyze*, *argue*, *classify*, *compare*, *criticize*, *define*, *describe*, *evaluate*, *narrate*, *recommend*, and *summarize*. Have you done what you were asked to do?
2. What is the thesis of your paper? Can you find a single sentence in your essay that sums up that thesis? If so, underline it. If not, write a one-sentence thesis statement.
3. How have you organized your paper? That organization ought to be conveyed in the way the paper has been paragraphed. Make an outline that contains only as many subdivisions as you have paragraphs.
4. Is each paragraph focused around a single idea? Is there an explicit statement of that idea? If so, underline it. If not, jot down in the margin the key word or words. Should that idea be specifically stated in the paragraph? Is that idea developed

adequately? Are there enough supporting details and examples?

5. What strategies did you use to begin and end your essay? Does your introduction seem likely to catch the reader's attention? Do you have a concluding paragraph, or do you just stop?

Only after you have asked and answered these kinds of questions about the larger elements of your paper should you move to questions directed toward style, grammar, and mechanics:

6. Is everything you punctuated as a sentence in fact a complete sentence? Check each sentence to make sure.
7. Look carefully at every mark of punctuation. Is it the right choice for this place in the sentence?
8. Check your choice of words. Are you certain of what each word means? Are there any words that might be too informal or too colloquial (words that are appropriate in a conversation with friends but not in academic writing)? Is every word spelled correctly? (If you have *any* doubt about *any* word, look it up in a dictionary.)

Keeping a Revision Log

Keeping a log of writing problems you most often encounter is an excellent way of promoting self-awareness. Your log should include subdivisions for a wide range of writing problems, not just grammatical and mechanical errors. The log will help you keep track of the areas that you know you have trouble with and those your instructor, peer readers, or writing tutors point out as needing improvement. Do you have a tendency to overparagraph? To stop rather than conclude? To have trouble with parallelism? Each time you discover a problem or one is pointed out to you, list it in your log. Then, as you revise your papers, look back through your revision log to remind yourself of these frequent problems and look closely for them in your current draft.

If a revision log seems a lot of trouble, remember that only you can improve your own writing. Improvement, in turn, comes with recognizing your weaknesses and working to correct them.

Using Peer Readers

Most of the writing you'll do in school is aimed toward only one reader—a teacher. Writing just for a teacher has both advantages and disadvantages. A teacher is a critical reader who evaluates your paper by a set of standards. But a teacher can also be a sympathetic reader, one who understands the difficulties of writing and is patient with the problems that writers have. Classmates, colleagues, or supervisors can be just as critical as teachers but less sympathetic.

Only in school, however, do you have someone who will read everything that you write and offer constructive comments. After you graduate, your letters and reports will be read by many different readers, but you will no longer have a teacher to offer advice or a tutor to conference with you. Instead, you will have to rely on your own analysis of your writing and on the advice of your fellow workers. For this reason, learning to use a peer reader as a resource in your revising process is extremely important. At first, you might feel a little uncomfortable asking someone other than your instructor to read your papers, but after some experience, you will feel better about sharing. Remember that every reader is potentially a valuable resource for suggestions.

Peer Editing

Many college writing courses use peer editing as a regular classroom activity. On a peer editing day, students swap papers with their classmates and then critique one another's work, typically using a list of peer editing guidelines. But you don't have to do peer editing in class to reap the benefits of such an arrangement. If your instructor approves, you can arrange to swap papers with a classmate outside of class, or you can ask a roommate or a friend to do a peer reading for you.

From the start, though, several ground rules are important. First, when you ask a peer to edit your paper, you are asking for criticism. You want advice; you want reaction. You cannot expect that your reader will love everything that you have written.

Second, peer editing is not proofreading. You should not ask your reader to look for misspelled words and missing commas. Rather, you want your reader to react to the whole paper. Is the thesis clear? Does the structure seem appropriate? Are there enough examples or details? Does the introduction catch the reader's attention and make him or her want to keep reading? You need to keep your reader's attention focused on these larger, significant issues. One good way to do so is to give your reader a checklist or a set of questions that reflect the criteria appropriate for evaluating this kind of paper.

Third, you want a peer reader to offer specific and constructive criticism. To get that type of response, you must ask questions that invite—or even require—a reader to comment in more than "yes" and "no" answers. For example, do not ask your reader, "Is the thesis clear?"; instead ask, "What is the thesis of this paper?" If your reader has trouble answering that question or if the answer differs from your own, you know that this aspect of your paper needs more work.

Group Editing

Sharing your writing in a small group is another good way to get reader reaction to your papers. Such an editing activity can take place either inside or outside of the classroom. In either case, you can prepare for a group editing session in the same way. Plan to form a group of four or five students, and make a copy of your paper for each group member. If possible, distribute those copies prior to the group editing session so that each member will have a chance to read and prepare some comments for the discussion. Then follow these guidelines:

Before the group editing session

1. Read each paper carefully, marking or underlining the writer's main idea and key supporting points. Make any other notes about the paper that seem appropriate.
2. On a separate sheet, comment specifically on one or two aspects of the paper that most need improvement.

At the group editing session

1. When it is your turn, read your own paper aloud to the group. Since you might hear problems as you read, keep a pen or pencil handy to jot down notes.
2. When you are finished, tell the group members what you would like them to comment on.
3. Listen to their remarks, and make notes. Feel free to ask group members to explain or expand on their observations. Remember, you want as much advice as you can get.

4. Collect the copies of your paper and the sheets on which the group members have commented on specific areas that need improvement.

After the group editing session

1. Carefully consider both the oral and written comments of your group. You may not agree with everything that was said, but you need to weigh each comment.
2. Revise your paper. Remember that you are responsible for your own work. No one else—not your instructor, your peer editors, or your group readers—can or should tell you *everything* that you need to change.

USING YOUR SCHOOL'S WRITING CENTER OR A WRITING TUTOR

Most colleges operate writing centers, writing labs, or writing tutor programs. Their purpose is to provide individual assistance to any student who has a question about writing. They are staffed by trained tutors who want to help you. In part, such services are intended to supplement the instruction that you receive in a writing class, since most writing teachers have too many students to be able to offer extensive help outside of class to everyone. These services also exist to provide advice to students writing papers for courses in other disciplines where writing might be required but not discussed.

If you are having trouble with grammar or mechanics, if you consistently have problems with beginnings or middles or ends of papers, if you are baffled by a particular assignment, do not be afraid to ask for help. After all, every writer can benefit from constructive advice or additional explanations, and writing centers and tutors exist to provide that help. Remember, though, that a writing tutor is a teacher whose job is to explain and to instruct. You do not drop off your paper at the writing center like you drop off your automobile at the service station. Your tutor will suggest ways that *you* can improve your paper or follow a particular convention. A tutor will not do the work for you.

Come to your appointment with a specific set of questions or problems. Why are you there? What do you want to discuss? What don't you understand? After all, when you have a medical problem, you make an appointment with a doctor to discuss a specific set of symptoms. A conference with a writing tutor should work in a similar way.

Finally, make sure that you keep some form of written record of your conference. Jot down the tutor's advice and explanations. Those notes will serve as a valuable reminder of what to do when you are revising your paper.

Using an OWL

For students who have access to the Internet and the World Wide Web—either from home or from school—another source of help in revising is an on-line writing lab, or OWL. Most OWLs are operated by traditional writing centers at colleges and universities. Although most provide help predominantly to students enrolled at those schools, many have services also available to students from anywhere who access the site through the Internet.

The services that OWLs provide range widely. Some offer e-mail tutoring; some provide access to MOOs ("multiple user dimensions, object-oriented"), where you can hold conversations with other writers. Most provide access to writing reference materials and extensive links to other related sites. One of the oldest OWLs is Purdue University's. Purdue's site offers information about writing based on reference materials and also maintains a listing of other OWLs and their e-mail addresses. A good place to start in a search for on-line revising help is the National Writing Centers Association List of Online Writing Labs and Centers. Visit the Reader's Website (www.prenhall.com/miller) for a list of hot-linked resources for revision.

Conferencing with Your Instructor

Your instructor in a writing class is always willing to talk with you about your writing. You can, of course, visit your instructor during scheduled office hours. In addition, many instructors, if their teaching schedule permits it, will schedule a set of regular conference times spaced throughout the semester. Whatever the arrangement, such a conference is an opportunity for you to ask questions about your writing in general or about a particular paper.

Whether you have asked for the conference or the instructor has scheduled it as a part of the class requirements, several ground rules apply. As with a tutoring session, you should always come to an instructor conference with a definite agenda in mind and a specific set of questions to ask. Writing these questions out is an excellent way to prepare for a conference. Generally, a conference is intended to be a dialogue, and so your active participation is expected. Do not be surprised, for example, if your instructor begins by asking you what you want to talk about. Since time is always limited (remember that your instructor might have to see dozens of students), you will not be able to ask about everything. Try to concentrate on the issues that trouble you the most.

Instructors like to use conferences as opportunities to discuss the larger issues of a paper: Is the thesis well defined? Is the structure as clear as it might be? Are there adequate transitions? Although your instructor will be happy to explain a troublesome grammatical or mechanical problem, do not expect your instructor to find and fix every mistake in your paper. A conference is not a proofreading session.

A conference is also not an oral grading of your paper. Grading a paper is a complicated task and one that frequently involves seeing your essay in the context of the other papers from the class. As a result, your instructor cannot make a quick judgment. Do not ask what grade the paper might receive.

As the conference proceeds, make notes for yourself about what is said. Do not rely on your memory. Those notes will constitute a plan for revising your paper.

Proofreading Your Paper

At one point or another, virtually everyone has had the injunction "proofread!" written on a paper. (*Proofreading* comes from printing terminology: a printer reads and corrects "proofs"—trial impressions made of the pages of set type—before printing a job.) You probably stared in dismay at those obvious slips that somehow managed to escape your eye. Why, you may have asked yourself, was I penalized for what were obviously just careless mistakes? In response, you could ask another question: why do businesses and industries spend so much money making sure that their final written products are as free from errors as possible?

Basically, the answer is related to an audience's perception of the writer (or the business). If a paper, letter, report, or advertisement contains even minor mistakes, they act as a form of "static" that interferes with the communication process. The reader's attention is shifted away from the message to some fundamental questions about the writer. A reader might wonder why you did not have enough pride in your work to check it before handing it in. Even worse, a reader might question your basic competence as a writer and researcher. As the number of errors in proportion to the total number of words rises, the reader's distraction grows. In college such static can have serious consequences. Studies conducted in New York City colleges, for example, revealed that readers would tolerate on the average only five to six basic errors in a three-hundred-word passage before assigning a student to a remedial English course. The point is that careless mistakes are rhetorically damaging to you as a writer; they undermine your voice and authority.

Once you have revised your paper thoroughly—considering the effectiveness of the thesis, the clarity of the organization, the strength of the opening and the conclusion, and any other problems in previous papers that you have listed in your revision log—you are ready to proofread. The secret of proofreading is to make sure that you read each word as you have written it. If you read too quickly, your mind often "corrects" or skips over problems. Force yourself to read each word exactly by moving a ruler or a piece of paper slowly down the page, reading aloud as you go. When you combine looking at the page with listening to the words, you increase your chances of catching mistakes that are visual (such as misspellings) and those that are aural (such as awkward phrasings).

Misspellings are so common that they need special attention. Everyone misspells some words; even the most experienced writer, teacher, or editor, has to check a dictionary for correct spellings of certain words. English is a particularly tricky language, for words are not always spelled the way in which they are pronounced. English has silent *e*'s as in *live; ph*'s and *gh*'s that sound like *f*'s as in *phone* and *tough;* silent *ough*'s and *gh*'s as in *through* and *bright.* It is easy to get confused about when to double consonants before adding *–ed* to the end of a word or when to drop the final *e* before adding *–able.* All of these difficulties are perfectly natural and common. No one expects you to remember how to spell every word in your speaking vocabulary, but people do expect that you will check your writing for misspelled words.

Most misspellings can be eliminated if you do two things. First, recognize the kinds of words you are likely to misspell; learn when not to trust your instinct, particularly with words that sound alike, such as *there* and *their* and *its* and *it's*. Second, once you have finished your paper, go back and check your spelling. If you have written your paper on a word processor that has a spell check function, be sure to run it. However, do not rely on that type of checking alone; for example, spell checkers won't show you that you've used *there* when you mean *their*. Always have a dictionary at hand. Go through your essay and look up every word that might be a problem. Doing these two things will go a long way toward eliminating misspellings in your papers.

Revisers at Work

To help you think about what is involved in revising and to help you see how it actually takes place, earlier chapters of this text include draft and final revised versions of student papers. In this chapter you can see professional writers at work revising their prose.

The first three selections in this chapter offer the final published version of a popular essay along with earlier drafts of sections of the essay. Just as writers use a variety of composing strategies, they also approach the problem of revising in vastly different ways. For some, the process of composition is so painstaking and logical that a single draft is sometimes sufficient. The revision has taken place in small steps as the writing occurred. For other writers, draft follows draft. One writer, when asked to contribute to this chapter, remarked, "Usually I take many, many drafts, even with simple-minded prose. But as I am sure you know, one cannot really just turn over actual drafts, not most of the time. . . . One would have to edit them and so forth."

In the three essays included here, you will see writers revising by adding paragraphs (M. Scott Momaday in "The Way to Rainy Mountain"), reworking an introduction (Nora Ephron in "Revision and Life"), and deleting paragraphs (Brent Staples in "Black Men and Public Space").

Finally, the chapter ends with a detailed case study of the evolution of Gordon Grice's essay on the black widow spider, a final version of which appears in Chapter 3. You can follow the evolution of that essay from its earliest journal entries through its first published form in *High Plains Literary Review* to its revised form in *Harper's*. The case study includes sample journal entries, an earlier version of the essay, and an interview with Grice in which he discusses how he revises his work and why he made some of the changes that he did in the course of revising.

Visualizing Revision

Robert Mankoff's cartoon does not really "visualize" revision, but it does remind us, as writers, that even when we have what we regard as a "final" draft, our writing task is not always over. Even though we have labored over every sentence, word, and mark of punctuation, now it is time to recruit friends, colleagues, and significant others for additional editing and proofreading tasks. "Does this make sense?" we ask. "Is my point clear? What do you think about my opening? Does my title work?" And, then, after we have cleared these hurdles, we still have one more: Published writing—books, essays, articles, advertisements—has all had the careful scrutiny of professional editors who, in turn, suggest changes, deletions, and additions to our "final" product. The process of revision is demanding (and yes, every writer gets tired and

"I like it—it's wonderfully editable."

frustrated), but every writer knows that the final product is that much better for all the attention that it has received.

Visit the Prentice Hall Reader's WebSite

When you have finished reading an essay, check out the additional material available at the *Reader's* Website at www.prenhall.com/miller. For each reading, you will find a list of related readings connected with the topic or the author; additional background information; a group of relevant hot-linked Web resources (just click your computer's mouse and automatically visit the sites listed); and still more writing suggestions.

Revising

Does your school have a Writing Lab or a Writing Center where you can get help with your papers? Does it have a Website? Can you get on-line help? Can you submit a draft by e-mail? The Web has extensive resources available for writers trying to revise. You can find advice, visit a "virtual" Writing Center, and discover what an OWL is. Check out the links on the *Reader's* Website.

THE WAY TO RAINY MOUNTAIN

N. Scott Momaday

Navarre Scott Momaday was born in Lawton, Oklahoma, in 1934. He earned a B.A. from the University of New Mexico and a Ph.D. in English from Stanford University. Professor of English, artist, editor, poet, and novelist, Momaday is above all a storyteller committed to preserving and interpreting the rich oral history of the Kiowa Indians. His work includes a book of Kiowa folktales, The Journey of Tai-me *(1967), which he revised as* The Way to Rainy Mountain *(1969), and the Pulitzer Prize-winning novel,* House Made of Dawn *(1968). His most recent book is* The Man Made of Words *(1997), a collection of essays, stories, and "passages."*

This essay originally appeared in the magazine The Reporter *in 1967, but Momaday revised it and used it as the introduction to* The Way to Rainy Mountain.

On Writing: *Momaday commented: "There's a lot of frustration in writing. I heard an interview with a writer not long ago in which the interviewer said, tell me, is writing difficult? And the writer said, oh, no . . . no, of course not. He said, 'All you do is sit down at a typewriter, you put a page in it, and then you look at it until beads of blood appear on your forehead. That's all there is to it.' There are days like that."*

BEFORE READING

Connecting: In what way does one of your relatives, perhaps a grandparent or a great-grandparent, connect you to a part of your family's past?

Anticipating: How and why does Momaday interlink descriptions of the landscape with descriptions of his grandmother?

REVISED DRAFT

1 A single knoll rises out of the plain in Oklahoma, north and west of the Wichita Range. For my people, the Kiowas, it is an old landmark, and they gave it the name Rainy Mountain. The hardest weather in the world is there. Winter brings blizzards, hot tornadic winds arise in the spring, and in summer the prairie is an anvil's edge. The grass turns brittle and brown, and it cracks beneath

your feet. There are green belts along the rivers and creeks, linear groves of hickory and pecan, willow and witch hazel. At a distance in July or August the steaming foliage seems almost to writhe in fire. Great green and yellow grasshoppers are everywhere in the tall grass, popping up like corn to sting the flesh, and tortoises crawl about on the red earth, going nowhere in the plenty of time. Loneliness is an aspect of the land. All things in the plain are isolate; there is no confusion of objects in the eye, but one hill or one tree or one man. To look upon that landscape in the early morning, with the sun at your back, is to lose the sense of proportion. Your imagination comes to life, and this, you think, is where Creation was begun.

I returned to Rainy Mountain in July. My grandmother had died in the spring, and I wanted to be at her grave. She had lived to be very old and at last infirm. Her only living daughter was with her when she died, and I was told that in death her face was that of a child. 2

I like to think of her as a child. When she was born, the Kiowas were living the last great moment of their history. For more than a hundred years they had controlled the open range from the Smoky Hill River to the Red, from the headwaters of the Canadian to the fork of the Arkansas and Cimarron. In alliance with the Comanches, they had ruled the whole of the southern Plains. War was their sacred business, and they were among the finest horsemen the world has ever known. But warfare for the Kiowas was preeminently a matter of disposition rather than of survival, and they never understood the grim, unrelenting advance of the U.S. Cavalry. When at last, divided and ill-provisioned, they were driven onto the Staked Plains in the cold rains of autumn, they fell into panic. In Palo Duro Canyon they abandoned their crucial stores to pillage and had nothing then but their lives. In order to save themselves, they surrendered to the soldiers at Fort Sill and were imprisoned in the old stone corral that now stands as a military museum. My grandmother was spared the humiliation of those high gray walls by eight or ten years, but she must have known from birth the affliction of defeat, the dark brooding of old warriors. 3

Her name was Aho, and she belonged to the last culture to evolve in North America. Her forebears came down from the high country in western Montana nearly three centuries ago. They were a mountain people, a mysterious tribe of hunters whose language has never been positively classified in any major group. In the late seventeenth century they began a long migration to the 4 south and east. It was a journey toward the dawn, and it led to a golden age. Along the way the Kiowas were befriended by the Crows, who gave them the culture and religion of the Plains. They acquired horses, and their ancient nomadic spirit was suddenly free of the ground. They acquired Tai-me, the sacred Sun Dance doll, from that moment the object and symbol of their worship, and so shared in the divinity of the sun. Not least, they acquired the sense of destiny, therefore courage and pride. When they entered upon the southern Plains they had been transformed. No longer were they slaves to the simple necessity of survival; they were a lordly and dangerous society of fighters and thieves, hunters and priests of the sun. According to their origin myth, they entered the world through a hollow log. From one point of view, their migration was the fruit of an old prophecy, for indeed they emerged from a sunless world.

5 Although my grandmother lived out her long life in the shadow of Rainy Mountain, the immense landscape of the continental interior lay like memory in her blood. She could tell of the Crows, whom she had never seen, and of the Black Hills, where she had never been. I wanted to see in reality what she had seen more perfectly in the mind's eye, and traveled fifteen hundred miles to begin my pilgrimage.

6 Yellowstone, it seemed to me, was the top of the world, a region of deep lakes and dark timber, canyons and waterfalls. But, beautiful as it is, one might have the sense of confinement there. The skyline in all directions is close at hand, the high wall of the woods and deep cleavages of shade. There is a perfect freedom in the mountains, but it belongs to the eagle and the elk, the badger and the bear. The Kiowas reckoned their stature by the distance they could see, and they were bent and blind in the wilderness.

7 Descending eastward, the highland meadows are a stairway to the plain. In July the inland slope of the Rockies is luxuriant with flax and buckwheat, stonecrop and larkspur. The earth unfolds and the limit of the land recedes. Clusters of trees, and animals grazing far in the distance, cause the vision to reach away and wonder to build upon the mind. The sun follows a longer course in the day, and the sky is immense beyond all comparison. The great billowing clouds that sail upon it are shadows that move upon the grain like water, dividing light. Farther down, in the land of the Crows and Blackfeet, the plain is yellow. Sweet clover takes hold of the hills and bends upon itself to cover and seal the soil. There the Kiowas paused on their way; they had come to the place where they must change their lives. The sun is at home on the plains. Precisely

there does it have the certain character of a god. When the Kiowas came to the land of the Crows, they could see the dark lees of the hills at dawn across the Bighorn River, the profusion of light on the grain shelves, the oldest deity ranging after the solstices. Not yet would they veer southward to the caldron of the land that lay below; they must wean their blood from the northern winter and hold the mountains a while longer in their view. They bore Tai-me in procession to the east.

A dark mist lay over the Black Hills, and the land was like 8
iron. At the top of a ridge I caught sight of Devil's Tower up-thrust against the gray sky as if in the birth of time the core of the earth had broken through its crust and the motion of the world was begun. There are things in nature that engender an awful quiet in the heart of man; Devil's Tower is one of them. Two centuries ago, because they could not do otherwise, the Kiowas made a legend at the base of the rock. My grandmother said:

> *Eight children were there at play, seven sisters and their brother. Suddenly the boy was struck dumb; he trembled and began to run upon his hands and feet. His fingers became claws, and his body was covered with fur. Directly there was a bear where the boy had been. The sisters were terrified; they ran, and the bear after them. They came to the stump of a great tree, and the tree spoke to them. It bade them climb upon it, and as they did so it began to rise into the air. The bear came to kill them, but they were just beyond its reach. It reared against the tree and scored the bark all around with its claws. The seven sisters were borne into the sky, and they became the stars of the Big Dipper.*

From that moment, and so long as the legend lives, the Kiowas have kinsmen in the night sky. Whatever they were in the mountains, they could be no more. However tenuous their well-being, however much they had suffered and would suffer again, they had found a way out of the wilderness.

My grandmother had a reverence for the sun, a holy regard 9
that now is all but gone out of mankind. There was a wariness in her, and an ancient awe. She was a Christian in her later years, but she had come a long way about, and she never forgot her birthright. As a child she had been to the Sun Dances; she had taken part in those annual rites, and by them she had learned the restoration of her people in the presence of Tai-me. She was about seven when the last Kiowa Sun Dance was held in 1887 on the Washita River above Rainy Mountain Creek. The buffalo were gone. In order to consummate the ancient sacrifice—to impale the head of a buffalo bull upon the medicine tree—a delegation of old men journeyed into

Texas, there to beg and barter for an animal from the Goodnight herd. She was ten when the Kiowas came together for the last time as a living Sun Dance culture. They could find no buffalo; they had to hang an old hide from the sacred tree. Before the dance could begin, a company of soldiers rode out from Fort Sill under orders to disperse the tribe. Forbidden without cause the essential act of their faith, having seen the wild herds slaughtered and left to rot upon the ground, the Kiowas backed away forever from the medicine tree. That was July 20, 1890, at the great bend of the Washita. My grandmother was there. Without bitterness, and for as long as she lived, she bore a vision of deicide.

10 Now that I can have her only in memory, I see my grandmother in the several postures that were peculiar to her: standing at the wood stove on a winter morning and turning meat in a great iron skillet; sitting at the south window, bent above her beadwork, and afterwards, when her vision failed, looking down for a long time into the fold of her hands; going out upon a cane, very slowly as she did when the weight of age came upon her; praying. I remember her most often at prayer. She made long, rambling prayers out of suffering and hope, having seen many things. I was never sure that I had the right to hear, so exclusive were they of all mere custom and company. The last time I saw her she prayed standing by the side of her bed at night, naked to the waist, the light of a kerosene lamp moving upon her dark skin. Her long, black hair, always drawn and braided in the day, lay upon her shoulders and against her breasts like a shawl. I do not speak Kiowa, and I never understood her prayers, but there was something inherently sad in the sound, some merest hesitation upon the syllables of sorrow. She began in a high and descending pitch, exhausting her breath to silence; then again and again—and always the same intensity of effort, of something that is, and is not, like urgency in the human voice. Transported so in the dancing light among the shadows of her room, she seemed beyond the reach of time. But that was illusion; I think I knew then that I should not see her again.

11 Houses are like sentinels in the plain, old keepers of the weather watch. There, in a very little while, wood takes on the appearance of great age. All colors wear soon away in the wind and rain, and then the wood is burned gray and the grain appears and the nails turn red with rust. The windowpanes are black and opaque; you imagine there is nothing within, and indeed there are many ghosts, bones given up to the land. They stand here and there against the sky, and you approach them for a longer time than you expect. They belong in the distance; it is their domain.

Once there was a lot of sound in my grandmother's house, a lot of coming and going, feasting and talk. The summers there were full of excitement and reunion. The Kiowas are a summer people; they abide the cold and keep to themselves, but when the season turns and the land becomes warm and vital they cannot hold still; an old love of going returns upon them. The aged visitors who came to my grandmother's house when I was a child were made of lean and leather, and they bore themselves upright. They wore great black hats and bright ample shirts that shook in the wind. They rubbed fat upon their hair and wound their braids with strips of colored cloth. Some of them painted their faces and carried the scars of old and cherished enmities. They were an old council of warlords, come to remind and be reminded of who they were. Their wives and daughters served them well. The women might indulge themselves; gossip was at once the mark and compensation of their servitude. They made loud and elaborate talk among themselves, full of jest and gesture, fright and false alarm. They went abroad in fringed and flowered shawls, bright beadwork and German silver. They were at home in the kitchen, and they prepared meals that were banquets. 12

There were frequent prayer meetings, and great nocturnal feasts. When I was a child I played with my cousins outside, where the lamplight fell upon the ground and the singing of the old people rose up around us and carried away into the darkness. There were a lot of good things to eat, a lot of laughter and surprise. And afterwards, when the quiet returned, I lay down with my grandmother and could hear the frogs away by the river and feel the motion of the air. 13

Now there is a funeral silence in the rooms, the endless wake of some final word. The walls have closed in upon my grandmother's house. When I returned to it in mourning, I saw for the first time in my life how small it was. It was late at night, and there was a white moon, nearly full. I sat for a long time on the stone steps by the kitchen door. From there I could see out across the land; I could see the long row of trees by the creek, the low light upon the rolling plains, and the stars of the Big Dipper. Once I looked at the moon and caught sight of a strange thing. A cricket had perched upon the handrail, only a few inches away from me. My line of vision was such that the creature filled the moon like a fossil. It had gone there, I thought, to live and die, for there, of all places, was its small definition made whole and eternal. A warm wind rose up and purled like the longing within me. 14

The next morning I awoke at dawn and went out on the dirt road to Rainy Mountain. It was already hot, and the grasshoppers 15 began to fill the air. Still, it was early in the morning, and the birds sang out of the shadows. The long yellow grass on the mountain shone in the bright light, and a scissortail hied above the land. There, where it ought to be, at the end of a long and legendary way, was my grandmother's grave. Here and there on the dark stones were ancestral names. Looking back once, I saw the mountain and came away.

QUESTIONS FOR DISCUSSION

1. What event triggers Momaday's essay?
2. How many "journeys" are involved in Momaday's story?
3. Why might Momaday have titled the essay "The Way to Rainy Mountain"? Why not, for example, refer more specifically to the event that has brought him back?
4. Why might Momaday retell the legend of the "seven sisters" (paragraph 8)? How does that fit into his essay?
5. How much descriptive detail does Momaday give of his grandmother? Go through the essay, and isolate each physical detail the reader is given.
6. What expectations might Momaday have of his audience? How might those expectations affect the essay?
7. Be prepared to define the following words: *knoll* (paragraph 1), *writhe* (1), *pillage* (3), *nomadic* (4), *luxuriant* (7), *lees* (7), *solstices* (7), *veer* (7), *tenuous* (8), *deicide* (9), *enmities* (12), *purled* (14), *hied* (15).

Note on Earlier Draft

Between the first appearance of "The Way to Rainy Mountain" in the magazine *The Reporter* in January 1967 and its publication as part of *The Way to Rainy Mountain* in 1969, Momaday made one major change: he added what are now paragraphs 6 and 7.

QUESTIONS ON THE REVISION

1. Why might Momaday have decided to add paragraphs 6 and 7? What do they contribute to the essay?
2. What is the effect of these other minor changes that Momaday made?
   a. Final: "They were driven onto the Staked Plains in the cold rains of autumn" (paragraph 3).

Earlier: "They were driven onto the Staked Plains in the cold of autumn."

b. Final: "As a child she had been to the Sun Dances; she had taken part in those annual rites" (paragraph 9).

Earlier: "As a child she had been to the Sun Dances; she had taken part in that annual rite."

c. Final: "In order to consummate the ancient sacrifice—to impale the head of a buffalo bull upon the medicine tree" (paragraph 9).

Earlier: "In order to consummate the ancient sacrifice—to impale the head of a buffalo bull upon the Tai-me tree."

WRITING SUGGESTIONS

1. **For Your Journal.** What memories do you have of a grandparent or a great-grandparent? When you think of that person, what comes to mind? In your journal, make a list of those memories—sights, sounds, smells, associations of any sort.
2. **For a Paragraph.** In a substantial paragraph, analyze the effects that Momaday achieved by adding paragraphs 6 and 7 to the essay.
3. **For an Essay.** Momaday once told an interviewer, "I believe that the Indian has an understanding of the physical world and of the earth as a spiritual entity that is his, very much his own. The non-Indian can benefit a good deal by having that perception revealed to him." What do such perceptions reveal to the non-Indian?

   Prewriting:

   a. Reread Momaday's essay carefully, looking for evidence of how he perceives the physical world. How does he describe the physical world? What does he seem to "see" in nature? How does his "seeing" differ from that of a scientist?

   b. On the basis of what he says, try to finish the following sentence, "Momaday sees nature as . . ."

   c. Brainstorm about the possible benefits to you from seeing things as Momaday sees them. Try to list a number of possibilities. What might you do differently?

Rewriting:

a. Look carefully at how you have structured the body of your essay. You probably either began with the most significant point or ended with it. Would the essay work better if the order were changed?

b. Look again at your introduction. Have you begun with something that might catch your reader's attention? Try to avoid beginning with just a thesis statement.

c. Carefully examine every sentence in your essay. Is each a complete sentence? Do the sentences have some variety in both structure and length?

4. **For Research.** What part have geography and other aspects of the natural world played in determining who you are? If you had to undertake a "pilgrimage" to a place or a geographical location or to retrack a migration, where would you go? What were the stages on the journey? Research part of your own family history, and write a research paper in which you trace out that journey for a reader. You might want to start by talking with your relatives. Then use research—in the library, in archives, in electronic databases, in atlases, in talks with people—to fill out the story for your reader. Be sure to acknowledge all of your sources.

Website Link

Among the Web resources for information about Momaday is a long, detailed interview with him that includes extensive audio clips—the link is at www.prenhall.com/miller.

Revision and Life: Take It from the Top—Again

Nora Ephron

Nora Ephron was born in 1941 in New York City. After she received her B.A. from Wellesley College in 1962, Ephron worked as a journalist and columnist for the New York Post, New York *magazine, and* Esquire, *where she developed her reporting and interviewing skills. She quickly established a reputation as a writer who brought snappy wit, cutting insight, and bare-all candor to any subject she wrote about. Ephron is also a successful screenplay writer and director. She wrote the screenplay for films such as* Silkwood *(1983),* When Harry Met Sally *(1989), and* Sleepless in Seattle *(1993), which she also directed. She has recently directed films such as* Michael *(1996),* You've Got Mail *(1998), and* Numbers *(2000). "Revision and Life," written in response to an invitation to participate in this textbook, was originally published in* The New York Times Book Review.

On Writing: *When asked about the autobiographical influences of her first novel, Ephron replied: "I've always written about my life. That's how I grew up. 'Take notes. Everything is copy.' All that stuff my mother [also a writer] said to us."*

BEFORE READING

Connecting: When it comes to writing, what does the word *revision* suggest to you?

Anticipating: When Ephron observes, "A gift for revision may be a developmental stage," what does she mean?

Revised Draft

I have been asked to write something for a textbook that is meant to teach college students something about writing and revision. I am happy to do this because I believe in revision. I have also been asked to save the early drafts of whatever I write, presumably to show these students the actual process of revision. This too I am happy to do. On the other hand, I suspect that there is just so much you can teach college students about revision; a gift for revision 1 may be a developmental stage—like a 2-year-old's sudden ability to place one block on top of another—that comes along somewhat later, in one's mid-20s, say; most people may not be particularly good at it, or even interested in it, until then.

2 When I was in college, I revised nothing. I wrote out my papers in longhand, typed them up and turned them in. It would never have crossed my mind that what I had produced was only a first draft and that I had more work to do; the idea was to get to the end, and once you had got to the end you were finished. The same thinking, I might add, applied in life: I went pell-mell through my four years in college without a thought about whether I ought to do anything differently; the idea was to get to the end—to get out of school and become a journalist.

3 Which I became, in fairly short order. I learned as a journalist to revise on deadline. I learned to write an article a paragraph at a time—and I arrived at the kind of writing and revising I do, which is basically a kind of typing and retyping. I am a great believer in this technique for the simple reason that I type faster than the wind. What I generally do is to start an article and get as far as I can—sometimes no farther in than a sentence or two—before running out of steam, ripping the piece of paper from the typewriter and starting all over again. I type over and over until I have got the beginning of the piece to the point where I am happy with it. I then am ready to plunge into the body of the article itself. This plunge usually requires something known as a transition. I approach a transition by completely retyping the opening of the article leading up to it in the hope that the ferocious speed of my typing will somehow catapult me into the next section of the piece. This does not work—what in fact catapults me into the next section is a concrete thought about what the next section ought to be about—but until I have the thought the typing keeps me busy, and keeps me from feeling something known as blocked.

4 Typing and retyping as if you know where you're going is a version of what therapists tell you to do when they suggest that you try changing from the outside in—that if you can't master the total commitment to whatever change you want to make, you can at least do all the extraneous things connected with it, which make it that much easier to get there. I was 25 years old the first time a therapist suggested that I try changing from the outside in. In those days, I used to spend quite a lot of time lying awake at night wondering what I should have said earlier in the evening and revising my lines. I mention this not just because it's a way

of illustrating that a gift for revision is practically instinctive, but also (once again) because it's possible that a genuine ability at it doesn't really come into play until one is older—or at least older than 25, when it seemed to me that all that was required in my life and my work was the chance to change a few lines.

In my 30's, I began to write essays, one a month for *Esquire* 5
magazine, and I am not exaggerating when I say that in the course of writing a short essay—1,500 words, that's only six double-spaced typewritten pages—I often used 300 or 400 pieces of typing paper, so often did I type and retype and catapult and recatapult myself, sometimes on each retyping moving not even a sentence farther from the spot I had reached the last time through. At the same time, though, I was polishing what I had already written: as I struggled with the middle of the article, I kept putting the beginning through the typewriter; as I approached the ending, the middle got its turn. (This is a kind of polishing that the word processor all but eliminates, which is why I don't use one. Word processors make it possible for a writer to change the sentences that clearly need changing without having to retype the rest, but I believe that you can't always tell whether a sentence needs work until it rises up in revolt against your fingers as you retype it.) By the time I had produced what you might call a first draft—an entire article with a beginning, middle and end—the beginning was in more like 45th draft, the middle in 20th, and the end was almost newborn. For this reason, the beginnings of my essays are considerably better written than the ends, although I like to think no one ever notices this but me.

As I learned the essay form, writing became harder for me. I 6
was finding a personal style, a voice if you will, a way of writing that looked chatty and informal. That wasn't the hard part—the hard part was that having found a voice, I had to work hard month to month not to seem as if I were repeating myself. At this point in this essay it will not surprise you to learn that the same sort of thing was operating in my life. I don't mean that my life had become harder—but that it was becoming clear that I had many more choices than had occurred to me when I was marching through my 20's. I no longer lost sleep over what I should have said. Not that I didn't care—it was just that I had moved to a new plane of late-night anxiety: I now wondered what I should have done. Whole areas of possible revision opened before me. What should I have done instead? What could I have done? What if I hadn't done it the way I did? What if I had a chance to do it over? What if I had a chance to do it over as a different person? These were the sorts of

questions that kept me awake and led me into fiction, which at the very least (the level at which I practice it) is a chance to rework the events of your life so that you give the illusion of being the intelligence at the center of it, simultaneously managing to slip in all the lines that occurred to you later. Fiction, I suppose, is the ultimate shot at revision.

7 Now I am in my 40's and I write screenplays. Screenplays—if they are made into movies—are essentially collaborations, and movies are not a writer's medium, we all know this, and I don't want to dwell on the craft of screenwriting except insofar as it relates to revision. Because the moment you stop work on a script seems to be determined not by whether you think the draft is good but simply by whether shooting is about to begin: if it is, you get to call your script a final draft; and if it's not, you can always write another revision. This might seem to be a hateful way to live, but the odd thing is that it's somehow comforting; as long as you're revising, the project isn't dead. And by the same token, neither are you.

8 It was, as it happens, while thinking about all this one recent sleepless night that I figured out how to write this particular essay. I say "recent" in order to give a sense of immediacy and energy to the preceding sentence, but the truth is that I am finishing this article four months after the sleepless night in question, and the letter asking me to write it, from George Miller of the University of Delaware, arrived almost two years ago, so for all I know Mr. Miller has managed to assemble his textbook on revision without me.

9 Oh, well. That's how it goes when you start thinking about revision. That's the danger of it, in fact. You can spend so much time thinking about how to switch things around that the main event has passed you by. But it doesn't matter. Because by the time you reach middle age, you want more than anything for things not to come to an end; and as long as you're still revising, they don't.

10 I'm sorry to end so morbidly—dancing as I am around the subject of death—but there are advantages to it. For one thing, I have managed to move fairly effortlessly and logically from the beginning of this piece through the middle and to the end. And for another, I am able to close with an exhortation, something I rarely manage, which is this: Revise now, before it's too late.

QUESTIONS FOR DISCUSSION

1. What links does Ephron see between revision and life?
2. How does Ephron structure her essay? What principle of order does she follow?

3. It would have been a simple matter for Ephron to omit the references to this textbook (paragraphs 1 and 8). *The New York Times* audience, for example, would not be interested in knowing these details. Why might she have chosen to include these references in her essay?
4. Why is fiction the "ultimate shot at revision" (6)?
5. What might Ephron mean by her final sentence ("Revise now, before it's too late")?
6. Be able to define the following words: *pell-mell* (paragraph 2), *extraneous* (4), *exhortation* (10).

Earlier Draft

These paragraphs correspond to paragraphs 1 and 2.

I have been asked to write something that will show college students something about writing and revision. I am happy to do this because I believe in revision. I have been asked to write something and save all the early drafts, which I am also happy to do. On the other hand, I believe there is just so much you can teach college students about revision, that an ability for revision is something (a Piaget stage, like a 2½-year-old's sudden ability to put one block on top of another) that is acquired slightly later, and that most people aren't particularly good at it or even interested in it until then. 1

When I was in college, I revised almost nothing. It seems to me (I know my memory isn't what it used to be but I'm fairly sure about this) I typed papers and pretty much turned them in. The same thing I might add applied in life: I pretty much went pell-mell through my four years of higher education without a thought about whether I ought to have done anything differently. The things I wrote were a means to an end—to turn in the assignment, I suppose—and so was the way I lived my life—to get out of school and become a journalist. 2

QUESTIONS ON THE REVISION

1. In the revised draft, Ephron omits the reference to Piaget (paragraph 1). Who was Piaget? Why eliminate the reference?
2. In the revised draft, Ephron suggests when it might be that people acquire an interest in revising ("in one's mid-20s, say"). Why add that detail?

3. What changes occur in the following passage from one draft to another? What is the effect of those changes?

   Earlier Draft:
   When I was in college, I revised almost nothing. It seems to me (I know my memory isn't what it used to be but I'm fairly sure about this) I typed papers and pretty much turned them in.

   Revised Draft:
   When I was in college, I revised nothing. I wrote out my papers in longhand, typed them up and turned them in. It would never have crossed my mind that what I had produced was only a first draft and that I had more work to do; the idea was to get to the end, and once you had got to the end you were finished.

4. What is the effect of changing "four years of higher education" to "four years in college?"

WRITING SUGGESTIONS

1. **For Your Journal.** What obstacles do you face when you try to revise something that you have written? Make a list of the ones that immediately come to mind. Add to your list as you finish each paragraph and essay during this course.
2. **For a Paragraph.** Study the two versions of the opening of Ephron's essay. Formulate a thesis about her revision strategy. In a paragraph, assert your thesis and support it with appropriate evidence.
3. **For an Essay.** On the basis of your own experience as a writer and as a student in this course, argue for or against *requiring* revision in a college writing course. Should a student be forced to do it? Does revision always produce a better paper?

   Prewriting:

   a. Remember that regardless of your stand, your argument should be based on solid, meaningful reasons. For example, you should not argue that revision is too much trouble or that it will please your instructor and get you a higher grade. Make a list of reasons.
   b. Interview classmates and friends for their experiences and opinions. Remember to take notes.
   c. Plan a possible organization for your essay. Does an inductive or a deductive approach seem better? In what

order will you arrange your reasons? Will you start or end with the strongest reason?

Rewriting:

a. Check your tone in the essay. Do you sound convincing? Reasonable? Ask a friend or classmate to read your essay and to characterize its tone.

b. Have you avoided emotionally charged language? Examine your word choice carefully. Underline any words that might seem distorted, inaccurate, or too emotional.

c. Titles are an important part of any essay. An effective title should clearly signal the essay's subject and should also arouse the reader's interest. Look carefully at your original title. Does it meet those tests? Try writing some alternative titles.

4. **For Research.** What role does revision play in the writing process of faculty and staff at your college or university? Interview a range of people—faculty (especially professors in disciplines other than English) and other professional staff members who write as a regular part of their job (for example, librarians, information officers, and admissions officers). Using notes from your interviews, write an essay about the revision practices of these writers. Your essay could be a feature article in the campus newspaper.

Website Link

Ephron is increasingly known as both a screenwriter and director. You can find detailed Web resources on all of her films, including stills, audio, and video clips. A list of places to start can be found at the Website.

Black Men and Public Space

Brent Staples

Born in Chester, Pennsylvania, Brent Staples graduated from Widener University in 1973 and earned a Ph.D. in psychology from the University of Chicago in 1982. He worked for the Chicago Sun-Times *as a reporter before moving to* The New York Times *in 1985. He is currently a member of* The Times' *editorial board, writing on politics and culture. In 1994 he published a memoir,* Parallel Time: Growing Up in Black and White, *which tells the story of his childhood in Chester, a mixed-race, economically declining town. The book focuses on his younger brother, a drug dealer who died of gunshot wounds at age twenty-two.*

"Black Men and Public Space" was originally published in the "Can Men Have It All?" section of Ms. *magazine under the title "Just Walk on By: A Black Man Ponders His Power to Alter Public Space." In revised and edited form, it was reprinted in* Harper's *with the new title "Black Men and Public Space."*

On Writing: *In* Parallel Time, *Staples describes how, in his early twenties, he began to explore his voice as a writer: "I was carrying a journal with me everywhere. . . . I wrote on buses and on the Jackson Park el—though only at the stops to keep the writing legible. I traveled to distant neighborhoods, sat on the curbs, and sketched what I saw in words. Thursday meant free admission at the Art Institute. All day I attributed motives to people in paintings, especially people in Rembrandts. At closing time, I went to a nightclub in The Loop and spied on the patrons, copied their conversations, and speculated about their lives. The journal was more than 'a record of my inner transactions.' It was a collection of stolen souls from which I would one day construct a book."*

BEFORE READING

Connecting: What precautions do you take if you have to walk at night in public spaces?

Anticipating: Why does Staples whistle melodies from classical music when he walks at night? What effect does that particular "cowbell" have on people?

Revised Draft

My first victim was a woman—white, well dressed, probably in her early twenties. I came upon her late one evening on a deserted street in Hyde Park, a relatively affluent neighborhood in an otherwise mean, impoverished section of Chicago. As I swung onto the avenue behind her, there seemed to be a discreet, uninflammatory distance between us. Not so. She cast back a worried glance. To her, the youngish black man—a broad six feet two inches with a beard and billowing hair, both hands shoved into the pockets of a bulky military jacket—seemed menacingly close. After a few more quick glimpses, she picked up her pace and was soon running in earnest. Within seconds she disappeared into a cross street. 1

That was more than a decade ago. I was twenty-two years old, a graduate student newly arrived at the University of Chicago. It was in the echo of that terrified woman's footfalls that I first began to know the unwieldy inheritance I'd come into—the ability to alter public space in ugly ways. It was clear that she thought herself the quarry of a mugger, a rapist, or worse. Suffering a bout of insomnia, however, I was stalking sleep, not defenseless wayfarers. As a softy who is scarcely able to take a knife to a raw chicken—let alone hold one to a person's throat—I was surprised, embarrassed, and dismayed all at once. Her flight made me feel like an accomplice in tyranny. It also made it clear that I was indistinguishable from the muggers who occasionally seeped into the area from the surrounding ghetto. That first encounter, and those that followed, signified that a vast, unnerving gulf lay between nighttime pedestrians—particularly women—and me. And I soon gathered that being perceived as dangerous is a hazard in itself. I only needed to turn a corner into a dicey situation, or crowd some frightened, armed person in a foyer somewhere, or make an errant move after being pulled over by a policeman. Where fear and weapons meet—and they often do in urban America—there is always the possibility of death. 2

In that first year, my first away from my hometown, I was to become thoroughly familiar with the language of fear. At dark, shadowy intersections, I could cross in front of a car stopped at a traffic light and elicit the *thunk, thunk, thunk, thunk* of the driver—black, white, male, or female—hammering down the door locks. On less traveled streets after dark, I grew accustomed to but never comfortable with people crossing to the other side of the street rather than pass me. Then there were the standard unpleasantries with policemen, doormen, bouncers, cabdrivers, and 3 others whose business it is to screen out troublesome individuals *before* there is any nastiness.

4 I moved to New York nearly two years ago and I have remained an avid night walker. In central Manhattan, the near-constant crowd cover minimizes tense one-on-one street encounters. Elsewhere—in SoHo, for example, where sidewalks are narrow and tightly spaced buildings shut out the sky—things can get very taut indeed.

5 After dark, on the warrenlike streets of Brooklyn where I live, I often see women who fear the worst from me. They seem to have set their faces on neutral, and with their purse straps strung across their chests bandolier-style, they forge ahead as though bracing themselves against being tackled. I understand, of course, that the danger they perceive is not a hallucination. Women are particularly vulnerable to street violence, and young black males are drastically overrepresented among the perpetrators of that violence. Yet these truths are no solace against the kind of alienation that comes of being ever the suspect, a fearsome entity with whom pedestrians avoid making eye contact.

6 It is not altogether clear to me how I reached the ripe old age of twenty-two without being conscious of the lethality nighttime pedestrians attributed to me. Perhaps it was because in Chester, Pennsylvania, the small, angry industrial town where I came of age in the 1960s, I was scarcely noticeable against a backdrop of gang warfare, street knifings, and murders. I grew up one of the good boys, had perhaps a half-dozen fistfights. In retrospect, my shyness of combat has clear sources.

7 As a boy, I saw countless tough guys locked away; I have since buried several, too. They were babies, really—a teenage cousin, a brother of twenty-two, a childhood friend in his mid-twenties—all gone down in episodes of bravado played out in the streets. I came to doubt the virtues of intimidation early on. I chose, perhaps unconsciously, to remain a shadow—timid, but a survivor.

8 The fearsomeness mistakenly attributed to me in public places often has a perilous flavor. The most frightening of these confusions occurred in the late 1970s and early 1980s, when I worked as a journalist in Chicago. One day, rushing into the office of a magazine I was writing for with a deadline story in hand, I was mistaken for a burglar. The office manager called security and, with an ad hoc posse, pursued me through the labyrinthine halls, nearly to my editor's door. I had no way of proving who I was. I could only move briskly toward the company of someone who knew me.

Another time I was on assignment for a local paper and killing time before an interview. I entered a jewelry store on the city's affluent Near North Side. The proprietor excused herself and returned with an enormous red Doberman pinscher straining at the end of a leash. She stood, the dog extended toward me, silent to my questions, her eyes bulging nearly out of her head. I took a cursory look around, nodded, and bade her good night. 9

Relatively speaking, however, I never fared as badly as another black male journalist. He went to nearby Waukegan, Illinois, a couple of summers ago to work on a story about a murderer who was born there. Mistaking the reporter for the killer, police officers hauled him from his car at gunpoint and but for his press credentials would probably have tried to book him. Such episodes are not uncommon. Black men trade tales like this all the time. 10

Over the years, I learned to smother the rage I felt at so often being taken for a criminal. Not to do so would surely have led to madness. I now take precautions to make myself less threatening. I move about with care, particularly late in the evening. I give a wide berth to nervous people on subway platforms during the wee hours, particularly when I have exchanged business clothes for jeans. If I happen to be entering a building behind some people who appear skittish, I may walk by, letting them clear the lobby before I return, so as not to seem to be following them. I have been calm and extremely congenial on those rare occasions when I've been pulled over by the police. 11

And on late-evening constitutionals I employ what has proved to be an excellent tension-reducing measure: I whistle melodies from Beethoven and Vivaldi and the more popular classical composers. Even steely New Yorkers hunching toward nighttime destinations seem to relax, and occasionally they even join in the tune. Virtually everybody seems to sense that a mugger wouldn't be warbling bright, sunny selections from Vivaldi's *Four Seasons.* It is my equivalent of the cowbell that hikers wear when they know they are in bear country. 12

QUESTIONS FOR DISCUSSION

1. What does Staples mean by the phrase "public space"? In what way is he capable of altering it?
2. What is the effect of Staples's opening sentences in the essay?
3. What type of evidence does Staples provide to illustrate his point—that black men alter public space?

4. What purpose might Staples have had in writing the essay?
5. Staples's essay originally appeared in *Ms.* magazine. What assumptions could Staples have made about his audience?
6. Be prepared to define the following words: *discreet* (paragraph 1), *dicey* (2), *errant* (2), *taut* (4), *warrenlike* (5), *bandolier* (5), *solace* (5), *entity* (5), *bravado* (7), *ad hoc* (8), *cursory* (9), *skittish* (11), *congenial* (11), *constitutionals* (12).

Earlier Draft

Paragraph A (in the *Ms.* version this appeared between paragraphs 4 and 5 of the *Harper's* version)

Black men have a firm place in New York mugging literature. Norman Podhoretz in his famed (or infamous) 1963 essay, "My Negro Problem—And Ours," recalls growing up in the terror of black males; they "were tougher than we were, more ruthless," he writes—and as an adult on the Upper West Side of Manhattan, he continues, he cannot constrain his nervousness when he meets black men on certain streets. Similarly, a decade later, the essayist and novelist Edward Hoagland extols a New York where once "Negro bitterness bore down mainly on other Negroes." Where some see mere panhandlers, Hoagland sees "a mugger who is clearly screwing up his nerve to do more than just *ask* for money." But Hoagland has "the New Yorker's quick-hunch posture for broken-field maneuvering" and the bad guy swerves away.

Paragraph B (in the *Ms.* version this appeared between paragraphs 6 and 7 of the *Harper's* version)

Many things go into the making of a young thug. One of those things is the consummation of the male romance with the power to intimidate. An infant discovers that random flailings send the baby bottle flying out of the crib and crashing to the floor. Delighted, the joyful babe repeats those motions again and again, seeking to duplicate the feat. Just so, I recall the point at which some of my boyhood friends were finally seduced by the perception of themselves as tough guys. When a mark cowered and surrendered his money without resistance, myth and reality merged—and paid off. It is, after all, only manly to embrace the power to frighten and intimidate. We, as men, are not supposed to give an inch of our lane on the highway; we are to seize the fighter's edge in work and in play and even in love; we are to be valiant in the face of hostile forces.

Unfortunately, poor and powerless young men seem to take all of this nonsense literally. . . .

QUESTIONS ON THE REVISED DRAFT

1. When the earlier draft was first published in *Ms.*, it was titled "Just Walk on By." When it appeared in *Harper's* (revised draft), it was retitled "Black Men and Public Space." Why might the title have been changed?
2. The whole of paragraph A in the earlier draft was deleted when the essay appeared in *Harper's*. Why? What does Staples do in that paragraph that he does not do elsewhere?
3. The whole of paragraph B in the earlier draft was also deleted when the essay appeared in *Harper's*. Why?

WRITING SUGGESTIONS

1. **For Your Journal.** Have you ever been frightened in a public space? Explore your memories or your recent experiences, and jot down a few such times. Try to capture a few details about each experience.
2. **For a Paragraph.** Select one of the experiences you entered in your journal for Suggestion 1, and narrate that experience in a paragraph. Why did you react as you did? Was your fear justified? You can also turn the topic around and describe a time when your presence frightened someone else while in a public space.
3. **For an Essay.** Regardless of our age or sex or color, we all provoke reactions from people who do not know us. Sometimes, in fact, we go out of our way to elicit a reaction—dressing in a certain way, driving a particular type of car, engaging in an unusual activity, wearing our hair in a peculiar style. Describe your image and behavior, and analyze how people react to you and why they react as they do.

   Prewriting:

   a. Think about the image that you either consciously or unconsciously project. Try to define that image in a couple of sentences. How do you create that image?

   b. Make a list of people's reactions to you. What have you noticed about their responses? What is typical? Make a list of those reactions, and then jot down next to each item a possible explanation for that reaction.

c. Ask some friends, or even some casual acquaintances, how they respond to you and why. Be sure to explain to them why you want to know—that might encourage them to respond in a helpful manner. Be prepared to be surprised.

Rewriting:

a. Try to find an effective incident with which to begin. Do not try to imitate Staples's introduction, especially his suspenseful example.
b. Be sure that you have offered explanations for why people react to you as they do.
c. Remember that your analysis of reactions needs to be organized in a logical manner. Why have you chosen the order you have? Is there any other way in which those reactions could be organized?

4. **For Research.** Who mugs whom? Research the problem of assault or mugging either in the country as a whole or in your own community. What are your chances of being mugged? Who is likely to do it to you? Where is it most likely to happen? If you decide to focus on your own community or college campus, remember to interview the local police.

Website Link

A Public Broadcasting Website offers video and audio clips of Staples; a list of his publications in *The New York Times* can be found at the newspaper's Website.

REVISION CASE STUDY

CAUGHT IN THE WIDOW'S WEB

Gordon Grice

Gordon Grice's essay on the black widow spider has a long history that involved substantial revision as it moved from conception to publication in several different forms. Grice began his essay in January 1993 in a journal. He wrote a series of consecutive entries through February, essentially drafting the essay from beginning to end. Then he put the essay aside for a year. "One day, when I was substitute-teaching a shop class in high school and the kids were all busy," Grice commented, "I took it out and rewrote the opening. The next journal I sent it to accepted it for publication." This published version, originally titled "The Black Widow," appeared in the High Plains Literary Review. *The essay was then rewritten and reprinted in* Harper's *magazine as "Caught in the Widow's Web" (that version is reproduced in Chapter 3). He continued to work on the piece for inclusion in his collection of essays,* The Red Hourglass: Inner Lives of the Predators *(1998).*

On Writing: *See the interview with Grice beginning on page 601.*

JOURNAL ENTRIES

Reproduced here are some of the original journal entries for the essay. Grice printed his entries in ink in a spiral-bound notebook. His revisions of those entries are preserved here. Crossed-out words are indicated by a line running through the word. Additions added above or to the side of the crossouts are reproduced here in brackets.

ENTRY 1

1/16/93

Idea for essay: What people have nightmares about. Paul dreamed 1
of people vomiting up human flesh, knew he was in hell.

1/16/93

The black widow has the ugliest web of any spider. The orb 2
weavers ~~have~~ make those seemingly delicate nets that poets have ~~turned~~ traditionally used as symbols of imagination (~~Dickinson~~),

order (~~Shakespeare~~), [and] perfection. The sheet-web ~~weavers make~~ spiders weave crisp linens ~~for the lawn~~ [on the lawn]~~—some of these have impressive looking underlayers and tunnels~~. But the widow makes messy-looking tangles in the corners and bends of things and under logs and debris. Often the web ~~has~~ is littered with leaves. Beneath ~~the web~~ it lie the ~~corpses~~ husks of insect prey, [their antenna stiff as gargoyle horns], cut loose and dropped; on them and the surrounding ground are splashes of the spider's white ~~dung~~ [urine], which looks like bird ~~urine~~ [guano] and smells of ammonia even at a distance of several feet. ~~If these spiders this ground is biolog~~ This fetid material draws scavengers—ants, sow bugs, crickets, roaches, and so on—which ~~walk into~~ become tangled in vertical strands of ~~web~~ [silk] reaching from the ground up into the web. The widow comes down and, with a bicycling ~~motion~~ of the hind [pair of] legs, throws [gummy] ~~liquid~~ silk onto this new prey.

Point of Comparison: Compare this entry with paragraph 6 in "The Black Widow," which follows in this chapter, and with paragraphs 2 and 3 in "Caught in the Widow's Web" in Chapter 3.

Entry 2

1/20/93

3 When the prey is seriously tangled but still struggling, the widow cautiously descends and bites the creature, usually on a leg joint. This is ~~the~~ a killing bite. ~~She will~~; it pumps neurotoxin into the victim. She will deliver a series of bites as the creature dies; these later bites inject substances that liquify the organs. And finally she will settle down to suck the liquified innards out of the prey, changing her ~~position~~ [place] two or three times to get [it] all.

Point of Comparison: Compare this entry with paragraph 7 in "The Black Widow" and paragraph 3 in "Caught in the Widow's Web."

Entry 3

4 The [architectural] complexit~~y~~[ities] of the widow-web ~~are beyond us. As a home~~ do not particularly impress the widow. ~~She~~ They move~~s~~ around in these webs ~~essentially~~ [almost] blind, yet they never snare themselves, misstep, or ~~lose their wa~~ get lost. In fact, a widow forcibly removed from her web and put back at a different

point does not seem confused; she will quickly return to her habitual resting place. ~~All this~~

> *Point of comparison: Compare this entry with paragraph 10 in "The Black Widow." This material does not appear in "Caught in the Widow's Web."*

Entry 4

2/3/93

The first thing people ask when they [hear] about my fascination 5
with the widow is why I~~'m~~ [am] not afraid. The truth is that my fascination is rooted in fear.

I know a man who as a child was frightened by ~~the~~ his 6
preacher's ~~claim that~~ invitation to eat the flesh of Jesus. The man's [worst] nightmares are about ~~cannibals. His hobby~~ vomiting up human meat. The thing he likes best to watch [horror] ~~movies~~ [films] about cannibals.

> *Point of comparison: Compare this entry with paragraph 15 in "The Black Widow" and with paragraph 6 in "Caught in the Widow's Web."*

Entry 5

2/4/93

~~There is, of course, one pragmatic reason for fearing the widow.~~ 7

~~These markings include a pair of triangles on the ventral side~~ 8
~~of the abdomen—the infamous "hourglass"~~

The widow's venom is, of course, a soundly pragmatic reason 9
for fear. The venom contains a neurotoxin that produces chills, [sweats], vomiting, ~~and~~ fiery pain, ~~sometimes~~ [and] convulsions and death. ~~Death It is [And]~~ Occasionally ~~a person~~ [people] die~~s~~ from ~~the~~ widow bites ~~but less than the~~ Some researchers ~~have theorized~~ [hypothesized] that the virulence of the venom was necessary for killing ~~scarab~~ beetles of the scarab family. This family contains thousands of ~~beetles~~ [species], including the june bug and the famous ~~Egyptian~~ dung beetle the Egyptians thought immortal. All the scarabs have thick, strong bodies and [unusually] tough exoskeletons, and ~~these~~ many of them are common prey for the widow.

> *Point of Comparison: Compare this entry with paragraphs 21 and 22 in "The Black Widow" and paragraphs 11 and 12 in "Caught in the Widow's Web."*

ENTRY 6

2/9/93

10 The widow, it was proposed, needs a strong venom to kill such thick-hided creatures. But this idea is yet another that owes more to ~~the widow's~~ dark romance ~~than~~ with the widow than to hard evidence. The venom is thousands of times too virulent ~~for this than~~ [for] this purpose. ~~We see~~ An emblem of immortality ~~trapped~~, killed by a creature ~~thing~~ whose most distinctive [blood-colored] markings people invariably describe as an hourglass: scientists, being human, want to see a deep causality.

11 But no one has ever offered a sufficient explanation for the ~~widow's~~ [dangerous] venom. It ~~has no~~ provides no evolutionary advantages: all of ~~its~~ [the widow's] prey items ~~are~~ would find lesser toxins fatal, and there is no particular ~~advantage to~~ benefit in harming or killing larger animals. A widow biting a human or other large animal is almost certain to be killed. Evolution does occasionally produce such flowers of [natural] evil—traits that are not functional, but vestiges of lost functions, but ~~pure~~ utterly pointless. ~~This~~ Such ~~things~~ [traits] come about because natural selection merely ~~works against~~ [favors] the inheritance of useful ~~traits~~ [characteristics] that arise from random mutation and extinguishes disadvantageous characteristics. All other characteristics, the ones that neither help nor hinder survival, are preserved [or not] (almost) randomly; when mutation links a useless but harmless trait to a useful one, both are preserved. Many people—even many scientists—assume that every animal is elegantly engineered for its ecological niche, that every bit of an animal's anatomy and behavior ~~can be~~ has a functional explanation. This assumption is false. Nothing in evolutionary theory sanctions it; fact refutes it. ~~It is in fact a lapse into magical thinking. But we want to order and explain things. But We all want order and order in the world and in the room of order In the ordered rooms~~

12 We want the world to be an ordered room, but in a corner of that room there hangs an untidy web ~~that says~~. Here the analytic mind finds an irreducible mystery, a motiveless evil in nature; [and] the scientist's vision of evil comes to match the vision of a religious woman with a ten-foot pole. No picture of the cosmos as elegant design accounts for the widow. No picture of a benevolent God explains the widow. She hangs in her haphazard web (that marvel of design) defying teleology.

Point of Comparison: Compare the entry with paragraphs 22–24 in "The Black Widow" and with paragraphs 12–15 of "Caught in the Widow's Web."

QUESTIONS FOR DISCUSSION

1. What thought or idea appears to trigger Grice's essay? Does he ever return to that idea in the sections of the journal reproduced here?
2. How does the black widow's web differ from those of most spiders?
3. What is puzzling about the widow's venom?
4. What associations do we have with the hourglass (paragraph 11)?
5. In what sense does the widow's web "defy teleology" (paragraph 12)? What is teleology?
6. What are the most common types of revisions that Grice makes in these journal entries?
7. Be prepared to define the following words: *gargoyle* (paragraph 2), *scavengers* (2), *neurotoxin* (3), *innards* (3), *habitual* (4), *pragmatic* (9), *exoskeletons* (9), *causality* (10), *vestiges* (11), *benevolent* (12).

WRITING SUGGESTIONS ON THE REVISIONS

1. **For Your Journal.** First, make a list of each revision that Grice made as he wrote in his journal. See if you can group these changes in any categories. Then make a list of the differences between one of the original entries in the journal and the corresponding paragraphs in either published version of the essay.
2. **For a Paragraph.** Formulate a thesis that explains one of the categories or types of revision that Grice made as he wrote in his journal. Use examples to support that thesis. Then formulate a thesis that explains the nature of the revision that Grice made from one of the journal entries to the corresponding paragraphs in either published version of the essay.
3. **For an Essay.** Using the evidence that you gathered for your journal entry, write an essay in which you analyze the revisions that Grice made as he wrote the first version of the essay in his journal. Alternatively, using the evidence that you gathered for your journal entry, write an essay in which you analyze the revisions that Grice made from the entries in the journal to either published version of the essay.

THE BLACK WIDOW

Gordon Grice

The essay was first published in High Plains Literary Review *in the fall of 1995, roughly a year and a half after Grice started it in his journal (see the preceding reading). This version of the essay is the longest; the primary difference between this version and the original one from the journal is the addition of the first five paragraphs.*

1 I hunt black widow. When I find one, I capture it. I have found them in discarded wheels and tires and under railroad ties. I have found them in house foundations and cellars, in automotive shops and toolsheds, in water meters and rock gardens, against fences and in cinderblock walls. I have found them in a hospital and in the den of a rattlesnake, and once on the bottom of the chair I was sitting in.

2 Sometimes I raise a generation or two in captivity. The egg sacs produce a hundred or more pinpoint cannibals, each leaving a trail of gleaming light in the air, the group of them eventually producing a glimmering tangle in which most of them die, eaten by stronger sibs. Finally I separate the three or four survivors and feed them bigger game.

3 Once I let several egg sacs hatch out in a container about eighteen inches on a side, a tight wooden box with a sliding glass top. As I tried to move the box one day, the lid slid off and I fell, hands first, into the mass of young widows. Most were still translucent newborns, their bodies a swirl of brown and cream. A few of the females had eaten enough to molt; they had the beginnings of their blackness. Their tangle of broken web clung to my forearms. They felt like trickling water in my arm hairs.

4 I walked out into the open air and raised my arms into the stiff wind. The widows answered the wind with new strands of web and drifted away, their bodies gold in the late sun. In about ten minutes my arms carried nothing but old web and the husks of spiderlings eaten by their sibs.

5 I have never been bitten.

6 The black widow has the ugliest web of any spider. The orb weavers make those seemingly delicate nets that poets have traditionally

used as symbols of imagination, order, and perfection. The sheet-web spiders weave crisp linens on the grass. But the widow makes messy-looking tangles in the corners and bends of things and under logs and debris. Often the web is littered with leaves. Beneath it lie the husks of insect prey, their antennae stiff as gargoyle horns, cut loose and dropped; on them and the surrounding ground are splashes of the spider's white urine, which looks like bird guano and smells of ammonia even at a distance of several feet. This fetid material draws scavengers—ants, sowbugs, crickets, roaches, and so on—which become tangled in vertical strands of silk reaching from the ground up into the web. The widow comes down and, with a bicycling of the hind pair of legs, throws gummy silk onto this new prey.

When the prey is seriously tangled but still struggling, the widow cautiously descends and bites the creature, usually on a leg joint. This is a killing bite; it pumps neurotoxin into the victim. The widow will deliver a series of bites as the creature dies, injecting substances that liquefy the organs. Finally it will settle down to suck the liquefied innards out of the prey, changing position two or three times to get it all. 7

Before the eating begins, and sometimes before the victim dies from the slow venom, the widow usually moves it higher into the web. It attaches some line to the prey with a leg-bicycling toss, moves up the vertical web strand that originally snagged the prey, crosses a diagonal strand upward to a higher point on a different vertical strand, and here secures the line. It has thus dragged the prey's body up off the ground. The whole operation is like that of a person moving a load with block and tackle. It occurs in three dimensions—as opposed to the essentially two-dimensional operations of orb weavers and sheet weavers. 8

You can't watch the widow in this activity very long without realizing that its web is not a mess at all but an efficient machine. It allows complicated uses of leverage and also, because of its complexity of connections, lets the spider feel a disturbance anywhere in the web—usually with enough accuracy to tell the difference at a distance between a raindrop or leaf and viable prey. The web is also constructed in a certain relationship to movements of air so that flying insects are drawn into it. This fact partly explains why widow webs are so often found in the face-down side of discarded car wheels—the wheel is essentially a vault of still air that protects the web, but the central hole at the top allows airborne insects to fall in. An insect that is clumsy and flies in random hops, such as a June beetle, is especially vulnerable to this trap. The widow often 9 seems to choose her building sites according to indigenous smells rather than creating her own stinking waste pile from scratch. The webs turn up, for example, in piles of trash and rotting wood. A few decades ago, the widow was notorious for building its home inside the works of outdoor toilets. Scraping around with a stick before using the toilet was a common practice.

10 The architectural complexities of the widow web do not particularly impress the widows. They move around in these webs almost blind, yet they never misstep or get lost. In fact, a widow forcibly removed from its web and put back at a different point does not seem confused; it will quickly return to its habitual resting place. Furthermore, widows never snare themselves, even though every strand of the web is a potential trap. A widow will spend a few minutes every day coating the clawed tips of its legs with the oil that lets it walk the sticky strands. It secretes the oil from its mouth, coating its legs like a cat cleaning its paws.

11 The human mind cannot grasp the complex functions of the web but must infer them. The widow constructs it by instinct. A brain smaller than a pinhead contains the blueprints, precognitive memories the widow unfolds out of itself into actuality. I have never dissected with enough precision or delicacy to get a good specimen of the black widow brain, but I did glimpse one once. A widow was struggling to wrap a praying mantis when the insect's forelegs, like scalpels mounted on lightning, sliced away the spider's carapace and left exposed the clear droplet of bloody brain.

12 Widows reportedly eat mice, toads, tarantulas—anything that wanders into that remarkable web. I have never witnessed a widow performing a gustatory act of that magnitude, but I have seen them eat scarab beetles heavy as pecans; carabid beetles strong enough to prey on wolf spiders; cockroaches more than an inch long; and hundreds of other arthropods of various sizes. Widows begin life by eating their siblings. An adult female will fight any other female; the winner often eats the loser. A popular game among Mexican children is to stage such fights and bet on the outcome. The children put the widows on a stick and pass it around so that everyone can see. Sometimes one female ties another up and leaves without killing her. I have come across such black pearls wrapped in silk and, upon peeling off the skin, seen the pearls unfold their legs and rush away.

13 The widow gets her name by eating her lover, though this does not always happen. He distinguishes himself from ordinary prey by playing her web like a lyre. Sometimes she eats him without first

copulating; sometimes she snags him as he withdraws his palp from her genital pore. Sometimes he leaves unharmed after mating; in this case, he soon withers and dies on his own. I have witnessed male and female living in platonic relationships in one web. The males' palps, still swollen with sperm, proved that these relationships had not been sexual.

Many widows will eat as much as opportunity gives. One aggressive female had an abdomen a little bigger than an English pea. She snared a huge cockroach and spent several hours subduing it, then three days consuming it. Her abdomen swelled to the size of a largeish marble, its glossy black stretching to a tight red-brown. With a different widow, I decided to see whether that appetite was really insatiable. I collected dozens of large crickets and grasshoppers and began to drop them into her web at a rate of one every three or four hours. After catching and consuming her tenth victim, this bloated widow fell from her web, landing on her back. She remained in this position for hours, making only feeble attempts to move. Then she died. 14

The first thing people ask when they hear about my fascination with the widow is why I am not afraid. The truth is that my fascination is rooted in fear. 15

I have childhood memories that partly account for my fear. When I was six my mother took my sister and me to the cellar of our farmhouse and told us to watch as she killed a widow. With great ceremony she produced a long stick (I am tempted to say a ten-foot pole) and, narrating her technique in exactly the hushed voice she used for discussing religion or sex, went to work. Her flashlight beam found a point halfway up the cement wall where two marbles hung together—one crisp white, the other a glossy black. My mother ran her stick through the dirty silver web around them, and as it tore it sounded like the crackling of paper in fire. This sound is unique to the widow's powerful web—anybody with a little experience can tell a widow's work from another spider's by ear. The black marble rose on thin legs to fight off the intruder. As the plump abdomen wobbled across the wall, it seemed to be constantly throwing those legs out of its path. The impression it gave was of speed and frantic anger, but actually a widow's movements outside the web are slow and inefficient. My mother smashed the widow onto the stick and carried it up into the light. It was still kicking its remaining legs. Mom scraped it against the sidewalk, grinding it to a paste. Then she returned for the white marble—the widow's egg sac. This, too, came to an abrasive end. 16

17 My mother's stated purpose was to teach us how to recognize and deal with a dangerous creature we would probably encounter on the farm. But of course we also took the understanding that widows were actively malevolent, that they waited in dark places to ambush us, that they were worthy of ritual disposition, like an enemy whose death is not sufficient but must be followed with the murder of his children and the salting of his land and whose unclean remains must not touch our hands.

18 The odd thing is that so many people, some of whom presumably did not first encounter the widow in such an atmosphere of mystic reverence, hold the widow in awe. Various friends have told me that the widow always devours her mate, or that her bite is always fatal to humans—in fact, it almost never is. I have heard told for truth that goods imported from the Orient are likely infested with widows and that women with bouffant hairdos have died of widow infestation. Any contradiction of such tales is received as if it were a proclamation of atheism.

19 The most startling contribution to the widow's mythical status I have ever encountered was *Black Widow: America's Most Poisonous Spider*, a book that appeared in 1945. Between genuine scientific observations, the authors present the widow as a lurking menace with a taste for human flesh. They describe the experiments of other investigators; one involved inducing a widow to bite a laboratory rat on the penis, after which event the rat "appeared to become dejected and depressed." Perhaps the most psychologically revealing passage is the authors' quotation from another writer, who said the "deadliest Communists are like the black widow spider; they conceal their *red* underneath."

20 We project our archetypal terrors onto the widow. It is black; it avoids the light; it is a voracious carnivore. Its red markings suggest blood. Its name, its sleek, rounded form invite a strangely sexual discomfort; the widow becomes an emblem for a man's fear of extending himself into the blood and darkness of a woman, something like the legendary Eskimo vampire that takes the form of a fanged vagina.

21 The widow's venom is, of course, a soundly pragmatic reason for fear. The venom contains a neurotoxin that can produce sweats, vomiting, swelling, convulsions, and dozens of other symptoms. The variation in symptoms from one person to the next is remarkable. The constant is pain. A useful question for a doctor trying to diagnose an uncertain case: "Is this the worst pain you've ever

felt?" A "yes" suggests a diagnosis of black widow bite. Occasionally people die from widow bites. The very young and the very old are especially vulnerable. Some people seem to die not from the venom but from the infection that may follow; because of its habitat, the widow carries dangerous microbes.

Some researchers hypothesized that the virulence of the venom was necessary for killing beetles of the scarab family. This family contains thousands of species, including the June beetle and the famous dung beetle the Egyptians thought immortal. All the scarabs have thick, strong bodies and unusually tough exoskeletons, and many of them are common prey for the widow. The tough hide was supposed to require a particularly nasty venom. As it turns out, the venom is thousands of times more virulent than necessary for this purpose. The whole idea is full of the widow's glamor: an emblem of eternal life killed by a creature whose most distinctive blood-colored markings people invariably describe as an hourglass. 22

No one has ever offered a sufficient explanation for the dangerous venom. It provides no evolutionary advantages: all of the widow's prey items would find lesser toxins fatal, and there is no particular benefit in killing or harming larger animals. A widow that bites a human being or other large animal is likely to be killed. Evolution does sometimes produce such flowers of natural evil—traits that are neither functional nor vestigial but utterly pointless. Natural selection favors the inheritance of useful characteristics that arise from random mutation and tends to extinguish disadvantageous traits. All other characteristics, the ones that neither help nor hinder survival, are preserved or extinguished at random as mutation links them with useful or harmful traits. Many people—even many scientists—assume that every animal is elegantly engineered for its ecological niche, that every bit of an animal's anatomy and behavior has a functional explanation. This assumption is false. Nothing in evolution theory sanctions it; fact refutes it. 23

We want the world to be an ordered room, but in a corner of that room there hangs an untidy web. Here the analytical minds find an irreducible mystery, a motiveless evil in nature, and the scientist's vision of evil comes to match the vision of a God-fearing country woman with a ten-foot pole. No idea of the cosmos as elegant design accounts for the widow. No idea of a benevolent God is comfortable in a world with the widow. She hangs in her web, that marvel of design, and defies teleology. 24

QUESTIONS FOR DISCUSSION

1. Grice begins his essay with a five-paragraph addition that is essentially autobiographical. What is the effect of adding this material?
2. What is the effect of the single-sentence paragraph 5?
3. When Grice writes, "They felt like trickling water in my arm hairs" (paragraph 3), what figure of speech is he using?
4. Beginning in paragraph 8, Grice describes how the black widow uses the web. Why?
5. In paragraph 11, Grice refers to the "blueprints" by which the spider builds a web as "precognitive memories the widow unfolds out of itself into actuality." What does he mean by this reference?
6. In paragraph 19, Grice mentions a 1945 book on the subject the black widow. To what extent does this paragraph contribute to the essay?
7. Be prepared to define the following words: *translucent* (3), *molt* (3), *guano* (6), *viable* (9), *indigenous* (9), *notorious* (9), *infer* (11), *precognitive* (11), *carapace* (11), *platonic* (13), *insatiable* (14), *abrasive* (16), *menace* (19), *archetypal* (20), *hypothesized* (22).

CAUGHT IN THE WIDOW'S WEB

Gordon Grice

The full text of the version of "The Black Widow" that appeared in Harper's *can be found in Chapter 3. "Caught" is substantially shorter. Although there are changes throughout the essay, the biggest differences can be found in the following paragraphs of "The Black Widow": 1 (a sentence deleted), 2–5 (all deleted), 6 (portions deleted), 8–11 (all deleted), 12 (about half deleted), 13 (deleted), 16 (substantial portions deleted), 19 (deleted), 22 (final sentence deleted). In addition, the final word of the original essay,* teleology, *was replaced by the word* reason.

QUESTIONS ON THE REVISION

1. The *Harper's* version deletes all of paragraphs 2 through 5 of "The Black Widow," the section that describes how Grice raised black widows and how one day he set some free. Why might those deletions have been made?
2. In the revised version of the essay, references to the spider as "bicycling" its hind legs (paragraphs 6 and 8 of "The Black Widow"), as working the web lines like "a person moving a load with block and tackle" (paragraph 8), and as licking its legs "like a cat cleaning its paws" (paragraph 10) have been omitted. Why might those references have been cut?
3. In the revised version of the essay, the story of the praying mantis slicing into the spider's brain (paragraph 11 in "The Black Widow") is omitted. Why might that reference have been cut?
4. Does the black widow always kill her mate? Compare the answer in the two versions.
5. In the original version, Grice describes the widow as trying to fend off the stick: "As the plump abdomen wobbled across the wall, it seemed to be constantly throwing those legs out of its path. The impression it gave was of speed and frantic anger, but actually a widow's movements outside the web are slow and inefficient" (paragraph 16). Those two sentences are omitted in the revised version. Why?
6. Paragraph 19 of "The Black Widow," devoted to the strange stories from the 1945 book on the spider, is deleted in the revised version. Why?
7. Why might the word *teleology* be replaced with *reason?*

WRITING SUGGESTION ON THE REVISION

1. **For an Essay.** Study the deletions and modifications that have been made from "The Black Widow" to "Caught in the Widow's Web." Formulate a thesis that accounts for at least most of those changes. In an essay, argue for a coherent strategy at work in the revision of the essay.

   Prewriting:

   a. Make a list of every change made from one draft to another.

   b. Write a thesis statement (or find one in the text) for "Caught in the Widow's Web." Does that thesis seem to be identical to that of "The Black Widow"? Given the thesis of "Caught," what types of details might Grice have chosen to omit as he moved to a newer, shorter version?

   c. Next to each item on your list, speculate on a possible reason why that item might have been deleted.

   Rewriting:

   a. Check your thesis statement about the revision strategy. Does it seem to account for most of the changes? Is it precise enough? Does it advance your hypothesis?

   b. Reexamine the evidence that you are presenting in support of your thesis. Have you managed to integrate it into your prose so that the transitions and introductions to quotations are smooth? Have you used enough examples? Too many?

   c. Look again at your title. Notice that "Caught in the Widow's Web" is far more effective than "The Black Widow" and more suggestive. Do you have an effective title for your essay?

WEBSITE LINK

Will you know a black widow spider when you see one? The Web can provide pictures to help you!

Revising "The Black Widow"

A Conversation with Gordon Grice

Q: "The Black Widow" began as a series of dated entries in a notebook. Is that your usual way of working?

A: No, I rarely use that technique. I don't use it when I have a good idea of where I'm going. Keeping a journal helps me when I don't really have a good subject in mind. I kept this one while I was taking a nonfiction workshop, because I had to turn in pieces on deadline and didn't really know how to start.

Q: An entry in your notebook mentioned a friend's nightmare about cannibalism and hell. This idea comes up again in the notebook draft of "The Black Widow," but you dropped it in the published versions.

A: That idea somehow launched me into the essay about the widow. It set me thinking on the subject of things that are simultaneously attractive and terrifying—for me, the widow is such a thing. I mentioned my friend in the essay to make this point about the widow. As soon as I brought the piece into the workshop, however, someone pointed out that the dream didn't fit in. I hated to drop it because I thought it was really interesting, but I realized it was distracting.

Q: In the notebook, you started with a section about the web. In the first printed version, that section comes later, after a new part about your personal experiences with black widows. Why did you add the new beginning?

A: I had tried to get the essay published, but I wasn't having any luck. I theorized that the opening wasn't catchy enough. I also thought the piece didn't quite fit any magazine I could think of—it was too arty for a science magazine, and most of the essays I saw in literary journals had more personal material than I had used. My idea was to let editors see right away that it was a personal essay and at the same time to jazz up the opening.

I wrote about getting young widows all over my arms because I thought the danger made it interesting. I carried the piece around with me until I got the chance to work on it. I was substitute-teaching a middle school shop class when I scribbled down the new opening. That was almost two years after I started the essay.

Q: Most of that new introduction was dropped when the essay was reprinted in *Harper's*. Why?

A: An editor at *Harper's* made that cut. I simple agreed to it. She was trimming for space and considered that part expendable.

Q: The *Harper's* version also changed the final word of the essay, from *teleology* to *reason*.

A: The editor at *Harper's* asked me to change *teleology* because she thought the word was too obscure. She thought a lot of readers wouldn't be familiar with it. Unfortunately, neither of us could come up with a good synonym. Our compromise was *reason*, which I didn't like. I reinstated *teleology* when I rewrote the piece for *The Red Hourglass*.

Q: What other changes have you made in the book version?

A: It's five or six times longer, so I covered a lot of new material. For example, I developed the section about the widow's venom with some case studies. I added details and changed the overall shape of the essay. I changed word choices and sentence structures as well.

Q: In general, how do you approach the job of revising?

A: It's different every time. Basically, I have a bag of tricks, and I try them until something works.

When I started revising the black widow piece, I went to a junkyard with an empty mayonnaise jar and caught a widow. I kept her on my desk as I wrote. I kept observing interesting things I had never thought of putting in the piece before. If I'm writing about something I can't catch in a jar, I find some other way to research it. I hit the library or interview people. This helps me find interesting details that will fire up a boring draft.

I try to figure out what's working in a draft and what's not. I put it away for a while so I can get some distance on it. I get other people to criticize it. I don't trust anybody who likes everything I write or anybody who hates everything I write.

I analyze a draft like this: I want something interesting in the first sentence. Usually my first draft begins badly, so my job on revision is to decapitate the essay. I cut until I hit something interesting. Or I may find an interesting part somewhere else in the draft and move it to the beginning. I move things around a lot. If I get frustrated trying to keep it all straight on the computer, I print it out and sit on the floor with scissors rearranging things.

I look for long sections of exposition or summary and try to break these up with vivid examples or details. If some part is boring, I try to think of ways to make it into a story.

I fiddle with the sentences as I go. I try to cut all the passive voice verbs and all the *be* verbs. I strike filler words like *very.* If it doesn't sound right without the filler, I take that as a clue that something's wrong with the ideas themselves. I aim for the prose to sound simple, even if the ideas are complex.

APPENDIX

Finding, Using, and Documenting Sources

Finding Sources

All effective writing involves some form of research. To write a laboratory report in chemistry, you use the information gathered from performing the experiment. To write an article for the student newspaper on your college's latest tuition increase, you include information gathered in interviews with those involved in making that decision. To answer a midterm examination, you marshal evidence from lecture notes and from required reading.

As these examples demonstrate, you may use a wide variety of sources when you research any particular topic.

- **Firsthand knowledge.** Your own observations and experiences play a major role in much of your writing. Such knowledge can be simple and acquired easily (before writing a review of a restaurant, you would sample the cuisine and service) or complex and gathered laboriously (scientists will study a virus for years, gathering information and testing out hypotheses by performing experiments).
- **Printed knowledge.** The bulk of your knowledge for the papers you will typically write in college comes from printed sources, including reference works such as dictionaries and encyclopedias, books, articles in magazines and journals, articles in newspapers, and government publications.

- **Electronic documents.** The Internet and the World Wide Web contain important sources of information. Many magazines, newspapers, and academic journals can be found in electronic form. Some journals, in fact, are available only electronically. Organizations and even individuals maintain home pages with valuable information. Our research in the future increasingly will be done through computers.
- **Interviewing.** On many topics, you can gather information by talking with the people involved. A newspaper reporter writing about the latest tuition increase, for example, would have to rely on information provided by administrators and budget analysts. Thanks to the increasing use of electronic mail (e-mail), interviewing no longer requires face-to-face contact or a telephone call.

Although all writing uses sources, not all writing meets the special considerations that we associate with a research paper. Not only does a research paper document its sources, but it also exhibits a particular approach to its subject. A research paper is not just a collection of information about a subject. Instead, a research paper poses a particular question or thesis about its subject and then sets out to answer that question or test the validity of that thesis.

In important ways, you should approach the research that you do for a college paper in the same way that a scientist sets about exploring a problem. The idea behind research—all research—is to isolate a particular aspect of a subject, to become an expert in that defined area, and to present an original or new conclusion about that material. Because research papers have a thesis, they differ significantly from the informational overviews that we find in encyclopedia articles. Many writers confuse the two forms of writing. The confusion probably dates back to grade school when a teacher assigned a report on, say, Jupiter. What most of us did was go to the encyclopedia, look up "Jupiter," and copy down the entry. That might have been an appropriate response for a grade school assignment, but such a strategy will never work for a college research paper.

Using Reference Books as a Starting Point: Encyclopedias and Dictionaries

If you do not already have a fairly detailed knowledge about your subject, encyclopedias and dictionaries can be good places to begin your research. Before using such reference works, however, you should remember three important points. First, encyclopedias and dictionaries are only good as *starting points*, providing just a basic overview of a subject. You will never be able to rely solely on such sources for college-level research. Second, encyclopedias and dictionaries range from general works that cover a wide range of subjects (such as the *Encyclopaedia Britannica*, *Encyclopedia Americana*, and *Collier's Encyclopedia*) to highly specialized works focused around a single area or subject. Third, although some encyclopedias are available in electronic formats (for example, the *Encyclopaedia Britannica* has version known as *Britannica Online*), the most detailed specialized encyclopedias and dictionaries are currently available only in print form.

Because general encyclopedias provide information about a variety of subjects, they can never contain as much information about a single subject as you can find in an encyclopedia that specializes in that subject. For this reason, you might begin any search with a specialized encyclopedia. The word *specialized* in this sense refers primarily to the more focused subject coverage that these works offer; most of the articles are still written in nontechnical language. The word *dictionary*, as it is used in the titles of these works, means essentially the same thing as *encyclopedia*—a collection of articles of varying lengths arranged alphabetically.

Your school is likely to have a wide range of specialized encyclopedias and dictionaries. To locate these reference tools, try the following steps:

1. Consult a guide to reference works. The following guides to reference books are widely available in college and university libraries. Use one or more of them to establish a list of possible works to consult.
   - Annie M. Brewer, *Dictionaries, Encyclopedias, and Other Word-Related Books* (3 vols), 3rd ed. (1982). Volume 1 is devoted to English-language sources.
   - Kenneth F. Kister, *Kister's Best Encyclopedias: A Comparative Guide to General and Specialized Encyclopedias*, 2nd ed. (1994). This provides detailed descriptions of over five hundred works.
   - Robert Balay, *Guide to Reference Books*, 11th ed. (1996).
2. Check in the library's catalog under the headings "Encyclopedias and Dictionaries—Bibliography," "[Your subject]—Dictionaries," and "[Your subject]—Dictionaries and Encyclopedias."

3. Ask a reference librarian for advice on the specialized sources likely to be relevant to your topic.
4. If your school's library maintains an electronic database, check to see any dictionaries or encyclopedias are networked into it.

Finding Books: Your Library's Catalog

Every library maintains an index or catalog that lists the material kept in its collections. The record for each item often provides a wide range of information, but it always includes the author's name, the title of the item, and a few of the most important subject headings. Most college and university libraries are now computerized. With all the information about each item contained in one large database, users can access holdings through a computer terminal, searching by author, by title, by subject, and often by date or place of publication. Most on-line catalogs not only display call numbers but also tell you whether the item you want has been checked out or is on the shelves. Often you no longer need to visit the library to search its catalog; it is accessible at home or in your dorm room via modem or network cabling.

When you start a search for books in your library's catalog, remember these key points:

- Always read the "help" menu the first time you use an on-line catalog. Do not assume that you know how the search functions work. Knowing *how* to search often makes the difference between disappointment and success.
- All catalogs—whether filed in drawers or stored on-line—list only material owned by that particular library or other libraries in the area or state. No library owns a copy of every book.
- Library catalogs list books (by author, title, and a few subject headings) and journals (*only* by title). Library catalogs never include the authors or titles of individual articles contained in journals or magazines.
- Much information on any subject—and generally the most current information—is found in journal articles, not in books. Remember as well that certain subjects may not be treated in books. For example, if a subject is very current or too specialized, no book may have been written about it. Therefore, a search for sources should *never* be limited to the references found in a library catalog.

- In initial searches for information, you are typically looking for subjects—that is, you do not yet have a specific title or author to look up. Searching for subjects in a library catalog can be considerably more complicated than it might initially seem since the subject headings used in library catalogs are often not what you might expect. Unless you use the subject heading or keyword that the catalog uses, you will not find what you are looking for. The next section offers some advice about subject headings.

Choosing the Right Subject Heading

The success of any research paper depends in part on finding reliable and appropriate sources of information. For most college papers, your information will come from *secondary* sources, typically books and articles that report the research done by others. Depending on your subject, you might also be able to use *primary* sources—original documents (historical records, letters, works of literature) or the results of original research (laboratory experiments, interviews, questionnaires).

Finding sources is not hard, no matter what your subject, but it does require knowing *how* and *where* to look. A quick tour of your college or university library, with its rows of shelves, or an hour on the World Wide Web will vividly demonstrate that you need a *search strategy.* The first step in that strategy is to find subject headings and keywords that can be used to retrieve information.

The subject headings used in library catalogs and periodical indexes are part of a fixed, interlocking system that is both logically organized and highly structured. The idea is not to list every possible subject heading under which a particular subject might be found but to establish general headings under which related subjects can be grouped. Most libraries use the subject headings suggested by the Library of Congress and published in the *Library of Congress Subject Headings* (LCSH), a five-volume set of books typically found near your library's catalog or in the reference area. In addition, most periodical indexes also use either the same system or one so similar that the LCSH headings will still serve your purpose. As a result, the most efficient way to begin a subject search is to check the LCSH for appropriate subject headings under which books and articles on your subject will be listed.

For example, suppose you were surprised to read that even today, women earn less than 80 percent of what men earn doing the same job. You want to research why that disparity exists and what is being done to remedy that inequity. Exactly what keywords or subject headings would you look under in a catalog, a database, or a periodical index to find appropriate sources: *Women? Work? Job discrimination? Salaries?* Unless you know where to begin, you might waste a considerable amount of time guessing randomly or conclude (quite wrongly) that your library had no information on the topic.

If you consulted the *Library of Congress Subject Headings*, you would find cross-references that would lead you to the following:

Equal pay for work of comparable value
  USE Pay equity
Equal pay for equal work *(May Subd Geog)*
    Here are entered works on equal pay for jobs that
  require identical skills, responsibilities, and effort.
  Works on comparable pay for jobs that require comparable skills, responsibilities, effort, and working
  conditions are entered under Pay equity.
  BT   Discrimination in employment
        Wages
  RT   Women—Employment
  —**Law and registration** *(May Subd Geog)*
    BT Labor laws and legislation
Equal pay for work of comparable value
  USE Pay equity

The LCSH use abbreviations to indicate the relationships among subjects. By following the cross-references, you can conduct a more thorough search. The relationships that are signaled include these:

Equivalence:	USE
Hierarchy:	BT (broader term)
	NT (narrower term)
Association:	RT (related term)

Having checked the key to using the headings, you know from these entries not to search under "Equal pay for comparable work" since the heading is not in bold type; instead, you are told to use "Pay equity." The best heading under which to search for books and articles related to your topic is **"Equal pay for equal work."** The abbreviation *May Subd Geog* indicates that the heading might be subdivided geographically, for example, "Equal pay for equal work—Delaware." The LCSH also suggests other possibilities: for a broader term, use "Discrimination in employment" or "Wages"; for a related term, use "Woman—Employment." You will find relevant information under all of these possible headings. In general, no one subject heading will lead you to all of the books your library has on a particular topic.

Here are a few cautions to keep in mind when using subject headings:

1. Always check the *Library of Congress Subject Headings* first to find the best headings to use for your subject. The quickest way to short-circuit your search strategy is to begin with a heading that you think will work, find nothing, and conclude that your library has no information on that topic.
2. Remember that the headings used might not be as specific as you want. You might need to browse through a group of related materials to find the more precise information you are seeking.

Subject headings use a *controlled vocabulary;* that is, all information about a particular subject is grouped under a single heading with appropriate cross-references from other related headings. For example, if your subject was "capital punishment," you would not also need to look under the headings "death penalty," "execution," or "death row." Controlled vocabularies do, however, place some restrictions on your search strategy. As we've mentioned, subject headings aren't always as precise as you would like them to be. Furthermore, timely or very recent subjects might not appear within the classification scheme for several years.

An on-line alternative to subject heading searches is *keyword* searching. A keyword is a significant word, almost always a noun, that is used in the titles (or someplace else in the computerized record) of books, reports, or articles. By combining keywords, you can conduct very precise searches. You will learn how to combine keywords and what "operators" to use (words such as *and*, *near*, and *or* that indicate the relationships between those keywords) only if you take the time to study the help menu. Keyword searches that do not specify the relationship between the words tend to produce unwieldy strings of "hits"—records that contain those words. The computer just lists every record that contains those words anywhere in it, even if the records themselves are completely unrelated to your topic or to each other.

Finding Sources on the World Wide Web

The Web is expanding at a prodigious rate—in 1997, it contained an estimated 320 million pages; in 1999, it had grown to 800 million pages; by the time you read this, it will probably be over a billion pages. Give that growth, it is not surprising that no single search engine (the term applied to software programs that index information on the Web) can retrieve it all. In fact, only about 40 percent of the Web is covered by search engines. Moreover, no one engine, as of this writing, can retrieve more than about 16 percent of the available information. What this means is that for the best results on a research project, you should use at least two different search engines. Unfortunately, every list of relevant sites retrieved is likely to contain some dead links—that is, the information is no longer available at the listed site. It's frustrating to encounter such links, but it's also common.

Retrieving relevant sites of information is only one problem. Anyone can post anything on the Web. Just because it is there, just because the Web pages look professional, does not mean that you can trust every document you retrieve. Evaluating Web sources is covered a little later in this appendix. Don't forget to look at the advice there (and on the *Reader's* Website at www.prenhall.com/miller) before you start using Web sources to write your research paper.

Choosing a Search Engine

In searching the Web, like searching most libraries' computerized catalogs, you have two initial choices: you can search by subject or by keyword. A number of sites offer indexes or catalogs of Web documents arranged by subject. A good place to start is Netscape's Search page, which contains an up-to-date index linked to the major commercial directories. One popular and effective subject organized site is Yahoo!, where human editors have selected the best information available on the Web and presented it in a large, comprehensive, and well-organized directory.

You can also search the Web by keywords or key phrases. Search engines such as AltaVista and Northern Light are both highly rated keyword engines. The problem with most keyword searches—like keyword searches in an on-line library catalog—is that they deliver a huge number of "hits" or references that are listed together only because each one contains—somewhere—the word or phrase you typed in. An initial search for a single word might turn up thousands of documents, the majority of which are irrelevant to the topic you want. Just as in the case of a keyword search in an on-line library catalog, you need to narrow your search by using precise terms and "operators." If your search turns up 100,000 seemingly relevant sites, don't just walk away from the computer in frustration. You need to learn how to tailor your requests to control the information you get back. For some starting tips, see the box "Web Searching Tips."

Web Searching Tips

A good place to start is to visit the Reader's Website at www.prenhall.com/miller. There you will find:

- A hot-linked list of the major research engines with comments on their strengths and weaknesses.
- Detailed suggestions for defining your Web queries more precisely.
- Advice on how to evaluate the accuracy of Web information, with some helpful hotlinks.
- Some tips on how searching on-line databases can help you better define your searches on the Web.
- How to find photographs or images on the Web using a search engine.

Some essentials:

1. As you research, develop a list of synonyms or related subjects. Vital resources might be irretrievable, if you don't enter the right key word or the exact subject heading. A good search generally involves searching multiple terms rather than searching a single word or phrase.
2. Use at least two search engines in every Web search. Remember different engines will retrieve different documents.
3. Read the help screens on each search engine to get the most precise advice on tailoring your search and organizing its results.
4. Learn to use *operators*—words or symbols that signal the relationship between words in a search entry. A large list of common ones can be found at the *Reader's* Website. Here are a few examples from that list that are particularly effective in Web searches:

" "	Place a phrase in quotation marks to find occurrences of that particular phrase in exactly that order rather than occurrences of each individual word in a phrase. *Disadvantage:* In finding names, such a query would not retrieve names where a middle name or initial intervened or where the first and last name were inverted.
+ or and	Attach the plus as a prefix to a word or the "and" between words to indicate that the word(s) must appear on a page.
– or and not	Attach the minus as a prefix to a word or the "and not" between words to indicate the second word cannot also appear on the page. Example: +Frankenstein +Dracula (both must appear on the same page, although not necessarily side by side) +Frankenstein –Dracula (only references to Frankenstein without references to Dracula.
* or ?	Most search engines have a symbol for truncation, sometimes called a wild card. Truncation symbols are essential when a word might have alternate spellings (theater or theatre) or alternate endings (theater, theaters, theatrical).

USING YOUR SEARCH FOR SUBJECT HEADINGS AND KEYWORDS TO REVISE YOUR TOPIC

Your search for subject headings and keywords is also a valuable tool in helping you sharpen and define your topic. Typically, despite the most diligent efforts to find a specific topic within a larger subject, you will begin your research strategy with a topic that is really still a subject, too large to research effectively or write about within the limits of a freshman English research paper. If the subject headings you use yield a mountain of published research, obviously you need to focus your topic more precisely.

Finding Magazines, Journals, and Newspapers

The greater amount of information on almost any topic will be found not in books but in magazines and journals. (College and university libraries generally do not use the term *magazine;* they refer to *periodicals* or *serials.* These two terms indicate that the publication appears periodically or that it is an installment of a larger series.) You'll find that most of the thousands of magazines sold at your local newsstand—whether issued weekly, biweekly, or monthly—cannot be found in your college or university library. Correspondingly, most of the journals found in your college's periodical room cannot be purchased on a newsstand. They are too specialized; they appeal to too limited an audience. Most, if not all, of your research for college papers should be done in the journals that your library holds.

Increasingly, the way in which libraries provide access to journals is changing. More and more libraries are discontinuing their subscriptions to printed copies of journals that do not have widespread use. Instead, they are providing electronic access to journals. The switch has some significant advantages. Many electronic databases include not just a bare bibliographical citation, or a short abstract, but also a full text of the essay. Some journals are exclusively available as electronic documents. In general, computer technologies have significantly increased our access to periodical literature, although that access is often through an electronic copy.

Increased access doesn't necessarily mean, however, that it is always easier to find the information that you need. For example, there is no single index to all periodical literature. (Similarly, many newspapers are not indexed at all). Instead, you have to consult a variety of indexes, depending on the particular subject that you are researching. Indexes to periodicals are found in two forms. Some come as printed volumes, with regular supplements, that are typically kept in the reference section of your library. Others are available in electronic formats and you search for information using a computer.

Printed indexes require that you search your subject through a series of separate volumes devoted to particular years. Once you have the citations you need, you then have to find the appropriate bound volume of the journals in your library. Admittedly, it can be a slow process. Electronic databases, on the other hand, allow you instantly to conduct a search of many sources published over a multiyear period. If the database includes full-text formats, you can retrieve on the computer screen the text of the article (sometimes even with illustrations). Electronic databases make the task of retrieving the articles simpler. Not surprisingly, printed indexes are gradually being replaced by electronic ones.

When you start your research, first visit your school's library and explore what types of indexes are available. Where they are located? How you can access them? Visit the reference section of the library. Are there printed indexes available? Check your library's computer network or Web page. Are the electronic databases listed there? How are they organized? What is available varies from school to school; there are no absolute certainties about what you will find.

For example, at my university, the library maintains a listing of 150 different databases that are available for searching. This listing includes some that are still only available in print and some that are only available in electronic form. The listing—which can be found on the library's Website—also indicates the date at which the databases started indexing and the subjects and periodicals included in it. The indexes are grouped so that you are first directed to general databases that are good places to start in any search. From here, the indexes are arranged in a series of subject areas: arts and humanities, business and economics, engineering, government, law, and politics, health sciences, life science, physical sciences, and social sciences.

The list of indexes that follows is representative. Your library might have all or only some of these. Different publishers market different databases, so the names might change as well, depending upon the service to which your library subscribes.

- *General Indexes: Good Places to Start.* These four sets of indexes are held by many libraries. Check to see if any or all are available at your school's library.

  Expanded Academic ASAP (Covers 1980–). Provides coverage of nearly every discipline. Also indexes national news magazines and newspapers. The largest version includes approximately 1,900 periodicals, 900 of which are offered in a full-text format.

  Lexus/Nexus Academic Universe (Coverage varies depending on the section). Composed of five sections—news, business, legal research, medical, and reference. Also has a detailed "Help" on how to use the different sections.

The Reader's Guide to Periodical Literature (Covers 1900–). Indexes about 240 popular periodicals, most of which can be purchased at newsstands. Available in both printed and electronic forms. Likely to be available in almost every library.

The New York Times Index (Covers 1851–). Indexes news and articles in the newspaper. Since many libraries subscribe to *The Times* and since it is a national newspaper, it can be a useful source of information. The *Index* and a group of other specialized indexes to *The Times* are available in both print and electronic formats.

- *Specialized Periodical Indexes: The Next Step.* About 200 different indexes to the periodical literature in specialized subject areas are available. Any library is likely to have a number of these; most will not have them all. Visit your library and ask what is available. In some cases, similar coverages are provided by indexes that have different names. The listing below includes those most widely held and used:

  Art Abstracts/Art Index (Covers 1929– for indexing; 1994– for abstracts). Indexes periodicals, yearbooks, and museum bulletins in art areas such as archaeology, architecture, art history, city planning, crafts, films, graphic arts, photography.

  Biography and Genealogy Master Index. The place to begin for biographical information about people living or dead. Indexes biographical dictionaries, encyclopedias, and other reference sources. Contains references to 12.7 million people. Widely available in print and also in an electronic format.

  Biological and Agricultural Index (Covers 1983–). Indexes articles on biology, agriculture, and related sciences in some 240 scholarly and popular periodicals.

  Computer Database (Covers 1996–). Indexes journals devoted to computer science, electronic, telecommunications, and microcomputer applications. Full-text format is available for about 100 journals.

  ERIC [U.S. Department of Education Resources Information Center] (Covers 1966–). Indexes, with abstracts, articles in professional journals in educations and other educational documents. Most libraries will also have print guides to ERIC materials as well.

General BusinessFile ASAP (Covers 1980–). Indexes and abstracts more than 900 periodicals on a broad range of business, management, trade, technology, marketing, and advertising issues. Full-text format is provided for 400 of the periodicals.

Health Reference Center (Covers 1995–). Indexes medical journals and consumer health magazines as well as health-related articles in more than 1,500 general interest magazines. Many essays are available as full-text.

MLA International Bibliography (Covers 1922– in print format; 1963– in electronic format). Indexes articles and books on modern languages, literature, linguistics, and folklore.

PsycINFO (Covers 1887–). Indexes and abstracts over 1,300 journals in areas such as psychiatry, nursing, sociology, education, pharmacology, and physiology.

Sociological Abstracts (Covers 1963–). Indexes and abstracts over 2,500 journals in sociology and related areas such as anthropology, economics, demography, political science, and social psychology.

Finding Government Documents

The United States government is the world's largest publisher of statistical information. On many research topics, government documents represent an excellent source of information. Most college libraries house collections of such documents, often located in a special area. Government documents are arranged by a Superintendent of Documents call number system that indicates the agency that released the document. Check with your reference or government documents librarian for help in locating relevant documents for your research. Depending on what indexes your library owns, the following are good starting points for research.

- *Marcive Web DOCS* (Covers 1976–). Indexes U.S. government publications cataloged by the Government Printing Office.
- *Statistical Universe* (Covers 1973–). Indexes and abstracts statistical publications produced by the federal and state governments, by international and intergovernmental organizations, and by private publishers. Includes a searchable version of the information contained within the *Statistical Abstract of the United States.*
- *Monthly Catalog of U.S. Government Publications* (Covers 1895–). Printed catalog held by most libraries.

INTERVIEWING

Depending on your topic, you may find that people—and not just books and articles—will be an important source of information. If you decide to interview someone in the course of your research, you must first choose a person who has special credentials or knowledge about the subject. For example, while working on an essay about campus drinking, you might realize that it would be valuable and interesting to include specific information about the incidence of drinking at your school. To get such data, you could talk to the dean of students or the director of health services. You might also talk to students who acknowledge that they have had problems with alcohol.

Once you have drawn up a list of possible people to interview, you need to plan your interviewing strategy. When you first contact someone to request an interview, always explain who you are, what you want to know, and how you will use the information. Whether you are doing the interview in person, on the telephone, or via e-mail, establish first any crucial guidelines for the interview—students who have problems with binge drinking, for instance, would probably not want to have their real names used in an essay. Once you have agreed on a time for an in-person or telephone interview, be on time. If you are using e-mail for the interview, make sure that your source knows when you will need a reply.

No matter what the circumstances of the interview, always be prepared—do some fairly thorough research about the topic ahead of time. Do not impose on your source by stating, "I've just started to research this problem, and I would like you to tell me everything you know about it." Prepare a list of questions in advance, the more specific the better. However, do not be afraid to ask your source to elaborate on a response. Take notes, but expand those notes as soon as you leave the interview, while the conversation is still fresh in your mind. If you plan to use any direct quotations, make sure that your source is willing to be quoted and that your wording of the quotation is accurate. If possible, check the quotations with your source one final time.

Quotations from interviews should be integrated into your text in the same way as quotations from printed texts—make sure they are essential to your paper, keep them short, use ellipses to indicate omissions, and try to position them at the ends of your sentences. When you are quoting someone who is an expert or an authority, it is best to include a reference to his or her position within your text, setting off that description or job title with commas:

> "We've inherited this notion that if it pops up on a screen and looks good, we think of it as fairly credible," said Paul Gilster, author at *Digital Literacy* (Wiley Computer Publishing, 1997).
>
> Tina Kelley, "Whales in the Minnesota River?" (Chapter 1)

Using Sources

Most researched writing—and virtually every college research paper—needs to be based on a variety of sources, not just one or two. A single source always represents only one point of view and necessarily contains a limited amount of information. In fact, a wide range of sources are available for any subject—encyclopedias and other reference tools; books; articles in specialized journals, popular magazines, and newspapers; pamphlets; government documents; interviews; research experiments or studies; electronic mail postings or documents from World Wide Web home pages. Your instructor might specify both the number and the nature of the sources that you are to use, but even if the choice is up to you, make sure that you have a varied set of sources.

Evaluating Sources

Primarily, you want your sources to be accurate, specific, up-to-date, and unbiased. Not every source will meet those criteria. Just because something is in print or posted on a Website doesn't mean that it is true or accurate—just think of the tabloids displayed at any supermarket checkout. In your search for information, you need to evaluate the reliability and accuracy of each source, because you don't want to base your paper on inaccurate, distorted, or biased information.

Obviously, evaluating sources is less difficult if you are already an expert on the subject you are researching. But how can you evaluate sources when you first start to gather information? The problem is not as formidable as it at first seems, for you regularly evaluate written sources when you try to answer day-to-day questions.

For example, if you are interested in information about the best way to lose weight, which of the following sources would you be most likely to trust?

- An article in the *National Enquirer* ("Lose 10 Pounds This Weekend on the Amazing Prune Diet!")
- An article in a popular magazine ("How to Lose a Pound a Week")
- A Web document urging the value of a particular weight reduction program (for example, electrotherapy treatments, a liquid diet plan, or wraps)
- A newspaper article offering advice on weight loss
- A magazine article published in 1930 dealing with diets
- A book written by medical doctors, dietitians, and fitness experts published in 2000
- The Website maintained by the American College of Sports Medicine

You would probably reject the *National Enquirer* article (not necessarily objective, accurate, or reliable), the Web document urging a particular program (potentially biased and likely to exaggerate the value of that particular treatment), and the article published in 1930 (out-of-date). The articles in the popular magazine and the newspaper might have some value but, given the limitations of space and the interests of their audiences, would probably be too general and too sketchy to be of much use. Presumably, the best source of information would be the new book written by obvious experts or the electronic information provided by a recognizable medical authority.

Evaluating printed sources for a research paper is pretty much a comparable activity. A good source must meet the following tests:

1. **Is the source objective?** You can assess objectivity in several ways. For example, does the language used in the work, and even in its title, seem sensational or biased? Is the work published by an organization that might have a special and hence possibly distorted interest in the subject? Does it contain documented facts? Are there bibliographical references, footnotes, and lists of works consulted? How reliable are the "authorities" quoted? Are their titles or credentials cited? The more scholarly and impartial the source seems, the greater the likelihood that the information it contains can be trusted.
2. **Is the source accurate?** Reputable newspapers and magazines make serious efforts to ensure that what they publish is accurate. Similarly, books published by university presses or by large, well-known publishing houses are probably reliable, and journals published by scholarly or professional organizations and the Websites they maintain very likely contain accurate information. For books, you could check reviews to see critical readers' evaluations. The *Book Review Index* and *Book Review Digest* can be found in your library's reference room.
3. **Is the source current?** In general, the more current the source, the greater the likelihood that new discoveries will be considered. Current information might not be crucial in discussing literary works, but it makes a great deal of difference in many other fields.
4. **Is the source authoritative?** What can you find out about the author's or sponsor's credentials? Are they cited anywhere? What does the nature of the source tell you about the author's expertise?

Knowing How Much Quotation to Use

Even though much of the information in a research paper—facts, opinions, statistics, and so forth—will be taken from outside sources, a research paper should never be just a cut-and-paste collection of quotations with a few bridge sentences written by you. The major part of your research paper should be in *your* own words. You can achieve this balance by remembering several points:

- Ask yourself if the quotation is really necessary. If something is common knowledge, you do not need to quote an authority for that information; any information that is widely known or that can be found in general reference works may be included in your own words.

- Keep your quotations as short as possible. Use large chunks of indented direct quotations sparingly, if at all.
- Avoid strings of quotations. You should never pile up quotations in a row. Rather, you should interpret and control the material that you are using and provide transitions for the reader that tie the quotations into your text.
- Learn to paraphrase and summarize instead of giving direct quotations. What is generally important is the idea or the facts that you find in your sources, not the exact words. Paraphrasing means putting the source material into your own words; summarizing goes even further in that you try to condense the quotation into the fewest possible words.
- Use ellipses to shorten quotations. An ellipsis consists of three spaced periods. It is used to indicate that a word, part of a sentence, a whole sentence, or a group of sentences has been omitted from the quotation.

Working Quotations into Your Text

Unless the quotation is only a few words long, try to place it at the end of your sentence. Avoid "sandwich" sentences in which a quotation comes between two parts of your own sentence. If you introduce a several-line quotation into the middle of a sentence, by the end of the sentence the reader will probably have forgotten how your sentence began.

When you place a quotation at the end of a sentence, use a colon or a comma to introduce it. The colon signals that the quotation supports, clarifies, or illustrates the point being made.

> One advice book, *Common Sense for Maid, Wife, and Mother*, stated: "Heated discussion and quarrels, fretfulness and sullen taciturnity while eating, are as unwholesome as they are unchristian."
>
> Joan Jacobs Brumberg, "The Origins of Anorexia Nervosa" (Chapter 7)

If the introductory statement is not a dependent clause, always use a comma before the quotation. For example, in the following sentence, the introductory clause ("As Brian Johnson . . . says") is not a complete sentence.

> As Brian Johnson, co-owner of the Dogwater Cafe, a fast-growing restaurant chain in Florida, says, "When I'm interviewing, I'm

looking for someone with a lot of energy who wants this job more than anything else."

Charlie Drozdyk, "Into the Loop" (Chapter 6)

If a complete sentence follows a colon, the first word after the colon may or may not be capitalized. The choice is yours, as long as you are consistent. However, if the colon introduces a quotation, the first word following that colon is capitalized.

Documenting Your Sources

Research papers require documentation—that is, you need to document or acknowledge all information that you have taken from your sources. The documentation serves two purposes. First, it acknowledges your use of someone else's work. Whenever you take something from a published source—statistics, ideas, or opinions, whether quoted or in your own words—you must indicate where it comes from (thereby acknowledging that it is not your original work). Otherwise, you will be guilty of academic dishonesty. Students who borrow material from sources without acknowledgment—that is, who plagiarize—are subject to some form of academic penalty. Writers and people in the business world who do so can be sued. Documentation is necessary for researchers to maintain their integrity. Documentation also serves a second purpose, however: it gives you greater credibility because your readers know they can consult and evaluate the sources that you used.

Different disciplines use different citation systems. In most introductory writing classes, you will be asked to use either the MLA or the APA form of documentation. MLA stands for the Modern Language Association, an organization of teachers of modern foreign languages and of English. A full guide to that system can be found in the *MLA Handbook for Writers of Research Papers* (5th edition, 1999). The APA is the American Psychological Association, and its style guide, *Publication Manual of the American Psychological Association* (4th edition, 1994) is widely used in the social sciences.

Documentation systems are standardized; that is, the systems have a fixed format in which the bibliographical information about the source is given. Even the marks of punctuation are specified. No one, however, expects you to memorize a particular citation system. The style guides are intended to serve as models. You should look at each of your sources, noting its particular features

(What type of source was it? How many authors did it have? In what type of book or journal did it appear?). You then look for a similar example in the style guide for the citation system that you are using, and use that sample as a model for your own citation. Citation formats for the types of sources most commonly used in a freshman English research paper are given on the next few pages. But because the range of possible sources on any topic is very large, you might have a source that does not match any of these common examples. For a complete guide, consult the *MLA Handbook* or the APA *Publication Manual.* Both can be found in the reference area of your school's library.

Acknowledging Sources in Your Text

Both the MLA and APA systems acknowledge sources with brief parenthetical citations in the text. The reader can then check the "List of Words Cited" (the MLA title) or "References" (the APA title) at the end of the paper for the full bibliographical reference. In the MLA system, the author's last name is given along with the number of the page on which the information appears. In the APA system, the author's last name is given along with the year the source was published and, for direct quotations, the page number. Notice in the following examples that the punctuation within the parentheses varies between the two systems.

Here is how a quotation from an article, "Immuno-Logistics," written by Gary Stix, that appeared in the June 1994 issue of *Scientific American* would be cited in the two systems:

MLA: The major vaccines—those for diphtheria, pertussis, tetanus, polio, measles, and tuberculosis—cost less to make than they do to distribute: "The United Nations Children's Fund, for example, spends a total of $1.50 on the vaccines. . . . A tenth of what a government then has to disburse for labor, transportation, training and refrigeration to get these vaccines to infants and young children" (Stix 102).

APA: The major vaccines—those for diphtheria, pertussis, tetanus, polio, measles, and tuberculosis—cost less to make than they do to distribute: "The United Nations Children's Fund, for example, spends a total of $1.50 on the vaccines. . . . A tenth of what a government then has to disburse for labor, transportation, training and refrigeration to get these vaccines to infants and young children" (Stix, 1994, p. 102).

Note that in both cases, the parenthetical citation comes before any final punctuation.

If you include the author's name in your sentence, you omit that part of the reference within the parentheses.

MLA: According to Gary Stix, the major vaccines—those for diphtheria, pertussis, tetanus, polio, measles, and tuberculosis—cost less to make than they do to distribute: "The United Nations Children's Fund, for example, spends a total of $1.50 on the vaccines. . . . A tenth of what a government then has to disburse for labor, transportation, training and refrigeration to get these vaccines to infants and young children" (102).

APA: According to Gary Stix (1994), the major vaccines—those for diphtheria, pertussis, tetanus, polio, measles, and tuberculosis—cost less to make than they do to distribute: "The United Nations Children's Fund, for example, spends a total of $1.50 on the vaccines. . . . A tenth of what a government then has to disburse for labor, transportation, training and refrigeration to get these vaccines to infants and young children" (p. 102).

Note that in the APA system the date in such cases goes in parentheses after the author's name in the text.

A quotation of more than four lines (MLA) or more than forty words (APA) should be indented or set off from your text. In such cases, the parenthetical citation comes after the indented quotation. Here is how a quotation from "A Weight That Women Carry" by Sallie Tisdale, which appeared in the March 1993 issue of *Harper's* magazine, would be cited in the two systems:

MLA: Sallie Tisdale points out the links between weight "reduction" and the "smallness" that society presses upon women:

> Small is what feminism strives against, the smallness that women confront everywhere. All of women's spaces are smaller than those of men, often inadequate, without privacy. Furniture designers distinguish between a man's and a

> woman's chair, because women don't spread out like men. (A sprawling woman means only one thing.) Even our voices are kept down. (53)

APA: Sallie Tisdale (1993) points out the links between weight "reduction" and the "smallness" that society presses upon women:

> Small is what feminism strives against, the smallness that women confront everywhere. All of women's spaces are smaller than those of men, often inadequate, without privacy. Furniture designers distinguish between a man's and a woman's chair, because women don't spread out like men. (A sprawling woman means only one thing.) Even our voices are kept down. (p. 53)

Note in both cases that the parenthetical citation comes after the final period.

If you are quoting material that has been quoted by someone else, cite the secondary source from which you took the material. Do not cite the original if you did not consult it directly. Here is how a quotation from an original source—a nuclear strategist writing in 1967—quoted on page 357 in a 1985 book written by Paul Boyer and titled *By the Bomb's Early Light: American Thought and Culture at the Dawn of the Atomic Age* would be cited.

MLA: Explaining how Americans' views of the atom bomb shifted during the 1950's, Albert Wohlstetter, a nuclear strategist, commented in 1967: "Bright hopes for civilian nuclear energy" proved to be "an emotional counterweight to . . . nuclear destruction" (qtd. in Boyer 357).

APA: Explaining how Americans' views of the atom bomb shifted during the 1950's, Albert Wohlstetter, a nuclear strategist, commented in 1967: "Bright hopes for civilian nuclear energy" proved to be "an emotional counterweight to . . . nuclear destruction" (cited in Boyer, 1985, p. 357).

In certain situations, you may need to include additional or slightly different information in your parenthetical citation. For example, when two or more sources on your list of references are by the same author, your citation will need to make clear to which of these you are referring; in the MLA system you do this by including a brief version of the title along with the author and page number: (Tisdale, "Weight," 53). (Note that this is generally not a problem in the APA system because works by the same author will already be distinguished by date.) For works that do not indicate an author, mention the title fully in your text or include a brief version in the parenthetical citation.

THE "LIST OF WORKS CITED" OR "REFERENCES"

At the end of your essay, on a separate sheet of paper, you should list all of those works that you cited in your paper. In the MLA system, this page is titled "List of Works Cited" (with no quotation marks); in the APA system, it is titled "References" (also no quotation marks). The list should be alphabetized by the authors' last names so that readers can easily find full information about particular sources. Both systems provide essentially the same information, although arranged in a slightly different order.

- *For books:* the author's or authors' names, the title, the place of publication, the publisher's name, and the year of publication
- *For articles:* the author's or authors' names, the title, the name of the journal, the volume number and/or the date of that issue, and the pages on which the article appeared
- *For electronic sources:* the author's or authors' names, the title, data of publication, the URL (Uniform Resource Locator, the electronic address) or other information on how the sources can be accessed, and the date on which you accessed the material (Dates are important in citing electronic sources because the source may change its URL or even disappear after a short period of time.)

Note in the following sample entries that in MLA style, the first line of each entry is flush with the left margin and subsequent lines are indented five spaces. Ask your instructor which of the APA's two recommended formats you should use: the first line flush left and subsequent lines indented five spaces (as shown here) or the first line indended five spaces and subsequent lines flush left.

Books

A book by a single author

MLA:

Boyer, Paul. By the Bomb's Early Light: American Thought and Culture at the Dawn of the Atomic Age. New York: Random House, 1985.

APA:

Boyer, P. (1985). By the bomb's early light: American thought and culture at the dawn of the atomic age. New York: Random House.

An anthology

MLA:

Ibieta, Gabriella, ed. Latin American Writers: Thirty Stories. New York: St. Martin's, 1993.

APA:

Ibieta, G. (Ed.). (1993). Latin American writers: Thirty stories. New York: St. Martin's Press.

A book by more than one author

MLA:

Burns, Ailsa, and Cath Scott. Mother-Headed Families and Why They Have Increased. Hillsdale, NJ: Erlbaum, 1994.

APA:

Burns, A., & Scott, C. (1994). Mother-headed families and why they have increased. Hillsdale, NJ: Erlbaum.

A book with no author's name

MLA:

Native American Directory. San Carlos, AZ: National Native American Co-operative, 1982.

APA:

Native American Directory. (1982). San Carlos, AZ: National Native American Co-operative.

An article or story in an edited anthology

MLA:

Quartermaine, Peter. "Margaret Atwood's Surfacing: Strange Familiarity." Margaret Atwood: Writing and Subjectivity. Ed. Colin Nicholson. New York: St. Martin's, 1994. 119-32.

APA:

Quartermaine, P. (1994). Margaret Atwood's Surfacing: Strange familiarity. In C. Nicholson (Ed.), Margaret Atwood: Writing and subjectivity (pp. 119-132). New York: St. Martin's Press.

An article in a reference work

MLA:

"Film Noir." Oxford Companion to Film. Ed. Liz-Anne Bawden. New York: Oxford UP, 1976. 249.

APA:

Film Noir. (1976). In L.-A. Bawden (Ed.), Oxford companion to film (p. 249). New York: Oxford University Press.

Articles

An article in a journal that is continuously paginated (that is, issues after the first in a year do not start at page 1)

MLA:

Meyer, David S. "Political Opportunity after the Cold War." Peace & Change 19 (1994): 114-40.

APA:

Meyer, D. S. (1994). Political opportunity after the cold war. Peace & Change, 19, 114-140.

Note: When each issue of a journal does begin with page 1, also indicate the issue number after the volume number. For MLA style, separate the two with a period: 9.2. For APA style, use parentheses: *9*(2).

An article in a monthly magazine

MLA:

Paine, Christopher E. "A Case against Virtual Nuclear Testing." Scientific American September 1999: 74-79.

APA:

Paine, C. (1999, Sept.). A case against virtual nuclear testing. Scientific American, pp. 74-79.

An article in a weekly or biweekly magazine

MLA:

Weaver, Mary Anne. "The Real bin Laden." New Yorker 24 January 2000: 32-38.

APA:

Weaver, M. (2000, Jan. 24) .The real bin Laden. New Yorker, pp. 32-38.

An article in a daily newspaper

MLA:

Nieves, Evelyn. "Many in Silicon Valley Cannot Afford Housing Even at $50,000 a Year." New York Times 20 Feb. 2000, Sunday National Edition, sec. 1: 16.

APA:

Nieves, E. (2000, Feb. 20). Many in Silicon Valley cannot afford housing even at $50,000 a year. New York Times, Sunday National Edition, sec. 1, p. 16.

An editorial in a newspaper

MLA:

"Reaching Drunk Drivers Early." Editorial. Chicago Tribune 8 June 1994, sec. 1: 12.

APA:

Reaching drunk drivers early. (1994, June 8). [Editorial]. Chicago Tribune, sec. 1, p. 12.

A review

MLA:

Tinder, Glenn. "Liberalism and Its Enemies." Rev. of The Anatomy of Antiliberalism, by Stephen Holmes. Atlantic Oct. 1993: 116-22.

APA:

Tinder, G. (1993, October). Liberalism and its enemies. [Review of The anatomy of antiliberalism, by Stephen Holmes]. Atlantic, pp. 116-122.

Other Sources

An interview

MLA:

Quintana, Alvina. Personal interview. 13 June 2000.

Worthington, Joanne. Telephone interview. 12 Dec. 1999.

Note: APA style does not include personal interviews on the Reference list, but rather cites pertinent information parenthetically in the text.

A film

MLA:

Silkwood. Writ. Nora Ephron and Alice Arden. Dir. Mike Nichols. With Meryl Streep. ABC, 1983.

APA:

Ephron, N. (Writer), & Nichols, M. (Director). (1983). Silkwood [Film]. Hollywood: ABC.

More than one work by the same author

MLA:

Didion, Joan. Miami. New York: Simon & Schuster, 1987.

---. "Why I Write." New York Times Book Review 9 Dec. 1976: 22.

APA:

Didion, J. (1976, December 9). Why I write. New York Times Book Review, p. 22.

Didion, J. (1987). Miami. New York: Simon & Schuster.

Note: MLA style lists multiple works by the same author alphabetically by title. APA style lists such works chronologically beginning with the earliest.

Electronic Sources

Increasingly the sources that we use for writing research papers are electronic—full-text articles taken from electronic databases available through libraries, journals that exist only in electronic form, documents taken from Websites, e-mail from people whom we have interviewed. Even books today are available—and sometimes only available—in an electronic format. The most recent edition of the *MLA Handbook for Writers of Research Papers* (5th edition, 1999) includes a section on citing electronic publications. Presumably the next edition of the *Publication of the American Psychological Association* (4th edition, 1995) will expand its coverage of citing electronic documents as well. What follows here is a guide to citing three of the most common types of electronic sources used in Freshman English research papers. For a fuller guide consult the *MLA Handbook*. For additional help, ask your instructor or the reference department in your library for assistance in locating a published style guide in your area of study.

An e-mail message

MLA:

Miller, George. "On revising." E-mail to Eric Gray. 7 March 2000.

APA:

Miller, G. (2000, March 7). On revising.

The crucial pieces of information in citing an e-mail include the name of the writer, the title of the message (taken from the subject line), the recipient, and the date on which the message was sent.

A full-text article from a periodical available through a library database

MLA:

Daniel, Caroline. "Monkey in Your Back." New Statesman 126 (17 January 1997): 22-23. On-line. Expanded Academic ASAP. 1 March 2000.

APA:

Daniel, C. (1997, Jan. 17). Monkey in your back. New Statesman, pp. 22-23. [On-line]. Available: Expanded Academic ASAP.

Information from a Website

MLA:

Hanson, David J. Alcohol: Problems and Solutions. 19 January 2000 <http://www2.potsdam.edu/alcohol-info>.

APA:

Hanson, David J. (2000, January 19) Alcohol: Problems and Solutions [On-line]. Available: <http://www2.potsdam.edu/alcohol-info>.

Annotated Sample Student Research Paper: MLA Documentation Style

The following paper was written to fulfill the research component of a freshman composition course and is documented according to guidelines of the Modern Language Association, as required by the instructor. Be sure to consult with your instructor to determine which documentation style you should follow.

This paper has been annotated to point out important conventions of research writing and documentation. Note that it does not begin with a title page. If, however, your instructor requires an introductory outline, your first page should be a title page (ask about the preferred format), and the next page should be headed with only the title of the essay.

Rubens 1 ① Page numbers in upper right corner, with author's last name.

Amy Rubens

ENGL 110

Instructor Dan Lane

② Double-spacing throughout.

③ Title centered.

Ecotourism: Friend or Foe?

Humans from all parts of the globe share a common feature: curiosity. While there are many ways to fulfill the urge to seek out the unknown, tourism is a way many people choose to satisfy this inquisitiveness. Every year, the number of plane tickets sold, hotel rooms booked, and tour packages put on the market increases, and many of these items are geared towards one of the fastest growing types of tourism: ecotravel. Ecotravel, also called ecotourism, is multifaceted. As Hector Ceballos-Lascurain notes, ecotourism involves "traveling to relatively undisturbed or uncontaminated natural areas with the specific objective of studying, admiring, and enjoying the scenery and its wild plants and animals" (qtd. in Boo XIV). Besides providing the traveler with breath-taking sights, ecotravel is a way to link tourism's economic benefits with environmental conservation because it can justify the "retention, enhancement, and enlargement of these areas in the face of

④ Definition of "ecotourism"

⑤ Quotation moved to the end of the writer's sentence.

⑥ Citing an indirect source

Rubens 2

competition" from forces that would otherwise halt or slow the conservation process (Carter 169). Researchers have proven that ecotourism is an effective means to preserve unique natural areas.

⑦ Citing a book—author's last name and page number

Despite the benefits of ecotourism, it does present some problems. Now more than ever before travelers are descending upon many protected areas of the world—especially marine environments. In particular, ecotourism is increasing drastically in the Caribbean areas because of their reputation, as Carter puts it, as "3-S" areas—places of sun, sand, and sea (160). The escalation of ecotourism has a direct correlation with an ecosystem's preservation and protection, but many of these environments and the animals that inhabit them are threatened. Thus, although ecotourism is mostly beneficial in that it boosts conservation and protection, there is a potential for environmental damage, especially in marine areas. To lessen the negative impacts of ecotourism, governments should devise plans and enact legislation to counteract the degradation of these environmental treasures.

⑧ Author's last name is in the sentence so parenthetical reference contains only page number.

⑨ Thesis statement

Marine environments through the world are popular tourist destinations. Countries in Latin and South America, like Costa Rica and

Rubens 3

Ecuador, are discovering different ways to market their coastlines' recreational capabilities and aesthetic values. One way to increase a nation's marketability to tourists is to exploit its most abundant resource. In the Caribbean area, for example, the ocean is more dominant than the land—tiny island nations seem to be swallowed up by the sea—and naturally these countries would try to take advantage of their largest resource. The main idea of this strategy is that most people come to tropical locations for "traditional" reasons, but some of these tourists may take an extra day or two out of their itinerary to explore natural areas. Therefore, tourists are not only spending money in resorts, but in other areas like national parks and preserves as well.

Many of these marine environments, ranging from beaches to wetlands to tidal pools to coral reefs, remain untouched by man and are thus prime destinations for developers who wish to capitalize on the booming ecotourism industry. Developers are planning and building beach resorts in Mexico and other countries. Along Costa Rica's Bahia Culebra, for example, an "ecodevelopment" venture called the Papagayo Project has plans for 1144 homes, 6270 condo-hotel units, and 6584 hotel rooms

⑩ Citation indicates that the statistics came from the source cited, but that the sentence is not a direct quotation.

Rubens 4

as well as a shopping center and a golf course (McLaren 105). In addition to the eco-developments, more eco-resorts, eco-lodges, and eco-marine parks are sprouting up in marine environments. This construction results from the countries' desire to entice more ecotourists to discover what their nations have to offer.

Most authorities of coastal communities believe that projects geared towards recreational and tourist-based interests are important to the financial health of a community (Heiman 13). The infrastructure ecotourism brings, for instance, creates jobs for local citizens. At the same time, the area is protected because the new jobs help slow the natives' destruction of the environment. A native who would probably employ the "slash and burn" technique to clear the land for crops would now have a new job and no longer a need to destroy the forest.

(11) Since the sentence has no quotation marks, the citation indicates that the ideas—and not the sentence itself—came from the source.

Development of natural areas to augment profits and increase infrastructure does come with some potentially disastrous effects. In Ecotourism: A Sustainable Option, Carter notes that among numerous other negative impacts, an influx of people brings pollution and can even change the behavior of wildlife (173). For

Rubens 5

ecotourism to truly attain its goal, the ecotourist must at least leave the area in the same condition as he or she found it (McLaren 98). Yet, this rarely happens. To illustrate, all types of transportation require potentially damaging fossil fuels; planes and cars that transport tourists, food, and other supplies such as building materials are dependent upon these kinds of fuels. Consequently, tourists often damage the natural environment. Moreover, tourists create a "transient but permanent population increase in destination sites . . . [that] creates monumental waste and pollution" (McLaren 98). Heiman, another expert on recreation's impact on marine environments, agrees with McLaren. Small marine towns must expand in order to accommodate the multitudes of tourists who flock to these communities each year and often damage delicate environments like dune systems (Heiman 33). Even when the number of incoming ecotourists is restricted, as it is in the Galapagos Islands of Ecuador, within a few years these limits are regularly surpassed. For example, in 1982, the Galapagos Islands allowed a maximum of 25,000 visitors, but in 1994 the number had crept to 60,000 who brought with them more cars, tourist boats, and pollution (McLaren 106).

⑫ Ellipses (the 3 spaced periods) are used to shorten the quotation.

Ecotourists also need support facilities in addition to the hotels, motels, and resorts where they stay during their trip. Waste disposal, parking, and roads are necessary to fully accommodate large groups of people touring the natural areas of a particular region, and all of these have negative impacts on the environment. Soil erosion caused by building activities, for example, leads to coral reef destruction by increasing the dirt particles in the water surrounding the reef and decreasing the amount of available light. Without an adequate supply of solar energy, the coral cannot obtain sufficient food from the water. Just as the dirt harms the coral, so does sewage from ecotourist facilities. In bays where tidal movement is limited, sewage will cause a thick growth of algae to spread over the coral reef. Since coral is a filter-feeding animal because it extracts nutrients from the ocean, the algae blanket prevents the coral from getting an adequate food supply. In addition, coral reefs act as breakwaters that help dissipate the intense energy of waves that pound the shore. Without coral reefs to lessen the continual blows of waves along the surf, one storm could wash the beach away. While no ecotourist or ecotourist facility has a direct intention of destroying coral reefs, it happens nonetheless. Coral reef destruction both deprives the visitor of seeing such a unique formation in a pristine state, and also exposes beaches to destructive erosion.

Another environmental consequences of sewage pollution from tourist areas is the excess growth of algae that results. This filamentous algae, also known as "blanket weed" because of its appearance, is a thick mass of slime that rests on the ocean's surface. It produces less than desirable swimming conditions and often ruins fishing lines and nets. The sewage can also cause an event called "water bloom," caused by the microorganisms mircocystis and anabaena that thrive in raw sewage and similar environments. These two nasty bacteria can afflict beach goers with rashes and stomach problems, and are poisonous to several species of fish (Edington 173). Edible refuse in the ocean is just as bad as non-edible refuse. Garbage thrown from ships into the ocean or left behind by beach goers who are staying in area hotels usually contain food scraps that can attract sharks, scavenging gulls, and rats to the beach.

Not every ecotourist facility turns away from its responsibility to preserve the

Rubens 8

environment. Located on the coast of Mexico's Yucatan Peninsula, the Hotel Eco Paraiso Xixim claims to be the paradigm of an earth-friendly tourist facility. Here, there is "no grass in the garden . . . and the beach is littered with sea shells, seaweed, and starfish" (Malkin). Not only are the creators of this ecotourist facility intent on preserving the natural marine setting of the region, they are also focused on reducing the impact of human by-products that inevitably result from these settlements: the hotel treats its waste water and sewage. Their conscientious efforts to improve the environment (combined with the investors' decision to leave a large portion of the surrounding land in its wild state) are expensive, though. Accordingly, many investors choose to perpetuate Mexico's current school of thought—megatourism—by choosing to construct large and more economical accommodations that are almost sure routes to financial success (Malkin). It is no surprise that environmentally supportive places like the Hotel Eco Paraiso Xixim are rare.

⑬ Citation to an article from an electronic database. Such sources do not have page numbers.

Since many ecotourism programs are designed to complement more traditional types of tourism, ecotourists often engage in activities other than viewing the local flora and fauna. One of the most popular types of tourist recreation is boating because it allows visitors access to marine areas other than the beach (Heiman 15), Guided boat tours are extremely popular, and this popularity does not come without problems. Large tour boats, for instance, allow gas and oil to enter the ocean, causing damage along the coastline and in sea caves. Similarly, exhaust produced from burning these fuels can disrupt sediments if the boat is in shallow water (Heiman 9) and, as has been previously pointed out, swirling sediment in the ocean is detrimental to coral reefs. Also, large boats frequently dump sewage into the water, threatening human health and destroying shellfish.

Cruise ships are also culprits in damaging the ocean. When guests disembark at ports of call, they engage in recreational activities that highlight the natural beauty of the region. By definition, these tourists are actually ecotravelers. Snorkeling near coral reefs, for example, often proves to be too much of a temptation, and snorkelers seldom refrain from stealing a small piece of the reef as a souvenir. Snorklers also threaten the local fishing economy because some of these underwater adventure seekers may spearfish. McLaren likens cruise ships to "mobile [resorts] that simply [float] away without any sense of obligation" to the preservation of the community's natural areas of wildlife (92-93). Popular ports of call for cruise lines often become the "dumping grounds" of inconsiderate tourists, and the local community is left to deal with the consequences of the environmental destruction.

Land development due to the booming ecotourism industry also negatively influences the aquatic animals that inhabit the marine environments. Road construction and the consequent influx of traffic to areas unaccustomed to human activity have profoundly affected the behavior of several species of marine turtles. The types of turtles affected are those who lay their eggs in nests located just above the high tide line on the beach. After two months of gestation, the turtles hatch and make their way to the sea. The turtles instinctively know where the ocean is, and they also rely on the moon's light over the ocean's horizon that acts as a signal for the direction in which to swim. Biologists have discovered that turtles associate a brighter horizon with the sea. Headlights of cars near the beach, however, can greatly "disorient [the] hatchlings and cause them to crawl inland rather than towards the sea" (Edington 170). Consequently, turtles that cannot find the ocean—their natural home—have a decreased chance of survival. Lights from streets, hotels, and floodlights can disorient turtles, too. Some coastal communities have recognized the plight of these marine turtles, and are using shrubs and trees to help screen the beach from artificial lights. Another threat to marine turtles are steep road embankments. Turtles that attempt to climb these embankments often find the task too challenging. The embankments are usually quite steep, and turtles can roll over easily. If the turtles remain upside-down, they will die.

Despite its detrimental effects, ecotourism is helping some animals to survive better. Environmentalists successfully convinced fishermen of Baja California to reduce their takes of certain kinds of fish. The fishermen responded by "[rolling] up their nets and [rolling] out the red carpet" to provide services for rich tourists who frequent the area (Padgett). The result: fish populations flourished, producing an increase in the number of gray and right whales off the coast of this part of Mexico. In 1996, Mexico expected 20,000 tourists to visit Baja California to participate in whale-watching activities (Padgett). Whale-watching is growing in popularity in other areas of the world, too. In the waters surrounding Spain's Canary Islands there are so many whale-watching expeditions that whales are often frightened by all the activity. To escape the commotion, whales retreat to the depths of the ocean for extremely long periods and could potentially run out of breathable air. While whales are hassled by ecotourists intent on glimpsing these magnificent creatures, the whales are still alive, and as they continue to make profits for natives, their fates do not include "blubber factories and jewelry shops" (Padgett).

It is unfortunate that ecotourism's main goal of preserving irreplaceable natural biospheres cannot be realized. Ecotourism was first conceived to help protect the environment, but its popularity has threatened these conservation goals. Ecotourism has also brought to certain areas of the world, particularly to marine and coastal regions, pollution, destruction, and harm to animals. Halting ecotourism, however, is not an adequate solution to this problem since

Rubens 13

ecotourism can be greatly beneficial to the environment. The governments of those countries where ecotourism is a main source of revenue should understand the need for reforms in ecotravel policies. In Coastal Recreation in California, Heiman argues that coastal communities should implement plans, as well as legislation, to limit things that are pleasing or that would harm or alter the environment (44). Already, developers planning new hotels in Costa Rica are spacing them farther apart. Officials should also consider the possibility of educating ecotourists (and tourists) about how their visit will impact the precious environment they will be visiting. The Canary Islands, for example, have already responded to this idea. A marine naturalist is on board each whale-watching vessel to help curtail any harassment of the creatures. The Cayman Island's new plan is an illustration of one of the most impressive attempts of ecotourism reform. Their new plan calls for an improvement of the visitor's awareness of the environment, a quota for visitors at specific marine sites, a reef management program that would regulate scuba diving activities, and new standards for all types of water recreation ("Cayman Islands").

Rubens 14

Ecotourism is effective in preserving the environment: it slows down the indigenous peoples' destruction of natural areas by providing jobs, and it has been successful in helping to preserve animal populations. However, ecotourism is becoming increasingly destructive. Ecotravel is quite popular in marine areas, but an increase of tourists has produced more damage to these special ecosystems. Rather than eliminating ecotourism (or allowing it to continue at its present state), countries should realize the need for reform. Above all, if countries and localities do not sufficiently protect the environment and the animals that inhabit it, tourists and ecotourists alike will not have the opportunity to visit or admire these unique treasures.

Rubens 15

Works Cited

Boo, Elizabeth. Ecotourism: The Potentials and Pitfalls. 2 vols. Washington, D. C.: World Wildlife Fund, 1990.

Carter, Erlet and Gwen Lowman, eds. Ecotourism: A Sustainable Option? New York: John Wiley and Sons, 1994.

"Cayman Islands Offers Five-Year Tourism Plan." Travel Agent Caribbean and Bahamas Supplement 15 July 1996: 5. Lexis-Nexis Academic Universe. U. of Delaware Library. 3 Nov. 1999 <http://web.lexis-nexis.com/universe>.

⑭ Citation to an article accessed through a library's database includes publication information and how and when it was accessed.

Edington, John M. and M. Ann Edington. Ecology, Recreation, and Tourism. Cambridge, England: Cambridge U P, 1986.

Heiman, Michael. Coastal Recreation in California. Berkeley: Institute of Governmental Studies, 1986.

Malkin, Elisabeth. "Betting on the Eco-Tourism Craze . . . And on Adventure and Travel, Too." Business Week 1 March 1999: 4. Lexis-Nexis Academic Universe. U. of Delaware Library. 3 Nov. 1999 <http://web.lexis-nexis.com/universe>.

Rubens 16

McLaren, Deborah. Rethinking Tourism and Ecotravel: The Paving of Paradise and What You Can Do to Stop It. West Hartford, CT: Kumarian Press, Inc., 1998.

⑮ Work by three authors lists all names.

Padgett, Tim, Sharon Begley, and Joshua Hammer. "Beware of the Humans." Newsweek 5 February 1996: 52. Lexis-Nexis Academic Universe. U. of Delaware Library. 3 Nov. 1999 <http://web.lexis-nexis.com/universe>.

Glossary

Abstract words refer to ideas or generalities—words such as *truth*, *beauty*, and *justice*. The opposite of an abstract word is a *concrete* one. Margaret Atwood in "The Female Body" (p. 476) explores the abstract phrase "female body," offering a series of more concrete examples or perspectives on the topic.

Allusion is a reference to an actual or fictional person, object, or event. The assumption is that the reference will be understood or recognized by the reader. For that reason, allusions work best when they draw on a shared experience or heritage. Allusions to famous literary works or to historically prominent people or events are likely to have meaning for many readers for an extended period of time. Martin Luther King Jr. in "I Have a Dream" (p. 497) alludes to biblical verses, spirituals, and patriotic songs. If an allusion is no longer recognized by an audience, it loses its effectiveness in conjuring up a series of significant associations.

Analogy is an extended comparison in which an unfamiliar or complex object or event is likened to a familiar or simple one in order to make the former more vivid and more easily understood. Inappropriate or superficially similar analogies should not be used, especially as evidence in an argument. See *Faulty analogy* in the list of logical fallacies on pp. 487–488.

Argumentation or *persuasion* seeks to move a reader, to gain support, to advocate a particular type of action. Traditionally, argumentation appeals to logic and reason, while persuasion appeals to emotion and sometimes prejudice. See the introduction to Chapter 9.

Cause and effect analyses explain why something happened or what the consequences are or will be from a particular occurrence. See the introduction to Chapter 7.

Classification is a form of division, but instead of starting with a single subject as a *division* does, classification starts with many items, and groups or sorts them into categories. See the introduction to Chapter 4.

Cliché is an overused common expression. The term is derived from a French word for a stereotype printing block. Just as many identical copies can be made from such a block, so clichés are typically words and phrases used so frequently that they become stale and ineffective. Everyone uses clichés in speech: "in less than no time" they "spring to mind," but "in the last analysis," a writer ought to "avoid them like the plague," even though they always seem "to hit the nail on the head."

Coherence is achieved when all parts of a piece of writing work together as a harmonious whole. If a paper has a well-defined thesis that controls its structure, coherence will follow. In addition, relationships between sentences, paragraphs, and ideas can be made clearer for the reader by using pronoun references, parallel structures (see *Parallelism*), and transitional words and phrases (see *Transitions*).

Colloquial expressions are informal words and phrases used in conversation but inappropriate for more formal writing situations. Occasionally, professional writers use colloquial expressions to create intentional informality. David Bodanis in "What's in Your Toothpaste?" (p. 207) mixes colloquial words *(gob, stuff, goodies, glop)* with formal words *(abrading, gustatory, intrudant)*.

Comparison involves finding similarities between two or more things, people, or ideas. See the introduction to Chapter 5.

Conclusions should always leave the reader feeling that a paper has come to a logical and inevitable end, that the communication is now complete. As a result, an essay that simply stops, weakly trails off, moves into a previously unexplored area, or raises new or distracting problems lacks that necessary sense of closure. Endings often cause problems because they are written last and hence are often rushed. With proper planning, you can always write an effective and appropriate ending. Keep the following points and strategies in mind:

1. An effective conclusion grows out of a paper—it must be logically related to what has been said. It might restate the thesis, summarize the exposition or argument, apply or reflect on the subject under discussion, tell a related story, call for a course of action, or state the significance of the subject.

2. The extent to which a conclusion can repeat or summarize is determined in large part by the length of the paper. A short paper should not have a conclusion that repeats the introduction in slightly varied words. A long essay, however, often needs a conclusion that conveniently summarizes the significant facts or points discussed in the paper.

3. The appropriateness of a particular type of ending is related to a paper's purpose. An argumentative or persuasive essay—one that asks the reader to do or believe something—can always conclude with a statement of the desired action—vote for, do this, do not support. A narrative essay can end at the climactic moment in the action. An expository essay in which points are arranged according to significance can end with the major point.

4. The introduction and conclusion can be used as a related pair to frame the body of an essay. Often in a conclusion you can return to or allude to an idea, an expression, or an illustration used at the beginning of the paper and so enclose the body.

Concrete words describe things that exist and can be experienced through the senses. Abstractions are rendered understandable and specific through concrete examples. See *Abstract*.

Connotation and **denotation** refer to two different types of definition of words. A dictionary definition is denotative—it offers a literal and explicit definition of a word. But words often have more than just literal meanings, for they can carry positive or negative associations or connotations. The denotative definition of *wife* is "a woman married to a man," but as Judy Brady shows in "I Want a Wife" (p. 449), the word *wife* carries a series of connotative associations as well.

Contrast involves finding differences between two or more things, people, or ideas. See the introduction to Chapter 5.

Deduction is the form of argument that starts with a general truth and then moves to a specific application of that truth. See the introduction to Chapter 9.

Definition involves placing a word first in a general class and then adding distinguishing features that set it apart from other members of that class: "A dalmatian is a breed of dog (general class) with a white, short-haired coat and dark spots (distinguishing feature)." Most college writing assignments in definition require extended definitions in which a subject is analyzed with appropriate examples and details. See the introduction to Chapter 8.

Denotation. See *Connotation.*

Description is the re-creation of sense impressions in words. See the introduction to Chapter 3.

Dialect. See *Diction.*

Diction is the choice of words used in speaking or writing. It is frequently divided into four levels: formal, informal, colloquial, and slang. Formal diction is found in traditional academic writing, such as books and scholarly articles; informal diction, generally characterized by words common in conversation contexts, by contractions, and by the use of the first person *(I)*, is found in articles in popular magazines. Bernard R. Berelson's essay "The Value of Children" (p. 232) uses formal diction; Judith Viorst's "How Books Helped Shape My Life" (p. 347) is informal. See *Colloquial expressions* and *Slang.*

Two other commonly used labels are also applied to diction:

- **Nonstandard** words or expressions are not normally used by educated speakers. An example would be *ain't.*
- **Dialect** reflects regional or social differences with respect to word choice, grammatical usage, and pronunciation. Dialects are primarily spoken rather than written but are often reproduced or imitated in narratives. William Least Heat Moon in "Nameless, Tennessee" (p. 168) captures the dialect of his speakers.

Division breaks a subject into parts. It starts with a single subject and then subdivides that whole into smaller units. See the introduction to Chapter 4.

Essay literally means "attempt," and in writing courses the word is used to refer to brief papers, generally five hundred to one thousand words long, on tightly delimited subjects. Essays can be formal and academic, like Bernard Berelson's "Value of

Children" (p. 232), or informal and humorous, like Suzanne Britt Jordan's "That Lean and Hungry Look" (p. 277).

Example is a specific instance used to illustrate a general idea or statement. Effective writing requires examples to make generalizations clear and vivid to a reader. See the introduction to Chapter 1.

Exposition comes from a Latin word meaning "to expound or explain." It is one of the four modes into which writing is sub-divided, the other three being *narration*, *description*, and *argumentation*. Expository writing is information-conveying; its purpose is to inform its reader. This purpose is achieved through a variety of organizational patterns including *division* and *classification*, *comparison and contrast*, *process analysis*, *cause* and *effect*, and *definition*.

Figures of speech are deliberate departures from the ordinary and literal meanings of words in order to provide fresh, insightful perspectives or emphasis. Figures of speech are most commonly used in descriptive passages and include the following:

- **Simile** is a comparison of two dissimilar things, introduced by the word *as* or *like*. Lynne Sharon Schwartz in "The Page Turner" (p. 366) describes the skin of the young woman turning pages as "an off-white like heavy cream or the best butter."
- **Metaphor** is an analogy that directly identifies one thing with another. After Scott Russell Sanders in "The Inheritance of Tools" (p. 185) accidentally strikes his thumb with a hammer, he describes the resulting scar using a metaphor: "A white scar in the shape of a crescent moon began to show above the cuticle, and month by month it rose across the pink sky of my thumbnail."
- **Personification** is an attribution of human qualities to an animal, idea, abstraction, or inanimate object. Gordon Grice in "The Black Widow" (p. 593) refers to male and female spiders as "lovers."
- **Hyperbole** is a deliberate exaggeration, often done to provide emphasis or humor. Margaret Atwood in comparing the female brain with the male brain (pp. 476–479) resorts to hyperbole: "[Female brains are] joined together by a thick cord; neural pathways flow from one to the other, sparkles of electronic information washing to and fro. . . . The male brain, now, that's a different matter. Only a thin

connection. Space over here, time over here, music and arithmetic in their sealed compartments. The right brain doesn't know what the left brain is doing."

- **Understatement** is the opposite of hyperbole; it is a deliberate minimizing done to provide emphasis or humor. In William Least Heat Moon's "Nameless, Tennessee" (p. 170), Miss Ginny Watts explains how she asked her husband to call the doctor unless he wanted to be "shut of" (rid of) her. Her husband, Thurmond, humorously uses understatement in his reply: "I studied on it."
- **Rhetorical questions** are questions not meant to be answered but instead to provoke thought. Barbara Ehrenreich in "In Defense of Talk Shows" (p. 219) poses a series of rhetorical questions toward the end of her essay: "This is class exploitation, pure and simple. What next—'homeless people so hungry they eat their own scabs'? Or would the next step be to pay people outright to submit to public humiliation? For $50 would you confess to adultery in your wife's presence? For $500 would you reveal your thirteen-year-old's girlish secrets on *Ricki Lake*?"
- **Paradox** is a seeming contradiction used to catch a reader's attention. An element of truth or rightness often lurks beneath the contradiction. John Hollander in "Mess" observes that "to describe a mess is to impose order on it" (p. 469), making it paradoxically not a mess.

Generalizations are assertions or conclusions based on some specific instances. The value of a generalization is determined by the quality and quantity of examples on which it is based. Bob Greene in "Cut" (p. 55) formulates a generalization—being cut from an athletic team makes men superachievers later in life—on the basis of five examples. For such a generalization to have validity, however, a proper statistical sample would be essential.

Hyperbole. See *Figures of speech*.

Illustration is providing specific examples for general words or ideas. A writer illustrates by using *examples*.

Induction is the form of argument that begins with specific evidence and then moves to a generalized conclusion that accounts for the evidence. See the introduction to Chapter 9.

Introductions need to do two essential things: first, catch or arouse a reader's interest, and second, state the thesis of the paper. In achieving both objectives, an introduction can occupy a single paragraph or several. The length of an introduction should always be proportional to the length of the essay—short papers should not have long introductions. Because an introduction lays out what is to follow, it is always easier to write after a draft of the body of the paper has been completed. When writing an introduction, keep the following strategies in mind:

1. Look for an interesting aspect of the subject that might arouse the reader's curiosity. It could be a quotation, an unusual statistic, a narrative, or a provocative question or statement. It should be something that will make the reader want to continue reading, and it should be appropriate to the subject at hand.
2. Provide a clear statement of purpose and thesis, explaining what you are writing about and why.
3. Remember that an introduction establishes a tone or point of view for what follows, so be consistent—an informal personal essay can have a casual, anecdotal beginning, but a serious academic essay needs a serious, formal introduction.
4. Suggest to the reader the structure of the essay that follows. Knowing what to expect makes it easier for the audience to read actively.

Irony occurs when a writer says one thing but means another. E. M. Forster ends "My Wood" (p. 387) ironically by imagining a time when he will "wall in and fence out until I really taste the sweets of property"—which is actually the opposite of the point he is making.

Metaphor. See *Figures of speech.*

Narration involves telling a story, and all stories—whether they are personal-experience essays, imaginative fiction, or historical narratives—have the same essential ingredients: a series of events arranged in an order and told by a narrator for some particular purpose. See the introduction to Chapter 2.

Nonstandard diction. See *Diction.*

Objective writing takes an impersonal, factual approach to a particular subject. Bernard Berelson's "Value of Children" (p. 232) is primarily objective in its approach. Writing frequently blends the objective and subjective together. See *Subjective.*

Paradox. See *Figures of speech.*

Parallelism places words, phrases, clauses, sentences, or even paragraphs equal in importance in equivalent grammatical form. The similar forms make it easier for the reader to see the relationships that exist among the parts; they add force to the expression. Martin Luther King Jr.'s "I Have a Dream" speech (p. 497) exhibits each level of parallelism: words ("When all God's children, black and white men, Jews and Gentiles, Protestants and Catholics"), phrases ("With this faith, we will be able to work together, to pray together, to struggle together, to go to jail together, to stand up for freedom together"), clauses ("Go back to Mississippi, go back to Alabama, go back to South Carolina, go back to Georgia, go back to Louisiana, go back to the slums and ghettos of our northern cities"), sentences (the "one hundred years later" pattern in paragraph 2), and paragraphs (the "I have a dream" pattern in paragraphs 11–18).

Person is a grammatical term used to refer to a speaker, the individual being addressed, or an individual being referred to. English has three persons: first (*I* or *we*), second (*you*), and third (*he, she, it*, or *they*).

Personification. See *Figures of speech.*

Persuasion. See *Argumentation.*

Point of view is the perspective the writer adopts toward a subject. In narratives, point of view is either first person *(I)* or third person *(he, she, it).* First-person narration implies a *subjective* approach to a subject; third-person narration promotes an *objective* approach. Point of view can be limited (revealing only what the narrator knows) or omniscient (revealing what anyone else in the narrative thinks or feels). Sometimes the phrase "point of view" is used simply to describe the writer's attitude toward the subject.

Premise in logic is a proposition—a statement of a truth—that is used to support or help support a conclusion. For an illustration, see p. 489.

Process analysis takes one of two forms: either a set of directions intended to allow a reader to duplicate a particular action or a description intended to tell a reader how something happens. See the introduction to Chapter 6.

Proofreading is the systematic checking of a piece of writing for grammatical and mechanical errors. Proofreading is quite different from revision; see *Revision.*

Purpose involves intent, the reason why a writer writes. Three purposes are fundamental: to entertain, to inform, or to persuade. These are not necessarily separate or discrete; they can be combined. An effective piece of writing has a well-defined purpose.

Revision means "to see again." Revision involves the careful, active scrutiny of every aspect of a paper—subject, audience, thesis, paragraph structures, sentence constructions, and word choice. Revising is more complicated and more wide-ranging than proofreading; see *Proofreading*.

Rhetorical questions. See *Figures of speech*.

Satire pokes fun at human behavior or institutions in an attempt to correct them. Judy Brady in "I Want a Wife" (p. 449) satirizes the stereotypical male demands of a wife, implying that marriage should be a more understanding partnership.

Simile. See *Figures of speech*.

Slang is common, casual, conversational language that is inappropriate in formal speaking or writing. Slang often serves to define social groups by virtue of being a private, shared language not understood by outsiders. Slang changes constantly and is therefore always dated. For that reason alone, it is wise to avoid using slang in serious writing.

Style is the arrangement of words that a writer uses to express meaning. The study of an author's style would include an examination of diction or word choice, figures of speech, sentence constructions, and paragraph divisions.

Subject is what a piece of writing is about. See also *Thesis*. Bruce Catton's subject in "Grant and Lee" (p. 283) is the two generals; his thesis is that the two represented or symbolized "two diametrically opposed elements in American life."

Subjective writing expresses an author's feelings or opinions about a particular subject. Editorials or columns in newspapers and personal essays tend to rely on subjective judgments. The editorial from *The New Yorker*, "Help for Sex Offenders" (p. 510), is an example of subjective journalism. Writing frequently blends the subjective and the objective; see *Objective*.

Syllogism is a three-step deductive argument involving a major premise, a minor premise, and a conclusion. For an illustration, see p. 489.

Thesis is a particular idea or assertion about a subject. Effective writing will always have an explicit or implicit statement of thesis;

it is the central and controlling idea, the thread that holds the essay together. Frequently a thesis is stated in a thesis or *topic sentence.* See *Subject.*

Tone refers to a writer's or speaker's attitude toward both subject and audience. Tone reflects human emotions and so can be characterized or described in a wide variety of ways, including serious, sincere, concerned, humorous, sympathetic, ironic, indignant, and sarcastic.

Topic sentence is a single sentence in a paragraph that contains a statement of *subject* or *thesis.* The topic sentence is to the paragraph what the thesis statement is to an essay—the thread that holds the whole together, a device to provide clarity and unity. Because paragraphs have various purposes, not every paragraph will have a topic sentence. The topic sentence is often the first or last sentence in the paragraph.

Transitions are links or connections made between sentences, paragraphs, or groups of paragraphs. By using transitions, a writer achieves *coherence* and *unity.* Transitional devices include the following:

1. Repeated words, phrases, or clauses
2. Transitional sentences or paragraphs that act as bridges from one section or idea to the next
3. Transition-making words and phrases

Transitional words and phrases can express relationships of various types:

- Addition: *again, next, furthermore, last*
- Time: *soon, after, then, later, meanwhile*
- Comparison: *but, still, nonetheless, on the other hand*
- Example: *for instance, for example*
- Conclusion: *in conclusion, finally, as a result*
- Concession: *granted, of course*

Understatement. See *Figures of speech.*

Unity is a oneness in which all of the individual parts of a piece of writing work together to form a cohesive and complete whole. It is best achieved by having a clearly stated *purpose* and *thesis* against which every sentence and paragraph can be tested for relevance.

Credits

Diane Ackerman, "Why Leaves Turn Color in the Fall" from *A Natural History of the Senses.* Copyright © 1990 by Diane Ackerman. Reprinted with the permission of Random House, Inc.

Maya Angelou, "Sister Monroe" from *I Know Why the Caged Bird Sings.* Copyright © 1969 by Maya Angelou. Reprinted with the permission of Random House, Inc.

Margaret Atwood, "The Female Body" from Good Bones and Simple Murders. Originally in Michigan Quarterly Review (1980). Copyright © 1983, 1992, 1994 by O. W. Toad, Ltd. A Nana A. Talese Book. Reprinted with the permission of Doubleday, a division of Random House, Inc. and Coach House Press.

Bernard R. Berelson, "The Value of Children: A Taxonomical Essay" from *The Population Council Annual Report, 1972.* Reprinted with the permission of The Population Council.

David Bodanis, "What's in Your Toothpaste" from *The Secret House* (New York: Simon & Schuster, 1986). Copyright © 1986 by David Bodanis. Reprinted with the permission of the Carol Mann Agency.

Judy Brady, "I Want a Wife" from "Why I Want a Wife" from *Ms.* (December 31, 1971). Copyright © 1971 by Judy Brady. Reprinted with the permission of the author.

Joan Jacobs Brumberg, "The Origins of Anorexia Nervosa" from *Fasting Girls: The Emergence of Anorexia Nervosa as a Modern Disease* (Cambridge: Harvard University Press, 1988). Copyright © 1988 by Joan Jacobs Brumberg. Reprinted with the permission of Georges Borchardt, Inc. for the author.

Robert Buderi, "The Virus Wars" from *The Atlantic Monthly* (April 1999). Reprinted with the permission of the author.

Fox Butterfield, "Why They Excel" from *Parade.* Copyright © 1991 by Fox Butterfield. Reprinted with the permission of *Parade* and the author.

Bruce Catton, "Grant and Lee: A Study in Contrasts" from *The American Story,* edited by Earl Schenk Miers. Copyright © 1956 by the United States Capitol Historical Society. Reprinted with the permission of the U.S. Capitol Historical Society. All rights reserved.

Judith Ortiz Cofer, "Marina" from *Silent Dancing: A Partial Remembrance of a Puerto Rican Childhood.* Copyright © 1990 by Judith Ortiz Cofer. Reprinted with the permission of Arte Publico Press. "The Myth of the Latin Woman" from *The Latin Deli: Prose and Poetry.* Copyright © 1993 by Judith Ortiz Cofer. Reprinted with the permission of The University of Georgia Press.

Diane Cole, "Don't Just Stand There" from "A World of Difference," a special supplement to *The New York Times* (April 16, 1989). Copyright © 1989 by The New York Times Company. Reprinted with the permission of the author.

Meghan Daum, "Virtual Love" from *The New Yorker* (August 25/September 1, 1997). Copyright © 1997 by Meghan Daum. Reprinted with the permission of International Creative Management, Inc.

Charlie Drozdyk, "Into the Loop: How to Get the Job You Want After Graduation" from *Rolling Stone* (March 23, 1995). Copyright © 1995 by Straight Arrow Publishers, Inc. Reprinted with the permission of *Rolling Stone*.

Gregg Easterbrook, "Watch and Learn" from *The New Republic* (May 17, 1999). Copyright © 1999 by The New Republic, Inc. Reprinted with the permission of *The New Republic*.

Barbara Ehrenreich, "In Defense of Talk Shows" from *Time* (December 4, 1995). Copyright © 1995 by Time, Inc. Reprinted with the permission of *Time*.

Lars Eighner, "Dumpster Diving" from *Travels With Lizbeth*. Copyright © 1991, 1993 by Lars Eighner. This essay first appeared in *The Threepenny Review* (Fall 1991). Reprinted with the permission of St. Martin's Press, LLC.

Nora Ephron, "Revision and Life: Take It from the Top—Again" from *The New York Times Book Review* (November 9, 1986). Copyright © 1986 by Nora Ephron. Reprinted with the permission of International Creative Management, Inc. and the author.

Susan Faludi, "Sold Out" from *Utne Reader* (January–February 2000). Originally published in *Stiffed: The Betrayal of the American Man*. Copyright © 1999 by Susan Faludi. Reprinted with the permission of HarperCollins Publishers, Inc.

E. M. Forster, "My Wood" from *Abinger Harvest*. Copyright 1936 and renewed © 1964 by Edward Morgan Forster. Reprinted with the permission of Harcourt, Inc., The Provost and Scholars of King's College, Cambridge, and The Society of Authors as the literary representative of the E. M. Forster Estate.

David Gelernter, "What Do Murderers Deserve?" from *Commentary* (April 1998). Copyright © 1999. Reprinted with the permission of the author and *Commentary*.

Bob Greene, "Cut" from *Esquire* (July 1984). Copyright © 1984 by Bob Greene. Reprinted with the permission of John Deadline Enterprises, Inc. "Adults Only" from *Chevrolet Summers, Dairy Queen Nights*. Copyright © 1997 by John Deadline Enterprises, Inc. Reprinted with the permission of Viking Penguin, a division of Penguin Putnam Inc.

Gordon Grice, "Caught in the Widow's Web" from *Harper's* (February 1996). Reprinted with the permission of the author.

Leslie Heywood, "One of the Girls" from *Pretty Good for a Girl*. Copyright © 1999 by Leslie Heywood. Reprinted with the permission of The Free Press, a division of Simon & Schuster, Inc.

John Hollander, "Mess" from *The Yale Review* 83 (April 1995). Copyright © 1995 by Yale University. Reprinted with the permission of the author and *The Yale Review*.

Evans D. Hopkins, "Lockdown" from *The New Yorker* (February 24/March 3, 1997). Copyright © 1997 by Evans D. Hopkins. Reprinted with the permission of the author.

Langston Hughes, "Salvation" from *The Big Sea*. Copyright © 1940 by Langston Hughes, renewal copyright © 1968 by Arna Bontemps and George Houston Bass. Reprinted with the permission of Hill and Wang, a division of Farrar, Straus and Giroux, LLC.

Suzanne Britt Jordan, "That Lean and Hungry Look" from *Newsweek On Campus* "My Turn" (October 9, 1978). Copyright © 1978 by Suzanne Britt. Reprinted with the permission of the author.

Jonathan Kellerman, "The Scapegoat We Love to Hate" from *Savage Spawn: Reflections on Violent Children.* Copyright © 1999 by Jonathan Kellerman. Reprinted with the permission of Ballantine Books, a division of Random House, Inc.

Tina Kelley, "Whales in the Minnesota River" from *The New York Times* (March 4, 1999). Copyright © 1999 by The New York Times Company. Reprinted with permission.

Martin Luther King, Jr., "I Have a Dream." Copyright © 1963 by Martin Luther King, Jr., renewed 1991 by Coretta Scott King. Reprinted with the permission of The Heirs to The Estate of Martin Luther King, Jr., c/o Writers House, Inc.

Elizabeth Larsen, "Buying Time" from *Utne Reader* (January/February 1994). Copyright © 1994 by Elizabeth Larsen. Reprinted with the permission of the author.

William Least Heat Moon, "Nameless, Tennessee" from *Blue Highways: A Journey into America.* Copyright © 1982 by William Least Heat-Moon. Reprinted with the permission of Little, Brown and Company (Inc.).

Eric Liu, "Po-Po" from *The Accidental Asian: Notes of a Native Speaker.* Copyright © 1999 by Eric Liu. Reprinted with the permission of Random House, Inc.

N. Scott Momaday, "The Way to Rainy Mountain" from *The Way to Rainy Mountain.* Copyright © 1969 by the University of New Mexico Press. Reprinted with the permission of the publisher.

Gloria Naylor, "A Word's Meaning Can Often Depend on Who Says It" from *The New York Times* (February 20, 1986). Copyright © 1986 by Gloria Naylor. Reprinted with the permission of Sterling Lord Literistic, Inc.

"Help for Sex Offenders" from *The New Yorker* (March 7, 1994). Copyright © 1994 by The New Yorker Magazine, Inc. Reprinted by permission. All rights reserved.

Mary Pipher, "Academic Selves" from *Reviving Ophelia.* Copyright © 1994 by Mary Pipher, Ph.D. Reprinted with the permission of Putnam Berkeley, a division of Penguin Putnam Inc.

Kyle Pope, "Network and Cable TV" from *Media Studies Journal* (Spring/Summer 1999). Copyright © 1999. Reprinted with permission.

Anna Quindlen, "The Name is Mine" from *The New York Times* (March 4, 1987). Copyright © 1987 by The New York Times Company. Reprinted by permission.

Richard Rodriguez, "None of This Is Fair" from *Politicks & Other Human Interests.* Copyright © 1977 by Richard Rodriguez. Reprinted with the permission of Georges Borchardt, Inc. for the author.

Barbara Katz Rothman, "The Potential Cost of the Best Genes Money Can Buy" from *The Chronicle of Higher Education* (June 11, 1999). Copyright © 1999 by Barbara Katz Rothman. Reprinted with the permission of the Carol Mann Agency.

Scott Russell Sanders, "The Inheritance of Tools" from *The Paradise of Bombs.* First published in the *North American Review* (1986). Copyright © 1986 by Scott Russell Sanders. Reprinted with the permission of the author and the Virginia Kidd Agency, Inc.

Lynne Sharon Schwartz, "The Page Turner" from *Face to Face: A Reader in the World* (Boston: Beacon Press, 2000). Copyright © 2000 by Lynne Sharon Schwartz. Reprinted with the permission of Sterling Lord Literistic, Inc.

Brent Staples, "Black Men and Public Space" from *Ms.* (September 1986) and *Harper's.* Copyright © 1986 by Brent Staples. Reprinted with the permission of the author.

Amy Tan, "Mother Tongue" from *The Threepenny Review* (1989). Copyright © 1989 by Amy Tan. Reprinted with the permission of the author and the Sandra Dijkstra Literary Agency.

J. J. Thompson, "Plugging the Kegs" from *U.S. News and World Report* (January 15, 1998). Copyright © 1998 by U.S. News and World Report. Visit us at our Website at www.usnews.com for additional information.

Susan Toth, "Cinematypes" from *Harper's* (May 1980). Copyright © 1980 by Harper's Magazine. Reprinted with the permission of *Harper's*. All rights reserved.

Bert L. Vallee, "Alcohol in the Western World" from *Scientific American* (June 1998). Copyright © 1998 by Bert L. Vallee. Reprinted with the permission of the author.

Judith Viorst, "How Books Helped Shape My Life" from *Redbook* (May 1980). Copyright © 1980 by Judith Viorst. Reprinted with the permission of Lescher & Lescher, Ltd.

Terry Tempest Williams, "The Village Watchman" from *Utne Reader* (March/April 1994). Copyright © 1994 by Terry Tempest Williams. Reprinted with the permission of the author.

Aline D. Wolf, "Advertising and Children" from *America* (August 1, 1998). Copyright © 1998 by America Press, Inc. Reprinted with the permission of *America*. All rights reserved.

William Zinsser, "Simplicity" from *On Writing Well, Sixth Edition* (New York: HarperCollins Publishers, 1994). Copyright © 1976, 1980, 1985, 1988, 1990, 1994, 1998 by William Zinsser. Reprinted with the permission of the author and Carol Brissie.

Index of Authors and Titles